Pĕsiḳta dĕ-Rab̲ Kahăna

Pĕsiḳta dĕ-Rab̲ Kahăna

R. Kahana's Compilation of
Discourses for Sabbaths and Festal Days

Translated from Hebrew and Aramaic by

William G. (Gershon Zev) Braude
and
Israel J. Kapstein

Jewish Publication Society of America, Philadelphia

First Edition

ISBN 0-8276-0051-8
Library of Congress Catalog Card Number: 74-6563
Manufactured in the United States of America

To my loving wife, Pen: For thirty years and more Midrash has been an obsession which she has had to put up with, wryly speaking of it from time to time as her husband's mistress. Her patience, her understanding, her readiness to sacrifice made it possible for me to continue these studies.

W. G. B.

My share in this work is dedicated
with love to the memory of my father,
Bernard Kapstein, and my mother,
Fanny Silver Kapstein

I. J. K.

CONTENTS

Introduction ix

I Contents ix

A. Origins, Uses, and Purposes ix
B. A Running Summary xi
C. The Basic Narrative xv
D. Doctrines xviii
E. Matters Biographical, Historical, and Factual xxiv

II Structure xxviii

A. The Methods of Discourse in the Piska xxviii
B. Norms of Exegesis xxxvii

III The Text xlv

A. The History of the Text and Its Compiler xlv
B. The Pĕsikta dĕ-Rab̲ Kahăna and Its Contemporary Midrashim xlix
C. The Translation li

Piska 1 3
Why God, having withdrawn from the earth, came back to it. Dwelling thereon in the Tabernacle, by His presence He sanctified it for ever

Piska 2 20
How did the children of Israel who had committed the sin of making the golden calf come to the merit of having the Tabernacle in their midst?

Piska 3 37
The role of Amalek

Piska 4 57
The mystery and paradox of the Red Heifer

Piska 5 86
Israel's reckoning of time by the moon; the advent of the new moon in Nisan as the time of Israel's redemption

Piska 6 122
Offerings serve men's needs, not God's

Piska 7 138
God's justice on the Passover midnight

Piska 8 153
The *'omer* as asserting that God alone is the source of substance

Piska 9 165
The infinite range of God's mercy

Piska 10 185
Tithe that you may be blithe

Piska 11 199
The awesome doings of God and the radiance of certain personages in Israel

Piska 12 223
Torah and its range of eternal meaning
Piska 13 251
Israel are to occupy themselves with matters right and proper for them, or else become wanderers
Piska 14 266
God's mild reproach of Israel, and the happy consequences of hearkening to Him
Piska 15 274
Lament for Jerusalem
Piska 16 286
The certainty of God's comforting
Piska 17 302
Why Zion should not despair
Piska 18 315
The comforting and rebuilding of Jerusalem
Piska 19 322
Israel's obedience to three basic commands makes her worthy of being God's own people
Piska 20 330
Jerusalem's ultimate distinction and glory
Piska 21 337
The radiance of Zion and God's bestowal of light
Piska 22 343
The universal joy and glory which will come at the time of Israel's vindication
Piska 23 350
From judgment to mercy
Piska 24 363
On repentance
Piska 25 385
God's acts of patience
Piska 26 390
On God's judgment
Piska 27 409
Lessons of the Feast of Sukkot
Piska 28 424
The Eighth-Day Festival as exemplifying God's gracious dealing with Israel

Supplement 1 445
Supplement 2 461
Supplement 3 474
Supplement 4 478
Supplement 5 480
Supplement 6 485
Supplement 7 489

Abbreviations 493
Glossary 500
Passages Cited 508
Authorities Cited 528
Subjects and Names 538
Plays on Words and Letters 585

INTRODUCTION

I. The Contents of the Pĕsiḳta dĕ-Rab̲ Kahăna

A. Origins, Uses, and Purposes

For a long time in Jewish history all interpretations of Scripture were handed down only by word of mouth, and it was not until the early centuries of the Common Era that Midrashim,[1] as the interpretations came to be called, were written down. The earliest, arranged according to chapter and verse in Scripture, were in effect running commentaries on certain books of the Bible. Other Midrashim did not, however, follow the order of chapter and verse, but focused instead on the close interpretation of selected passages in Scripture. These passages came from the Biblical lessons which were read as part of the order of service in the synagogue on regular Sabbaths, special Sabbaths, and festal days.

Midrashic discourse on these select passages was of two kinds: one kind was devoted to the regular Sabbath service of the year and concerned itself with the lessons in the three-year cycle during which the entire Pentateuch was read;[2] the other kind was derived from passages in the Biblical lessons read in the service for special Sabbaths or festal days, passages considered suitable for such occasions. Each such passage, usually brief, was termed a *piska*, meaning "section." By extension the term came to be applied to Midrashic discourse on a single Scriptural "section" or passage; the plural *pĕsiḳta* (sometimes written *pĕsiḳat̲a*)[3] came to be applied to compilations of

1. The term *midrash*, derived from the root *drš*, means "to seek out" the hidden meaning of a text, as opposed to the term *pašuṭ* or *pĕšaṭ* which means to read that which is "spread out, plain" or "obvious in meaning." What Midrash seeks out is the secret chambers of Torah, or the mysteries of Torah. See H. A. Wolfson, *The Philosophy of the Church Fathers* (Cambridge, 1956), *1*, 24; Shalom Spiegel's Introduction in Louis Ginzberg, *Legends of the Bible* (New York, 1956); and William G. Braude, "The Relevance of Midrash," *Yearbook of the Central Conference of American Rabbis, 65* (1955), 133–42; and "Open Thou Mine Eyes," *Central Conference of American Rabbis Journal, 11* (1963), 44–49.

2. The Pentateuch was divided into either 154 or 175 *sĕd̲arim*, "lessons for the regular Sabbaths." Unlike passages in Scripture read on festal days or special Sabbaths, these passages were read not annually but once every three years.

3. The root *psḳ* means "to cut into sections" and by extension came to mean "to cut up Scripture into Sections for annual use." *Pisḳaṭa* would be the correct form of the plural of *Pisḳa*. See Friedmann's Introduction in his edition of Pĕsiḳta

such discourses. The Pĕsiḳta dĕ-rab̲ Kahăna, made up of twenty-eight discourses, is just such a compilation: an English approximation of the title would be *R. Kahana's Compilation of Discourses on Select Passages Drawn from the Scriptural Lessons for Special Sabbaths and Festal Days.* The work is attributed to R. Kahana,[4] because it was presumably he who gathered, compiled, and edited the Piskas that comprise the work. A later editor or editors appended seven supplementary discourses to the text,[5] and these are included in the two editions of the Pĕsiḳta.

Just when an important portion of this kind of Midrash, the portion known as the *pĕt̲iḥah*,[6] had been made part of the synagogue service, we do not know. The *pĕt̲iḥah* was a brief dramatic sermon or homily which on a Sabbath or a feast day preceded the reading of the lesson for the day in the Torah Scroll. Sometimes as much as half or more than half of each Piska in R. Kahana's *Compilation* is given over to homilies of this kind. The *pĕt̲iḥah* began with the theatrical declamation by the preacher or his aide of a verse which seemed to have no bearing on or connection with the day's Scriptural lesson, and the congregation waited in suspense for the connection to be made. When the preacher or his aide succeeded in demonstrating the verse's relevance to the lesson, having brought his *pĕt̲iḥah* to a climax with citation of the lesson's first verse, the congregation responded with the amazement and delight that are evoked by the ingenious and logical resolution of a mystery. Obviously, the *pĕt̲iḥah* was an oratorical device intended to capture and hold the congregation's attention to the theme of the discourse. It was for just such a congregation that at a New Year's Day assembly in Jerusalem (*ca.* 458 B.C.E.) Ezra and his associates *read in the Book, in the Law of God distinctly; gave the sense and moved* [*the people*] *to understand the reading* (Neh. 8:8).

Rabbati, pp. 25–26; and J. Theodor in *JE*, *8*, 550–54, *s.v.* "Midrash Haggadah."

"The . . . form *hap-Pĕsiḳta*, viz. that the so-called Pĕsiḳta contained sections on the readings that interrupted the regular *sĕd̲arim*, is apparently the original designation of this Midrashic work." Jacob Mann, *The Bible as Read and Preached in the Old Synagogue* (Cincinnati, 1940–66), *2*, 111, n. 124.

4. For extended discussion of the attribution of the Pĕsiḳta and date of compilation, see Section III-A of this Introduction.

5. These editors also added shorter supplements: Piska 3, a–e, 22.[5a], 28. a–g.

6. The term *pĕt̲iḥah*, from the root *ptḥ*, "to open," may mean "the opening or beginning of a discourse," or "the opening, the disclosing, of meaning not readily apparent." For detailed analysis of the *pĕt̲iḥah* and other portions of Midrashic discourse as they appear in the Pĕsiḳta, see Section II-A of this Introduction. The presentation herein owes much to Joseph Heinemann's *Dĕras̆ot̲ bĕ-ṣibbur bi-tĕḳufat̲ hat-T̲almud* (Jerusalem, 1970), 7–10. See also his "The Proem in the aggadic Midrashism," *Scripta Hierosolymitana* (Jerusalem, 1971), *22*, 100–22, in which he endeavors to work out the history of the *pĕt̲iḥah*.

Not that the discourses which make up the Pĕsiḳta dĕ-Rab̲ Kahăna are given over entirely to the *pĕṯiḥah* as a teaching device. On the contrary, though each Piska begins with a *pĕṯiḥah* and sometimes presents three or four in succession, a very substantial portion of every discourse is given over to less oblique and less dramatic kinds of exegesis[7] of the Scriptural lesson in hand. These are not as striking, but in their variety and their insights they are just as significant as the *pĕṯiḥah*. One wonders, indeed, whether such more direct interpretation may not also have been used in public discourse along with the *pĕṯiḥah* for the instruction of congregations and other kinds of assemblies.

As the purpose of the dramatic *pĕṯiḥah* was simultaneously to entertain and edify its hearers, and the purpose of close exegesis was to instruct them, so the purpose of the brief peroration that follows upon the exegesis and brings each Piska to a close was to reassure them of God's concern for them. The theme of the peroration grew naturally out of the occasion that the special Sabbath or the festal day celebrated, so that, for example, the peroration of the Piska dealing with New Year's Day or the Day of Atonement turns upon the theme of repentance and God's eagerness to forgive the penitent transgressor. Other such perorations affirm God's response to prayer, or His determination to do away with the forces of evil, or His promise to rebuild Jerusalem and the Temple, or His redemption of Israel in the days of the Messiah.

B. A Running Summary

Since R. Kahana's *Compilation* follows the order of the special Sabbaths and the festal days as they come along in the calendar year, each of the Piskas has its own unifying theme, a theme appropriate to the Scriptural reading that the Piska accompanies. Piska 1, accompanying Numbers 7:1, begins the work with a theme appropriate for Hanukkah: God, having returned His presence to the Tabernacle, will never again forsake the world.

Piskas 2–6 are made up of discourses for five consecutive special Sabbaths. Piska 2 is concerned with Sabbath *Šĕḳalim*, so called because its lesson, Exodus 30:12, deals with Israel's giving of half-shekels for the maintenance of the Tabernacle; the aim of the Piska is to explain how Israel came to the merit of having the Tabernacle in their midst; Piska 3, based on Deuteronomy 25:17, the lesson for Sabbath *Zaḵor*, so called because it has to do with the remembrance (*zaḵor*) of Amalek, Israel's enemy, considers Amalek as having been sent by God to make Israel expiate their sins; Piska 4, a discourse for Sabbath *Parah*, whose lesson, Numbers 19:2, deals with

7. For a full account of the norms used in the *pĕṯiḥahs* and in the exegetical passages that follow them, see Section II-B of this Introduction.

the ash of the Red Heifer (*parah*), concerns itself with the ritual use of the ash for Israel's purification; the purification of Israel, so that they will be ready for redemption in a Nisan of the future, is the theme of Piska 5 which accompanies Exodus 12:2, the lesson for Sabbath *ha-Ḥodeš*, dealing with the command that Nisan be the first of the months; the last Piska of the group, Piska 6, whose lesson, Numbers 28:2, concerns itself with the offerings on the altar for the New Moon of Nisan, takes as its theme Israel's true offerings—obedience and good deeds—to God.

The next group of discourses, Piskas 7–11, accompany the lessons for *Šabbaṯ hag-Gadol*, which is the Sabbath preceding Passover, and for Passover. Piska 7, based on Exodus 12:29, focuses on the recurrence in Jewish history of deliverance at the midnight of Passover. Piskas 8 and 9 are given over to discussion of the offerings to God on Passover; Piska 8, accompanying Leviticus 23:11, is concerned with the offering of a sheaf of barley as asserting that God alone is the source of substance; Piska 9, based on Leviticus 22:27, is concerned with the offering of lambs, an offering exemplifying God's mercy and love. Piska 10, commenting on Numbers 14:22, adjures Israel that to tithe is to be blithe, for God will reward them with prosperity. The first part of Piska 11, the climactic Piska of the Passover group, takes as its theme from Exodus 13:17 God's awesome deeds in His judgment of the heathen, in His deliverance of Israel from Egypt, and in His ministry to them in the wilderness; the latter part of the Piska, anticipating the thirty-third day of 'Omer whose hero is R. Simeon ben Yoḥai, tells stories about him and his son R. Eleazar.[8]

Piska 12, a discourse on Exodus 19:1, the lesson for Pentecost, celebrates Torah and its many levels of eternal meaning.

Piskas 13, 14, and 15 make up a group on the readings from the Prophets, the haftarahs of Rebuke and Admonition, preceding the Fast of the Ninth of Ab. Piska 13, accompanying Jeremiah 1:1, admonishes Israel to occupy themselves with words of Torah lest they become wanderers. Accompanying Jeremiah 2:4–5, Piska 14 declares that though God's reproach of Israel is mild, it is persistent and makes Israel hearken even after death. When Jerusalem fell, God himself lamented, Piska 15, based on Lamentations 1:1, asserts, and goes on to say that neglect of study of Torah was the ultimate cause of Jerusalem's destruction.

Further discourse in connection with the Fast of the Ninth of Ab is pursued in Piskas 16–22. These Piskas are based on the haftarahs, the readings from the Prophets devoted to the seven Sabbaths of Consolation which follow the Fast. In Piska 16, treating of Isaiah 40:1, God assures Israel that Isaiah and other Prophets will bring true comfort and consolation to Israel

8. See Abraham Goldberg, *Kirjath Sefer*, *43* (1967), 76.

and Zion. Zion is not to despair, Piska 17, accompanying Isaiah 49:14, says again and again: God is still the merciful and gracious protector of Israel; even the punishment He inflicts upon Israel is for beneficent ends. Israel has had to suffer, continues Piska 18, accompanying Isaiah 54:11, because of her lack of knowledge of Torah and her lack of good deeds and righteous men; but vindication and comfort will come to Israel and Jerusalem. In the meantime, however great the suffering, says Piska 19, based on Isaiah 51:12, Israel is to remember that study of Torah, deeds of kindness, and offerings to God for ever qualify her as God's own people. Accordingly, declares Piska 20, accompanying Isaiah 54:1, when Zion is restored, the boundaries of Jerusalem will rise up to the very throne of glory. Indeed, continues Piska 21, commenting on Isaiah 60:1, the glory of Zion's restoration will surpass the glory of the revelation on Sinai. Israel's greatest joy, however, concludes Piska 22, accompanying Isaiah 61:10, will be that God their King will have come back to Zion.

The themes of Piskas 23–26 are drawn from the lessons for New Year's Day, for the Fast of Gedaliah, for the Sabbath of Repentance, and for the Day of Atonement. Piska 23, accompanying Leviticus 23:24, tells us that on New Year's Day God judged Adam and Eve and granted them clemency, and that ever since on New Year's Day God judges the world and Israel. Piska 25 is concerned with the Fast of Gedaliah, which commemorates the assassination of Gedaliah, Judea's last Jewish leader (2 Kings 25:22); the Piska declares that as God enhances the strength of the righteous to do His will, so His own strength is enhanced by righteous men. Piska 24, a discourse on repentance based on Hosea 14:2, points out that the ten days between New Year's Day and the Day of Atonement are particularly suitable for repentance; even if repentance is only half-hearted, God accepts it. The reading for the Day of Atonement, Leviticus 16:1, is concerned with the death of Aaron's two sons, and evokes in Piska 26 a discourse on the likeness of the fate that befalls the good and the wicked. Pointing out that everywhere grief is mingled with joy, the Piska concludes that the death of the righteous is a means of atonement for Israel's sins.

Sukkot and the Eighth-day Festival are the concerns of Piskas 27 and 28. Piska 27, accompanying Leviticus 23:40, stresses instruction in Torah and obedience to Torah's precepts, explains the symbolic significance of the lulab and ethrog, and concludes with God's promise not to hold Israel's past transgressions against her, but to commence a new reckoning from Sukkot on. Piska 28, whose companion lesson is Numbers 29:35, begins by saying that unlike the nations of the earth who observe holidays riotously, Israel observes them tranquilly, in prayer. As a reward for such decorous conduct, Israel was given an additional day for rejoicing, the Eighth-Day Festival that follows upon the seven days of Sukkot. The conclusion of the Piska points to the rebuilding of the Temple and to the keeping of all the ordinances connected with it.

The seven supplementary Piskas, though not an intrinsic part of the Pĕsiḳta dĕ-Raḇ Kahăna, have some general connections with the themes of the body of the work and were added because of these connections. Supplement 1, for example, takes up the lesson, Deuteronomy 33:1, for Śimḥaṯ Torah, a holiday not discussed in the preceding Piskas; in connection with Moses' receiving of the Torah, the Supplement stresses his blessings of Israel as well as the blessings bestowed upon Israel by those who came after him.

Supplement 2, another discourse on Sukkot, takes its theme from Isaiah 4:6, and declares that living in a sukkah—that is, living in awareness of the presence of God—will shelter a man from fire on the Day of Judgment and will earn him a sukkah of transcendent beauty in the world-to-come.

The Inclination to evil and the Inclination to good are the subject of Supplement 3, the discourse on Ecclesiastes 4:13; the Inclination to evil is born with an infant as it leaves its mother's womb and grows as the child grows; on the other hand, the Inclination to good is not born until a child reaches the age of thirteen and must continuously struggle against the resistance of the body to right conduct.

Supplement 4, accompanying Deuteronomy 14:22, deals with tithing and exhorts Israel to give tithes to God for the harvests He bestows; it was, in part, because of their willingness to tithe that the Fathers attained the highest merit.

Supplement 5, deriving its theme from Isaiah 52:7, describes the miraculous events ushering in and accompanying Zion's redemption. Supplement 6, after quoting the words of comfort that Isaiah and other Prophets spoke to Israel following upon their previous words of reproach, goes on to God's rejoicing at the rebuilding of Jerusalem and His requital of Edom, and concludes with Israel's hymn of praise of the Messiah.

The alternation of God's willingness to respond to Israel's prayer and His unwillingness to do so is the subject of the first part of Supplement 7; its conclusion stresses the power of repentance, particularly just before the Day of Atonement, to secure God's response to prayer.

The seven supplements, despite their difference in structure—they have no *pĕṯiḥahs*—and despite their loose connection with the main body of the Pĕsiḳta dĕ-Raḇ Kahăna, form a fitting finale to the Midrash; they begin with the blessing of Moses in connection with the giving of Torah whose words are, after all, the main concern of the Midrash; they go on to man's capacity to struggle with his Inclination to evil, to repent for his transgressions, and to prevail over the evil side of his nature; and triumphantly conclude with Israel's glory in the days when the Messiah will have come to the world.

C. The Basic Narrative

From the foregoing survey it might appear that each Piska, pursuing a different theme for each Sabbath or festal day, stands independently of all the other Piskas, so that any unity the *Compilation* as a whole may lay claim to is provided by no more than the chronological sequence it follows. But the work does possess a deeper unity than is obvious on the surface, an organic unity such as the seemingly diverse branches of a plant derive from the invisible root that holds them together and sustains them all. The root of the Pĕsiḳta dĕ-Rab̲ Kahăna is Torah—not only its interwoven narrative and doctrine, but the rich medley of fable and legend, of history and tradition, of speculation and interpretation that over the centuries had accumulated around Scripture. Hence what we discover beneath each Piska's preoccupation with its special theme is the broader theme threaded through all the Piskas and binding them together—the theme of man's, particularly Israel's, spiritual journey from the creation to the coming of the Messiah.

Earth's creation, we are told, started on the twenty-fifth day of Elul, but the spiritual creation as distinguished from the physical creation did not start until six days later, on the day, the first of the month of Tishri (Piska 23.1), when God created Adam whose stature reached heaven (Piska 4.4). After Adam's sin, however, God withdrew from the world, Adam's stature was diminished and his splendor taken away (Piska 1.1, 4.4). Not disobedience, however, but ingratitude was Adam's egregious sin (Piska 4.4).

In the days of Abraham, God returned to earth and went forth with Abraham to war against the four kings (Piska 7.8). God helped Abraham because he was gentle in speech (Piska 14.1), because he and his family were scrupulous in tithing (Piska 10.6), because his wife Sarah was chaste (Piska 11.6). On account of her pure conduct, God saw to it that she gave birth to Isaac. He, the first child to be circumcised as prescribed by the Torah, symbolizes the first stage in the redemption of mankind. Consequently, at his birth, certain events occurred which forecast some of the events attendant upon the coming of the Messiah: barren women everywhere became fecund, and those unfortunates who were mad or blind or dumb were cured of their afflictions (Piska 22.1).

God's return to earth, however, was marred by the wickedness of certain men: by the people of Sodom, for example, which before its destruction was like the Garden of the Lord (S2.3), by Esau, progenitor of Amalek (Piska 3.1), by Reuben who sinned with Bilhah. Having repented, however, Reuben was to be the forebear of Hosea the prophet, who was the first to call Israel to repentance (Piska 24.9).

Abraham's direct descendant, Joseph, was endowed with both knowledge —he knew seventy languages (Piska 4.3)—and virtue, as shown by his resistance to the temptation as well as to the threats of Potiphar's wife

(S3.2). His conduct toward his brothers, furthermore, was marked by nobility (Piska 16.5). No wonder, then, that Moses raised Joseph's coffin from the bottom of the Nile for the children of Israel to take with them in their exodus, and that in the wilderness the ark containing his bones accompanied the Ark of Him who lives for ever (Piska 11.12).

In Egypt, where the family of Jacob became the people of Israel, Ephraim's descendants, having rebelled prematurely against the Egyptians, lost 180,000 in battle (Piska 11.10). When Israel's deliverance from Egypt finally came, it came for four reasons: they had not changed their names; they had not changed their language; they had not informed on one another; and they had not been wanton (Piska 11.6). As for the Egyptians, when the plague of the first-born befell them, even the statues of their first-born were smashed and even the first-born of their cattle perished: of all the first-born Egyptians, only Bithiah, Pharaoh's first-born daughter, who had saved Moses, survived (Piska 7.6/9).

Notable among those who had come to Egypt with Jacob was Serah, daughter of Asher. In her own person she experienced so many of Israel's travails and triumphs that her name is taken to signify "one whose years for long endured." Upon coming down into Egypt, she had been enslaved and compelled to do forced labor (Piska 7.6/9). At the time of the exodus, she told Moses where Joseph was buried (Piska 11.12). It was her counsel which brought to an end the civil war that followed Absalom's rebellion. And from her place in the Garden of Eden it was she who told R. Johanan that the waters of the Red Sea, rising up like a wall for Israel, shone because of the radiance of such personages as Moses and Aaron, who had drunk deep of Torah's waters (Piska 11.13). According to one opinion, however, most Israelites in Egypt had become very much like their masters, so that at the exodus no more than one Israelite out of every five hundred was willing to leave (Piska 11.11). And with those who did leave, a graven image passed over the Red Sea (Piska 10.8). Nevertheless, to protect the Israelites from the arrows of Pharaoh's pursuing hosts, God enclosed the fugitives with clouds of glory (S2.2; 2.6). Just the same, because the Israelites at Rephidim doubted God's presence among them, He allowed Amalek to penetrate the encompassing clouds and attack Israel (Piska 3.9). From time to time thereafter, as in the past, Israel's misdeeds were to bring the scourge of Amalek upon them. Ultimately, however, Amalek is to receive his punishment, a punishment represented symbolically in the threefold requital of Agag, Amalek's king, at the hands of Samuel (Piska 3.6).

When the time came to give the Torah, God went around among all the peoples of the world and offered it to them, but they would not accept it (S1.5; 2.1). Then, when Israel chose to accept it, God gave them the splendor He had taken away from Adam (Piska 12.19). Moses, the intermediary between God and Israel, was called "spouse of God" because he had the authority over the Shekinah that a spouse has over his wife (S1.9, 13), an authority which Moses unhesitatingly exercised. For that matter, no prophet in Israel ever hesitated to demand from God what Israel required (Piska 12.1). Still, although Moses served for forty years as High Priest in the Tabernacle, the Presence came into it not through his agency, but through Aaron's (Piska 4.4).

At the end of Moses' life, he seized and bound the angel of death and cast him down at his feet; then, in the very presence of the angel, he blessed the people of Israel and thus saved them from death's dominion (S1.10). Moses died in the wilderness so that the generation of the wilderness, which had worshiped the golden calf, will be allowed, because of his merit, to enter the Promised Land at the time of the Resurrection (Piska 24.9).

God mourns the death of the righteous and sees to it that they are rewarded. He mourned the death of Aaron's sons, Nadab and Abihu (Piska 26.4), who were not guilty of dissolute practices as it was alleged (Piska 26.8). Their death, as well as the death of Aaron, was as grievous to God as was the breaking of the Tablets (Piska 26.11). He rewards the righteous convert as well as the righteous born Israelite: for example, the descendants of Jethro, a convert, were to sit in the Sanhedrin (Piska 3.d). Among the descendants of such righteous converts as Rahab and the Gibeonites were the prophets Jeremiah, Ezekiel, and Uriah (Piska 13.4, 12). And in reward for its righteousness, the Tribe of Levi was entrusted with the perfect Scroll of Torah by which the correctness of the text could be maintained everywhere in the world (S1.8). Righteous, too, were the princes of Israel in the wilderness who, when they were taskmasters of the children of Israel in Egypt, had earned their rank by protecting their charges (Piska 1.7). It was these princes who provided marvelously wrought wagons for conveying the Tabernacle and its appurtenances through the wilderness (Piska 1.8).

The kings of Israel in the Land were judged not by their success or failure in war but by their righteousness or lack of righteousness; Saul, we are told, was a meek and humble man, a scholar in Torah (Piska 5.3); David would rise at midnight to occupy himself with Torah (Piska 7.4). Whenever Solomon ascended his throne, a herald would recite to him the commandments against accumulation of worldly things (Piska 1.7). Because Solomon disregarded these admonitions, however, an angel in Solomon's guise seated himself upon the throne, and when Solomon insisted to the people that he was king, he was deemed crazy (Piska 26.2). King Hezekiah is singled out for mention because he instituted ritual baths for women (Piska 6.2). Though king Manasseh turned to God only after having called in vain upon every idol, his repentance was accepted. King Jeconiah was to have been the last of David's line, and thus the hope of Israel's restoration would have ended, but because of Jeconiah's repentance for his transgressions, God forbore to extirpate his line (Piska 24.11).

Even heathen kings honor Israel's God and His righteousness. Thus, in the sacrifice of his son, king Mesha was emulating Abraham, who would have sacrificed Isaac at God's command (Piska 2.5). In a letter to Hezekiah, king Merodach took care to salute Hezekiah's God first and then saluted Hezekiah (*ibid.*). King Nebuchadnezzar long heard in his palace a Divine Voice commanding him to destroy the Temple, and finally he did so (Piska 5.9). But whether the Temple stands or not, upon its site the Presence continues to dwell (Piska 26.4; 5.8).

Whosoever obeys the command to dwell in a sukkah—that is, live in awareness of the presence of God—will dwell in the world-to-come in a sukkah made of the Leviathan's skin and will feast upon the Leviathan's head (S2.4)—in short, serenity and joy will be the lot of the righteous. Living in the radiance of the Messiah, Israel will exclaim: "Blessed is the hour in which the Messiah was created! Blessed is the womb whence he came! Blessed is the generation whose eyes behold him! Blessed is the eye which is given the privilege of seeing him whose lips open with blessing and peace, whose diction is pure delight, whose garments are glory and majesty, who is confident and serene in his speech, the utterance of whose tongue is pardon and forgiveness, whose prayer is a sweet savor, whose supplication during his study of Torah is purity and holiness" (S6.5).

D. Doctrines

Accompanying the narrative of Israel's journey through history to eternity, a narrative that begins with the creation of Adam and comes to its climax in the coming of the Messiah, are the religious and ethical doctrines of Judaism. The narrative and the doctrine are, in fact, inextricably entwined and complement each other: the narrative gives dramatic force and a sense of everyday reality to such general ideas as justice, righteousness, sin, and the like; on the other hand, the doctrines give significance and assign value to what would otherwise be a mere record of a variety of persons and what befell them.

As narrative and doctrine are entwined in the Torah, so are they entwined in such discourses on Torah as the Pĕsiḳta dĕ-Raḇ Kahăna, which in its account of the creation of Adam unmistakably links man's acts with the idea of divine justice as a living force in man's daily life (Piska 1.1). The Rabbis who speak to us in the Pĕsiḳta simply take it for granted that God created man in the person of Adam as capable of understanding moral ideas and values, capable of discriminating between good and evil, and responsible not only for his own good but the good of his fellows. So, on the very first day of Adam's life, as we are told, God commanded Adam's obedience to six laws: he was instructed to refrain from idolatry, from blasphemy, from bloodshed, from unchastity, from theft, and in order to make him exercise justice as well as experience it, had been instructed to set up civil courts (Piska 12.1). Hence, when Adam and his descendants—Cain, the generation of the flood, the people of Sodom, and so on—were punished for their transgressions, they were punished as violators of the moral responsibility God had entrusted to them.

Why had they violated His trust? Because, the Rabbis tell us, they had yielded to their Inclination to evil, or rather because their Inclination to good had been overcome by their Inclination to evil. In this view, man's conduct is the consequence of a never-ending inner struggle between the two opposing forces in human nature. It is no easy matter for man to win in this struggle, because the Inclination to evil is born with him even as he comes out of the womb and stays with him for a lifetime, whereas the Inclination to good does not come to life in him until he has reached man's estate at the age of thirteen (Piska 11.1; S4).

Those in whom the Inclination to good is victorious are the righteous: they live in obedience to the will of God and His precepts as revealed in the Torah. God does not, however, delight so much in those who study Torah diligently and meditate upon its teachings as He does in those who act upon its precepts in their day-to-day living. Thus to a Jew who says, "I have no learning in Torah, have not meditated upon its wisdom—am I then worthless?" God replies, "All study of Torah, all wisdom, is but a small matter: he who fears Me and carries out Torah's precepts—in the heart of such a man is the entire Torah and entire wisdom" (S1.2). Hence, in the Temple offerings that God requires of Israel, what He truly requires and what delights Him is the obedience and good deeds that the offerings represent (Piska 6.1).

Besides the righteous conduct enjoined upon Adam the day he was created, a number of good deeds are specifically urged upon his descendants. They are to live chastely (S3.2), tithe scrupulously (Piska 10), give generously to the poor (Piska 28.3), use honest weights and measures (Piska 3.4), study Torah diligently (Piska 15.5), show respect for the teacher of Torah (Piska 26.8; 12.5), emulate the righteousness of the Patriarchs and of the devout generally (Piska 10.6, 9, 10), and observe decorum in the celebration of festivals (Piska 28.1).

For their good deeds the righteous are rewarded not only in this world but in the world-to-come in the days of the Messiah. Because Sarah hedged herself in against unchastity, she and Abraham were blessed with the child they had long yearned for (Piska 11.6), the child at whose birth wondrous events took place (Piska 22.1) by way of forecasting what is to take place at the coming of the Messiah. Job, too, in spite of his being of Amalek's stock, was a righteous man and so was rewarded—indeed, doubly rewarded (Piska 16.6). Abraham and Jacob were blessed with abundance because of their scrupulous tithing, and all who emulate them prosper in the world (Piska 10.6).

What holds for the individual holds for the entire people of Israel. The reward of their righteousness when they were slaves in Egypt was their deliverance (Piska 11.6). Their security, their prosperity, their happiness throughout history have always come from their obedience to God's precepts, just as their affliction and suffering at the hands of Amalek are the punishment they have brought upon themselves by their transgression of His precepts (Piska 3.4, 12).

Eventually the people of Israel will have gained so much merit by their righteousness that God will redeem them. And when the Gentile nations will also have learned to live righteously, they, too, may expect to be redeemed (Piska 5.5). With redemption and the coming of the Messiah, the righteous will receive their final reward: they will dwell in sukkahs of transcendent beauty made from the skin of the Leviathan, and they will feast upon the Leviathan's head, the greatest of delicacies. This, like the manna which Israel ate in the wilderness, will give them the capacity to receive instruction in Torah from God Himself (S2.4).

As the righteous are rewarded both in this world and in the world-to-come, the wicked are punished not only in this world, but in the underworld of Gehenna. Since the people of Israel are themselves responsible for their transgression of divine law, they are themselves responsible for the punishment that God inflicts upon them. For their sins He gives them measure for measure (Piska 11.4), and so they suffer for their forsaking of the covenant (Piska 17.4), for their surrender to idolatry (Piska 13.2; 15.6), for their skepticism concerning Him (Piska 3.12), and for such sinful conduct as unchastity (Piska 17.6), niggardliness in tithing (Piska 10.3), hypocrisy and double-dealing (Piska 10.1; 15.9), slander and calumny (Piska 4.2), and the like.

The Pĕsiḳta gives scant space to Gehenna as a place for punishment of the wicked. Gehenna is divided into two regions, one of extreme heat and the other of extreme cold, and the souls of sinners suffer alternately in one or the other (Piska 10.4). But the Rabbis do not linger on details of the sinners' suffering—we are given no picture of souls writhing in agony. What the Rabbis stress finally is that Gehenna and the Garden of Eden are not a whole world apart, but that they are directly adjacent to each other (Piska 28.3), so that the distance from one to the other is but one step. The one step from the Garden to Gehenna is transgression; the one step from Gehenna to the Garden is repentance.

As God punishes individuals in Israel, so He punishes Israel as a people. Throughout Israel's history, her punishment for her transgressions has been the suffering that slavery, poverty, war, and oppression inflict. Hence, the specific events in Israel's history—her times of freedom or slavery, of prosperity or poverty, of joy or sorrow—are not the effects of social or political or economic circumstances she cannot control: rather are the circumstances the consequences of Israel's obedience or disobedience to religious and moral law. Transgression brings on Amalek, Israel's most evil oppressor, as God's scourge of Israel (Piska 3.8).

If the events of history have a moral basis, they also have a moral force. To God, punishment is not an end in itself, but a goad to repentance (Piska 14.3) and hence a means of redemption. Redemption is God's hope for Israel, and redemption is to be won by the resolve of the people of Israel to turn to Him in repentance for their transgressions. Once they turn to Him, they find that He is not only the God of justice: He is also the God of mercy, full of tender concern for all His creatures and anxious to spare them suffering. Since His presence is everywhere in the world, even in the lowliest thorn bush (Piska 1.2), He knows and feels the plight of every one of His creatures. In different ways He shows His concern for all of them: for example, Scripture does not identify the tree from which Adam ate, for the tree was in no way responsible for Adam's transgression (Piska 20.6); because many Egyptians perished during Passover, God gave Israel no command to rejoice as at all other festivals (S2.8); so as to spare Abraham the pain of witnessing the heinous transgressions of his grandson Esau, He took away from Abraham the last five years of his life (Piska 3.1).

Such is His mercy that He gives even the most flagrant sinners a chance to repent. Only when they are utterly unwilling to mend their ways does He exercise summary justice (Piska 3.3). Even so, when justice requires the extreme penalty, the taking of their lives, He puts off as long as possible the execution of the sentence (Piska 7.10). Furthermore, in His punishment of the unrepentant who deserve nothing less than death, He imposes punishment only a little at a time (Piska 24.17), so as to make the sinner suffer as little as possible (Piska 25.1).

But it is not vengeance that God seeks—it is repentance. He delights in "broken vessels" which have been mended (Piska 24.5). The children of Israel must remember always that if they repent, God will bear them no grudge for their past sins, for He is their merciful Father in heaven (Piska 23.16). "Make for Me an opening in you as narrow as the eye of a needle," God pleads, "and I shall make the opening so wide that camps full of soldiers and siege engines can enter it. Vow repentance for as little time as it takes to wink an eye, *and you will be aware that I am God*" (Piska 24.12). Even when sinners offer Him no more than a semblance of repentance as did Cain, Ahab, the people of Nineveh, and their like, He accepts it. He even accepted the repentance of Manasseh who, at death's door, called in vain upon every idol in the world, and in the end, taking a last desperate chance, so to speak, turned to God (Piska 24.11).

In fact, despite their most grievous provocation of Him, God manages to find extenuation for the misconduct of the children of Israel (Piska 9.7, 8). Thus, after they made and worshiped the golden calf, He forgave them because, as He said, at the Red Sea they had proclaimed Him their ruler, at Sinai they had taken on the yoke of His rule, and finally because they are the people through whom He will ultimately be glorified by all the world (Piska 2.7). Hence, even though now and again they despair of His deliverance of them, He will not forsake them—they are to endure like heaven and earth even though one oppressor intent upon extirpating them follows fast upon the other (Piska 19.5).

In creating man, in bestowing the power to choose between right and wrong upon one in whom the Inclination to good is constantly at war with the Inclination to evil, God risked the possibility of the world's destruction. He took a further risk when He chose Israel as the people He hoped to redeem, the people through whom He hoped to redeem ultimately all mankind. True, the people of Israel came from good stock, the stock of Abraham, Isaac, and Jacob, righteous men whom God hoped they would emulate; true, too, that during their enslavement in Egypt, the conduct of Israel in a number of ways had been exemplary (Piska 12.6, 7). On the other hand, they had also taken on some Egyptian ways: like the Egyptians they did not practice circumcision, and like the Egyptians they worshiped idols (Piska 5.11). Accordingly, if God should deliver them from Egypt, the prospect that Israel would be a people righteous enough for His need or purpose was uncertain. Indeed, were it not for the oath whereby God had bound Himself to deliver them, He might not have done so. But the merit of the Fathers (Piska 2.1; 5.8; 9.9) and the chastity of Israel's men and women (Piska 11.6) helped finally to bring about their deliverance.

The ideas just outlined—ideas of good and evil, of righteousness and its rewards, of wickedness and its punishment, of God's mercy and Israel's repentance—are all embraced in the doctrine of Israel's destiny as God's chosen people. His purpose in choosing Israel, an act which set Israel off from the other nations of the world, is not the good of Israel alone, but the good of all mankind (Piska 5.5). When the other nations, following Israel's example, accept the rule of the Holy One and the guidance of the Torah, they, too, may expect redemption. The Torah, we must note, was not intended for Israel alone; it was given under the zodiacal sign of Twins by way of indicating that the nations, the descendants of Jacob's twin brother Esau, were also asked to accept it (Piska 12.20). That they chose not to, does not mean, however, that kind and honorable men are not to be found among them; on the contrary, even those among them who are not kind and honorable are capable of turning to Him (Piska 3.3).

God's choice of Israel is irrevocable (Piska 1.3), and thus in different guises—as a mighty man waging war, for example, or as an elder teaching Torah—He seeks to preserve them in the world and bring them to redemption. Whatever His guise, however, He is one and the same (Piska 12.24). From Him comes all substance (Piska 8.2). The heeding of His commandments sustains the world and Him who made it (Piska 12.1). Hence, when the children of Israel study Torah, it bestows such strength that no nation in the world can overcome Israel in battle (Piska 15.5). Indeed, if Jews do no more than gather in synagogues and in houses of learning, even if they do not pray or study Torah in these places, God gathers with them (Piska 28.8), for by being in such places, they may come to a change of heart and end up in prayer and study (Piska 15.5). God delights, of course, in those who study Torah and meditate upon its teachings, but He delights even more in those who live by its precepts (S1.2; Piska 6.1).

Because they are His chosen people, whenever the children of Israel have cried out to Him, "Come hither! Come hither!" He has come running towards them like a gazelle (Piska 5.8). Indeed, long ago He brought Himself to surrender to them, shrinking His Presence, so to speak, in order to dwell among them in the Tabernacle (Piska 1.3). Even with Tabernacle and Temple gone, the Presence still abides on the bare crag of rock which is the site of the Temple, the "foundation" upon which the world is set (Piska 26.4). Though the Temple is destroyed, its Western Wall, according to His promise, will stand for ever as visible proof of the abiding of His Presence there (Piska 5.8). Even in ruins, the Temple, because of His Presence, has brought righteous men to the fore, more righteous men, in fact, than when the Temple stood intact (Piska 20.5). As the Presence dwells in the Temple for the sake of His chosen people, so, for their sake, the Presence also dwells in the Land of Israel, the land which among all the lands of the world God loves most (Piska 23.10). So strong is the bond between the Land and the children of Israel that it moves them to righteousness while they dwell in it (Piska 23.10), and when they are exiled from it and God goes into exile with them (Piska 13.9), it becomes so desolate that no birds fly over it (Piska 13.10).

The redemption of His chosen people and through her the redemption of all mankind—this has been God's aim from the beginning of the history of the human spirit, a history that began on the sixth day of creation when He made Adam and Eve and brought them to judgment (Piska 23.1). To realize His aim, God gave Israel the Torah for a guide and has rewarded or punished her on her journey through history according to her obedience or disobedience to His commands. When she has sinned, He has punished her—has brought Amalek and Edom to oppress her (Piska 3.a, 4), has sent her into exile and captivity (Piska 13.7, 8), has reduced her to poverty (Piska 14.3), but in all His affliction of her has never forsaken her (Piska 17).

He has not forsaken Israel because the merit of the Fathers has interceded for her (Piska 2.1; 3.c; 5.8; 9.9). He has not forsaken Israel because the Prophets have ever reminded Him of His mercy (Piska 12.1). He has not forsaken Israel because righteous men have died to atone for her sins (Piska 26.11). He has not forsaken Israel because her righteous men have studied Torah diligently and have lived by its precepts (Piska 11.14, 16, 22). He has not forsaken Israel because sinful men have repented of their transgressions and turned to Him (Piska 24.8, 9). And He has not forsaken Israel for His own sake: when Israel does not do His will, they weaken Him; when Israel does His will, He is strengthened (Piska 25.1).

By the doing of God's will, Israel grows in righteousness (Piska 19.6) and brings ever closer the coming of the Messiah, he whom we bless again and again (S6.5). His advent will be preceded by times of terrible affliction (Piska 5.9), but they are the sure signs of Israel's redemption (S5.3). In the blessed world-to-come the Temple will be rebuilt on Zion, and the boundaries of Jerusalem will extend upwards to the very throne of glory (Piska 20.7). The "Holy One will create us anew" (Piska 27.3), and mankind will live in beauty and delight (S2.4), in serenity and peace (Piska 18.6).

E. Matters Biographical, Historical, and Factual

As we have previously noted, the matters of the Pĕsiḳta dĕ-Rab̲ Kahăna are not limited to Biblical narrative and doctrine but range freely into the traditions, legends, anecdotes, and so on that had accumulated around the special concerns of the work up to the time that it was put together by its compiler. Hence, in citing the individual Rabbis whose exegetical comments over the centuries make up the bulk of the Pĕsiḳta, the work often does something more than give them their rightful credit for the ingenuity or accuracy or profundity of their insights; it also includes stories of the more notable Rabbis—biographical anecdotes, accounts of miracles, and the like. These stories show that the Rabbis were not scholarly recluses, but that they practiced what they preached, and thus are exemplars of piety and righteousness whom the children of Israel are to emulate as they are to emulate the Patriarchs and the Prophets and all the righteous men and women of Torah. Indeed, the Pĕsiḳta searches out the righteous everywhere, for it also tells us stories of the piety of the wives and mothers of the Rabbis, of the good deeds of men and women in Israel, and even of heathen notable for their exemplary conduct. In this connection, it is again worth noting how these stories of individual persons in the specific situations of experience convey to us with dramatic liveliness a sense of religious doctrines being lived out in everyday life. The stories are intended, in their own way, to exert a didactic force such as are intended by the religious and ethical doctrines that the Rabbis expound in the Pĕsiḳta.

Many of the stories simply illustrate chaste or pious conduct in observing the precepts of Torah or in performing good deeds. We are told, for example, how Kimḥith (first century, B.C.E.) was so modest a woman that not even the beams of her house had ever beheld the hair of her head (Piska 26.10); how R. Zadok (first century, B.C.E.) and R. 'Aḳib̲a (second century, C.E.)

resisted sexual temptation (S3.2); how Simeon the Just (second century, B.C.E.) built two runways for the two Red Heifers prepared during his ministry (Piska 4.7); how R. Simeon ben Yoḥai (*fl.* 140–65 C.E.) was so aglow with Torah that in his own person he was the rainbow, the token of the covenant between God and earth (Piska 11.15); how R. Simeon's son, R. Eleazar, found himself drained of his extraordinary physical strength once he had given himself to the study of Torah (Piska 11.22); how radiant was the face of R. Abbahu (late third century, C.E.) when he came upon a new insight in his study of Torah (Piska 4.4); how deference to masters of Torah was such that R. Tanḥum bar R. Jeremiah (late third century) would not venture to render legal decisions when he learned that his teacher lived nearby (Piska 26.7); how the mother of R. Tanḥum bar R. Ḥiyya (late third century), whenever she set out to buy food for her son, would end up by buying a double amount, one portion for him and an equal portion for the poor (Piska 27.3); how a heathen king, more or less contemporary with the Rabbis, was exemplary in his dispensing of justice (Piska 9.1).

A number of stories tell of encounters of one kind or another between Rabbis and heathen, skeptics, or heretics. R. Johanan ben Zakkai (10–80 C.E.), for example, sought to explain to a heathen the mystery of the Red Heifer (Piska 4.7); Rabban Gamaliel II (*fl.* 80–120 C.E.) told a heathen why God once revealed Himself in a lowly thorn bush (Piska 1.2); R. Meir (*fl.* 140–65) put down a Cuthean who questioned Jacob's way of tithing (Piska 10.6); R. Jose ben Ḥalafta (*fl.* 140–65) made it clear to a Roman lady how God's matchmaking differed from hers (Piska 2.4); Levi ben Sisi (early third century, C.E.) made marauding soldiers vanish into thin air (Piska 24.18); R. Johanan (died 279 C.E.) rebuked a heretic who expressed doubt of the glory of Jerusalem rebuilt (Piska 18.5).

Other stories and allusions are of particular interest because they throw light on Israel's experience of other peoples and nations and hence of other customs, other beliefs, other religions. It should be noted, however, that these stories and allusions, while they give us glimpses of the political and social circumstances of Israel in the time of the Rabbis, are, in fact, no more than glimpses because the Rabbis were not writing history or politics or economics or tracts against customs, beliefs, or religions different from their own; the stories or allusions connected with these matters are incidental to the Pĕsiḳta's primary purpose—the religious instruction and edification of Israel. Thus, when we are told that for eighteen years Nebuchadnezzar hesitated, despite the bidding of a Divine Voice, to proceed against Jerusalem, the intention is not to reveal some aspect of Nebuchadnezzar's character, but to indicate the awe in which Israel's holy city was held even by a powerful heathen king. And when he finally moved upon Jerusalem, he is held to be not an independent political figure, but an instrument chosen by God as a scourge of Israel for her transgressions (Piska 5.9). Nebuzaradan, Nebuchadnezzar's general, was used by God for the same purpose; his bloody acts were requital for the iniquities—trickery, venality, heartlessness—which the inhabitants of Jerusalem had sought to hide (Piska 15.9). When Alexander the Great visited a principality whose king dispensed true equity rather than Alexander's highhanded brand of justice (Piska 9.1), the story means to say little about Alexander and much about the arbitrary exercise of power. Similarly, Alexander's conviction that whenever he saw the face of Simeon the Just before a battle, he would be victorious, is not mentioned out of deference to Alexander's military prowess but in recognition of the charisma of Simeon's virtue (Piska 4.9). The only detail we are given of Vespasian's devastation of Jerusalem is that the city's 480 synagogues, each of which had a school for younger students and one for older students, were destroyed (Piska 15.7), and we are given this detail not to illustrate the Emperor's ruthlessness but rather to show that for Israel the supreme deprivation is the loss of opportunity to study Torah.

Allusions to Israel's subjugation to Rome are fairly common in the Pĕsiḳta, but again these allusions, revealing as they may be, are used to give dramatic force to moral and religious teachings. We are told, for example, of the summary operation of Roman courts of law in order to explain why Samuel in proceeding against Agag, king of Amalek, dispensed with the precautions in behalf of the accused, precautions which mark judicial procedure in Jewish courts (Piska 3.6; 24.8–10). An allusion to Hadrian's persecution in the second century C.E. is brought in for the purpose of extolling Jewish martyrs who died to hallow God's name (Piska 11.4). So, too, the intention of the allusion to Rome's rapacious taxation of Israel is the contrast to God's modest levy upon Israel for funds to maintain the religious and municipal services of Jerusalem (Piska 2.2).

As for the Rabbis' reaction to the other religions of their day, the Pĕsiḳta reveals throughout their abhorrence of idolatry as well as their conviction that in God's good time it will disappear from the face of the earth and all mankind will be united in worship of the Holy One alone (Piska 3.2, 15). It is to be wondered naturally whether the Pĕsiḳta argues against Christianity, but nowhere in the work is there any direct allusion to Christian doctrines. It is barely possible that in two places in the text there are oblique allusions to such doctrines, but if they are such, they are not argumentative, and the greater likelihood by far is that they are meant to do no more than stress Jewish doctrines. Hence, when we read in Piska 1.1–4 of God's withdrawal from the earth because of man's sinfulness and then of His gradual return, which began in the time of Abraham and culminated in the time of Moses, it is plain that God's return to earth and His "inhabitation" of it is essential to man's redemption. But it is straining the point to consider His "inhabitation" of the world as a Jewish polemic against the idea of God's incarnation as a human being. At another place in the Pĕsiḳta, the significance of the Passover lamb and the two lambs offered daily in the Temple is that they remind God of Israel's willingness to offer up their lives for the sake of their covenant with Him (Piska 5.17). Again, it would be straining to assume that the reference to the Passover lamb is directed against the idea of the "Passover lamb" (1 Corinthians 5–7) as representing an individual: the Rabbis appear to have used the phrase simply as a common and convenient metaphor for the entire people of Israel.

We can conclude this sampling of biographical and historical matters in the Pĕsiḳta by observing once more that the Rabbis did not live in scholarly seclusion and that this fact in itself explains much of the work's appeal to the modern reader. Intense as was the Rabbis' devotion to the study of Torah, they were well aware of what was going on in the world around them. They did not separate their religious life from their secular life, for life to them was all of a piece, to be lived from day to day in accordance with God's precepts.

Zealous to make these precepts living realities in the day-to-day life of Israel, they rarely talk in fleshless abstractions, but turn to vivid presentation and illustration of these realities at work in the events of history and in the lives of historical personages. We see further evidence of the Rabbis' skill in communicating moral truths in their ready resort to Greek terms current in Palestine in their time and in their extensive use of specific, concrete images, homely details, drawn from a variety of everyday activities—farming, fishing, grape growing, sheep herding, fish mongering, diamond trading, money lending, produce selling, flour refining, metal working, and the like. The otherwise unkown Greek word *nikologos,* "one regularly victorious in courts" (Piska 23.7), is used in reference to Abraham, Isaac, and Jacob as Israel's advocates before God. The term [*ta hiera*] *hilaria* (Piska 28.f) signifies "an occasion for a king's rejoicing." In reference to gladiatorial contests, the spectators are spoken of as *theoretai* and the gladiator who fought the beasts as *kynēgos* (Piska 28.3). It is worth noting that the Rabbis' employment of Greek terms preserves in a number of instances meanings which other sources do not always record.

As for references to everyday activities and matters, we are told, for example, that the larvae of certain harmful beetles which deposit their eggs on the roots of trees are killed by exposure to air (Piska 23.8); that a field growing thistles, if sown to wheat, will produce a good crop, and that a field growing cockles, if sown to barley, will likewise produce a good crop (Piska 10.8); that the wood of the *šiṭṭim* trees used in the building of the Tabernacle was a variety of cedar that grew in Lebanon (Piska 1.2); that heavy rains in the region of Sharon caused houses to collapse, burying their inhabitants (Piska 23.4); that when Israel went into exile in Babylon, hundreds of species of kosher fish also went into exile, all of which came back, except for the carp (Piska 13.10).

Elsewhere the Pĕsiḳta praises men of the East who do not kiss on the mouth, but on the hand; who do not tear their food with their teeth, but eat it with a knife; and who in order to prevent eavesdropping, take counsel only in an open field (Piska 4.3). We are told further of a tame snake which warns its master of danger (Piska 11.11); of six characteristics which typify a horse (Piska 3.3); of gourmet food cooked in vessels standing on tripods (Piska 6.1); of the devices by which women attract men (Piska 17.6; 18.3); of six signs of improving health in a person who is ill (Piska 19.5); of a lamp wherein oil and water work together (Piska 1.3); of reckoning the calendar by the phases of the moon (Piska 5.15); of how the Leviathan's scales are held together (S2.4); of God's use of Roman military tactics in His proceeding against the Egyptians (Piska 7.11).

As we have observed, the great many details of everyday life that attend the religious truths advanced in the Pĕsiḳta serve to reinforce these truths. The presence of these details, it may therefore be concluded, is not the result of a kind of naiveté in literary composition. Nor, on the other hand, is their presence the result of a self-conscious literary sophistication. They are in the Pĕsiḳta, rather, because of the very origin of the work. It is a work which is rooted in Scripture and which grew out of Scripture, and so in its multiplicity of detail it is a spontaneous and unconscious imitation of Scripture whose precepts are interwoven with and inseparable from the events and circumstances, small and large, ordinary and extraordinary, painful and joyous, in the life of Israel.

II. The Structure of the Work

A. The Methods of Discourse in the Piska

The Pĕsiḳta dĕ-Raḇ Kahăna, as we have already observed, is a compilation of discourses inspired by the Biblical lessons read in the order of the synagogue service for special Sabbaths and festal days in the Jewish year. The compilation, made sometime in the fifth century C.E., is attributed to R. Kahana, who presumably collected the Rabbinic homilies and comments on the lessons and arranged each of the Piskas as well as the entire work in the order in which we read them today. His task could not have been an easy one, for he had to collect comments that had been made over a period of five hundred years beginning with the Schools of Hillel and Shammai about the first century B.C.E. and ending, to the best of our knowledge, about the fourth century C.E. It is possible that some of these comments had been committed to writing, but we have no definite evidence to this effect.[9] What seems to be more likely is that the comments, transmitted orally from genera-

9. See below, Section III-B.

ion to generation, were gathered by R. Kahana from his contemporaries—Rabbis, scholars, students of Torah in general—wherever he found them in synagogues, in schools, and in houses of study.

He undertook not only to collect the materials, but to arrange them in chronological order, citing the earliest comment and its author first and continuing with subsequent comments on the verse by later Rabbis, who often began their own comments by citing their predecessors on the verse in hand. R. Kahana's arrangement of the comments was both chronological and topical: he assigned the comments not only to the Piska whose discourse was inspired by the Biblical lesson for a special Sabbath or festal day, but also grouped the comments around the particular topics derived from the Rabbis' explication of words, phrases, and verses within the lesson.

The number of comments that had accumulated over five centuries was considerable. Hence it is not uncommon to find a Piska that begins with three or four brief dramatic homilies (*pĕṯiḥahs*) composed by different preachers at different times over the years, most of the homilies leading up to the same verse, usually the first one in the lesson, and each homily taking a different approach to the verse. Likewise, following upon the *pĕṯiḥahs*, one finds extended exegesis, accumulated from century to century, of the meaning of certain words, or phrases, or verses in the Biblical lesson. The compiler of the work is himself invisibly present in it though he never cites himself; one is aware, however, of his hand joining comments together and making connections wherever necessary in order to maintain the force and clarity of the discourse in the Piska and bring it to its concluding peroration.

What we have in each Piska, then, is no mere string of undifferentiated comments, but a carefully arranged sequence beginning with one or more *pĕṯiḥahs*, going on to precise and extended exegesis of certain words, phrases, and verses that present special problems of interpretation, and coming to a climax with a reassuring peroration, derived from the theme of the Piska, of God's concern for Israel.[10]

It is of particular interest to note at this point that the practice of interpreting Scripture for the pleasure and instruction of congregations and assemblies led to remarkable skill in public discourse, a skill in which Sages such as Shemaiah and Aḇtalyon (*ca.* 50 B.C.E.), Ben Azzai and Ben Zoma (90–130 C.E.), R. Eliezer ben R. Simeon (*ca.* 200 C.E.), Levi ben Sisi (*ca.* 200 C.E.), R. Johanan (*ca.* 250), R. Levi and R. Samuel bar Isaac[11] are said to have excelled. We are told of R. Johanan, for example, that people ran to make certain they could get into the synagogue or house of

10. For a masterly analysis of the structure of Piskas, see Abraham Goldberg, *Kirjath Sefer*, *43* (1967), 68–79.

11. See B. Pes 70b; Soṭ 49b; Piska 27.1, 24.18; P. Hor 3:7, 48b; Piska 23.12, 24.11.

study where he was to hold forth.[12] Audiences often broke into applause at the skill of the preachers or their aides, and their appearance at synagogues and houses of study frequently outdrew the attendance at Roman theaters and circuses. Indeed, the preachers and their audiences were sometimes so carried away as to make it appear, according to Chrysostom's (345?–407 C.E.) acidulous remark, that "there was no difference between a synagogue and a theater."[13] Jews as well were occasionally critical of the way in which the preachers' aides performed, saying that they "raised their voices in sing-song style to make the people listen."[14] Despite such criticism, it would seem that preachers or interpreters of Scripture enjoyed greater public favor than did civic leaders, scribes, scholars, Sages, and even Prophets.[15]

It is possible that the *pĕṯiḥah* originated in houses of study as a product of the diligent study and interpretation which all Midrashim demonstrate, and the fact that it came to be part of the service in the synagogue may have been due to the zeal of the scholars to make known to the public at large what new or deeper meanings they had discovered in their study of Scripture. The striking method of the *pĕṯiḥah* was no doubt a dramatic teaching device, but it is not mere ingenuity that it displays, for it turns on the absolute conviction that every letter and syllable, every word and phrase of Torah is charged with infinite, and therefore inexhaustible, meaning because their composer was God himself. They shine out not only with their own divine light, but throw their light upon every other part of Torah. Hence, two verses, no matter how far apart from each other and no matter how seemingly unrelated, are taken by the Rabbis to throw light on each other when they are brought into conjunction and their connection is sought out.

If we come now to an examination of Piska 1, we can find ample illustration not only of the *pĕṯiḥah* but of the extended exegesis and peroration typical of all the discourses in R. Kahana's *Compilation*. The Piska, inspired by Hanukkah, begins with a *pĕṯiḥah* whose climax is the first verse of the Biblical lesson read for the day: *And it came to pass on the day that Moses*

12. See P. Hor 3:7, 48b.

13. Chrysostom, *Orations Against the Jews*, 1, Sec. 3, end; 2, beginning. Professor Morton Smith of Columbia University provided the references.

14. "The preacher's aide" was the *mĕturgĕman*. See Tos Meḡ 3, end (Lieberman, *TFK, Mo'eḏ*, 364); and Heinemann, *Dĕrašoṯ bĕ-ṣibbur*, etc., 10–11. Generally, a preacher "did not impart instruction in his own person. He gave an aide the gist of his subject, and the latter conveyed it in an amplified form to the congregation." See Eccles. Rabbah 7:12 (Soncino tr. 179, n. 3). See also Gen. Rabbah 80:1 (TA, 951), and A. A. Hal-lewi, *Ša'are ha-Ăgaḏah* (Tel Aviv, 5724/1963), p. 8.

15. See *The Fathers according to R. Nathan*, 31 (YJS, *10*, 126), B. Sanh 38b, AZ 5a, and MTeh 139.6 (YJS, *13*, 2, 347). In other passages—such as B. Suk 38b and BB 119b—we are told that preachers came last in public esteem.

had made an end of setting up the Tabernacle, and had anointed it and sanctified it, etc. (Num. 7:1). The *pĕṯiḥah* itself begins by citing a verse from the Song of Songs, *I am come into my garden, my sister, my bride* (5:1). As is typical of the *pĕṯiḥah*, this verse seems to have little or no connection with the verse from Numbers cited just above, but as we have already observed, the choice of just such an apparently unrelated verse was an oratorical device calculated to provoke the hearers' attention and drive home the point of the *pĕṯiḥah*. Having cited the verse from the Song of Songs, the *pĕṯiḥah* leaves it hanging and with no transition whatever turns to tell a parable of a queen who had been expelled from royal estate. Before consenting to return, she demanded that all the perquisites she had formerly enjoyed be restored to her. The application of the parable follows: like the queen, mankind at the beginning of time in the Garden of Eden had enjoyed royal estate, the greatest of its perquisites being God's presence on earth. But Adam's transgression and the transgression of succeeding generations of men made God withdraw His presence from the earth, this withdrawal amounting, in effect, to the expulsion of mankind from royal estate. With the coming of good men, however—men such as Abraham, Isaac, and Jacob—God began His gradual return to earth, and Israel, speaking for mankind, was then emboldened to say, *Let my Beloved come* [*back*] *into His garden* (Song 4:16)—that is, let Him restore the perquisites which mankind had once enjoyed when God walked in the Garden of Eden (Gen. 3:8). And because of the rise of good men, God consented to return, saying to Israel, *I am come* [*back*] *into My garden, My sister, My bride* (Song 5:1).

Thus far, the *pĕṯiḥah* has made no connection between this verse and the first verse of the lesson from Numbers, and we are still in suspense: what we have at this point, however, is an allegorical reading of the verse from the Song of Songs, a reading which identifies the "I" of the verse as God and the "bride" of the verse as Israel. The *pĕṯiḥah* now goes on to ask: "When did the great event of God's coming back to earth take place?" The answer is "in the days of Moses," whose merit was such as to bring to a conclusion God's return. The day of His return was Israel's bridal day, the day when the King restored to His spouse her former perquisites, the greatest of these being His presence on earth.

We have still to wait for the final link that connects the first verse of the *pĕṯiḥah* (*I am come into My garden*, etc.) with the first verse from Numbers (*And it came to pass on the day that Moses had made an end of setting up the Tabernacle*, etc.). Nevertheless, we have come very close now to the solution of the mystery, for Moses has been introduced into the allegory of God's return by way of his setting up the Tabernacle, God's dwelling place on earth. What all this has to do with Hanukkah now becomes clear. Hanukkah is the festival that celebrates the Maccabees' restoration of the Temple, God's dwelling place on earth, and thus signifies His return to His spouse,

Israel, just as Moses' setting up of the Tabernacle had also signified His return through Israel to mankind. Hence, the *pĕṯiḥah* not only connects logically its two seemingly unrelated verses, but justifies the connection rhetorically, for the climactic verse is read by an exegetical mode—in this instance by way of puns, not readily apparent in the verse—so that instead of the usual reading, *And it came to pass on the day that Moses had set up the Tabernacle*, etc., we are to read: *It was on* [*Israel's*] *bridal* (*klt*) *day that Moses brought to a conclusion* (*klwt*) [*the coming back to earth that God had begun in the days of Abraham*]. It would seem, indeed, that the Hebrew pun on the words *klt* ("bridal") and *klwt* ("brought to a conclusion") was the seed from which the *pĕṯiḥah* grew like an elaborate plant.

The import of the parallel between Moses' setting up of the Tabernacle and the Maccabees' restoration of the Temple goes beyond mere ingenuity. What the *pĕṯiḥah* is stressing finally is God's Love of Israel and, through Israel, of mankind. Though He may remove Himself from time to time because of men's transgressions, their good deeds will ever induce Him to return and dwell among them.

On the way to establishing the connection between its two verses, the *pĕṯiḥah* concerns itself with a number of other related matters. For example, we are told that Torah teaches us good manners, as that a groom is not to come to his bride until she gives him leave. We are to infer this rule of conduct, says R. Ḥanina, from the two verses cited from the Song of Songs, the first of which, *Let my beloved come into his garden* (Song 4:16), is the bride's invitation to her groom, while the second, *I am come into my garden* (Song 5:11), is his acceptance.

With regard to God's presence on earth at the beginning of time, R. Tanḥuma asks us to note that the Song of Songs does not say, "I am come into a garden," but *I am come into My garden*, and then states that for *ganni* ("My garden") we are to read *ginuni* ("My bride's bower")—that is, My and mankind's dwelling place at the beginning of time. That God's presence dwelt on earth at the beginning of time is proved, says R. Abba bar Kahana, by the verse *They used to hear the voice of the Lord as* [Adam] *would walk in the garden* (Gen. 3:8). The verse does not really say "would walk in," but "walked away from"; hence, concludes the Rabbi, the verse refers not to Adam but to God who, in His anger at Adam's sin, walked away from him towards heaven. To confirm this reading, R. Aibu points out that in the same verse the words *Adam and his wife were all but hid* (*ibid.*) indicate that the instant God walked away Adam was deposed from his high place, and his stature was reduced to no more than a hundred cubits.

As to those whose sins after Adam's gave God additional cause to withdraw further and further from earth and those whose good deeds gave Him cause to return, the Rabbis are explicit. Concerning the righteous, R.

Isaac cites the verse, *The righteous shall inherit the earth and dwell thereon in eternity* (Ps. 37:29), and giving it a characteristic Rabbinical turn takes it to signify that it is the righteous who will cause the Eternal to dwell on earth. It was Moses who brought to a culmination the righteousness of the good men who from Abraham on had preceded him: hence, *It was on [Israel's] bridal day that Moses brought to a conclusion [the coming back to earth that God had begun in the days of Abraham]*.

The second and third *pĕṯiḥahs* of the Piska proceed in much the same fashion as the first. The second also takes its first verse from the Song of Songs—*King Solomon made himself a pavilion* (3:9)—but is somewhat less mystifying than the first *pĕṯiḥah*, for we are told at once that by *pavilion* is meant the Tabernacle, the Pavilion of God, and that by King Solomon is meant the King of the universe. With typical attention to the possibilities of hidden meaning in Scripture, the commentator takes the Hebrew words for *King Solomon made himself* to signify that the King of the universe, requiring a means of private communication with Israel, made the Tabernacle for Himself. This idea is stressed in the *pĕṯiḥah* by means of a conversation between Rabban Gamaliel and a heathen, as well as by a parable and other modes of exegesis, and is further supported by citation of the verse *And when Moses went into the Tent of Meeting that God might speak with him*, etc. (Num. 7:89).

Then, by pointing to the similarity in the materials used for Solomon's pavilion and in Moses' Tabernacle, the *pĕṯiḥah* demonstrates the identity of the two, even as it proves that no part of the Tabernacle was devoid of the divine Presence—indeed, the comment concludes, nothing on earth, not even the lowliest thorn bush is devoid of His presence. The *pĕṯiḥah*, still stressing the omnipresence of God, finishes with a striking analogy: as a cave at the shore is filled by the sea without the sea's being diminished elsewhere, so the Tabernacle was filled with God's presence without His presence being diminished elsewhere. We are then brought again to the climax of the *pĕṯiḥah*, the citation of the first verse from the Scriptural reading for Hanukkah. In this *pĕṯiḥah* the Tabernacle is pointed up as God's own dwelling place on earth, and His presence in it and hence everywhere else in the world is, in a sense, reestablished by the Maccabees through their restoration of His Temple.

The third *pĕṯiḥah*, longest of the three in the Piska, also opens with a verse from the Song of Songs that is usually read *Go forth, O ye daughters of Zion, and gaze upon king Solomon*, etc. (3:11). But the *pĕṯiḥah* finds special hidden significance in the puns that are interwoven in the words of the verse, so that it is read *Go forth, O younglings, whose name Zion indicates that you bear a sign*, and again we are left to wonder, as doubtless did the preacher's audience long, long ago, what light this verse can throw on the verse with which the *pĕṯiḥah* will conclude: *And it came to pass on the day that Moses had made an end of setting up the Tabernacle*, etc. The *pĕṯiḥah* begins its movement towards this verse by taking the word *sign* from the verse cited above as referring to the sons of Israel who, for the sake of the Holy One, bear the sign of circumcision, the sign upon head and face of hair unshaved, and the sign of fringes upon the corners of their garments. These children of Israel are bidden to *gaze upon King Solomon* whose name means peace: this is to say, according to the commentator, that by *King Solomon* is meant the King of the universe, He who has the power to make peace by bringing all the different things and beings in His creation to surrender to one another. *All things in creation are at peace with Him* (Job 25:2), says R. Johanan, because He has set all things each in its own place, and though they are all different, they dwell with one another and do no harm to one another. These observations the Rabbis amply illustrate by reference to the elements of nature, the make-up of angels, the working of a lamp, and by the parable of two mutually hostile legions of the king who made up their differences and joined together to fight for him. Indeed, God's love of peace is so strong that He even brings Himself to surrender to His people Israel—and at this point we first see clearly the movement of the *pĕṯiḥah* towards its climax—surrendering His infinity, so to speak, and shrinking His presence in order to dwell in the finite limits of the Tabernacle that Moses built for His dwelling place.

The climax of the *pĕṯiḥah* is put off, however, by the Rabbi's turning to comment at some length on the Tabernacle itself—its colors, we are told, were suggested to Moses by God Himself, and it was modeled after the Tabernacle in heaven above so as to be a fit dwelling place for Him. That He was willing to shrink His presence and dwell in the earthly Tabernacle proves, says R. Eleazar, His great love for Israel.

At this point we become aware that the long previous section of the *pĕṯiḥah*, dealing with God's love and His making all things surrender to one another for the sake of peace, is an elaborate prelude in explanation of His surrender to Israel, an act of love. To convey a sense of this love, the *pĕṯiḥah* uses, as does the Piska throughout, the marriage imagery of the Song of Songs. Thus a comment tells us that *the day of His espousals* (Song 3:11) means the day of God's betrothal of Israel, and *the day of the gladness of His heart* (*ibid.*) means the day He entered the Tabernacle. Hence, says the *pĕṯiḥah*, citing its climactic verse, *It was on* [*Israel's*] *bridal day that Moses brought to a conclusion* [*God's coming back to earth*, etc.] (Num. 7:1). We are to conclude, then, in connection with the celebration of Hanukkah that God's dwelling in the Temple restored by the Maccabees is, like His dwelling in the Tabernacle built by Moses, an act of self-surrender that proves His love of Israel.

The first three *pĕṯiḥahs*, each in its own way, make much the same point: God's love of His people. But the fourth and final *pĕṯiḥah*, much the shortest of the four, takes a different turn and stresses the idea of God's power. The *pĕṯiḥah* gets under way by quoting Proverbs 30:4, *Who ascends up into heaven, and descended? Who gathers the wind in his fists? Who binds the waters in his garment? Who raises up all those who have come to their end upon the earth? What is his name, and what is his son's name, if thou knowest?* He is the Holy One, answers the commentator, and in proof cites appropriate verses from Scripture, concluding with the answer to the question, *What is his son's name?* "His son's name is Israel, My first-born" (Exod. 4:22).

Following upon this identification of God and of Israel, however, is a set of other answers to the questions. The "who" of the verse is successively identified, first, as the man who tithes generously, then as Elijah, and finally as Moses, each identification being supported by quotation of appropriate verses from Scripture. These other identifications are not to be taken as mere digressions. Their presence in the *pĕṯiḥah* simply shows the Rabbis' absolute conviction of the limitless depths of Torah—the word of God is as infinite as He and to the searching eye and mind of mortal man yields up meaning upon meaning upon meaning. This is not to say that the multiple meanings of some word, phrase, or verse can be inconsistent with one another or even opposed to one another. On the contrary, one of the aims of the Rabbis is to explain or reconcile apparent inconsistencies or seeming contradictions and to show the absolute consistency, coherence, and harmony of meaning throughout Torah. Thus the four different identifications of the "who" in the verse from Proverbs are not only considered to be correct—they are unified by the idea of the power of righteousness, whether it is God Himself who is exercising this power or a nameless mortal who tithes generously.

The *pĕṯiḥah* chooses, however, to focus on Moses because his building of the Tabernacle is the subject of the Scriptural lesson for Hanukkah, the festival that celebrates the Maccabees' restoration of the Temple. The climax of the *pĕṯiḥah*, the citation of the first verse in the lesson, is preceded, therefore, by a repetition of the question from Proverbs, *Who hath established all the ends of the earth?*, the answer of the commentator being, "Moses, by means of the Tent of Meeting." The climactic verse, *It was on the day that Moses brought to a conclusion the setting up of the Tabernacle* (Num. 7:1), is thereupon given, but R. Joshua ben Levi, citing R. Simeon ben Yoḥai, gives the verse a surprising turn, and we see that the climax of the *pĕṯiḥah* is yet to come. R. Joshua points out that the text does not simply say "setting up of the Tabernacle" but says *setting up of* [*another*] *along with the Tabernacle*. This other, set up along with the Tabernacle, the Rabbi goes on, was the earth: until the Tabernacle was set up, the earth was unstable; it became stable only when the Tabernacle was set up. Hence, the first verse of the Scriptural lesson climaxing the *pĕṯiḥah* is to be read *It was on the day that brought to a conclusion the setting up of* [*another*] *along with the Tabernacle* (Num. 7:1).

The *pĕṯiḥah* must have left its audience to draw some obvious inferences. With the Tabernacle set up and God's presence in it, the earth was set on a firm foundatiom: with the restoration of the Temple and God's presence in it, the Maccabees, like Moses, brought stability to the earth. Thus, it is God's presence in the world that we celebrate on Hanukkah.

The four *pĕṯiḥahs* take up about two-thirds of Piska 1; the concluding third is given over to a variety of exegetical comments on individual words and phrases in the Scriptural lesson. In the first verse the word *klt*, for example, usually taken to mean "brought to an end," is spelled defectively in the text, thus permitting it to be read *kallat*, "bridal," and hence as referring to the day that Israel entered the bridal chamber as God's bride. But taking it in its usual sense, the Rabbis speculate as to just what Moses "brought to an end," suggesting variously that he brought to an end his daily setting up and taking apart of the Tabernacle, that he brought to an end the existence of demons in the world, that he brought to an end the enmity in the world, that he brought to an end the instability of the world by setting up the Tabernacle. The commentary then goes on to consider why there were two anointings, referred to in the words, *Moses . . . had anointed it* (the Tabernacle) *and sanctified it* (Num. 7:1b) and *Moses anointed them* (the vessels in the Tabernacle) *and sanctified them* (ibid.). Like consideration is given to a similar repetition in the two verses, *Thou shalt couple the curtains* (Exod. 26:6) and *Thou shalt couple the Tent together* (Exod. 26:11).

The next comment is concerned with the princes of Israel, mentioned in the second verse of the Scriptural lesson, and explains why they were named princes and what they did for the children of Israel. The offering of the princes to the Lord was six wagons (Num. 7:3) in which to carry the parts of the Tabernacle, and this number is variously explained as corresponding to the six days of creation, to the six orders of Mishnah, to the six Matriarchs, to the six firmaments, to the six commandments which a king is bound to obey. Mention of the king and his throne leads to description of the throne's decoration. The wagons themselves are described as *ṣaḇ,* and this word, according to its various etymologies, can mean that the outer surface of the wagons' frames was reticulated like a lizard's skin; that the wagons were gaily decorated; that they were fully equipped; that the body of the wagons was shaped like a bent bow.

From discussions of the meanings of words and phrases concerning the wagons, the exegesis passes to Scripture's account of the oxen that drew the wagons. We are informed that each pair of princes contributed one wagon and that the prince of each Tribe provided one ox. These oxen were to become by purchase the property of the congregation of Israel, and in connection with their purchase it is explained by citation of a number of verses from different sections of Torah how it was that the Tribe of Issachar suggested to the princes the construction of the wagons for carrying the Tabernacle's parts. The exegesis concludes with consideration of how long the oxen remained alive and when and where they were finally sacrificed to the Lord.

From what has just been said, it is plain that the *pĕṯiḥahs* on the one hand and the exegetical commentary on the other follow two different approaches. Intent upon the dramatic impact of making a connection between the first verses of the Scriptural lesson and a verse remote from it in the Torah and apparently having no bearing upon it, the *pĕṯiḥah* advances step by step towards its climax. This is the method of the orator-preacher, and it is indeed striking in contrast to the matter-of-fact, analytical method of the scholar-Rabbi who searches out the meaning of words and phrases which, because of apparent irregularities in spelling and sound, or seeming anomalies or contradictions, require close examination and explanation. What we have in both approaches is an anomaly, in a sense: an oratorical device joined to an analytical method, though as we have seen, the oratorical device itself within its own confines also makes use of exegetical analysis. Actually, the two approaches complement each other: as we have seen, the *pĕṯiḥahs* stress general ideas, themes, or concepts as guides to the understanding of the Piska as a whole; the exegetical commentary that follows the *pĕṯiḥahs* clears up the particulars that, if left unexamined, would weaken the force of the *pĕṯiḥahs* and the significance of the Piska as a whole.

To return to our oxen: it is from their presence in the Scriptural lesson that the Piska's peroration comes. Brief as the peroration is, scarcely a half dozen lines, it makes its point and rounds off neatly the discourse of the Piska. It is a short sermon, uncluttered with commentary, simple and direct: if the life of oxen, for doing no more than cleaving to their task of conveying the Tabernacle about, was extended for many, many years, how much more life is to be given to Israel for cleaving to the Holy One! *But ye that cleave unto the Lord your God are alive, every one of you this day* (Deut. 4:4).

B. Norms of Exegesis

The question may be asked in regard to the Rabbis' exegesis of Scripture, whether they read their interpretations into it or read them out of it.[16] The Rabbis' own answer would unquestionably be that it would be a

16. For Maimonides' view, see William G. Braude, "Maimonides' Attitude to Midrash," *Kiev Jubilee Volume* (New York, 1971), pp. 75–82.

kind of blasphemy on their part to read any notions of theirs into what Scripture is saying, and that they were doing no more than uncovering to public view what is already there in Scripture but is not visible without diligent search. Nor are the procedures the Rabbis employ in their quest for meaning a matter of personal choice: they must obey a canon of interpretation, a specific set of norms, long established by tradition and custom, for sanction of their readings of Scripture.

As we have already noted, the Rabbis are particularly diligent in searching out the significance of seeming anomalies, irregularities, or contradictions in the text, for their sure belief is that in the word of God there can be no anomalies, irregularities, or contradictions, and that their responsibility is to demonstrate the absolute harmony of Scripture, any appearance to the contrary notwithstanding. What often draws their close attention, then, is the word whose spelling is defective, or presents a variety of meanings, or seems unnecessary in its context. The Rabbis' diligence goes further, of course—goes to the study of phrases that present similar problems of interpretation, and extends further still to lengthy exegesis of verses that appear to contradict each other, or entire passages whose meaning, on the one hand, appears obscure, or, on the other, seems superficially obvious.

Before we come to definition and illustration of the norms of interpretation, we can take a look at some examples of the Rabbis' working procedure. Consider, first, how seriously the pun is viewed in the following exchange and how it leads to rich interpretation of what is otherwise a verse of little import. When R. Huna bar Nathan asked R. Ashi, "What's the point of the verse *Kinah and Dimonah and Adadah*?" (Josh. 15:22), R. Ashi replied: "The verse is listing some towns in the Land of Israel." Whereupon R. Huna said: "Isn't it obvious that the verse is listing towns? The point I want to make is the lesson that R. Gebihah from [Be] Argiza got out of the names of the towns: Whosoever has cause for resentment [*ḳin'ah*] against his neighbor and yet holds his peace [*domem*], He that abides for all eternity [*'aḏe 'aḏ*] shall espouse his cause."[17]

Or consider the quest for meaning in a verse whose significance in its usual translation is in itself dramatically satisfying and seems to require little if any elucidation. Isaiah 49:14–15 reads: *But Zion said, "The Lord hath forsaken me, and the Lord hath forgotten me."* [Whereupon God replied]: *"Can a woman forget her sucking child, that she should not have compassion on the son of her womb? Yea, these may forget, yet will not I forget thee."* As the verses read, Zion is presented metaphorically as a wife who complains that her husband has forsaken and forgot-

17. B.Giṭ 7a.

ten her. God's response is oblique: He can no more forget Zion than a mother can forget her child. The change in metaphor from God as husband and Zion as wife to God as mother and Zion as child caught and held the searching, wondering Rabbinical eye, and so did the apparent mistake in the reference of the pronoun *these* to one person. The mind that went with the searching eye did not take these seeming errors in composition as errors: how could the word of God be in error? Evidently they were intended to serve as pointers to meanings hidden below the surface of the verses. So when Iḳa came to construe the words *Can a woman ('iššah) forget her sucking child ('ulah)*, he construed them by way of two key puns not as God's reassurance of Zion, but as Zion's reiteration of her anguish at being forsaken, and so took the verse to be saying: "Canst Thou forget the offerings made by fire (*'iššeh*), the whole burnt offerings (*'olah*)? Canst Thou have forgot the offerings Israel used to bring to Thee?" Then, Iḳa continued, God took this reference to past offerings made to Him as applying to Israel's good deeds, for He replied: "Evil deeds I forget, but good deeds I do not forget. I forget evil deeds, such as are alluded to in the words, 'These are thy gods, O Israel!' (Exod. 32:4), words which thou didst utter of a calf; but I do not forget good deeds, such as are alluded to in thy saying to me at Sinai 'All that the Lord hath spoken we will do, and obey'" (Exod. 24:7) (Piska 17.7). Thus Iḳa does not accept the plural *these* of the verse from Isaiah as an incorrect pronominal reference to a singular noun; on the contrary, simply because it cannot refer to a singular noun, the plural it refers to is to be found elsewhere in Scripture—is found, indeed, in a verse which uses the demonstrative *these* in reference to such evil deeds as worship of the golden calf. The Rabbis have thus led us by way of two puns from the metaphor of God and Zion as a woman and her sucking child to the burnt offerings made to God,[18] these offerings themselves being symbolic of Israel's good deeds while the *these* of the verse is taken to refer to Israel's evil deeds. Accordingly, Iḳa reads the conclusion of the verse—God's reply to Zion—as follows: *Yea, thy 'these' I shall forget, but [thy response to Me] at Sinai, I shall not forget.* The implication of the verse is consolatory: "It is true, O Zion," God is saying, "that I have forsaken you for the time being, but I have not forgotten you. What I have forgotten is your one great transgression, your worship of the golden calf: what I shall never forget is your wholehearted surrender to Me on Sinai." Thus, in

18. In a parallel comment the phrase *son of her womb* is construed as referring to the first-born males hallowed to God's service and to the first-born of animals brought as offerings. So Resh Laḳish in B.Ber 32b. See *Kiṯḇe MaHaRaL Mip-Prag*, ed. Abraham *Ḳariḇ* (Jerusalem 5704/1944), 2, 278–81.

explaining away what seems to be the incorrect reference of a single word, the Rabbis deepen the significance of the verse from Isaiah by uncovering in it a dialogue between God and Israel that encompasses millennia of Jewish experience.

Interpretations of Scripture such as those we have just examined could have no legitimacy unless their proponents arrived at them by following established norms of procedure. These may be put in four categories: (1) interpretation based on such methods of logic as inference, deduction, analogy, and the like; (2) interpretation derived from the context of words, phrases, verses, or passages and from certain peculiarities of composition and style; (3) interpretation derived from seeming irregularities or oddities of grammar and syntax; and (4) interpretation based on the conviction that every word—indeed, every syllable and letter—of Scripture is charged with significance that goes far beyond what the ordinary mortal eye sees in it.

The first category, which consists of norms that work by ordinary logic, R. Jose bar Ḥanina makes use of as he seeks to find out why in the first of the Ten Commandments God says, *I am the Lord thy God*, rather than "I am the Lord your God." The Rabbi's answer is that by using *thy*, God was addressing individually each man, woman, and child in Israel, and did so in order to suit His words to the capacity of each person to understand them. To prove his point, R. Jose shows from verses in Scripture that every person in Israel, young or old, tasted the manna that God provided in the wilderness according to each person's capacity in tasting. Hence, concludes the Rabbi, "If each and every person was enabled to taste the manna according to his particular capacity, how much more and more was each and every person enabled, according to his capacity, to hear the Divine Word" (Piska 12.25).[19]

For illustration of the second category of norms—definition or extension of meaning according to context—consider the verse in Scripture that follows upon the statement of Rebekah's death: God *appeared unto Jacob again . . . and blessed him* (Gen. 35:9). Scripture does not say what the blessing was, but, declares R. Aḥa, the context plainly indicates that it was the blessing of consolation spoken to mourners (Piska 3.1). The full meaning of a word or phrase is also arrived at by its use in a different context. So, when Moses tells Joshua on the day before Joshua was to defend the Israelites against Amalek's onslaught, *Tomorrow I will be standing on the peak* (Exod. 17.9), the statement appears to have merely incidental significance and is certainly not one likely to reassure or inspire Joshua. However, says an anonymous commentator, the word *standing* in

19. The argument here is *a fortiori*: for its use in demonstrating Israel's capacity to endure, see Piska 1.8; 16.1,5; 22.1,2; S3.2.

other contexts means "standing in prayer," a fitting and meaningful posture for Moses on the eve of Israel's battle (Piska 3.c).[20] The Rabbis in their quest for meaning scrutinize not only the context of words and phrases, but also the context of entire passages. Thus, says R. Berechiah in commenting on Proverbs 15:24, *The eye of the wise man goeth upward*, the verse is to be read *The eye of the wise man* [who studies Torah] *goeth upward* [on the Scroll as he reads it]—that is, his eye goes upward on the Scroll to see what has been said just before the passage he has in hand, and consequently he comes to ponder upon the sequence of the passages in Torah and why they follow in the order they do(Piska 23.5). If the passage in hand, says an anonymous commentator, happens to be the one that enjoins upon Jews the observance of New Year's Day, when the wise man's eye goes upward on the Scroll to the passage just above, he reads there that Jews are to practice charity when they harvest their crops. Because his eye has gone upward on the Scroll—that is, because he has read the passage in hand in its context—he comes to understand that on New Year's Day, the day of judgment, his and all Israel's obedience to such precepts of conduct as the giving of charity brings God not to destroy them[21] for their transgressions but only to chastise them. The repetition of the same words in different contexts also asks for extended interpretation. In nearly identical words, for example, both Leviticus 23:24 and Numbers 29:1 enjoin the observance of New Year's Day. God does not repeat Himself[22] without reason: hence, concludes another anonymous commentator, one of the two verses, the one from Leviticus, is "available" for special interpretation and is construed as intimating to Israel that in their prayers on New Year's Day they should invoke the merit of the Fathers (Piska 23.7).[23] A further illustra-

20. For another example of this norm, sometimes called verbal analogy, see Piska 3.1.

21. By means of the norm of juxtaposition of passages and the enlargement of context, it is inferred that the scourge of Amalek came after Israel questioned God's providence (Piska 3.2), and was guilty of using false weights and measures (Piska 3.4); it is further inferred that Amalek mutilated live Israelites (Piska 3.6). By means of this norm it is likewise inferred that eating untithed food is like eating carrion (Piska 6.9), and that for God the death of Aaron was as grievous as the breaking of the Tablets (Piska 26.11).

22. By the same token the notion of Biblical parallelism is inadmissible. See Piska 3.4 for the Rabbinic exposition of Micah 6:11.

23. So, too, the passage requiring that he-lambs be offered daily is found both in Exodus and in Numbers. Hence the "superfluous" passage considered "available" for interpretation is construed as hinting at the significance of the offering of the he-lambs; they put Israel's iniquities out of sight. They do more, according to Ben Azzai: "They cleanse the sins of the people of Israel and make them as innocent as an infant in its first year" (Piska 6.4).

tion of the force of context is to be found in the interpretation of a word whose presence in a sentence seems unnecessary, indeed baffling. Thus, in the account of the Temple's destruction at the time that Jeremiah was being taken captive, one would expect Scripture to say, "When Nebuzaradan had taken him, he was bound in chains" (Jer. 40:1), but the verse actually reads, *When Nebuzaradan had taken him—and he was bound in chains.* The apparently intrusive and puzzling *and* in *and he* is brilliantly construed by R. Aḥa, who reads the words as *and He* and so takes the verse to be saying that God Himself along with Jeremiah was bound in chains (Piska 13.9) and that He went into exile with him. A similar kind of contextual force is exerted upon a word which seems inappropriate not only in its application but also in its grammatical form. For example, the term *Lord* (YHWH) is always taken to stand for "God in His aspect of mercy," yet Psalm 94:1 describes Him as "Lord of vengeances"—in the plural. How can vengeance, let alone vengeances it is asked, be attributed to the God of mercy? To be thought truly merciful, replies R. Isaac, He must have vengeances attributed to Him, for God does not take vengeance mercilessly—that is, He inflicts punishment for transgression not all at once but only a little at a time, taking small vengeances so that the suffering of the sinner be not too great (Piska 25.1).

The third category of norms works by interpretation derived from the pressure of the context upon an apparent irregularity of grammar or syntax. The two-letter particle *'t*, for instance, usually serves grammatically as no more than a sign of the accusative before nouns, but because it may be dispensed with, the Rabbis find its presence as hinting at further meaning to be sought for in a verse. Thus, in the verse, *It was on the day that Moses brought to an end the setting up of ('t) the Tabernacle* (Num. 7:1), R. Simeon ben Yoḥai takes the *'t* as intimating that something other was set up along with the Tabernacle. "What was this other?" the Rabbi asks, and answers, "It was the earth." Before the Tabernacle was set up, the earth was unstable; when the Tabernacle was set up, the earth became stable. From its context, then, R. Simeon understands the particle *'t* to be intimating that the moral teachings symbolically represented by the setting up of the Tabernacle are the very foundation of man's life on earth. In much the same way as *'t* points to hidden significance, so does the particle *'k* ("howbeit" or "only"). Thus, in the account of Noah and the ark (Gen. 7:23), R. Jose the Galilean construes the particle as a form of the verb *nkh* ("to smite" or "to spring upon"), and so assumes that on the ark Noah was sprung upon by a lion and was mutilated (Piska 26.1).[24]

24. For another limiting particle, *rḳ*, likewise suggesting grave mishap, see Piska 7.10, where R. Ḥama (*fl.* middle third century) infers from the use of the particle that the only one of Job's herdsmen who escaped, escaped at the cost of having his limbs broken and his body beaten.

The fourth category of norms takes every word, every phrase—in fact, every syllable and letter—of Scripture as a self-contained unit of divine radiance, shedding the light of its meaning around it and illuminating the sense of the verse or passage in which it occurs. Consider, for example, a phrase in regard to the exodus from Egypt, a phrase which R. Levi, citing R. Ḥama bar Ḥanina, construes in the verse *God led* [*Israel*] *not by the way of the earth of the Philistines* (Exod. 13:17). The illuminating phrase is *not by the way of the earth*, which is taken to signify something more than the literal *not by way of the land of the Philistines*—is taken, in fact, to signify "not in the usual manner." In short, say the commentators, God led Israel in His own way—miraculously—out of Egypt, and they go on to cite eight dramatic examples of the miraculous ways by which God led Israel through the wilderness (Piska 11.8). Names, too, in themselves indicate dramatic meaning: the name of Abraham's child Isaac, harbinger of revelation and redemption, means "joy" (Piska 22.1); the name of her who was witness of Israel's humiliation in Egypt, Miriam, means "bitterness" (Piska 5.11). Two prophets, Amos and Micah, whom Israel did not heed, bore names which meant respectively "tongue-heavy" and "one who is smitten" (Piska 16.4). The name of Jeremiah, who prophesied and witnessed the Temple's destruction, signified variously "void and destitute" (Piska 13.8), "desolation" (Piska 13.12), and "one during whose lifetime the Presence journeyed up and away from Jerusalem" (Piska 13.11). Kolaiah, the name of a false and lecherous prophet, means both "one accursed" and "roasted in fire" (Piska 24.15), and Shealtiel, the name of the person through whom David's royal line was miraculously continued, means "a sapling newly set out" (Piska 24.11). As words and names radiate significance, so do the elements of which they are composed—syllables and letters. The order of letters in a word, or the anomalous spelling of a word, even the size of letters or their numerical value—all have the power to throw light on the text in which they occur. Thus Rephidim, the name of the place where Amalek attacked Israel, when divided into its syllables signifies the moral lapse on Israel's part that was responsible for the attack (Piska 3.a); likewise, the name Amalek, when read syllable by syllable, is taken to signify "a people which like a kind of locust swooped down swiftly," or "like a dog come from afar to lick up Israel's blood" (Piska 3.8).[25] An anomalous spelling, such as is found in the account of the setting up of the Tabernacle, is also taken to be meaningful: thus, the word *klt*, defectively spelled, signifies "on that day Israel became God's bride";[26] given its full spelling,

25. For other examples of words construed by means of the syllables which make them up, see Piska 10.4, 11.7.

26. For other examples of this kind of interpretation, see Piska 10.1, 7.10, 25.1.

klwt, it signifies "the setting up of the Tabernacle was concluded" (Piska 1.5). So, too, the letters of which a word is composed may be read in different order to make up a different word, an anagram whose meaning is added to the meaning of the word in the usual order of its letters. For example, the letters of the word *hbr'm* (Gen. 2.4), which signifies the creation, are rearranged to make the word *'brhm* (Abraham), and the two words conjoined, *hbr'm-'brhm*, are taken to intimate that the world was created because of Abraham—for the purpose, that is, of having men like him populate the world (S1.20). The sum of the numerical values of the letters in a word can also illuminate the word's context. Thus, in the verse *Abraham shall surely become* (*yhyh*) *a great nation* (Gen. 18:18), the numerical value of the letters in *yhyh*—*yod̲*, 10; *he'*, 5; *yod̲*, 10; *he'*, 5—add up to thirty, and from this sum it is inferred that the verse, beside telling us that Abraham is to be the progenitor of a great nation, is also assuring us that the world is never to be without at least thirty men of the likes of Abraham (Piska 11.15)[27]—in short, the righteousness of thirty men guarantees the continuation of the world. The meaning of a word, phrase, or verse is extended not only by the numerical value of its letters, but also by the number of letters it contains. For example, Deuteronomy 4:34, which speaks of God's deliverance of Israel from Egypt, contains seventy-two letters, the same number as in the ineffable name of God; hence, concluded R. Berechiah, God, aside from what the measure of His justice required, arbitrarily delivered Israel with the plenitude of His power (Piska 5.11). Charged with its own illuminating power, a letter in a word under the closely scrutinizing Rabbinic eye can change itself enough to supplement the meaning of the verse it is found in. Thus, the letter *śin*, read as a *šin* in a word whose context asks Jews to be generous in giving tithes, yields God's adjuration, "Tithe that you may be blithe" (Piska 10.10).[28] Even variations in the size of letters in Scripture are regarded as significant. For example, in two verses concerning God's strength (Num. 14:17; Deut. 32:18), the presence of an oversize letter and an undersize letter is understood as suggesting that when men do God's will His strength is increased, and when they do not, His strength is diminished (Piska 25.1). Finally, the Rabbis' use of Greek and Arabic words in interpreting Scripture reflects their conviction of the interrelation

27. The amount of water in a ritual pool and the fact that Eliezer was the sole companion of Abraham in his battle against the four kings are inferences likewise drawn from the numerical value of letters. See Piska 6.2 and 8.2.

28. For other instances of such changes, see Piska 10.3 and 24.11. In keeping with the idea of the protean character of letters, there are also ciphers like *Atbash*, in which the first letter of the Hebrew alphabet is interchanged with the last letter, the second with the next to last, and so on, such interchanging resulting in supplement to the meaning of the word in its original form. See Piska 24.19.

of Greek, Arabic, and Hebrew and their further conviction that even as every word in Scripture may radiate multiple meanings, so all the words of Scripture may simultaneously speak "in tongues"[29]—not only in a few tongues, but in the world's seventy languages.[30]

R. Eliezer ben Jose the Galilean, a great man of Midrash, counted thirty-two norms for the interpretation of Scripture, a number remarkably apt, for thirty-two is the sum of the letters in *lḇ*, the Hebrew word for "heart." And one key to Scripture's heart is what a Midrash such as the Pĕsiḳta dĕ-Raḇ Kahăna provides.

III. The Text

A. The History of the Text and Its Compiler

Of the teachers whose utterances R. Kahana set down in his compilation, the earliest were disciples from the Schools of Hillel and Shammai (*ca.* first century B.C.E.). The latest, such as R. Tanḥuma, lived in the second half of the fourth century C.E. The country of a few of the Rabbis cannot be determined; a few came from Babylonia to live in Palestine; the greater number by far came from Palestine.[31] Since Palestinian Rabbis are cited more frequently than Babylonian and since no Rabbis who lived

29. See Piska 9.6, 14.5, and 24.6.

30. Cf. "When the Holy One . . . gave forth the Divine Word, the voice divided itself into voices, and from the seven voices passed into the seventy languages of the seventy nations, so that all men understood it. Hence it is said *Great was the company of those that published it.*" See MTeh 68:6 (YJS, *13*, 2, 541).

31. Many teachers are identified by reference to cities or towns in Palestine where they lived or came from. Thus: Abba of Acco, Abba bar Hoshaia of Teria, Abdimi of Haifa, Azariah of Kefar Ḥiṭṭaya, Dostai of Kokaba, Ḥiyya of Jaffa, Huna Rabbah of Sepphoris, Issachar of Kefar Mindu, Jacob of Nubrai, Jacob of Kefar Ḥanin, Jonah of Boṣrah, Jose of Mimlaḥ, Jonathan of Beth Gubrin, Joshua of Siḵnin, Luliani of the South, Mani of Shaab, Menahem of Gallia [Eglaim], Nisa of Caesarea, Nunya of Caesarea, Shela of Kefar Tamarta, Taḥalifa of Caesarea, Tanḥum of Jaffa, Yudan of Gallia [Eglaim], and Zakkai of Kebul.

In the telling of stories or anecdotes, specific cites in Palestine are referred to, e.g. the great academy of Lydda (Piska 18.5), synagogues in Magdala (Piska 11.17) and Sepphoris (Piska 18.5), and a synagogue whose congregation consisted of people who had come from Babylonia to Palestine (Piska 25.1); also referred to is a beach in Haifa (Piska 18.5); a banquet in Kokaba (Piska 6.2); scholars' residences in Caesarea (Piska 4.4, 11.12), in Tiberias, Sepphoris (Piska 26.1), and Hefer (Piska 26.8); and finally burial places in Giscala and Meron (Piska 11.13).

later than the fifth century C.E. are cited, the work is believed to have been compiled in Palestine sometime during the fifth century C.E. Further support for this dating comes from the fact that recently discovered liturgical compositions by Yannai (*fl.* sixth century) are unmistakably based on a redacted text of *Pĕsiḳta dĕ-Rab̲ Kahăna.*[32]

The known manuscripts of the text are as follows: Oxford MS, dating from the thirteenth century; Parma MS, from the thirteenth or fourteenth century; $Oxford_2$ MS, from the fifteenth century; $Oxford_1$ MS, from the sixteenth century; Carmoly MS, from the late fifteenth or early sixteenth century; Safed MS, from the sixteenth; and Casanata MS, from the early seventeenth.[32a]

The work was frequently referred to from the days of Saadiah Gaon (882–942) to those of Azariah dei Rossi (1513–1578).[33] Saadiah Gaon speaks of it as Pĕsiḳta,[34] and Nathan ben Jehiel of Rome (eleventh century), referring to it as Pisḳot̲, cites individual passages and identifies them as coming from Piska *Comfort Ye* or Piska *And Zion Said*, these being the opening phrases, respectively, of the two Piskas. In a comment on Psalms 30:12, Rashi (1040–1105) makes mention of the work as *Pĕsiḳta zuṭa*, "the short Pesikta," perhaps to distinguish it from Pesikta Rabbati, "the long Pesikta." R. Eleazar ben Judah of Worms (*ca.* 1176–*ca.* 1238) refers to the work as "Midrash."[35]

During the latter half of the sixteenth century, however, despite the existence of manuscripts dating from about this time, the *Compilation* seems to have been lost sight of, and except for quotations from it embedded in earlier writings, it remained unknown until 1832. In that year Leopold Zunz published his *Gottesdienstliche Vorträge der Juden*, in which he reconstructed the content and the order of the Piskas by close examination of quotations from them found in the *'Aruḳ* and the *Yalḳuṭ*. Zunz's brilliant reconstruction led to diligent search in libraries for manuscripts of the *Compilation*, a search which culminated in 1868 with the publication of Solomon Buber's edition of the work. Buber collated the Safed manuscript with three others, and these four, in the main, confirmed Zunz's reconstruction. The major difference between the two versions is that Buber's begins with the Piska based on the Scriptural lesson for

32. See Ṣĕb̲i Meir Rabinowitz, *Halaḳah wĕ-'ăḡad̲ah bĕ-fiyyuṭe Yannai* (Tel Aviv, 5725/1965), 162–63.

32a. For further details on the MSS of PRK, see PRKM, *1*, 8–13, and *2*, xii–xiii.

33. See his *Mĕ'or 'enayim*, ed. Cassel (Berlin, 1867), p. 166.

34. In his "Ten Reasons for Blowing the Shofar," cited by Abudirham (ed. Jerusalem, 5719 [1959]), 270.

35. *Roḳeaḥ* (Jerusalem, 5723 [1963]), Sec. 219.

Hanukkah, while Zunz's begins with the Piska based on the lesson for New Year's Day.[36]

A new edition of the Pĕsiḳta was not forthcoming until nearly a hundred years later when in 1962 Bernard Mandelbaum published his edition, using the Oxford manuscript as his *Grundtext.* This edition, an admirable achievement, in which a group of scholars collaborated with Mandelbaum, was published with an apparatus which provides all the variants from the six other manuscripts, including those used by Buber, as well as variants from Genizah fragments. On the whole, Mandelbaum's edition is superior to Buber's because it is based on a better manuscript to begin with, and because it is more accurately and more amply edited.[37] There seems good reason, however, to disagree with Mandelbaum's argument that Zunz in his reconstruction was right to make the Piska for New Year's Day the first one.[38] The evidence appears to favor Buber's order of the Piskas, making the Piska for Hanukkah the first one, if only because the Pĕsiḳta, in following the cycle of annual readings for special Sabbaths and festivals in the calendar year, would naturally begin with the Sabbath during Hanukkah, the first special Sabbath in the year for which an annual reading in the Pentateuch was prescribed.[39] Two internal pieces of evidence, one derived from Piska 10, the other derived from the perorations of Piskas 1 and 28,[40] also warrant the assumption that the Piska for the

36. In Buber's edition Piska 1 is based on Num. 7:1, the lesson in Scripture for Hanukkah. And so, since the Piskas for the four—or possibly five—special Sabbaths which follow and the Piskas for Passover and Pentecost, as well as the Piskas for the three Sabbaths of Rebuke and for the seven Sabbaths of Consolation, precede the one for New Year's Day, listed as first in Zunz's reconstruction, Zunz's Piska 1 is Piska 23 in Buber's edition.

37. Buber introduced into his text variants from other manuscripts and even variants from parallel sources without telling the reader that such liberties were being taken. Still, the commentary which Buber provided remains useful, particularly since Mandelbaum's very brief commentary often takes no note of difficult passages. Where Mandelbaum does provide an explanation, he is generally helpful, and of course Professor Saul Lieberman's supplementary notes are invariably illuminating. Mandelbaum's edition has made possible an analysis of the original structure of Piskas in the Pĕsiḳta dĕ-Rab̲ Kahăna. See Abraham Goldberg, *Kirjath Sefer, 43* (1967), 74–79.

38. See his Introduction, p. xvii.

39. See Abraham Goldberg, *Kirjath Sefer, 43* (1967), 72.

40. Num. 14:22, on which Piska 10 is based, used to be read—as is now known —on the Sabbath during Passover and on the Sabbath during Sukkot. Had the Piska for New Year's Day been the initial Piska, the one on Deut. 14:22 would have been placed not in the Passover cycle but in the cycle of Sukkot, specifically

Sabbath during Hanukkah was intended to be the first in the *Compilation.*

There are two early attributions of the work to a R. Kahana as its compiler. R. Meshullam bar Moses of Mayence (died 1096) designates a part of the work, the Piskas for the three Sabbaths of Rebuke and for the seven Sabbaths of Consolation (Piskas 13–22), as having been drawn together by R. Kahana;[41] and R. Eliezer ben Joel of Bonn (*ca.* 1160) refers to the entire work as the Pĕsiḳta dĕ-Rab̲ Kahăna.[42]

But just who R. Kahana was cannot be established with any certainty. In modern times both Zunz and Buber maintained that he was the Palestinian Amora, R. Abba bar Kahana (*fl.* first half of the fourth century C.E.), who is cited at the beginning of Piska 13. The puzzling fact that it is R. Abba bar Kahana who is thus cited whereas the entire work is attributed simply to R. Kahana, Zunz explains by saying that Pĕsiḳta dĕ-Rab̲ Kahăna is an abbreviated or corrupt form of the full title, which should read Pĕsiḳta dĕ-Rab̲ Abba bar Kahăna.[43] According to Meir Friedmann, however, the work was compiled by a R. Kahana who lived in post-Talmudic times (after the sixth century C.E.) and whose name was attached to the ten Piskas (13–22) for the Sabbaths preceding and following the Ninth of Ab.[44] Mandelbaum, agreeing with Zunz that the work should be ascribed to R. Kahana, identifies him as an Amora who must have flourished at the beginning of the fifth century C.E. The attribution of the work to this R. Kahana came about, Mandelbaum argues,

---

between Sukkot and the Eighth-Day Festival (see Goldberg, *ibid.*). Then, too, in the Buber edition Piskas 1 and 28 conclude with perorations based on the same verse, *Ye that cleave unto the Lord your God will be alive every one of you this day,* (Deut. 4:4). In Piska 1 the peroration asserts that because Israel cleave to the Lord they live on and on. In Piska 28 the peroration asserts that even after the Temple's destruction God, continuing to look forth from His holy habitation upon the people of Israel so long as they cleave unto Him, sees to it that they remain alive.

The people of Israel are thus possessed of strength, *kḥ* (20+8=28) a word whose letters represent the numerical value of the 28 Piskas in Pĕsiḳta dĕ-Rab̲ Kahăna. The disguised cipher for the number 28 may also be taken as the signature for the final Piska in the work.

41. In R. Meshullam's responsum quoted in *Sefer hap-Pardes*, ed. Ehrenreich (Budapest, 5684 [1924]), pp. 344–45.

An attribution such as this may have been due—Joseph Heinemann suggests—to the statement in the Talmud "R. Kahana was expounding a portion of Scripture before Rab" (B.Shab 152a).

42. *Sefer Rabyah*, ed. Aptowitzer (2nd ed. Jerusalem 5724 [1964]), 2, 274 (Sec. 55b).

43. See Zunz, *had-Dĕrašot̲*, pp. 82, 85; and PRKB, p. iv.

44. *Bet̲ Talmud̲*, 5, 6.

because of the ascription at the beginning of Piska 23 which, according to Mandelbaum, was Piska 1 in the original sequence of the Piskas. The ascription reads: "The opinion of R. Kahana coincides with what R. Eliezer taught in a Baraita," etc.[45] In any event, the evidence is so slight that the attribution of the work to one R. Kahana or another cannot be made with any certainty, though perhaps with greater certainty to a R. Kahana than to any other Rabbi.

B. The Pĕsiḳta dĕ-Rab̲ Kahăna and Its Contemporary Midrashim

In purpose and in some of its content, the Pĕsiḳta dĕ-Rab̲ Kahăna resembles the Pĕsiḳta Rabbati. Both are compilations of discourses for special Sabbaths and festal days in the Jewish year, and the two works have ten Piskas that duplicate, or come very close to duplicating, one another.[46] Since the compilation of the Pĕsiḳta dĕ-Rab̲ Kahăna was done in the fifth century and the compilation of the Pĕsiḳta Rabbati no earlier than the sixth century, it is very likely that the latter borrowed from the former the Piskas they have in common.

More complicated is the relation of the Pĕsiḳta dĕ-Rab̲ Kahăna to Leviticus Rabbah, a compilation of discourses based on the first verses of the lessons in Leviticus that are read on the regular Sabbaths of the year. In each of the two works, five Piskas based on the lessons for the same festal days duplicate, or come close to duplicating, one another: concerned with Passover are Piskas 8 and 9 of the Pĕsiḳta dĕ-Rab̲ Kahăna and chapters 27 and 28 of Leviticus Rabbah; concerned with New Year's Day are Piska 23 of the Pĕsiḳta dĕ-Rab̲ Kahăna and chapter 29 of Leviticus Rabbah; concerned with the Day of Atonement are Piska 26 of the Pĕsiḳta dĕ-Rab̲ Kahăna and chapter 20 of Leviticus Rabbah; concerned with Sukkot are Piska 27 of the Pĕsiḳta dĕ-Rab̲ Kahăna and chapter 30 of Leviticus Rabbah.

Fairly recent Genizah finds, already alluded to, of some liturgical compositions by Yannai (*fl.* sixth century) have helped to confirm the date of the compilation of both works in the fifth century,[47] and the question as to which one borrowed from the other has been actively debated with

45. In O and O_2. Further evidence that Piska 23 was Piska 1 in the original order Mandelbaum finds in the *'Aruḵ* (*svv. ms's'* and *msḳyd*) where Nathan of Rome speaks of it as *Roš Pisḳot̲*, a phrase which Mandelbaum takes to mean "the first of the Pisḳot̲." However, *Roš Pisḳot̲* may also mean "the one among the Piskas which deals with the year's beginning."

46. Piskas 4–8 in PRK parallel 14–18 in PR; Piska 16 parallels 29/30A and 29/30B; 32 parallels 18; 27 and 28 parallel 18 and 52.

47. See Ṣĕb̲i Meir Rabinowitz, *Halaḵah wĕ-'ăḡad̲ah bĕ-fiyyuṭe Yannai* (Tel Aviv, 5725/ 1965), 178.

some notable scholars ranged against one another.[48] But Mordecai Margulies believes that the question of priority need not be posed, arguing that both works may have come from the same house of study—indeed, may have been compiled by the same person, who simply brought into them Piskas and fragments of Piskas dealing with subjects common to both.[49] Joseph Heinemann suggests a similar answer, maintaining that the two works were compiled at about the same time in the fifth century and that soon after their compilation other editors transposed parts from one compilation to the other and from the other to the one.[50]

Aside from such duplications as those referred to above, Rabbinic works in general have so much in common that it is not always easy to discern the special characteristics that set off the Pĕsiḳta dĕ-Rab̲ Kahăna, Leviticus Rabbah, and the Pĕsiḳta Rabbati from one another. We can make out, however, specific differences in their attitudes towards some themes of major importance. For example, all three works reveal their expectations of the coming of the Messiah, expectations aroused and strengthened no doubt by a steady worsening of the situation of the Jews in the Byzantine empire during the fifth and sixth centuries. The Byzantine government, we are told, sought "to isolate the Jews . . . to demean them, and by liquidating central and local organizations to wipe out Judaism altogether."[51] As the plight of the Jews grew, the deepening intensity of their hopes of the Messiah's coming to deliver them is revealed by the three Midrashim. In Leviticus Rabbah their expectations are voiced mildly, in the Pĕsiḳta dĕ-Rab̲ Kahăna they are expressed with greater yearning, and in the Pĕsiḳta Rabbati, a later work than the two others, they anticipate the ordeal of the Messiah and celebrate his ultimate triumph.[52] It is possible that in the Pĕsiḳta Rabbati, Nebuchadnezzar's siege and capture of Jerusalem (Piska 26) and the valor of Abikah during Vespasian's siege of Jerusalem (Piska 29/30B)[53] are recalled by way of

48. Solomon Buber, Julius Theodor, Abraham Epstein, and Meir Friedmann believe that Leviticus Rabbah took these chapters from Pĕsiḳta dĕ-Rab̲ Kahăna (see *JE*, *8*, 560). On the other hand, Leopold Zunz, Isaac Hirsh Weiss, and Chanoch Albeck ("Midraš Way-yiḳra' rabbah," *Ginzberg Jubilee Volume* [New York, 5706/1945], Hebrew part, 36–39) and Abraham Goldberg (*Kirjath Sefer*, *43* [1967], 73a) believe that Pĕsiḳta dĕ-Rab̲ Kahăna took these chapters from Leviticus Rabbah.

49. Lev. Rabbah M, *5*, xxxii.

50. See his "Parašiyyot̲ bĕ-Way-yiḳra' rabbah," etc., in *Tarb̲iṣ*, *37* (5728/1968), 339–54; and " 'Omanut̲ haḳ-ḳompoziṣyah bĕ-midraš Way-yiḳra' rabbah" in *has-Sifrut̲*, Tel Aviv, *2*, 809–34.

51. Michael 'Abi-Yonah, *Bi-yĕme Romah u-Bizanṭiyon* (Jerusalem, 5706/1946), 152, quoted in Ṣĕb̲i Meir Rabinowitz, ibid., 26.

52. See Heinemann, " 'Omanut̲," p. 826.

53. *YJS*, *13*, 588–89.

an oblique reminder that Jews are capable of taking up arms against an oppressor.

Besides such difference in their treatment of specific subjects, we can also see a marked difference in the tone of these Midrashim. The Pĕsiḳta dĕ-Rab̲ Kahăna and Leviticus Rabbah seem more philosophical, more aware of the complexity and irony of the human condition than the Pĕsiḳta Rabbati, and use fewer parables, homely folk materials, and other simple rhetorical means of appeal. Unlike the compiler of the Pĕsiḳta Rabbati, who begins the Piska of the Red Heifer (Piska 14) with two stories,[54] the compiler of the Pĕsiḳta dĕ-Rab̲ Kahăna starts its Piska of the Red Heifer (Piska 4) with a meditative passage puzzling out the paradox that out of the unclean can come that which is clean, and finally leaving the paradox, not resolvable by man, to God.

The same sort of acceptance of paradox as a fact of man's existence is to be found in the Pĕsiḳta dĕ-Rab̲ Kahăna's discussion of the fate of Aaron's two sons, the same fate which befalls all men—the good, the bad, the indifferent (Piska 26.1). This discussion is followed by the almost stoic adjuration that human beings, though human enough to be distracted by grief, are not to let grief entwine itself permanently in their lives (Piska 26.3).

Perhaps even the contradictory statements with regard to Aaron's part in the making of the golden calf are likewise due to the awareness of the Pĕsiḳta dĕ-Rab̲ Kahăna's compiler of the gap between human weakness and human aspiration, between what man is capable of doing and what God requires him to do. On the one hand, we are told that Aaron's two sons were taken away from him by God by way of punishing him for his transgression (Piska 26.6–7) and, on the other, that in the making of the golden calf there was no guilt on his part because converts from Egypt were responsible for its making (Piska 9.7). On the one hand, it is said that when Israel were in Egypt they did not change their language (Piska 11.6) and, on the other, that they had so thoroughly forgotten Hebrew as to make God talk to them in Egyptian (Piska 12.24).

It may indeed be that the Pĕsiḳta's awareness, reflecting Scripture's awareness, of the eternal conflict that rages in human nature, of the depths to which man can descend and the heights to which he can rise, of man's need of God and God's need of man, is what makes the Midrash something more than mere commentary and entitles it to be spoken of as part of Torah.

C. The Translation[55]

Translation would be an easy task if all it required were taking each word

54. *Ibid.*, 259–64.

55. The text on which the translation in hand is based is an eclectic one. In the main, the Oxford manuscript has been relied on, except where variants in other

as it came along in the text and replacing it by its equivalent in another language. But every language has idioms peculiar to itself, its own way of combining words, its own grammar and syntax for indicating connections among the elements of a sentence, its own idea of the sequence of elements in the sentence. If one were to translate simply by following along from one word to the next, one would be changing what is natural and logical in one language to what is unnatural and illogical in another. Hence, the responsibility of the translator is to make his translation as natural and logical as the original; in short, in order to be faithful to the spirit of the language he is translating from, he must be faithful to the spirit of the language he is translating into. This is not to say, of course, that the translator has the right to be as free as he likes. He must, after all, work within the limits prescribed by the meaning of the words in the text he is translating. He must translate *angel* as "angel," *demon* as "demon," *white* as "white," *black* as "black," *terrify* as "terrify," *soothe* as "soothe," *swiftly* as "swiftly," *slowly* as "slowly."

Yet this matter of finding equivalents is not as simple as it appears at first glance. The language of the marketplace is not the same as the language of the lecture hall; the language of everyday conversation among men is not the same as the language of prayer. The difference in these instances is not merely one of vocabulary, but of what is appropriate for the occasion. Is the Hebrew word for *male parent* to be translated always "father"? If a child is speaking, would not "daddy" or "papa" be more appropriate? If the Hebrew refers to a man who does not speak the truth, is the fact to be translated into English by the everyday word *lying* or the learned word *mendacious*? If a man's head is taken off in Hebrew, in English is he "decapitated" or "beheaded"? In every instance of this sort, the translators have sought the word or phrase that seems the most appropriate one for the occasion. So, too, if two tradesmen are in conversation in the marketplace, if a Rabbi is debating with a heathen, if a king is speaking to a servant who replies to him, the translators have tried not only to find words that reflect the social or intellectual rank of the speakers, but have ventured to use colloquial constructions of a kind not to be found in Hebrew—such contractions, for example, as "don't" for *do not* or "I'll" for *I shall.*

Laboring still further to be faithful to the spirit of the original, the translators have often been compelled by the essential differences between Hebrew

---

manuscripts or in parallel sources have supplied more precise or ampler meaning.

August Wünsche translated the entire text into German in his *Pesikta des Rab Kahana* (Leipzig, 1885); and Philipp Bloch translated three Piskas in "Uebersetzungsprobe aus der Pesikta derab Kahana, Die Piskoth für die drei Trauersabbathe *Dibre, Šimĕ'u, 'Eykah*," in *Festschrift zum achzigsten Geburtstage Moritz Steinschneiders* (Leipzig, 1896), 41–71.

and English to add words or omit words or even to re-define words. Sometimes an exact one-word equivalent does not exist for the word they are translating, and so they have had to use two or three words whose equivalents are not to be found in the text, and sometimes, they have had to go so far as to add not only a word or two but an entire phrase or even a sentence where the failure to add would lead to a serious lapse in the clarity or coherence of the thought. Sometimes a word entirely at home in the original had to be omitted in the translation so as not to impede the flow of thought; sometimes a meaning not usually attributed to a word in the original had to be substituted to convey precisely the force of the word in its context.

By way of illustration of the liberties translators must take for the sake of accuracy, consider the fact that Hebrew depends greatly upon the context of words, phrases, sentences, and even of entire passages to make clear the meaning of any one of these, and so lacks the variety of connective words and phrases that by contrast are so common in English. The particle *w*, whose most common meaning is "and," is used not only for coordination but also to indicate disjunction, consequence, contradiction, and so on. Since the pressure of the context in one language does not always carry over into another, then the translator's duty is to supply the exact sense of *w* as determined by its Hebrew context and to translate it by whatever English word or phrase is necessary for clear understanding. Indeed, Hebrew relies so strongly on context to convey grammatical or syntactical connections that, apart from its loose use of *w* to indicate a relationship of some kind between the elements of a clause or sentence, it makes little or no use of such directive words and phrases as English *however, on the contrary, as a result of, in addition*, nor even of such ordinary coordinating or subordinating terms as *as, but, for, if, when, although*, and the like.

Such transitional words or phrases need particularly to be supplied by the present translation not only because of the nature of Hebrew, but also because of the kind of work the Pĕsiḳta dĕ-Rab̲ Kahăna is. Because it is a compilation, it lacks, to begin with, the continuity between section and section of its Piskas that a literary work concerned with development of a single theme supplies as a matter of course. Again, because the Pĕsiḳta is a compilation made up of many separate pieces brought together from a variety of sources, each of the pieces more or less maintains its original independence of the others.[56] Finally, because the compiler of the work took it for granted that his audience was familiar with the materials he was drawing together—was, at the very least, familiar with the Scriptural citations and allusions in the work—he did not presumably think it necessary always to supply connectives between sentence and sentence or between section and section of a Piska. In any event, therefore, in order to make clear to the reader the

56. See e.g. the beginning of Piska 1.4, 9.4, 16.4, and elsewhere.

development of the themes in the Midrash, the English translation supplies, wherever necessary, connective words or phrases, entire sentences, and even paragraphs. Interpolations of this kind are indicated in the translation by square brackets, and the reader can decide for himself whether these interpolations are justified by leaving them out as he reads.

In the translation of certain set phrases and locutions, some justifiable liberties have also been taken. For example, the statement *zehu še'amar hakkaṯuḇ*, literally translated means "This is what Scripture says," but the literal meaning does not indicate precisely what the commentator had in mind. Generally, the statement is used as a connective between two verses quoted from Scripture brought together to throw light on each other. Where the connection between the two verses is apparent, the statement has been slightly amplified to read "Elsewhere this is what Scripture says," the added "elsewhere" indicating, according to the context, either a parallel or a contrast in the thought of the two verses. Where the intermediate context does not supply such an apparent connection, the translation of the statement is extended to read, "These words are to be considered in the light of what Scripture says elsewhere." Frequently also, in quoting verses from Scripture, the Rabbis use such formulas as *šene'ĕmar* ("as is said"), *diḵĕṯiḇ* ("as is written"), *wĕ'omer* ("and says"), or *minnayin* ("whence?"), and these terms, too, for complete clarity need sometimes to be extended in translation. So *šene'ĕmar*, besides "as is said," is translated also "as Scripture says," or "as the text states," or "and again," and so on. For *wĕ'omer*, "and says," phrases such as "the text continues" or "Scripture goes on to say" are used. *Minnayin*, "whence," is sometimes rendered "Whence the proof?" or "And the proof?"[57]

The translators have also ventured to abbreviate certain other phrases and to supply pronominal references where English usage requires them. For example, "the Holy One, blessed be He" appearing again and again in the Pĕsiḳta,[58] in the translation has been shortened to "the Holy One." "Israel"

57. Besides paraphrasing technical terms and expanding compact utterances, certain liberties had to be taken in reproducing the names of Rabbis which in the original appear at times in the same passage in different forms or spellings. Generally the manuscripts give variants which permit a translator to be consistent in spelling the names of the Rabbis. Thus in Piska 1.5 the same Rabbi is referred to as "Simeon ben Laḳish" and "Resh Laḳish." To avoid confusion in the translation, the form "Simeon ben Laḳish" was chosen. In Piska 11.6 the form "R. Ḥiyya bar Abba" instead of "R. Ḥiyya bar Bah" was chosen. In Piska 12.10 the form "R. Aḥa" instead of "R. Aḥwh" was chosen; in Piska 12.11, the form "R. Samuel ben Ḥalafta" instead of "R. Samuel ben Ḥalfuṭah" was chosen; in Piska 21.3 the form "R. Huna" instead of "R. Ḥuma" was chosen; and the same elsewhere.

58. Not generally in Supplements 1–7.

has been translated as a singular noun when it refers to the people of Israel as an entity, but has been treated as a plural when the context intimates that the commentator has in mind the individuals who make up the people of Israel. Israel's gender is also determined in the translation by the context: when Israel is referred to as a people, its pronominal designation is "it"; when Israel is referred to as God's bride, the pronominal designation is "she." The sense of the term "the world-to-come" is also determined by its context. Standing alone, the phrase is an ambiguous one, for it can refer either to the time of the Messiah or to the time following the resurrection.[59] In some places, even the context is of no help in determining exactly which of its meanings is intended, and consequently, the translation, accepting the ambiguity as it stands, makes no attempt to supply an unequivocal meaning.

The exegetical work of the Rabbis has often compelled re-translation of Scriptural verses and passages in the light of the Rabbis' own understanding of them. While the translators in quoting Scripture use, for the most part, the Jewish Publication Society's translation, the Rabbis' approach to certain verses and passages, differing sometimes to a marked degree from the Publication Society's translation, has led to consultation and quotation of other English versions. Often, however, no one of the English versions seems to represent adequately the Rabbis' interpretation of a particular verse or passage, and in such instances, the present translation of the Pĕsiḳta renders it anew in line with what the Rabbis understand the verse or passage to be saying. Where such a rendering differs substantially from the usual translation, a footnote quotes the usual translation. Occasionally, in order to give the special sense of a verse as the Rabbis understood it, the translators have found it necessary to resort to interpolation, treating the interpolation as part of the Scriptural verse or passage, but setting off the interpolated matter in brackets. Finally, because the men who composed Midrash were aware that their audiences knew Scripture by heart, they sometimes quote only the beginning of a verse, even though their comment deals with the latter part of the verse, and so in this situation, for the sake of the modern reader's understanding of the comment, the entire verse or most of it is quoted by the translation in hand.

One of the most difficult problems of the translation was posed by the *pĕṯiḥahs* which take up half or more of each Piska. The fact that the *pĕṯiḥah* was an oratorical device depending for its effect upon the preacher's making a surprising connection between two apparently unrelated verses, seems to

59. The time when God Himself will teach Torah to Israel (Piska 12.21) is probably the time of the Messiah. On the other hand, the time when God will have the righteous dwell in sukkahs made of the impervious skin of the Leviathan in order to protect them from the fire of the Day of Judgment (S2.4), may refer to the time following the resurrection.

have led the preacher to suppress or to put off as long as possible the clues to the connection, so that his audience would be properly amazed and edified when he reached the climactic verse of the *pĕṯiḥah*. Hence, for the modern reader's understanding of many of the *pĕṯiḥahs*, it is necessary for him to know in advance, so to speak, what the preacher discovered in the introductory verse that could be startlingly connected with whatever hidden significance he had also found beneath the surface of the climactic verse. The translation in hand, consequently, often renders the introductory and the climactic verses in such terms as to make explicit what is hidden below the surface, sometimes far below the surface, of the two verses. Such re-translation, it goes without saying, stretches the content and hence the meaning of the verses far beyond what is conveyed in their usual translations, but at the same time it is faithful to the Rabbis' understanding of the verses.

The third *pĕṯiḥah* in Piska 1,[60] which is based on the Scriptural lesson for Hanukkah, provides representative illustration of how the *pĕṯiḥah* goes about building the bridge between its introductory and its climactic verses. It opens with a verse from the Song of Songs that is usually rendered *Go forth, O ye daughters of Zion and gaze upon king Solomon* and concludes with a verse from Numbers, usually rendered *And it came to pass on the day that Moses had made an end of setting up the Tabernacle*, etc. What connection there can be between these two verses so remote from each other in Scripture and so seemingly remote from each other in the sense of what they are saying is gradually, almost grudgingly, revealed to us. The preacher exploiting the puns in both verses does succeed in bridging the apparent gap between the two verses, but to help the modern reader see what transformation has been effected in both verses by ingenious exegesis, the hidden meanings of both, meanings which make possible their union, are herein re-translated—with some stretching, to be sure—as follows: the introductory verse, *Go forth, O ye daughters of Zion and gaze upon king Solomon*, is rendered *Go forth, O younglings, whose name Zion indicates that you bear a sign, and gaze upon the King who has the power to make peace*; and the climactic verse is rendered *It was on* [Israel's] *bridal day that Moses brought to a conclusion* [*God's coming back to earth*], etc. It is the hope of the translators that by way of these re-translations, not arbitrarily arrived at but based on the Rabbis' close scrutiny and skilled interpretation of the Hebrew originals, the reader can more comfortably follow, step by step, the ingenious structure of the bridge that the *pĕṯiḥah* is building.

It is the translators' larger hope that their rendering into English of the Pĕsiḳta dĕ-Raḇ Kahăna will also serve as a bridge, a bridge between the Jewish past and the Jewish present, a bridge between Jewish thought and the world's understanding of Judaism, a bridge between Jews and all those who

60. The *pĕtiḥah* has been analyzed in detail in Section II-A of this Introduction.

are not Jews but share with them the heritage of Jewish Scripture and the teachings of the Rabbis.

Leon Nemoy read the manuscript and gave it precision and consistency. Professor Saul Lieberman of the Jewish Theological Seminary of America and Professor Jakob J. Petuchowski of the Hebrew Union College resolved many textual difficulties. Mrs. Philip Kaplan, an ever loyal secretary, meticulously typed and retyped the work, and prepared the index of Authorities. Mrs. Harold Organic provided the index of Subjects and Names; Gladys (Mrs. Sherwin) Kapstein read copy, and together with Lillian Blotcher made up the index of Passages Cited; and Rabbi Gerald Serotta prepared the index of Plays on Words and Letters. The B'nai B'rith Hillel Foundations granted a stipend from The Merrill Trust. In ways both implicit and explicit, the people of Beth-El showed patience, understanding, and generosity. To all our gratitude.

William G. Braude
Israel J. Kapstein

Erev Yom Kippur 5732

Pĕsiḳta dĕ-Rab̲ Kahăna

PISKA 1

SUMMARY

Why God, having withdrawn from the earth, came back to it. Dwelling thereon in the Tabernacle, by His presence He sanctified it for ever.

The Tabernacle is the visible sign of God's having come back to His world. He had withdrawn from it because of men's wicked deeds, beginning with Adam's, but came back because of men's good deeds beginning with Abraham's and culminating in Moses' (Sec. 1). In having Moses build the Tabernacle, God showed His respect for Israel as a people come of age with whom He would converse in the privacy of their Sanctuary. His presence is not confined to the Tabernacle alone, however, for He is present everywhere, even in the lowliest thorn bush (Sec. 2). He makes His presence known by making peace between His creatures and His creations. His chosen people gazes with awe upon the harmony that He establishes everywhere in the universe, for He brings to mutual surrender even those diverse elements of His creation that are hostile to one another. Indeed He even brings Himself to surrender—He surrenders to His people Israel, for their sake shrinking His presence, so to speak, in order to dwell among them in the Tabernacle (Sec. 3). Nevertheless, though God dwells in the Tabernacle, He does not confine His presence to it—He comes and goes as He likes: His power is endless. The verse in Proverbs (30:4) that celebrates His power is also interpreted to be speaking of ordinary men—of those who are generous with their tithes or of those who are not; the verse is also read as applying to Prophets like Elijah and Moses, particularly in regard to Moses' setting up of the Tabernacle and the significance and consequences of his doing so (Secs. 4–6). The princes of Israel, as they had served their people in Egypt and in the desert, also served them in providing the oxen and wagons that carried about the Tabernacle and its appurtenances. The number of wagons was fixed not at seven but at six—seven would have stood for the days of the earth's creation and the setting up of the Tabernacle, both symbols of eternity—to parallel the six days of man's work, the six orders of the Mishnah, the six Matriarchs and their chastity, and so on (Sec. 7). The oxen themselves, cleaving, as it were, to their task of conveying the Tabernacle about, were rewarded with many, many years of life—how much more and more life, then, is to be Israel's reward for cleaving unto God! (Sec. 8).

PISKA 1

It was on [Israel's] bridal (klt) day that Moses brought to a conclusion (klwt) [the coming back to earth that God had begun in the days of Abraham] (Num. 7:1).[1]

1. *I am come [back] into My garden, My sister, My bride* (Song 5:1). R. Azariah, citing R. Judah bar[2] R. Simon, told the parable of a king who became so angry at his wife that he deposed her and cast her out of his palace. After a time when he was willing to bring her back and restore her to her place,[3] she said: Let him first renew for my sake his former practice [of accepting from my hand whatever I offered him], then let him bring me back and restore me to my place.[4] Thus in the past [when the Holy One had withdrawn far from men into heaven], yet from above He would still accept their offerings, as it is said of Noah's offering [*From above*] *the Lord smelled*[5] *the sweet odor* (Gen. 8:21). Now, however, He will renew His ancient practice of accepting their offerings while close to them here on the earth below: *I am come [below] into My garden, My sister, My Bride.* Thus incidentally, according to R. Ḥanina, Torah teaches one good manners, as that a groom is not to enter the bridal bower until his bride gives him leave: *Let my Beloved come into His garden* (Song 4:16), and only after that *I am come into My garden* (Song 5:1).

[With regard to God's presence on earth at the beginning of time], R. Tanḥum, the son-in-law of R. Eleazar ben Abina, citing R. Simeon ben Yosne, noted that Song does not say "I am come into a garden" but *I am come into My Garden.* [For *gnni*, "My garden"], read *ginuni*,[6] "My bride's

1. In the comments which follow, the verse is apparently so construed. The word *klt* is thus read in two senses: as if spelled *kallaṯ*, "bridal"; and as spelled in MT, *klwt*, "brought to a conclusion." JV: *It came to pass on the day that Moses had made an end of*, etc. The passage is the lesson for the Sabbath during Hanukkah. See Meḡ 3:6.

2. "R. Judah bar"—O_1.

3. *Hḥzyr* is here read in two senses: "bring back," as well as "restore to one's place."

4. Here, too, the verb *hḥzyr* is read in two senses.

The preceding verse *Let my Beloved come [below] into His garden* (Song 4:15) is construed as Israel's request of God. Thereupon, in token of His choice of Israel as the agent whereby man who forced God out of Eden is to be redeemed, God says, *Let them make Me the Sanctuary that I may dwell among them* (Exod. 25:8).

5. The only such reference to God in Scripture.

6. The change involves only vocalization.

power," My and man's dwelling place where at the beginning of time the Divine Root was implanted—yes, originally the root of the Presence was fixed in the regions of the earth below. The verse *They used to hear the voice of the Lord God as* [*Adam*] *would walk in the Garden*[7] (Gen. 3:8) proves God's presence on the earth at the beginning of time, for, as R. Abba bar Kahana noted: The text does not really say "would walk in" but "walked away from" [and refers not to Adam] but to God who, [after Adam had sinned, was angered], yet in reluctance[8] walked away from [him towards heaven]. Thereupon *Adam and his wife were all but hid* (*ibid.*) because, as R. Aibu explained, in that instant Adam was deposed from his high place and his stature was diminished to no more than a hundred cubits (*ḳomah*).[9]

[As to who brings about God's return to the earth], R. Isaac said: It is written *The righteous shall inherit the earth, and dwell thereon in eternity* (Ps. 37:29). And where will the wicked dwell? Are they to fly about in the air? The concern of the verse, however, is not the dwelling place of the righteous or the wicked: by *shall . . . dwell thereon in eternity* is meant that the righteous bring it about that the Eternal shall dwell[10] on the earth.

At the beginning of time, accordingly, the root of the Presence was fixed in the regions of the earth below. After Adam sinned, the Presence withdrew to the first heaven. The generation of Enosh arose: they sinned; the Presence withdrew from the first heaven to the second. The generation of the flood arose: they sinned; the Presence withdrew from the second heaven to the

7. JV: *And they heard the voice of the Lord God walking in the garden.* But see PR 15:3; and Targum Jonathan on Gen. 3:24.

8. Ordinarily—so Rabbi Mordecai Savitsky avers—the verb *ḳpṣ* means "jump down" (see B.BḲ 21b). Hence the addition of *slyḳ*, "ascended," is a way of saying that here "jump" means not "down" as generally intimated by *kpṣ*, but "up." God's "jumping up" however in this instance was in short leaps, the precise connotation of the intensive *mĕḳappeṣ*. Hence "in reluctance."

9. The reduction in Adam's height from what is assumed to have been two hundred cubits to one hundred cubits (see B. Sanh 100a) is regarded as symbolic of the reduction in his, and hence of all mankind's, moral stature as a consequence of his sin. This reduction in man's moral stature and its subsequent elevation to the grandeur of human nature before Adam's sin is represented symbolically in Jewish history by the heights of the two Temples; the one which was twice destroyed in the past is taken as representative of man's lowered moral stature and hence is regarded as having been only one hundred cubits high (see Maimonides' Code VIII, I, iv, 3 [YJS, *12*, 18]); the other, the never-to-be-destroyed Temple of the future to be built in the time of the Messiah is regarded as representative of the heightening of mankind's moral stature in the Messiah's time and hence will be two hundred cubits high.

The idea of the greater height of the Temple and of mankind's greater moral stature in the time of the Messiah is derived from Leviticus 26:11: *I will set My Temple among you . . . and I will* [*again*] *walk among you . . . I have broken the*

third. The generation of the dispersion of the races of man arose: they sinned; the Presence withdrew from the third heaven to the fourth. The Egyptians in the days of our father Abraham arose: they sinned; the Presence withdrew from the fourth heaven to the fifth. The Sodomites arose: they sinned; the Presence withdrew from the fifth heaven to the sixth. The Egyptians in the days of Moses arose: from the sixth heaven to the seventh.

Over against these wicked men, seven righteous men arose and brought it about that the Presence came back to the earth. Our father Abraham arose: the merit he earned brought it about that the Presence came back from the seventh heaven to the sixth.[11] Isaac arose: the merit he earned brought it about that the Presence came back from the sixth heaven to the fifth. Jacob arose: the merit he earned brought it about that the Presence came back from the fifth heaven to the fourth. Levi arose: the merit he earned brought it about that the Presence came back from the fourth heaven to the third. Kohath arose: the merit he earned brought it about that the Presence came back from the third heaven to the second. Amram arose: the merit he earned brought it about that the Presence came back from the second heaven to the first. Moses arose: the merit he earned brought it about that the Presence came back to the earth. Hence [the reference to Moses] in the verse *It was on Israel's bridal (klt) day that Moses brought to a conclusion (klwt) [the coming back to earth that God had begun in the days of Abraham]*[12] (Num. 7:1).

2. *King Solomon made Himself a Pavilion* (Song 3:9). By *Pavilion* is meant the Tabernacle; *King Solomon (Šĕlomoh) made Himself*:[12a] that is, the King of the universe needing a means of private communication [with

---

bars of your yoke, and made you go upright (ḳomĕmiyyṯ). *Ḳomĕmiyyṯ*, a *hapax legomenon*, usually read "go upright" is here, in regard to Israel's moral stature, construed as *ḳom me'oṯ*—that is, "a height of hundreds." In keeping with Rabbinic practice, when no specific number is given, a plural is taken to refer to no more than two of a kind; hence, "a height of hundreds" is taken to signify two hundred cubits, the grand height to which the Temple and mankind will be raised in the time of the Messiah.

10. By a slight change in vowels, *yiškĕnu*, "shall dwell," may be read *yaškinu*, "shall cause to dwell." *'Aḏ*, "in eternity," taken as a noun, is rendered "the Eternal," or "the Eternal presence."

11. In parallels, such as PR 5:7, Cain is charged with having driven the Presence to the second heaven. Thus the anachronism of the Presence's anticipating in Abraham's time the Egyptians' sin in Moses' time is done away with. Accordingly, in Abraham's day the Presence had already removed itself to the seventh heaven.

12. Since it was Moses who brought God back to earth, he, and not the architect Bezalel, is credited with completing the Tabernacle in which God was to dwell.

12a. "Whenever Solomon (*Šĕlomoh*) is mentioned in Song of Songs the name is sacred" (B. Sheḇu 35b), referring as it does to God to whom peace (*šalom*) belongs.

Israel] (*haš-šillum*[13] *šello*), *made* [*it for*] *Himself.* In explanation of the verse, R. Judah bar Il'a'i told the parable of a king who had a young daughter. Before she was old enough to show the signs of puberty, he felt free to talk to her wherever he saw her—whether in the market, in alleys or in lanes, he felt free to talk to her. But after she came of age and showed the signs of puberty, he said: It does not suit the deference owed to my daughter that I speak to her in public. Make a pavilion for her, and I will speak to her in privacy within the pavilion. So [was it between God and Israel]. At the beginning *When Israel was a child in Egypt, then in My love of him, I used to cry out* [wherever I saw him], *"O son of Mine"* (Hos. 11:1). Thus it came about that the children of Israel saw Me in Egypt when I said *I will go through the land of Egypt* (Exod. 12:12); they saw Me at the Red Sea, *when Israel saw the great Hand* (Exod. 14:31); they saw Me at Sinai when, according to Scripture, *The Lord spoke with you face to face* (Deut. 5:4). But once they accepted the Torah and hence were regarded by Me as a people come of age, I said, It no longer suits the deference owed to My children that I speak to them in public. Make ye the Tabernacle for Me, and then I shall speak to them[14] [in privacy] from within the Tabernacle. Thus Scripture: *And when Moses went into the Tent of Meeting that He might speak with him*, etc. (Num. 7:89).

The requirement that the pavilion be made *of* [*cedar*] *wood of Lebanon* (Song 3:9) parallels "And thou shalt make the boards of the Tabernacle of *shittim* cedars[15] standing upright" (Exod. 26:15). The statement that *He made the pillars thereof of silver* (Song 3:10) parallels "The hooks of the pillars and their fillets shall be of silver" (Exod. 27:10). The phrase *The top thereof of gold* (Song 3:10) parallels "And thou shalt overlay the boards with gold" (Exod. 26:29). The phrase *The covering*[16] *of it of purple* (Song 3:10) parallels "[To cover] the Holy of Holies thou shalt make a veil of blue and purple" (Exod. 26:31). What, then, parallels the term *love* in the statement *The inside thereof being inlaid with love* (Song 3:10)? While R.

13. Cf. "We shall communicate (*nĕšalmah*) with our lips offerings of oxen" (Hos. 14:3 literally).

14. "to them"—C, Cas, Yalḳuṭ. After the revelation at Sinai, the only way of communication between God and Israel. So KY; see also PR 5:10.

15. A variety that grew in Lebanon (Mah on Num. Rabbah 12:4). Jacob and his sons planted these trees in Egypt; and when the children of Israel left Egypt they took them along for use in the building of the Tabernacle (Ginzberg, *Legends*, *3*, 164).

Lebanon, "the whitener," is an epithet for the Tabernacle which "whitens" Israel's dark sins (Sif Deut., ed. Finkelstein, p. 45).

16. *The covering*—Septuagint; JV: "The seat." Rashi construes *the covering* as the veil which is stretched between posts standing in front of the Holy of Holies and shields it.

Yudan took the term to mean merit of study of Torah and merit of righteous men, R. Azariah, citing R. Judah bar R. Simon, asserted that by *love* is meant the Presence. For, according to R. Abba[17] bar Kahana, the verse *And there*[18] *I will meet with thee* (Exod. 25:22) proves that even the Tabernacle area that was west of the Ark-cover[19] was not devoid of the Presence.

A heathen put the following question to Rabban Gamaliel: Why did the Holy One reveal Himself to Moses in a thorn bush? Rabban Gamaliel replied: Had He revealed Himself high in a carob tree or high in a fig tree, what would you have said? [Would you not have argued that He shunned the lowly thorn bush]?[20] As it is, you see that no place on earth is devoid of the Presence.

R. Joshua of Siḵnin said in the name of R. Levi: With what is the Tent of Meeting to be compared? With a cave situated on the edge of the sea. When the sea rises and floods it, the cave, of course, is filled by the sea, yet the sea is not diminished. Likewise, the Tent of Meeting was filled with the splendor of the Presence, an event, according to Scripture, which took place when *On* [*Israel's*] *bridal day Moses brought to a conclusion* [*the coming back to earth that God had begun in the days of Abraham*] (Num. 7:1).

3. *Go forth, O younglings whose name Zion indicates that you bear a sign* (*ṣywn*)[21] (Song 3:11): O sons of Israel, you who for My sake bear the sign of circumcision, the sign upon head and face of hair unshaved,[22] and the sign of fringes on the corners of your garments, *gaze upon King Solomon* (*Šĕlomoh*) (*ibid.*)—upon the King of the universe who has the power to make peace (*hišlim*) by making His creations surrender to one another and even by making Himself surrender (*haš-šillum šello*).

The words *Upon King Solomon* (*Šĕlomoh*) mean that the sons of Israel are bidden to gaze upon the King of the universe who has the power to make His creations surrender (*hišlim*) to[23] His creatures—He made fire surrender to Abraham; He made the sword's edge surrender to Isaac; He made an angel surrender to our father Jacob.[24]

17. "R. Abba"—O_1, C, Cas; S: "R. Aḥa."

18. The word *there* is construed as implying the Tabernacle's entire area.

19. The back chamber west of the Ark-cover contained no sacred vessels, only documents concerning such matters as priestly lineage. See Mid 1:1, and Lieberman, *HJP*, 172.

20. See MhG Exod., p. 45.

21. JV: *Go forth, O ye daughters of Zion.*

22. See Lev. 19:27.

23. "surrender to"—O_1, and parellels in Num. Rabbah 12:8; O: "make peace with."

24. The fire did not even singe Abraham when he was thrown into the furnace; the knife touched Isaac's throat, yet he was saved; the angel who fought Jacob had to admit defeat and beg for peace.

Or the words *Upon King Solomon* (*Šĕlomoh*) mean that the sons of Israel are bidden to gaze upon the King of the universe who [without enforcing surrender] makes peace (*šalom*) among His creatures. In reference to this comment R. Johanan cited [*Merciful*] *dominion and fear are* [*at peace*] *with Him* (Job 25:2), and, in keeping with R. Jacob of Kefar Ḥanan's identification of [*Merciful*] *dominion* as Michael and *fear* as Gabriel,[25] asserted that the words *are* [*at peace*] *with Him*[26] imply the surrender of both angels to God so that one does not injure the other. R. Johanan said further: [*All things in creation are at peace with Him* (Job 25:2) because He has given each one its specific place]. Thus the sun has never seen the black, unshining face of the moon;[27] no planet rises out of its turn before another; no planet beholds the one above it, for all the planets revolve, so R. Levi[28] said, as on a spiral stairway.[29]

With regard to the verse *Who layest the beams of Thine upper chambers in the waters, who makest the flaming fires Thy ministers* (Ps. 104:2–3), R. Simeon ben Yoḥai taught: The firmament is water, and the stars are fire, yet they dwell with each other and do no harm one to the other. The firmament is water, the ministering angel is fire, yet they live with each other and do no harm one to the other. R. Abin added: Nor is the peace between one angel and another the end of the matter! For each angel is himself part fire and part water, and between the two He makes peace. Indeed the verse [*The angel's*] *body was like the beryl, and his face as the appearance of lightning, and his eyes as torches of fire, and his arms and his feet like in color to burnished brass, and the voice of his words like the voice of a roaring multitude* (Dan. 10:6) indicates that within each angel there are five elements all different from one another, yet not one harms the others.[30]

[That hostile elements can even work together is illustrated by the verse] *So there was hail, and fire flashing continually amidst the hail* (Exod. 9:24). R. Judah's explanation of this verse was that phials made of hail and filled with fire [came down]. R. Nehemiah said: Fire and hail, mingling, were made to work together. R. Judah's explanation, said R. Ḥanin, brings to mind the pomegranate within whose pulp the seeds are visible; while R. Nehemiah's explanation, R. Ḥanin went on to say, brings to mind a crystal lamp wherein

25. The opposition set up in this verse is between God's mercy and God's judgment. God's continuing dominion of man depends upon His mercy which is represented by the angel Michael; God's judgment, of which man stands in terror, is represented by Gabriel (see Num. Rabbah 12:8).
26. The verse goes on to say *He maketh peace in His high places.*
27. That the moon might not be humiliated.
28. "R. Levi"—O_1, C, Cas, and Yalḳuṭ; S: "R."
29. See Saul Lieberman in Lev. Rabbah M, 871.
30. "Yet not one harms the others"—C.

equal amounts of water and oil work together to keep the flame of the wick burning above the water and oil.[31]

In the verse just cited, namely, *So there was hail and fire mṯlḳhṯ* (Exod. 9:24), what is the precise meaning of *mṯlḳhṯ*? R. Judah bar Simon, dividing the word into two, said: Both the fire and the hail were resolved to die (*myta*) in their determination (*lhḳt*)[32] to carry out God's charge [that they work together for Him]. R. Aḥa illustrated their action by the parable of a king who had two fierce legions that were hostile to each other, but when the king's own war had to be fought, they made peace with each other [and fought for him]. So, too, fire and hail are hostile to each other, yet when the war of the Holy One had to be fought in Egypt "It came to pass that hail and fire resolved to die . . . [for Him]" (Exod. 9:24)—a double miracle [for each of the two willingly surrendered its own being to the other].

In comment upon the verse *Even upon the crown wherewith his mother hath crowned him in the day of his espousals* (Song 3:11), R. Isaac said: We went through all of Scripture, from first to last, and did not find that Bathsheba had made a crown for her son Solomon. Hence it must be concluded that by *the Crown* is signified the Tent of Meeting because, like a crown, it is topped with blue, purple, and scarlet. [Seeking another explanation, however], R. Simeon ben Yoḥai, according to R. Ḥunya, asked R. Eleazar bar R. Jose:[33] Have you perhaps heard from your father an interpretation of the verse *Even upon the crown wherewith his mother hath crowned him?* R. Eleazar replied: The verse may be understood by the parable of a king who

31. [The simile is of a rather deep lamp, filled half with water and half with oil, the oil, being lighter, floating above the water. The wick is short, so that it does not extend below the level of the oil, and the light fed by the oil burns above both the oil and the water. When all the oil is gone, the wick is automatically doused by the water, and so the earthenware lamp is prevented from heating up and cracking and perhaps burning down the house. L. N.]

32. Saul Lieberman's reading and explanation are followed here (PRKM, p. 473). Cf. "These last (lightning and thunderbolts) provided a most marvelous spectacle, for they ran through the hail, their natural antagonist, and yet did not melt it nor were quenched by it, but unchanged coursed up and down and kept guard over the hail" (Philo, *The Life of Moses*, *1*, 118; ed. Colson, *6*, 337).

33. R. Simeon ben Yoḥai turned to R. Eleazer because R. Eleazer's father, R. Jose ben Ḥalafta the historian, was the best judge of the range of meaning in any verse in the Song of Songs. That R. Simeon turned to R. Eleazer would indicate that the Song's interpretation had long been linked with the crossing of the Red Sea, the revelation at Sinai, and the building of the Tabernacle. The Song was systematically interpreted as symbolizing each of these events, and it was for this reason that R. Simeon asked R. Eleazar how Song 3:11 was to be construed in reference to the building of the Tabernacle (see Saul Lieberman's Appendix D in Scholem, Gershom G., *Jewish Gnosticism, Merkabah Mysticism, and Talmudic Tradition* [New York, 1960], pp. 118–26).

had a daughter whom he loved inordinately. He did not stop calling her endearing names until he had called her "my sister"; even then, he did not stop his endearment of her but went on to call her "my mother." So at first, in His endearment of Israel, the Holy One called her "My daughter"—*Hearken, O daughter, and consider* (Ps. 45:11). He did not stop His endearment of her but went on to call her "My sister"—*My sister, My bride* (Song 5:1). Even then He did not stop His endearment of her but went on to call her "My mother," as is indicated by the verse *Attend unto Me, O My people, and give ear unto Me, O My nation* (Isa. 51:4), where *u-lĕ-'ummi*, "My nation," is spelled defectively so that it may read *u-lĕ-'immi*, "My mother."[34] [Upon hearing this interpretation of *Even upon the crown*, etc.], R. Simeon ben Yoḥai rose, kissed R. Eleazar on the brow, and said to him: Had I come and heard nothing but this interpretation, I would have been content.

R. Joshua of Sik̲nin taught in the name of R. Levi that when the Holy One said to Moses: "Make the Tabernacle for Me," Moses might simply have brought four poles and stretched skins over them to form the Tabernacle. Since he did not do so, we may infer from the verse cited below that while Moses was on the Mount, the Holy One showed him red fire, green fire, black fire, white fire, and said to him: Make the Tabernacle for Me [in these fiery colors]. Moses asked the Holy One: Master of universes, where am I to get red fire, green fire, black fire, and white fire? The Holy One replied: AFTER *the pattern which is being shown thee in the Mount*[35] (Exod. 25:40).

In the name of R. Levi also, [in further reference to the building of the Tabernacle], R. Berechiah cited the parable of a king who appeared before his steward in a garment covered entirely with precious stones and said to him: Make one like this for me. The steward replied: My lord king, how am I to get the materials with which to make a garment covered entirely with precious stones? The king replied: Follow the pattern with whatever materials you have, and I will still reign in my glory. Even so the Holy One said to Moses: If you pattern the Tabernacle here below after the one in heaven above, I will leave My heavenly counselors, come down, and so shrink My presence as to fit into your midst below. Even as *Seraphim stand* (Isa. 6:2) above, so the Tabernacle's *boards of shittim cedars stand* (Exod. 26:15)

34. The defective spelling of *u-lĕ-'ummi* does indeed occur in O_1 and in C. R. Jose read Song 3:11 as "The crown wherewith He crowned Himself [in calling Israel] 'His mother'."

35. The Tabernacle was to be made in these colors of fire, not out of fire itself. Cf. the conclusion of Exod. 25:9, *Even so shall ye make it*, with Exod. 25:40 which merely requires that the general pattern be followed. Although the latter verse seems to speak only of the lampstand, it is construed, nevertheless, as referring also to the Tabernacle, details of whose construction follow.

here below. Even as the stars are above, so the Tabernacle's clasps are here below, a parallel which proves, according to R. Ḥiyya bar Abba, that the Tabernacle's golden clasps looked like stars fixed in the firmament.

By the words *In the day of His espousals* (Song 3:11) is meant the day of God's betrothal of Israel [at Sinai];[36] and by the words *in the day of the gladness of His heart* (*ibid.*) is meant the day He entered the Tent of Meeting.

Or by the words *In the day of His espousals* is meant the day He entered the Tent of Meeting; and by the words *in the day of the gladness of His heart* is meant His gladness at Israel's building of the eternal Habitation.[37] Hence it is said *It was on [Israel's] bridal day that Moses brought to a conclusion [God's coming back to earth,* etc.] (Num. 7:1).

4. [Yet, as Scripture affirms, He comes and goes as He likes—indeed, His power is endless]: *Who ascends up into heaven, and descended? Who gathers the wind in His fists? Who binds the waters in His garment? Who raises up all those who have come to their end upon*[38] *the earth? What is His name, and what is His son's name, if thou knowest?* (Prov. 30:4). *Who ascends up into heaven?* The Holy One, of whom it is written "God ascends amidst [man's trembling, a trembling like] the tremolo (*tĕru'ah*) [of the shofar that bespeaks man's fear of God's judgment]" (Ps. 47:6).[39] *And descended*? "And the Lord came down upon Mount Sinai" (Exod. 19:20). *Who gathers the wind?* "In His hand is the soul of every living thing, and the breath of all mankind" (Job 12:10). *Who binds the waters?* "He bindeth up the waters in His thick clouds" (Job 26:8). *Who raises up all those who have come to their end upon the earth?* "The Lord killeth, and maketh alive" (1 Sam. 2:6). *What is His name?* His name is "Rock"; His name is "Shaddai"; His name is "Lord of Hosts." *And what is His son's name?* His son's name is "Israel, My first-born" (Exod. 4:22).

In further comment [the verses are taken as referring successively to different kinds of men. Thus] the first part of the first verse is read *Who ascends up into heaven and brings down?* and is taken to be asking: Who is he whose prayer goes up to heaven and causes rain to come down? The man who bestows his tithes in generous fistfuls; it is he who causes dew and rain

36. "at Sinai"—parallels in Num. Rabbah 12:8, and Song Rabbah 3:11.

37. For even though the Temple was destroyed twice, God never left the site upon which it had been built. See MTeh 11:3, and PR 15:10.

38. The commentator will take *'fsy*, "ends of," in its other meaning of "those who have come to naught in." So David Luria on Num. Rabbah 12:11. Strashun, in the addenda to his Novellae on Num. Rabbah 12:11, reads, by a transposition of letters, *'sfy*, that is "those who have been gathered into [the earth]." JV: *Who hath established all the ends of the earth.*

39. See PR 40:5.

to come down upon the world.[40] *Who gathers the wind in his fists? Who binds the waters in his garment? Who raises up all that betokens an end of the earth?* In other words, who is the one [whose actions are fruitless], whose prayer does not go up to heaven and does not cause rain to come down? The man who does not bestow his tithes in generous fistfuls: it is he who keeps the heavens from bringing dew and rain to the world.[41]

In another comment the questions are taken to refer to Elijah: *Who hath ascended up into heaven?* Elijah, as is said "Elijah went up by a whirlwind into heaven" (2 Kings 2:11). *And descended?* "The angel of the Lord said to Elijah: "Go down with him; be not afraid" (2 Kings 1:15). *Who hath gathered the wind*[42] *in his fists?* [Elijah, who said]: "As the Lord, the God of Israel, liveth . . . there shall not be dew nor rain these years" (1 Kings 17:1). *Who hath bound the waters?* Elijah, who "took his mantle and wrapped it together, and smote the waters, and they were divided" (2 Kings 2:8). *Who hath raised up all those who have come to their end upon the earth?*[43] Elijah, who said: "See, thy son liveth" (1 Kings 17:23).

In another comment the questions are taken to refer to Moses: *Who hath ascended up into heaven?* Moses, as is said "And Moses went up unto God" (Exod. 19:3). *And descended?* "And Moses went down from the Mount" (Exod. 19:14). *Who hath gathered the wind in his fists?* [Moses]: "As soon as I am gone out of the city, I shall spread forth my hands unto the Lord"[44] (Exod. 9:29). *Who hath bound the waters in a garment?* [Moses, at whose bidding] "The floods stood upright as a heap" (Exod. 15:8). *Who hath established all the ends of the earth?* Moses, by means of the Tent of Meeting. For the verse *It was on the day that Moses brought to a conclusion the setting up of the Tabernacle* (Num. 7:1), signifies that through the Tabernacle the stability of the earth was achieved. As R. Joshua ben Levi, citing R. Simeon ben Yoḥai, pointed out: The text does not simply say "setting up of the Tabernacle," but actually says *setting up of [another] along with*[45] *the Tabernacle.* What was the "other" set up along with the Tabernacle? It was the earth that was set up with it. Until the Tabernacle was set up, the

40. See Mal. 3:10.

41. Cf. *The Lord will make the rain of thy land powder and dust* (Deut. 28:24).

42. During the rainy season in the Land of Israel, gusts of wind precede the fall of rain.

43. See Piska 1, note 38. It may also mean—as the late Professor Mordecai Margulies suggested in a private communication—"Who raised wonder and astonishment in the hearts of all the earth's inhabitants?"

44. And hold back the hail.

45. The Rabbis frequently treated the accusative particle *'t*—here rendered "[another] along with"—as an extending particle which adds to the text something that is not explicitly stated therein.

earth was unstable. After the Tabernacle was set up, the earth became stable. Hence Scripture: *It was on the day that Moses brought to a conclusion the setting up of* [*another*] *along with the Tabernacle* (Num. 7:1).

5. Further comment on the word *klt* in the verse *It was on the day that Moses brought to a conclusion* (*klt*) (Num. 7:1). Comment above on *klt* has pointed to its defective spelling as permitting it to be read *kallaṯ* meaning "bridal,"[46] and hence referring to the day that [Israel] entered the bridal chamber as God's bride. In what follows, however, *klt* is read in the sense of "brought to an end." As to what was brought to an end, R. Eleazar and R. Samuel bar Naḥmani differ. R. Eleazar said: The verse *It was on the day that Moses brought to an end* (Num. 7:1) refers to the day he ended his daily setting up of the Tabernacle, concerning which we have the following Baraita: On each of the [seven] days [of the priests' investiture] Moses used to set up the Tabernacle, bringing his offerings therein each and every morning and then taking it apart; on the eighth day, however, Moses set it up but did not take it apart.[47] That Moses thought it necessary to set up the Tabernacle in the light of day, implies, according to R. Ze'era, that the altar's being set up the night before did not qualify it for offerings to God on the following day.[48] R. Samuel bar Naḥmani disagreed with R. Eleazar, saying: On the eighth day also Moses set it up and took it apart.[49]

Whence do we know that the taking apart of the Tabernacle occurred daily? From the verse *It was on the day that Moses brought to an end the setting up of the Tabernacle* (Num. 7:1) which suggests, as R. Ze'era pointed out, that the daily setting up had come to an end [and hence that the daily taking apart had also come to an end].

46. The word *klt* is usually translated "made an end of," as though spelled *klwt*, which is the spelling in MT. But *Minḥaṯ šay* on Num. 7:1 cites several references to the defective spelling of this word.

47. Possibly to show the priests and Levites how their service was to be performed. For the same reason, seven days before the Day of Atonement, the High Priest himself used to perform the daily tasks in the Sanctuary. See Yoma 1:2.

48. Scripture might have read "It was when Moses," etc. The fact that it reads *It was on the day*, etc. is taken to indicate that the Tabernacle's being set up the preceding night did not qualify it for sacrificial service on the following day.

49. According to R. Eleazar, at the end of the seventh day, Moses had completed his instruction of the priests and the Levites. But, according to R. Samuel bar Naḥmani, on the eighth day, Moses instructed Aaron and his sons in the burning of incense on the golden altar within the Tabernacle (see Rashi on Lev. 10:23). Inasmuch as during the preceding seven days Aaron and his sons were enjoined to remain at the entrance of the Tent of Meeting and thus were denied access to its interior (Lev. 8:33), they had no previous opportunity to learn how such a rite was to be carried out. And so, since on the eighth day also Moses ministered at the rites in the Tabernacle, he, according to R. Samuel, not only had to set up the Tabernacle on that day, but also had to take it apart.

In regard to this same verse, R. Eleazar and R. Johanan had a difference of opinion. R. Eleazar took the words *It was on the day that Moses brought to an end* (Num. 7:1) as proving it was on this day that demons came to an end in the world. And his proof? The verse *There shall no evil thing befall thee, neither shall any demon come nigh by reason of thy Tent* (Ps. 91:10)[50] —in short, once the Tent of Meeting was set up, demons came to an end in the world. But R. Johanan said: Why need I draw such proof at such a remove in Scripture when I may draw it from the passage in hand? *The Lord bless thee, and keep thee* (Num. 6:24)—keep thee from demons, of course.

R. Johanan also differs with R. Simeon ben Laḳish, for R. Johanan took the words *It was on the day that Moses brought to an end* as proving it was on this day that enmity came to an end in the world. Until the Tabernacle was set up, there was enmity,[51] jealousy, rivalry, wrangling, and dissension in the world. But after the Tabernacle was set up, love, affection, friendship, mercy, and peace were bestowed upon the world. And the proof? The verse *He will speak peace unto His people . . . when [by means of the Tabernacle, God's] glory is made to dwell in our Land* (Ps. 85:9–10). But Simeon ben Laḳish said: Why draw such an implication at such a remove in Scripture when I may draw it from the passage in hand? *The Lord . . . give thee peace* (Num. 6:26) immediately precedes *It was on the day that Moses brought to an end the setting up of the Tabernacle* (Num. 7:1). for, as R. Joshua [ben Levi], citing R. Simeon ben Yoḥai, pointed out: The text does not simply say "setting up of the Tabernacle," but actually says *setting up of [another] along with*[45] *the Tabernacle*. What was the "other" set up along with the Tabernacle? It was the earth that was set up with it. Until the Tabernacle was set up, the earth was unstable. After the Tabernacle was set up, the earth became stable.

6. *Moses . . . had anointed it and sanctified it* (Num. 7:1). After saying *had anointed it and sanctified it*, for what purpose does Scripture go on to say in the same verse *had anointed them and sanctified them* (*ibid.*)? According to R. Aibu, R. Taḥalifa of Caesarea and Resh Laḳish differ in their explanations. One said: After Moses had anointed each vessel in the Tabernacle one at a time, he then anointed all of them together. The other disagreed, saying: The addition of the phrase *he anointed them* means that Moses' anointing of the vessels one at a time was an anointing for the world as we know it and that his anointing them all together was an anointing for the world-to-come.[52]

A like repetition occurs in the verse *Thou shalt . . . couple the Tent*

50. Moses is said to have written Psalm 91 directly after he set up the Tabernacle. See Rashi on B.Sheb̲u 15b.

51. Between God and Israel because of the golden calf. See Num. Rabbah 12:1.

52. So that there would be no need ever again to anoint these vessels. Cf. Num. Rabbah 14:13.

together (Exod. 26:11), which is preceded by *thou shalt couple the curtain* (Exod. 26:6). R. Yudan, R. Levi, and R. Taḥalifa of Caesarea took sides against Resh Lakish in their interpretation of the verses. One side said: After coupling each group of five curtains into two sets, Moses was to couple the two sets, [thus bringing the Tent together].[53] The other side took the second verse to mean "thou shalt couple the curtains together . . . and it shall be one" (ibid.)—that is, the dimensions of the Tabernacle's curtains will remain one and the same for ever, just as the one anointing of the Tabernacle's vessels will endure for ever.[54]

7. *The princes of Israel . . . offered. They were named princes* (Num 7:2) [because as officers appointed by the Egyptians they let themselves be beaten] *with rods*[55] (*ibid.*) [to protect the Israelites put in their charge]. *These are they that were over* [*the Israelites*] *that were numbered* (*ibid.*)—that is, these princes were presently put in charge of [Israel's] four standards in the wilderness.[56]

And [*the princes*] *brought their offering before the Lord, six wagons*, etc. (Num. 7:3), corresponding to the six days of creation; six, corresponding to the six orders of the Mishnah; six, corresponding to the six Matriarchs: Sarah, Rebekah, Rachel, Leah, Bilhah, and Zilpah. According to R. Johanan, the six correspond to the six commandments which a king is bound to obey: *He shall not multiply wives to himself* (Deut. 17:17); *he shall not multiply horses to himself* (Deut. 17:16);[57] *neither shall he greatly multiply to himself silver and gold* (Deut. 17:17); *thou shalt not wrest judgment; thou shalt not respect persons; neither shalt thou take a gift* (Deut. 16:19). In further comment, the six correspond to the six steps of the king's throne.[58] What significance did each step have? When the king set foot on the first step as he was going up to his seat, a herald came forth and cried: *He shall not multiply wives to himself*. When the king set foot on the second step as he was going up to his seat, a herald came forth and cried: *He shall not multiply horses to himself*. When the king set foot on the third step, a herald came forth and cried: *Neither shall he greatly multiply to himself*

53. "Moses was to couple the two sets . . . together]"—Cas. S is obscure.

54. Subsequent Tabernacles or Temples, such as Solomon's, required no new anointing (see Maimonides' *Code*, VIII, II, i, 12 (YJS, *12*, 45). Nor did wrinkles or creases in the Tabernacle's curtains when they were joined together result in any altering of the original dimensions. See Num. Rabbah, ed. A. A. Hal-lewi (Tel Aviv, 1963), p. 509.

55. See Rashi. JV: *these had become princes of the Tribes*. But *maṭṭoṯ* may mean "Tribes" or "rods."

56. During and following the census which was to be taken on the first of Iyyar, a month after the dedication of the Tabernacle. See Num. 1:5–15, and 2:1–31.

57. The verses are listed in the order in which they are cited in Sanh 2:4.

58. See 1 Kings 10:19.

silver and gold. When he set foot on the fourth step, a herald came forth and cried: *Thou shalt not wrest judgment.* When he set foot on the fifth step, a herald came forth and cried: *Thou shalt not respect persons.* When he set foot on the sixth step, a herald came forth and cried: *Neither shalt thou take a gift.* And when he was about to sit down, after having set foot on the seventh step, he was told: Know before Whom you are about to sit down.

And the top of the throne was round behind (1 Kings 10:19) means, according to R. Aḥa, that the throne resembled the seat of Moses:[59] *And there were arms on either side of the throne*[60] *by the place of the seat* (*ibid.*) How was the throne decorated? A golden scepter was suspended behind it, and on top of the scepter was a dove. In the dove's mouth there was a crown of gold, and when the king sat under it on the seat of the throne, the crown all but touched his head.[61]

Finally, the six wagons are taken to correspond to the six firmaments. But are there not seven firmaments? [The seventh firmament], R. Abin explained, is where the King resides and as royal property [is not to be counted with this world's property].

8. [The wagons the princes brought are described as] *ṣab̲*[62] (Num. 7:3), a word which can be read variously as follows: read as *ṣab̲*, "lizard," it signifies that the outer surface of the wagons' frames was as delicately reticulated as the skin of a lizard; [as *ṣb'*, "decorated"], it signifies that the wagons were gaily decorated; [as *ṣb'*, "equipped"], it signifies that the wagons were fully equipped; and finally, [as *ṣbh,* "bent"],[63] it signifies, taught R. Nehemiah, that the body of the wagons was shaped like a bent bow.

And twelve oxen: a wagon for every two of the princes, and for each one an ox (*ibid.*): that is, every two princes together brought one of the wagons, and [the prince] of each and every Tribe brought one ox apiece.[64]

And they offered [*the oxen*] *before the Tabernacle* (Num. 7:3). [Where-

59. The particular place in the synagogue where the elders used to sit was known metaphorically as the seat of Moses or as the throne of Torah, symbolizing the succession of teachers of Torah down through the ages. See Jacob Mann, *Texts and Studies* (Cincinnati, 1931–35), *1*, 237.

60. *"of the throne"* is not in MT.

61. The weight of the crown was too much for the king to bear.

62. EV: *covered.* In the comments that follow, the biliteral *ṣb* will be taken to stand for two letters of three triliteral verbs.

63. So that the holy vessels in them should not split from the sun's heat. R. Nehemiah associates *ṣb* with *ṣbh*, "swell," hence, "arched, bent." See Song Rabbah 6:4.

64. Unless the words *a wagon for every two of the princes, and for each one an ox* (Num. 7:3) had been added to the previous statement that the princes *brought six wagons, and twelve oxen* (*ibid.*), it might have been assumed that six princes brought the six wagons, and that the other six princes brought the twelve oxen,

upon God said to Moses: *Purchase*[65] (Num. 7:5) on behalf of the congregation.

That is, the oxen were to become the property of the congregation so that they could be used for pulling the Tabernacle. If they had not become the property of the congregation, then the princes, despite their good will in dedicating the oxen to the Tabernacle, would have been guilty of violating the regulation, "He who dedicates things unblemished for the Temple's maintenance violates a positive as well as a negative command" (Tos Tem 1:13). To make the oxen the property of the congregation], the princes had the oxen assessed for their monetary value, and then having given the amount of the assessment to the congregation, sold the oxen to the congregation.[66]

In reference to the words which just precede *Purchase* (Num. 7:5), namely, *Thereupon the Lord told Moses to say* (Num. 7:4), what was Moses told to say?[67] According to R. Hoshaia, the Holy One told Moses: Go out and speak soothing[68] words of praise, words of cheer, to the princes[69] [who are distraught because up to now they have contributed nothing to the building of the Tabernacle].[70]

At the same time Moses was distraught, but for a different reason. He said: The holy spirit must have departed from me, and having come to rest upon the princes, [inspired them to bring the wagons and the oxen]. Whereupon the Holy One said: "Moses, if I had wanted the princes to bring their offerings, I would have asked you to tell them so. But what I now tell you is *Purchase; it is of them* (Num. 7:5): The idea of offerings came from the 'them' [referred to elsewhere in Scripture, and not from the princes]." Who, then, are meant by "them"? The Tribe of Issachar who gave the idea to the princes, the Tribe of whom Scripture says, *And of the children of Issachar came men who had understanding of the times* (1 Chron. 12:33). What is meant by *the times*? The right times for doing what should be done, according to R. Tanḥuma; intercalary days and months, according to R. Jose bar Ḳaṣri. Concerning the Tribe of Issachar, Chronicles goes on: *the heads of them were two hundred* (*ibid.*), that is, over the years the Tribe of Issachar was to provide two hundred heads of courts of justice. *And all their brethren were at their commandment* (*ibid.*) implies that their brethren in Israel were to conduct themselves in keeping with the practical advice given them by Issachar. It was the Tribe of Issachar, then, [and not the holy spirit] which

---

each prince bringing a pair of them. Thus each prince would have brought an entire offering—not just a part of one.

65. JV: *Take*.

66. Professor Saul Lieberman has supplied the interpretation of this passage.

67. In Scripture there is no mention of what Moses was to say.

68. The word "say" (*'mr*) is often taken to mean soothing speech.

69. "to Israel" which is in O does not occur in S, C, Cas, or Yalḳuṭ.

70. See Num. Rabbah 12:16.

said to the princes: "This Tent of Meeting that you see being made—how is it to move about? Is it to fly in the air? Make wagons for it and carry its parts therein."[71]

[Though Moses was reassured for himself], he now became fearful [in the princes' behalf], saying: One of the wagons may break down, or one of the oxen may die, and the offering of the princes will thereby come to naught.[72] The Holy One said to Moses: *They shall be to do the service of the Tent of Meeting* (Num. 7:5)—that is, these oxen shall be given being which abides, and they will remain alive for a long, long time.[73] How long did these oxen remain alive? R. Yudan in the name of R. Samuel bar Naḥman, and R. Ḥunya in the name of Bar Ḳappara, said: *In Gilgal they sacrificed the oxen*[74] (Hos. 12:12) [some forty years later]. "Where did they finally offer them?" R. Abba bar Kahana asked and then answered: "In Nob[74] they offered them." But according to R. Abbahu, they offered them in Gibeon.[74] And according to R. Ḥama bar R. Ḥanina, they offered them in the eternal Habitation. R. Levi suggested that R. Ḥama bar Ḥanina's proof was the verse *King Solomon offered a sacrifice of the oxen* (2 Chron. 7:5), where it is not written "a sacrifice of oxen," but *a sacrifice of the oxen*—that is, a sacrifice of the oxen that the princes had brought for carrying the Tabernacle.[75] For in R. Meir's name it is taught: Until the time of Solomon the oxen remained alive, had no offensive odor or appearance, had not grown old—indeed, had no disease whatever.[76]

Now cannot we draw an inference from the oxen's remaining alive? These oxen, made to cleave to no more than the task of conveying the Tabernacle about—if being which abides was given to them, so that they remained alive for many, many years, how much more and more is given to Israel who cleave to the Holy One! *But ye that cleave unto the Lord your God are alive every one of you this day* (Deut. 4:4).

71. See Ginzberg, *Legends*, *3*, 193–94.

72. "come to naught"—C; O: "become unfit."

The Tabernacle had permanence. But what of the oxen and wagons provided by the princes—were these to be eventually discarded?

73. At times the word *lĕʿolam* means "for a long time." See B.Er 54a, and Maimonides, *Guide*, *2*, (Eng. tr., Pines [Chicago, 1963], 334–35), chap. 28.

74. Apparently the commentator uses the verse without reference to its context. JV: *In Gilgal they sacrifice unto bullocks.*

Gilgal (Josh. 4:19), Nob (1 Sam. 21–22), and Gibeon (2 Kings 3:4, 2 Chron. 1:3) were sites where the Tabernacle was set up temporarily before the Temple was built in Jerusalem. See Zeḇ 14: 5–8.

75. "*King Solomon offered* . . . carrying the Tabernacle"—parallel in MTeh 101:4. PRK reads "*Solomon offered for the sacrifice of peace offerings which he offered unto the Lord, two and twenty thousand oxen* (1 Kings 8:63)," a verse from which it is difficult to derive proof for R. Ḥama bar Ḥanina's opinion.

76. Cf. B.Beḵ 41a.

PISKA 2

SUMMARY

How did the children of Israel who had committed the sin of making the golden calf come to the merit of having the Tabernacle in their midst?

Because of the merit of the Fathers, God gave Israel the joy of lifting their heads high again (Sec. 1). Then, too, as a result of Moses' intercession in behalf of Israel—Moses who had been the target of Israel's vile effrontery—God transmuted and purified the offensive "this" by which Israel had contemptuously designated Moses in the phrase *"this" man Moses* (Exod. 32:1) into the redemptive "this" of the phrase *"This" they shall give* (Exod. 30:13), "this" designating here the ransom that Israel gave in expiation of their reprehensible conduct (Secs. 3–4). Moreover, Israel's generosity—so great that within two days they provided all that was needed for the Tabernacle—helped them procure God's forgiveness (Sec. 5). Not at all concerned with the respect due Him, He is ever ready to bestow forgiveness (Sec. 6), particularly upon Israel in whose behalf Moses had asked for His forbearance. Indeed, Moses himself set a human example of forbearance through his bringing back of Reuben into Israel's midst. And so God forgave Israel because, after all, Israel did cleave to Him; because at the Red Sea they were the first to proclaim Him ruler; because at Sinai they took upon themselves the yoke of His rule; and because when all is said and done it is only through Israel that He will ultimately be glorified (Sec. 7). And so in order to assure the continuous flow of His blessings upon Israel, God is reluctant to number Israel since His blessings, bestowed in His own mysterious way, are freely given only to those whose number remains unknown (Sec. 8).

Israel's loss in numbers is mysteriously made up by God again and again, even as a pit dug in the sand in the evening is filled up the following morning (Sec. 9).

In proof of His forbearance God brought forth from under His throne of glory something like a coin of fire, showed it to Moses, and said *This*—the half-shekel—*they shall give* (Exod. 30:13) as their ransom: the half-shekel, whose value is equal to six small coins, is to remind Israel that they worshiped the golden calf in the sixth hour of the day; even as the half-shekel itself, offered as though it were fire in Israel's hand, is meant to evoke dread of what they did and dread of sinning again.

The precise character of the ransom demanded for Israel's soul was one of three commandments which at first startled Moses who felt that no man could possibly comply with any of the three. But God reassured him by saying that He makes demands upon Israel not commensurate with His majesty, but commensurate with Israel's capacity (Sec. 10).

PISKA 2

When thou liftest the heads of the children of Israel (Exod. 30:12)[1]

1. *How great are they that say of my soul: "There is no help for him in God ever"*[2] (Ps. 3:3). R. Samuel bar Ammi and the Rabbis differ as to whom David meant by "they." R. Samuel bar Ammi, identifying them as Doeg and Ahithophel, asserted: Since the *they* of *How great are they that say of my soul* are [the reprobates] Doeg and Ahithophel, why did David call them *great*? Because they were great in knowledge of Torah.[3] *That say of my soul*—It was they who said in reproach of David: A man who seized a ewe lamb, murdered her shepherd, and caused Israelites to die by the sword[4] —can such a man expect God's help? *There is no help for him in God ever.* In these words David acknowledged his guilt: Though Thou, O Lord, dost agree with Doeg and Ahithophel—for in Thy Torah Thou didst write "Both the adulterer and the adulteress shall surely be put to death" (Lev. 20:10)—yet *Thou . . . art a shield about me* (Ps. 3:4). Because of the merit of my fathers Thou didst encompass me as with a shield and thus shielding *my glory* (*ibid.*), Thou didst restore me to kingship. And Thou wast *the lifter up of my head* (*ibid.*). What I deserved from Thee was the removing of my head rather than its lifting up, but through Nathan the prophet Thou didst tell me "The Lord also hath put away thy sin; thou shalt not die" (2 Sam. 12:13), and didst allow me a lifting up of the head.

The Rabbis read the beginning of the verse *How many are they that say* (Ps. 3:3), etc., and identified the "they" as the nations of the earth. Why did David call them *many*? Because the nations are so designated in the verse "Ah, the uproar of many peoples" (Isa. 17:12). *That say of my soul* (Ps. 3:3), that is, they say of Israel: A people who on Mount Sinai heard from its God "Thou shalt have no other gods before Me" (Exod. 20:4), and then, forty days later, said of a calf "This is thy God, O Israel" (Exod. 32:4)—can such a people expect God's help? *There is no help for it in God ever* (Ps. 3:3). Israel replied: Though Thou, O Lord, dost agree with the nations—for in Thy Torah Thou didst write: "He that sacrificeth unto any god, save unto the Lord only, shall be utterly destroyed" (Exod. 22:19)—yet *Thou . . . art*

1. Exod. 30:11–16 is the supplementary lesson (*mafṭir*) in the Pentateuch for Sabbath *Šĕḳalim*—first of the four special Sabbaths—during which the injunction to levy the head-tax for the Temple is read. See Meḡ 3:4.
2. In Rabbinic exegesis, *slh* is generally rendered "ever."
3. See B.Sanh 106:2.
4. The ewe was Bath-sheba, and the shepherd, Uriah. See 2 Sam. 11:12.

a shield about me (Ps. 3:4): solely because of the merit of my Fathers Thou didst encompass us as with a shield. Nay more, *Thou art become my glory* (*ibid.*), for Thou didst cause Thy presence to dwell amidst Israel: "Let them make Me the Sanctuary that I may dwell among them" (Exod. 25:8). *And the lifter up of my head* (Ps. 3:4). What we deserved from Thee was a removing of our heads rather than a lifting up of them, but through Moses to whom Thou didst say *When thou liftest the heads of the children of Israel* (Exod. 30:2), Thou didst give us the joy of lifting our heads high.

2. [It was this joy] R. Jacob bar Yuda, citing R. Jonathan of Beth Gubrin, had in mind when he began his discourse with the verse *The wide road of him who is slothful is like a prickly hedge; but the narrow path of one whose uprightnesses are many is made easy*[5] (Prov. 15:19). *The wide road of him who is slothful*—it is Esau [Rome] who is here referred to as slothful to obey God—*is like a prickly hedge*: Its thorns though plucked away from one side of the road will yet jab a man from the other side. So, [like a prickly hedge], Esau keeps jabbing away at a man: "Bring your head tax, bring your general tax, bring the levies upon your crops and herds." When a man cannot produce the tax, Esau exacts heavy fines and imposes drastic penalties upon him. *But the narrow path of one whose uprightnesses are many is made easy* (*ibid.*). The *one whose uprightnesses are many* is the Holy One, so identified in the verse "The many ways of the Lord are upright" (Hos. 14:10). [He is the one who made it easy for Israel to support the House of God by narrowing down their obligations to a single head tax.[6] And even with this single obligation God is not demanding—indeed He makes it an occasion for exalting Israel]: Moses was to say,[7] *When Thou dost accept the head tax from the children of Israel, Thou also liftest their heads*[8] (Exod. 30:12).

5. JV: *The way of the slothful is as though hedged by thorns; but the path of the upright is even.* But see Elijah of Wilno, Commentary on Proverbs, Wilno, 1885.

Throughout Scripture, the wicked, Ibn Ezra notes, is designated as "slothful" or "sluggardly." See MhG Gen., p. 27.

6. All of Jerusalem was considered as the House of God. Hence the single head-tax—the half-shekel—also provided wages for judges who sat permanently in the Temple, wages for those who examined the accuracy of Torah Scrolls, provided also the cost of maintaining Jerusalem's walls, towers, and water channels, as well as a number of other public services. See Shek 4:1–2; and B.Ket̲ 105a, 106a–b.

7. Literally "He so framed the words Moses was to utter [as to endow them with the promise of exaltation]." In order to provide an intelligible transition, however, between R. Jonathan's comment on Prov. 15:19 and Exod. 30:12, it is necessary to expand the cryptic original into "He is the one who made it easy for Israel . . . Moses was to say."

8. *Tiśśa'* means both "accept" and "lift," the latter meaning inhering in the promise in the same verse that the half-shekel tax asked for is to insure Israel

3. R. Jonathan in his discourse [on the lifting up of the heads of the children of Israel] cited the verse *When the common man bowed down, the great man was humbled,* etc. (Isa. 2:9). By *the common man* is meant Israel of whom it is written "Ye, My sheep, the sheep of My pasture, are common men." (Ezek. 34:31). In *the great man was humbled* it is Moses who is referred to, for of him it is written "Now the man Moses was much humbled" (Num. 12:3). [In behalf of Israel], Moses said bluntly to the Holy One: I know that when Israel bowed down to the golden calf, I, too, was humbled. [Now that Thou hast lifted up my head], *wilt Thou not do as much for them and lift up their heads*? (Isa. 2:9). God replied: *When thou liftest the heads of the children of Israel* (Exod. 30:12), I will do as much for them.

4. R. Jonah of Bozrah beginning his discourse [on the lifting up of the heads of the children of Israel] with the verse *When God judges, He putteth down this one, and lifteth up that one* (Ps. 75:8) told of a Roman lady who asked R. Jose bar R. Ḥalafta: In how many days did the Holy One create His world? R. Jose replied: In six days, for it is written *In six days the Lord made heaven and earth,* etc. (Exod. 31:17). She asked: And what has He been doing since?[9] R. Jose replied: He has been busy making matches: the daughter of Such-and-such to So-and-so, the widow of Such-and-such to So-and-so, the dowry of Such-and-such to [the possessions of] So-and-so. The Roman lady said: If that is all He does, I can do the same thing. How many manservants, how many maidservants have I? In no time at all, I can match them up. R. Jose said: Matchmaking may be a trivial thing in your eyes; but for the Holy One it is as awesome an act as dividing the Red Sea.

Thereupon R. Jose bar R. Ḥalafta left the Roman lady and went away. What did she do? She took a thousand manservants and a thousand maidservants, lined them up in row upon row facing one another, and said: So-and-so shall marry Such-and-such, and Such-and-such shall be married to So-and-so, and thus matched them all up in a single night. In the morning the ones thus matched came to the lady, one with his head bashed in, another with his eye knocked out, still another with his leg broken, this man saying "I don't want that woman," and this woman saying "I don't want that man."

Thereupon the Roman lady sent and had R. Jose bar R. Ḥalafta brought to her. She said to him: Your Torah is unerring and completely right, meriting praise far beyond what you claim. What you said is exactly so. R. Jose replied: Did I not tell you that though matchmaking seems a trivial thing to

against the plague (P. Shek 2:4, 46b; and PR 10:12): thus Israel's heads are lifted high, even as the horns of the altar referred to in the preceding verse are lifted high.

9. Apparently an ironical shaft directed at the Jewish idea that creation was a single act of God in the distant past.

you, for the Holy One it is as awesome an act as His dividing of the Red Sea? What does the Holy One do? Even if they are not happy with each other, He sees to it that they stay together. Of this practice of God's, Scripture says, *When God bringeth single people to dwell together in marriage, it is as awesome as when He brought forth the imprisoned* [*Israelites*] *out of Egypt bakkošaroṯ* (Ps. 68:7). What is meant by *bakkošaroṯ*? Read as made up of the words *bĕḵi*, "weeping," and *široṯ*, "song," it implies that he who accepts the match God makes for him will break out in song, while he who does not accept it, will be constrained to weep.[10]

R. Berechiah, in differing with R. Jonah's version of R. Jose bar R. Ḥalafta's reply to the Roman lady's question about what God has been doing ever since His creation of the world, said that R. Jose's reply was as follows: The holy One has been busy making ladders, having this one ascend and that one descend, lifting this one up and putting that one down—[in short, He has been judging mankind]. Scripture says, *When God judges, He putteth down this one, and lifteth up that one* (Ps. 75:8).

[In another comment the verse is read *When God judges, "this" putteth down, and "this" lifteth up* (*ibid.*), with] R. Jonah of Bozrah and the Rabbis differing as to the person designated by the word "this." The Rabbis said that the verse designates Aaron, who was put down through his using of the word "this" and then was lifted up through God's using of the word "this." Aaron was put down through his using of the word "this": *I cast it into the fire, and there came out "this" calf* (Exod. 32:24). [The contemptuous "this" of *"this" calf* specifies the abomination by which Aaron was degraded, but] this very "this," transmuted and purified by God, also specifies His exaltation of Aaron's and his sons' offering on the day he was anointed High Priest: *"This" is the offering of Aaron and his sons*[11] (Lev. 6:12). On the other hand, R. Jonah of Bozrah said that the verse designates Israel who were put down through their using of the word "this" and then were lifted up through God's using of the word "this." They were put down by using the word "this": *As for "this" man Moses* (Exod. 32:1). [The contemptuous "this" of *"this" man Moses* specifies the vile effrontery towards Moses by which Israel degraded themselves, but] this very "this," transmuted and purified by God, also specifies the ransom Israel gave in expiation of their conduct, the ransom for which God exalted them: *"This" they shall give, every one that passeth among them that are numbered* (Exod. 30:13).[12]

10. Likewise, the Israelites broke out in song while the Egyptians were constrained to weep. See Meḵ, *1*, 140.

11. "The contemptuous 'this' . . . *and his sons*" is a paraphrase of the more literal "On the other hand he was lifted up when God used the word 'this': '*This* *is the offering of Aaron and his sons*.'"

12. "The contemptuous 'this' . . . *that are numbered*" is a paraphrase of the

5. *Charity exalteth the nation; but lovingkindness* (*ḥesed*) *is a sin for* [*other*] *peoples* (Prov. 14:34). R. Eliezer, R. Joshua, and [several other teachers], as well as the Rabbis differ in their interpretations of this verse. R. Eliezer said: *Charity exalteth the nation*—that is, Israel; *but lovingkindness is a sin for* [*other*] *peoples*—even deeds of lovingkindness become a sin for heathen peoples because they boast of such deeds. R. Joshua read the verse as follows: *Charity exalteth the nation*—that is, Israel; *but sin is a boon* (*ḥesed*) *for* [*other*] *peoples*: That is, when Israel sin, it is a boon for the peoples of the world because they can then again impose bondage upon Israel. Rabban Gamaliel read the verse as follows: *Charity exalteth the nation*—that is, Israel; *but lovingkindness is a sin for* [*other*] *peoples:* even an act of lovingkindness—when the peoples of the earth perform one—masks a sin on their part,[13] as Daniel knew when he said to Nebuchadnezzar: *Break off thy sins by almsgiving . . . that there may be a lengthening of thy prosperity* (Dan. 4:24), [saying, in short, that Nebuchadnezzar's true purpose in almsgiving was the increase of his own prosperity]. In his construing of the verse, Rabban Gamaliel thus followed R. Eleazar ben 'Araḵ's transposition of the word *lovingkindness*, reading the verse *Charity and lovingkindness exalt the nation*—that is, Israel; whereas seeming acts of charity and lovingkindness by the peoples of the earth are really sins [because they are performed for private gain]. Concerning R. Eleazar ben 'Araḵ's transposition of *lovingkindness*, Rabban Johanan ben Zakkai is reported to have remarked [to R. Eliezer and R. Joshua]: I prefer Eleazar ben 'Araḵ's exegesis to yours, for he justly attributes both charity and lovingkindness to Israel and attributes sins to the peoples of the earth.

Construing *ḥesed* (Prov. 14:34) not as "lovingkindness" but as "reprimand," Abin bar R. Judah[14] interpreted the verse in Proverbs as follows: *Righteousness exalts the nation*—that is, Israel; *but sin* [in Israel] *provides* [*heathen*] *peoples with* [occasions for] *reprimand*, for when Israel sin, they receive harsh reprimand from the heathen peoples of the earth. Thus the heathen Rab-shakeh found occasion to say to Hezekiah: *Am I now come up without the Lord against this place to destroy it? The Lord said unto me: Go up against this land, and destroy it* (2 Kings 18:25). And the heathen Nebuzaradan found occasion to say to Jeremiah: *The Lord hath brought it, and done according as He spoke, because ye have sinned against the Lord,*

---

more literal "On the other hand they were lifted up when God used the word 'this': '*This' they shall give, every one that passeth among them that are numbered.*" Cf. Piska 4.1, 2.10, and 6.4.

13. Augustine characterizes the pagan virtues as "splendida vitia" = glittering vices (*De civitate dei*, 19.25). Thanks are due to Professor William Schoedel for the analogy.

14. Or, better as in O_1, "R. Judah bar R. Judah."

therefore—the verse now follows the *kĕṯiḇ* in its conclusion—*what He spoke*[15] *is come upon you* (Jer. 40:3).

R. Neḥunya ben hak-Ḳanah taking the word *ḥeseḏ* to mean "pious act" interpreted the verse as follows: *Righteousness exalteth the nation*—that is, Israel; while a *pious act of* [*heathen*] *peoples is deemed a failing*: the pious acts of heathen peoples serve to set off Israel's failure [to match such acts]. How do we come to such a conclusion? From the story of Mesha: *Now Mesha king of Moab was a noḳeḏ* (2 Kings 3:4). What is meant by *noḳeḏ*?[16] It means literally "one who dots" and hence signifies here that his flocks were so many as to dot all the landscape.[17] From these, as Scripture tells us, *He was forced to render unto the king of Israel a hundred thousand fatted lambs and a hundred thousand wool-bearing rams* (*ibid.*)—[not simply "the wool of a hundred thousand rams," as the verse might be read], R. Abba bar Kahana explained, but the rams themselves full-grown and unshorn[18] [—too many even for sheep-rich Mesha to give up]. What did he finally do? He summoned all his astrologers and said to them: Do you maintain that were I to wage war against any other people [than the Jews], I would be victorious, but that if I were to wage war against the Jews, they would be victorious? The astrologers replied: Yes. It is so because of a certain elder they had. He asked: And who was that elder? They replied: Abraham. He asked: What did he do? They replied: At the age of one hundred, having been given an only son, he brought this only son as a sacrifice. Mesha asked: Did he, in fact, offer him up? They replied: No. Thereupon Mesha said to them: If Israel's miraculous victories are won because of Abraham even though he did not actually sacrifice his son, how many more and more miraculous victories would Israel have won had he in fact sacrificed his son! Well, then, a certain person hereabouts has an only son who was meant to rule in his place—but that person will now go and offer his son so that miraculous victories will be won for him as they were for Israel. Of Mesha's act it is written *Then he took his eldest son that should have reigned in his stead, and offered him for a burnt offering upon the wall* (2 Kings 3:27). Since the word *ḥmh,* "wall," is written defectively—without the *waw*—it may be read *ḥammah*, "sun," a reading which implies that Mesha worshiped the sun. [Does Israel match the pious acts of heathen such as Mesha who are so unaware of God as to worship the sun? No]. Therefore Scripture at once goes on to say: *And there came great wrath upon Israel* (*ibid.*). In His wrath the Holy One said to Israel: My children, the nations of the earth, who are

15. The *keṯiḇ* may be read *dibber*, "He spoke"; the *ḳeri is had-daḇar*, "the thing." See Ḳimḥi.

16. In the Septuagint the word is left untranslated, possibly indicating that its special meaning was widely known.

17. Or translated literally in another way, "A raiser of sheep in large numbers."

18. See PR 16:6 (YJS, *18*, 352–53, note 42).

not aware of My strength, in their ignorance do not heed Me, but you, who are aware of My strength, show in your failure to perform pious acts that you do not heed Me either.

R. Mana noted: Israel would have been destroyed in that hour of God's wrath were it not for the merit of Obadiah's wife. And the proof? The verse which follows directly: *Now there cried a certain woman of the wives of the sons of the Prophets unto Elisha, saying: "Thy servant, my husband,"* etc. (2 Kings 4:1), [for in agreement with her husband Obadiah they had pledged their children in return for money they had borrowed[19] to maintain Prophets in hiding].

R. Ze'ira sent word to R. Ze'ir: Have you heard the gem of a comment which R. Huna made on the verse *Righteousness exalteth the nation, but sin is a reproach (ḥesed̲) to any people* (Prov. 14:34)? R. Ze'ir replied: "No. What was it?" Thereupon R. Ze'ira reported R. Huna's construing of the verse: *Righteousness exalteth the nation*—that is, Israel; *but [heathen] peoples' piety (ḥesed̲) brings [punishment for] sin [to Israel]*—that is, a pious act which peoples of the world perform is stored up to harm Israel much as the venom of a serpent can be stored up for harm. From whose pious act does one make such inference? From Merodach's. Merodach-baladan was in the habit of eating at midday and sleeping until three in the afternoon. When, in the days of Hezekiah, the orb of the sun went back ten degrees,[20] Merodach had gone to sleep as usual, but when he rose and found it was morning, he was about to slay all his servants, saying accusingly to them: You have let me sleep all day and all night! They replied: Sire, you ate at your usual time and you slept your usual time: but the orb of the day went backwards [while you slept]. He asked: Which God made it go backwards? They replied: Hezekiah's God made the orb of day go backwards. He asked: Can there be a God greater than my gods? They replied: Hezekiah's God is greater than your gods.

Thereupon he sent letters and a gift to Hezekiah, as is written *At that time Merodach-baladan the son of Baladan, king of Babylon, sent letters and a present to Hezekiah* (Isa. 39:1). What did he write in the letters? "Peace to Hezekiah, peace to his God, peace to Jerusalem." No sooner were the letters despatched, than he bethought himself, saying, "I have not done right: I have put my salutation of Hezekiah before my salutation of his God."

Forthwith he rose from his throne, took three steps, had the letters brought back, and indited other letters in their stead. How did he order the salutations in them? "Peace to the God of Hezekiah, peace to Hezekiah, peace to Jerusalem the holy city."

19. From king Joram, the creditor in 2 Kings 4:1, at a high rate of interest. See Ginzberg, *Legends*, 4, 189–90.

20. See Isa. 38:8.

Thereupon the Holy One said to Merodach: "Thou didst rise from thy throne and take three steps in My honor. By thy life I swear that I will raise up from thee three kings, Nebuchadnezzar, Evil-merodach, and Belshazzar, world-conquerors [in whom will be stored up the venom which will lead to the destruction of Jerusalem]: they will be rulers from world's end to world's end." But finally when they rose up to blaspheme Him, the Holy One extirpated their line and made others rise in their stead.

The Rabbis construed the first part of the verse [previously read *Charity exalteth the nation*] as *Free-giving lifteth the nation* (Prov. 14:34) and said that because of the generous freewill offering which Israel brought for the furnishing of the Tabernacle and the Tent of Meeting,[21] the joy of lifting their heads high was given them through Moses who said: *When Thou liftest the heads of the children of Israel* (Exod. 30:12).

6. R. Yudan began his discourse with the verse *The tongue of the righteous is as choice silver; the heart of the wicked is little worth* (Prov. 10:20). The words *The tongue of the righteous is as choice silver* refer to Jedo the prophet;[22] and the words *the heart of the wicked is little worth* refer to Jeroboam. [As Jeroboam went up to offer upon an altar in a manner his wicked heart had devised], *Behold*—so Scripture tells us—*there came* [*Jedo*] *a man of God out of Judah by the word of the Lord*, etc. *And he cried out against the altar by the word of the Lord, and said: "O altar, altar"* (1 Kings 13:1–2). Why did Jedo repeat the word *altar*? He had in mind—so said R. Abba bar Kahana—the altar at Beth-el as well as the altar at Dan. What did Jedo proclaim would take place upon the altar which Jeroboam had built at Beth-el and at Dan?[23] That *A son shall be born unto the house of David, Josiah by name, and* [*that*] *upon thee,* [*O altar*], *shall he sacrifice the priests of the high places who offer upon thee* (*ibid.*). But note that Jedo went on to say *A certain man's bones shall they burn upon thee* (*ibid.*). The verse shows that in choosing his words carefully so as not to name Jeroboam as the man whose bones would be burned upon the altar, Jedo was according Jeroboam the respect due to royalty. That Jedo had Jeroboam in mind may be inferred from the verse which follows: *And it came to pass when the king heard the saying of the man of God, which he cried out against the altar in Beth-el, that Jeroboam put forth his hand from the altar, saying: "Lay hold on* [*Jedo*]" (1 Kings 13:4). From what follows in Scripture, said R. Huna in the name of R. Idi, we learn that He who is everywhere has greater regard for the respect due to a righteous man than for the respect due to Him. For when Jeroboam was in the act of offering to an idol, his hand did not dry up, but the moment he put forth his hand against a righ-

21. See Exod. 36:3–7.
22. 2 Chron. 9:29.
23. I Kings 12:28–29.

teous man, at once his hand dried up. Thus it is written *And his hand dried up because he put* [*it*] *forth against* [*Jedo, a man of God*][24] (*ibid.*). *Thereupon the king spoke up and said unto the man of God: "Entreat now the favor of the Lord thy God, and pray for me"* (1 Kings 13:6). Concerning Jeroboam's use of the expression *thy God*, two Amoraim differ. One, [having in mind the words of the verse *The heart of the wicked is little worth* (Prov. 10:20)], maintained that [the unregenerate] Jeroboam meant: Thy God, but not my God. The other Amora asked, however: By what brazenness could Jeroboam have spoken of the Lord as "my God?" After all, since he had just been in the act of offering to an idol, how could he have called Israel's Lord "my God?" Whatever Jeroboam may have meant by saying "my God," in his behalf *The man of God entreated the Lord, and the king's hand was restored him; nevertheless it was as before*[25] (*ibid.*). What is meant by *it was as before*? R. Berechiah [and] R. Judah bar R. Simon said in the name of R. Joshua ben Levi: Though you pound a fool in an artisan's mortar, you cannot make anything worthwhile out of him. Thus with Jeroboam [*it was as before*]: even as he had previously made offerings to an idol, so afterwards he kept on making offerings to an idol.

A final comment on [*When Thou liftest*, etc.]: *The tongue of the Righteous is as choice silver* (Prov. 10:20). This is to say that the Holy One, [not at all concerned with the respect due to Him], saw to it that Moses chose words [as precious as choice silver and as dazzling in the unexpected favor they showed to Israel]: *When Thou liftest the head tax from the children of Israel,* [*Thou also liftest their heads*].[26]

7. What verse directly precedes the Sabbath lesson? The verse *Aaron shall make atonement upon the horns of* [*the altar*] *once in the year* (Exod. 30:10). What verse comes next? The verse *When Thou liftest* (*tiśśa'*) *the head of the children of Israel* (Exod. 30:12), where the *kĕṯiḇ*, *taššeh*,[27] "lend," is to be understood as in the verse "When thou lendest (*taššeh*) thy neighbor any manner of loan" (Deut. 24:10). Therefore Moses, in saying *When Thou lendest* (Exod. 30:12), was telling the Holy One bluntly: Master of universes, when Israel have [the merit of having atonement made for them upon the altar], Thou, of course, lettest Israel alone; but when Israel do not have such merit, then, if I dare speak thus, extend credit to them every year on Atonement Day; hence when the Day comes it will in itself procure atonement,[28] *For through this day shall atonement be made for you*, etc. (Lev. 16:30).

24. JV: *And his hand which he put forth against him dried up.*

25. JV: *and became as it was before*, which appears to be redundant. Hence the comment that follows.

26. See Piska 2.2, and note 6.

27. Not in MT.

28. See Sif, ed. Finkelstein (Codex Assemani LXVI), New York, 5716/1956,

In the phrase *the head* (Exod. 30:12), so said R. Jose bar R. Ḥanina, it is intimated that Moses would bring back into Israel's midst the head—that is, the oldest one—of the Tribe Fathers. Who was that? Reuben, of course, of whom at the end of Moses' life, Moses was to say, *Let Reuben live*: [let his sin in lying with Bilhah be remembered no more] *and his people be reckoned in the numbering* [*of Israel*][29] (Deut. 33:6).

In comment on the phrase *children of Israel* (Exod. 30:2), [which occurs so frequently in Scripture], R. Yudan, citing R. Samuel bar R. Naḥman, told the parable of a king who had a particular undergarment concerning which he kept giving commands to his servant, saying to him: Shake it out; fold it up; give it constant care. The servant spoke up: My lord king, of all the undergarments you have, you keep giving me commands only about this one. The king replied: Quite so, because this is the undergarment I wear close to my body. Likewise Moses spoke up to the Holy One: Master of universes, of the seventy sovereign nations which are Thine in the world, it is only concerning Israel that Thou continually commandest me: *Thou shalt say to the children of Israel* (Lev. 20:2); *Thou shalt speak unto the children of Israel* (Exod. 30:31); *Say unto the children of Israel* (Exod. 33:5); *Speak . . . unto the children of Israel* (Exod. 31:13); *Command the children of Israel* (Lev. 24:2); *Thou shalt command the children of Israel* (Exod. 27:20); *When thou liftest the heads of the children of Israel* (Exod. 30:12). The Holy One replied: [I keep commanding thee concerning them] because Israel cleave close unto Me, as is written *As the girdle cleaveth to the loins of a man, so have I caused to cleave unto Me the whole house of Israel*, etc. (Jer. 13:11). R. Abin told the parable of a king who had a purple cloak concerning which he kept giving commands to his servant, saying to him: Shake it out; fold it up; give it constant care. The servant spoke up: My lord king, of all the purple cloaks you have, you keep giving me commands only about this one. The king replied: It is because I had this one on when I was made ruler. Likewise Moses spoke up to the Holy One: Master of universes, of the seventy sovereign nations Thou hast in Thy world, it is only concerning Israel that Thou continually commandest me: *Thou shalt say to the children of Israel; Thou shalt speak unto the children of Israel; Say unto the children of Israel: Speak . . . unto the children of Israel; Command the children of Israel; Thou shalt command the children of Israel; When thou liftest the heads of the children of Israel.* The Holy One replied: I keep giving them commands through thee because Israel

---

p. 453; and R. Judah's opinion in B.Ker 7a. In keeping with other Tannaitic opinion, however, such as found *ibid.*, as well as in P.Yoma 8:8, 45 b–c, and B.Yoma 86a, Maimonides rules that unless there is repentance, the Day itself does not procure atonement. See *Code I*, v, i, 8.

29. See Rashi on Deut. 33:6, and Gen. 35:22.

proclaimed Me ruler at the Red Sea, saying "The Lord shall reign for ever and ever" (Exod. 15:18). R. Berechiah told the parable of an elder who had a headdress concerning which he kept issuing commands to his servant, saying to him: Shake it out; fold it up; give it constant care. The servant spoke up: My lord elder, of all the headdresses you have, you keep giving me commands only about this one. The elder replied: I do so because I wore it when I was first appointed elder. Likewise Moses said to the Holy One: Master of universes, of the seventy sovereign nations that exist in Thy world, it is only concerning Israel that Thou continually commandest me: *Thou shalt say to the children of Israel; Thou shalt speak unto the children of Israel; Say unto the children of Israel; Speak . . . unto the children of Israel; Thou shalt command the children of Israel; When thou liftest the heads of the children of Israel.* The Holy One replied: I keep giving them commands through thee because they took upon themselves the yoke of My kingship at Sinai, saying: "All that the Lord hath spoken, we will do, and hearken" (Exod. 24:7).

R. Yudan said: Come and see how much the Holy One loves Israel, for in a single verse He mentions them five times: *And I have given the Levites—they are given to Aaron and to his sons from among the children of Israel, to do the service of the children of Israel in the Tent of Meeting, and to make atonement for the children of Israel, that there be no plague among the children of Israel, through the children of Israel coming nigh unto the Sanctuary* (Num. 8:19). [Rabbi Yudan's comment was in keeping with] the Baraita wherein R. Simeon ben Yoḥai told the parable of a king who entrusted his son to a tutor. The king, after giving the tutor specific instructions, kept inquiring: "Has my son eaten? Has my son had something to drink? Did my son go to school? Has my son returned from school?" So, too, [R. Yudan concluded], the Holy One covets occasions to keep mentioning the children of Israel.

R. Judah bar R. Simon told the parable of a man who sat making a crown for the king. A passerby saw him and asked him: What are you making? The man replied: A crown for the king. The passerby said: Set in it as many emeralds as you can possibly set; set in it other precious stones—pearls, too—since the crown will be put on a king's head. So the Holy One said to Moses: Moses, praise Israel as much as you can; praise them to Me; glorify Israel as much as you can; glorify them since I am to be glorified through them: *And He said unto me: "Thou art My servant, Israel, in whom I will be glorified"* (Isa. 49:3).

8. In commenting on *according to their number* (Exod. 30:12), R. Joshua bar R. Nehemiah taught: When the Holy One said to Moses: "Moses, go count Israel," Moses said bluntly to the Holy One: Master of all the universes, it is written of Israel *Thy seed shall be as the dust of the earth* (Gen. 28:14), and *I will multiply thy seed as the stars of heaven* (Gen. 26:4), and *The number of the children of Israel shall be as the sand of the*

sea (Hos. 2:1), [verses which I take to mean that since the dust and the sand and the stars cannot be counted, so Israel cannot be counted].[30] And yet Thou sayest to me, "Count Israel." The Holy One replied: Moses, I do not mean to have them counted one by one, as thou supposest. If thou wouldst ascertain Israel's number, thou needest only take the first letters of the names of the Tribes and thus ascertain Israel's number in thousands. The letter *reš* in Reuben is 200,000; the *šin* in Simeon is 300,000; the *nun* in Naphtali, 50,000; [the *yods* in] Judah, Joseph, and Issachar add up to 30,000;[31] the *zayin* in Zebulun, 7,000; the *dalet* in Dan, 4,000; the *gimel* in Gad, 3,000; the *bet* in Benjamin, 2,000; the *'alef* in Asher, 1,000. You thus have 597,000. [But since the number of the people in the Tribes was originally 600,000], what happened to the other 3,000? They were the ones who fell in the days which followed the making of the calf: *The sons of Levi did according to the word of Moses; and there fell of the people that day about three thousand men* (Exod. 32:28).

[In explanation of God's commanding Moses to count Israel at this particular time], R. Menaḥema cited R. Bebai's parable of the king who had a flock of sheep which wolves came to rend. Thereupon the king said to the shepherd: Number my flock to find out how many are gone. Even so the Holy One said to Moses: Count Israel to find out how many are gone.

According to Scripture, Israel were counted on ten occasions. Once when they came down into Egypt: *Thy fathers went down into Egypt with threescore and ten persons* (Deut. 10:22). And once when they came up out of Egypt: *The children of Israel journeyed from Rameses to Succoth about six hundred thousand men on foot* (Exod. 12:37). And twice in the Book of Numbers: the first time at the setting up of the four standards in the wilderness (Num. 2:2); the second time in preparation for the division of the Land among the Tribes (Num. 26:19–56). And twice in the days of Saul: *Saul . . . numbered them by "lambs"* (Telaim) (1 Sam. 15:4); *And he numbered them by "pebbles"* (Bezek) (1 Sam. 11:8). (When the children of Israel were rich, Saul numbered them by having them give lambs to him; when they were poor, he had them give pebbles to him). And once in the days of David, of which it is said *Joab had to hand over the* [*total*] *sum, the* [*incomplete*]

30. "He who counts Israel, so said R. Eliezer, violates a negative commandment, the one which declares, *The number of the children of Israel . . . may not be measured nor numbered* (Hos. 2:1)" (B.Yoma 22b). Such numbering, it is believed, might halt the flow of blessing God intends for Israel, since blessing is freely available only for that which is hidden from the eye (Piska 10.6, B.Ta 8b, and BM 42a). Thus before the miracle of vessels being filled with oil was performed in behalf of Obadiah's widow (2 Kings 4:2, and Piska 2.5), Elisha asked her to *go in, and shut the door* (2 Kings 4:4). See *Torat ḥayyim* on 'En Ya'akob B.BM 42a.

31. The letter *yod* stands for 10.

enumeration of the people (2 Sam. 24:9). If a [*total*] *sum*, how [an *incomplete*] enumeration? And if an [*incomplete*] *enumeration*, how a [*total sum*? Joab had two reports, however, a larger one [total], and a smaller one [incomplete]. The smaller one he showed to David; he did not show him the larger one, yet in the end *Joab had to hand over* [to David] *the* [*total*] *sum* [*instead of*] *the* [*incomplete*] *enumeration* [(*ibid.*)][32] And once in the days of Ezra: *The whole congregation together was forty . . . thousand* (Ezra 2:64). And once in the time-to-come: *The flocks shall again pass under the hands of him that counteth them* (Jer. 33:13). And, of course, once in the present context: *When thou takest the sum*, etc. (Exod. 30:12).

9. R. Menaḥema, R. Bebai, and the elder R. Ḥiyya said in the name of R. Eliezer bar Jacob: Israel are said to be like sand. Why like sand? You dig a pit in it in the evening and in the morning you find that the pit has filled itself up. Likewise, all the thousands that were lost in the days of David were made up in the days of Solomon, as is said *Judah and Israel increased as the sand*, etc. (1 Kings 4:20).

R. Eliezer taught in the name of R. Jose ben Zimra: As long as Israel are counted when there is need for such counting, there is no decrease in their number; but when no need exists, the counting is followed by a decrease. At what particular time were they counted where there was need? In the days of Moses. And at what particular time were they counted where there was no such need? In the days of David.

In the name of R. Jonathan, R. Samuel bar Naḥmani [differed with R. Eliezer], citing the verse *They shall give every man a ransom for his soul* (Exod. 30:12) as Israel in the days of Moses gave such ransom in order *that there be no plague among them, when thou numberest them* (*ibid.*), as was to happen in the days of David [when no such ransom was given].

10. *This they shall give, every one that passeth among them that are numbered*, etc. (Exod. 30:13). According to R. Meir, the Holy One brought forth from under His throne of glory something like a coin of fire, showed it to Moses, and said to him: *This*[33] *they shall give*—as though the half-shekel Israel give for their ransom were a burning reminder of their sinning in the past and a fiery warning against their sinning in the future.[34]

Concerning the meaning of *Every one that passeth* (*ibid.*), R. Judah and

32. On Joab's reluctance to take the census, see PR 11:3 (YJS, *18*, 204–07).

33. The verse should have read "A half-shekel they shall give" (Exod. 30:13), the demonstrative *This* at the verse's beginning being unnecessary. Hence R. Meir assumes that in saying *This*, God actually pointed to a coin of fire.

34. The words "as though the half-shekel Israel give . . . against their sinning in the future" paraphrase the literal "something like this they are to give." R. Meir apparently takes the word *zeh*, "this," in Exod. 30:13 as a derivative of the root *'z*,' "to fire, to make hot" (Dan. 3:19, 22). Cf. MTeh 68:5, and PR 10:12 (YJS, *18*, 190, n. 86).

R. Nehemiah differ. According to R. Judah the words mean, "Every one that passed over the waters of the Red Sea."[35] According to R. Nehemiah, the words refer only to the lay members of the congregation who were counted as they passed by.

Concerning the import of *Half a shekel* (*ibid.*), R. Judah and R. Nehemiah differ. R. Judah said: Since Israel's sin began when half the day was gone, each one of them had to bring half a shekel for ransom. R. Nehemiah said: Since Israel's sin began in the sixth hour of the day,[36] each one had to bring half a shekel—there are six *grammata* in a half-shekel—for ransom. R. Joshua bar Nehemiah, citing Rabban Johanan ben Zakkai, said: Because Israel transgressed the Ten Commandments, each man in Israel had to give ten gerah for ransom.[37]

R. Berechiah and R. Levi said in the name of R. Simeon ben Laḳish: Because the Tribe Fathers sold Rachel's first-born for twenty pieces of silver,[38] each and every man in Israel has to redeem his own first-born with twenty pieces of silver.[39] Furthermore, said R. Phinehas in the name of R. Levi: Because the Tribe Fathers sold Rachel's first-born for twenty pieces of silver, a *ṭeḇa'* (half a shekel) falling to each Tribe father as his share,[40] therefore each and every man in Israel must give a *ṭeḇa'* for ransom

R. Judah bar Simon said in the name of R. Johanan: From the Divine Power, Moses heard three commandments which startled him and made him recoil. The first was when God said: *Let them make Me the Sanctuary, and I shall dwell among them* (Exod. 25:8). In reply Moses said bluntly to the Holy One: Master of the universe, behold! The heavens, not even the heavens above the heavens, can contain Thee, and yet Thou sayest, *Let them make Me the Sanctuary*! Thereupon the Holy One reassured Moses: Moses, it is not as thou thinkest; though the Sanctuary is to be only twenty boards wide in the north and only twenty boards wide in the south and only eight boards wide in the west, I shall go down to the earth and shrink My presence into your midst below, as is said *And there will I meet with thee* (Num. 25:22).

Again, when God said: *My food which is presented unto Me for offerings made by fire, shall ye observe to offer unto Me* (Num. 28:2), Moses said

35. Including priests and Levites who had not been counted in the census (Num. 1:49). R. Judah thus reads the words "Every one that passeth, as well as those that were numbered."

36. Cf. PR 10:12 (YJS, *18*, 189–90).

37. *The shekel is twenty gerahs* (Exod. 30:13).

38. *They . . . sold Joseph to the Ishmaelites for twenty pieces of silver* (Gen. 37:28).

39. The five shekels used in redeeming a first-born (Num. 3:47), a shekel being the equivalent of four denar, which are twenty pieces of silver.

40. A *ṭeḇa'* = 2 denar = ½ shekel. Since Benjamin was not with the brothers, their number was ten.

bluntly to the Holy One: Master of the universe, if I were to bring all the beasts of the earth, would they be enough for a single offering? Or the wood of all the trees of the world—would they be enough for one altar fire? For it is said *Lebanon is not enough for altar fire, nor the beasts thereof enough for burnt offerings* (Isa. 40:16). The Holy One reassured Moses: Moses, it is not as thou thinkest. *Say unto them: This is the offering made by fire . . . he-lambs of the first year without blemish, two day by day* (Num. 28:3), an offering of not even two at a time, but only one in the morning and one at dusk, as is said *The one lamb shalt thou offer in the morning, and the other lamb shalt thou offer at dusk* (Num. 28:4).

Finally, when God said: *They shall give every man a ransom for his soul* (Exod. 30:12), Moses bluntly replied to the Holy One: Master of the universe, who can give a ransom for his soul? *No man can by any means redeem his brother . . . for too costly is the redemption of men's souls* (Ps. 49:8–9). The Holy One reassured Moses: It is not as thou thinkest, but *This they shall give* (Exod. 30:13), *this* being the coin of fire looking something like a half-shekel that He showed to Moses.

(R. Huna said in the name of Rab:[41] The verse *Almighty—we cannot find Him out—O great One in strength* [Job 37:23] means that we cannot find out the full might of the Holy One, for the Holy One makes demands upon Israel not commensurate with His majesty [but commensurate with Israel's capacity]).

And when Moses heard God's answers to his three blunt questions, he proceeded to congratulate Israel, saying *Happy is the people whose God is the Lord, yea, happy is the people that is in such a case* (Ps. 144:15); *Happy is he whose help is the God of Jacob* (Ps. 146:5).[42]

41. "Rab"—O_1, C, Cas; O: "Rabbi."
42. Cf. PRKM 6.4.

PISKA 3

SUMMARY

The role of Amalek

Because Israel had let go both Torah and commandments at Rephidim, Amalek was able to launch upon Israel an attack (Sec. a) which Joshua, who sprang from the Tribe destined to destroy Esau's brood, was called upon to resist (Sec. b). Still, Moses had to invoke the merits of the Patriarchs and the Matriarchs, as well as the merit of the rod upon which God's seventy names were emblazoned, to sustain Israel in its combat with Amalek (Sec. c). After his victory Joshua refrained from slaying all the Amalekites, choosing to slay only those upon whom death-lots fell.

Upon hearing of Joshua's victory, Jethro came and was converted. Because of his conversion, his descendants were to sit as judges in Jerusalem's Chamber of Hewn Stones (Sec. d). The privilege accorded to Jethro's descendants was God's dramatic way of showing His willingness to give sinners an opportunity to repent, even such flagrant sinners as Egyptians and Edomites. It is when such sinners show utter unwillingness to mend their ways that He proceeds against them summarily (Sec. e). Hence only because of the many kinds of affliction that Esau, Amalek's progenitor, brought upon his kin, and only because as early as the age of fifteen Esau was already guilty of such transgressions as rape, murder, and theft—in short only because of Esau's heaping up of such enormities did God say of Amalek, Esau's most sinful descendant, *Remember what Amalek did unto thee* (Deut. 25:17) (Sec. 1). Still, whenever they proceed against Amalek, Israel must repent of their own sins. Otherwise, Amalek will again impose servitude upon Israel (Sec. 2). In proceeding against Esau's brood, Israel must be mindful of those among them who are occasionally kind and must remember that only Amalek is totally evil (Sec. 3). Israel must also be ever mindful of the fact that their own misdeeds, such as using false weights and measures, bring on the scourge of Amalek (Sec. 4). It is noted that the wicked in Israel are not as incorrigibly wicked as Amalek, whose very name Israel is therefore bidden to blot out (Sec. 5). What were some of Amalek's enormities? Amalek cut the circumcised organ of generation from live Israelites and taunted God with it. Amalek tore up Scrolls of Torah; he cut away the Sanctuary to its very foundations. In precise and symbolic requital of what Amalek had done and was to do, Samuel—so commentators say—cut off Agag's male member; or, as others say, having tied Agag between four pikes set in the ground, had him pulled in four different directions so that he was torn apart; or, as still others say, cut olive-sized pieces from live Agag—Amalek's king (Sec. 6).

In the comments that follow, Israel reminds God that He before whom there is no forgetfulness ought to be more immediately mindful of what Esau's brood did to Jerusalem, God's own city (Sec. 7). The root of the word Amalek is taken to suggest the kind of locust which swoops down swiftly, or to suggest a hound which licks up blood, or a fly greedy to get at an open wound (Sec. 8). But the remembrance of Amalek is also meant to remind Israel of their own moral breach at Rephidim shortly after their departure from Egypt, a breach which served to bring on the hound—Amalek (Sec. 9) who thereupon resorted to all kinds of evil tricks. Having managed to get hold of Israel's genealogical records stored in Egyptian archives, he was able by use of the precise information in the records to lure Israelites from the safety of their camp, and then either slew them or polluted them by pederasty. Subsequently, encouraged by Amalek's successful example, other nations dared attack Israel (Sec. 10). Amalek was the first nation which resorted to obscene forms of blasphemy (Sec. 11). It is noted, however, that those smitten by Amalek were sinners in Israel—the enfeebled ones in the rear, such as the idolaters of the Tribe of Dan whom the cloud had flung out; and also the skeptics in Israel, such as those who whispered among themselves about God, saying: *Is the Lord among us, or not?* (Exod. 17:7) (Sec. 12). Hence only a descendant of Joseph who feared God and made little of himself, who grew up with Pharaoh and Potiphar but did not emulate their deeds, is always selected as the one at whose hand Amalek is to fall (Sec. 13).

Upon their entrance into the Land, Israel were commanded not only to set up a king over themselves and to build the Temple, but also to destroy Amalek and blot out remembrance of him—his very name (Sec. 14)—a task which God Himself had also undertaken once it was clear that Amalek put forth his hand against God's very throne (Sec. 15). No wonder that no proselytes are to be accepted from Amalek.

While Amalek endures, it is as though a pennon were hiding God's face: His name is not complete, His throne is not whole. Only when Amalek's seed perishes from the earth will God's name be complete and God's throne whole (Sec. 16).

PISKA 3

Remember (Deut. 25:17)

a. [1]In comment on *Remember what Amalek did unto thee* (Deut. 25:17)[2] is ited the verse *When thou smitest a scorner, the simple will become prudent* Prov. 19:25). By *scorner* in the words *When thou smitest a scorner* is ıeant Amalek; and by *simple* in the words *the simple will become prudent* is ıeant Jethro.[3]

When Amalek came to fight against Israel, what does Scripture say? *Then ame Amalek, and fought with Israel on account of Rephidim*[4] (Exod. 7:8). [*Rephidim*, made up of *rfh* meaning "let go" and *ydym* meaning hands," is taken here not as a place-name but as designating a moral lapse n Israel's part],[5] for before Amalek's attack Israel's hands had let go both 'orah and commandments.[6] The actual name of the place was Massah-and-Aeribah (Trying-and-strife), as revealed by the verse just preceding: *He Vho Is Everywhere called the name thereof Massah-and-Meribah*[7] (*Trying-nd-strife*) (Exod. 17:7). The Holy One had so named it in His anguished rying out *At the striving of the children of Israel* [*against Him*], *and be-ause they tried Him* (*ibid.*). At that time Moses likewise had cried out in

1. The passage beginning "In comment on *Remember what Amalek*" and end-ng "Hence . . . Scripture says *Remember* (Deut. 25:17)" (Sections a–e) occurs nly in S. According to BM, the passage is not an authentic part of PRK. How-ver, even if Sections a–e differ somewhat in form from other parts of PRK, hematically they belong to the Piska.

2. Deut. 25:17–19 is the supplementary lesson (*maftir*) in the Pentateuch for Sabbath *Zakor*—second of the four special Sabbaths—the Sabbath of remembering Amalek. See Meg 3:4.

3. According to R. Joshua, the tidings of Israel's successful war against Amalek reported in Exod. 17:14–18:1 made Jethro come to Moses (Mek, 2, 162).

4. JV: *in Rephidim*.

5. The commentator seems also to regard Rephidim in Exod. 17:1 not as a place name, but as a deliberately oblique reference to Israel's moral lapse as set forth in the verses that follow. See B.Sanh 106a.

6. At Marah (Exod. 15:23–25), the children of Israel were said to have been given the following ten commandments: (1) to abstain from idolatry, (2) from adultery, (3) from murder, (4) from robbery, (5) from cutting flesh from a living animal, (6) from emasculating men or animals, (7) from crossbreeding plants or animals, (8) to institute civil courts, (9) to observe the Sabbath, and (10) to honor one's parents. See B.Sanh 56b.

7. JV: *And the name of the place was called Massah and Meribah*. But at times *Place* is construed as *Topos*, a name of God. Hence: *He Who Is Everywhere*.

anguish saying *Why strive ye with me? Wherefore do ye try the Lord?* (Exod 17:2). R. Levi said: What parable applies here to Israel? The parable of man who had a son whom he placed on his shoulder and took to the marke There, when the son saw a desirable object, he said to his father, "Buy it fo me," and his father bought for him what he wanted the first time he asked, th second time, and the third. But then, when the son saw someone whom h asked, "Have you seen my father?" the man said to his son: You fool, yo are astride my shoulder, whatever you wish I buy for you, and yet you as that man, "Have you seen my father?" What did the father do then? H threw his son from his shoulder, and a dog came and bit the son.

So, too, after Israel went out of Egypt, the Holy One, [like a lovin father], encompassed them with seven clouds of glory, as is said *He com passed him about, He cared for him* (Deut. 32:10). They asked for manna He gave it. For quail: He gave them. After He gave all that they asked, the proceeded to ruminate *Is the Lord among us, or not?* (Exod. 17:7). Th Holy One said to them: You ruminate as to My presence in your midst? A you live, I shall make you aware of it. Here is a dog to bite you. And wh was the dog? Amalek, for the very next verse in Exodus says, *Then cam Amalek* (Exod. 17:8). Hence *Remember* (Deut. 25:17).

b. It is written *And Moses said to Joshua* (Exod. 17:9). Why to Joshu in particular? Because he was of the Tribe of Joseph;[8] and Scripture declare "The house of Jacob shall be a fire, and the house of Joseph a flame . . . an they shall kindle in them, and devour them" (Ob. 1:18), which is to say tha out of the house of Joseph was to go forth the flame that would devour th stubble of the house of Esau: the flame was Joshua who slew Amalek, as i said *Joshua discomfited Amalek* (Exod. 17:13).

c. The words *Behold, I will be standing* [in the verse *Behold, I will be standing on the peak, on the hill, with the rod of God in my hand*] (Exod 17:9) intimate that, like Moses, righteous men rise early and stand ready and willing to serve the needs of the community. Furthermore, the word *standing* in the verse intimates that Moses was saying: "I, Moses, will be standing in prayer," for in another verse in Exodus the context of the word *standing* defines it as "standing in prayer": "The Lord descended in the cloud, and standing there with Moses, invoked [in His prayer] the name o the Lord" (Exod. 34:5). The phrase *on the peak* that follows *I will be standing* (Exod. 17:9) intimates that Moses was saying "I, Moses, invoke the merit of Israel's Patriarchs, Patriarchs indeed of the entire world"; to these Balaam also alludes in the following words: "Because of the peak"—that is the towering merit of the Patriarchs—"I see [Israel] as strong as the rocks"[9] (Num. 23:9). The next words from the verse in Exodus, *on the hil*

8. See Num. 13:8.

9. JV: *From the top of the rocks I see him, and from the hills I behold him.* But see Rashi.

(Exod. 17:9), intimate: "I, Moses, invoke as well the merit of the Matriarchs"; to these Balaam likewise alludes in the same verse from Numbers, "And because of the hills"—that is, the merit of the Matriarchs, only a little less high than that of the Patriarchs—"I behold Israel['s strength]" (Num. 23:9). As for *the rod* in *With the rod of God in my hand* (Exod. 17:9), it is the one with God's seventy names emblazoned upon it.[10]

After Moses had spoken, Joshua said: How many notables there are in this generation!—Aaron, Hur, and the seventy elders. Yet Moses enjoined no one except me. Nor did he enjoin me without good cause[11]—he saw that Amalek would fall by my hand. At once *Joshua did as Moses had said to him, and fought with Amalek* (Exod. 17:10).

d. *Moses, Aaron, and Hur went up to the "peak," to the "hill"* (*ibid.*). These words tell us that three men are required, [in keeping with the words *out of the depths I call Thee, O Lord* (Ps. 130:1)], to go down before the Holy Ark, the one who is the congregation's emissary for prayer, and the other two who go down to assist him.

And Joshua cast lots[12] (*way-yaḥălos̆*) (Exod. 17:13). Our Masters [construing *way-yaḥălos̆* to be a form of *ḥeles̆*, "lot"], as in the Mishnaic dictum "Priests may cast lots (*ḥălas̆im*) . . . for their portions" (Shab 23:2), read the verse "Joshua cast [death-]lots upon the Amalekites." In Scripture "lot" has four designations, *ḥeles̆*, *pur*, *goral*, *ḥeḇel*. By means of these four lots, [only the utterly wicked] descendants of Esau [but not their less guilty allies], are smitten. Thus by the lot called *ḥeles̆*—*Joshua cast lots* (*way-yaḥălos̆*) (Exod. 17:13)—only Amalek was smitten.[13] After a *goral*, also termed *pur*—*They cast pur, that is, the goral which was to fall upon Haman*[14] (Esther 3:7)—only Haman was smitten. After the *ḥeḇel of the time that is to be shall come upon him*[15] (Hos. 13:13), only [utterly

10. See Song Zuṭa, ed. Buber (Berlin, 1894), p. 8.

11. "not without good cause"—parallel in Yalḳuṭ, *Bĕs̆allaḥ*, 264. S misreads "without good cause" (*ḥinnom*) as "the people" (*ha'am*).

12. JV: *discomfited.*

13. Amalek—so R. Jose ben Ḥalafta maintained—gathered together other nations with whose aid he waged war against Israel (see Meḳ, 2, 136; Mĕḳilta de-R. Simeon ben Yoḥai, ed. Epstein-Melamed [Jerusalem, 5715/1955], p. 119; Zohar, S̆ĕmoṯ 66a). And so after Joshua's victory, Joshua cast lots to make certain that only Amalekites—no others—would be slain. Professor Saul Lieberman has supplied the interpretation of this passage.

14. "When Haman cast lots in order to destroy the holy nation, a heavenly voice was heard saying: 'Fear not, O congregation of Israel, if thou turnest in repentance to God, the lot will fall upon Haman instead of upon thee' " (2 Targum Esther 3.7, as quoted in Ginzberg, *Legends*, 6, 465). JV: *they cast pur, that is, the lot, before Haman.* But *lifne*, "before," also means, "in the face of," and so, "upon."

15. Presumably the punishment visited upon the utterly wicked in Ephraim will, at the end of time, be visited upon utterly wicked Edom. JV: *The throes of a*

wicked] Edom will be smitten. Such is the import of *And Joshua cast lots* (Exod. 17:13).

As soon as Jethro heard of all the miracles which the Holy One worked against Egypt and Amalek, he came at once and was converted: *When thou smitest a scorner the simple will become prudent* (Prov. 19:25). What was Jethro's reward? His descendants had the privilege of sitting as judges in the Chamber of Hewn Stones and to be reckoned as part of Israel: it was *They who sat before Jabez: the Tirathites, the Shimeathites, the Sucathites. These are the Kenites,*[16] etc. (1 Chron. 2:55).

e. [That God conducts Himself in His own special way is shown by the contrast between] one verse that reads *Remember what Amalek did unto thee* (Deut. 25:17), and another that reads *Thou shalt not abhor an Edomite, for he is thy brother!* (Deut. 23:8). Come and see that the way of the Holy One is not the way of flesh-and-blood. The way of flesh-and-blood: When a man has done <an injury> to his fellow, the bitter memory never departs from his fellow's heart. Not so with the Holy One. Even though [His people] Israel were in bitter servitude in Egypt, as is said *They made their lives bitter with hard service* (Exod. 1:14), and even though Amalek of wicked Esau's seed appeared after Israel had left Egypt and inflicted one injury after another upon Israel [His people], nevertheless, the Holy One declared: *Thou shalt not abhor an Edomite, for he is thy brother,* etc. (Deut. 23:8). R. Levi said: By what parable may God's way be explained? By that of a king who prepared a feast. He had two foes whom he invited, saying to those reclining at the feast, "Receive these foes of mine with pleasant mien." And the king's guests did so. Yet after the two foes had eaten and drunk, they seized two iron axes and set about to demolish the king's palace. <The king said to the two foes:> "Instead of battering away at my palace, should you not have been content that in your behalf I commanded Israel to honor you? Do you not appreciate the honor I bestowed on you?" Thereupon the king's men removed the two foes and hanged them—one opposite the other. So you find that after all the injuries that Egypt and Edom had inflicted upon Israel, God commanded in their behalf, *Thou shalt not abhor an Edomite, for he is thy brother; thou shalt not abhor an Egyptian,* etc. (Deut. 23:8). Yet these were the two who arose to demolish His House, as is said *Remem-*

---

travailing woman shall come upon him. But *ḥeḇel*, "throe," also means "line," or "lot" (see 2 Sam. 8:2); and *yoleḏah*, "[woman] in travail," can also mean "[time] in travail," hence, "time that is to be."

16. The commentator seems to construe 1 Chron. 2:55 to read as follows: "The men in the gates of justice (*Tirathites*) who won the privilege of hearing God on Sinai (*Shimeathites*) were originally meant because of their ancestry to have remained dwellers of booths in the wilderness (*Sucathites*): these men—the Kenites—are descendants of Jethro the convert." See Meḵ, 2, 187; Sif Num. 78 (ed. Horovitz, p. 73); and B.Sanh 104a.

ber, O Lord, against the children of Edom, the day of Jesusalem['s destruction] (Ps. 137:7), and as is also said, *Egypt gave a hand against us*[17] (Lam. 5:6). Israel said reproachfully: Master of the universe, see what they of whom it is said *Thou shalt not abhor an Edomite . . . thou shalt not abhor an Egyptian* (Deut. 23:8) have done to us. Thereupon the Holy One replied: Have them hanged, one opposite the other: *Egypt shall be a desolation, and Edom shall be a desolate wilderness* (Joel 4:19).

Hence [it is only because of the enormity of Egypt's and Edom's behavior that] Scripture says *Remember* (Deut. 25:17).

1. *Remember what Amalek did unto thee* (Deut. 25:17). [These words are to be considered in the light of the verse] *Let the iniquity ('ăwon) of his*[18] *fathers be brought to remembrance unto the Lord* (Ps. 109:14). But were Esau's fathers wicked men? Were not his grandfather Abraham and his father Isaac completely righteous men? Yet Scripture says, *Let the iniquity of his fathers be brought to remembrance!* However [the word *'ăwon* is to be construed not as "the iniquity of his fathers]," but as "the affliction[19] he brought upon his fathers." And what affliction did Esau bring upon his fathers? [Upon Abraham, to begin with]. You know, of course, that Isaac got all his vitality from Abraham, yet Isaac was to live 180 years[20] while Abraham lived only 175 years.[21] According to R. Yudan citing R. Aibu, and R. Phinehas citing R. Levi, [the reason Abraham did not live as long as Isaac was that] during the five years which were taken from Abraham, [the last five years of his life], wicked Esau was to commit two grievous transgressions: he was to rape a maiden who was betrothed and he was to murder a human being. Of the first of these transgressions it is written *And Esau came in from the field* (Gen. 25:29). That Esau was guilty of rape is shown by the fact that the verse specifying his coming in *from the field* is linked with another verse also specifying "field," the verse from Deuteronomy that states the penalty for rape: "If the man find the damsel that is betrothed in the field" (Deut. 22:25). That he was guilty of murder is inferred from the linking of the conclusion of the verse in Genesis that says Esau *was faint* (Gen. 25:29) with the verse in Jeremiah that declares fainting to be characteristic of the souls of murderers: "Woe is me now for my soul fainteth as [the souls] of murderers" (Jer. 4:31).

According to the elder R. Zakkai, Esau was also guilty of theft, for the

17. So apparently, Septuagint. JV: *We have given the hand to Egypt.*
18. Identified as Esau who in the same Psalm in verse 17 is described as one who *delighted not in blessing.*
19. See Ibn Ezra on Gen. 4:13.
20. Gen. 35:28.
21. Gen. 25:7.

verse *If thieves come to thee* [*O Esau*] (Ob. 1:5) [shows that he was an intimate of thieves].[22]

[To spare Abraham the suffering that knowledge of Esau's transgressions would have caused him], the Holy One said: I promise, Abraham, *thou shalt go to thy fathers in peace; thou shalt be buried in a good old age* (Gen. 15:15). Could it have been a good old age for Abraham if he had lived to know of his grandson's transgressions—rape, murder, and theft? Can anyone say that such knowledge would have given him a good old age? It was better for such a righteous man to have been gathered in peace: hence it is said God's *lovingkindness is better than life* (Ps. 63:4).

And what was the affliction Esau brought upon his father? He caused his father's eyes to grow dim.[23] Hence people say that he who rears a wicked son or a wicked disciple will have his eyes grow dim. Such the outcome for our father Isaac because of a wicked son: *And it came to pass, that when Isaac was old, his eyes grew dim, so that he should not see* (Gen. 27:1). And what should he not see? That in Esau he had reared a wicked son. Such the outcome for Ahijah of Shiloh[24] because of a wicked disciple: *Ahijah could not see; for his eyes were set by reason of his age* (1 Kings 14:4). And what was he kept from seeing? That he had reared a wicked disciple. And who was the disciple? Jeroboam son of Nebat who sinned and caused Israel to sin. It was only because of Jeroboam that Ahijah's eyes grew dim.

And what affliction did Esau bring upon his mother?[25] [According to] R. Tanḥum bar Abun, R. Judah, R. Nehemiah, and the Rabbis differ. R. Judah said: At his going forth from his mother's belly he ripped her womb so that she bore no more children. Of this act it is written *Because he pursued his brother as with a sword, he destroyed the womb whence he came*[26] (Amos 1:11). You are not to suppose, R. Berechiah pointed out, that what Esau did was merely an accident resulting from the effort to emerge from his mother's womb. The fact is that as he was leaving his mother's womb, his fist was stretched out against his brother [thus rupturing his mother's womb]. And the proof? The verse *The wicked are fisted*[27] *from the womb; the speakers of lies go astray as soon as they are born* (Ps. 58:4). R. Nehemiah said: It was Esau who kept Rebekah from bringing forth the twelve Fathers of the

22. "for the verse *If thieves* . . . intimate of thieves]"—O_1, Cas, S, C. The "proof" is no more than a toehold in Scripture to support a tradition that Esau was a thief. See *Yĕfeh to'ar* on Gen. Rabbah 63:12.

23. A man who is blind is considered as though dead. See B.Neḏ 4b.

24. See B.Sanh 102a.

25. The comment is based on *Let not the sin against his mother be blotted out* (Ps. 109:14).

26. JV: *Because he did pursue his brother with the sword, and did cast off all pity.*

27. The word *zoru* may be derived from *zar*, "stranger," or *zeyrta'*, "fist, span."

Tribes,[28] although, as R. Huna proved, Rebekah deserved to bring forth the twelve Fathers of the Tribes. He counted the twelve as follows: two, according to the words, *Two nations are in thy womb;* [two, according to the words], *two peoples shall be separated from thy bowels*—thus far four; [two, according to the words], *one people shall be stronger than the other people*, making six; [two, according to the words], *the elder shall serve the younger*, making eight. [Two, according to the verse], *And when her days to be delivered were fulfilled, behold, there were twins in her womb,* making ten. [Finally two, according to the verse], *And the first came forth . . . And after that came forth his brother* (Gen. 25:23–26), making twelve.[29] Some find in an earlier passage a hint of the twelve sons that Rebekah deserved to bring forth, for she says, *If this is the way my childbearing is to go, why should I bear that many (zh)?* (Gen. 25:22): since the word *zh* is made up of the letter *zayin* whose numerical value is seven and the letter *he'* whose value is five, you have a total of twelve.[30]

As a further instance of Esau's wickedness, the Rabbis said: Esau brought it about that no public funeral was given to Rebekah. You find that after Rebekah died, people asked: Who is to walk before her bier? Abraham is dead. Isaac whose eyes have grown dim has to stay at home. Jacob has fled from Esau. If the wicked Esau walk before her bier, mortals will say: "Cursed be the dugs that gave suck to such a one." What did the people do? They took her out at night. Because the body of Rebekah was taken out at night and thus received no public funeral, R. Jose ben R. Ḥanina used to say, Scripture records her death obliquely by stating that it was *Deborah, Rebekah's nurse,* [*who*] *died* (Gen. 35:8), and *was buried below Beth-el under the oak. And the name of it,* the verse continues, *was called Allon-bacuth* (*ibid.*). [It is by way of the word *Allon* that we know the verse is really alluding to Rebekah's death]. What is meant by *Allon*? According to R. Samuel bar R. Naḥman who cited R. Jonathan, *allon* is a Greek word meaning "another occasion." [Since *bacuth* means "weeping," the phrase *Allon-bacuth* means "another occasion for weeping"]. For even while Jacob was observing the period of mourning for Deborah who had been his mother's nursemaid, the tidings of his mother's death reached him, as intimated in the verse which follows directly *God appeared unto Jacob again, when he came from Paddan-aram, and blessed him* (Gen. 35:9). What was the blessing He bestowed upon him? He bestowed upon him—so said R. Aḥa

28. A privilege which she deserved because of her virtue and piety.

29. God's long and precise response to Rebekah suggests to the commentator that the six phrases contrasting such striking types also point to six pairs of brothers—the twelve Fathers of the Tribes—who like the twelve signs in the Zodiac represented highly striking individuals.

30. In this comment Rebekah is understood to be asking: If I suffer thus in bearing two children, how can I possibly bear twelve?

citing R. Jonathan—the blessing of consolation given to mourners [and it was then that Jacob knew his mother was dead].[31]

Thereupon the Holy One said: Esau's father had ample cause to requite him with evil. Esau's mother had ample cause to requite him with evil. His brother had ample cause to requite him with evil. His grandfather had ample cause to requite him with evil. You, Israel, have ample cause to requite him with evil. I, too, have ample cause to requite him with evil. And so even as you remember his [iniquitous] name on the earth below, I expunge his name in heaven above: [*His iniquities*] *are before the Lord continually, and therefore He will cut off the name of* [*Amalek and his brood*] *from the earth* (Ps. 109:15). Hence *Remember what Amalek did unto thee* (Deut. 25:17).

2. [In comment on God's command to remember Amalek], R. Tanḥum bar R. Ḥanila'i began his discourse by citing the following verse: *Your acts of remembering* [*Amalek, followed by repentance for your sins*], *will be like "ashes"; but when you deserve visitation* [*for sin*], *visitation in "clay" shall be your punishment*[32] (Job 13:28). The Holy One said to Israel: My children, I inscribed in Torah two references to Amalek that you are to remember—heed them: *Thou shalt blot out the remembrance of Amalek* (Deut. 25:19); *I will utterly blot out the remembrance of Amalek* (Exod. 17:14). But let *your acts of remembering* [*be followed by repentance for your sins so that you*] *will be like "ashes"*—that is, if through repentance[33] you gain merit,[34] you will be true children of Abraham who spoke of himself as "ashes," saying "I am . . . but dust and ashes" (Gen. 18:27). If you do not gain such merit, however, [because when you remembered Amalek you did not repent of your own sins], then a deserved *visitation, visitation in "clay" shall be your punishment* (Job 13:12): You will have to prepare yourselves for another servitude like that in Egypt. What is written of the servitude in Egypt? The Egyptians "made their lives bitter with hard service, in clay," etc. (Exod. 1:14). [Hence, *Remember what Amalek did unto thee* (Deut. 25:17).]

3. R. Judah, citing R. Aibu, began his discourse [on repayment in kind] as follows: *Be not as the horse or the mule which have no understanding,* etc. (Ps. 32:9). Six things are said of a horse: he eats much and excretes little, he loves copulation, loves battle, despises sleep, and has a haughty spirit. Some say that in battle he even seeks to slay his master. *Be not as the*

31. See B.Soṭ 14a; and Nahmanides on Gen. 35:8.

32. JV: *Your memorials shall be like unto ashes, your eminences to eminences of clay*. But the word *ḡaḇ*, "eminence," may also be construed as a form of *gbh*, "collect, impose or visit punishment for sin."

33. See Piska 3.a; and PR 13:7.

34. Now the word *ziḵroneḵem*, "your acts of remembering," seems to be taken by the commentator to contain *zĕḵiṯem*, "you gain merit."

ıorse or the mule. When you put a bit on him, he kicks; when you pat him, ıe kicks; when you bedeck him with ornaments, he kicks; when you feed him ›arley, he kicks. Even if you do not come near him, he kicks. Be not like the ıorse: when people are kind to you take care to repay them with kindness; ›nly the totally evil are you to repay with evil. Repay with kindness those vho are now and then kind—*Thou shalt not abhor an Edomite*, etc. (Deut. 23:8). Repay the totally evil with evil—*Remember what Amalek did unto thee*[35] (Deut. 25:17).

4. R. Banai, citing R. Huna, began his discourse [on remembering Amalek] with the verse *A false balance is an abomination to the Lord*, etc. (Prov. 11:1). And R. Banai, citing R. Huna, proceeded: When you see a generation whose measures and balances are false, you may be certain that a wicked kingdom will come to wage war against such a generation. And the proof? The verse *A false balance is an abomination to the Lord*, etc., which is immediately followed by a verse that says, *The insolent* [*kingdom*] *will come and bring humiliation*[36] [*to Israel*] (Prov. 11:2). Citing R. Abba bar Kahana, R. Berechiah said: It is written *Shall I be pure* (*zkh*) *with wicked balances*? (Micah 6:11). How can a man ask such a question as "Shall I be pure with false balances?" Dare one even suggest that a man who uses false balances can be pure? [But because the word *zkh* has the sense of "profit" as well as "pure," the verse is also asking whether a man can really profit by using false balances], and the verse itself answers: *If gemstones got through deceit,* [*by false balances*], *are in a man's purse, he will find himself deceived* [*as to their value*][37] (*ibid.*). According to R. Levi, Moses intimated to Israel that the specific consequences of not keeping honest measures and balances are to be inferred from the following four verses in Torah, beginning with these two: *Thou shalt not have in thy pouch diverse weights, a great and a small. Thou shalt not have in thy house diverse measures, a great and a small* (Deut. 25:13–14). If you do have diverse weights and measures, know that a wicked kingdom will come and wage war against your generation. And the proof? The third verse: *All that do such things . . . are*

35. [Generally vengeance is deprecated and regarded as a usurpation of God's own prerogative (*Vengeance is Mine*, etc.). Moreover, while the sinner is living, he may yet repent and then should be forgiven by those whom he had wronged. In regard to Amalek, however, God foreknew that his wickedness was to be absolute and enduring and would never be tempered by repentance. Hence, for such as Amalek, vengeance, both divine and human, is just and proper. L. N.]

36. JV: *When pride cometh, then cometh shame.*

37. JV: *Shall I be pure with wicked balances, and with a bag of deceitful weights.* But the word *'eḇen* means "weight" as well as "gemstone"; and the word *mirmah* is used in a dual sense, "deceit" as well as "deceitful"—hence *he will find himself deceived.*

an abomination unto the Lord thy God (Deut. 25:16). What warning against the abomination of using false measures and balances follows in the fourth verse? *Remember what Amalek did unto thee* (Deut. 25:17).

5. R. Levi began his discourse with the verse *Thou wilt castigate the heathen, Thou wilt destroy the wicked, Thou wilt blot out their name for ever and ever* (Ps. 9:7). The words *Thou wilt castigate the heathen* apply to Amalek, of whom it is written "Amalek was the first of the heathen [to attack Israel]" (Num. 24:20). The words *Thou wilt destroy the wicked* apply to wicked Esau, of whom it is said "Edom . . . shall be called the border of wickedness" (Mal. 1:4). If it be suggested, "Some of you, Jacob's descendants, must also be included among the wicked," say in reply: The verse says *Thou wilt destroy the wicked* [*one*] (Ps. 9:7)—not the wicked ones, but the wicked one, the wicked Esau. *Thou wilt blot out* [*the*] *name* [*only of the wicked heathen*] *for ever and ever* (*ibid.*): "Thou shalt blot out the name of Amalek" (Deut. 25:19).

6. [In comment on repayment of the wicked Amalek in kind, the following verse is cited]: *Render unto our neighbors sevenfold into their bosom their taunt, wherewith they have taunted Thee, O Lord* (Ps. 79:12). R. Judah bar Gurya[38] said: The phrase *into their bosom their taunt* pleads that what the Amalekites did to the circumcised organ of generation set in Abraham's middle—in his bosom, so to speak—be remembered against them. This interpretation of the verse's plea is in agreement with what R. Ḥanina bar Šilḳa, R. Joshua of Siḵnin, and R. Levi used to say in the name of R. Johanan: Just what did the retinue of Amalek use to do? They would cut off the circumcised organ of generation from live Israelites and would fling it heavenwards, taunting God: "Is this what Thou hast chosen? Here is what Thou didst choose for Thyself." But R. Joshua ben Levi said: The expression *sevenfold into their bosom their taunt* (Ps. 79:12) pleads that what the Amalekites did[39] in [tearing up Scrolls of] Torah, which Scripture speaks of as "refined sevenfold" (Ps. 12:7), be remembered against them: Render unto the Amalekites sevenfold into their bosom—what they did to "the sevenfold." And the Rabbis said: The verse pleads that what the Amalekites did[39] in [cutting all the way down to the foundation of] the Sanctuary, which is set in the bosom of the earth, be remembered against them. That the Sanctuary is referred to by the word "bosom" is plain, as R. Huna taught, from the verse that, speaking of the Sanctuary, says "from the bosom of the earth[40] to the lower settle shall be two cubits" (Ezek. 43:14).

When Samuel the prophet came, he requited the Amalekites: *Because of*

38. "Gurya"—O, Cas; O_1 and C—"Gadya."

39. "To us" is omitted as in C and Yalḳuṭ. In the Rabbis' lemma, "to us" is omitted only in C.

40. JV: *from the bottom upon the ground.*

[*Amalek's taunting of*] *the Lord, Samuel cut Agag apart in Gilgal*[41] (1 Sam. 15:33). Just what did Samuel do to Agag? [In requital for Amalek's cutting all the way down to the Sanctuary's foundation], said R. Abba bar Kahana, Samuel cut many olive-sized pieces of flesh from live Agag and fed them to ostriches: "Pieces of his body shall be devoured, yea, the first-born of death shall devour pieces of his flesh"[42] (Job 18:13)—that is to say, Samuel devised a kind of death first in the degree of its cruelty.[43]

[In requital for Aamalek's tearing up of Torah Scrolls], say the Rabbis, Samuel set up four pikes in the ground, bound Agag to them, and had him pulled in four different directions [so that he was torn apart]—a form of execution hinted at in Agag's asking Samuel *Is this most bitter of deaths proper for a prince?*[44] (1 Sam. 15:32). Do you execute princes in such cruel ways?

R. Samuel bar Abdimi said: In passing such harsh and peremptory judgment upon Agag, Samuel followed the procedure of the nations of the earth, which, [unlike Jewish procedure], does not require two witnesses who actually saw the crime committed and further, [unlike Jewish procedure], does not require that the acused man receive warning in advance of the consequences of his crime.[45]

[In requital for Amalek's cutting off the circumcised organ of generation from live Israelites], said R. Isaac, Samuel cut off Agag's member. In proof of his assertion, R. Isaac cited the verse from 1 Sam. 15:33 which is usually read *Samuel said: As thy sword hath made women childless, so shall thy mother be childless among women.* But, according to R. Isaac, the word *'immeḵa*, "thy mother," is to be read *'ammeḵa*,[46] "thy member," namely, Agag's member, and hence the verse is to be construed: "As thy sword

41. JV: *Samuel cut Agag apart before the Lord in Gilgal.*

42. In Job 18 the commentator finds an intimation of Agag's fate because the chapter describes the punishment of the wicked; and verse 17 in it declares that *His remembrance*—a phrase linked with Amalek—*shall perish from the earth.*

43. In this comment, Agag would be understood as saying *Surely the Lord of deaths is at hand* (1 Sam. 15:32). *Mar*, generally rendered "bitterness" means in Aramaic, "lord, prime, first."

44. JV: *Surely the most bitter of deaths is at hand.* But the commentator apparently gives the word *sr*, "is at hand," a dual interpretation: (1) *sr*, as an abbreviated form of *srs*, "pull, tear apart"; (2) *sr* as though spelled with a *śin*, hence "prince."

45. *Agag came unto him cheerfully. And Agag said, Surely the bitterness of death is departed* (AV and ERV), thinking that Samuel being a prophet would exercise mercy. Agag had not realized that, as one of a proscribed people, justice meted out to him would be swift, severe, and arrived at in keeping with procedures followed in non-Jewish courts which make confession alone sufficient ground for imposition of sentence. See P.Ḳid 1:5, 58c.

46. Actually *'ammatĕḵa.*

[cutting off Israel's male parts] hath made their women childless, so shalt thou, [Amalek], thy member [cut off], keep thy women childless." [Having thus spoken, at once then, as the verse concludes, Samuel cut off Agag's male parts].[47]

R. Levi added: Indeed Moses hinted at Agag's cutting the circumcised organ of generation from live Israelites as something that might be inferred from Torah, for the verse *When men strive together one with another, and the wife of one draweth near to deliver her husband out of the hand of him that smiteth him . . . and seizes him by his genitals* (Deut. 25:11–12) is shortly followed by the words *Remember what Amalek had done unto thee* (Deut. 25:17)—[that is, had cut off thy genitals].

7. *Remember* (Deut. 25:17). R. Berechiah taught: Thou sayest to us *Remember.* Do Thou remember. Forgetfulness is frequent with us, but seeing that with Thee there is no forgetfulness, do Thou remember what Edom's brood has done to Thee. As R. Isaac pointed out, [the children of Israel were asking]: Has Edom done evil only to us? Has he not also done evil to Thee? *Remember, O Lord, against the children of Edom the day of Jerusalem['s destruction, the day] they said: 'aru, 'aru*[48] (Ps. 137:7), which R. Abba bar Kahana took to mean "raze it, raze it," as in the verse "The broad walls of Babylon shall be utterly razed (*'ar'er*)" (Jer. 51:58). R. Levi took *'aru, 'aru* to mean "empty it, empty it," as in the verse "She hastened and emptied (*tĕ'ar*) her pitcher into the trough" (Gen. 24:20). According to R. Abba bar Kahana who said the words mean "raze it, raze it," the verse in the Psalm implies that the Edomites razed the city to its foundations—did not stop until they had got down to its very foundations. But according to R. Levi who said the words mean "empty it, empty it," the verse implies that [in plundering the city], they cut away its foundations—the very foundations were taken away.[49]

8. *Amalek* (Deut. 25:17) is made up of the words *'am*, "people," and

47. On special Sabbaths the practice in Palestine was to suspend the regular Sabbath lesson and instead have the passage prescribed for the particular Sabbath read, if necessary, again and again by the seven people called to the Torah. In this instance since the passage beginning *Remember what Amelek had done unto thee* (Deut. 25:17) had only three verses, the minimum required for each reader, Deut. 25:17–19 was repeated seven times by the seven readers. Hence the *pĕtiḥah*'s opening verse, *Remember unto our neighbors sevenfold into their bosom* (Ps. 79:12), had ironic aptness. Hence, too, the recital of Amalek's three kinds of enormity to explain and account for Samuel's cruel execution of Agag, as set forth in 1 Sam. 15, the haftarah for Sabbath *Zakor*—the Sabbath of remembering Amalek.

48. JV: *Raze it, raze it.*

49. See Piska 20.2.

yeleḳ, "locust," for, like the kind of locust known as *zaḥla*, Amalek swooped down swiftly [upon the people of Israel].

Another comment: The word is made up of *'am*, "people," and *laḳ*, "lick" —hence a people which, like a dog, came to lick up Israel's blood. This comment is in line with what R. Levi said in the name of R. Simeon ben Ḥalafta: With what may Amalek be compared? With a fly greedy to get at an open wound. Hence the comment that Amalek was like a dog greedy to get at Israel. Indeed, as R. Nathan taught, Amalek [was so greedy to get at Israel that he] was willing to travel a distance of four hundred parasangs[50] when he came to make war against Israel in Rephidim.

9. *Remember what Amalek did unto thee by the way as ye came forth out of Egypt* (Deut. 25:17). R. Levi said: Like a highwayman he came upon you from the wayside. In this connection is told the parable of a king who had a vineyard which he had enclosed with a fence and in which he had put a dog who was a biter. The king said: If any one should come and breach the fence, the dog will bite him. When the king's own son came and breached the fence, the dog bit him. Thereupon, whenever the king wished to remind his son of his sin—what he had done in the vineyard—he would say to him, "Remember how the dog bit you." So, too, whenever the Holy One wished to remind Israel of their sin at Rephidim in querying one another, *Is the Lord among us, or not?* (Exod. 17:7), He would say to them *Remember what Amalek did unto thee* (Deut. 25:17).[51]

10. [The next verse, Deut. 25:18, is usually read *How Amalek met thee by the way, and smote the hindmost of thee, all that were enfeebled in thy rear, when thou wast faint and weary; and he feared not God*]. On the interpretation of the word *ḳrk*, usually translated *How he met thee*, in *How he met thee by the way* (Deut. 25:18), R. Judah, R. Nehemiah, and the Rabbis differ.[52] For *ḳrk*, R. Judah read *ḳyrk*, meaning "How he took advantage of the mischance which befell thee"—that is, the mischance of thy nocturnal emission of semen which required thee, [in obedience to Scripture], to leave the camp—*Any man, that is not clean by reason of that which mischanceth him (mḳrh)*[53] *by night shall go abroad out of the camp* (Deut.

50. He came from the mountains of Seir. Meḵ, 2, 137. A parasang is about 4,000 yards.

51. Cf. PR 12:12.

52. *How he met thee by the way* appears to imply that Amalek's coming upon Israel was accidental. That there was anything fortuitous or accidental in Amalek's attack upon Israel is regarded by the three commentators as inconceivable. Hence the comments which follow.

53. *Mḳrh* is understood as a form of *ḳry*, a word which means "the mischance of nocturnal emission."

[R. Judah interpreted *ḳrk* as meaning "he befouled thee with his (Amalek's)

23:11). [Thus it was that Amalek got the opportunity to seize thee and pollute thee by pederasty].

R. Nehemiah, however, read *ḳrk* as *ḳr'k*, meaning "how he read up on thee," and took the verse to be saying "*How he read up* (*ḳr'k*) *in records that go away back*" (*bdrḵ*)[54] (Deut. 25:18). What deed of Amalek's did R. Nehemiah have in mind? That Amalek having managed to get into Egypt's archives and taken from them the Tribes' genealogical rolls wherein were recorded the names of the Israelites, stationed himself just beyond the cloud of glory [that protected Israel] and called out names he had read in the rolls: "Reuben! Simeon! Levi! Judah! I am your brother. Come forth because I want to transact a matter of business with you." And when one of the Israelites whose name was thus called out went forth, Amalek slew him.

But our Rabbis [read the verse "How he cooled thee" (ḳyrḵ) (Deut. 25:17)]: that is, Amalek made Israel appear lukewarm in battle in the eyes of nations. As R. Huna said: What Amalek did may be understood by the parable of a pool of scalding water into which no living creature dared to descend. Then one vile person came and, though he knew he would be scalded, sprang right into the pool, so that in the eyes of others it appeared lukewarm. So, too, when Israel went out of Egypt, fear of their burning zeal fell upon all the nations of the earth: *Then were the chiefs of Edom affrighted . . . Terror and dread falleth upon them* (Exod. 15:15–16). But after Amalek came and waged war against Israel, though he got from them the scalding he deserved, still he made Israel appear lukewarm in battle in the eyes of the nations of the earth.

11. The word *way-yězanneḇ*, usually translated *how he smote the hindmost of thee* (Deut. 25:18), is here taken to mean "how he smote the hinder part of thee"—that is, smote thy male member. That such is the meaning of *way-yězanneḇ* is in agreement with what R. Ḥanina bar R. Šilḳah, R. Joshua of Siḵnin, and R. Levi citing R. Johanan said: For what did the retinue of Amalek use to do? From live Israelites they cut off the circumcised organs of generation and threw them heavenward, saying: "Is this what Thou hast chosen for Thyself? Here Thou hast what Thou didst choose."

The fact is that the children of Israel had not at first known of the mode of derision wherein the male member is used, although it is suggested by Scrip-

---

semen (by subjecting thee to sodomy)," and in proof cites Deut. 23:11 where *ḳrh* does indeed refer to emission of semen. R. Judah clearly makes no reference to the Israelites themselves having been made ritually unclean by their own semen (which is but a minor pollution compared with the dreadful sin of sodomy practiced by Amalek). I would therefore rephrase: "R. Judah interpreted *ḳrk* in the sense of 'he befouled thee (with his semen),' as in the verse *Any man, that is not clean by reason of the emission of semen* (*mḳrh*) *by night*," etc. (Deut. 23:11). L. N.]

54. "*records—away back*" is an attempt to match the pun in the Hebrew of *bdrk*, "away," and *bd'rky*, "records" or "archives."

ure's saying of Judah's abominations *Lo, they put the branch—the phallus —to My*[55] *nose* (Ezek. 8:17). Actually, it was Amalek who, when he came [to Rephidim], first showed this mode of derision to the children of Israel. And from whom had Amalek learned it? From his grandfather Esau who derisively said of Jacob: *Is not* (*haki*)[56] *he rightly named Jacob* (Gen. 27:36)—that is, Esau hawked up phlegm and exhibited his member [by way of expressing his contempt of Jacob who was born circumcised].[57]

12. On the words *All that were enfeebled in thy rear* (Deut. 25:18), R. Judah, R. Nehemiah, and the Rabbis differ. R. Judah said: Every one who hung back feebly from obeying [God's commands] found himself cast[58] [outside the cloud of glory that protected Israel]. R. Nehemiah said: Every one whom the cloud of glory expelled[59] was cast outside of its shelter. The Rabbis said: It was the Tribe of Dan whom the cloud of glory expelled, for all Danites served idols.[60] And R. Isaac said: In keeping with comments made by R. Judah, R. Nehemiah, and the Rabbis, the verse refers to all [the backbiters] who whispered *in Thy rear*.[61] For, according to R. Judah, the backbiters among the Israelites whispered: If He is Lord over all His works,[62] even as He is Lord over us, we will serve Him; but if He is not Lord over all, we will rebel against Him. According to R. Nehemiah, they also whispered: If He provides us with sustenance[63] in the manner of a king who resides in his own capital city and therefore insures that it lacks nothing at all, we will serve Him; but if He does not, we will not serve Him. According to the Rabbis, they also whispered: If in our hearts we ask for things, and He knows what we ask for, we will serve Him; but if He does not know, we will rebel against Him. R. Berechiah, citing R. Levi, said: Actually, the Israelites in their hearts did ask for things, and the Holy One granted their

55. MT: *their*. This is one of the instances in Scripture where the Scribes, out of reverence for God, modified the text. See Mek, 2, 43–45.

56. If *haki* means "hawking," then the contempt could be in the spitting of phlegm.

57. The commentator may find a suggestion for this inference from the name Jacob, "One that takes by the heel," hence, seizes the end, i.e. the male organ. Jacob was born circumcised. See *The Fathers According to R. Nathan*, tr. Judah Goldin, chap. 2 (YJS, *10*, 23).

58. *Nḥšlym*, "enfeebled," is thus taken to be made up of *nḥ*, "easy" or "feeble," and *šl*, "cast out."

59. *Nḥšlym* is construed as though it were *nḥšrym*, "distilled, discharged." See 2 Sam. 22:12; and B.Ta 9b.

60. *In thy rear* (Deut. 25:18) is taken to suggest the Tribe of Dan who journeyed at the rear (Num. 2:31). See Targum Jonathan on Exod. 17:8; and PR 12:13 (YJS, *18*, p. 240, n. 105).

61. *Nḥšlym* is read by metathesis as *mlḥšym*, "whisperers."

62. They were thus dubious concerning the range of God's power. See RH 3:8.

63. See Exod. 16:3, 17:2.

requests. And the proof? The verse *They tested God in their hearts by asking food for their craving* (Ps. 78:18). And what verse follows? The verse *So they did eat, and were well filled; for He gave them that which they craved* (Ps. 78:29).

13. *When thou wast faint and weary* (Deut. 25:18)—the verse goes on—that is, when Israel [in the desert] was faint from thirst and weary from the road. In connection with the continuation of the verse, *And he*—[Amalek]—*feared not God* (*ibid.*), an 'Ăḡaḏah transmitted from generation to generation tells us—so said R. Phinehas, citing R. Samuel bar R. Naḥman—that Amalek, the seed of Esau, will fall at the hands of none other than Rachel's children: *Surely the youngest of the flock shall drag them* [*of the seed of Esau*] *away* (Jer. 49:20). And why does Scripture call Rachel's children the youngest of the flock? Because they were the youngest of the Tribe Fathers. The one was called "lad," and the other was called "least." The one was called "lad"—*Joseph . . . being . . . a lad* (Gen. 37:2); and the other was called "least": [*O Edom*], *I make thee least*—[that is, of least worth *among the nations*] (Ob. 1:2). The other grew up with two righteous people,[64] but did not act in keeping with their deeds; and the one grew up with two wicked people,[64] but did not act in keeping with their deeds. Let the other fall at the hand of the one. One had consideration for the honor of his Maker, and the other despised the honor of his Maker. Let the other fall at the hand of the one. Of the other it is said *for he feared not God* (Deut. 25:18); while the one is quoted as saying *I fear God* (Gen. 42:18). Let the other fall at the hand of the one.

14. [The next verse in Deuteronomy has an allusion to the fate of Amalek]: *Therefore it shall be, when the Lord thy God hath given thee rest from all thine enemies*, etc. (Deut. 25:19). R. Azariah and R. Judah bar R. Simon citing R. Judah bar R. Il'a'i taught: Upon their entrance into the Land, Israel were commanded to do three things: to set up a king over themselves (Deut. 17:15), to build themselves the Temple—*Let them make Me the Sanctuary* (Exod. 25:8)—and to wipe out the remembrance of Amalek (Deut. 25:19).

15. R. Joshua ben Levi said in the name of R. Alexandri: One verse says *thou*, [*Israel*], *shalt blot out the remembrance of Amalek* (Deut. 25:19); and another verse quotes God as saying *I will blot out the remembrance of Amalek* (Exod. 17:14). How are the two verses to be reconciled? Before Amalek put forth his hand against God's throne, Scripture said that thou, [Israel], art to blot out the remembrance of Amalek. After Amalek had put forth his hand against God's throne, God is quoted as saying *I will utterly blot out the remembrance of Amalek* (Exod. 17:4). But is it possible for flesh-and-blood to put forth a hand against the throne of the Holy One? Yes,

64. Respectively, Isaac and Rebekah, Pharaoh and Potiphar.

ince by "God's throne," Jerusalem is meant. And because Amalek was to ise up to destroy Jerusalem of which it is written *at that time they shall call Jerusalem The throne of the Lord* (Jer. 3:17), God said: *I will utterly blot out the remembrance of Amalek from under heaven* (Exod. 17:14).

16. *And he said, "The hand upon the throne of the Lord: the Lord will have war with Amalek from generation to generation"* (Exod. 17:16). In a Baraita, it is taught in the name of R. Eliezer: The Holy One swore a solemn oath, "By My right hand and again by My right hand,[65] by My throne and again by My throne, I swear that if would-be proselytes come from any of the nations of the earth I will receive them, but if from the seed of Amalek I will never receive them." Nor would David receive them: *David asked the young man that told him* [of the deaths of Saul and Jonathan]: *"Whence art thou?" And he answered: I am the son of an Amalekite proselyte*[66] (2 Sam. 1:13). According to R. Isaac, the young man who brought the tidings was the son of Doeg[67] the Edomite, to whom David said *Thy blood be upon thy head* (2 Sam. 1:16). Now the *kĕṯiḇ*, as R. Isaac pointed out, is *thy bloods*,[68] for David meant to say to the young man: Much blood have you shed in Nob the city of priests.[69]

From generation to generation (Exod. 17:14). The Holy One said: I keep tracking[70] Amalek from generation to generation. R. Eliezer, R. Joshua, and R. Jose differ concerning the length of the period during which God would be tracking Amalek. R. Eliezer said that the period was to be from the generation of Moses to the generation of Samuel. R. Joshua said it was to be from the generation of Samuel to the generation of Mordecai and Esther.[71] And R. Jose said it was to be from the generation of Mordecai and Esther through the generation of the king Messiah which is to endure as long as three ordinary generations, as is said *They will fear Thee while* [*the Messiah's*] *sun endures, so long, that is, as* [*the reign of a scion of David symbolized by*] *the moon, continues, a generation and generations*[72] (Ps.

65. "Wherever 'hand' is mentioned, it refers to the right." B.Zeḇ 24a.

66. JV: *stranger*. In Rabbinic Hebrew, however, *stranger* is taken to mean "proselyte," or "would-be proselyte."

67. "The son of"—Tanḥuma, *Ki ṯeṣe'*, end. This reading is adopted because David knew Doeg (1 Sam. 21:8, 22:9) and so would not have asked him "Who art thou?"

68. *dmyk*, not *dmk*, "thy blood" (singular).

69. See 1 Sam. 22:18–19. Presumably Doeg's son helped his father in carrying out the massacre which Saul had ordered.

70. *Mdr dr*, "from generation to generation," written defectively, permits the reading *mdrdr*, "roll after, track," and the consequent play on words.

71. Moses, Samuel, Mordecai, and Esther had to fight Amalek.

72. JV: *They shall fear Thee while the sun endureth, as long as the moon, throughout all generations* (Ps. 72:5). Here Rashi's interpretation of the verse as given in B.Sanh 99a is followed.

72:5): since a *generation* is one and *generations* implies at least two more, you thus have three generations.

R. Berechiah said in the name of R. Abba bar Kahana: As long as Amalek's seed endures in the world, it is—if one dare speak thus—as though a pennon hid God's face. Once the seed of Amalek perish, *Thy Teacher shall not hide Himself* [*as with a pennon*] *any more, but thine eyes shall see thy Teacher* (Isa. 30:20).

R. Levi said in the name of R. Ḥama[73] bar R. Ḥanina: The name of the Lord will not be complete, and the throne of the Lord will not be whole as long as Amalek's seed endures in the world; but when Amalek's seed perishes from the world, the Name will be complete and the throne will be whole. And the proof? The verse *The destructions of the enemy are come to a perpetual end, and their cities Thou didst uproot, their very memorial is perished* (Ps. 9:7). What does the text at once go on to say? *The Lord is enthroned; He hath prepared His throne for judgment* (Ps. 9:8).[74]

73. "Ḥama"—Yalḳuṭ and PR; O: "Huna."

74. Cf. MTeh 9:10, where R. Levi's statement ends with the words: "Here, behold, the Name is complete, and the throne is whole." That is, the spelling is no longer defective, the Hebrew words for *Lord* and *throne* being given in full. See also PR 12:9 (YJS, *18*, 235).

PISKA 4

SUMMARY

The mystery and paradox of the Red Heifer

Bringing forth out of the unclean that which is clean is a mysterious act which only God, the Unique One of the universe, can perform (Sec. 1). His concern with purity is so great that to avoid unseemly terms He speaks in a roundabout way. In His eyes slander is an impurity even more hateful than unseemly speaking. Therefore, in Saul's generation, even though children were thoroughly versed in Torah—in that which is most pure—still, because the children's elders were informers, the people of that generation fell in battle. On the other hand, the men of Ahab's generation worshiped idols and presumably did not study Torah. Nevertheless, they were victorious in battle because knowing that Obadiah was hiding one hundred Prophets whom Ahab had proscribed, they did not denounce them to Ahab.

Slanderers slaying men who are far away are more evil than a serpent who can slay only those close by. Slander may be active as was Doeg's, and may be passive—by innuendo—as was Abner's.

To rid Israel of every kind of impurity—such as impurity in words which are unseemly or slanderous—God set down prescriptions concerning the Red Heifer which by its power to refine *seven times seven* brings purity out of men's impulse to impurity (Sec. 2).

The mystery of the Red Heifer is such that not even Solomon, privy to every kind of wisdom, could fathom it. Solomon's wisdom exceeded the wisdom of the children of the east, as is proved by his uncovering of a hoax which Pharaoh sought to perpetrate upon him. Solomon was wiser than Adam who named everything that exists, including God on high; wiser than Abraham, than Moses, than Joseph who knew seventy languages; wiser than the generation of the wilderness. So great was Solomon's wisdom that he had three thousand parables to illustrate each and every verse he uttered and a thousand and five interpretations for each and every parable. Solomon knew the reasons for the manner of cleansing a leper; knew the reasons for the differing requirements for the slaughter of beasts and fowl; knew why he who hunted certain creeping things on the Sabbath was not culpable; why fish do not require ritual slaughtering. By way of contrast to Solomon's wisdom is cited the wrongheaded teaching that fish require ritual slaughtering and that the son of a Gentile woman married to a Jewish man may be circumcised on the Sabbath. Great as was Solomon's wisdom, however, he could not understand the section concerning the Red Heifer (Sec. 3).

Among those described as "*the* wise," namely, God, Adam, Israel, and disciples of scholars, Moses also is included, not on account of his sundry attainments but solely because the command concerning the Red Heifer was vouchsafed to him (Sec. 4).

Such is the importance of the passage concerning the Red Heifer that its being linked for ever with Aaron is deemed as great an honor as though an entire Book of Torah were inscribed with his name (Sec. 5). Still the Impulse to evil finds it possible to impugn the rite of the Red Heifer: all that take part in its preparation have their garments defiled, yet its ash mixed with water makes garments ritually clean (Sec. 6). The Red Heifer's mystery known only to Moses will in time-to-come be as clear as crystal to all.

So great is God's concern for Israel's purification as achieved through the Red Heifer's ash that in heaven the voice of God engaged in the study of the passage of the Red Heifer was heard by Moses.

No wonder that High Priests such as Simeon the Just spent as much as sixty talents of gold on the runway for the Red Heifer in order to lend solemnity to the preparation of its ash.

Though the rite of the Red Heifer may in some ways resemble the mixing of medicines, it has no human origin but is divine, established by a decree of God which must be obeyed without cavil. Differing with this significance of the rite, another commentator sees the Red Heifer as a symbolic expiation for Israel's misdeed in regard to the golden calf (Secs. 7–8).

Finally, other commentators, by means of allegorical interpretation, see in the rites of the Red Heifer a prefiguring of Israel's experience in Egypt, Babylon, Media, Greece, and Rome, and a prefiguring of Rome's ultimate destruction. Still others see Israel unruly as a heifer and so punished and exiled, but finally, through the merit of Israel's devout men, delivered, cleansed by God Himself, and restored to Jerusalem. There, in the time-to-come, God, dispensing with the Red Heifer, will Himself cleanse Israel of their sins (Secs. 9–10).

PISKA 4

The Red Heifer (Num. 19:2)[1]

1. *Who can bring forth a clean thing out of an unclean thing? Is it not the ne*[2] (Job 14:4), He who brought forth Abraham out of Terah, Hezekiah ıt of Ahaz, Mordecai out of Shimei,[3] Israel out of the nations,[4] the world--come out of this world?[5]

Who other than the One can do so?
Who other than the One can so ordain?
Who other than the One can so decree?
Is it not the One?
Is it not the Unique One of the world?

ı a Mishnah we learn [of His mysterious decrees]: If a man has on his body a right spot no larger than a grain of bean grits, he is considered unclean; but the spot spreads over his entire body, he is considered clean.[6]

Who other than the One can prescribe such things?
Who other than the One can ordain them?
Who other than the One can decree them?
Is it not the One?
Is it not the Unique One of the world?

ıgain in a Mishnah we learn [of His mysterious decrees]: "If an embryo dies ı its mother's womb, and the midwife puts in her hand and touches the inant, she becomes ritually unclean for seven days,[7] but the mother is conidered clean until the embryo is expelled" (Ḥul 4:3). As long as the dead ıfant is in the house—in the womb—the house is clean, but as soon as the lead embryo comes out of the house—out of the womb—the woman is ınclean.

Who other than the One can prescribe such things?
Who other than the One can ordain them?

1. Num. 19:1–22 is the supplementary lesson (*mafṭir*) in the Pentateuch on Sabbath Parah (see Table of Scriptural Lessons, p. xv)—Sabbath of the Heifer, he third of the four special Sabbaths (see Meḡ 3:4).
2. JV: *not one.*
3. *Mordecai the son of Jair the son of Shimei* (Esther 2:5), the latter being dentified as the Shimei who was David's contemporary. See 2 Sam. 16:5, and B.Meḡ 12a.
4. See Deut. 4:34.
5. Only he who accumulates good deeds in this world will be rewarded with life in the world-to-come. See David Luria on Num. Rabbah 19:1.
6. See Lev. 13:2, and Neḡ 8:2.
7. Num. 19:11.

Who other than the One can decree them?
Is it not the One?
Is it not the Unique One of the world?

And in another Mishnah we learn of one more instance of [His mysterio decrees]: "All that have the care of a Red Heifer make their garments ritual unclean,[8] but the Red Heifer itself makes clean the unclean" (Par 4:4 [With regard to the foregoing paradoxes], there is but one explanation: [the are what He has decreed]. The Holy One says: Whatever statute I set dow or whatever decree I issue, you are not permitted to disobey My bidding. *Th is the statute of the Torah which the Lord hath commanded* (Num. 19:2).

2. R. Tanḥum bar Ḥanila'i began his discourse by citing the verse *Th words of the Lord are words pure as silver, tried in a crucible on the eart refined seven times* (Ps. 12:7). And R. Tanḥum continued his discourse b exclaiming *The words of the Lord are Words*—the words of the Lord ar deathless, but the words of mortals are themselves mortal. It is the way c the world that when a king of flesh-and-blood enters a province and th people of the province praise him, their praise may please him so much as t make him say, "Tomorrow I shall build you bathhouses,[9] tomorrow I sha bring in drainage ditches for you." Thereupon, he goes to sleep—and rise no more. Where is he then, and where are his promises? But the Holy On does not act thus, for *The Lord is the God of* [*everlasting*] *truth* (Je 10:10). Jeremiah's reason for declaring *The Lord is the God of* [*everlast ing*] *truth* is found, according to R. Abun, in the conclusion of the verse *H is the living God, and therefore an everlasting King* (*ibid.*).

Pure (Ps. 12:7). R. Judah citing R. Johanan, R. Berechiah citing R Eleazar, and R. Jacob of Kefar Ḥanin, who, according to some, cited R Joshua ben Levi, joined in saying: We find Scripture speaking in a round about way so as to avoid an unseemly term. Thus it is written *Of every clea beast thou shalt take to thee seven* (Gen. 7:2). But the text does not go o to say "and of the unclean beasts." Instead it says *and of the beasts that ar not clean*[10] *two* [*and two*], *each with his mate* (*ibid.*).

R. Judah bar R. Manasseh said: Even when the Holy One was about t point out to the children of Israel the signs by which animals that are unclea are to be distinguished, He began by pointing to those signs of clean animal

8. "All that have the care of a Red Heifer make their garments ritually un-clean—O_1; O: "All that have the care of a Red Heifer become ritually unclean i they wear garments." Not, accordingly, if they are naked. See Saul Lieberman's explanation in PRKM, 473.

9. The Hebrew for "and lavatories" is taken to be a gloss meant to explain "public bathhouses," a word of Greek origin. Indeed, C, O_2, and Yalḳuṭ do not have the conjunction "and" precede "lavatories."

10. Scripture could have used the one word "unclean" but avoids it and instead uses three words, "that [are] not clean."

which the unclean ones also have. Thus He did not begin by saying "The camel, because he parteth not the hoof," [the sign of uncleanness]; instead He began with *Because he cheweth the cud* (Lev. 11:4), [a sign of cleanness]. Not with "the rock-badger, because he parteth not the hoof," but with *because he cheweth the cud* (Lev. 11:5). Not with "the hare, because he parteth not the hoof," but with *because he cheweth the cud* (Lev. 11:6). Not with "the swine because he cheweth not the cud," but with *because he parteth the hoof* (Lev. 11:7).

R. Jose of Mimlaḥ,[11] and R. Joshua of Sik̲nin, citing R. Levi, said: Even before they knew anything about sexual desire, children[12] who lived in the days of David[13] knew those subtle distinctions of the law that elaborate forty-nine arguments by which a thing may be proved unclean and forty-nine[14] other arguments by which the very same thing may be proved clean. It was in behalf of these children that David prayed, saying *Keep them,*[15] *O Lord* (Ps. 12:8)—keep their understanding of Torah in these children's hearts; *preserve them out of this generation, ever* (*ibid.*)—preserve the children out of this generation which deserves complete destruction. For, despite their superior learning, when the men of the generation of David's time went into battle, they perished. Whenever they went into battle, they perished because so many of them had foul tongues. Of the foul-tongued men of this generation David said: *My soul is among lions; I lie down among them that would lap up*[16] (Ps. 57:5). By *lions,* David meant Abner and Amasa who were mighty as lions in their understanding of Torah [yet did not speak up in behalf of David when they should have].[17] In saying *I lie down among them that would lap up,* David meant Doeg and Ahithophel whose delight was lapping up slander [and passing it on].[18] By the words *sons of men, whose teeth are spears and arrows* (*ibid.*), he meant the men of Keilah,

11. In Galilee. See Lev. Rabbah M, 5, map facing p. xxviii.

12. The comment apparently takes *ʿalil,* "crucible," as though written *ʿolal,* "young child," and thus renders the phrase *in a crucible in the earth* (Ps. 12:7) as "in young children in the Land."

13. While Saul, still alive, was persecuting him. See Lev. Rabbah M, 3, 589.

14. JV: *seven times* (Ps. 12:7). But *šbʿtym,* the dual form of *šbʿ,* "seven," is here taken to mean "seven-seven," that is, seven times seven, or forty-nine.

[Rather, "knew how to interpret the Torah in forty-nine ways so as to prove a thing unclean, and in forty-nine other ways so as to prove the very same thing clean." L.N.]

15. *The words of the Lord* (Ps. 12:7) are understood as the object of *them.* Hence the children's "understanding of Torah" in the comment.

16. JV: *among them that are aflame.*

17. Hence, *The faithful fail from among the children of men* (Ps. 12:2).

18. Doeg informed on David and Nob the city of priests (1 Sam. 22:9). As for Ahithophel, even though his being an informer is not mentioned in Scripture, the Rabbis apparently had a tradition that he also was one.

concerning whom he asked "Will the men of Keilah deliver up me and m men into the hand of Saul?" [and concerning whom the Lord replied: "The will deliver thee up"] (1 Sam. 23:12). And by the phrase *Their tongue sharp sword* (Ps. 57:5), David referred to the Ziphites who "came and sai to Saul: 'Doth not David hide himself with us?' " (Ps. 54:2). At that tim David questioned the Holy One: Master of universes, with such slande spoken, how can Thy presence possibly abide on the earth?[19] *Be Thou exalted, O God, above the heavens* (Ps. 57:6)—remove Thy presence fron men's midst.

But though the men of Ahab's generation, all of them, worshiped idols they were victorious[20] when they went into battle because there were no foul-tongued informers among them. It was because of this fact that Obadiah was able to say to Elijah: *Was it not told, my lord, what I did when Jezebel slew the Prophets, how I managed to hide a hundred men of the Lord's Prophets by fifty in a cave, and fed them with victuals,*[21] *and water* (1 Kings 18:13). If Obadiah provided them with victuals, what need to mention water? To indicate that water was even more difficult to find than bread,[22] [and hence that many people must have known of Obadiah's hiding of the Prophets]. Therefore, when Elijah called out to the people on Mount Carmel: *I, even I only, am left a prophet of the Lord* (1 Kings 18:22), though all the people knew otherwise, none made it known to the king [that there were a hundred Prophets whom Obadiah had hidden].

Concerning slander, R. Samuel bar Naḥman taught: If a serpent be asked, "Why are you found among fences?" it is likely he will answer, "Because I made a breach in the fence of the world."[23] [If asked], "Why do you slither along with your tongue close to the dust?" the serpent is likely to answer, "Because the tongue brought me to this fate." [If asked], "Why is it that when other animals, wild or domestic, bite, they do not kill but when you bite, you kill?" the serpent is likely to answer, "*Does the serpent bite unless there be a whisper?*[24] (Eccles. 10:11). Is it conceivable that I do anything

19. "Whenever a man speaks slander, he causes the Presence to depart from earth to heaven." R. Mona in Deut. Rabbah 5:10. See also Piska 1.1; and MTeh 7:7.

20. Ahab is said to have been one of three potentates who ruled over the entire space beneath the vault of heaven (see B.Meḡ 11a).

21. JV: *bread.* But *lḥm* may have the more comprehensive meaning of "victuals," which would include water. Obadiah (see Piska 2.5) was a member of Ahab's court.

22. The period was one of severe and prolonged drought. See 1 kings 17:1, and 18:1–12.

23. In tempting Eve to eat of the forbidden tree, he opened the way to all kinds of breaches in God's law.

24. JV: *If the serpent bite before it is charmed.*

t all unless it be whispered to me from Above?" [If asked], "And why, hen you bite one limb, do all other limbs feel the poison at once?" the rpent is likely to reply, "Are you asking me? Ask the man of evil tongue ho may utter slander here [in the land of Israel] and manage thereby to ay someone as far away as Rome."

Why is the foul tongue of slander called a triple-slaying tongue? Because it ays three persons: the person speaking, the person spoken to, and the erson spoken of. Indeed, in the days of Saul an evil tongue killed four ersons: Doeg who spoke slander,[25] Saul who heeded it,[26] Ahimelech of hom it was spoken,[27] and Abner. Abner—why was he killed? R. Joshua en Levi, R. Simeon ben Laḳish, and the Rabbis differ in their explanations. According to R. Joshua ben Levi, it was because Abner put his own name efore David's. With reference to Abner's presumption, Scripture says, *Abner ent messengers to David* [*with a letter*] *in which David's name was put ast*—the letter began "from Abner to David"—*saying,*[28] *"Whose is the Land?"* (2 Sam. 3:12). According to R. Simeon ben Laḳish, it was because Abner made of young men's blood something to play with, as is written *Abner said to Joab: "Let the young men, I pray thee, arise and play before us"* (2 Sam. 2:14)—[that is, engage in a sword-fighting contest]. According to the Rabbis, however, it was because Abner did not let Saul be reconciled with David when David said to Saul: *My father, see, yea, see the skirt of thy robe in my hand*, etc. (1 Sam. 24:12)—[that is, David could have killed Saul in the cave in En-Gedi but instead cut off the skirt of Saul's robe; and later having followed Saul out of the cave, showed Saul the skirt as proof that he had refrained from killing him]. Thereupon Abner said to Saul: "Why pay attention to this one's boastful lie? The skirt of your robe was probably torn away by a thorn bush." And afterwards, [when David took away the spear and the cruse of water from near Saul's head][29] in the barricade where Saul lay, David cried to Abner: *Wilt thou not speak up, Abner?* (1 Sam. 26:14), as if to say, "Are you not he who declared: 'The skirt of Saul's robe was probably torn away by a thorn bush?' The spear and the cruse—were they also torn away by a thorn bush?" Finally there are some who say that Abner was killed because [as one of Saul's guards] he

25. Against Nob, the city of priests (1 Sam. 22:15); and he was slain, if we identify the Amalekite proselyte whom David slew as Doeg (2 Sam. 1:15, and Piska 3.15).

26. See 2 Sam. 1:9 and Rashi who, citing a Midrash, says that Saul was slain because he had slain the priests of Nob.

27. See 1 Sam. 22:16.

28. JV: *Abner sent messengers to David straightway, saying*, etc. But the word *taḥtaw*, "straightway," may also be rendered "under," meaning "after him," after Abner, that is. The proper form of address was "To David from Abner."

29. See 1 Sam. 26:5, 12.

had an opportunity to protest [the slaying of the priests of Nob], but di not protest.[30]

R. Ḥanan bar Pazzi read the verse concerning the purity of the Lord' words as follows: *The words of the Lord are purifying words . . . they refin by means of instructions* (Ps. 12:7) [concerning the Red Heifer]. Thes instructions number *seven times seven*[14] (*ibid.*): They contain seven refer ences to the Heifer [or to its ash mingled with water];[31] seven reference to burning;[32] seven references to sprinklings;[33] seven references to seve persons who are to wash their garments;[34] seven references to seven person who become unclean because of their handling of the Heifer;[35] seven refer ences to lustration;[36] and seven references to the priests engaged in the rit of the Heifer.[37] If anyone say to you, "Seven such references to priests ar not to be found here—[only five]," say in reply: Both Moses and Aaron are also to be counted in the references to priests, *The Lord spoke unto*

30. See I Sam. 22:17, and Rashi.

31. Num. 19:2, 5, 6, 9 (two references), 10, 17. The seven are taken to allude to the seven Red Heifers which, since the days of Moses, had been burned for lustration (see Par 3:5).

32. Of her skin, her flesh, her blood, her dung, cedarwood, hyssop, and scarlet.

33. *Eleazar the priest shall take of her blood . . . and sprinkle of her blood toward . . . the Tent of Meeting seven times* (Num. 19:4).

34. *The priest shall wash his clothes* (Num. 19:7), following the three stages in the rite of the Heifer prescribed in (1) *Ye shall give her unto Eleazar the priest* (Num. 19:3), (2) *Eleazar the priest shall take of her blood with his finger* (Num. 19:4), and (3) *The priest shall take cedarwood* (Num. 19:6). Four additional commands to wash clothes are given in (1) *He that burneth her shall wash his clothes in water* (Num. 19:8); (2) *he that gathereth the ash of the Heifer shall wash his clothes* (Num. 19:10); (3) *the clean person shall sprinkle upon the unclean . . . and he*—the person being cleansed—*shall wash his clothes* (Num. 19:19); and (4) *he who sprinkled the water of lustration shall wash his clothes* (Num. 19:21).

35. When a person dies in a tent, (1) whoever enters the tent, (2) whoever is in the tent, (3) and every open vessel in the tent. In the open field, (4) anything that touches a person who was killed, (5) or who died naturally, (6) or a human bone, (7) or a grave (see Num. 19:16).

36. A person who is clean shall take hyssop, dip it in the Heifer's ash mixed with water, and sprinkle it (1) on the tent, (2) and on the vessels, (3) and on people who were there, (4) or on him who touched the bones, (5) or on the person who was killed, (6) or died naturally, (7) or on the grave (Num. 19:18).

37. (1) *You shall give the Heifer to Eleazar the priest*; (2) *Eleazar the priest shall take some of its blood*; (3) *the priest shall take cedarwood*; (4) *the priest shall be unclean*; and (5) *the priest shall wash his clothes* (Num. 19:3, 4, 6, 7).

oses and unto Aaron,[38] *saying: This is the statute of the Torah* (Num. :1–2).[39]

3. R. Isaac began his discourse [on the wisdom required to understand e purifying strength of the Red Heifer's ash by quoting Solomon]: *All this ve I proved in wisdom; I say, "Would I could get wisdom"; but it is far om me* (Eccles. 7:29). Yet Scripture itself says, "God gave Solomon wis- om and understanding exceeding much . . . even as the sand that is on the ashore" (1 Kings 5:9). As to the meaning of "as the sand that is on the ashore," R. Levi and the Rabbis differ. According to the Rabbis, God gave olomon wisdom equal in scale to all of Israel's.[40] According to R. Levi, as e sand is a wall that holds back the sea, so was wisdom the wall that held ack Solomon's turbulent desires. There is a proverb: "If you have acquired isdom, what do you lack? If you lack wisdom, what have you acquired?" When a man lacks wisdom, he is like] a city broken into, left without a all—*Like a city broken down and without a wall, so is he whose spirit is ithout* [*wisdom's*] *restraint* (Prov. 25:28).

Scripture says, *Solomon's wisdom excelled the wisdom of all the children f the east*, etc. (1 Kings 5:10). What was the wisdom of the children of the ast? They were expert in casting horoscopes and skillful in ornithomancy. R. Simeon ben Gamaliel said: For three things I praise the men of the east: hey do not kiss on the mouth, but on the hand; they do not tear their food vith their teeth, but cut it with a knife; and [to prevent eavesdropping] they ake counsel only in an open field, as is said of our father Jacob "Jacob sent and called Rachel and Leah to the field unto his flock" (Gen. 31:4)—that s, called them to an open space. [*Solomon's wisdom*] *excelled all the wisdom of Egypt* (1 Kings 5:10). What, for example, was the wisdom of Egypt? You find that when Solomon was about to build the Temple he sent word to Pharaoh-the-lame,[41] saying: Since I am about to build the Temple, send me craftsmen: I will pay them a good wage. What did Pharaoh-the-lame do? He assembled all his astrologers, and they gazed into the future and saw what craftsmen were destined to die that year. These he sent to Solomon. As soon as they came to Solomon, he saw by the power of the holy

38. *Moses and Aaron among His priests* (Ps. 99:6). Then, too, in the wilderness Moses served as High Priest (PR 14:11 [YJS, *18*, 286–87]).

39. For the explanation of the above seven categories, Elijah of Wilno's commentary *'Adderet 'Eliyyahu* on Num. 19 is followed.

40. In a parallel version the text continues "who are likened to sand, as in the verse *The number of the children of Israel shall be as the sand of the sea* (Hos. 2:10)." See PR 14:8 (YJS, *18*, 270–71).

41. Taken here to be Shishak, Solomon's father-in-law. See Ginzberg, *Legends*, *6*, 378.

spirit that they would die that very year. So he gave them shrouds and s[ent] them back to Pharaoh with a written message which said: Apparently y[ou] had no shrouds in which to bury your dead. Here they are, and here are th[e] shrouds as well.

He was wiser than he who contained within himself all mankind[42] [(1] Kings 5:11), that is to say, wiser than Adam, the first man. Wherein was t[he] wisdom of Adam? You find that when the Holy One was about to create t[he] first man, He consulted the ministering angels and asked: *Shall we ma[ke] man?*[43] (Gen. 1:26). They spoke right up to Him: Master of universe, *What is man that Thou art mindful to him*, etc.? (Ps. 8:5). The Holy O[ne] replied: "This being whom I desire to create in My world—his wisdom w[ill] be greater than yours." Then what did the Holy One do? He assembled a[ll] domestic animals, all wild beasts and fowl, and had them pass before th[e] angels. He asked: What are the names of these creatures? The angels did n[ot] know.

When He created the first man, again He assembled all domestic animal[s,] all wild beasts and fowl, and had them pass before him. He asked Adam[:] What are the names of these creatures? Adam replied: This one—the nam[e] "horse" fits him. This one—the name "lion" fits him. And this one—"camel." And this one—"ox." And this one—"eagle." And this one—"ass." Thus it is written *And the man gave names to all cattle*, etc. (Gen. 2:20).

God asked him: "And thou, what is thy name?" He replied: "Adam." God asked: "Why?" "Because I was fashioned out of the earth (*'ădamah*)." God asked: "And I, what is My name?" Adam replied: "Lord." God asked[:] "Why?" Adam replied: "Because Thou art Lord over all Thy works."

According to R. Aḥa, the Holy One said: *I am the Lord, that is My name* (Isa. 42:8). That is My name, the name by which *'adon*—that is Adam[44] who was the first lord of the earth—called Me. That is My name, the name I have consented to be called by. That is My name which I have consented to be called by when I am with the ministering angels.[45]

[*Solomon . . . was wiser . . . than Ethan the Ezrahite, and Heman, and Calcol, and Darda, the sons of Mahol* (1 Kings 5:11)]. By *Ethan* is meant our father Abraham, [who was author of the Psalm headed] "Maschil of Ethan the Ezrahite [—the mighty one who came from the east]"[46] (Ps.

42. JV: *than all men.*

43. JV: *Let us make man.*

44. *'Adon*, "lord," spelled *'Adn* with a change in the final consonant becomes *'Adm.*

45. Cf. MTeh 8:2.

46. See PR 6:5; MTeh 1:6; and B.BB 15a. The commentator assumes that Solomon is compared with the most famous Sages of all past time—with Abraham who gazed at the stars (see Gen. 15:5), with Moses who heard God speak, with Joseph who surpassed in the art of government.

1). By *Heman*, "the trusted one," is meant Moses, [of whom God d]: "He is trusted in all My house" (Num. 12:7). By *Calcol*, "the tainer," is meant Joseph: "And Joseph sustained his father and his thren," etc. (Gen. 47:12). [At the time Pharaoh set Joseph over all the d of Egypt], the Egyptians said: "Is it for any reason other than the dom ascribed to him that a slave has been made king over us?" What did y do to test him? They took seventy tablets, wrote phrases in seventy guages upon them, and tossed them to him: Joseph read each and every rase in each language. Besides, he could speak the sacred tongue[47] the yptians did not understand at all. [That the Egyptians tested him in venty languages is intimated in the verse] *At the time the news went forth it he had been set over all the land of Egypt, Jehoseph,* [*confronted with test of seventy languages, exclaimed*]*: I understood languages which I d never heard* (Ps. 81:6).[48] The *kĕṯiḇ*, however, is [not *'ešma'*, "I under-ood," but] *'ašmia'*, "I make myself understood in"—[that is, not only uld he understand, but he could also speak the seventy languages].

Solomon was *Wiser . . . than Darda,* which was the generation of the lderness. And why does Scripture speak of it as Darda? Because it was a neration (*dor*) of men, everyone of whom was filled with knowledge *e'ah*).

Solomon was *Wiser . . . than . . . the sons of Mahol,* another name for rael, a people to whom the Presence gave pardon (*moḥlah*) for the making the golden calf.[49]

47. Hebrew, spoken by Israel, a "nation unique in the earth," is not reckoned being one of the seventy languages spoken by the nations of the earth.

48. JV: *This He ordained in Jehoseph for a testimony when he went out rough the land in Egypt; where I heard a language that I understood not.* Be-use this verse as usually translated is not very clear, the commentator construes as referring to Joseph at the time he was made head over all the land of Egypt.

The legend that at that instant Joseph became master of seventy languages (see .Soṭ 36b) is said to be based on the fact that the verse (Ps. 81:6) begins and nds with the letter *'ayin* whose numerical value is seventy.

The name "Joseph" appears in this verse as *Jehoseph*, a letter being added. It is e letter *he'* which stands for that part in God's name (YH) with which He reated heaven and earth (PR 21:21). The added letter is construed by the com-entator as implying that because Joseph overcame his own lusting eye (*'ayin*), s he resisted Potiphar's wife's attempts to seduce him, he thereby made himself eady for the kind of wisdom which caused Pharaoh to say of him: *Can we find uch a one as this, a man in whom the spirit of God is?* (Gen. 41:38). See Samuel dels on B.Soṭ 36b.

49. That the phrase *sons of Mahol* is to be construed as the generation which eceived pardon for making the golden calf is in keeping with a Rabbinic norm which assumes that identical series of names in two passages in Scripture must be consistent. In this instance, Ethan, Heman, Calcol, etc. are identified in a genea-

[50]*And he spoke three thousand parables* (1 Kings 5:12). R. Samuel Nahmani said: We went through all of Scripture, from first to last, and fou that Solomon was inspired to utter no more than about eight hund verses,[51] and yet it is said that he spoke three thousand parables. But fact is that each and every verse which he was inspired to utter admits of t or three [or more] parables implicit in it, as is shown by the verse *As earring of gold, and also as an ornament of gold, so is the wise reprove* (Prov. 25:12).

The Rabbis said, however: Solomon had three thousand parables to ill trate each and every verse; and a thousand and five applications for each a every parable, for the verse does not conclude as one might expect wi "Solomon's songs were a thousand and five," but with *each song of (šyryw) was a thousand and five* (1 Kings 5:12). The word *šyryw*, "song is here read as *šyyrw*, meaning "application," hence implying a thousand a five applications of each one of Solomon's parables.

And he spoke upon[53] *trees, from the cedar that is in Lebanon even un the hyssop that springeth out of the wall* (1 Kings 5:13). Is it likely, as t verse seems to say, that a man would speak while perched upon treetop What the verse really says, however, is that in the course of his speculatio Solomon spoke upon the uses of trees, upon the *cedar that is in Lebano* and upon *the hyssop that springeth out of the wall* (*ibid.*). Asking wh Scripture requires that in the ritual cleansing of a leper both the cedar, talle of the trees, and the hyssop, lowest of the herbs, be used, his answer wa Because when a man exalts himself like a cedar, he is smitten with lepros but when he humbles himself like hyssop, he is healed with hyssop.[54]

He spoke also upon[53] *beasts, and upon fowl* (*ibid.*). But is it likely, a the verse seems to say, that a man would speak astride beasts and astrid

logical list in 1 Chron. 2:6 as being "the sons of Zerah," whereas in 1 Kings 5:1 the same individuals are identified as "sons of Mahol." Hence the conclusion th "sons of Mahol" intimates the people which received pardon.

50. The examples which follow are meant to illustrate how Solomon, goin beyond the generation which received the Torah in the wilderness, knew how t draw on his own divers inferences from the written text of Torah. *'Eṣ Yosef*, citin *Kĕli yĕḳar*, on Num. Rabbah 19:3.

51. According to the Masoretic text, Proverbs has 915 verses, Song of Song has 117 verses, and Ecclesiastes has 222. R. Samuel may have counted, howeve only those verses which present similes. Ḳimḥi says that some of Solomon's para bles may have been lost in the course of Israel's wanderings.

52. The reprover is Solomon himself, and since the reproof is compared to a earring as well as to an ornament, the inference is drawn that every verse lend itself to several nuances in interpretation.

53. JV: *of*.

54. See Lev. 14:4.

wl? What the verse really says, however, is that Solomon spoke upon the bject of ritual slaughter of beasts and fowl. Speculating on why Scripture quires that in the slaughtering of an animal both the windpipe and the ıllet be cut, but that in the slaughtering of fowl it is enough that either one cut,[55] his answer was that beasts were created out of dry earth, but that wl, according to one verse, were created out of dry earth, and according to nother verse, out of waters of the sea. Since one verse speaks [of fowl] as aving been created out of earth—*Out of the ground the Lord God formed . . every fowl of the air* (Gen. 2:19)—and another verse speaks of them as aving been created out of waters of the sea—*God said: Let the waters bring rth abundantly . . . fowl that may fly above the earth,* etc. (Gen. 1:20)—fowl are therefore considered in regard to ritual slaughter as being in a ategory between beasts which are slaughtered by cutting of both windpipe nd gullet, and fish which require no slaughtering at all].[56]

In a comment on this matter, Bar Ḳappara said that fowl were created out f sea mud [and so are beast-like]. But R. Abun said in the name of R. amuel of Cappadocia: Maybe so, but the skin of chickens' feet resembles he scale-covered skin of fish, [and so fowl are considered fish-like].

And upon creeping things (1 Kings 5:13). But is it likely, as the verse eems to say, that a man would speak astride creeping things? What the verse eally says, however, is that Solomon was meditating upon this question: In egard to the eight creeping things mentioned by name in the Pentateuch,[57] why is it that he who hunts them or wounds them on the Sabbath is culpable, whereas in regard to other creeping things which are likewise forbidden for food he who hunts them or wounds them is not culpable?[58] Solomon's answer was that he who hunts the former is culpable because they have skins, [the breaking or bruising of which makes a man guilty of working on the Sabbath].[59]

And upon fishes (*ibid.*). But is it likely, as the verse seems to say, that a man would speak astride fish? What the verse really says, however, is that Solomon was speculating upon the following question: Why is it that all kinds of animals, wild and domestic, as well as fowl require ritual slaughtering, but that fish do not?

55. See Ḥul 2:1, and B.Ḥul 27b.

56. See B.Ḥul 27b.

57. The weasel, the mouse, the great lizard, the gecko, the land crocodile, the lizard, the sand lizard, the chameleon. See Lev. 11:29–30.

58. See Shab 14:1, and Ḥul 9:2.

59. Since he breaks the skin by wounding them or suffuses the skin with blood by bruising them, he is guilty of working on the Sabbath, for breaking the skin comes under the category of "threshing," and bruising the skin comes under the category of "dyeing." See Bertinoro on Shab 7:2.

Concerning fish, Jacob of Kefar Nibburin[60] taught in Tyre that th require ritual slaughtering. When R. Haggai heard of this teaching he ha him summoned, and he asked him: On the basis of what verse do you teac thus? Jacob replied: On the basis of the verse which reads, *God said: "L the waters bring forth abundantly the moving creature that hath life, an fowl that may fly,"* etc. (Gen. 1:20)—that is, [since the waters bring fort both fish and fowl, both belong to the same category, and hence] even a fowl require ritual slaughtering, so fish require ritual slaughtering. Where upon R. Haggai said: Have him lie down that he may be lashed. [Jaco asked]: Shall a man who tries to prove a point by citing a verse fror Scripture be lashed? R. Haggai replied: The verse you cite does not apply Jacob asked: Then what verse does apply? R. Haggai replied: The one whic reads, *Shall the flocks and the herds be slaughtered for them? Or shall all th fish of the sea be gathered for them?* (Num. 11: 22). Note that in speaking o fish, the verse does not say "be slaughtered," but merely *gathered*. Jacob said: Keep on beating me—you are beating some sense into me.

In regard to the circumcision of the son of a Gentile woman [and a Jewish man], Jacob of Nubrai taught in Tyre that the son may be circum- cised on the Sabbath. When R. Haggai heard of this teaching, he summoned Jacob and asked him: Upon what authority do you teach thus? Jacob re- plied: Upon the authority of the verse which reads, *They declared their pedigrees after their families, by their fathers'*[61] *houses* (Num. 1:18); and also upon the authority of the verse which reads, *And he that is eight days old shall be circumcised . . . even one who is not of your seed* (Gen. 17:12). R. Haggai said: Have him lie down that he may be lashed. Jacob asked: Shall a man who tries to prove a point by citing verses from Scripture be lashed? R. Haggai said: The verses you cite do not apply. Jacob asked: What verses do apply? R. Haggai replied: First, lie down; then hearken. And he went on to say: If a man of any one of the Gentile nations comes to you and says, "I will become a Jew on condition that I be circumcised on the Sabbath or on the Fast Day of Atonement," shall the Sabbath or the Day of Atonement be profaned on his account? It goes without saying that neither the Sabbath nor the Day of Atonement may be profaned on his account: an exception is made only for the son of a Jewess.[62] Jacob said: Yes, but what verse applies? R. Haggai replied: The verse which reads, *Now therefore let*

60. A town in Galilee.

61. Jacob deduces therefrom that the child is reckoned after the father, who in this case is a true Israelite.

62. The words "And he went on to say: If a man of any one of the Gentile nations . . . only for the son of a Jewess" are not found in the parallels in P.Yeb 2:6, 4a and Ḳid 3:14, 64d, since even the circumcision of a native born Jew does not set aside the Sabbath if for some reason the circumcision had to be postponed beyond the eighth day from birth.

us make a covenant with our God to put away all the wives, and such as are born of them,[63] *according to the counsel of the Lord* (Ezra 10:3)—[that is, the verse is referring to the heathen wives of Jews and to the fact that their children are also considered heathen and therefore may not be circumcised on the Sabbath or the Day of Atonement, though they may be circumcised on other days].

Jacob asked: And would you have me lashed on the strength of that which is not in the Pentateuch?[64] R. Haggai answered: This very text goes on to say, *And let it be done according to the Pentateuch* (*ibid.*). Jacob asked: But according to what particular verse in the Pentateuch? R. Haggai replied: According to the one which R. Johanan cited in the name of R. Simeon ben Yoḥai: *Neither shalt thou make marriages with them: thy daughter thou shalt not give unto his son* (Deut. 7:3). Why this particular prohibition? *For* [*the heathen son-in-law*] *will turn away thy* [*grand*]*son from following Me* (Deut. 7:4). Thus Scripture uses *thy* [*grand*]*son* only in speaking of a son born of [*thy daughter*]—a Jewess, that is. Whereas of a son born of [thy son who is wed to] an idolatress or a heathen maidservant, Scripture would not say *thy* [*grand*]*son* but "her son."[65] Thereupon Jacob said: Keep on beating me—you are beating some sense into me.

Solomon said: All the foregoing subject-matters I understood—[all except one]. The one passage concerning the Heifer, whenever I grapple with it, I struggle to get at its meaning, I go over it word by word, but finally am forced to say, *"Would I could get wisdom; but it is far from me"* (Eccles. 7:23).

4. *Who is as the wise? and who knoweth the interpretation of a thing? A man's wisdom maketh his face to shine, and the strength of his face is changed* (Eccles. 8:1).

Who is as the wise?—that is, wise as the Holy One, of whom it is said "The Lord by wisdom founded the earth; by understanding He established the heavens" (Prov. 3:19). *And who knoweth the interpretation* [*pšr*] *of a thing?* No one but Him who interpreted [*prš*][66] the written Torah to Israel [in the light of the Oral Law]. *A man's wisdom maketh His face to shine.* R. Yudan said: Very wise in the power of language are the Prophets who, in order to make the children of Israel aware of God's shining presence, speak

63. That is, the requirement that a child be circumcised on the eighth day does not apply to children of heathen mothers.

64. Hebrew *Ḳabbalah*, i.e. the Scriptural books excluding the Pentateuch.

65. A conclusion derived from the fact that the text does not read "she, [thy heathen daughter-in-law]," etc., but *he,* [*thy heathen son-in-law*], *will turn away thy* [*grand*]*-son,* implying that the son of a heathen daughter-in-law is not considered a Jewish grandson. See Tosafoṯ on B.Yeḇ 17a, top.

66. The Aramaic for that which is dissolved is *pšr'*. See Targum Onkelos on Lev. 11:3.

of the likeness of the Almighty as though of the likeness of a man, as Daniel did when he said "And I heard the voice of a man[67] between the banks of Ulai" (Dan. 8:16). R. Yudan bar R. Simon said: There is a verse in Ezekiel which speaks of such a likeness even more explicitly: "And upon the likeness of the throne was the likeness as the appearance of a man" (Ezek. 1:26). The verse from Ecclesiastes goes on: *And the [terrifying] strength of His face is changed* from the measure of justice to the measure of mercy toward Israel [because the children of Israel accept the Torah and the teaching of the Prophets].

Another comment: *Who is as the wise?* (Eccles. 8:1)—that is, as wise as Adam, to whom it was said, "Thou seal most accurate, full of wisdom and perfect in beauty" (Ezek. 28:12).[68] *And who knoweth the interpretation of a thing?* Adam. For it was he who gave names interpretive of their natures to all creatures, as is said "Adam gave names to all cattle, and to the fowl of the air" (Gen. 2:20).[69] *Man's*—Adam's—*wisdom maketh his face to shine* (Eccles. 8:1). R. Levi said in the name of R. Simeon ben Menasya: The very round of Adam's heel outshone the globe of the sun. And do not wonder at this! Human nature is such that when a man has two salvers made for him, one for himself and one for his steward, whose salver does he have made the more beautiful? Not his own? So Adam was created for the service of the Holy One, and the globe of the sun was created for the service of creatures. Does it not follow, then, that the very round of Adam's heel outshone the globe of the sun? And if the round of Adam's heel outshone the globe of the sun, how much more brightly shone the countenance of his face!

R. Levi said in the name of R. Ḥama bar R. Ḥanina: The Holy One joined together thirteen canopies[70] over Adam in the Garden of Eden, as is evident from the verse "Thou wast in Eden, the Garden of God;[71] every kind of precious stone was thy covering; the carnelian, the topaz, and the emerald, the beryl, the onyx, and the jasper, the sapphire, the carbuncle, and

67. Since here "the voice of a man" directs the angel Gabriel, it is understood as being the voice of God.

68. See B.BB 75a and Samuel ben Meir *ad loc.*

69. See Piska 4.3.

70. Either canopied seats (cf. PR 37:1) or bridal canopies, which God provided for Adam and Eve in the Garden of Eden, the canopies symbolizing the glory and splendor of the world as it might have been had Adam and Eve not listened to the serpent and fallen into sin. After their sin the canopies disappeared, the light of Adam's countenance was gone, and his height, which made him tower above all creatures, was diminished (see PR 15:3).

71. Though the words are addressed to the Prince of Tyre, the reference to "Eden the Garden of God," with which Tyre is compared, permits the commentator to regard the passage as an account of the distinctions lavished by God upon Adam in the Garden of Eden.

the smaragd, and gold," etc. (Ezek. 28:13). According to R. Simeon ben Lakish, it was eleven canopies, and according to the Rabbis, ten. The Amoraim do not differ [as to the verse from which the numbers are inferred, but differ only as to the numbers themselves]. For he who maintains that the canopies were thirteen understands the phrases "every kind," "precious stone," and "was thy covering" as intimating that [out of precious stones not specified by Ezekiel but listed in the Book of Exodus], God made three more canopies [in addition to the one of gold].[72] He who maintains that the canopies were eleven takes the phrase "every kind of precious stone" as implying one more canopy[73] [in addition to the canopy of gold]. And he who maintains that the canopies were ten understands "every precious stone" as a general phrase not implying any additional canopy.[74] Yet despite all the splendor that was bestowed upon Adam, [he was told] "For dust thou art, and unto dust shalt thou return" (Gen. 3:19). *The [impudent] strength of his face was changed* (Eccles. 8:1). After Adam had sinned and said, "The woman whom THOU gavest[75] to be with me, she gave me of the tree" (Gen. 3:12), the Holy One did in fact change [the impudence of] his face as He banished him from the Garden of Eden, as is said "Thou changest his countenance and sendest him away" (Job 14:20). As Scripture says, "The Lord God sent him away from the Garden of Eden" (Gen. 3:23).

Another comment: *Who is as the wise man?* (Eccles. 8:1)—that is, as wise as Israel, of whom it is said "Surely this great nation is a wise and understanding people" (Deut. 4:6). *And who knoweth the interpretation of a thing?* It is Israel who know how to interpret the Torah with its forty-nine

72. Thirteen in all: nine canopies made out of the nine stones mentioned by Ezekiel; three more which God made out of the jacinth, agate, and amethyst, listed among the twelve stones in the High Priest's breastplate (Exod. 39:12), these three, according to R. Levi, being alluded to in the vague phrase "every kind of precious stone"; and a thirteenth canopy made out of the "gold." So Friedmann (see PR 14:10 [YJS, *18*, 281, n. 57]).

73. Perhaps he understands the phrase to say that one canopy was made out of a combination of the nine precious stones which Ezekiel lists.

[This view seems to take *wĕ-kol 'eḇen yĕḳarah*, with *'eḇen* in the singular, as indicating one kind of jewel in addition to the nine named. In other words, according to this view, the verse should be rendered "a certain kind of precious stone was thy complete (*kol*) covering, in addition to other coverings made, respectively, of carnelian," etc. L.N.]

74. He regards the phrase "every kind of precious stone" as intended to introduce the detailed specifying of stones which follows. See Lev. Rabbah 20:2 M, 446–47.

75. The implication is, If Thou hadst not given the woman to be with me, I would not have been seduced into sin, hence the blame for it is Thine, not mine. B.AZ 5a.

modes of determining what is ritually unclean and its forty-nine modes of determining what is ritually clean.

A man's wisdom maketh his face to shine (Eccles. 8:1). R. Zakkai of Shaab taught in the name of R. Samuel bar Naḥman: You find that when Israel stood at Mount Sinai and said: *All that the Lord hath spoken, we will do, and obey* (Exod. 24:7), something of the splendor of God's presence was bestowed upon them, as is said "And thy renown went forth among the nations for thy beauty; for it was perfect, through My splendor which I had put upon thee" (Ezek. 16:14). But when they said of that [odious] thing they made, "This is thy God, O Israel, which brought thee up out of the land of Egypt" (Exod. 32:8), and thereby became haters of the Holy One, then, as Scripture says, *The* [*splendid*] *strength of his face was changed* (*yšwn'*)[76] (Eccles. 8:1)—that is, the face of Israel "became that of a hater" (*yśwn'*), the letter *šin* in *yšwn'* being read as the letter *śin*. And it was then that the Holy One, [after having said "Ye are godlike beings (Ps. 82:6) who will live forever]" changed His intentions toward them and concluded by saying "Surely ye shall die like men" (Ps. 82:7).[77]

Another comment: *Who is as the wise man?* (Eccles. 8:1). He who is a disciple of wise men. *Who knoweth the interpretation of a thing?* (*ibid.*)—that is, he knows how to explain what he has learned. *A man's wisdom maketh his face to shine* (*ibid.*) when he is asked a question and is able to answer. *And the strength of his face is changed* (*ibid.*) when he is asked a question and is unable to answer it.

When, from his teacher's seat, Rabbi [Judah] posed the problem, "What is the proof from Scripture that a negative command is violated when a substitute is designated for a firstling?"[78] the face of [R. Judah] bar

76. The Biblical spelling *yšwn'* (as given in O_1) for *changed* is an uncommon one—the regular spelling is *yšwnh*; hence the inference.

77. See PR 1:2, and Mek̲, 2, 272.

78. When a man substitutes one unblemished animal for another already designated as an offering for the altar, both animals are considered holy. The substituted animal cannot, however, be offered on the altar as an offering and is to be kept in pasture until it suffers a blemish, at which time it may be used for the general maintenance of the Temple. In the meantime, the man who made the substitution has violated a negative command since animals which are not blemished may not be given for general maintenance of the Temple. Such may be given only as offerings for the altar. See Lev. 27:9–11 and 22:17–20; Tem 1:1, B.Tem 7b; Lev. 22:23 and B.Pes 42a.

But Scripture does not clearly prohibit the substitution of another animal for a firstling as it clearly prohibits substitution for an animal designated as an offering.

In P.Naz 5:1, 53d, however, where the encounter between Rabbi [Judah] and Bar Pedaiah is given in fuller form, Rabbi [Judah] says that the word *l'mr*, "saying," at the end of Lev. 22:17 is to be construed as though it read *l'w 'mwr*, meaning "a

Pedaiah lighted up and shone. Thereupon Rabbi [Judah] said: This man senses the special reading of the verse which deals with the problem I posed from my teacher's seat.

A heathen saw R. Judah bar R. Il'a'—saw him with his face aglow—and said: "One of three things is true of that man: Either he lends money upon interest, or he raises pigs,[79] or is drunk with wine." R. Judah bar R. Il'a', overhearing the heathen's remark, said to him: "May the breath of life in such a man as you be blown out, for not one of these things is true of me. I do not lend money upon interest, for it is written *Thou shalt not lend upon interest to thy brother: interest of money, interest of victuals, interest of any thing that is lent upon interest* (Deut. 23:20). I do not raise pigs, since it is forbidden for a Jew to raise pigs, as we are taught in a Mishnah, 'A man may not raise pigs anywhere'[80] (BḲ 7:7). Nor am I drunk with wine: indeed the four cups of wine which I drink on the eve of Passover make me feel [during the forty-nine days] from Passover to the Feast of Weeks as though I had a tight cord around my head."[81] (For the same reason R. Mana used to feel from Passover to Sukkot that there was a tight cord around his head). The heathen asked R. Judah: "Why, then, does your face shine?" He replied: "It is instruction in Torah which makes my face shine, as is written *A man's wisdom maketh his face to shine*" (Eccles. 8:1).

R. Abbahu went to Caesarea and returned thence, his face shining. The disciples saw him and came and told R. Johanan: "Can you believe it? R. Abbahu has found a treasure!" R. Johanan asked: "What makes you say so?" They replied: "Because his face is shining." He said to them: "May it not well be that he has heard a new interpretation of a passage in Torah?" And [without hesitation], when R. Abbahu came in to see him, R. Johanan asked him: "What new interpretation of a Torah passage have you heard?" R. Abbahu replied: "Something I came upon in an ancient Tosefta." Thereat R. Johanan applied to him the verse *A man's wisdom maketh his face to shine* (Eccles. 8:1).

Another comment: *Who is as the wise man?* (Eccles. 8:1). The wise Moses, of whom it is said "A wise man scaleth the city of the mighty"[82] (Prov. 21:22). *And who knoweth the interpretation of a thing?* (Eccles. 8:1). Moses, for he interpreted the written Torah to Israel [in the light of

---

negative prohibition [of the attempt to substitute for a firstling] is here intended." When R. [Judah] saw Bar Pedaiah's face aglow, he surmised that Bar Pedaiah was aware of this subtle, exegetical turn of the verse.

79. Both immensely profitable occupations.

80. Whether in or out of the Land of Israel.

81. Literally "my head is tied up."

82. The verse continues *and bringeth down the strength wherein it trusteth*, the strength being the Torah which Moses obtained in heaven despite the angels' objections (PR 20:4 [YJS, *18*, 409]; and MTeh 8:2).

Oral Law]. *A man's wisdom maketh his face to shine* (*ibid.*). R. Mani of Shaab said in the name of R. Joshua of Sik̲nin who said in the name of R. Levi: With each and every command which God uttered to Moses, He told him under what circumstances persons or objects could become ritually unclean and how they could be purified. When He reached, however, the passage of Scripture that reads *Speak unto the priests the sons of Aaron . . . There shall none defile himself for the dead* (Lev. 21:1), Moses asked God bluntly: "But, Master of the universe, what if a priest becomes ritually unclean through touching a dead person: by what means can he be purified?" God gave him no answer, and in that instant the face of Moses our teacher grew pale.[83] As Scripture says, *The strength of his face was changed* (Eccles. 8:1). When God reached the passage of Scripture dealing with the Red Heifer (Num. 19), however, the Holy One said to him: When I gave thee the command, *Speak to the priests . . . There shall none defile himself* (Lev. 21:1), thou didst ask Me, "Master of universes, if a priest becomes ritually unclean, by what means can he be purified?" and I did not answer thee. Now, however, I give thee the answer: *And for the unclean* [the one about whom thou didst previously inquire], *they shall take of the ash of the burning of the purification from sin* (Num. 19:17)—[ash that is, of the Red Heifer]. And how does the passage containing God's answer to Moses begin? With the words *This is the statute of the Torah* (Num. 19:2).

5. *Moses and Aaron among His priests, and Samuel among them that call upon His name* (Ps. 99:6). R. Yudan citing R. Joseph bar R. Judah, and R. Berechiah citing R. Joshua ben Ḳorḥa, said: During all the forty years that Israel were in the wilderness, Moses did not hesitate to perform the functions of the High Priest, for Scripture says, *Moses and Aaron among His priests.* That Moses served as High Priest, R. Berechiah, going on to cite R. Simon, inferred from the verse *The sons of Amram: Aaron and Moses; and Aaron was separated, that he should be sanctified as most holy* (1 Chron. 23:13). And what does Scripture tell us next? [That up to the time Aaron was set apart to become High Priest, the High Priest was] *Moses the man of God. His sons, however, are named as being merely of the Tribe of Levi* (1 Chron. 23:14). R. Eliezer bar R. Joseph taught: [There is no need to seek out the inference from Scripture]. We have a tradition[84] that Moses, wearing a priestly white linen garment, served as High Priest in the wilderness.[85] However, said R. Tanḥum bar R. Yudan, a Baraita[86] tells us that during the seven days of the priests' investiture when Moses was serving as High Priest,

83. Because he thought he was unworthy of a reply (*Mattĕnot̲ Kĕhunnah* on Eccles. Rabbah 8:5).

84. So rendered in Lev. Rabbah M, p. 227.

85. See Rashi on B.AZ 34a.

86. See Glossary.

the Presence did not, through Moses' agency, come down to dwell in the world. It was [only on the eighth day] when Aaron also began to serve as High Priest that through Aaron's agency the Presence came down to dwell in the world. Hence [on the eighth day, when Moses summoned Aaron to serve with him in the office of High Priest] Moses, [with Aaron's agency in mind], declared *Today, [O children of Israel], the Lord appeareth unto you* (Lev. 9:4).[87]

Moses and Aaron . . . and Samuel . . . called upon the Lord, and He answered them (Ps. 99:6). Moses called upon the Lord and was given an answer, and Aaron called upon the Lord and was given an answer. *He spoke unto them in the pillar of cloud* (Ps. 99:7). We hear of Moses that God in the pillar of cloud conversed with him, as is written *The Lord descended in the cloud, and stood with him there* (Exod. 34:5), and also *The Lord came down in the cloud, and spoke unto [Moses]* (Num. 11:25); and of Aaron also that God in the pillar of cloud conversed with him, as is written *The Lord came down in a pillar of cloud, and stood at the door of the Tent, and called Aaron* (Num. 12:5). But we have not heard such a thing said explicitly of Samuel. In what verse do we hear it said indirectly? In the verse *And they answered them, and said, he is; behold, He is before thee* (1 Sam. 9:12). According to R. Yudan who cited Mari bar Jacob, [when Saul and his servant asked some young women where Samuel could be found, and the young women in their reply finished by saying *He is before thee*, they meant that Samuel could be found where God in the cloud was conversing with him]. "Do you not see," they asked, "the cloud which always hovers above Samuel's courtyard?" The word *yš*, "He is," in the words *Behold, He is before thee*, points to God's presence in the cloud,[88] for the same word is used in the verse *And so He was (yš) when the cloud was . . . upon the Tabernacle* (Num. 9:20).

Moses, Aaron . . . and Samuel . . . kept His testimonies, and the statute [Book] that He gave them (Ps. 99:7). We hear of Moses that the Torah was inscribed to him with his name, as is said *Remember ye the Torah of Moses My servant* (Mal. 3:22). And of Samuel, too—a Book of Torah was inscribed to him: *Samuel's name . . . was inscribed in a book which was laid up before the Lord*[89] (1 Sam. 10:25). But we have not heard of such an inscription to Aaron. We are taught, however, that the passage concerning the Red Heifer was dedicated to him, so as never to be removed from

87. See Sif, *Šĕmini, Mĕkilta dĕ-millu'im, 14* (ed. Weiss, 44c).

88. As 1 Sam. 9:15 goes on to say, *The Lord had revealed unto Samuel the day before Saul came*, etc.

89. In the translation of the verse David Luria on PR 14:12 is followed. JV reads: *Samuel . . . wrote it in a book, and laid it before the Lord.*

connection with him—not from him, nor from his children, nor from his children's children, until the end of all generations.[90] And what is the passage? It is the one beginning with the words *This is the statute of the Torah* (Num. 19:2), [the statute which commands that only Aaron and his descendants may prepare the ash of the Red Heifer].

6. According to R. Joshua of Sik̲nin speaking in the name of R. Levi, the statute concerning the Red Heifer is one of four statutes that the Impulse to evil impugns. [Since a statute is by definition an absolute, divine decree that admits of no exception, the Impulse to evil seeks to discredit the word of God by pointing to those verses in Scripture that take exception to, or contradict, the statute]. The first one of the four statutes is concerned with a man's marrying his brother's wife; the second is concerned with mixtures of "diverse kinds";[91] the third is concerned with the scapegoat; and the fourth is concerned with the Red Heifer.

The first statute absolutely prohibits marriage between a man and a woman who was formerly his brother's wife: *Thou shalt not uncover the nakedness of thy brother's wife* (Lev. 18:16). Yet, as the Impulse to evil points out, Scripture says elsewhere: *Her husband's brother shall go in unto her*, etc. (Deut. 25:5)—that is, as long as the man she was first married to is alive, [even though she is legally divorced from him], she may not marry his brother. But if the man she was first married to dies without issue, the man's brother is allowed, [may even be obliged], to marry her. Scripture does not resolve the contradiction between the statute and the verse which takes exception to it: it simply includes the prohibition *Thou shalt not uncover the nakedness of thy brother's wife* in the general injunction *Ye shall keep My statutes* (Lev. 18:5).

The second of the four statutes absolutely proscribes the mixture of "diverse kinds": *Thou shalt not wear a mingled stuff, wool and linen together* (Deut. 22:11), and yet, as the Impulse to evil points out, Scripture says elsewhere that a linen cloak with wool fringes (*ṣiṣit̲*) is permitted.[92] Here, too, Scripture does not acknowledge the exception to the statute, but again simply enjoins obedience to all the statutes: *Ye shall keep My statutes* (Lev. 19:19).

The third of the four statutes declares the uncleanness of the scapegoat: *He that letteth go the goat of Azazel shall wash his clothes* (Lev. 16:26), and yet, as the Impulse to evil points out, the goat itself is the means whereby men are washed clean of their sins. Without regard to the incon-

90. An authorization taken by the commentator to be intimated in the concluding words of the Psalm verse *the statute that He gave them* (Ps. 99:7)—gave the priests, that is.

91. *Kil'ayim*, specifically, in this passage, the proscription of wearing cloth made out of mixed wool and linen. See Jastrow, 638b.

92. See Num. 15:38–39, and B.Yeb̲ 4b.

sistency, Scripture simply asserts the uncleanness of the goat as an everlasting statute: *And this shall be an everlasting statute unto you* (Lev. 16:29).

The fourth statute asserts the uncleanness of the Red Heifer. A Mishnah teaches: "All those who take any part in the preparation of the Red Heifer from beginning to end have their garments defiled" (Par 4:4). Yet, as the Impulse to evil points out, the Heifer's ash when mixed with water makes garments ritually clean. Without regard to the inconsistency, Scripture simply asserts that the defilement of the garments of those who prepare the Red Heifer is a statute: *This is a statute of the Torah* (Num. 19:2).[93]

7. *The Lord spoke unto Moses . . . That they bring [the Red Heifer] unto thee* (Num. 19:2). *[The Red Heifer] unto thee*, so Lulianos bar Tiberius taught in the name of R. Isaac means that God said: "With thee, Moses, is the rite of the Red Heifer to begin."[94] However, R. Azariah, in the name of R. Isaac, and of R. Jose bar R. Ḥanina taught the following two interpretations of *unto thee*: [The first, according to R. Isaac, was as follows]: the Holy One said to Moses, "Moses, I reveal unto thee[95] the reasons for the statute concerning the Red Heifer, but to others [for the time being] it is a statute [I choose not to explain]." For, as R. Huna taught, [God said], *When I take up My pledge of a world-to-come I shall give My reasons for the statutes I ordained*[96] (Ps. 75:3). God's pledge is to be found in the verse *And it shall come to pass in that day that there shall not be light; but heavy clouds and thick* (*wḳp'wn*) (Zech. 14:6). Actually, [according to the Masorah], the last word in this verse is written *yḳp'wn* ("will be perspicuous"), [so that the verse is to be read *there shall not be light; yet precious things will be perspicuous*][97]—that is, explanation of things con-

93. See B.Yoma 67b, and Rashi on Num. 19:2.

94. *K'ṭryḳw*, at Ephraim E. Urbach's suggestion, is derived from the Greek *Katarchou*, "you initiate the rite." See his *Lašon wĕ-'inyan* in *Lĕšonenu, 32* (5728[1968]), 122–24. Thus R. Isaac takes *unto thee* which in the context appears to be superfluous to mean "with thee"—that is, the rite is to begin with thee, Moses.

Buber in PRKB, 39a, n. 168 construes *k'ṭryḳw* as a corruption of "of Carthage."

95. The initial verse is read *that they bring the Red Heifer, [the reason for which is revealed] unto thee*. It is so read because Moses was not the one who prepared the ash of the Heifer, nor was it prepared solely for his use.

96. JV: *When I take up the appointed time I Myself will judge with equity*. The word *šfṭ*, however, is taken in the sense of "give reasons," and *myšrym* in the sense of "statutes I ordained." Cf. MTeh 75:1; and PR 8:4.

97. This reading is arrived at in the following way: the word *wḳp'wn*, literally "and thickness," may be taken, as JV takes it, to be a noun whose meaning is coordinate with that of the previous phrase "heavy clouds." But as actually written, *yḳp'wn* is the verb in the clause of which "heavy clouds" is the subject. As a verb, its meaning is derived from *ḳp'*, "to be perspicuous." Since the noun *yḳr*, previously

cealed from you in this world [things such as the Red Heifer], will in the time-to-come be as clear to you as crystal. Nevertheless, note that in the verse *I will bring the blind by a way they knew not. I will make darkness light before them . . . These things have I done* (Isa. 42:16), Scripture does not say "These things will I do," but *have I done*—that is, I have already done them for R. 'Akiba.[98] "As a matter of fact," said R. Aha, "things which had not been revealed even to Moses were revealed to R. 'Akiba, so that to R. 'Akiba apply the words *And his eye seeth every precious thing*" (Job 28:10).[99]

[In the second interpretation, R. Azariah went on—] R. Jose bar R. Ḥanina['s—the verse is to be read as follows: *That they* (*will continue to*) *bring thee a Red Heifer* (Num. 19:2) and means that] God intimated to Moses, "The ash of all other Red Heifers will disappear, but the ash of thy heifer, Moses, will endure [even to the time when the Temple will be rebuilt."[100] Not only would the ash of Moses' Red Heifer endure: his teaching concerning the Red Heifer would be continued through the teaching of a Sage who was to be a lineal descendant of his. For, R. Azariah went on], R. Aḥa taught in the name of R. Jose bar R. Ḥanina that when Moses went up to the heights of heaven, he heard the voice of the Holy One, as He sat engaged in the study of the passage on the Red Heifer, citing a law in the name of the Sage who stated it: "R. Eliezer taught: The heifer whose neck is to be broken must be [not more than] one year old;[101] and the Red Heifer [not more than] two years old" (Par 1:1).

Moses dared to say bluntly to the Holy One: Master of universes, worlds above and worlds below are in Thy domain, yet Thou sittest and citest a law ascribed to flesh-and-blood!

The Holy One replied: Moses, there will arise in My world a righteous man who, [in his concern for the purification of Israel], will begin his instruction in the Oral Law with the passage on the Red Heifer, and so I, [also concerned for the purification of Israel], say, "R. Eliezer taught: The

---

rendered "heavy clouds," does not make good sense as the subject of this predicate, it is read as meaning "precious things"—hence, *precious things* [*which are now concealed*] *will be perspicuous.*

98. "and his colleagues" deleted as in C.

99. Elsewhere in Rabbinic literature, Job 28:11 is construed as alluding to R. 'Akiba. See *The Fathers According to R. Nathan*, tr. Judah Goldin, chap. 6, (YJS, *10*, 42); and B.Men 29b.

100. Ash of the Heifer prepared in the days of Moses continued to be used for the sanctification of all Heifers prepared in subsequent years and is divinely stored within the Temple's rampart to be used again in the time-to-come (Mah on Deut. Rabbah 19:6; and Num. 19:9).

101. See Deut. 21:1 ff.

heifer whose neck is to be broken must be [not more than] one year old; and the Red Heifer [not more than] two years old."[102]

Moses said: Master of universes, may the [Divine] Will decree that Eliezer spring from my loins!

The Holy One replied: As thou livest, it is decreed that Eliezer be from thy loins. The words *And the name of the one Eliezer* (Exod. 18:4) intimate that R. Eliezer, [a lineal descendant of Moses], was the Sage foreordained [to begin his instruction in the Mishnah with the section on the Red Heifer].[103]

[Concerning the Red Heifer] we are taught in [another] Mishnah: "Abba Saul said: The High Priests used to build the runway for the Red Heifer at their own expense" (Shek 4:2). Not one of them would lead his Red Heifer out on the runway built by his predecessor. Each one would demolish his predecessor's runway, then build a new one at his own expense, even though, as R. Aḥa said in the name of R. Ḥanina, the High Priests without exception being ostentatious men, it cost him more than sixty talents of gold. "But" [said a questioner], "in a Baraita we are told of Simeon the Just who, [during his term of office], led out two Red Heifers,[104] that even

102. R. Jose bar R. Ḥanina assumes that its being the first Mishnah in Parah, i.e. in the Tractate of the Red Heifer, shows that R. Eliezer actually began his instruction with this Mishnah. The late Professor Mordecai Margulies elucidated this passage.

103. Since Eliezer was the second son of Moses, one would expect the verse to read "And the name of the second Eliezer." But the text reads, instead, *And the name of the one Eliezer*. R. Jose bar R. Ḥanina assumes, therefore, that in this context the word *one* points to R. Eliezer who lived some 1600 years later in the first century C.E. Basing his inference on the phrase *the one Eliezer*, R. Jose bar R. Ḥanina concludes that R. Eliezer was not only *the one* who was deeply concerned like Moses with the matter of the Red Heifer, but was also *the one* who, according to Scripture, was a lineal descendant of Moses.

R. Jose bar R. Ḥanina's exegetical *tour de force* seems intended to indicate God's comforting of Moses for his disappointment in his immediate descendants. Moses, like God Himself, is understood to have meditated deeply on the Red Heifer as a means of purifying Israel. Thus, after Israel had defiled themselves with idolatry, Moses used the powder of the golden calf, an anticipation, as it were, of the use of the ash of the Red Heifer, to begin Israel's purification (see Exod. 32:20; and PR 14:14), for he was passionately concerned with the extirpation of idolatry. His remote descendant R. Eliezer, likewise concerned, began his instruction in the Oral Law with regulations pertaining to the ash of the Red Heifer, in striking contrast to Moses' own children who, in their lack of concern for God's prohibition of idolatry, were a grievous disappointment to Moses. One grandson, Jonathan, may have actually served as priest before Micah's graven image (see Judg. 18:30).

104. See Par 3:5.

he deemed it necessary not to lead out the second on the same runway upon which he had led out the first. Do you dare say that such a righteous man was ostentatious?" "Indeed not," as R. Abin explained in the name of R. Eleazar, "the fact is that all the High Priests built new runways in order to demonstrate their scrupulous concern for the ritual purity of the Red Heifer."[105]

A heathen questioned Rabban Johanan ben Zakkai, saying: The things you Jews do appear to be a kind of sorcery. A heifer is brought, it is burned, is pounded into ash, and its ash is gathered up. Then when one of you gets defiled by contact with a corpse, two or three drops of the ash mixed with water are sprinkled upon him, and he is told, "You are cleansed!"

Rabban Johanan asked the heathen: "Has the spirit of madness ever possessed you?"[106] He replied: "No." "Have you ever seen a man whom the spirit of madness has possessed?" The heathen replied: "Yes." "And what do you do for such a man?" "Roots are brought, the smoke of their burning is made to rise about him, and water is sprinkled upon him until the spirit of madness flees."

Rabban Johanan then said: "Do not your ears hear what your mouth is saying? It is the same with a man who is defiled by contact with a corpse—he, too, is possessed by a spirit, the spirit of uncleanness, and, [as of madness], Scripture says, *I will cause [false] prophets as well as the spirit of uncleanness to flee from the Land*" (Zech. 13:2).

Now when the heathen left, Rabban Johanan's disciples said: "Our master, you put off that heathen with a mere reed of an answer, but what answer will you give us?"

Rabban Johanan answered: "By your lives, I swear: the corpse does not

105. Since all the runways were immovably fixed on the ground, they could not possibly have become ritually unclean (Shebu 6:6, and Ṭoh 5:8). Nevertheless, the High Priests built new runways by way of demonstrating to the Sadducees their scrupulous concern for the purity of the ash of the Red Heifer—a concern which the Sadducees were wont to dispute because according to them the ritual purity of the High Priest preparing the Red Heifer had to be even more punctilious than was required by the Rabbis. Thus, if on the day he was to prepare the Red Heifer, the High Priest's ritual cleanness happened to be unblemished, the Rabbis deliberately had the runway diminished (see Par 3:7 and B.Yoma la), and, consequently, opened themselves to the Sadducees' charge of marring or even belittling the rite of the Red Heifer. Hence in all other matters concerning the Red Heifer, e.g. the runway for it, the High Priests went to lengths which might have been deemed unnecessary to demonstrate that in fact they were as scrupulous with regard to the Red Heifer as were the Sadducees. See Maimonides' Code, X, II, i, 13–14 (YJS, *8*, 99–100); and Lieberman, TKF, *5*, 682.

106. [Literally "possessed that man," a courteous turn of phrase, in order not to connect misfortune with the person directly addressed. L. N.]

have the power by itself to defile, nor does the mixture of ash and water have the power by itself to cleanse. The truth is that the purifying power of the Red Heifer is a decree of the Holy One. The Holy One said: 'I have set it down as a statute, I have issued it as a decree. You are not permitted to transgress My decree. *This is the statute of the Torah*' " (Num. 19:1).

8. Why are male animals used for all other [communal][107] sacrifices, whereas a female is used for the rite of the Red Heifer? R. Aibu said: "Consider this analogy: There was a maidservant's child who defecated in the king's palace. The king said: 'Let his mother come and wipe up the excrement—the excrement of the excrement she nursed at her bosom.' In the same way the Holy One said: 'Let the mother of a calf come and atone for the making of the calf'—[that is, for the nursing of such excrement as the golden calf]."

9. By *heifer* (Num. 19:2), Egypt is meant: "Egypt is a very fair heifer" (Jer. 46:20). By *red* (Num. 19:2), Babylon is meant, its king having been told, "Thou art the head of [red] gold" (Dan. 2:38). By *faultless* (Num. 19:2), Media is meant: what the kings of Media did was not—so said R. Ḥiyya bar Abba—their fault; the Holy One had nothing against them, for the idols they worshiped were no other than those they had received from their ancestors.[108] By *wherein is no blemish* (*ibid.*) is meant the kingdom of Greece:[109] Alexander of Macedon, whenever he saw Simeon the Just, would stand up and say, "Blessed is the God of Simeon the Just." When his retinue reproached him, "Do you stand up in the presence of a Jew?" he would reply, "If I see his visage before I go down into battle, I win."

By *upon which never came yoke* (*ibid.*)is meant wicked Edom—Rome—which never accepted the yoke of the Holy One. And Edom was not content not to take His yoke upon itself—it mocked and blasphemed, saying: "Whom have I in heaven [to bother with]?" (Ps. 73:25). *And ye shall give* [*Edom*] *unto the priest Eleazar* (Num. 19:3)—[here *unto . . . Eleazar* is read as *unto 'El 'ozer*, "unto the God who helps"], the God who ministering like a priest will help [Israel]; *and* [*Edom*] *will be brought forth outside the camp* (*ibid.*). That is, God will begin His help by thrusting Edom's prince out [of heaven], out of His encampment. *And then* [*Edom*] *shall be slain before His face* (*ibid.*): "For the Lord hath a sacrifice in Bozrah,[110] and a great slaughter in the land of Edom" (Isa. 34:6). The words "great slaughter," according to R. Berechiah, may be read "slaughter of the great one" [and hence refer to the fate of Edom's—that is, Rome's—princely counterpart in

107. See Tem 2:1.

108. See B.Ḥul 13b.

109. The comment may also refer to the "unblemished" beauty associated with Japheth, forebear of Greece. See B.Meḡ. 9b.

110. Bozrah, where the prince of Edom, mistaking the place for Bezer, a city of refuge, will flee. See B.Mak 12a.

heaven]. *And the heifer*—Rome—*shall be burnt in His sight* (Num. 19:5), as Scripture says: "The [fourth] beast . . . was given to be burnt with fire" (Dan. 7:11)—*her skin, her flesh, her blood, with her dung shall be burnt* (Num. 19:5), by *her dung* being meant, her captains, her prefects, and her commanders-in-chief. Elsewhere, Scripture speaks in different imagery of Rome's fate, saying to her: "Thy riches and thy wares . . . thy calkers, and the exchangers of thy merchandise, and all thy men of war, that are in thee, with all thy company which is in the midst of thee, shall fall into the heart of the seas in the day of thy ruin" (Ezek. 27:27).[111] By "all thy company," said R. Samuel bar R. Isaac, God meant the following: Those who were once of My company, but then went and attached themselves to thy company, they, too, "shall fall into the heart of the seas" (*ibid.*).

10. Another comment: By *A . . . heifer* (Num. 19:2), Israel is meant: "Israel is now stubborn like a stubborn heifer" (Hos. 4:16). *Red* (Num. 19:2): "[The princes of Israel] were once more ruddy in body than rubies" (Lam. 4:7). *Faultless* (Num. 19:2): Israel—"My dove, My faultless one, was once unique" (Song 6:9). *Wherein was no blemish* (Num. 19:2): Israel—"thou wert all fair, My love; and there was no blemish in thee"[112] (Song 4:7). *Upon which the yoke did not long rest* (Num. 19:2): that is, in the days of Jeremiah,[113] Israel chose no longer to take upon herself the yoke of the Holy One. *Therefore ye shall give her unto Eleazar the priest* (Num. 19:3), that is, unto [*'El 'ozer*, "God's adjutant," the priest] Jeremiah, for, "of the priests in Anathoth" (Jer. 1:1), he was the one who would predict God's punishment of Israel. In fulfillment of his prediction, *The heifer shall be brought forth without the camp* (Num. 19:3)—that is, "Nebuchadnezzar . . . carried the people"—just referred to as *the heifer*—"away into Babylon" (Ezra 5:12). *She shall be slain before his eyes* (Num. 19:3): "They slew the sons of Zedekiah before his eyes" (2 Kings 25:7): [their death, ending the dynasty of David, is here taken to symbolize the death of Israel herself]. *And the heifer shall be burnt in his sight* (Num. 19:5): "And he burnt the House of the Lord as well as the king's house (2 Kings 25:9). *Her skin, and her flesh* (Num. 19:5): "All the houses of Jerusalem, also the entire house of the Great One burnt he with fire" (2 Kings 25:9; Jer. 52:13). But why does Scripture use the phrase "house of the Great One?" Because it is referring to a house of a particular kind such as was to be the

111. These words addressed to Tyre are understood as referring to Rome. See PR 15:25, and 17:8.

112. Song of Songs is construed allegorically as God's courtship of Israel. See PR 7:7.

113. The statement in Jer. 11:15, *the hallowed flesh is passed from thee*, is construed by Rashi and and Ḳimḥi as implying that Jeremiah's contemporaries had discontinued even the rite of circumcision whereby their flesh had been hallowed. See PR 15:13 (YJS, *18*, 325, n. 79); and B.Men 53b.

study house of R. Johanan ben Zakkai, where [by probing the doctrines of creation and God's throne-chariot] his disciples extolled the greatness of the Holy One.[114]

And . . . shall take (Num. 19:6)—that is, the wicked Nebuchadnezzar shall take *cedarwood, and hyssop, and scarlet* (*ibid.*), men as choice as Hananiah, Mishael, and Azariah. *And cast into the midst of the burning of the heifer* (*ibid.*)—[that is, those Jews who cast Hananiah, Mishael, and Azariah into the fiery furnace[115] were cast in as well]: "The flame of the fire slew those men" (Dan. 3:22). *But the man that is clean shall gather up all the ashes of the heifer* (Num. 19:9)—[all of them]. That is, the Holy One will gather them up, for of Him it is written "He will set up an ensign for the nations, and will gather up the dispersed of Israel" (Isa. 11:12). By *the man* is meant the Holy One of whom it is written "The Lord is the Man of war, [Master of all]" (Exod. 15:3). By *that is clean* (Num. 19:9) is meant the Holy One: "Thou that art of eyes too pure to behold evil" (Hab. 1:13). *The ashes of the heifer* (Num. 19:9) are the dispersed of Israel. *And lay them up without the camp in a clean place* (*ibid.*)—that is to say, Israel will be gathered up in Jerusalem which is ritually clean.[116]

And [the mixture of ash and water] shall be kept for the congregation of the children of Israel (*ibid.*). In this world things are pronounced ritually clean or unclean by the mouth of a priest. But in the time-to-come the Holy One Himself will pronounce Israel clean, as is said "I will sprinkle clean water upon you, and ye shall be clean; from all your uncleannesses, and from all your idols, will I cleanse you" (Ezek. 36:25).

114. So *Yĕfeh 'anaf* on Lam. Rabbah, end of *pĕtiḥah* 12. Professor Judah Goldin has supplied the note and the reference.

115. Presumably, they were forced to act in such a capacity. See PRF 14, n. 119.

116. Jerusalem's houses never became defiled through leprosy, and the city's ritual cleanness was scrupulously maintained. See B.BḲ 82b.

PISKA 5

SUMMARY

Israel's reckoning of time by the moon; the advent of the new moon in Nisan as the time of Israel's redemption

According to R. Johanan, when the world was made, the orb of the sun was created to give light while the moon was created to enable Israel to determine thereby the incidence of New Moons and of New Years' Days. R. Ḥanina [ben Ḥama], while agreeing that when the world was created, only the sun was intended to give light, maintains that the moon was created to divert the nations from worshiping the sun.

R. Simon, however, said that both luminaries were created to give light, for God intended from the beginning that the nations of the earth should reckon the year by the sun and that Israel should reckon it by the moon (Sec. 1).

The *pĕtiḥah*'s introductory verse, *Thy wonderful works . . . and Thy thoughts which are to us-ward* (Ps. 40:5), is construed in several ways as referring to God's purpose in a number of things He did: (1) His purpose when He showed the future of Israel to Abraham was to make Abraham choose the yoke of the kingdoms. If Abraham had not chosen this yoke, Israel might not have endured in the world at all. (2) His purpose in intensifying sexual desire was to assure the continuation of the race. (3) Though His purpose in offering the Torah to the nations was frustrated by their rejection of it, the result was that Israel's acceptance of it brought them a double reward. (4) His purpose, after 2448 years of His reckoning of time, was to turn over to Israel the task of reckoning it (Sec. 2).

In connection with the long awaited new moon of Nisan, whose advent begins the time of Israel's redemption, the introductory verse of the next *pĕtiḥah*, *Hope deferred maketh the heart sick; but desire fulfilled is a tree of life* (Prov. 13:12), is also interpreted in several different ways: (1) The verse is taken as referring to a man who betroths a woman and weds her some time later and to a man who betroths a woman and weds her right away. (2) It is taken as referring to David who had been anointed king, but began to rule only after a number of years, and to Saul who was anointed king and at once began to rule—a privilege vouchsafed to him because of his many virtues. The listing of Saul's virtues leads to a meditation on the consequences of sin: as long as a man refrains from sin, he is an object of fear and awe. The moment he sins, he is subject to fear and awe. In proof of this apothegm, instances are cited from the life of Adam, from the experience f Israel, and from the life of David, of Solomon, of Saul. Finally the verse *Iope deferred,* etc. is taken as referring to Israel before and after the advent f the new moon of Nisan—that is, before and after redemption (Sec. 3).

God's messengers of redemption were Moses and Aaron, whom Israel sked for in the words *O send out Thy light and Thy truth* (Ps. 43:3) (Sec.). The redemption of Israel, which led to Israel's separation from the ations, is intended for the nations' good. When the nations improve and aise themselves up, they, too, may expect to be redeemed. In the meantime, ll Israel's activities are unique in comparison with the corresponding activiies of the peoples of the earth (Sec. 5). The themes of Israel's recurring eparation from God through sin, of God's enduring feeling of kinship with srael, of His unremitting call to Israel, of Israel's response, and of God's dew of revelation at Sinai are found in allegorical interpretation of *I sleep, yet my heart waketh; Hark! My beloved knocketh: Open to Me, My sister . . . Yea, My head is filled with dew* (Song 5:2) (Sec. 6).

The introductory verse of the next *pĕṯiḥah, My beloved! . . . he cometh, leaping upon the mountains* (Song 2:8), is construed in a number of ways as referring to the first and last of Israel's redemptions. Thus in the days of Moses, the "leaping over the mountains" is interpreted as God's shortening of the period before redemption, or as His disregard of the "mountains" of idolatry, or as leaping with joy upon the "mountains" which stand for the courts of the righteous. In reference to the days of the Messiah, the "leaping over the mountains" is interpreted as God's reckoning lands like Barbaria or Sarmatia, lands beyond the mountains, whither a single Jew might have been banished, as making up the total of seventy nations that Israel must serve in slavery as a prerequisite to redemption (Sec. 7).

Even as Israel, yearning for redemption, plead with God "Come hither! Come hither!" *like a gazelle* (Song 2:9) He comes leaping towards them and looks down through the windows of heaven waiting to enter into Israel's encampment and say "I am the Lord thy God." Again, God leaps *like a gazelle* from synagogue to synagogue, from schoolhouse to schoolhouse, where His glory stands ready to receive and to answer Israel's prayers, where His glory *looketh in through the windows* (*ibid.*), through the openings, that is, that are formed by the arms of the priests when they say "May the Lord bless thee and keep thee."

The Messiah, too, will be *like a gazelle,* appearing to Israel and then disappearing. As Moses disappeared from Israel for three months, so the Messiah will disappear for forty-five days. In the meantime, *like a young hart* God stands behind the western wall of the Temple which will never be destroyed. Of Him in the time before the coming of the Messiah, it is said *He looketh in through the windows,* which alludes to the merit of the Patriarchs, and *He showeth Himself through the lattice,* which alludes to the merit of the

Matriarchs. Then, at the new moon's advent, in some Nisan of the future, He will say again *This month shall be unto you the beginning of months* (Exod. 12:2)—that is, the time of your redemption (Sec. 8).

The text goes on with accounts of the words and actions of God's messengers of redemption, beginning with Moses and Aaron, continuing with Joshua and Eleazar, with Daniel and Ezra, and ending with Elijah and the Messiah. The signs of the Messiah's coming will be pestilence and all kinds of other afflictions, culminating in the reviling of God by generation after generation (Sec. 9). The price of Israel's redemption is obedience to the precepts set down by Moses in groups of sixty, or, according to another opinion, in groups of seventy (Sec. 10).

According to some authorities, however, when Israel were redeemed from Egypt, they were just as heathenish as the Egyptians, so that Israel's redemption was unprecedented in human history. It was an arbitrary act of God, requiring the plenitude of God's power residing in the seventy-two letters of His name. Only because God had bound Himself by an oath and also because Israel came of goodly stock, did He redeem them. Indeed, because of Israel's goodly stock, God made a record of His nuptials with Israel at the advent of the new moon in Nisan—*This month shall be unto you the beginning of months* (Exod. 12:2)—even as a king marrying a woman of noble lineage orders in her behalf a record of the nuptials and of the date of her marriage (Sec. 11). If Israel are worthy of God's love, the days that they count will be days of their waxing stronger and stronger like the moon's waxing to the full. But if Israel are not worthy, the days that they count will be days of their waning like the moon's waning (Sec. 12).

The keeping of the calendar, Israel's responsibility after their redemption from Egypt, is a task such as a king entrusts to a son only after he is grown up. God's turning over of the responsibility for the calendar is so complete that He Himself abides by Israel's calendrical decisions (Sec. 13). Israel being a small nation, it is natural that she count by the moon. It is natural that large nations, such as Rome, count by the sun. The implications of reckoning time by the two heavenly bodies are considered in connection with the destiny of Israel and the destiny of the nations of the earth (Sec. 14). The mystery of the moon's changes was one of three things which baffled Moses, and God Himself explained it and showed him the procedure whereby the new moon's advent is to be determined (Sec. 15).

In another comment on the verse *This month shall be unto you the beginning of months*, certain similarities between the redemption from Egypt and the redemption in the time-to-come are considered (Sec. 16).

Since lambs were regarded as divinities in Egypt, when Israel took them for the Passover offering, Israel acted with a daring which was to stand by them at the crossing of the Jordan even as it was to stand by them in the days of Haman. By their daring in taking the lambs sacred to Egypt, Israel took od unto themselves, an act symbolized in subsequent years by the two mbs offered daily in the Temple (Sec. 17).

Israel's servitude under Babylon, Media, Greece, and Rome is prefigured Exod. 12:2. From these several servitudes, Naṭrona, the Supreme Guardn, has delivered Israel and will deliver them again—but not in haste, as in gypt, for in the time-to-come *Ye shall not go out in haste, neither shall ye o by flight, for the Lord will go before you, and the God of Israel will be our rearguard* (Isa. 52:12) (Secs. 18–19).

PISKA 5

This, [the determination of time by the] moon, is to be yours (Exod. 12:2).[1]

1. *He appointed the moon for [lunar] seasons; yet by the sun is the tim of its departure reckoned* (Ps. 104:19). R. Johanan taught: When the worl was created, only the orb of the sun was intended to give light. The defectiv spelling of the word *lights* in Gen. 1:14 indicates, as a matter of fact, tha only one light was intended, for the verse actually reads, *Let there be light.*[2] Why, then, was a moon created? To determine thereby the incidenc of New Moons and New Year's Days. Nevertheless, because the verse in th Psalm goes on to say, *yet by the sun is the time of its departure reckone* (Ps. 104:19), one is to set the instant of a month's departure—so taught R Shela of Kefar Tamarta[3] in the name of R. Johanan—not at the moon' conjunction, [which often takes place during the day], but at the [first o second] sunset that follows.[4] In support of such reckoning, Justa,[5] companion of scholars, cited in the name of R. Berechiah the verse *They journeyed from Rameses in the first month, on the fifteenth day of the first month; on the morrow after the Passover the children of Israel went out* (Num. 33:3). Now if one reckoned from the time of the moon['s conjunction, there would have been fifteen days prior to the day on which they went out]. Actually there were only fourteen days.[6] The fact [that the text

1. JV: *This month shall be unto you.* Exod. 12:1–20 is the lesson for Sabbath ha-Ḥod̲eš, the fourth of the four special Sabbaths (see Table of Scriptural Lessons in JV, p. xv; and Meḡ 3:4). The portion which declares Nisan the first of the months of the year was appropriately read either on the last Sabbath in Adar or on the New Moon of Nisan if the new moon fell on a Sabbath. *Mishnah Megillah*, ed. Joseph Rabbinowitz, (London, 1931), p. 101.

2. One would have expected *m'wrwt*, the full spelling of "lights"; instead the spelling is *m'rt*, which makes possible the reading "a light." After all, the commentator seems to say, it is only the sun which gives light.

3. A village in Judea, B.Ḥul 62a.

4. Professor Abraham Sachs of Brown University has elucidated the passage.

5. Justa was an unordained scholar. The name is an abbreviation of Justus or Justinus.

6. There is a tradition that the first of Nisan, the month during which the children of Israel left Egypt, fell on [a Wednesday evening and] Thursday, while the actual conjunction occurred after the noon hour on Wednesday; it is further assumed that when this conjunction occurs, the moon will not be visible until the second evening following, i.e. the evening of Friday. Hence, if the month's beginning is counted from the instant the conjunction occurred—that is, Wednesday afternoon—and made the second day of Nisan Wednesday evening and Thursday,

peaks of the day on which they journeyed from Rameses as the fifteenth day of the first month] proves that we set the instant of a month's departure not at the moon['s conjunction] but at the [first or second] sunset that follows.

R. Ze'era said in the name of R. Ḥanina [ben Ḥama]: When the world was created, only the orb of the sun was intended to give light. The defective spelling of the word *lights* in Gen. 1:14 plainly indicates that only one luminary was intended, for the verse actually reads, *Let there be a light.* Why, then, was a moon created? Because the Holy One foresaw that the nations of the earth were to arise and worship heavenly luminaries as deities, and so He said: If the nations of the earth are to worship luminaries as deities, let them at least divide their worship between a sun and a moon, for if there were only one luminary to worship, how much greater would their acclamation of it be!

No, said R. Berechiah in the name of R. Simon, [from the beginning] both luminaries were created for the sole purpose of giving light, as is said *Let there be lights* (Gen. 1:14), and *Let them be for lights* (Gen. 1:15), and Scripture goes on to say, *God set them in the firmament of the heaven to give light upon the earth* (Gen. 1:17). Then let them both serve a second purpose, says Scripture: *Let them be for signs and for appointed times* (Gen. 1:14)—that is, for Sabbaths, described as "a sign between Me and you" (Exod. 31:13); *and for appointed times* (Gen. 1:14)—that is, times appointed for festivals; *and for days* (*ibid.*)—that is, for days designated as first in the month; *and years* (*ibid.*)—that is, for New Year's Days, for God's intention from the beginning was that the nations of the earth reckon the year by the sun and that Israel reckon it by the moon: *The* [*determination of time by the*] *moon is to be yours* (Exod. 12:2).

2. *Many, O Lord our God, are Thy wonderful works which Thou hast done, and Thy thoughts which are to us-ward* (Ps. 40:5). R. Ḥanina bar Papa read two implications in this verse. [The first implication was this]: All Thy wonderful works and Thy thoughts were intended to make our father Abraham accept the yoke of the kingdoms—*Thy works . . . and Thy thoughts . . . us-ward* were for our sake that we might endure in the world.

---

then the day on which the children of Israel left Egypt should have been designated by Scripture as the sixteenth day, even as the preceding day, on which the Passover was offered, should have been designated by Scripture as the fifteenth day. If, on the other hand, we counted time solely when the new moon is visible, then by the Thursday on which they left, a fortnight after, there would have been only thirteen sunsets. Since, however, the day they left Egypt is called the fifteenth of the month, we conclude that the month was calculated from the first sunset after the conjunction. See the parallel in Gen. Rabbah 6:1. TA, p. 40, reads, "but if you count by the moon, there were only thirteen sunsets." See also MTeh 104:16; and PR 15:21.

For our sake, the Holy One—so taught Simeon bar Abba in the name of R. Johanan—showed four things to our father Abraham: Torah, Temple offerings, Gehenna, and the yoke of the kingdoms. Torah: *a torch of fire* (Gen. 15:17);[7] offerings: *Take Me one heifer for threefold use*[8] (Gen. 15:9); Gehenna: *Behold a smoking furnace* (Gen. 15:17); the yoke of the kingdoms: *Lo, a dread, even a great darkness* (Gen. 15:12).[9] The Holy One said to our father Abraham: As long as thy children busy themselves with the first two of these, they will be saved from the other two. As long as thy children busy themselves with Torah and with offerings, they will be saved from Gehenna and from the yoke of the kingdoms. Since it is ordained, however, that the Temple will be destroyed and offerings will cease, how wouldst thou have thy children chastised—in Gehenna or by the kingdoms? [According to Simeon bar Abba], R. Ḥanina bar Papa suggested that, of his own volition, Abraham chose the yoke of the kingdoms. And the proof? The verse *How should one chase a thousand, and two put ten thousand to flight, except their rock had given them over?* (Deut. 32:30), *the rock* being Abraham, of whom it is said "Look unto the rock whence ye were hewn" (Isa. 51:2). And since the verse in Deuteronomy concludes with the words *and the Lord had delivered them up,* the implication is that the Holy One agreed with Abraham's choice.

[Differing with Simeon bar Abba that Abraham of his own volition chose the yoke of the kingdoms], R. Berechiah in the name of R. Levi said: All that day Abraham sat wondering to himself and asking: "Which shall I choose for my children? Gehenna or the yoke of the kingdoms, each more cruel than the other?" The Holy One said: "Abraham, how long wilt thou sit and wonder? Cut short the indecision in thy heart." Of God's declaration to Abraham it is written, *In that day the Lord cut short Abram* [*in the matter of*] *a covenant,* [*commanding him*] *to say*[10] (Gen. 15:18). To say what?

7. "*Torch* clearly refers to Torah, of which it is said 'All the people saw the thunderings, and the torches' (Exod. 20:15)." See MTeh 52:8.

8. JV: *Take Me a heifer of three* [*years old*]. But the Hebrew *mšlšt* can also be construed as "one [heifer] for threefold use," namely, for use as an offering on the Day of Atonement, for use as an offering when the correct interpretation of a precept escaped the leaders of the nation (Lev. 4:13), and for use when a heifer's neck had to be broken in connection with the finding of a man's unidentified body (Deut. 21:4). The phrases one *goat for threefold use* and one *ram for threefold use* which follow in Gen. 15:9 are likewise construed as referring to three kinds of offerings. See Gen. Rabbah 44:6 (TA, pp. 436–37).

9. See PR 33:6; and MTeh 38:2, 52:8.

10. According to R. 'Aḳiḇa, whenever the term "saying" occurs unnecessarily a second time in a chapter, as here, it is to be taken as having a special meaning, "requiring exposition." See Sif, *Naśo'*, 2, ed. Horovitz, p. 5, and note.

[According to R. Berechiah], R. Ḥanina bar Papa suggested that God told Abraham to say that the yoke of the kingdoms was his choice.

We are now brought to a difference of opinion [as to the verses in Scripture that serve to indicate whether it was Abraham or God who made the choice of the yoke of the kingdoms]. For R. Yudan, R. Idi, and R. Ḥama bar Ḥanina, [in the name of] a certain elder who cited Rabbi also maintained that the Holy One Himself chose for Abraham the yoke of the kingdoms,[11] but cited as proof the verse *Thou hadst caused men to ride over our heads* (Ps. 66:12)—that is, Thou, O God, hadst brought it about that the nations who rode over us subjugated us to the yoke, a subjugation as painful as if *we went through fire and through water* (*ibid.*), [through Gehenna].

The second implication which R. Ḥanina bar Papa found [in the verse, *Many . . . are Thy wonderful works . . . and Thy thoughts which are to us-ward* (Ps. 40:5)], was this: Many are all the wonderful works and thoughts which Thou, O God, dost employ to have a man feel desire for his wife. Of this feeling it is written *Adam knew his wife yet more* (Gen. 4:25). What is implied by Scripture's saying *yet more*? That his desire had been increased by so much more desire than formerly: formerly he had not felt desire when he did not see his wife, but now he felt desire for her whether he saw her or did not see her.[12]

It is such stronger desire which compels traveling merchants and seafarers —so said R. Abba bar Yudan in the name of R. Aḥa—to be reminded of their wives and to return to them.

R. Simon said: The verse in the Psalm refers to all the wonderful works and thoughts which Thou didst employ not to have the nations of the earth accept Thy Torah. Since it was already known and revealed to Thee that they would not accept it, why, then, didst Thou go through the motions of seeking them out and pressing it upon them?[13] In order, [concluded R. Simon], to double the reward we are to get for accepting it.

Another comment[14] of R. Simon's: The verse speaks of Thy thoughts

11. In the following verses, ten nations are listed as being under the rule of the children of Abraham, three more than the seven in the land of Canaan. The surrender of the three additional ones is understood as taking place at the end of time. Previously, however, these three would have oppressed Israel, their oppression of Israel being tantamount to Gehenna from which Israel through God's intercession were to escape. The commentator thus demonstrates the wonderful works and thoughts *which are to us-ward.*

12. See Gen. Rabbah 23:5. Until such stronger desire had been added, Adam—according to Rabbinic tradition—was able to live apart from Eve for a hundred and thirty years.

13. See PR 21:3.

14. "Another comment"—Pa.

which are to us-ward (Ps. 40:5) in matters of calendrical reckoning. Duri each of the two thousand and four hundred and forty-eight years before t children of Israel went out of Egypt, the Holy One used to sit thinking o the calendar, making intercalations, proclaiming the days on which the ne years were to commence and announcing the beginning of months, but whe Israel went out of Egypt, then He turned these matters over to them, as said *And the Lord spoke unto Moses and Aaron . . . saying: This mon shall be unto you* (Exod. 12:1–2). What is implied in the word *saying* That He said to them: Henceforth all calendar matters are turned over t you, and your management of these matters begins this month, as is sai *This month shall be unto you the beginning of months* (Exod. 12:2).[15]

3. R. Ḥiyya bar Abba began his discourse by quoting *Hope deferre maketh the heart sick; but desire fulfilled is a tree of life* (Prov. 13:12). Th saying *Hope deferred maketh the heart sick* applies to a man who betroths woman and weds her some time later; *but desire fulfilled is a tree of lif* applies to a man who betroths a woman and weds her right away.

Another comment: *Hope deferred,* etc., applies to David who had bee anointed king but had to wait two[16] years before beginning to rule. *Bu desire fulfilled is a tree of life* applies to Saul who was anointed king and a once began to rule. Through what merit? Through the merit of the goo deeds he accumulated. For he was a meek and humble man;[17] he observe the Levitical precautions of purity even when he ate common food;[18] h spent his own money freely in order to save money for Israel;[19] he deeme the honor of his servant equal to his own honor.[20] Besides, taught R. Judah bar Naḥman in the name of R. Simeon ben Laḳish, Saul was a scholar i Torah: *By me*, says Torah, *princes come to reign* (Prov. 18:16); *By me kings come to reign* (Prov. 8:15).

R. Ishmael taught: As long as man refrains from sin, he is an object of fear and awe. The moment he sins, he is subject to fear and awe. So, before Adam sinned, God's voice sounded familiar to him; after he sinned, it

15. Since in the same verse Nisan is identified as *the first month of the year* (Exod. 12:2), the phrase *the beginning of months* is considered in this comment and in subsequent ones as "available" for further exposition.

16. Parallel in PR 15:3: "after a number."

17. Of Saul it is said *Behold, he hath hid himself among the baggage* (1 Sam. 10:22).

18. See MTeh 7:2.

19. *He took a yoke of oxen, and cut them in pieces and sent them throughout . . . Israel* (1 Sam. 11:7). See MTeh *ibid.*

20. Saul said to his servant: *Lest my father leave caring for the asses, and become anxious concerning us* (1 Sam. 9:5), thus putting himself and his servant on a par.

unded frighteningly strange to him. Before Adam sinned, it was usual for m to stand erect while he was listening to God's voice. Of this is it written *ey used to hear the voice of the Lord God as [Adam] walked in the rden*[21] (Gen. 3:8). After Adam sinned, as soon as he heard God's voice crouched to hide himself, as is said *Adam and his wife hid themselves bid.*). In that instant—so taught R. Aibu—Adam's height diminished and came only one hundred cubits.[22]

Before the children of Israel sinned, what does Scripture say of them? *he appearance of the glory of the Lord was like devouring fire on the top of e Mount in the eyes of the children of Israel* (Exod. 24:17). The phrase *vouring fire,* according to R. Abba bar Kahana, means that seven seas of re[23] seemed to be devouring one another on the top of the Mount. And rael beheld them and had no fear and felt no terror. But after they sinned, ey could not gaze even upon the face of God's intermediary Moses.[24] Of eir fear it is written *When Aaron and all the children of Israel saw Moses . . they were afraid to come nigh him* (Exod. 34:30).

R. Phinehas bar Abun said in the name of R. Ḥanin: Even God's inter- ediary suffered from Israel's sin. [Speaking of the time of the revelation at inai, Scripture says]: *Kings of [heavenly] hosts do flee, do flee* (Ps. 8:13). The text, as R. Yudan pointed out in the name of R. Aibu, does not ay, "angels of [heavenly] hosts," but *Kings of [heavenly] hosts,* that is o say, before Israel sinned, kings of heavenly kings—even Michael, even Gabriel—could not gaze upon the face of Moses. But after Israel sinned, Moses could not gaze even upon the faces of angels of lowly rank: *For I,* aid Moses, *was in dread of [the angels of] anger and hot displeasure* Deut. 9:19).

Before the unspeakable business [with Bath-sheba] happened to David, what does Scripture quote him as saying? *The Lord is my light and my salvation; whom shall I fear?* (Ps. 27:1). But after the unspeakable business happened to him, Scripture quotes Ahithophel as saying of David during Absalom's rebellion *I will come upon him while he is weary and weak-handed* (2 Sam. 17:2).

Before Solomon sinned, fearlessly he ruled even over male and female

21. JV: *And they heard the voice of the Lord God walking in the garden.* See Piska 1.1, note 7.

22. Cf. Piska 1.1; and PR 46:2.

23. Literally "areas" or "realms of fire." Mah on Num. Rabbah 11.3 cites the relevant phrases in Deuteronomy which suggest that the seas of fire were seven.

24. Moses said of himself: *I stood between the Lord and you at that time, to declare unto you the word of the Lord; for ye were afraid because of the fire, and went not up into the Mount* (Deut. 5:5).

demons, saying *I got me . . . Adam's progeny,*[25] *demons and she-demons* (Eccles. 2:8). For what was his purpose in getting the demons and sh demons sprung from Adam if not to rule over them? But after he sinne such was his dread of them that he summoned threescore mighty men for th guarding of his litter: *Behold, it is the litter of Solomon; threescore migh men are about it . . . they all handle the sword and are expert in war . . because of the dread in the night* (Song 3:7–8).

Before Saul sinned, what does Scripture say of him? *So Saul took th kingdom over Israel . . . and whithersoever he turned himself, he put them t the worse*[27] (1 Sam. 14:47)—that is, *whithersoever he turned himsel* [etc.], he overcame the Philistines simply by his fearlessness. But after h sinned, what does Scripture say? *When Saul saw the host of the Philistines he was afraid, and his heart trembled greatly* (1 Sam. 28:5).

Another comment: *Hope deferred maketh the heart sick* (Prov. 13:12) R. Ḥiyya bar Abba said: Here the allusion is to the children of Israel befor they were redeemed. You find that after Moses came to Israel and told them "The Holy One said to me, Go tell Israel, *I will surely remember you*" (Exod. 3:16), they kept asking him: Moses, our master, merely anothe promise of remembering? *What is my strength, that I should keep on waiting? And what is the time set for my redemption that I should keep on being patient? Is my strength the strength of stones? Or is my flesh of brass?* (Job 6:11–12). So, like Job, Israel asked: Is our strength the strength of stones? Or is our flesh made of brass? But as soon as God said: "In this month ye shall be redeemed," they said: "A definite time at last!—*Desire fulfilled is a tree of life*" (Prov. 13:12). *This month shall be unto you the beginning of months* (Exod. 12:2)—[the beginning of your redemption].

4. R. Judah bar Naḥman began his discourse in the name of R. Simeon ben Laḳish: *O send out Thy light and Thy truth; let them lead me; let them bring me unto Thy holy mountain, and to Thy dwelling places* (Ps. 43:3). *Thy light* is Moses, of whom it is said "The skin of his face sent forth beams" (Exod. 34:29). And *Thy truth* is Aaron, of whom it is said "The law of truth was in his mouth" (Mal. 2:6), and "Thy Thummim—truth—and Thy Urim be with Thy holy [priest]" (Deut. 33:8).

There are some, however, who shift these meanings about:[28] *Thy light,*

25. "Throughout the entire one hundred and thirty years during which Adam held aloof from Eve . . . female demons inflamed by Adam bore offspring" (Gen. Rabbah 24:6).

26. JV: *women very many*. But the difficult Hebrew is variously rendered. On the use Solomon made of demons, see MTeh 78:12.

27. "that is, *whithersoever he turned himself*, [etc.]"—C; O: "that is, *he put them to the worse*."

28. [Literally "And there are some who offer an interpretation different from the preceding one." L.N.]

ey say, is Aaron, as is shown by "Thy Thummim and Thy Urim—lights— with Thy holy [priest]" (Deut. 33:8); and *Thy truth* is Moses, of whom od said, "My servant Moses . . . is trusted in all My house" (Num. :7).

R. Isaac said: At the Red Sea, Moses saw—"seeing is the custom of his usehold"[29] (Prov. 31:27)—that he was [to go up only to the boundaries the Land of Israel, but] not to enter the Land of Israel. Hence he did not y, "Thou shalt bring us in and plant us," but said, as Scripture tells us, *hou shalt bring them in and plant them* (Exod. 15:17). Accordingly, in raying elsewhere *Let them bring me unto Thy holy mountain, and to Thy welling places* (Ps. 43:3),[30] Moses was consoling himself for his not being ermitted to enter the Land with the fact that Israel's boundaries—of which e *holy mountain* and the *dwelling places* are a part—are as holy as the and of Israel itself.

Another comment: *O send out Thy light and Thy truth* (Ps. 43:3). That , send Moses and Aaron, through whom the Holy One sent light to Israel to edeem them from Egypt. Redeem them when? This month of Nisan, the nonth referred to in the verse *This month shall be unto you the beginning of nonths* (Exod. 12:2).

5. R. Levi began his discourse: *Ye shall be holy unto Me; for I the Lord m holy, and have set you apart from the peoples, that ye should be Mine* Lev. 20:26). [As for the latter part of this verse, R. Levi continued, it hould be noted that] R. Yudan taught in the name of R. Ḥama bar Ḥanina, nd R. Berechiah taught in the name of R. Abbahu: Had God said "I have et apart the heathen peoples from you," the heathen peoples would have no ope of ever elevating themselves. For just this reason Scripture points up he separation of Israel from the heathen rather than the separation of the heathen from Israel: *and have set you apart from the peoples, that ye should be Mine*. The point is that one who sets apart the good from the bad is likely to go back and seek to set apart more of the good. But once one sets apart the bad from the good, one is not likely to go back and seek to find the good by picking over the bad that have already been set apart.

[In regard to the first part of the verse concerning Israel's holiness to God], R. Levi went on to say: All Israel's activities are unique in comparison with the like activities of the peoples of the earth—in their plowing, in their sowing, in their harvesting, in their gathering the sheaves, in their threshing, in furnishing their servants liberally from their granaries and from their wine presses, in their counting of time, and in their reckoning of it. In their plowing: *Thou shalt not plow with an ox and an ass together* (Deut. 22:10).

29. The members of Abraham's household were said to have been seers. See Gen. Rabbah 45:7. JV: *She looketh well to the ways of her household.*

30. Unlike the anonymous teacher in the comment that follows, R. Isaac seems to ascribe to Moses this verse in Psalm 43.

In their sowing: *Thou shalt not sow thy vineyard with two kinds of se* (Deut. 22:9). In their harvesting: *Neither shalt thou gather the gleaning thy harvest* (Lev. 19:9). In their gathering the sheaves: *When thou reape . . . in thy field, and hast forgot a sheaf in the field, thou shalt not go back fetch it* (Deut. 24:19). In their threshing: *Thou shalt not muzzle the when he treadeth out the corn* (Deut. 25:4). In furnishing their servan liberally from their granaries and from their wine presses: *Thou shalt furni [the Hebrew servant] liberally . . . out of thy threshing floor and out of tl wine press* (Deut. 15:14). And finally in their counting of time and the reckoning of it. For the nations of the earth count the passage of time by th sun, but Israel count it by the moon: *This month shall be unto you th beginning of months* (Exod. 12:2).

6. *I sleep; nevertheless, my heart waketh; Hark! My Beloved knocket "Open to Me, My sister, My delight, My dove, My undefiled." Yea, m head is filled with dew*, etc. (Song 5:2). The congregation of Israel spoke u to the Holy One: Master of worlds, *I sleep*—in lack of the Temple I ar numb [as though asleep]; *nevertheless, my heart waketh* in houses o prayer and in houses of study. *I sleep*—in lack of Temple sacrifices; *never theless, my heart waketh* through acts of mercy and charity. *I sleep*—in lac of God's commandments;[31] *nevertheless, my heart waketh*, ready to obe them. *I sleep*—in ignorance of the time set for redemption; *nevertheless, m heart waketh* for the time of redemption. *I sleep*—in lack of redemption *nevertheless, the heart* [*of the Holy One*] *waketh* to redeem me. Indeed asked R. Ḥiyya bar Abba, where do we find that the Holy One is actuall identified as the heart of Israel? In the verse *God is the rock, my heart, an my portion for ever* (Ps. 73:26).

Hark! My beloved knocketh (Song 5:2)—that is, Moses knocks, declar ing, "Thus saith the Lord: About midnight will I go out into the midst o Egypt" (Exod. 11:4). By *Open to Me* (Song 5:2), according to R. Asi, the Holy One was saying: Make an opening for Me in you, an opening as narrow as the eye of a needle, and I shall make the opening so wide that camps full of soldiers and siege engines could enter it. By *My sister* (*ibid.*), God was saying: Israel, My own, My kin—you who bound yourselves irrevocably[32] to Me in Egypt by two covenants of blood, the blood of Passover and the blood of circumcision. By *My love* (*ibid.*), He was referring to Israel at the Red Sea—at the Red Sea where Israel showed their love of Him, saying "The Lord shall reign for ever and ever" (Exod. 15:18). By *My dove*

31. That is, such of the commandments as have been suspended for the duration of the exile.

32. Play on the word *'aḥoṯ*, "sister," and *'aḥuy*, "akin," or "stitched together," two stitches being regarded as a completed act of sewing if done on the Sabbath. See David Luria on Song Rabbah, and Shab 13:1. See also PR 15 (YJS, *18*, 322, n. 67).

bid.), He was referring to Israel at Marah where Israel through receiving [additional] commandments came to have the iridescence of a docile dove.[33] By *My undefiled* (*tammaṯi*), He was referring to Israel at Sinai—at Sinai, where they became pure (*nittammu*) in My sight when they said to Me [in perfect trust], "We will do, and then hear" (Exod. 24:7).

R. Yannai said: For the word *tammaṯi*, read *tomyiaṯi*—[that is, "My twin," "My equal"]: "I the Lord am not greater than Israel, nor is Israel greater than I".[34] But R. Joshua of Siḵnin added in the name of R. Levi: As with twins, when the head of one of them aches, the other also feels an ache, so the holy One feels Israel's pain saying: "I am with him in trouble" (Ps. 91:15).

[After the revelation at Sinai, Israel said]: *Yea, my head is filled with dew* (Song 5:2)—that is, [morning's heavenly dew, the Written Torah, of whose revelation to Israel], Scripture says, "The heavens dropped [dew upon me]" (Judg. 5:4). The remainder of the verse in Song of Songs speaks of *My locks with the drops of the night* (Song 5:2), [the heavenly drops of Oral Law, that is, of whose revelation to Israel], Scripture says, "Yea, [in the night] the clouds dropped water" (Judg. 5:4).[35]

At what point in Scripture [does the sequence of themes, commencing with Israel's kinship with God (*My sister*) and ending with the revelation at Sinai (*My head is filled with dew*), begin]? With the words *This month—This month shall be unto you the beginning of months* (Exod. 12:2)—[that is, this month of Nisan is the month wherein began Israel's kinship with God].

7. *Hark! My beloved! behold, he cometh, He leaps upon the mountains, He skips upon the hills* (Song 2:8). R. Judah, R. Nehemiah, and the Rabbis differ in their comments on this verse [though all agree that the first "he" of the verse refers to Moses].

33. Cf. Ps. 68:13. With regard to Marah, the parallel in Song Rabbah 5:2 goes on to quote "There He set forth to them statutes and ordinances" (Exod. 15:29), which the commentator construes as meaning that at Marah, besides the seven commandments already given to the descendants of Noah (see Gen. 9:17), God gave Israel three more commandments: namely, to institute civil courts, to observe the Sabbath, and to honor parents. According to the scheme in this passage, the seven commandments previously given to the descendants of Noah proscribed idolatry, adultery, murder, robbery, cutting flesh out of a living animal, castrating men or animals, and crossbreeding plants or animals. See B.Sanh 56b; and Piska 3, note 6.

34. The glory of the righteous being equal to the glory of God. See Gen. Rabbah 77:1, where the verse *There is none like unto God, O Jeshurun* (Deut. 33:26) is rendered, "There is none like God save Jeshurun"—save the upright.

35. Scripture is to be studied in the day and Oral Law in the night. See MTeh 19:7.

According to R. Judah, the words *Hark! My beloved! behold, he come* (*ibid.*) refer to the coming of Moses. When he came and said to Israel, "Y are to be redeemed this month," they replied: Moses, our master, how c we expect to be redeemed now? Did not the Holy One say clearly to o father Abraham, *Thy seed . . . shall serve them; and they shall afflict the four hundred years* (Gen. 15:13)? According to our reckoning, we ha served only two hundred and ten years.[36] Moses replied: Since He desir your redemption, He does not heed your reckonings. Instead *He leaps upo the mountains, He skips upon the hills* (Song 2:8)—that is, he contracts t limits of the period before redemption and spurns your reckonings of yea and times, saying, "It is My will that in this month you shall be redeeme *This month shall be unto you the beginning of months* (Exod. 12:2), [th beginning of your redemption]."

R. Nehemiah said: *Hark! My beloved! behold, he cometh* (Song 2:8)– that is, behold, Moses cometh. When he came and said, "In this month yo shall be redeemed," they asked: Our master Moses, how can we be re deemed, seeing that the land of Egypt is filled with the filth of our idolatry He replied: Inasmuch as God desires your redemption, He will overloo your idolatrous deeds. Instead, *He leaps over the mountains, He skips ove the hills*—that is, [He will overlook] the *mountains*, here signifying temple of idolatry, as in the verse *They sacrifice upon the tops of the mountains, an offer upon the hills* (Hos. 4:13).

And the Rabbis also said: *Hark! My beloved! behold, he cometh* mean "Moses cometh." When he came and told Israel, "In this month you shall b redeemed," they asked: Our master Moses, how are we to be redeemed since we own no good deeds? Moses replied: "Inasmuch as He desires you redemption, He regards not your wicked deeds. But what does He regard The righteous in your midst, such as Amram and his court."[37] [Here it i intimated that God leaps with joy upon the mountains], for *mountains* an *hills* stand for the courts [of the righteous], as in the verse spoken by th daughter of Jephthah: *That I may depart and seek out upon the mountain* (Judg. 11:37), [that is, seek out the Sanhedrin, the heights of justice].[38]

36. Jochebed, Moses' mother, was born at the time Jacob and his family entered Egypt; she was 130 years old when she gave birth to Moses who was 80 years old when he came to deliver Israel.

37. That is, the court founded by Amram who was Moses' father. See PR 43:4.

38. [JV: *go down upon* (variant reading: *to*) *the mountains*. The literal meaning of this phrase is obviously somewhat contradictory, since one usually goes up upon mountains. Hence the suggestion that *mountains* means "the heights where justice is dispensed," that is the Sanhedrin, which is empowered to absolve Jephthah from his unfortunate vow, and save his daughter's life. L.N.]

Here a play may also be intended on *harim*, "mountains," and *horim*, "the Sanhedrin whose decisions instruct men as to what is just." Cf. Yalkut.

R. Yudan said: From the words *In a land that is not theirs . . . four ndred years* (Gen. 15:13) we arrive at the following reckoning: Israel was servitude [two hundred and ten years]; to these are added the [one ndred and ninety] years when Israel, though aliens, were not in servitude. ence the total [period of the stay in Egypt] includes even those years en Israel were at ease in Egypt.[39]

R. Yudan taught in the name of R. Eliezer ben R. Jose the Galilean, and Huna taught in the name of R. Eliezer ben Jacob: *Hark! My beloved! hold, he cometh.* That is, the king Messiah cometh. When he comes and ys to Israel, "In this month you shall be redeemed," they will ask: "Our aster, O king Messiah, how can we be redeemed? Has not the Holy One id that He will reduce us to servitude among seventy nations?" Then the essiah will make exactly clear by two illustrations what God meant by His atement: (1) If only one of you is banished to Barbaria[40] and only nother one of you is banished to Sarmatia,[41] He will consider it as though l of you had been banished. (2) Moreover, since this wicked kingdom—Rome]—levies troops from each and every nation, if a Cuthean[42] comes nd forces even only one of you into military service, He will consider it as ough the entire people of Israel were conscripted. If an Ethiopian comes nd forces even only one of you into military service, He will consider it as ough the entire people of Israel were conscripted. Hence, in whatever onth circumstances such as these occur, you shall be redeemed. *This month hall be unto you the beginning of months* (Exod. 12:2)—[the beginning of our redemption].

8. *My Beloved is like a gazelle or a young hart* (Song 2:9). In *My eloved* (*Dwdy*) *is like a gazelle*, R. Isaac pointed out, the word *Dwdy*, when separated into two parts, *dw* and *dy*, makes two Greek words: *dw* tanding for *Deui*, "come hither," and *dy* standing for *theos*, "God." Hence] n the first part of *Dwdy*, Thou, O God, sayest to us, "*Deui, deui,*[43] come ither!" In the second part of *Dwdy*, Israel replies to Thee: "*Dy*,[44] God, Thou comest to us before we stir."[45] Indeed, R. Isaac observed, as a gazelle

39. The word *'ysptlyyh* is derived from *spatalē*, "rest," or "leisure." See Lieberman, *GJP*, p. 62. It may also be read *isopoliteia*, "civil equality granted to strangers." So Jastrow, 53a.

40. Germania Barbara, or Barbary, the East African coast. So Jastrow, 190a.

41. The country extending from the Vistula to the Rha (Volga). So Jastrow, 999a.

42. I.e. Goth?

43. The Greek *deui* or *deuro* means "come hither."

44. Or *Thee, Thee*, the vocative of *Theos*, "God," in Greek.

45. The explanation given by Mah on PR 15:8, and by B. Z. Bacher in his *'Aggadat 'Amora'e 'Ereṣ Yiśra'el* (Tel Aviv, 5685/1925), 2, 244, n. 4 is followed here. Cf. also PR 44:7 (YJS, *18*, 776).

leaps and skips from tree to tree, from thicket to thicket, from grove grove, so the Holy One leaped from Egypt to the Red Sea and from the R Sea to Sinai. The children of Israel saw Him in Egypt, as is said *I will through the land of Egypt in that night* (Exod. 12:12). They saw Him at t Red Sea: *And Israel saw the great work* (Exod. 14:31). They saw Him Sinai: *Moses . . . said, The Lord came to Sinai,*[46] *after having first risen Seir unto the people thereof* (Deut. 33:2).

My Beloved is like . . . a young hart (Song 2:9)—like the young of t gazelle, said R. Jose bar R. Ḥanina. *Behold, He standeth behind our w* (*ibid.*), [waiting to enter into our encampment], as is said "For the thi day the Lord will come down in the sight of all the people upon Mou Sinai" (Exod. 19:11). *He looketh out through the windows* (Song 2:9 [of heaven, waiting to come down]: "And the Lord came down upon Mou Sinai, to the top of the Mount" (Exod. 19:20). *He sings out*[47] *through t lattice* (Song 2:9), as when He said, "I am the Lord thy God" (Exo 20:2), and goes on, as we are told, *My Beloved spoke, and said un me: "Rise up, My love, My fair one, and come away"* (Song 2:10). Ar before saying, "*Come away* . . . [Return ye to your tents" (Deut. 5:27) what words did He speak to me? The words "I am the Lord thy Go (Exod. 20:2).[48]

Another comment: *My Beloved is like a gazelle* (Song 2:9). R. Isaa said: As a gazelle leaps and skips from tree to tree, from thicket to thicke and from grove to grove, so the Holy One leaps from synagogue to syna gogue, from schoolhouse to schoolhouse. Why? In order to bless Israe Through whose merit? Through the merit of Abraham who, while he wa sitting down [at prayer and study] by the terebinths of Mamre [was told b God when He appeared to him, not to stand up but to keep sitting, becaus he was sitting at prayer and study]. Note well how in the following vers

---

Saul Lieberman suggests that Israel's reply is "*Deuro, deuro,* do Thou come t us before we stir." See *Tarbiṣ*, 27 (1958), 187. See also Shalom Spiegel, in *Studie of the Research Institute for Hebrew Poetry in Jerusalem*, 5, 284, note 30.

46. JV: *The Lord came from Sinai, and rose from Seir unto them.* But se PR 21 (YJS, *18*, 417, n. 11).

47. ERV: *He showeth Himself.* JV: *He peereth.* But the commentator derive *mṣyṣ* from *ṣwṣ*, "chirp."

48. After hearing God's voice say out of the fire *I am the Lord thy God*, th children of Israel, afraid that they would be unable to hear His voice because th fire attendant upon His uttering subsequent commandments would consume them asked Moses to act as intermediary between God and themselves in subsequen revelations. Thereupon God said: "May they always be of such mind to revere Me and to follow all My commandments"; and told Moses, "Go say to them, Return to your tents" (Deut. 5:26–27). See PR 22:3.

Scripture makes the point: *When the Lord appeared unto him by the terebinths of Mamre, he sat down at the door of the tent* [*of prayer and study*] (Gen. 18:1). For, according to the *kĕṯiḇ*, as R. Berechiah taught in the name of R. Levi, the last phrase is not to be translated "when he was sitting" but "he sat down [even though he was in God's presence]."[49] Of course, when the Holy One appeared to him, Abraham stood up, and it was only when God said to him, "Sit down," that Abraham sat down. Then the Holy One went on to say, "Abraham, whenever thy children come into houses of prayer or houses of study, they, too, may sit,[50] even though My glory remains standing." And the proof? The verse *God standeth* (*niṣṣaḇ*) *in the congregation of* [*Israel who at the times set for prayer aver the sovereignty of*] *God*[51] (Ps. 82:1). Note—so said R. Haggai in the name of R. Isaac—Scripture does not merely say that God stands (*'omeḏ*), but that God stands ready (*niṣṣaḇ*)—ready to receive and to answer prayer.

R. Samuel bar Ḥiyya bar Judah [differs], saying in the name of R. Ḥanina: At each and every praise with which Israel praise the Holy One, He has His presence abide among them. And the proof? The verse *Thou art holy, O Thou that abidest in the praises of Israel*[52] (Ps. 22:4).

Or a young hart (Song 2:9)—He is like the young of the gazelle, said R. Jose bar R. Ḥanina. *Behold, He standeth behind our wall* (*ibid.*)—outside the walls of houses of prayer and houses of study. *He looketh in through the windows* (*ibid.*)—that is, through the openings that are formed by the arms of the priests [when they raise their hands in blessing]. *He showeth Himself through the lattice* (*ibid.*)—that is, through the openings between the fingers of the priests [when their fingers are spread out in the bestowal of blessing]. *My Beloved spoke and said unto me* (Song 2:10)—how do the priests phrase what He said to me? "May the Lord bless thee, and keep thee" (Num. 6:24).

Another comment: *My beloved is like a gazelle* (Song 2:9). R. Isaac said: As a gazelle appears and then disappears, so [Moses], the first Messiah, appeared among Israel and then disappeared from among them. For how long a time did he disappear? R. Judah Berabbi said: For three months.

49. The *kĕṯiḇ*—the traditional spelling of Scripture—is not the present participle *yošeḇ*, which would imply that Abraham continued sitting, but *yašaḇ*, which is taken to imply that when the Lord appeared unto him, Abraham, who had been sitting, was about to stand up, but sat down again at God's behest.

The commentator may have construed the expression *in the heat of the day* (Gen. 18:1) as referring to the time of day when the *Shĕma'* is to be recited.

50. In the Temple they had to stand. See B.Yoma 25b, and elsewhere.

51. That is, recite the Shĕma' at the times set for prayer. See Song Rabbah on 2:9, 2, and Ber 1:1–3.

52. That is, at whatever time they pray to Him. Cf. MTeh 18:29, 22:19.

With reference to his absence and his reappearance it is written *And they met Moses . . . who stood [unexpectedly] in the way*[53] (Exod. 5:20).

Or a young hart (Song 2:9)—that is like the young of the gazelle, according to R. Jose bar R. Ḥanina. *Behold, He standeth behind our wall* (*ibid.*)—that is, by the western wall of the Temple which will never be destroyed. *He looketh in through the windows* (*ibid.*)—that is, His presence is among us through the merit of the Patriarchs. *He showeth Himself through the lattice* (*ibid.*)—that is, His presence is among us through the merit of the Matriarchs. Take note that just as there is a difference between a window and a lattice, so is there a difference between the merit of the Patriarchs and the merit of the Matriarchs.[54]

R. Berechiah said in the name of R. Levi: Like the first redeemer, so the last redeemer; as the first one appeared among Israel and then disappeared from among them, so the last redeemer will appear among Israel and then disappear from among them. And for how long will he disappear from among them? R. Tanḥuma said in the name of R. Ḥama who said it in the name of R. Hoshaia, [and] R. Menaḥema said it in the name of R. Ḥama bar R. Ḥanina: For forty-five days. With reference to this period Scripture says, *From the time that the continual burnt offering shall be taken away, and the destestable thing that causeth appalment set up, there shall be a thousand two hundred and ninety days* (Dan. 12:11), and then goes on to say, *Happy is he that waiteth, and cometh to the thousand three hundred and five and thirty days* (Dan. 12:12). These days, forty-five above the number given in the previous verse, to what do they refer? They refer to the period of forty-five days during which the Messiah, who will have appeared among the children of Israel will disappear from among them again. [By way of testing their faith], where will he have them go? To the wilderness of Judah, some say; and some say, to the wilderness of Sihon and Og. Concerning the place he will have them go to, it is written *Therefore, behold, I will allure [Israel], and bring her into the wilderness*, etc. (Hos. 2:16).[55] There he who believes in the Messiah will be content to eat saltwort and the roots of the broom and will remain alive, for in the wilderness *They pluck saltwort with wormwood; and the roots of the broom are their food* (Job 30:4). But he who does not believe in him, will forsake Israel and attach himself to the heathen nations who will eventually slay him.

R. Isaac bar Marion said: At the end of the forty-five days, the Holy One will appear to the children of Israel and bring down the manna [for them]. How do we know? Because *that which hath been is that which shall be, for*

53. After Pharaoh issued the decree that no straw be provided for the making of bricks, Moses is said to have gone back to Midian (see Exod. Rabbah 5:19).

54. See PR 12:5.

55. The context of the passage is Messianic.

there is nothing new under the sun (Eccles. 1:9), [and so Israel will again dwell in the desert]: *I am the Lord thy God from the land of Egypt; I will yet again make thee to dwell in tents, as in the days of the Feast* [*of Booths*] (Hos. 12:10), and, [again in the desert], *As in the days of thy coming forth out of the land of Egypt, will I show unto Israel marvelous things*[56] (Micah 7:15).

9. *My Beloved spoke* (*'anah*), *and said unto me: Rise up, My love, My fair one, and come away* (Song 2:10). R. Azariah asked: Do not the words *spoke* and *said* mean the same thing? No, here the word *'anah* means not "spoke" but "answered," that is, [at the Red Sea] He answered me at Moses' bidding, and then through Aaron *said* [encouraging things] *unto me*.[57] And what did He say to me? *Rise up*, make thyself ready, O Israel, *thou who didst cause Me to be loved*,[58] thou daughter of Abraham who made Me beloved in the world; *who madest Me fair*,[58] thou daughter of Isaac who made My name fair throughout My world when his father bound him on the altar; *and go away*, thou daughter of Jacob, he who hearkened to his father and his mother, as is said "Jacob hearkened to his father and his mother, and went to Paddan-aram" (Gen. 28:7). *For lo, the winter is past, the rain is over and gone* (Song 2:11). The words *For lo, the winter is past* refer to the entire four hundred years decreed for our ancestors' stay in Egypt. And the words *the rain is over and gone* refer to their two hundred and ten years [of servitude].

In another comment the words *For lo, the winter is past* are taken to refer to the two hundred and ten years [of our ancestors' stay in Egypt]; and the words *the rain is over and gone* to the time of their most bitter servitude in those years. But do not the words *winter* and *rain* convey the same idea? R. Tanḥuma explained: The bitter part of the winter season is the cold rain [which lasts about eighty-six days];[59] the period of most bitter servitude lasted exactly eighty-six years, beginning at the time Miriam was born. Why, in fact, was she named Miriam? Because, as R. Isaac said, Miriam means "bitterness" (*mrwr*), as in the verse "And they made their lives bitter (*mrr*) with hard service in mortar" (Exod. 1:14).

[*The flowers appear on the earth; the time of singing is come, and the voice of the turtle is heard in our land* (Song 2:12)]. *The flowers appear on the earth*—[the fame of] Moses and Aaron flourishes. By the words *The time of singing is come* is meant [the season when plants are pruned or cut

56. "As in the days . . . marvelous things"—C.

57. The translation is based on analogy with B.Ta, ed. Malter (Philadelphia, 1930), p. 54, n. 3; and Lieberman, TKF, *Mo'ed*, 327, line 65. Professor Saul Lieberman provided the interpretation of the passage.

58. JV: *My love, My fair one.*

59. Beginning with the seventeenth of Heshvan and ending on the fifteenth of Shevat. See B.RH 14a; and *Hašmaṭoṯ* of David Luria's Novellae on Song Rabbah.

back[60]—hence, metaphorically speaking], the time has come for the foreskin to be cut;[61] the time has come for the Egyptians to be cut down; the time has come for their idols to be cut out of the world: "Against all the gods of Egypt I will execute judgments: I am the Lord" (Exod. 12:12); the time has come for the Red Sea to be cut in two: "And the waters were divided" (Exod. 14:21). The time has come for singing the song at the Red Sea: "Then sang Moses and the children of Israel this song" (Exod. 12:1); the time has come for the Torah to be given: "O Lord, my strength is a song"[62] (Exod. 15:2), a verse interpreted by R. Bebai as implying "[The strength of] Thy statutes has been my songs" (Ps. 119:54), and by R. Tanḥuma as implying that the time has come for Israel to raise their voices in song to the Holy One: "My strength is a song to the Lord" (Exod. 15:2). *And the voice of the turtle (twr) is heard in our land* (Song 2:12). R. Johanan said: This verse means that the voice of Moses, the one who led us with great care through the turnings[63] (*tyyr*) of our journey, was heard in the land: "And Moses said, Thus saith the Lord: About midnight will I go out into the midst of Egypt" (Exod. 11:4).

[*The fig tree drops (as into a grave) her unripe and sickly figs, whilst the young grapes just formed from the blossoms on the vines*[64] *give forth their fragrance. Arise, my love, my fair one, and come away* (Song 2:13).] In the words *The fig tree*, [that is, the house of Israel], *drops* [*as into a grave*] *her unripe and sickly figs*, the phrase *unripe and sickly figs* refers to what happened in the three days of darkness (Exod. 10:22) when the lives of Israel's wicked ones [who spurned redemption] were brought to an end by God, [and, without the Egyptians knowing it, the bodies of the wicked of Israel were dropped into graves].[65] The rest of the verse, namely, *whilst the young grapes just formed from the blossoms on the vines give forth their fragrance*, refers to those among the children of Israel [whose deeds, though far from acceptable], had, nevertheless, the fragrance of repentance so that those Israelites were received by God[66] and remained alive [during the three

60. The word *zamir* means both "song" and "pruning."

61. There is a tradition that after Joseph died, the children of Israel, determined to be like the Egyptians, gave up the practice of circumcision. Before they left Egypt, however, Moses circumcised them. See Exod. Rabbah 1:8.

62. The Torah is often called "strength." See Mek̲, 2, 22; and PR 5:3.

63. "turtle . . . turnings" is an attempt to reproduce the Hebrew pun *twr*, "turtle," and *tyyr*, "guide."

64. JV: *The fig tree putteth forth her green figs, and the vines in blossom*, etc. See Rashi.

65. Cf. Song Rabbah on this verse, and Exod. Rabbah 14:3.

66. Cf. Exod. Rabbah 15:1 where *the young grapes just formed from the blossoms* are described as being between the completely righteous and the entirely wicked.

days of darkness]. Thereupon Moses said to the children of Israel: You are in such good odor, and yet you are still here [in Egypt]: *Arise, my love, my fair one, and come away.*

Another comment: *My Beloved spoke* (*'anah*), *and said unto me* (Song 2:10). R. Azariah asked: Do not the words *spoke* and *said* mean the same thing? No, here the word *'anah* means not "spoke" but "answered"—that is, [at Gilgal] He answered me at Joshua's bidding, and then through Eleazar *said* [encouraging things] *unto me.* And what did He say to me? *Rise up, My love, My fair one, and come away* (Song 2:10). *For lo, the winter is past* (Song 2:11)—the forty years Israel spent in the wilderness. *The rain is over and gone* (*ibid.*)—gone is the bleak period of thirty-eight years, [the life span of the generation of the golden calf, a period] in which God in His wrath at Israel's sin [did not speak to Moses].[67] *The flowers appear on the earth* (Song 2:12)—that is, the fame of the princes[68] flourishes: "one prince of every Tribe to take possession of the Land" (Num. 34:18). By the words *The time of singing is come* (Song 2:12) is meant [the season when plants are pruned or cut back—hence metaphorically speaking], the time has come for the foreskin to be cut;[69] the time has come for the Canaanites to be cut down, the time has come for the Land of Israel to be cut up: "Unto these the Land shall be divided," etc. (Num. 26:52). *And the voice of the turtle* (*twr*) *is heard in our land* (Song 2:12) means, according to R. Johanan, that the voice of him who turned us (*tyyr*) with great skill towards the Land of Israel was heard in the land, that is to say, the voice of Joshua: "Then Joshua commanded the officers of the people, saying . . . Go in to possess the Land" (Josh. 1:10). *The fig tree putteth forth her green figs* (Song 2:13), which are put on top of the baskets of first fruits.[70] *And the vines in blossom give forth their fragrance* (*ibid.*)—that is, the fragrance given off by the drink offerings.

Another comment: *My Beloved spoke* (*'anah*), *and said unto me* (Song 2:10). R. Azariah asked: Do not the words *spoke* and *said* mean the same thing? No, here the word *'anah* means not "spoke" but "answered," that is, [in the lions' den] He answered me at Daniel's bidding, and then through Ezra *said* [encouraging things] *unto me.* What did He say to me? *Rise up, My love, My fair one, and come away* (Song 2:10). *For lo, the winter is past* (Song 2:11)—the seventy years' rule of the kingdom of Babylon is past; *the rain is over and gone* (*ibid.*), the fifty-two years' rule of the king-

67. See Deut. 2:14, 16–17. During this period, according to Rashi on B.Ta 30 b, God spoke to Moses only in visions or dreams.

68. "the princes"—Yalḳuṭ; PRK: "the spies." Cf. Piska 1.7.

69. Joshua circumcised the children of Israel when they entered the Land of Israel (Josh. 5:2).

70. See Tos Bik 2:8. According to R. Jose, the fruit Adam ate was the fig. See Piska 20.6.

dom of Media is over and gone.[71] Another comment: *For lo, the winter is past* (*ibid.*), the period of seventy years Israel spent in exile is past. But, in fact, was it not a period of fifty-two years?[72] R. Levi explained: Take into account the eighteen years [during which Israel's exile was impending],[73] years when a Divine Voice came forth and reverberated in the palace of Nebuchadnezzar, commanding him: Wicked servant, go forth, destroy the House of thy Master, for the children of thy Master do not hearken to Him. *The rain is over and gone* (*ibid.*)—the enslavement is over and gone. *The flowers appear on the earth* (Song 2:12)—that is, the fame of such as Daniel and his companions, of such as Mordecai and his company, of such as Ezra and his company flourishes. By the words *The time of singing is come* (*ibid.*) is meant [the season when plants are pruned or cut back—hence, metaphorically speaking], the time has come for the foreskin to be cut;[74] the time has come for the wicked to be broken and cut down, the time of which it is written "The Lord hath broken the staff of the wicked" (Isa. 14:5); the time has come for the Babylonians to be cut down; the time has come for the Temple to be rebuilt: "The glory of this latter House shall be greater than that of the former" (Haggai 2:9). *And the voice of the turtle* (*twr*) *is heard in our land* (Song 2:12), that is, said R. Johanan, the voice of Cyrus, the voice of the one who turned us (*tyyr*) with great skill towards the Land of Israel was heard in the land: "Thus saith Cyrus king of Persia: All the kingdoms of the earth hath the Lord, the God of heaven, given me; and He hath charged me to build Him a House in Jerusalem, which is in Judah" (Ezra 1:2). *The fig tree putteth forth her green figs* (Song 2:13), which are put on top of the baskets of first fruits brought as offerings. *And the vines in blossom give forth their fragrance* (*ibid.*)—that is, the fragrance given off by the drink offerings.

Another comment: *My Beloved spoke* (*'anah*) *and said unto me* (Song 2:10). R. Azariah asked: But do not the words *spoke* and *said* mean the same thing? No, here the word *'anah* means not "spoke" but "answered," that is, [on Mount Carmel], He answered me at Elijah's bidding, and then through the Messiah He will say [encouraging things] to me. What will He say to me? *Rise up, My love, My fair one, and come away* (*ibid.*). *For lo, the winter is past* (*ibid.*)—that is, said R. Azariah, the wicked kingdom which enticed mortals into a wintry way[75] has passed on, the wicked kingdom

71. See Seḏer 'olam zuṭa (London, 5760/1910), p. 26.

72. See *JE*, *4*, 68, *s.v.* "Chronology."

73. Beginning with the subjection of Jehoiakim. See 2 Kings 24:1, and B.Meḡ 11b.

74. Toward the end of the First Commonwealth, the people of Israel were so sinful that they even gave up the practice of circumcision. See PR 14:15 (YJS, *18*, 294, n. 105); and B.Men 53b.

75. In the Hebrew, there is a play on the words *stw*, "winter," and *syṯ* and *t'h*,

alluded to in the verse "If thy brother [Esau, from whom came Edom and Rome], the son of thy mother [Rebekah] . . . entice thee . . . saying: 'Let us go and serve other gods' " (Deut. 13:7). *The rain is over and gone* (Song 2:11) refers to the enslavement [under Edom] that is over and gone. *The flowers appear on the earth* (Song 2:12), the flowers standing metaphorically, as R. Isaac said, for the craftsmen in the verse "And the Lord showed me four craftsmen [who wreak deliverance for Israel]" (Zech. 2:3). These craftsmen are Elijah, the king Messiah, Melchizedek, and the priest who was anointed in time of war [to exhort the armies of Israel].[76] By the words *The time of singing is come* (Song 2:12) is meant [the season when plants are pruned or cut back—hence metaphorically speaking], the time has come for the foreskin to be cut; the time has come for the wicked to be broken and cut down: "The Lord hath broken the staff of the wicked" (Isa. 14:5); the time has come for the wicked kingdom to be rooted out of the world; the time has come for the kingdom of heaven to be revealed: "And the Lord shall be king over all the earth," etc. (Zech. 14:9). *And the voice of the turtle* (*twr*) *is heard in our land* (Song 2:12), words which mean, according to R. Johanan, that the voice of the king Messiah, the voice of the one who will lead us with great care through the final turnings (*tyyr*) of our journey is heard in the land: "How beautiful upon the mountains are the feet of the messenger of good tidings" (Isa. 52:7). *The fig tree drops* [*as into a grave*] *her unripe and sickly figs* (Song 2:13). R. Ḥiyya bar Abba said: In the days of the Messiah a great pestilence will come, and the lives of the wicked will come to an end. *And the vines in blossom give forth their fragrance* (Song 2:13). This verse refers to the ones that are left to live: "And it shall come to pass, that he that is left in Zion, and he that remaineth in Jerusalem shall be called holy" (Isa. 4:3). Of the particular seven-year period at the end of which [the Messiah], the son of David, will appear,[77] the Rabbis taught as follows: In the first year "I will cause it to rain upon one city and cause it not to rain upon another city" (Amos 4:7). In the second year arrows of famine will be launched [upon Israel]. In the third year there will be a general famine;

"entice," the "enticing [into a wintry way]," may refer to the missionary activity of Rome after its conversion to Christianity, or in general, to the political policy it pursued.

76. See PR 8:4.

77. According to Yĕhudah 'Eben Shĕmu'el, the idea of a seven-year period at the end of which the Messiah was to come is linked with the calculation that at the end of 85 Jubilee periods—that is, after Anno Mundi 4250—the Messiah was to be expected. A.M. 4250 corresponded to 447 C.E., a year which many believed would mark the end of Rome (in 433 C.E. Attila the Hun made himself ruler of Rome). In one of the seven-year periods, accordingly, in the eighty-sixth Jubilee, the Messiah was expected. See Yĕhudah 'Eben Shĕmu'el, *Midrĕše gĕ'ulah*, 2d. ed. (Jerusalem-Tel Aviv, 5714/1954), p. 45. See also PR 1:7 (YJS, *18*, 46–47, n. 51).

during the year, men, women, and little children will die, and [because of Israel's hunger] the Torah will be forgotten in the Land of Israel. During the fourth year, there will be a scarcity of one thing and a surplus of another.[78] During the fifth, there will be great plenty, and people will eat and drink and rejoice, and the Torah will again shine for Israel as when it was newly given.[79] During the sixth, there will be rumors [of war];[80] and during the seventh, wars. And with the departure of the seventh year, the son of David will appear.

Abaye exclaimed: How many such seven-year periods have come, and yet the son of David has not come! [Seven-year periods have nothing to do with his coming]. The signs of his coming will be those that R. Johanan indicated: In the generation in which the son of David comes, disciples of the wise will die out; and as for those who remain alive, their eyes will be consumed with sorrow and sighing [as they weep]; and many agonies will afflict the entire people as harsh decrees are added one to the other—indeed, while one is still in force, another will be proclaimed and added to it.

R. Abun said: In the generation during which the son of David comes, the chamber where scholars are wont to meet for study will be used for harlotry, Galilee will be laid waste, the Gaulan region[81] will be made desolate; the men of Galilee will go about from town to town and find no pity, men of truth will perish, and truth, rejected, will go hence. Whither will it go? According to the School of R. Yannai, it will go and dwell among bands [of hermits] in the desert, as it is said *Truth shall be among bands*[82] (Isa. 59:15).

R. Nehorai said: In the generation in which the son of David comes, the young will insult their elders, and the elders will wait upon the young:[83] "The daughter will rise up against her mother, the daughter-in-law against her mother-in-law; a man's enemies will be the inmates of his own house"[84] (Micah 7:6); and a son will feel no shame before his father.[85] The wisdom of the Scribes will be deemed a stench. The vine will yield its fruit, yet wine will be costly.

78. Literally "scarcity and no scarcity, plenty and no plenty."

79. Joseph Klausner (*The Messianic Idea in Israel* [New York, 1955], pp. 449–50) suggests that the temporary disappearance of the Torah from Israel is among the pangs suffered by Israel during the time preceding the Messiah's coming.

80. Cf. Mark 13:7; Matthew 24:6. Or "[of thunderings]" or "rumors [that the Messiah is on his way]." So Rashi on B.Sanh 97a.

81. East of the Sea of Galilee and of the upper Jordan. See I. Epstein's note in the Soncino tr., B.Sanh 97a.

82. JV: *Truth is lacking*. In this comment, *'dr*, "lack," is taken in its other sense of "flock" or "band."

83. [Literally "the young will cause their elders to go pale (with shame), and the elders will rise (in deference) before the young." L.N.]

84. See Matthew 10:35–36, and Luke 12:53.

85. Cf. Amos 2:7.

R. Abba bar Kahana said: The son of David will not come except in a generation whose every member deserves extermination. R. Yannai said: The son of David will not come except in a base, a dog-faced,[86] generation.

R. Levi said: "When you see generation after generation revile God, look for the feet of the king Messiah." By what verse did he justify his comment? By the verse *When Thine enemies have reviled Thee, O Lord, when they have reviled Thee—[then are] the footsteps of Thine anointed* (Ps. 89:52). And what words immediately follow? *Blessed be the Lord for evermore. Amen, and Amen* (Ps. 89:53)—[that is, when the Messiah comes, the Lord's glory will be evident to all the world all the time].

10. R. Johanan[87] began his discourse by quoting the verse *I bought her to me for fifteen pieces of silver, a homer of barley, and a half homer of barley* (Hos. 3:2),[88] [and then continued: Even as Hosea "bought," that is, provided his wife with silver and barley, whereby sustaining herself, she could resist a life of harlotry, so God spoke of His "buying"—i.e. providing —Israel with precepts, whereby sustaining themselves, they could resist straying from God]. Accordingly, R. Johanan read the verse as follows: *I bought [Israel so that she stay loyal] to Me for fifteen pieces of silver*—fifteen pieces; *a homer of barley*, thirty measures;[89] *and a half homer of barley*—[fifteen measures], making a total of sixty, a figure favored by Moses who set down precepts[90] in groups of sixty[91] in the Torah. For, as R. Johanan, citing R. Simeon ben Yoḥai, went on to point out, Moses set down for us in the Torah three passages, each of which is made up of sixty precepts:[92] the passage concerning the Passover sacrifice, the passage concerning damages, and the passage concerning holiness. According to R. Levi who cited R. Shela of Kefar Tamarta, each of the three is made up of a total of seventy, not sixty, precepts. R. Tanḥuma, however, stated that there was no real difference of opinion. For he who considers the passage concerning

86. Brazen-faced and brutalized. Cf. Soṭ 9:15, and PR 1:7.

87. "R. Johanan"—O_1, C; O: "R. Jonah."

88. According to Leon Nemoy, R. Johanan interprets the Masoretic *w'ḵrh* as "supplied her with *kor*-measures," and then proceeds to calculate how many such measures (each *kor* being equal to 30 *sĕ'ah*) there were. Loyalty is thus not under discussion here.

89. A *homer* is the equivalent of thirty *sĕ'ah* [and so is a *kor*. L.N.].

90. "Silver" is taken to stand for deeds of such excellence as to be termed "sterling"—hence precepts which lead to such deeds; and *śĕ'orim*, the Hebrew for "barley," is understood as an acronym for *sar 'awon*, "keep from iniquity"—hence, precepts which keep from iniquity. See B.Ber 57a.

91. See Rödelheim *Maḥzor* for the evening service of Passover, where, in comments on *'Ezkĕrah šĕnoṯ 'olamim*, the sixty precepts are counted. For a critique and correction of Rödelheim's enumeration see *'En Ḥanoḵ*, in comment on Lev. Rabbah, chap. 24 (Midrash Rabbah, ed. 'Ănafim [New York, 5717/1957], *1*, end).

92. Exod. 12:1–13:10; 21:1–22:23; and Lev. 19:1–20:23.

the Passover sacrifice as made up of seventy precepts includes within it the passage concerning tefillin; he who considers the passage concerning damages as made up of seventy precepts includes within it the passage concerning release from debt in the Sabbatical year; and he who considers the passage concerning holiness as made up of seventy precepts includes within it the passage on forbidden sexual relations.[93]

In another comment the verse is read [*Precious to Me on account of the forty-five*] *sterling men*[94] [*who are ever to be in her midst*], *I bought Me*—[i.e. *covenanted with Israel*] *on the fifteenth* (Hos. 3:2)—that is, on the fifteenth of Nisan. For when, [according to what Torah hints to us, did these forty-five sterling men begin to be an ever-present part of Israel]? On this very day in this very month: *This month shall be unto you the beginning of months* (Exod. 12:2).

11. *This shall be a new* [*experience*][95] *unto you* (*ibid.*). According to R. Berechiah, citing R. Yudan bar R. Simeon, the Holy One said to Israel: My children, here in Egypt you are to have a new and unprecedented experience in redemption.[96] In times gone by I redeemed no nation from the midst of another nation. But now I shall redeem a nation out of another nation, as is said of Me in the verse *God hath assayed to go and take him a nation from the midst of another nation* (Deut. 4:34). R. Joshua bar R. Nehemiah, citing R. Johanan bar Pazzi, called particular attention to the phrase *a nation from the midst of another nation*, and declared that by not saying "a people from the midst of another nation," Scripture intimates that it was "one heathen nation from the midst of another heathen nation." For at that time the Jews were uncircumcised even as the Egyptians were uncircumcised; at

93. Here Friedmann's emendation (*'rwh*) in PRF 15:16 is followed, even though all PRK MSS read, "the passage on the fruit of trees in the first three years (*'rlh*)." In the Hebrew a slight change in the form of a letter could account for the error.

Those who count seventy precepts thus include the previously cited passages in Exodus and Leviticus, together with the adjoining passages in Exod. 13:16; Exod. 23:10–19; and Lev. 18:7–18.

94. Literally *silver*, which in this comment is taken to suggest, as does silver when it is designated as sterling, the sterling qualities of the righteous men in Israel, who never being fewer than forty-five, account for Israel's survival despite Israel's persistent disregard of God's precepts. The number "forty-five" is arrived at by adding the thirty measures represented by the *homer of barley* (Hos. 3:2) to the fifteen measures represented by the *half-homer of barley* (*ibid.*). These forty-five measures stand metaphorically for the righteous men whose ongoing merit made God enter into and keep His covenant with Israel (see above, note 90). In B.Ḥul 92a, and in Yalḳuṭ Hosea, R. Johanan, citing R. Simeon ben Jehozadak, offers the same comment in a more extended form. In his own behalf, however, in Piska 12.4, he gives a different comment. See also B.Sanh 96b.

95. *Ḥdš* may mean "month" or "new [experience]."

96. The words "in the time-to-come" are deleted, as in MC.

that time the Jews grew locks even as the Egyptians grew locks [to be shorn off at puberty and offered to the deity]. Accordingly, the measure of justice would never have allowed Israel to be redeemed out of Egypt. Indeed, as R. Samuel bar Naḥman said, had not the Holy One previously bound Himself by an oath, Israel would never have been redeemed out of Egypt. And the proof of the oath? The verse *Therefore say unto the children of Israel . . . I will bring you out from under the burden*, etc. (Exod. 6:6); here *therefore* implies an oath, as in the parallel instance *Therefore I have sworn unto the house of Eli*, etc. (1 Sam. 3:14).

Thus, R. Berechiah concluded, the statement *Thou hast redeemed Thy people with Thine arm* (Ps. 77:16) means, Thou hast redeemed them arbitrarily, [in spite of what the measure of justice requires], with the plenitude of Thy power. [The presence of God's power], as R. Yudan pointed out, [is implicit] in the passage beginning with *to go and take Him a nation*, and ending with *and by great terrors* (Deut. 4:34), a passage containing seventy-two letters, [the same number as in the name of God].[97] And if anyone says to you: "There are actually seventy-five," say in reply: You are to exclude the letters of the word *gwy*, "nation," in its second occurrence, which, [since it refers to Egypt], obviously cannot be included in the count.

R. Abin went on to say: God redeemed them with the full glory of His name, the name of the Holy One, with its seventy-two letters.

[*This month shall be unto you the beginning of months* (Exod. 12:2).] R. Joshua ben Levi said: In connection with this verse consider the analogy of a king whose son was captured. The king, wearing the cloak of vengeance, went forth and forcibly freed his son. Thereupon he commanded: Count ye the years of my reign as beginning with the forcible freeing of my son. Even so the Holy One commanded: Count ye the years of My reign as beginning with the exodus from Egypt. R. Levi said in the name of R. Ḥama bar R. Ḥanina: Consider likewise the analogy of a king who married many women, but did not order in their behalf records of the nuptials or of the dates of the marriages. As soon as he married a woman of goodly stock, however, yea, one of noble lineage, he ordered in her behalf a record of the nuptials and of the date of her marriage. So, too, in regard to all the women whom Ahasuerus married, he did not order in their behalf records of the nuptials or of the dates of the marriages. But when he married Esther, a woman of goodly stock, yea, of noble lineage, he ordered in her behalf a record of the nuptials and of the date of her marriage. The record of her nuptials: *So Esther was taken . . . into his house royal in the tenth month, which is the month Tebeth* (Esther 2:16); also the year of her marriage: *In the seventh year of his reign* (*ibid.*).

Just so, the Holy One said: When I created My world and the nations of

97. See *JE*, 9, 164, *s.v.* "Names of God."

the earth began to come into existence, I gave them no record of either month or week. But when Israel came into existence, I gave her both new moons and leap years. Hence it is said *This month shall be unto you*[98] (Exod. 12:2).

12. With reference to *This month shall be unto you,* R. Berechiah said: The moon in its waxing and waning is to be a sign for you: *David's seed . . . shall be established for ever as the moon* (Ps. 89:38): If you are worthy, the days you count will be days [of Israel's waxing stronger and stronger] like the moon's waxing to the full. But if you are not worthy, the days you count will be days [of Israel's waning] like the moon's waning. [When you are worthy], the days wax through Abraham, Isaac, Jacob, Judah, Perez, Hezron, Ram, Amminadab, Nahshon, Salmon, Boaz, Obed, Jesse, and David to Solomon: *Then Solomon sat on the throne of the Lord as king* (1 Chron. 29:23). Lo, the moon in its fullness! [But when you are not worthy], then you count the days [of Israel's waning] as the moon wanes into darkness—the days wane through Rehoboam, Ahijah, Asa, Jehoshaphat, Jehoram, Ahaziah, Joash, Amaziah, Uzziah, Jotham, Ahaz, Hezekiah, Manasseh, Amon, and Josiah down to Zedekiah:[99] *And they put out the eyes of Zedekiah* (2 Kings 25:7). Lo, the moon in utter darkness!

13. *This reckoning of the month shall be unto you* (Exod. 12:2)—that is, the reckoning of time will be turned over to you. Consider, said R. Joshua ben Levi, the analogy of a king who had a timepiece and turned the timepiece over to his son when the son grew up; or the analogy, said R. Jose bar R. Ḥanina, of a king who had an arm ring[100] and turned the arm ring over to his son when the son grew up; or the analogy, said R. Aḥa, of a king who had a finger ring and turned the ring over to his son when the son grew up; or the analogy, said R. Isaac, of a king who had treasuries, each with a key, and who turned over the keys to his son when the son grew up; or the analogy, said R. Ḥiyya bar Abba, of a carpenter who had a tool he wrought with and who turned the tool over to his son when the son grew up; or the analogy,

98. "Just so, the Holy One said . . . *unto you*" added as in the parallel, Yalḳuṭ, *Bo'*, 190.

99. Zedekiah, the sixteenth king, thus corresponds to the 31st day of the month—the first day in the succeeding month—when the moon is in utter darkness.

Jehoahaz, who ruled for only three months, is not included; neither are Jehoiakim and Jehoiachin, both of whom were put in power in Jerusalem by the kings of Egypt and Babylon respectively (*Zayyiṯ ra'anan* on Yalḳuṭ, *Bo'*, 190).

100. *Šwmyrh* is thus equated with *šemeru*, the Akkadian for the arm ring which was worn around the biceps as a sign of authority and high rank (see Joseph Perles in *Festschrift Adolf Schwarz* [Berlin-Wien, 1917], p. 309). Traditional Jewish commentators define *šwmyrh* as a watchtower.

said the Rabbis, of a physician who had a medicine cabinet and turned the cabinet over to his son when the son grew up.[101]

[In keeping with the interpretation that God turned the reckoning of time over to Israel], R. Hoshaia taught: When a court on earth decrees and says, "New Year's Day is today," the Holy One tells the ministering angels: "Raise up the dais.[102] Summon the advocates. Summon the clerks. For the court on earth has decreed and said: New Year's Day is today."

But if the witnesses are delayed in coming, or if, for any reason, the court decides to put off the beginning of the year by one day, the Holy One tells the ministering angels: "Remove the dais, dismiss the advocates, dismiss the clerks, since the court on earth has decreed that the New Year will not begin till tomorrow." And the proof from Scripture? *When it is a decree of Israel it is an ordinance for the God of Jacob* (Ps. 81:5): therefore what is not a statute for Israel is not—if one be permitted to speak thus—an ordinance for the God of Jacob.

R. Phinehas and R. Hilkiah taught in the name of R. Simon: When all the ministering angels gather before the Holy One and ask Him, "Master of universes, when does the New Year begin?" He replies: "Are you asking Me? Let us, you and I, ask the court on earth."[103] And the proof? The verse *The Lord our God is [near] whensoever we on His behalf proclaim*[104] (Deut. 4:7)—proclaim, that is, the set feasts on His behalf. Here the word "proclaim" refers to set feasts, as in the phrase *holy proclamation* (Exod. 12:16). Such feasts, according to R. Ḳrispa, citing R. Johanan, were in times gone by proclaimed by God Himself, as shown by the verse *These are the feasts set by the Lord, even holy proclamations* (Lev. 23:4). Now and hereafter they shall be the ones *which* YE *shall proclaim* (*ibid.*). Hence, if you proclaim them, they will be considered *feasts set by the Lord*. But if you do not proclaim them, they will not be considered *feasts set by the Lord*.

14. *This month shall be unto you* (Exod. 12:2). You reckon the month

101. The timepiece represents the calendar (cf. Piska 23.1); the watchtower situated on a height gives the watchman, Israel, that is, the capacity to see all things, high and low, alike; the ring symbolizes the authority given to Israel; in the heavenly treasuries rain is stored and the key to its release is given to men such as Ḥoni the Circle-Drawer (see B.Ta 19a); the tool is the Torah with which God made the world (see Gen. Rabbah 1:1); and the medicine cabinet contains secrets of healing and restoration of life given to men such as Elijah and Elisha (1 kings 17; 2 Kings 4). See *Ḳorban ha-'edah* on P.RH 1:3.

102. A heavenly court to examine all men's deeds comes into session on New Year's Day, and its verdicts are set down nine days later on the Day of Atonement.

103. Cf. MTeh 81:6.

104. JV: *whensoever we call upon Him.*

of Nisan [as the beginning of the year], but the heathen nations do not reckon it as such.[105]

R. Levi said in the name of R. Jose bar Il'a'i: It is but natural that the large should reckon by the large, and the small by the small. Esau—[Rome]—who is large reckons by the sun which is large; Jacob who is small reckons by the moon which is small, and indeed, as R. Naḥman said, this difference is a happy sign. Just as the larger luminary rules by day but does not rule by night, so wicked Esau rules in this world but will not rule in the world-to-come. And just as the smaller luminary rules by day and by night,[106] so Jacob will rule in this world and will also rule in the world-to-come.

R. Naḥman said: As long as the light of the larger luminary shines in the world, the light of the lesser one is not noticeable; but when the light of the larger one declines, the light of the lesser one becomes noticeable. Even so, as long as the light of Esau shines brightly in the world, the light of Jacob cannot be made out; but when the light of the wicked Esau declines, the light of Jacob is made out, as is said *Arise, shine, for thy light is come, and the glory of the Lord is risen upon thee. For behold, darkness shall cover the earth, and gross darkness the peoples; but upon thee the Lord will arise, and His glory shall be seen upon thee* (Isa. 60:1–2).[107]

15. [108]R. Simeon ben Yoḥai taught that Moses was baffled by three things: he could not grasp the complicated instructions concerning the making of the candlestick for the Tabernacle; he did not know how to identify the reptiles forbidden as food; he did not understand the mystery of the moon's changes. With His finger, if one may speak thus, God indicated each of the three to Moses, saying of the candlestick, THIS *is the work of the candlestick* (Num. 8:4); of the reptiles, THIS *is what is unclean unto you among the creeping things that creep upon the earth* (Lev. 11:29); and of the moon's changes, THIS *stage of the moon's renewal shall be the time when months begin.*[109]

[It was necessary for God to indicate the mystery of the moon's changes to Moses because, as] R. Simlai taught in the name of Samuel, on any day that the conjunction of the new moon does not take place before noon,[110]

105. "Sabba *Bo'* 71b quotes from an unknown source the statement that the Jewish calendar was introduced as a protest against the Egyptian one, which was a part of the Egyptian system of idolatry." Ginzberg, *Legends*, 5, 432.

106. The moon is often visible by day as well as by night, whereas the sun is always hidden at night. Exod. Rabbah 15:27.

107. See Gen. Rabbah 6:3.

108. The *incipit* in the translation differs from PRKM where it is set at the beginning of the next paragraph.

109. JV: *This month shall be unto you the beginning of months.*

110. Literally "before six hours."

the moon cannot possibly be seen [in the evening] by any human eye [such as Moses'].

In this connection, R. Samuel bar Yeba and R. Aḥa in the name of R. Samuel bar R. Naḥman explained that in the year when Israel went forth out of Egypt, the lunar month as well as the spring season[111] began on the same day of the week.[112]

[Through the following procedure]—so said R. Ḥiyya bar Abba citing R. Johanan—[with His finger, if one may speak thus, God indicated to Moses how to determine the arrival of the new moon]: The Holy One wrapped Himself in a prayer shawl with woolen fringes and placed Moses on one side of Him and Aaron on the other. Then He summoned Michael and Gabriel, who, as if they were messengers dispatched by an [earthly] court,[113] were to report their witnessing the arrival of the new moon, and He asked them: "In exactly what position did you see the moon? Turned towards the sun? Away from it? To the north? To the south? How high in the sky was it? Towards what point in the compass did it incline? How thick was the crescent?"

God then said to Moses and Aaron: In just the manner that you have observed here shall My children on earth reckon the calendar throughout the year: the presence of an elder, of witnesses, and of a prayer shawl with woolen fringes[114] are all required.

111. The year is divided into four seasons (*tĕḳufoṯ*): the summer and winter solstices, the vernal and autumnal equinoxes. See MTeh 19:10.

112. PRK reads "the months of the year and the months of the seasons were equal," which seems to say that the lunar months as well as each of the four seasons of the year began on the same day of the week. But according to Professor Abraham Sachs such an incidence is impossible; and so, at his suggestion, the emendation of the passage as set down by Edgar Frank in his *Talmudic and Rabbinical Chronology* (New York, 1956), p. 52, n. 81 is followed.

In a letter, Rabbi Saul Leeman, dissenting from the above, writes "The months of the year—(i.e. the lunar months) and the months of the season—(i.e. the solar months) were equal. Why did the Lord arrange for this? Quite simple. The . . . purpose of intercalation is to take care of the discrepancies between the lunar months and the solar months. Up until the year of the exodus the Lord took care of this Himself; after the year of the exodus Israel was in charge. But during the transitional year, the year of the exodus itself, the lunar and solar months were made to correspond so that no intercalation was called for."

113. Such messengers were employed by the court and sent out whenever witnesses who sighted the arrival of the new moon failed to come.

114. The fringes were blue, a color which "has the appearance of the sea; the sea, the appearance of grass; grass, the appearance of heaven; heaven, the appearance of a rainbow; a rainbow, the appearance of a cloud on a rainy day; a cloud on a rainy day, the appearance of the throne of glory; and the throne of glory, the appearance of the glory of the Lord." See MTeh 24:12, and 90:18.

16. [*This shall be a new experience for you* (Exod. 12:2)]. R. Naḥman, [and jointly] R. Eleazar bar R. Jose and R. Aḥa commented on this passage. According to the one, the Holy One said to Israel: My children, here [in Egypt] you are to have a new and unprecedented experience in redemption.[115] And according to the others: Soon after your exodus you are to have a completely new experience which you will have again only in the time-to-come. As in the time-to-come *The eyes of the blind shall be opened* (Isa. 35:5), so, too, after your exodus, for Scripture says, ALL *the people saw the thunderings* (Exod. 20:15). As in the time-to-come *The ears of the deaf shall be unstopped* (Isa. 35:5), so, too, after your exodus, for Scripture says, *All the people . . . said "*ALL *that the Lord hath spoken we will do as we hear"* (Exod. 24:7). As in the time-to-come *Then shall the lame man leap as a hart* (Isa. 35:6), so, too, after your exodus, for Scripture says, *Moses brought forth the people out of the camp to meet God; and they,* [*even the lame*] *stood at the nether part of the Mount* (Exod. 19:17). As in the time-to-come *The tongue of the dumb shall sing* (Isa. 35:6), so, too, after your exodus, for Scripture says, ALL *the people sang out together,* etc. (Exod. 19:8).

17. *Speak unto all the congregation of Israel, saying: In the tenth day of this month they shall take to them every man a lamb* (Exod. 12:3). R. Johanan asked: But is not a lamb fit for an offering only when newly taken out of the fold? Why then, is it said *In the tenth day?*[116] Because from the tenth day on, the lambs were tied to the legs of bedsteads in Israel's households, and when the Egyptians came in and saw them so tied, their souls fled in shock at the sight [of what they considered blasphemy].[117]

In this connection, note the comment of R. Ḥiyya bar R. Adda of Jaffa, on the verse *Draw out, and take you lambs according to your families, and kill the passover lamb* (Exod. 12:21): Each of you is to draw out—that is, drag out an Egyptian's [lamb, which is his] god, and kill it before his very eyes, even as the Egyptian, in his anxiety for it, speaks up in protest.[118]

R. Ḥelbo, citing R. Johanan, called attention to the fact that here Scripture says *In the tenth day of this month*[119] (Exod. 12:3), and, in reference to the crossing of the Jordan, says *The people came up out of the Jordan on the tenth day of the first month*[119] (Josh. 4:19). The point of the parallel,

115. The words "in the time-to-come" are deleted, as in MC. See Piska 4.11.

116. To be kept, as the text goes on to say, for four days, since the Passover lamb was to be slaughtered on the fourteenth day of the month. See Kel 19:2.

117. Lambs were objects of worship to the Egyptians. See Rashi on Exod. 8:22; Piska 7.9; PR 17:5; and Exod. Rabbah 16:3.

118. Leon Nemoy provided the interpretation of R. Ḥiyya's comment.

119. The verse in Exodus continues with *they shall take to them every man*; and Josh. 4:20 reads: *Those twelve stones which they took out of the Jordan did Joshua set up in Gilgal.*

s R. Ḥiyya taught in the name of R. Johanan, is that Israel's daring in aking the lambs in Egypt also stood by them at the Jordan, even as Israel's laring in eating the lamb [on the night preceding the fifteenth of Nisan] was to stand by them in the days of Haman: *They shall eat the flesh in* THAT *night* (Exod. 12:8); *On* THAT *night, when the king could not sleep* (Esther 5:1).[120]

According to R. Berechiah, citing R. Abbahu, Nahum bar R. Simai, discoursing in Tarsus, took the verse to read *They shall take unto them the Man* (Exod. 12:3), that is, take the Holy One, of whom it is said "The Lord is the Man—[that is, the manager]—of war"[121] (Exod. 15:3). How do you take Him? With the two lambs offered up daily in the Temple, [even as you took God unto yourselves when you daringly took the lambs in Egypt. This parallel is intimated by the two verses in each of which lamb is twice specified: *The one lamb thou shalt offer in the morning, and the other lamb thou shalt offer at dusk* (Exod. 29:39)]; *The one lamb in the ancestral House, the other lamb in [that House], in the Temple*[122] (Exod. 12:3).

[Because of the daily offerings of the lambs brought by a community daily repenting its misdeeds], said R. Yudan in the name of R. Simon, no man who lodged in Jerusalem for a full day could stay possessed of his sin. How so? The morning offering made expiation for transgressions done in the nighttime; and the offering at dusk made expiation for transgressions done in the daytime. No matter what, no man who lodged in Jerusalem for a full day could stay in possession of his sin. And the proof from Scripture? *Righteousness lodged in her* (Isa. 1:21)—[that is, "He who lodged in Jerusalem was made righteous"].[123]

18. [*There must be a cleansing—otherwise you will be afflicted by "the*

120. The Targum on Esther *ad loc* identifies the night as the night when the first-born of Egypt were slain, the night, that is, when the children of Israel ate of the Passover lamb. Cf. Esther 3:12; and Piska 8.3 and note 38 thereon.

121. He makes wars come out as He wants them to.

122. In JV, Exod. 12:3 reads *They shall take to them every man a lamb according to their fathers' houses, a lamb for a household.* Thus the Passover lamb as well as the two lambs offered daily in the Temple were meant to remind God of an entire people's willingness to risk life for the sake of making its covenant with God, of taking Him unto itself. The daily offering of the lambs, the act of "taking God," had, according to R. Nahum, expiatory effect, for it was a reliving, as it were, of Israel's boldness in rejecting Egypt's divinities, a boldness which within four days was followed by Israel's entering into a covenant with the true God.

The passage may obliquely be directed against Christianity: No one individual can be "the Passover lamb" (1 Corinthians 5:7); only the entire people of Israel can be the Passover lamb as Israel was ready to be in Egypt. In a subsequent time, Israel's willingness to sacrifice itself was symbolized by the daily offering of two lambs in the Temple.

123. "[that is . . . righteous]"—parallel in PR 15:24. A slight change in spelling

head"; there must be many cleansings—otherwise you will be afflicted b *"the first"* (Exod. 12:2).][124] R. Berechiah said in the name of R. Isaac *There must be a cleansing*—that is, you are to make your deeds clean o evil: otherwise, he who is spoken of as *the head* and he who is spoken of as *the first* are sure to come upon you. *The head* is wicked Nebuchadnezzar who is addressed in Scripture, "thou art the head of gold" (Dan. 2:38); *th first* is wicked Esau, of whom it is written "And the first came forth" (Gen 25:25). Who, O Israel, will eventually requite *the first* on your behalf? "I the Lord, [shall requite] 'the first' [of the Esaus who will afflict you]; anc I am He, the same [who will requite] subsequent [Esaus]" (Isa. 41:4) Who will requite Media on your behalf? [I the Lord]. Media is the kingdom alluded to in the phrase *by a sum of ten*[125] (Exod. 12:3). The phrase, according to R. Abin, refers to [the sum—ten thousand silver talents—to be paid into Ahasuerus' treasury when] Haman and his ten sons come into the world.[126] Who will requite them on your behalf? Two mortal guardians,[127] Mordecai and Esther—Mordecai outside the palace, Esther inside.[128] Who will requite Greece on your behalf? The descendants of the Hasmoneans, who, every day, [even in times of affliction and famine], offered up the two lambs in the Temple.[129]

Who will settle for you with Edom? *Naṭrona*,[130] the Supreme Guardian: *And He shall be unto you a guard*[131] [*against Esau*] (Exod. 12:6). Of Esau, the Holy One said: His father called him great: *Isaac . . . called Esau his great son*[132] (Gen. 27:1); and his mother called him great: *Rebekah*

---

turns *ṣdḳ*, "righteousness," into *ṣdyḳ*, "righteous." The change makes for a better parallel with the concluding clause of the verse, *but now murderers*. See Piska 15.7.

124. So the verse must be translated to fit R. Berechiah's comment which follows. JV: *This month shall be unto you the beginning of months; it shall be the first month of the year to you.*

125. JV: *in the tenth.*

126. See Esther 3:9.

127. *Klḳṭr* is taken to be a miswriting of *blḳṭr*, a form of the Greek *phylakter*, "watchman" or "guardian."

128. Friedmann (PRF 15, n. 140) suggests that the words *a lamb, according to their fathers' houses, a lamb for a household* (Exod. 12:3) provide the Scriptural basis for this comment, Mordecai being the lamb of the "fathers' house," and Esther being the lamb within the "household."

129. See B.BḲ 82b. Friedmann (PRF 15, n. 141) suggests that the Scriptural basis for this comment is the words *Your lamb shall be without blemish* (Exod. 12:5), in reference to the two lambs without blemish which priests were to offer up daily.

130. Aramaic for "guardian."

131. JV: *And ye shall keep it.*

132. JV: *elder*. But *ḡaḏol* means literally "large" or "great."

ook *the garments of Esau her son, the great one* (Gen. 27:15); neverthe-ess, I call him small: *Behold I make thee small among the nations* (Ob. :2). Still, seeing that his father and mother call Esau great, I shall see to it hat the size of the slaughterer is in keeping with the size of the ox: *The Lord ath a sacrifice in Bozrah, and a great slaughter in the land of Edom* (Isa. 4:6), that is, according to R. Berechiah, the slaughterer in the land of Edom—of Esau—will be the Great One,[133] [God Himself].

19. *Eat not of it raw* (Exod. 12:9). Desire not to see Edom only half-consumed or merely *sodden with water* (*ibid.*); *but roasted with fire; its head with its legs and with the inwards thereof* (*ibid.*)—in short, see it all con-sumed, together with its rulers, governors, and commanders, in keeping with the words spoken to Tyre,[134] *Thy riches, and thy wares, thy merchandise, thy mariners, and thy pilots, thy calkers, and the exchangers of thy mer-chandise, and all thy men of war that are in thee, with all thy company which is in the midst of thee, shall fall into the heart of the seas in the day of thy ruin* (Ezek. 27:27). According to R. Samuel bar R. Isaac, in the conclusion of the verse, beginning with the words *All thy company,* God was saying: Even those who were once of My company but went and attached themselves to thy company, they, too, in the day of thy ruin shall fall into the heart of the seas.

And thus ye shall eat it: with your loins girded, your shoes on your feet, and your staff in your hand; and ye shall eat it in haste—it is the Lord's Passover (Exod. 12:11). R. Samuel bar Naḥman said: Seeing that in this world you had to eat the roasted flesh in haste, lo, what is said of the manner of your deliverance in the world-to-come? *Verily ye shall not go out in haste, neither shall ye go by flight; for the Lord will go before you, and the God of Israel will be your rearguard* (Isa. 52:12).

133. R. Berechiah translates the word *ṭebaḥ*, "slaughter," as though it were written *ṭabbaḥ*, "slaughterer." See PR 14:5.

134. That is, Rome. On the identification of Tyre as Rome see PR 14:14, 17:8; and Gen. Rabbah 61:7 end.

PISKA 6

SUMMARY

Offerings serve men's needs, not God's

Since God is merciful and man is cruel, if God were hungry, He would not ask cruel man to provide food for Him. In asking for animal sacrifices, He does not make inordinate demands, for it is not to satisfy hunger that He asks for sacrifices. If His angels require no food or drink, God certainly does not require them. If Moses required no food or drink on Sinai, certainly God does not require them. Besides, if no one of God's creations requires to be fed by what it creates, does God the Creator require to be fed by His creation? No. Yet we are told that only a small wine offering is enough to fill, satiate, and even intoxicate Him. How are we to understand such a statement, since man is unable to feed the Behemoth, much less the Behemoth's Creator? The Behemoth feeds on the produce of a thousand mountains, and its need for drink is so huge that the waters of the Jordan are only enough to moisten its mouth. To satisfy its thirst it requires the limitless waters of Yubal, a river that comes forth out of Eden. Similarly, man cannot supply the requirements of the Ziz or of the Leviathan. As for the people of Israel, they could barely provide Solomon's measure of food, or even the food required by Nehemiah, a governor whose needs were modest. Therefore, when God speaks to them of *food . . . presented unto Me for offerings* (Num. 28:2), it is really the fragrance of their obedience and good deeds which He truly requires and in which He delights (Sec. 1).

Consider: righteous persons like Eliezer, Ruth, and Hezekiah required very little to satisfy their wants. Only the wicked like Esau, Rezin, and Remaliah's son stuffed food into their mouths, the wicked like Mesha, king of Moab, whose desire for more and more sheep knew no restraint. All the wicked who are insatiable receive their just deserts in the end (Sec. 2).

Now that the daily offering to God is no more, the study of the ordinances pertaining to the offering is considered the equivalent of the offering itself. Children, who are pure, are to study Leviticus which has to do with the purity of things such as the daily offering.

The fact that God asked Israel to bring a burnt offering continually shows that He was pleased with the manner of Israel's presenting it to Him (Sec. 3). The daily offerings cause God to put Israel's iniquities out of sight or, according to some, to cleanse them of iniquities of long standing. Several comments follow concerning the place on the altar in Jerusalem where the two lambs are to be offered and the beneficial effects of such offerings—for xample, no man who lodged in Jersualem for a full day could stay possessed f his sin.

The precise character of the daily offering was one of the three commandments which startled Moses who felt that man could not possibly fulfill them, ntil God reassured him by saying that He did not come to Israel with emands commensurate with His majesty, but with Israel's capacity (Sec.).

PISKA 6

My food which is presented unto Me for offerings (Num. 28:2).[1]

1. *If I were hungry, I would not speak to thee of it; for the world is Mine and the fullness thereof* (Ps. 50:12). Of the words *I would not speak to thee of it*, R. Simon said: Thirteen qualities of mercy are attributed in Scripture to the Holy One, as indicated in the verse *The Lord passed by before him, and proclaimed: "The Lord, the Lord, God, merciful and gracious, long-suffering, and abundant in goodness and truth; keeping mercy unto the thousandth generation, forgiving iniquity, and passing over transgression and sin, clearing [those who repent"]*[2] (Exod. 34:6–7). Do you think it likely, then, that One so merciful would entrust the providing of His sustenance to man who is cruel? Hence, *If I were hungry, I would not speak to thee of it* (Ps. 50:12).

According to R. Judah bar R. Simon, the Holy One said to Israel: [My children], I have made available ten clean beasts as food for you—three of these subject to your control, and seven not subject to your control. Subject to your control: *The ox, the sheep, and the goat* (Deut. 14:4); not subject to your control: *the hart, the gazelle, the roebuck, the wild goat, the ibex, the antelope, and the mountain sheep* (Deut. 14:5). Have I so burdened you that you need to go over mountains and hills to fetch Me an offering out of those that are not subject to your control? Have I not told you to fetch only such as are subject to your control, such as those reared at your trough? Hence, *Suppose I were hungry, I am not asking too much of thee* (Ps. 50:12).

R. Isaac said that in the words *My food which is presented unto Me for offerings* (Num. 28:2), God raises the question: Does My person require food or drink? If you think My person requires food or drink, then learn otherwise from My angels, learn otherwise from My ministers. Of them it is written *His ministers are a flaming fire*[3] (Ps. 104:4). And how is their fire

1. In PRF 16, n. 1, Friedmann suggests that Num. 28:1–8 used to be the lesson on the fifth Sabbath—following the four special Sabbaths—which can fall in the first week of Nisan.

According to B.Meğ 21b, however, Num. 28:1–8 is the lesson for the New Moon, specifically—so Abraham Goldberg—for a New Moon which falls on a weekday (see his "Pĕsiḳta dĕ-Rab̲ Kahăna," *Kirjath Sefer, 43* [1967], 69).

2. JV: *forgiving iniquity and transgression and sin, and that will by no means clear.* In this comment, however, the latter phrase is rendered literally "clearing [those who repent], but not clearing [those who do not]." See Rashi.

3. Apparently the conclusion of the verse in Num. 28:2, the phrase, rendered for the purpose of this comment "take heed of My fiery ones," provides the link with Ps. 104:4. JV: *made by fire.*

ourished? By the flame-like splendor of God's presence, for it is written *In he light of the King's countenance is life* (Prov. 16:15). And further on this oint, R. Haggai, citing R. Isaac, said: It is written *Thou hast made heaven, he heaven of heavens . . . their [angelic] host . . . and Thou preservest hem all* (Neh. 9:6)—with Thee is the preservation of life.[4] [Hence, *If I vere hungry, I would have no reason to speak to thee* (Ps. 50:12)].

R. Simeon ben Laḳish said that in the verse *It is to be a continual burnt offering, [like that] which was offered on Mount Sinai, for a sweet savor,*[5] *an offering made by fire unto the Lord* (Num. 28:6), Scripture suggests that God is asking: Does My person require food or drink? Learn the answer rom the statement in Scripture, *And [Moses] was there with the Lord orty days and forty nights; he did neither eat bread, nor drink water* (Exod. 34:28). Did he see Me eat, did he see Me drink? It may therefore be argued *a fortiori*: If Moses, when he went on a mission for Me, ate no bread and drank no water for forty days and forty nights,[6] do you suppose My person requires food or drink? Hence, *If I were hungry, I would have no reason to speak to thee* (Ps. 50:12).[7]

According to R. Ḥiyya bar Abba, the Holy One said: My creatures do not require for their sustenance the things which in accordance with My command they create. Do I, for My sustenance, require the things which I have created? Have you ever in all your life heard anyone say, "Give some wine to this vine to drink so that it will create much more wine," "Give some olive oil to this olive tree to drink so that it will create much more oil?" My creatures do not require for their sustenance the things which in accordance with My command they create. Shall I, then, require for My sustenance that which I have created? Hence, *If I were hungry, I would not speak of it to thee [who art My creature]* (*ibid.*).

R. Yannai said: Human nature being what it is, would a man walking alongside a stream be likely to feel that he has quenched his thirst by drinking no more than two or three *loḡ*[8] of water? The Lord, however, says of a

4. Leon Nemoy suggests that the commentator intends a distinction between *mĕḥayyeh 'eṯ kullam* and *mĕḥayyeh lĕkullam*; the former means "Thou keepest them alive," the latter "Thou providest them with livelihood (=food)."

5. JV: *It is a continual burnt offering, which was offered in Mount Sinai, for a sweet savor*. But apparently R. Simeon understands the verse to say that the experience of Moses *on Mount Sinai* proved that the continual daily offering, a "sweet savor," so to speak, was only to please God by doing His will. *On Mount Sinai* is thus taken to refer to the experience of Moses; since no offering was presented on the Mount, it was presented on the altar built "under the Mount" (Exod. 24:4). See David Luria's Novellae on Num. Rabbah 21:16.

6. "and forty nights"—O_1.

7. Cf. PR 48:3.

8. A *loḡ* is the equivalent of one fourteenth of a gallon.

log̃ of wine [or so[9]] that makes up the daily drink offerings: "I drink, I a filled, I am satisfied." For, as R. Ḥiyya taught, in the words *In the holy plac shalt thou pour out a drink offering of filling, intoxicating drink unto th Lord* (Num. 28:7), His drinking, His satiety, and His intoxication are im plied.[10]

As a matter of fact, said Jose ben Menasya in the name of R. Simeon be Laḳish, when the drink offerings were poured upon the altar, its cup-like[11] drains had to be stopped up [so that the wine overflowing the altar woul make it appear that God could not swallow the wine fast enough].[12] Ac cording to R. Jose bar Bun, if the practice which R. Simeon ben Laḳis spoke of is not followed, the drink offering is not valid.

[*If I were hungry, would I ask sustenance of thee?* (Ps. 50:12). Why], gave you just one head of a certain kind of cattle whose measure of food yo could not possibly provide! What one was that? *The Behemoth*[13] *upon a thousand mountains* (Ps. 50:10). On the precise meaning of these words R Johanan, R. Simeon ben Laḳish, and the Rabbis differ as follows: According to R. Johanan, the Behemoth, the only one of its kind of cattle, is couched upon a thousand mountains, and the thousand mountains bring forth for him the food which he eats. And the proof? The verse *Behold now Behemoth which I made*[14] . . . *Surely the mountains bring him forth food* (Job 40:15, 20). According to R. Simeon ben Laḳish also, the Behemoth, the only one of its kind of cattle, is couched upon a thousand mountains. And the thousand mountains produce all kinds of food [for him, food], adds R. Simeon, which in the time-to-come will be eaten by the righteous. And the proof? The verse *And Sharon which had been a fold for* [*Behemoth, huge as innumerable*] *flocks, and the valley of Achor which had been a place for* [*Behemoth, huge as many*] *herds, to couch upon, shall be for My people that have sought Me* (Isa. 65:10). And according to the Rabbis also, the Behemoth, the only one of its kind of cattle, is couched upon a thousand mountains, and the thousand mountains, the Rabbis go on to say, produce a supply of cattle for him which he eats. And the proof? The verse *Behold now Behemoth . . . for him all the beasts of the field are ground up there*[15] (Job 40:15, 20). But is such a thing possible, that cattle should eat other cattle?

9. Three *log̃*, to be exact. See Num. 15:7.
10. See PR 48:3.
11. [Literally "basin-like." L.N.]
12. See B.Suk 49b.
13. JV: *cattle.*
14. On the sixth day of creation. See PRE, chap. 11.
15. In this comment the verb *śḥḳ*, "to play," is read *šḥḳ*, "to be ground"—ground up, that is, for food.

. Tanḥuma, quoting *The works of the Lord are many* (Ps. 111:2), said: ow diverse are the works of the Holy One!

And where does Behemoth drink from? R. Joshua ben Levi said: [From e Jordan]—in a single draught he drinks up all [the water] that it brings own in six months. And the proof? The verse *Behold now Behemoth . . . he confident, because the Jordan rushes forth*[16] *to his mouth* (Job 40:15, 3). And the Rabbis said: He makes a single draught of all [the water] that e Jordan brings down in twelve months. And the proof? The verse *He is onfident, because the Jordan rushes forth to his mouth.*[17] And yet this raught is only enough to moisten the Behemoth's mouth.[18] R. Huna said in e name of R. Jose: "There is not even enough to moisten his mouth."[19] hen where does he drink from? [R. Jose thereupon quoted the answer of] . Simeon ben Yoḥai: "*Out of Eden there goes forth a river* (Gen. 2:10) hose name is Yubal, named in the verse *That spreadeth out its roots by ubal*[20] (Jer. 17:8), and from its limitless waters he drinks." [God's ower is such]—so it is taught in the name of R. Meir—[that if He equired food He would not need to ask man for it]: *But ask now the ehemoth*—"the Behemoth of a thousand hills" (Ps. 50:10)—*and he*[21] *hall teach thee* (Job 12:7); *and* THE *fowl of the air* (*ibid.*)—that is, "the iz" (Ps. 50:10), [a bird so huge that it darkens the sun with its wings]—*nd it shall tell thee* (Job 12:7); *or speak to the earth* (Job 12:8)—the part hat is the Garden of Eden[22]—*and it shall teach thee; and* THE *fish*[23] *of the ea*—that is, the Leviathan—*shall declare unto thee* (*ibid.*). *Who knoweth ot among all these, that the hand of the Lord hath wrought this?* (Job 2:9).

[Indeed, could you provide for Me]? I gave you a unique king, and you

16. Since Scripture says "rushes," it implies, according to R. Joshua, the six months of the rainy season when the Jordan is full.

17. The Rabbis say that since the time is not delimited clearly in the verse, a year's flow of the Jordan may be assumed.

18. Since Scripture does not say "to his throat"—only *to his mouth.*

19. Since Scripture says *to* (not *into*) *his mouth* it seems to imply that the waters of the Jordan do not even wet his mouth.

20. JV: *the river.* That the river is in Eden is inferred from the fact that the text in Jeremiah speaks of the abode of the righteous and of the tree of life. See Rashi on B.Beḳ 55b.

21. JV: *the beasts, and they.*

22. Since Behemoth, Ziz, and Leviathan, marvelous creatures, are referred to in the other parts of the verse, the commentator assumes that the marvelous part of the earth, namely, the Garden of Eden, is the one referred to in this part of the verse.

23. JV: *fishes.* But apparently he construes the plural as intimating the gigantic size of this particular fish.

were barely able to provide his measure of food. Which king was tha Solomon, son of David. *And Solomon's provision for one day was thir measures of fine flour, and threescore measures of meal* (1 Kings 5:2 According to R. Samuel bar R. Isaac, these measures were only enough t provide him with honey cakes [to nibble on]. As for his regular meals, a ordinary mortal was barely able to provide them. *Ten fat oxen* (1 King 5:3)—fattened with fodder; *and twenty oxen out of the pasture, and hundred sheep* (*ibid.*)—also out of the pasture; *besides harts, gazelles, roe bucks, and fatted barburim*[24] (*ibid.*). What are *fatted barburim*? Accordin to R. Berechiah, citing R. Judah, they are various kinds of game so calle because they come from the vivarium. But according to the Rabbis, *barburim* is the name of a large bird, renowned and choice, which was brough every day and served at Solomon's table.[25] R. Judah bar R. Zebida said Solomon had a thousand wives,[26] and each of them used to prepare banquet, such as the one described just above, thinking that he might choos to dine with her. Hence, *If I were hungry, I would not ask sustenance of the* (Ps. 50:12).

I gave you a unique person, the one who was once held captive.[27] Hi measure of food you could barely provide. What person was that? Nehemia the governor, who said: *Now that which was prepared for one day was one ox and six choice sheep, also fowls were prepared for me; and once in ter days store of all sorts of wine; yet for all this I demanded not the usual fare provided for the governor, because the service was heavy upon this people* (Neh. 5:18). *What is meant by fare . . . for the governor*? R. Huna bar Yeḳo said: It means, "gourmet food carefully cooked in vessels standing upon tripods." [Hence, because you could not provide even enough for the governor, *If I were hungry, I would not ask sustenance of thee* (Ps. 50:12)].

"When fragrant spices sprinkled on coals are brought in after the banquet is over" (Ber 6:6), do the guests enjoy anything more of the spices except the fragrance? So the Holy One said to Israel: My children, of all the offerings which you bring before Me, do I enjoy any part of them other than the fragrance? *It is the fragrance which is My own delight that ye are to . . .*

24. Usually rendered *fowls.*

25. A parallel passage in Eccles. Rabbah 2:7 goes on to say that the bird came from Barbaria—a term applied to countries outside the Roman Empire.

26. For the number see 1 Kings 11:3.

27. Nehemiah is described as having been held captive either because he lived part of his life in exile in Babylon, or because he had been enslaved by Artaxerxes. [Note the descending sequence: Israel cannot feed God; indeed, they cannot feed a king; as a matter of fact, they cannot even feed a lowly governor. L.N.]

fer unto Me (Num. 28:2)[28]—[that is, the fragrance of your obedience[29] d good deeds].[30]

2. *The righteous eateth to the satisfying of his desire* (Prov. 13:25). Such as Eliezer the servant of Abraham who said to our mother Rebekah: "Give e to drink, I pray thee, a little water of thy pitcher" (Gen. 24:17)—one rink satisfied him. *But the belly of the wicked shall want* (Prov. 13:25). uch was the wicked Esau who said to our father Jacob: "Stuff me, I pray ee, with this red, red pottage" (Gen. 25:30). R. Isaac bar R. Ze'era xplained: This wicked man opened his mouth wide as though he were a amel and said, "I have my mouth open, keep putting food into it." The ords "stuff me"[31] are associated with the feeding of a camel, as we read in Mishnah: "On the Sabbath you must not make a manger of the camel's omach, nor push food into his gullet, but you may stuff it into his mouth" Shab 24:3).

Another comment: *The righteous eateth to the satisfying of his desire* Prov. 13:25). Such was Ruth the woman of Moab, of whom it is written And she did eat and was satisfied, and left thereof" (Ruth 2:14). R. Isaac aid: From this verse you may infer one of two possible meanings: Blessing welt in the hand of the righteous Boaz [who gave her corn to eat]; or lessing dwelt in the stomach of the righteous Ruth [who required so little]. But since the verse says, "And she did eat and was satisfied, and left thereof," t is more probable that the blessing dwelt in the stomach of this righteous woman.[32] *But the belly of the wicked shall want* (Prov. 13:25). These

28. JV: *of an odor of delight unto Me shall ye observe to offer unto Me.* In the Rabbinic paraphrase the entire verse seems to be read as follows: *As for My offering, My food, consider My fiery angels.* [*Since they require no food, would I*]*? It is the fragrance which is My own delight that ye are to observe to offer unto Me.*

29. With reference to the phrase "the fragrance which is My own delight," Rashi on B.Zeḇ 46a says that it means "It is pleasing to Me that I spoke and My will was done." See also B.Men 110a; and MhG Num., p. 179.

30. The parallel in Num. Rabbah 21:19 reads: "My children! It is not because I eat or drink that I told you to offer sacrifices, but on account of the savor which should remind you that you must be sweet and pleasing to Me like a sweet savor." See also PR 48:3.

31. A *hapax legomenon* in Scripture.

32. Since all Ruth was given to eat was only as much parched corn as Boaz could hold between his finger tips, it follows, according to R. Isaac, that by giving Ruth so little corn, Boaz intimated that she belonged to the stock to whose members was vouchsafed the power of increasing whatever portion of food was offered them.

Abraham was aware that his stock was endowed with such power. Hence he could send Hagar and Ishmael into the wilderness with no more than a loaf of

wicked are [heathen of] the nations of the earth. R. Meir said: A certa Dosetai of Kokaba[33] asked me: What is meant by *The belly of the wick shall want*? I replied: In our city there was a heathen who prepared banquet for all the elders of the city, and he invited me along with them. H meant to set before us all [the kinds of food] that the Holy One creat during the six days of creation, and indeed, his table lacked nothing at a except soft-shelled nuts.[34] [When the heathen saw that they were wanting what did he do? He removed from before us the table top we had eate from—it was worth something like six talents of silver—and broke it. asked him: Why did you do this? The heathen replied: "Rabbi, you say th world is ours and the world-to-come is yours. So if we cannot eat now [a much as we want to], when shall we eat at all?" To him I applied the vers *The belly of the wicked shall want* (Prov. 13:25).

Another comment: *The righteous eateth to the satisfying of his desir* (Prov. 13:25). Such was Hezekiah, king of Judah. It is said that only tw bunches of greens and one pound of meat were brought in and set befor Hezekiah for his daily fare. And Israel spoke disrespectfully of him, saying This one calls himself a king, but Rezin—and the son of Remaliah also—i really a king [for he consumes much gourmet food]: "And they rejoice over Rezin and Remaliah's son"[35] (Isa. 8:6). Of this contrast in kingl behavior it is written *Forasmuch as this people hath refused the waters o Shiloah that go to 'Aṭ,*[36] *and rejoiceth with Rezin and Remaliah's son* (Isa 8:6). How can it be said that the waters of Shiloah went to " 'Aṭ," since Ba Ḳappara stated: We went through all of Scripture, from first to last, bu found no place named " 'Aṭ?" Hence, in its connection with Hezekiah, king of Judah, the word must be explained in a different way. It was he whc instituted for women the practice of immersion after their menstrual periods[37] in a pool of forty *sĕ'ah*,[38] and forty corresponds to the word *lĕ-'at*, this number being the sum of the numerical value of the letters that compose

---

bread and a skin of water, knowing that for the members of his household food and drink would miraculously become plentiful. See Gen. Rabbah 53:13, and Yiṣhaḳ Vartski, *Lĕšon ham-Midrašim* (Jerusalem, 5730/1970), 30–35; and Piska 16.1.

33. Near Jotapata in Galilee.

34. See PR 11:2 (YJS, *18*, 200, n. 14).

35. To speak of nothing else, the dessert served before Pekah, Remaliah's son, king of Samaria, consisted of forty *sĕ'ah* of young pigeons. See Rashi, and B.Sanh 94b.

36. JV: *that go softly*; Hebrew: *lĕ-'aṭ* (spelled *l'ṭ*).

37. Isa. 8:6 is thus read: *The waters of Shiloah which* [*Hezekiah caused to*] *go to pools of cleansing.*

38. A *sĕ'ah* is the equivalent of 2.83 gallons. Forty *sĕ'ah* is the minimum required for such a pool.

ɜ word.[39] [The point is that by instituting immersion for women Hekiah brought sexual purity and restraint to the people of Israel]. Hence ɜ Holy One said apropos of Israel's rejoicing at Rezin's and Remaliah's n's lack of restraint: Is it the greatly gluttonous that you are out to praise? *·hold, the Lord bringeth up . . . the waters of the River, mighty and many, en the king of Assyria, and all his glory; and he shall come up over all his ·annels, and go over all his banks,* [*and will devour you as would a utton*] (Isa. 8:7).

But the belly of the wicked shall want (Prov. 13:25). Such was Mesha ng of Moab, as is said *Now Mesha king of Moab was a noḳeḏ*[40] (2 Kings :4). (What is meant by *noḳeḏ*? A raiser of sheep in large numbers, yet one hose desire for more and more sheep knows no restraint).[41] *But he was nally forced to render unto the king of Israel a hundred thousand fatted ımbs and a hundred thousand wool-bearing rams* (*ibid.*)—[not "the wool f a hundred thousand rams," as the verse might be read], R. Abba bar ahana explained, but rams full-grown and unshorn.[42]

Another comment: *The righteous eateth to the satisfying of his desire* Prov. 13:25). Such were the kings of Israel and the kings of the house of)avid. *But the belly of the wicked shall want* (*ibid.*). These wicked were the ings of the east. [Concerning the amount of meat these kings consumed], ₹. Yudan and R. Huna differ. According to R. Yudan, a hundred sheep and ;oats were served to each king every day. According to R. Huna, a thousand heep and goats were served to each every day.

39. l = 30, ' = 1, ṭ = 9.

40. Professor Saul Lieberman calls attention to the fact that in the Septuagint he word *noḳeḏ* is transliterated but not translated.

41. Professor E. E. Urbach has suggested that the term *r'y* be translated "evil ɜye which knows no restraint." The word is taken here to have two meanings, the ɔne just given as well as "raiser of sheep in large numbers."

[*Noḳeḏ* was a rare and obscure word already in the Septuagint period, and what the Hebrew does, very sensibly, is provide a perfectly well-known synonym for it. (I would suppose the correct reading is *r'y* ending with an apostrophe = *ra'aya*, the apostrophe easily likely to drop out after a *yoḏ*.) I would stick to the Hebrew in the translation, and consign Dr. Urbach's interesting tie with *'ayin ha-ra'* to the note, for the reader's delectation: "What is meant by *noḳeḏ?* A sheepraiser. But he was," etc. L.N.]

42. Professor Baruch Levine helped explain the point of R. Abba bar Kahana's comment. He also called attention to the reference in Gesenius' *Hebrew Grammar* (2d ed., Oxford, 1910, reprint 1960), pp. 423–24, where an explanation for the anomalous form *'elim ṣamer* can be found.

[Since *'ayil* has any number of variant meanings (cf. Gesenius-Brown), R. Abba indicated the precise Greek synonym in this context. *Probata*, according to Liddell-Scott, is used in Attic Greek for small cattle (sheep and goats), and in Ionic and Doric Greek for all four-footed animals, both big and small cattle. L.N.]

In another comment the verse is read *The Righteous One eateth His fill that which is in a man's soul*[43] (Prov. 13:25). Such a Righteous One is t Holy One. The Holy One said to Israel: My children, of all offerings whi you present to Me, I delight to eat only of those with the fragrance [obedience and good deeds], as is said *It is the fragrance which is My ov delight*[44] (Num. 28:2).

3. *In Numbers Thou didst* [*again*] *ordain* (Ps. 119:4). Where did Gc again ordain? In the Book of Numbers. What did He again ordain? *T observe due season*[45] (*ibid.*), words which echo *Ye shall* [*continuall observe to offer unto Me in its due season* (Num. 28:2). Since the passage Exodus 29:38–42 setting forth the ordinance is exactly like the passage Numbers 28:2 that sets it forth, why does Scripture set it forth once and the again [at the time Israel were about to enter the Land]? R. Judah, I Nehemiah, and the Rabbis differ in their answers. According to R. Judah, was because Israel said: In the past, [during our wanderings in the wilde ness], when camp had to be moved from place to place, the continual burn offering could rightly be required at each new site. But now [that we ar about to enter the Land], even as the moving of camp from place to place about to cease, so should the continual burnt offering cease.[46] Therefore th Holy One instructed Moses: Go tell Israel to keep on with the continua burnt offering.

According to R. Nehemiah, [as they were about to enter the Land], th children of Israel took to making light of the continual burnt offering, [say ing, "Since the Land itself makes expiation for our sins,[47] there will be nc

43. The Hebrew word *nfš* may mean either "desire" or "soul."

44. [What the Hebrew says, grammatically, is "of all the offerings which you present to Me, do I enjoy any benefit other than the mere fragrance thereof?" The Hebrew doesn't say, as far as I can see, that God discriminates between sincere and insincere offerings. Hence the following quotation from Num. 28:2 should be cited according to JV. L.N.]

45. By means of a play on *piḳkudim*, "precepts," which can also mean "Numbers," and on *mĕ'oḏ*, "diligently," which may be read *mo'eḏ*, "season," the commentator apparently suggests that Ps. 119:3–4 be rendered as follows: "Though they do no unrighteousness, [though] they walk in His ways, yet in Thy Numbers Thou didst [again] ordain to observe [that which is to be offered daily in its] due season"—the daily round of offerings brought in a spirit of adoration. JV: *Yea, they do no unrighteousness; they walk in His ways. Thou hast ordained Thy precepts (piḳkuḏeḳa) that we should observe them diligently (mĕ'oḏ).*

46. Continuing adoration of God was unnecessary. A one-time offering in the Temple in Jerusalem should be sufficient for the God of the permanent site. See *Zayiṯ ra'anan* on Yalḳuṭ, *Pinḥas*, 776–77.

47. *His Land shall make expiation for His people* (Deut. 32:43). See PR 1:6 (YJS, *18*, 45).

rther need for burnt offerings]."[48] Therefore the Holy One said to [oses: Go tell Israel not to make light of the continual burnt offering.[49]

According to the Rabbis, the preceding passage in Exodus enjoins udy;[50] this passage enjoins performance.[51]

According to R. Aḥa, in the name of R. Ḥanina bar Papa, the ordinance as repeated in order that Israel might not say: In the past, [before the emple was destroyed], we used to bring offerings and so we concerned urselves with study of the pertinent ordinances; but now, since we do not ring offerings, why concern ourselves with such study? The Holy One said) them: When you concern yourselves with such study, it is as though you ring offerings.

In this connection, R. Ḥuna said two things. R. Ḥuna first said: The exiles vill be gathered in only through the merit of studying the entire corpus of the Mishnah.[52] And the proof? The verse *Yea, if among the nations they engage n oral learning,*[53] *I will forthwith gather them up* (Hos. 8:10).

R. Ḥuna then said another thing: *From the rising of the sun even unto the going down of the same My name is great among the nations; and in every lace offerings are presented unto My name, even pure oblations* (Mal. :11). But [since sacrifices were offered only in the Land of Israel], how could there have been an oblation to God in Babylonia? What the Holy One meant was: Since you are engaged in the study of the pertinent ordinances, it s as though you bring oblations.

But Samuel cited the verse *And if they be ashamed of all that they have done, make known unto them the form of the House, and the fashion*

48. The words "saying, Since the Land itself . . . no further need for burnt offerings" are interpolated on the basis of the comment in *Zayit ra'anan* on Yalkuṭ, *Pinḥas.*

49. For, regardless of the Land's sanctity, the continuing adoration of God symbolized by the daily burnt offering is required. On *mglglym* in the sense of "make light of," or "ridicule," see H. Yalon in *Tarbiṣ, 6* (1935), 228.

50. There is a theory that no offerings were brought in the wilderness. See Ibn Ezra on Num. 28:6; and Sif Num. 67.

[In such a context, I would suppose *lĕtalmud* means rather "formulates the rule" for future observance. L.N.]

51. In Exodus Scripture merely says, *This is that which thou shalt offer*, implying the possibility of postponing action. In Numbers, however, Scripture implies that obedience is to be immediate: *Command . . . Israel and say unto them . . . Ye shall observe to offer unto Me.* See Sif Num. 142.

52. Those parts which have practical use as well as those which have not. See David Luria on Lev. Rabbah 7:3.

53. In Biblical Hebrew and often in Rabbinic Hebrew the word *ytnw* from *tnh* (which, according to EV, here means "hire") sometimes means "recount," "rehearse," "learn, or teach, by word of mouth." See Judg. 5:11, and Ps. 8:2 (cf. B.BB 8a).

thereof, and the goings out thereof, and the comings in thereof, and all th forms thereof . . . and write it in their sight; that they may keep the who form thereof (Ezek. 43:11). But was there at that time a form of the Hou of God? The Holy One replied: When you concern yourselves with the for of the House, it is as though you build the House.

R. Jose said: Why do we have young children begin their study with th Book of Leviticus?[54] We should, instead, have them begin with Genesis. Th Holy One replied: As sacrifices are pure, so young children are pure; le the pure come and begin by occupying themselves with study of things that ar pure.[55]

R. Abba bar Kahana and R. Ḥanin, both of them, said in the name of R Azariah of Kefar Ḥiṭṭaya:[56] Consider the parable of a king who had tw cooks. The first cooked a dish for him, and he ate it and it pleased him. Th second cooked another dish for him, and he ate it and it pleased him. But w do not know directly which pleased him more. We may infer, however, tha since the king enjoined the second cook, saying to him, "Prepare the sam dish for me," the dish of the second pleased him more. Even so Noal brought an offering and the Holy One was pleased, as is said *And the Lor smelled the sweet savor* (Gen. 8:21). Israel also brought an offering, and i also pleased the Holy One, but we do not know directly which offerin pleased Him more. Since He enjoined Israel, however, saying to them: *My food . . . of a sweet savor unto Me, shall ye observe to offer unto Me in its due season* (Num. 28:2), we know that Israel's offering pleased Him more.

R. Abin said two things. R. Abin first said: Consider a parable of a king reclining upon his dining couch. They brought him the first dish, he ate it, and it pleased him; then they brought him the second dish which he ate, and it also pleased him, pleased him so much that he licked the plate clean. Hence *I offer unto Thee burnt offerings,* [*even their*] *remnants*[57] [pleasing to Thee] (Ps. 66:15), as the remnants of the king's second dish were so pleasing to him that he licked the plate clean.

R. Abin said another thing: Consider a parable of a king who was journeying along the highway. He came to the first rest station, where he ate and drank; to the second station, where he not only ate and drank but also spent

54. Literally "The Torah of Priests."

55. Unlike Genesis which speaks of the guile of the serpent, of Cain's slaying of Abel, and of Lamech's two wives, the Book of Leviticus reads: *If anyone sin, and commit a trespass,* etc. (Lev. 5:30). See Meir Friedmann in *Beṯ Talmuḏ*, *1*, 265.

56. Hattin, near Tiberias.

57. JV: *I will offer unto Thee burnt offerings of fatlings* (*mḥym*). But apparently the commentator finds inadmissible the emphasis on "fatlings," and so he associates *mḥym* with *mḥh*, "wipe clean"—hence, "remnants," which in a burnt offering are also consumed on the altar.

he night. [In regard to the burnt offering] God did likewise. Else why would the Torah make repeated reference to the burnt offering, saying *Aaron's sons shall make the fat of the peace offerings] smoke on the altar upon the burnt offering* (Lev. 3:5); *This is the law of the burnt offering, it is the burnt offering on its burning place upon the altar all night unto the morning* (Lev. 6:2)? By such lingering repetition the Torah teaches that the burnt offering is to be given over wholly to the flames [which will spend the entire night consuming it].[58]

4. Concerning the meaning of *kĕḇaśim*, "he-lambs" (Num. 28:3), the disciples of Shammai and the disciples of Hillel differ. The disciples of Shammai read *kĕḇaśim* as though written *kabbašim*, "they that put out of sight."[59] That is, the daily offering of the lambs brings it about that God puts Israel's iniquities out of sight, as the verse tells us, *He will turn again and have compassion upon us; He will put our iniquities out of sight* (*yiḵboš*) (Micah 7:19). But the disciples of Hillel said:[60] The phrase *kĕḇaśim bĕne šanah*, "he-lambs of the first year" (Num. 28:3), is to be understood as though written *kabbasim bĕne šanah*, "they that cleanse the things which are of many a year." That is, the daily offerings cleanse the sins of Israel, as is said *Though your sins be as of many a year,*[61] *they shall be as white as snow* (Isa. 1:18). And Ben Azzai said: The phrase *kĕḇaśim bĕne šanah* means that they cleanse the sins of the people of Israel and make them as innocent as an infant in its first year.

The phrase *two with the day* [in the verse *he-lambs . . . two with the day for a continual burnt offering* (Num. 28:3) signifies that the two he-lambs are to be offered respectively on the northeast and southwest corners of the altar] in keeping with the sun's course during the day.[62]

[In another comment the phrase *two with the day* is read] *two for the day*: Each lamb will serve as an advocate for Israel on *the* day, [the Day of Judgment that burneth as a furnace]: *They shall be Mine, saith the Lord of hosts, on the day that I do this, even Mine own treasure; and I will spare them, as a man spareth his own son that serveth him* (Mal. 3:17).

Two for the day: The two he-lambs are to be offered in behalf of the

58. God is thus understood as spending the entire night with the children of Israel.

59. Since the passage in Numbers is a repetition of what had already been set down in Exodus, it is considered "available" for allegorical interpretation.

60. Apparently reasoning that whatever is put out of sight may come into sight again.

61. EV: *scarlet.* But *šanim* can also mean "years." See B.Shab 89b.

62. For *gll* in the sense of "course," see Job 20:7 and Ibn Janah, *Sefer haš-šorašim* (Berlin, 1893), p. 92; "day" can have the meaning of "sun." See Sanh 10:3. For interpolated words see Sif Num. 142. [A more literal interpretation is "for the sake of the day," that is, "to atone for the sins committed during the day." L.N.]

children of Israel [from day to day] and no more than two for any particular day.[63]

Two for the day. It is to be determined in advance[64] which lamb is to be slaughtered in the morning and which is to be slaughtered in the evening.

The burnt offering is for continuing [intercession][65] (Num. 28:6). R. Judah bar R. Simon said: No man who lodged in Jerusalem for a full day could stay possessed of his sin. How so? The morning offering made expiation for transgressions committed in the nighttime; and the offering at dusk made expiation for transgressions committed in the daytime. Hence, no matter what, no man who lodged in Jerusalem for a full day could stay possessed of his sin. And the proof from Scripture? *Righteous lodged in her* (Isa. 1:21).[66]

R. Judah bar R. Simon said in the name of R. Johanan: From the Divine Power, Moses heard three commandments which startled him and took him aback. First, when He decreed: *Let them make Me the Sanctuary, and I shall dwell among them* (Exod. 25:8), Moses said bluntly to the Holy One: Master of universes, "Behold, not even heaven and the heaven of the heavens can contain Thee" (1 Kings 8:27), and yet Thou sayest: *Let them make Me the Sanctuary.* Thereupon the Holy One reassured Moses: Moses, it is not as thou thinkest; though the Sanctuary is to be only twenty boards wide in the north and twenty boards wide in the south and eight wide in the west, yet I shall go down to the earth below and shrink My presence into their midst, as is said *And there I will meet with thee* (Exod. 25:22).

Second, [when the children of Israel sinned, and God commanded]: *They shall give every man a ransom for his soul* (Exod. 30:12), Moses asked: Master of universes, who can give a ransom for his soul? *No man can by any means redeem his brother . . . for too costly is the redemption of men's souls* (Ps. 49:8–9). The Holy One replied: Redemption of the soul is not reckoned as thou thinkest! But *This they shall give* (Exod. 30:13)—[a half-shekel]—as if to say, "They need give only as much as this," and then, according to R. Meir, the Holy One brought forth from under His throne of glory something like a coin of fire and showed it to Moses and said to him:

63. So that if the burnt offerings have been omitted on any day the omission cannot be made up on a subsequent day.

64. There were never to be less than six lambs approved for the offering in the Chamber of Lambs of the Sanctuary, and they were to be available four days before being offered (Maimonides' Code, VIII, VI, i, 9 [YJS, *12*, 253–54]). The four days were prescribed by analogy with the Paschal lamb (Sif Num. 142).

65. A sin offering is intercessory, whereas a burnt offering is a gift—a purely devotional act. Still, when the burnt offering alone is presented, it also has intercessory power. See Ginzberg, *CPT*, *3*, 42.

66. See PR 15:24, where the commentator reads the verse "He who lodged in her was made righteous." See also Piska 5.17.

This[67] *they shall give*—as though the half-shekel Israel give for their ransom were a burning reminder of their sinning in the past and a fiery warning against their sinning in the future.[68]

And third, when He said: *My food . . . of a sweet savor unto Me, shall ye observe to offer unto Me in its due season* (Num. 28:2), Moses asked: Master of universes, [if I were to bring all the beasts of the earth, would they be sufficient for a single offering? Or] all the trees of the world—would they be sufficient for one altar fire? For it is written *Lebanon is not sufficient for an altar fire, nor the beasts thereof sufficient for burnt offerings* (Isa. 40:16). The Holy One reassured Moses: It is not as thou thinkest. But *he-lambs of the first year without blemish, two day by day* (Num. 28:3) suffice. Not even two at a time; but one *in the morning, and the other lamb shalt thou offer at dusk* (Num. 28:4).

(R. Huna said in the name of Rab: The verse *Almighty, we have not found Thee out,*[69] *O Great One in strength* [Job 37:23] means that we cannot find out the full extent of the might of the Holy One, for the Holy One makes demands upon Israel not commensurate with His majesty [but commensurate with Israel's capacity]).

And when Moses heard this he began congratulating Israel, saying: *Happy is the people that is in such a case, yea, happy is the people whose God is the Lord* (Ps. 144:15).[70]

67. The verse should have read "A half-shekel they shall give" (Exod. 30:13), the demonstrative *this* at the verse's beginning being unnecessary. Hence R. Meir assumes that in saying *this,* God actually pointed to a coin of fire.

68. The words "as though the half-shekel Israel give . . . against their sinning in the future" paraphrase the literal "something like this they are to give." R. Meir apparently takes the word *zeh,* "this," in Exod. 30:13, as a derivative of the root *'z'*, "to fire, to make hot" (Dan. 3:19, 22). Cf. MTeh 68:5, and PR 10:12 (YJS, *18*, 190, n. 86).

69. MT: *whom we cannot find out.*

70. "though the Sanctuary is to be only twenty boards wide in the north . . . whose God is the Lord"—O_1. O reads: "The rest of the passage is as in *Ki tiśśa'*, the only difference being that the other passage ends with *They shall give every man a ransom for his soul* (Exod. 30:12); whereas this one ends with *My food . . . of a sweet savor unto Me* (Num. 28:2)." Cf. Piska 2.10.

PISKA 7

SUMMARY

God's justice on the Passover midnight

Since only the Lord can know the exact instant of midnight, since only He can distinguish between the drop of sperm from which a first-born is conceived and the drop of sperm from which a subsequent offspring is conceived, Scripture says that *At midnight* THE LORD *smote all the first-born* (Exod. 12:29) (Secs. 1–2). Because Moses predicted that at midnight God would go out into the midst of Egypt, God, whose wont it is to confirm the word of His servants, acted precisely at midnight (Sec. 3).

It was at midnight, therefore, that David would rise to occupy himself with Torah and to thank God for the judgments brought at Passover's midnight upon the Pharaoh who seized Sarah. David would also thank God for His judgments upon the Moabites and the Ammonites; thank Him for His mercies in Egypt to Israel's forebears; and finally thank Him for Boaz' restraining his desire for Ruth, since if he had not restrained himself, the seed of David might have been accursed (Sec. 4).

It was on a Passover midnight also that Abraham pursued the four kings who had invaded the land of Canaan and defeated them. Indeed, God went forth at midnight to war in behalf of Israel in Egypt as a reward to Abraham for his boldness in going to war on the same midnight many years before. Contradictory passages seeming to indicate that during the day the princely counterpart of Egypt in heaven was felled and the first-born of Egypt died, are reconciled (Sec. 5).

The term "first-born" is interpreted as having applied to children first born to males as well as to children first-born of females. The term is also taken to have applied to heads of households and to the first-born of maidservants. The term applied even to the statues of first-born who had died, and so the statues were smashed. It applied even to the first-born of cattle, worshiped by the Egyptians, and so the cattle died. Sensing the imminence of disaster, the first-born of the Egyptians pleaded with their fathers and with Pharaoh to let the Hebrews go. At the denial of their plea, the first-born turned upon their fathers and slew sixty myriads of them. The only first-born who did not die was Pharaoh's daughter, Bithiah (Secs. 6–9).

In His exercise of justice God puts off taking human life, as is seen from the way He proceeded against Job and against Mahlon and Chilion, and as is seen also from the plagues which He first brings upon the property of Israelites before inflicting them upon the Israelites themselves. In Egypt also,

God first took toll of the Egyptians' goods and property and only afterwards smote their first-born (Sec. 10).

The plagues in Egypt followed military tactics: water conduits were shut off, arrows shot, legions mustered, sources of food cut off, burning stuff flung, catapults set up, scalers of walls mobilized, imprisonment and executions ordered. Punishments over and above those visited upon Egypt will in the time-to-come be visited upon Edom (Rome) (Sec. 11): Darkness was called upon to serve in Egypt; whereas dark chaos and emptiness will be called into service in Rome. But upon Israel, who accepted the Torah that was given out of darkness over Sinai, upon them God's glory shall be seen (Sec. 12).

PISKA 7

And it came to pass at midnight, that the Lord smote all the first-born in the land of Egypt (Exod. 12:29).[1]

1. R. Tanḥum of Jaffa, in the name of R. Nunya of Caesarea, began his discourse by citing the verse *When I pondered how I might apprehend this, it proved too difficult for me* (Ps. 73:16). By these words David meant that no creature could be so knowing as to apprehend the exact instant of midnight—only the Holy One could. For the likes of me, said David, it is too difficult. And so because no creature can be so knowing as to apprehend the exact instant of midnight—only the Holy One can—therefore Scripture says, *And it came to pass [precisely] at midnight that* THE LORD *smote*.

2. R. Aḥa began his discourse by citing the verse *I am the Lord, that is My name; and My glory I do not give to a delayed one,*[2] *neither My renown to things hewn out* (Isa. 42:8). *I am the Lord, that is My name* (*ibid.*) means, according to R. Aḥa, that the Holy One said: I am the Lord, that is My name, the name which Adam called Me; that is My name, the name I have consented to be called by; that is My name which I have consented to be called by when I am with the ministering angels. *And My glory I do not give to a delayed one* (*ibid.*) means, according to R. Menaḥema citing R. Abin, that God did not give [any kind of independent power] to the demons, [whose creation was delayed to the end of the sixth day of creation].[3]

But R. Nehemiah, citing R. Mani, [read the end of the verse in Isaiah *And My glory I do not give to another*, and] understood by it that God was saying: No other being in the world is able to distinguish between the seed of a first birth and the seed which is not that of a first birth—only the Holy One can so distinguish. For my part, said Moses, making a distinction of this kind is utterly beyond me. And because, by the same token, no other being can be so knowing as to apprehend the exact instant of midnight—only the Holy

1. Exod. 12:21–51 is the lesson in Scripture on the first day of Passover. According to Professor Joseph Heinemann, Ezra Fleischer found evidence that in some localities in the Land of Israel, Exod. 12:21–51 was read on *Šabbaṯ hag-gaḏol*.

2. EV: *another*; but in this comment the word *'ḥr* is apparently rendered in the sense of "delay."

Leon Nemoy suggests, however, that *'hr* refers not to delay in the creation of demons, but rather to their nature—they are the "other ones" who have gone astray from goodness and become evil.

3. See Ab 5:6. For the preternatural power of demons, see MTeh 78:12.

One can—therefore Scripture says, *And it came to pass* [*precisely*] *at midnight, that* THE LORD *smote all the first-born.*

3. *It is He that confirmeth the word of His servant, and performeth the counsel of His messengers, each of whom says of Jerusalem: "She shall be inhabited"; and of the cities of Judah: "They shall be rebuilt, and I will raise up the waste places thereof"* (Isa. 44:26). R. Berechiah said in the name of R. Levi: Since we know of an instance in which God confirmed the word of a servant of His,[4] is it not certain that He will [confirm the word] and *perform the counsel of His* [*many*] *messengers, each of whom says of Jerusalem: "She shall be inhabited"; and of the cities of Judah: "They shall be rebuilt"?* The instance [R. Berechiah had in mind] was God's confirmation of the word of His angelic servant who appeared from on high to Jacob our father and said to him: *"What is thy name?" And he replied "Jacob." And he said: "Thy name shall be called no more Jacob, but Israel"* (Gen. 32:28–29). Whereupon the Holy One from on high appeared to Jacob our father and confirmed the word of the angelic servant: *God said to Jacob, "Thy name shall not be called any more Jacob, but Israel shall be thy name"* (Gen. 35:10). Hence all the more certain is it that Jerusalem will be rebuilt, for all prophetic messengers predict that it will be rebuilt, [and God will confirm their words].

Another comment: In the phrase *confirmeth the word of His servant* (Isa. 44:26), the word of Moses, [he whom God called] "My servant Moses" (Num. 12:7), is meant; and in the words *performeth the counsel of His messengers*, Moses is again referred to, [for it said of him that the Lord] "sent a messenger and brought us forth out of Egypt" (Num. 20:16). Thus the Holy One said to Moses: Go tell them, tell Israel, *I will go through the land of Egypt in that night* (Exod. 12:12). And Moses went, but specified an exact time, saying to Israel: *Thus saith the Lord: At the time of*[5] *midnight will I go out into the midst of Egypt* (Exod. 11:4). Whereupon the Holy One said to Himself: I declared My trust in Moses long ago when I said of him: *He is trusted in all My house* (Num. 12:7). Shall My servant Moses be made out to be a liar? Since Moses said *At the time of midnight*, I will act *at midnight*[6] (Exod. 12:29). Hence *And it came to pass* [*precisely*] *at midnight* (*ibid.*).

4. *At midnight I will rise to give thanks unto Thee because of Thy judgments, of Thy mercy*[7] (Ps. 119:62). In regard to this verse, R. Phinehas

4. R. Berechiah thus reads the verse in Isaiah as follows: *He that confirmeth the word of His servant will surely perform*, etc.

5. So Rashi; EV: *about.*

6. Cf. PR 3:1.

7. Since the word *mšpṭ* means "judgment" and the word *ṣdḳ*, "mercy," the commentator finds the two notions together inconsistent, and the phrase an oxymoron; and so instead of rendering it "Thy judgments of mercy" he divides the

said in the name of R. Eleazar bar R. Menahem: What did David use to do? He used to take a psaltery and a harp, put them at the head of his couch, and rising at midnight would play upon them. Thereupon the studious in Israel, upon hearing the sound of David's playing, used to say: "If David, the king, occupies himself [at midnight] with Torah, so much the more should we." And so it turned out that all in Israel occupied themselves with Torah.

R. Levi said: A window to the north side was left open above David's couch, and over against the window was hung the harp. When the north wind came up at midnight it blew through the strings, and the harp then played of itself. Hence the text *when [the instrument] played* (2 Kings 3:15). Note that the text does not say "when the minstrel played," but *when the instrument played*, meaning that the harp played of itself.[8] Thereat all in Israel, upon hearing David's voice [accompanying the harp], used to say: If David, the king, so occupies himself, all the more should we. And so it turned out that all in Israel occupied themselves with Torah.

It was of this rising at midnight that David sang: *Awake, my glory; awake, psaltery and harp; I will awake the dawn* (Ps. 57:9), as if to say: Let my glory—the glory of a king—awake for the sake of my Maker's glory, for my glory is nothing at all before my Maker's glory. *I will awake the dawn*: that is, "I will awake the dawn, the dawn shall not awake me." For his Inclination to evil, inciting David, would say to him: "David! It is the imperious way of kings to let the dawn awake them. Yet thou declarest *I will awake the dawn.* It is the imperious way of kings to sleep three hours into the day.[9] Yet thou sayest humbly *At midnight I will rise to thank Thee because of the judgments, because of Thy mercy*" (Ps. 119:62). What did David mean by *because of the judgments, because of Thy mercy*? He meant: Because of the judgments Thou didst bring upon the wicked Pharaoh and because of the mercy Thou didst show to my grandmother Sarah, as is said *And the Lord plagued Pharaoh . . . with great plagues because of Sarai, Abram's wife* (Gen. 12:17).[10]

Or, by *because of the judgments, because of Thy mercy*, David meant: Because of the judgments which Thou didst bring upon certain nations of the earth, [such as the Ammonites and the Moabites[11]]; and because of the

phrase into its constituents, and renders it "Thy judgments, Thy mercy." JV: *Thy righteous ordinances.*

8. Following a marginal correction cited by Dr. Mandelbaum, Leon Nemoy prefers to translate 2 Kings 3:15 "*it was as if the minstrel played,*" the words "as if" implying that the harp played of itself.

9. Till nine o'clock in the morning. See Ber 1:2.

10. See PR 15:23. "The view that many important events in the history of the Patriarchs and that of Israel took place during the first night of Passover, is very old and is a favorite topic with Paitanim." See Ginzberg, *Legends*, 5, 221, n. 76.

11. Ruth Rabbah 6:1 reads "judgments which Thou didst bring upon the

mercy which Thou didst show to my grandfather [Boaz] and to my grandmother [Ruth]. Had Boaz, [giving in to his sexual desire], permitted himself to slip into her as she lay at his feet, whence would I have had my origin?[12] Instead Thou didst put a blessing into his heart so that, [restraining his sexual desire], he said: *Blessed be thou of the Lord, my daughter* (Ruth 3:10).

Or, by *because of the judgments*, etc. (Ps. 119:62), David meant: Because of the judgments which Thou didst bring upon the Egyptians in Egypt; and because of the mercy Thou didst show our fathers in Egypt at a time when they had not the merit of obedience to Thy various commandments, obedience whereby they might have won redemption; for at that time they were obedient to only two of Thy commands,[13] those concerned with the blood of Passover and the blood of circumcision. Of His mercy then, it is written *When I passed by thee, and saw thee wallowing in thy blood, I said unto thee: In thy bloods,*[14] *live* (Ezek. 16:6)—through thy bloods, that is, through the blood of the Passover lamb and the blood of circumcision.

5. [*And it came to pass in the* (*precise*) *middle of the night*, etc. (Exod. 12:29)]. R. Simeon ben Yoḥai taught: Moses did not know the exact duration of an *'et̲*, of a *rega'*, or a *zěman*[15] in the night. Therefore he said *about midnight* (Exod. 11:4). But the Holy One knows the exact duration of an *'et̲*, of a *rega'*, or of a *zěman* in the night. Therefore with hairbreadth precision He could smite the first-born at the very middle of the night.

Ammonites and the Moabites," who could not be admitted into the community of the Lord (Deut. 23:4). Here there may be an allusion to the incestuous origin of the Ammonites and Moabites; the two daughters of Lot, thinking that the world had come to an end, contrived through drink to make their father have intercourse with them (see Gen. 19:31 ff., and PR 42:3). In a sense, Ruth's stratagem was not dissimilar. Boaz, having eaten and drunk, was taking rest by a pile of sheaves; then Ruth crept near, turned back the end of Boaz' mantle, and lay down (Ruth 3:7). But for God's mercy, as the commentator goes on to say, the outcome for Ruth's progeny might have been as fateful as it was for the progeny of the daughters of Lot.

12. Such an unhallowed union between Boaz, a man of eighty, and Ruth, a woman of forty, might have brought no progeny at all; or the seed might have been accursed seed like that of the Ammonites and Moabites.

13. See Piska 5.6, and PR 15:17. At one time the Hebrews in Egypt worshiped idols, filled the theaters and circuses of the land, and behaved much like the Egyptians (Tanḥuma B, 2, 4; and Ginzberg, *Legends*, 5, 395).

14. JV: *blood*; the Hebrew word, however, is in the plural, which permits the ensuing comment.

15. All these are measures of time, each 1/24th of the one preceding. An *'et̲* is 1/24th part of an *'onah* which is 1/24th part of an hour; a *rega'* is 1/24th of an *'et̲*, a *zěman* is 1/24th of a *rega'*. See Tos Ber 1:1, ed. Lieberman; *Piske tosafot̲*, AZ 1:4; and H. Y. Borenstein, in *hat-Těḳufah*, 6, 270. In his *CPT* (*1*, 59), Ginz-

[Another comment on an event which took place on the same midnight many years before, when *The night was divided* (for Abraham and his servants while they were pursuing the marauding kings) (Gen. 14:15)]. How did the division of that night come about?[16] R. Benjamin bar Japheth said in the name of R. Johanan: It just happened that way. But the Rabbis said: Its Creator divided it, for in the light of the verse *And it came to pass at the time of [God's] dividing of the night* (Exod. 12:29), the verse in Genesis is to be read not *"The night was divided,"* etc., but *He divided the night* [for Abraham and his servants], etc. (Gen. 14:15).[17] According to R. Tanḥuma, the Holy One said: Your father Abraham went forth to war at midnight; I, with his sons, will likewise go forth to war at midnight.[18] And according to the Rabbis, the Holy One said: Your father went forth with Me from nightfall until midnight; and I will go forth with his sons from midnight until dawn.

[In seeking to reconcile the statement that *At midnight . . . the Lord smote all the first-born in the land of Egypt* (Exod. 12:29) with the contradictory statement *On the day that I smote all the first-born in the land of Egypt* (Num. 3:13)], R. Johanan construed the latter verse as asserting that it was the princely counterpart of Egypt in heaven—[symbolic of Egypt's pride in her power as a nation]—who was smitten in the daytime [as distinguished from the Egyptians on earth who were smitten at night]. And the proof? The verse *At Tehaphnehes also the day shall withdraw itself, when I shall break there the yokes of Egypt, and the pride of her power shall cease in her*, etc. (Ezek 30:18).[19] In further proof [that *on the day* refers

---

berg maintains that the division of the hour into diminishing time units of twenty-fourths is not found among other peoples.

16. Cf. Lev. Rabbah 6:5 (M, p. 138 and notes thereto). In a comment on *And Moses took half the blood* (Exod. 24:6) a similar question is asked: How did the division of the blood come about? How, that is, could a mortal make such an exact division?

17. In the comment of the Rabbis *wyḥlḳ* is vocalized not *wayyĕḥaleḳ*, "and was divided," but *wayyaḥălok*, "and He divided."

18. Abraham's fight against the four nations is understood as prefiguring Israel's age-old battle against the four Kingdoms, Egypt, Babylon, Greece, and Rome.

19. The translation follows Friedmann's interpretation in PRF 17, note 33. According to David Luria, however, R. Johanan asks a question: Since Egypt is described as falling during the day, what can be meant by the statement that at midnight the first-born were smitten? This question is answered in keeping with R. Johanan ben Zakkai's teaching that "day" can be taken as a general term, including in its reference the hours of darkness as well as hours of light; and in keeping with R. Joshua's teaching that for God night and day are one and the same.

to the smiting of Egypt's pride in her power as a nation], R. Johanan cited another verse [which likewise says of the time-to-come] *In that day there shall be five cities in the land of Egypt that speak the language of Canaan, and swear to the Lord of hosts; one shall be the city of Heres*[20] (Isa. 19:18)—[a name which signifies either the "city of sherds" or "city of the sun"]. (By what names are the five cities known now? R. Hilkiah said in the name of R. Simon: No is Alexandria; Noph is Memphis; Tehaphnehes[21] is Hupianas; the "city of sherds" is Ostracena;[22] and the "city of the sun" is Heliopolis.)

R. Johanan ben Zakkai explained away the apparent contradiction, saying: We find in Scripture that the day and the night together are spoken of as a day, as is said *And there was evening and there was morning, one day*[23] (Gen. 1:5).

R. Joshua bar R. Nehemiah resolved the apparent contradiction on the basis of the following verse: *Even the darkness is not too dark for Thee; the night shineth as the day; the darkness is even as the light* (Ps. 139:12). The verse intimates that God is saying: The darkness, which is the same as light to Me, is night only so far as its use to mortals is concerned.

Another comment: In one place in Scripture it is written *And it came to pass at midnight that the Lord smote all the first-born in the land of Egypt* (Exod. 12:29); but elsewhere Scripture says, *On the day that I smote all the first-born in the land of Egypt* (Num. 8:17),[24] a verse which leads one to suppose that the first-born of Egypt died during the daytime. How are the two verses to be reconciled? As follows: At nightfall the first-born were smitten with a death-stroke, so that they were in convulsions throughout the night and died on the following day. And the proof? Scripture does not say, "We are all dead men," but *We are all dying men* (Exod. 12:33), that is, dying hour by hour.

As for the repetition of the verse *On the day that I smote all the first-born in the land of Egypt* (Num. 8:17) in the verse *On the day that I smote all the first-born in the land of Egypt I hallowed unto Me all the first-born in Israel* (Num. 3:13), you may say that God meant: On the day that the first-

20. JV: *destruction*. But the word can also mean "sun."

21. No, Noph, and Tehaphnehes are mentioned in Ezek. 30:13, 14, and 18.

22. So Krauss, *Lehnwörter*, p. 414. Apparently a play on *ḥeres* in the sense of "sherd."

23. Accordingly, even an incident which took place in the night could be spoken of as having occurred on the day, [that is, the twenty-four hours beginning with the sunset through the following day, to the next sunset. L.N.]

24. "Another comment . . . *the land of Egypt*"—parallel in Yalḳuṭ, *Bĕha'alotĕḳa*, 720, where, however, the verse from Num. is cited before the verse from Exod.

born of Egypt died, that was the day on which I hallowed unto Me all the first-born [of Israel to minister as My priests].[25]

6/9. *The Lord smote all the first-born in the land of Egypt* (Exod. 12:29)—"the first-born" signifying every kind of first-born: a man's first-born or a woman's first-born, whether the first-born was a male or the first-born was a female. How so? If one man had cohabited with ten women and each of them had had a son by him, then all of the sons were considered the women's first-born; or if ten men had cohabited with one woman and she had had a son by each of the men, then all of the sons were considered the men's first-born.

Now suppose that in a household there was no first-born, belonging either to a man or a woman, how would then the verse *There was not a house where there was not one dead* (Exod. 12:30) be justified? R. Abba bar Aḥa explained: The one who had charge of the household was smitten, such a one as is referred to in the verse *Shimri the one in charge—for though he was not the first-born, yet his father put him in charge* (1 Chron. 26:10).

[Not only was the one in charge smitten]. It is taught in the name of R. Nathan: There was a custom in an Egyptian household that when a first-born died, a statue of him was wrought for the house he had lived in. Hence, on the day the Lord smote the first-born, this statue, too, was smashed, broken up into fragments, and scattered. And for the father of the dead first-born, the statue's destruction was as grievous as though he had buried his first-born that very day.[26]

R. Yudan went further, saying: Since the Egyptians buried their dead inside their houses, [on the day the first-born were smitten], dogs, entering through sewer pipes,[27] dragged from among the dead the bodies of the first-born and sported grotesquely with them. For the fathers of the dead first-born, the dogs' sport was as grievous as though they had buried their first-born that very day.

25. That is, they were hallowed on that day; but first-born born after that day were not hallowed again during their sojourn in the wilderness. Whether during their sojourn in the wilderness, subsequently born first-born were hallowed or not, is a controversy between R. Johanan and Resh Laḳish, the latter holding that in the wilderness there was no hallowing of first-born. See B.Bek̠ 4b and 5a. See also Yalḳuṭ Num. 8:17, and MhG Num., pp. 184–85.

26. According to Egyptian belief, a dead man "retained some form of life as long as his image existed." The Egyptian father, therefore, regarded the destruction of the first-born's statue as his son's second death. See Saul Lieberman in "After Life in Early Rabbinic Literature," *Harry Austryn Wolfson Jubilee Volume* (Jerusalem, 1965), 2, 523, n. 72.

27. The word *kwk*, "sepulchral niche," is emended to read *byb*, "sewer-pipe," which is the reading in O_1 and in the parallel account in Mĕk̠ilta de-R. Simeon, ed. Epstein-Melamed, p. 29; see also, Mĕk̠ilta de-R. Ishmael, ed. Horovitz-Rabin, p. 44, n. 12.

At midnight . . . the Lord smote all the first-born . . . from the first-born of Pharaoh that was to sit on his throne[28] (Exod. 12:29). From this verse it is assumed that Pharaoh himself was a first-born.

All the first-born gathered around their fathers and pleaded with them: "Now that Moses has said *All the first-born in the land of Egypt shall die* (Exod. 11:5) and all that he had predicted heretofore concerning the Egyptian people has befallen them, we must bestir ourselves and get these Hebrews out of our midst,[29] else the Egyptian people will die." The fathers replied: "Each one of us has ten sons: let one of them die, just so that the Hebrews be not permitted to get out."[30] The first-born then said: "There is but one way to settle the matter: let us go to Pharaoh, himself a first-born, who may take pity upon himself and let these Hebrews get out of our midst."

They went to Pharaoh and said to him: "Since Moses has said *All the first-born . . . shall die* and since all that he had predicted heretofore concerning the Egyptian people has befallen them, rise up and let these Hebrews get out of our midst, else the Egyptian people will die."

But Pharaoh said [to his servants]: "Get going and beat these poltroons until they are humpbacked"; and to the first-born he said: "I have sworn: 'My life or the lives of the Hebrews!' And you dare speak thus!"

At once the first-born went out and slew sixty myriads of their fathers. Of this it is written *To Him that smote Egypt with their first-born* (Ps. 136:10). Scripture does not say here "To Him that smote the first-born of Egypt," but says, *To Him that smote Egypt with their first-born*, which is to say, it was the first-born of Egypt that slew sixty myriads of their fathers.

R. Abun said in the name of R. Judah ben Pazzi: Bithiah the daughter of Pharaoh was a first-born. By what merit did she escape death? Through the merit of Moses' prayer for her. Of her it is written "She perceived that [Moses], who was called a goodly child,[31] was a shield, and that therefore her lamp—her soul—had not gone out by night"[32] (Prov. 31:18). Since the

28. The words *that was to sit on his throne* are unnecessary, according to the commentator, unless construed as indicating that every Pharaoh had to be a first-born. The Pharaoh of the exodus, however, though first-born, did survive, in keeping with the purpose stated in the verse *But in very deed for this cause have I made thee to stand, to show thee My power, and that My name may be declared throughout all the earth* (Exod. 9:16). Cf. Mek, *1*, 97, 99–100; and MhG Exod., p. 207.

29. "out of our midst"—O_1; O: "out of your midst."

30. Here Yalkuṭ, which has *ypḳwn* is followed. As the text stands, it might be translated "just so [freedom] shall not be given to the Hebrews."

31. Cf. Exod. 2:2.

32. JV: *She perceiveth that her merchandise is good; her lamp goeth not out by night.* See Exod. Rabbah 18:3. The word *sḥrh*, usually rendered "her merchandise," may also be understood as "shield."

word for "night" is spelled here not, as is customary, *laylah*, but *layil*, the verse is to be read in the light of another verse where *layil* is also exceptionally used. This other verse, *It was a night* (*layil*) *of watching unto the Lord* (Exod. 12:42), refers to the night when the first-born of Egypt were smitten. [Hence it is assumed that on this night Bithiah's lamp did not go out—that is, her life was spared].[33]

Even unto the first-born of the maidservant that is behind the mill (Exod. 11:5). R. Huna and R. Aḥa [taught] in the name of R. Eleazar ben R. Jose the Galilean: Smitten even were the first-born of Egyptian maidservants, who, bent over mills in forced labor, used to say, "We are glad to remain in slavery so long as Israel remains in slavery, [particularly so long as Israel's well-born women remain in slavery]." The Egyptian maidservants were alluding to women such as Serah daughter of Asher,[34] who, upon coming down into Egypt, was enslaved and compelled to bend over a mill in forced labor. So said R. Judah ben Pazzi citing a traditional 'Āḡaḏah transmitted from generation to generation.

And all the first-born of cattle (Exod. 11:5). Men sinned, to be sure; but how can cattle be said to have sinned? Since the Egyptians worshiped the ram,[35] however, [the first-born of their cattle were smitten] in order that the Egyptians should be unable to say: It is our deity who has brought this punishment upon us. Our deity is strong and can stand up for himself, as is shown by the fact that this punishment did not come upon such animals as represent him.

10. R. Huna and R. Joshua bar Abin, the son-in-law of R. Levi, taught in the name of R. Levi: The Master of Mercy [in His exercise of justice] puts off taking human life. From whose experience can you learn this? From Job's—[his oxen and asses were smitten before he was. Scripture begins the story of Job by saying]: *There came a messenger unto Job and said: The oxen were plowing, and the asses feeding beside them* (Job 1:14). How is it possible that while the oxen were plowing the asses should be feeding beside them? R. Ḥama explained: Something of an anticipation of the world-to-

33. The Scriptural proof for the tradition that Bithiah escaped death on the night of the plague of the first-born seems to run as follows: Bithiah was one of twenty-two women whose virtues matched the virtues of "the woman of valor" described in Prov. 31 (see Ginzberg, *Legends*, 5, 258). Accordingly, a reference to Bithiah may properly be sought in that chapter. This reference, it is believed, occurs in the words *Her candle goeth not out by night.*

34. Of Jacob's immediate family Serah was the only one who not only came to Egypt but lived through the entire period up to the exodus (see Ginzberg, *Legends*, index, *s.v.*), and even beyond it (see Piska 11.13). Her experience thus symbolizes the travail of her people.

35. [The ram was the symbol of the Egyptian God Amon, whom the Greeks identified with Zeus. L.N.]

come was provided for Job, as it is said "Behold, the days come, saith the Lord, when one that ploweth shall come near one that reapeth."[36] (Amos 9:13).

[Apropos of Job's herds, *The Sabeans made a raid, and took* (*the oxen and the asses*) *away—yea, they smote the servants with the edge of the sword* (Job 1:15).] The oxen and the asses taken away by the Sabeans from the village of Karnaim, [the home of Job], were led through the district of Abela in its entirety, and, according to R. Abba bar Kahana, when they got to Magdala of the Dyers[37] they died there.[38]

[*And I only am escaped alone* (*ibid.*).] Since, according to R. Ḥama, the word "only" (*raḳ*), denoting limitation, here implies "at the expense of," Scripture is suggesting that he who escaped, escaped at the cost of having his limbs broken and his body beaten.

R. Yudan said: The words *And I only am escaped alone to tell thee* mean that even he who managed to escape died immediately after he had told his tidings, as is intimated in the words which follow: *This one had enough strength left in him to speak*[39] *until there came also another* (Job 1:16), who reported that *The Chaldeans set themselves in three bands*, etc. (Job 1:17). As soon as Job heard this news, he began to draw up his armies for battle, but reconsidered, saying, *I was about to break a great multitude and the most contemptible of families which would terrify me; but then I kept silence, and went not out of the door* (Job 31:34). Job meant that the Chaldean nation was the most contemptible in the entire family of nations:[40] "Behold, the land of the Chaldeans—this is the people that was not" (Isa. 23:13), [of whom God Himself said], "Would that it had not been!" "This is the nation that would cast its terror upon me?" said Job, [but at the same moment realized the full meaning of the words previously

36. [That is, corn will ripen within moments after the seed is planted, so that browsing animals will follow in the tracks of the plowing animals. L.N.]

37. Karnaim, just south of Sheikh Sa'ad in the Peraea, was said to have been the home of Job. Abela was south of the Yarmuk, the northernmost tributary of the Jordan. Magdala of the Dyers lay southeast of Tiberias, near Geder, one of the cities in the Decapolis, the region east of the Jordan. See Lev. Rabbah 17:4 (M, p. 379, note 3; map, *ibid.*, part 5, p. xxix); Lev. Rabbah, Soncino tr., p. 218, n. 4; and Ginzburg, *Legends*, 5, 385–86.

38. Concerning the oxen and the asses, the text simply says that they were taken away. To obviate the suggestion that Job might have got other servants and recovered his oxen and asses, the commentator states that it was impossible for Job to do so, since the oxen and the asses had died.

39. JV: *while he was yet speaking.*

40. Since "they do not possess a tongue or a script" (B.AZ 10a). "Greek remained the spoken and written language throughout the East even after the establishment of the Eastern Roman Empire to which allusion is here made" (Jacob Obermeyer, *Die Landschaft Babylonien* (Frankfurt am Main, 1929), p. 263, n. 2.

reported to him, namely] *A fire of God is fallen from heaven* (Job 1:16), and so he went on: "Since this is God's exercise of justice, what can I do? Thereupon *I kept silence, and went not out of the door*" (Job 31:34).

Immediately thereafter, as the text says, [Job was smitten with sore boils from the sole of his foot even unto his crown], *And he took him a potsherd to scrape himself therewith* (Job 2:8).

In the exercise of His justice God's reluctance to take human life is shown also in His treatment of Mahlon and Chilion, for first their horses died, and then their camels and their asses; after that the father died, *And Elimelech, Naomi's husband, died* (Ruth 1:3); and then his two sons died: *And Mah- and Chilion died, both of them* (Ruth 1:5).[41]

In similar fashion God exercises justice in the order of the divine plagues which are visited upon men. God begins first with a man's house. If the man repents, the requirement is no more than that the stones of the house, stones discolored by the plague, be taken out: *Then the priest shall command that they take out the stones* (Lev. 14:40). If the man does not repent, the requirement is that the stones [and the house itself] be broken down: *And he shall break down the house, the stones of it* (Lev. 14:45). Next, God begins on the man's garments. If the man repents, the requirement is no more than that the part of the garment spotted by the plague be rent out: *The priest . . . shall rend it out of the garment or the skin* (Lev. 13:56). But if the man does not repent, the requirement is that the garment be burnt: *And he shall burn the garment* (Lev. 13:52). Then God begins on the man's body. If the man repents, [he will be cured of his leprous-like scalls] and will be free to go where he likes; but if he does not repent, [stricken with leprosy], *he shall dwell alone; without the camp shall his dwelling be* (Lev. 13:46).[42]

And it was likewise in Egypt. First, God's measure of justice took toll of the Egyptians' property: *He smote their vines also and their fig trees* (Ps. 105:33); *He gave over their cattle also to the hail, and their flocks to fiery*

41. C and Friedman (PRF 17, n. 57) delete the words "And after that she also died" which follow.

Mahlon, Chilion, and Elimelech had incurred guilt because they failed to return to the Land of Israel. See B.BB 91a.

42. See Tos Neḡ 6:7; Saul Lieberman, *Tosefeṯ rišonim* (Jerusalem, 1939), *3*, 193; and Maimonides' Code, X, III, xvi, 10 (YJS, *8*, 203–04).

The order of the verses from Leviticus cited in the text does not seem to sustain the Rabbinic inference with regard to the order in which divine plagues are visited upon men. There is a hermeneutic rule, however, which declares that "There is neither prior nor posterior in Torah," that is, the textual sequence of verses does not necessarily correspond to the temporal sequence of the events described in them. See MhG Gen., p. 38.

bolts (Ps. 78:48). And it was only at the last that *He smote all the first-born in Egypt* (Ps. 78:51).[43]

11. R. Levi bar Zechariah taught in the name of R. Berechiah: Employing the tactics of warrior kings, God set upon the Egyptians. First, He shut off their water conduits. Then He brought up loud voices to confuse them. After that He shot arrows at them. Then He brought the legions upon them. Then He deprived them of their source of food.[44] After that He flung burning stuff upon them. After that He shot stones at them from catapults. After that He arrayed the scalers of walls against them. After that He put them in prisons. And then He led forth each and every one of the most cherished among them and slew him. First, He shut off their water conduits —*turned their rivers into blood* (Ps. 78:44). Then He brought up loud voices to confuse them—the croaking of frogs which, according to R. Jose bar Ḥanina, was harder for the Egyptians to bear than their disgust at the sight of them. After that He shot arrows at them—gnats.[45] After that He brought the legions upon them—swarms of wild beasts. Then He deprived them of their source of food—*a very grievous murrain* (Exod. 9:3) [befell their cattle]. After that He flung burning stuff upon them—boils. After that He shot stones at them from catapults—hail. After that He arrayed the scalers of walls against them—locusts. After that He put them in prisons—threw them into darkness. After that He led forth each and every one of the most cherished among them and slew him—the plague of the first-born.

[In further comment on the measure of God's justice], R. Levi the son-in-law of R. Zechariah, taught in the name of R. Berechiah: *As at the report concerning Egypt, so they shall be startled at the fall of the Adversary* (*ṣr*) (Isa. 23:5). Whenever the word *ṣr* is spelled in full [with the *waw* in the middle] it refers—so taught R. Eliezer—to the principality of Tyre; and whenever, as here, it is spelled defectively, Scripture has reference to wicked Rome [the Adversary].

R. Levi said in the name of R. Ḥama bar R. Ḥanina: With the very means by which He punished the former He will punish the latter. As He punished Egypt with blood, so, too, He will punish Edom—[Rome], for it is written *I will show wonders in the heavens and in the earth, blood, and fire, and pillars of smoke* [*over Edom*] (Joel 3:3). As Egypt, frogs; so, too, Edom:

43. The verses cited from Psalms thus construe *The hail . . . smote both man and beast and every herb of the field* (Exod. 9:25) as meaning that the actual order of smiting was first herbage, then beast, and finally man.

44. Literally "wrought destruction [upon their source of food]." *Drwlmsyy'* may—so Professor Saul Lieberman suggests—represent the Greek *dorilēpsia*, "capture by spear," or *dorialōsia*, "capture by storm," during which none of the inhabitants are spared.

45. These penetrated into human beings. See Exod. 8:13.

The sound of an uproar from the city [*of Rome*], *an uproar because of the Temple* [*which Rome destroyed*], *an uproar of the Lord who rendereth recompense to His enemies* (Isa. 66:6). As Egypt, gnats; so, too, Edom with gnats: *The streams* [*of Bozrah*] *shall be turned into pitch, and the dust thereof into brimstone, and the land thereof shall become burning pitch* (Isa. 34:9);[46] *Smite the dust of the earth, that it may become gnats* (Exod. 8:12). As Egypt, all kinds of wild beasts; so, too, Edom: *The pelican and the bittern shall possess it*, etc. (Isa. 34:11). As Egypt, pestilence; so, too, Edom: *I will plead against* [*Gog*] *with pestilence and with blood* (Ezek. 38:22). As Egypt, boils; so, too, Edom: *This shall be the plague wherewith the Lord will smite all the peoples that have warred against Jerusalem: Their flesh shall consume away while they stand upon their feet* (Zech. 14:12). As Egypt, hail; so, too, Edom: *I will cause to rain upon* [*Gog*] . . . *an overflowing shower and great hailstones* (Ezek. 38:22). As Egypt, locusts; so, too, Edom: *And thou, son of man, thus saith the Lord God: Speak unto the birds of every sort . . . The flesh of the mighty shall ye eat . . . blood shall ye drink . . . ye shall eat fat till ye be full, and drink blood till ye be drunken* (Ezek. 39:17–19). As Egypt, darkness; so, too, Edom with darkness: *He shall stretch over* [*Edom*] *the line of* [*dark*] *chaos and the plummet of emptiness* (Isa. 34:11). As with Egypt He took each of the chiefest among them and slew them, so, too, with Edom: *A great slaughter in the land of Edom, among them to come down shall be the Remim*[47] (Isa. 34:6–7), that is, as R. Meir expounded it—among those to come down shall be the Romans, [pre-eminent among all the peoples of Edom].

12. *Behold, darkness shall cover the earth, and gross darkness the peoples; but upon thee the Lord will arise, and His glory shall be seen upon thee* (Isa. 60:2). R. Aḥa bar Kahana said: For three days darkness and thick darkness were called upon to serve in Egypt. And the proof? The verse *And there was a thick darkness in all the land of Egypt three days* (Exod. 10:22). On the other hand, dark chaos and emptiness have never been summoned to serve in this world. And where will dark chaos and emptiness be called into service? In the great city of Rome: *He shall stretch over it the line of* [*dark*] *chaos, and the plummet of emptiness* (Isa. 34:11).

And the Rabbis say: The nations of the earth which have not accepted the Torah that was given out of darkness [over Sinai], of them Scripture says, *Behold, darkness shall cover the earth, and gross darkness the peoples* (Isa. 60:2). But Israel, who accepted the Torah that was given out of darkness [over Sinai], of them Scripture says, *But upon thee the Lord will arise, and His glory shall be seen upon thee* (*ibid.*).

46. Whose touch upon human skin will sting and burn like the sting of a gnat.
47. JV: *wild oxen.*

PISKA 8

SUMMARY

The ʿomer *as asserting that God alone is the source of substance*

The Sages were about to suppress the Book of Ecclesiastes because they found in it ideas such as *What profit hath a man of all his labor wherein he laboreth under the sun?* (Eccles. 1:3), ideas which smacked of heresy. But they decided otherwise after probing more deeply into the meaning of the text.

Comments on the phrase *under the sun* include observations concerning the unnoticed work of God who causes winds to blow, clouds to rise, rains to come down, dews to bespangle plants, plants to spring up, and fruits to grow plump. In appreciation of His work—for example, in acknowledgment of His gift of crops in the field—Jews exercised great care in offering the sheaf of barley on the second day of Passover. For His part, when God gave Israel the *ʿomer* of manna in the wilderness, He gave one to each of them, whereas all He asks in return is one *ʿomer* from all of them together (Sec. 1).

Substance comes ultimately from the Lord, and when He chooses, He takes it away, as is seen from what happened to Amraphel (Nimrod), who acquired his substance through violence; to Pharaoh, who acquired his through trade; to Sihon and Og, who got theirs through hard work; to Sisera, who got his through good fortune; to Sennacherib—through wisdom; to Haman—through happenstance; to the thirty-one kings of Canaan—through inheritance. The offering of the *ʿomer* is intended to give expression to the faith that God alone is the source of substance (Sec. 2).

The intent in waving the *ʿomer* toward the four points of the compass and up and down is set forth (Sec. 3).

The importance of the precept of the *ʿomer* is emphasized through the following examples: because of his obedience to the precept of the *ʿomer*, Abraham won the right of possessing the land of Canaan; by the tenth part of an ephah of barley meal, the same amount as in the *ʿomer*, God brings peace between a husband and his wife who has been proved innocent of infidelity; the offering of the *ʿomer* stood Israel in good stead in the days of Gideon, in the days of Hezekiah, in the days of Ezekiel, and in the days of Haman (Sec. 4).

PISKA 8

Ye shall bring the sheaf, [an 'omer], *of the first fruits of your harvest unto the priest* (Lev. 23:10).[1]

1. *What profit hath a man of all his labor wherein he laboreth under the sun?* (Eccles. 1:3). R. Benjamin bar Levi said: The Sages were about to suppress the Book of Ecclesiastes,[2] having found in it ideas which smacked of heresy. They said: Should Solomon have given utterance to such a thought as *What profit hath a man of all his labor wherein he laboreth under the sun?* This question might imply—might it not?—that Solomon meant to include labor in the study of Torah. But then the Sages decided otherwise, declaring: Had Solomon said *What profit hath a man of all labor* and refrained from being more precise, we might have suspected that he also meant to include labor in the study of Torah. However, by saying *of all* HIS *labor,* Solomon implied that there is no profit for a man in laboring for himself, but that there is profit in his laboring at the study of Torah.

R. Samuel bar R. Isaac also said: The Sages were about to suppress the Book of Ecclesiastes, having found in it ideas which smacked of heresy. They asked: Should Solomon have given utterance to advice such as *Rejoice, O young man, in thy youth; and let thy heart cheer thee in the days of thy youth, and walk in the ways of thy heart, and in the sight of thine eyes* (Eccles. 11:9)? For, though Moses had declared, *Go not about after your own heart and your own eyes* (Num. 15:39), Solomon said, *Walk in the ways of thy heart, and in the sight of thine eyes,* as though all restraint were removed and there were neither justice nor Judge. Since Solomon went on to say, however, *But know thou that for all these things God will bring thee into judgment* (Eccles. 11:9), [the Sages decided that] Solomon had spoken well after all.

Another comment on *What profit hath a man of all his labor . . . under the sun?* R. Yudan said: [The man who is concerned with things] under the sun will have no profit therefrom; but the man who is concerned with what is higher than the sun, [namely, with Torah], will have profit. For, both R. Huna and R. Aḥa citing R. Ḥilfo said: Though the man who is concerned with Torah labors under the sun, his treasure is above the sun.

R. Levi and the Rabbis [read the verse *What profit hath a man of all his labor? . . . That he is under the sun*]. According to R. Levi, the verse implies that no matter how greatly men in this world extend themselves in the

1. At one time, so Friedmann (PRF 17, n. 1) maintains, Lev. 23:9–14 was the lesson for the second day of Passover, the day the first sheaves of barley were harvested and waved as an offering. See *JE*, 9, 398–99, *s.v.* "*'Omer.*"

2. To exclude it from the Biblical canon.

performance of religious duties and good deeds, it is reward enough for them that the Holy One causes the sun to shine for them, *That the sun ariseth, and the sun goeth down* (Eccles. 1:5). According to the Rabbis, the verse implies that no matter how greatly men in this world extend themselves in the performance of religious duties and good deeds, it is reward enough for them that [in the world-to-come] the Holy One will renew their countenances as the disk of the sun [is renewed each day]—*They that love Him will be as the sun when he goeth forth in his might* (Judg. 5:31).[3]

R. Yannai said: The way it is with mankind, when a man buys a pound of meat in the marketplace, how much trouble he goes to, how much time, money, and strength he must give in order to sit down to his cooked meat![4] Yet while mortals are asleep in their beds, the Holy One causes winds to blow, clouds to rise, rains to come down, dews to bespangle plants, plants to spring up, fruits to grow plump—and you are asked to give Him in return no more than the *'omer* of barley![5]

R. Phinehas said: The way it is with mankind, when a man washes his cloak during the rainy season, how much trouble he goes to with it and how much he puts himself out in tending it until he succeeds in drying the cloak. Yet while mortals are asleep in their beds, the Holy One causes winds to blow, clouds to rise, rains to come down, dews to bespangle plants, plants to spring up, fruits to grow plump—and you are asked to give Him in return no more than the *'omer* of barley!

R. Abin said:[6] Come, behold what care Israel exercised in obedience to the precept of the sheaf of barley! As we learn in a Mishnah, "they reaped it, put it into baskets, and brought it to the Temple court. [And in order to prepare it for grinding], they used to expose it to fire in keeping with the ordinance that it be *parched with fire* (Lev. 2:14). So R. Meir. But the Sages say: They used to beat it with reeds and with the stems of plants[7] so that the

3. Cf. Lev. Rabbah 30:2, and MTeh 11:6.

4. "how much time . . . to his cooked meat" paraphrases the more literal "how much he puts himself out because of it, until he succeeds in cooking it." Meat was expensive in those days, and a luxury for most people.

5. R. Ammi and R. Phinehas seem to interpret the verse in Ecclesiastes: *For any man, what does the tenth,* [*the 'omer*] (*'śrwn,* "tenth," instead of *ytrwn,* "profit"), *amount to, compared to all of God's work wherein He labors under the sun.*

6. R. Abin seems to interpret the verse in Ecclesiastes as follows: *What is the tenth* (*'śrwn,* "tenth," instead of *ytrwn,* "profit") *given* [*by Israel to the Lord, the tenth*] *in whose preparation Israel* [*in their use of fire, fire*] *that comes from the sun, exercise such care.*

In the play on *ytrwn* and *'śrwn* R. Abin may also find Biblical proof for translating *'omer* not a "sheaf," as the Septuagint translates it, but "measure," specifically a tenth of an ephah, about a quart.

7. Instead of flails.

grains should not be crushed. Then they put it into a [copper] pipe, a perforated pipe, so that the fire might get at all of the grains" (Men 10:4). Immediately afterwards, as we learn in the same passage in the Mishnah: "They spread it out in the Temple courtyard so that the wind blew over it. Then they put it into a grist mill[9] and took therefrom a tenth [of an ephah of flour] which was then put through thirteen sieves" (*ibid.*).

R. Levi said: Behold, [God says], you have labored—you have plowed, sown, weeded and pruned, hoed and reaped, bound the sheaves, threshed and stacked the sheaves; still, if I brought not forth a little wind to winnow for you, how would you or any one else stay alive? And will you not pay Me a wage for the wind? After all, *What profit would there be [for a man] if he were to labor to make the wind blow?*[10] (Eccles. 5:15).

R. Eleazar[11] taught: It is written *Neither say they in their heart: Let us now fear the Lord our God that hath given the former rain, and the latter in due season; [neither say they], He is the one who for weeks must maintain in our behalf conditions suitable for the harvest*[12] (Jer. 5:24). *That hath given*, that is, God gave you all [the rain needed]; and do you think that henceforth you have no further need of Him? Remember *He is the one who for weeks must maintain in our behalf conditions suitable for the harvest*—no scorching heat, no blasting winds, and no noxious dews[13] for the seven full weeks between Passover and Pentecost. In this connection R. Ḥiyya, citing the verse *Seven weeks shall they be—full ones* (Lev. 23:15),[14] taught: When are the weeks considered full? When the period between Passover and Pentecost is completed by the priestly watch of Jeshua alone, whose watch is the ninth one, so that Shecaniah's watch, which is the tenth one, is not needed to fill out the period.[15]

According to R. Joshua ben Levi, [God] said: I am thy watchman: and wilt thou not give Me the wage for watching over thee?

8. In order to cool the grains and dry them.

9. Which grinds very coarsely, so that only the husk is separated from the grain.

10. [Literally "Therefore, (if) you do not pay Him a wage for the wind (by laboring also in the study of Torah), *What profit*," etc. Mere plowing, sowing, etc., is not enough to earn you wind. You must also do the labor of studying Torah, specifically in this case, the rules concerning the sheaf of barley. L.N.]

11. "R. Eleazar"—O_1, C, and Yalḳuṭ; O: "R. Levi."

12. The rainy season ends on Passover. The wheat harvest follows about seven weeks later at the time of Pentecost. JV: *that keepeth for us the appointed weeks of the harvest.*

13. "and no noxious dews"—O_1 and C; not in O.

14. The first part of the verse reads: *And ye shall count you from the morrow after the day of rest* (Hebrew *Sabbath*), *from the day that ye brought the sheaf of waving.*

15. Full weeks are, paradoxically, not "full," that is not weeks that begin on

According to R. Berechiah, [God said]: I am thy cook, the one who spices thy food, and wilt thou not let Me taste the dish prepared for thee, that I may know what is needed [for its seasoning]?[16]

God's attention to the rain is what David had in mind when he said: *As for rain, it was bounteous; now wave down*[17] *[dew], O God, whereby Thou mayest give support to [Israel] Thine inheritance when it is weary* (Ps. 68:10). When the Land needed rain Thou gavest it bounteously; now that it needs dew, *wave down [dew],*[18] *O God, whereby Thou mayest give support to Thine inheritance when it is weary.*

According to R. Benaiah, the Holy One said to Israel: My children, when I used to give you the *'omer* [in the wilderness], I gave an *'omer* to each one of you—*An 'omer a head* (Exod. 16:16). But now that you are giving Me the *'omer*, you are to give Me no more than one *'omer* from all of you together. And not only this: the *'omer* is to be not of wheat but only of barley.[19]

Therefore, for all the reasons given above, Moses enjoins Israel, saying to them: *Ye shall bring an 'omer of the first fruits of your harvest unto the priest* (Lev. 23:10).

2. *I have seen the foolish [and licentious] taking root; but suddenly . . . their harvest the hungry eateth up, and taketh it, though without bucklers; and the allies trample upon their substance*[20] (Job 5:5). By *their harvest*

Sunday. The reference is to a year when the new moon of Nisan is not on the Sabbath, so that the waving of the *'omer* is not on a Sunday, thus disproving the Sadducees' contention that the *'omer* is to be waved on Sunday. See PR 18 (YJS, *18*, 382, n. 14).

16. According to R. Berechịah, delicate blending of atmosphere and dew is required for a successful harvesting. The *'omer* is thus a prayer to God to maintain conditions suitable for the harvest. See Nogah ha-Rĕ'ub̲eni, *Ṭeb̲a' ha-'areṣ bĕ-tiḳse miḳdaš wĕ-ḥag̅*, Proceedings of the American Academy for Jewish Research *37* (1969), 25–31.

17. JV: *A bounteous rain didst Thou pour down.*

18. The waving of the sheaves of barley is thus taken to symbolize the prayer for the waving down of dew.

19. R. Benaiah seems to interpret Eccles. 1:3 as saying, *What a profit hath man of all his labor wherein he laboreth under the sun*, the point being of course that "so far as any of the commandments are gifts, as it were, rendered to God, they are far smaller than God's gifts to man." See Montefiore, *RA*, p. 192.

20. JV: *and taketh it even out of the thorns, and the snare gapeth for their substance.* But *'el,* "out of," read *'al*, can also mean "without"; *ṣinnim*, "thorns," can also mean "shield" or "buckler"; *ṣammim*, "snare," as a form of *ṣamat̲*, can mean "to meet, to join," whence "allies" or "associates"; and *ša'af*, "gapeth," may be derived from *šuf*, "bruise, crush," whence "trample upon." See Judah J. Slotki's notes in Lev. Rabbah 28:4, Soncino tr., pp. 361, 362.

the harvest of one such as Nimrod is meant.[21] The phrase *the hungry eateth up* refers to our father Abraham, [hungry for the word of God]. The words *taketh it though not with bucklers* imply that Abraham took Nimrod's power away not with a weapon nor by blocking it with a shield, but with prayer and supplications to the Lord, as is said "When Abram heard that his brother was taken captive, he led forth his trained one,[22] born in his house—three hundred and eighteen—and pursued as far as Dan" (Gen. 14:14). Actually, as R. Simeon ben Laḳish explained, citing Bar Ḳappara, [it was not three hundred and eighteen men that] Abraham led forth but one man, Eliezer, in whose name the numerical value of the letters is three hundred and eighteen.[23] *And the allies trample upon their substance.* Who was it that trampled upon Nimrod's substance? Abraham, [Eliezer being] all he had in the way of an ally.

Another comment: By *their harvest* (Job 5:5) a harvest such as Pharaoh's is meant. The phrase *the hungry eat up* refers to Moses and Aaron, [hungry for the word of God]. The words *take it though not with bucklers* imply that they took Pharaoh's power away not with weapons nor by blocking it with a shield, but with prayer and supplications to the Lord, as is proved by the text "The Lord said unto Moses: Wherefore criest thou unto Me?" (Exod. 14:15). *And the allies trample upon their substance.* Who was it that trampled upon the wicked Pharaoh's substance? Moses and Aaron and all who were allied with them.

Another comment: By *their harvest* (Job 5:5) is meant Sihon's harvest and Og's harvest. The phrase *the hungry eat up* refers to Moses and Aaron, [hungry for the word of God]. And the words *take it though not with bucklers* imply that they took away the power of Sihon and Og not with weapons nor by blocking it with a shield, but with prayer and supplications to the Lord, as is proved by the text "The Lord said unto Moses: Fear him not; for I have delivered him into thy hand" (Num. 21:34). *And the allies trample upon their substance.* Who was it that trampled upon Og's and Sihon's substance? Moses and Aaron and all that were allied with them.

Another comment: By *their harvest* (Job 5:5) a harvest such as Sisera's is meant. The phrase *the hungry eat up* refers to Deborah and Barak, [hungry for the word of God]. The words *take it though not with bucklers* imply that they took Sisera's power away not with weapons nor by blocking it with a shield, but with prayer and supplications to the Lord, as is proved by the text

21. Nimrod is identified as Amraphel, the leading king among the four whom Abraham defeated. See Rashi on Gen. 14:1.

22. JV: *trained ones*. But the *kĕṯiḇ* is "trained one." See Leḳaḥ Ṭoḇ and Rashi.

23. Eliezer was Abraham's chief steward (see Gen. 15:2). The Hebrew letters *'alef* = 1, *lameḏ* = 30, *yoḏ* = 10, *'ayin* = 7, *zayin* = 7, *reš* = 200 add up to 318. Since four armies were thus destroyed by two men, Abraham and Eliezer, it inescapably follows that only through prayer did Abraham win his victory.

They fought from heaven, the stars in their courses fought against Sisera" Judg. 5:20). *And the allies trample upon their substance.* Who was it that trampled upon Sisera's substance? Deborah and Barak and all that were allied with them.

Another comment: By *their harvest* (Job 5:5) a harvest such as Sennacherib's is meant. The phrase *the hungry eat up* refers to Isaiah and Hezekiah, [hungry for the word of God]. The words *take it though not with bucklers* imply that they took Sennacherib's power away not with weapons nor by blocking it with a shield, but with prayer and supplications to the Lord, as is proved by the text "Hezekiah the king, and Isaiah the prophet son of Amoz, prayed because of this, and cried to heaven" (2 Chron. 32:20). *And the allies trample upon their substance.* Who was it that trampled upon Sennacherib's substance? Hezekiah and Isaiah and all that were allied with them.

Another comment: By *their harvest* (Job 5:5) a harvest such as Haman's is meant. The phrase *the hungry eat up* refers to Mordecai and Esther, [hungry for the word of God]. The words *take it though not with bucklers* imply that they took Haman's power away not with weapons nor by blocking it with a shield, but with prayer and supplications to the Lord, as is proved by the text "And many lay in sackcloth and ashes" (Esther 4:3). *And the allies trample upon their substance.* Who was it that trampled upon Haman's substance? Mordecai and Esther and all that were allied with them.

Another comment: By *their harvest* (Job 5:5) is meant the harvest of the thirty-one kings. The phrase *the hungry eat up* refers to Joshua and Caleb, [hungry for the word of God]. The words *take . . . though not with bucklers* imply that they took away the power of the thirty-one kings not with weapons nor by blocking it with a shield, but with prayer and supplications to the Lord, as is proved by God's command to Joshua, "Get thee up; wherefore now art thou fallen upon thy face?" (Josh. 7:10). *And the allies trample upon their substance.* Who was it that trampled upon the substance of the thirty-one kings? Joshua and Caleb and all that were allied with them.

By what merit did Israel earn the privilege of having the land of Canaan given to them? By the merit of harvesting the sheaf [and bringing the *'omer* which is Israel's prayer and supplication to the Lord]. Hence Moses bids Israel: *Ye shall bring the sheaf of the first fruits of your harvest unto the priest* (Lev. 23:10).[24]

24. Substance comes from the Lord is the point of the homily. Accordingly, though Israel came to a goodly land, its goodliness cannot remain Israel's unless God maintains it in Israel's hands. There are seven other ways whereby one may acquire substance: (1) through robbery and violence, as Nimrod got his; (2) through trade, as Pharaoh acquired it, enlarging his fortune during the years of famine; (3) through diligence and hard work, as exemplified by Sihon and Og,

3. *And he shall wave the 'omer* [*of barley*] *before the Lord to be ac-cepted* (Lev. 23:11). How was the *'omer* waved? R. Ḥami bar R. 'Oḳba said in the name of R. Jose bar Ḥanina: It was waved toward the four points of the compass to nullify blasting winds, and it was waved up and down to nullify noxious dews. However, R. Simon said in the name of R. Joshua ben Levi: It was waved toward the four points of the compass in recognition of Him to whom the whole world belongs, and up and down in recognition that to Him belong the regions above and the regions below.

According to R. Abin, the difference of opinion in regard to the waving of the *'omer* was [not between R. Jose bar Ḥanina and R. Joshua ben Levi but] between R. Judah and R. Nehemiah.

4. R. Jacob bar Abaye said in the name of R. Judah bar R. Simon that R. Johanan and R. Simeon ben Laḳish had each his own teaching about the *'omer*. R. Johanan taught: Let the precept of the *'omer* of barley never seem trivial in your eyes. Because of obedience to the precept of the *'omer* of barley Abraham won the right of possessing the land of Canaan, as is said: *And I will give unto thee, and to thy seed after thee, the land of thy sojourn-ings, all the land of Canaan* (Gen. 17:8), on condition that *thou shalt keep the covenant* (Gen. 17:9). And what was the covenant? The precept of the *'omer* of barley.[25] R. Simeon ben Laḳish taught: Let the precept of the *'omer* of barley never seem trivial in your eyes. By the tenth part of an ephah of barley meal, the same as makes up the *'omer*, the Holy One brings peace between a husband and a wife [who has been cleared of suspicion of infidel-ity]: *Then shall the man bring his wife unto the priest, and shall bring her offering for her, the tenth part of an ephah of barley bread* (Num. 5:15).[26]

R. Abbahu—according to some it was R. Simon, according to others it was R. Joshua ben Levi—taught: It was this offering of the *'omer* that stood

---

whose people hired themselves out as soldiers to keep order (for this reason Sihon and Og, who had committed themselves to the kings of Canaan, did not permit the children of Israel to go through their lands); (4) through good fortune, enjoyed by Sisera, in whose behalf, prior to his engagement with Barak, even the stars fought in their courses; (5) through wisdom, in which Sennacherib excelled; (6) through happenstance, which was the way of Haman, whom the king chanced to single out for preferment; and (7) through inheritance, which the 31 kings of Canaan possessed. But the ultimate source of substance is the Lord, faith in whom the *'omer* gives utterance to. See *Yĕfeh to'ar* on Lev. Rabbah 28:4.

25. The phrase *thou shalt keep the covenant* is apparently construed as referring to the sacrificial cult; and Israel's offering upon their entrance into Canaan (see Josh. 5:11) of an *'omer* of barley as the first performance of a cultic act in the Land of Israel. See *Torah šĕlemah*, Gen., *3*, 701.

26. In PRF 18, note 26, Friedmann explains that according to the Rabbis, the barley grain is symbolic of the heathen who have no self-restraint; the wheat grain, on the other hand, being cleft, is symbolic of the circumcised, of Israel. See PR

[Is]rael in good stead in the days of Gideon, as is said *When Gideon was [c]ome, behold, there was a man telling a dream to his fellow and saying: Behold, I dreamed a dream, and, lo, ṣĕlil,*[27] *but then a barley bread tumbled [in]to the camp of Midian, and came unto the tent, and smote it that it fell, [a]nd turned it upside down, that the tent lay flat"* (Judg. 7:13). What is [m]eant by *ṣĕlil*? The Rabbis explain that the generation of Gideon was bare [(]*ṣĕlil*) of righteous men.[28] By obedience to what one precept was it saved? [B]y obedience to the precept symbolized by the barley bread[29] [in the [d]ream]. And just what is the precept? The precept of the *'omer* of barley.[30]

R. Samuel bar Naḥman taught: It was this offering of the *'omer* that stood [I]srael in good stead in the days of Hezekiah: *In every place where the [a]ppointed staff will pass, [the staff] which the Lord will lay upon [Asshur], [i]t shall be with tabrets and harps; and in battles of tĕnufah will He fight along [w]ith them* (Isa. 30:32). But was Hezekiah's generation able to wage *battles of [t]ĕnufah?*[31] No, but then waving, *tĕnufah*, of the *'omer* in obedience to the [p]recept of the *'omer* brought about the wielding, *tĕnufah*, of God's power in Israel's behalf.[32]

And the Rabbis taught: It was this *'omer* of barley that stood them in [g]ood stead in the days of Ezekiel: *Take thou also unto thee wheat, barley,*

10:3 (YJS, *18*, 172). And so, coming into the Land, Israel was called upon to offer the barley, to give up, as it were, its living without self-restraint. In the relations of husband and wife, the giving of the barley is symbolic of the giving up of unrestrained sexual desire.

27. EV: *and lo, a cake of barley bread*. But *ṣĕlil*, translated "cake," is a *hapax legomenon* whose precise meaning is unknown. The disjunctive accent over *ṣĕlil* tends to support R. Joshua ben Levi's rendition.

28. For even Gideon's father, one of the foremost men in his generation, had an altar of Baal. See Judg. 6:25, and Rashi on Judg. 7:13.

29. The word *ṣĕlil* is omitted as in O_1 and in PRKB.

30. The night when the dream was told was the night of the 16th of Nisan, the night of harvesting the sheaves of barley for the *'omer* offering. See Rashi on Isa. 9:3.

31. The generation of Hezekiah was too weak to wage wars on a large scale. See 2 Kings 18:23, and Mah on Lev. Rabbah 28:6.

[I would say, "What *battles of tĕnufah* were there in that generation, other than the waving—*tĕnufah*—of the *'omer*?" L.N.]

32. "No, but then waving . . . of God's power in Israel's behalf" is a paraphrase of the more literal "No, but [God fought along with Israel], because of their obedience to the precept of the *'omer*."

The *'omer* when offered had to be waved. The verb "to wave" is the same as the verb "to wield." Hence the analogy. The deliverance from Sennacherib is said to have taken place on the night of the 16th of Nisan. See Rashi on Isa. 9:2. The phrase *bmlḥmwt tnwfh*, usually translated *battles of wielding,* is construed in this comment as "[barley] bread of waving." See Lev. Rabbah M, p. 661, n. 4.

Following the offering of the *'omer* of barley, which serves as food for animals,

beans, lentils, millet, and spelt, and put them in one vessel, and make th bread thereof[33] (Ezek. 4:9). In order to make *bread thereof*, which of th three grains, wheat, barley, or spelt did Ezekiel use most of?[34] Into th dough—so taught R. Ḥama bar R. Ḥanina—he put most of barley,[35] a excess of which, according to R. Samuel bar Naḥman, brings on the run Samuel said: Over in Babylonia it is told that out of dough with an excess o barley they made a cake for a dog, but he would not eat it.

A Roman lady, in speaking to R. Jose ben Ḥalafta, exclaimed: "Wha pain that righteous Ezekiel must have endured! And to think that every on of the great number of manservants and maidservants he had, looked dow upon him because of the food and drink he chose to live on!" R. Jose be Ḥalafta replied: "Ezekiel's pain was meant to make you understand tha whenever Israel are in pain, the righteous are in pain with them."[36]

R. Levi taught: It is this *'omer* of barley which stood Israel in good stea in the days of Haman. We are told that when Mordecai saw Haman come toward him leading a horse,[37] he said: I have a feeling that this wicked man is coming to kill me. And he said to his disciples: "Flee that you be no scorched by the coal meant for me." They replied: "Whether for life or fo death, we are with you." What did Mordecai do? He wrapped himself in his prayer shawl and stood up to pray. The wicked Haman came and sat down with Mordecai and his disciples—right in the midst of them, and asked "What are you so busy with?" They replied: "With the precept of the *'omer,*[38] which Israel used to offer in the Temple." He asked: "And what was that *'omer* made of—silver? gold? wheat? barley?" They replied: "Bar-

fifty days are counted to the next festival, celebrating the giving of Torah which is food for man and for his spirit. R. Samuel bar Naḥman thus dwells on the precept of the *'omer* as intended to inspire Israel to give up brutish ways of living and seek instead the ways of Torah—the kind of life in which the generation of Hezekiah excelled. See PR 16:6; MTeh 87:5; and *Yĕfeh to'ar* on Lev. Rabbah 28:6.

33. Upon which Ezekiel was to sustain himself for 390 days.

34. "In order to make . . . most of?"—O_1, C.

35. If it were to be called bread, the mixture had to have more of wheat, or barley, or spelt. See Friedmann's note 32 in PRF 17; and P.Ḥal 1:1.

36. The Rabbis who cite R. Jose ben Ḥalafta's reply to the Roman lady seem to regard the *'omer* of barley as a symbol of the suffering and self-denial which a great man willingly took upon himself, thereby to divert God's wrath from Israel: otherwise His wrath might have consumed Israel altogether. See B.Sanh 39a and Samuel Edels.

37. See Esther 6:11.

38. The day was the 16th of Nisan, on which day the *'omer* used to be ceremoniously reaped, waved, and brought as a meal offering (Lev. 23:10–11). See Esther Rabbah, chap. 10.

y." He asked: "And what was its value? twenty talents?[39] ten talents?" hey replied: "Ten farthings at most." He said to them: "Arise, for your ten rthings have prevailed over my ten thousand talents of silver."[40] Then, as oon as Mordecai finished praying, Haman said: "Come, put on this gar- ent." Mordecai replied: "Would you insult royalty? Would a person put on oyal robes without bathing first?" So Haman went to seek a bath attendant, ut could not find one. What did he do? He tied a menial's apron on himself, et to, and bathed Mordecai.[41] After Mordecai came out of the bath, laman said: "Come, put on this crown." Mordecai replied: "Would you nsult royalty? Would a man put on a royal crown without having first had a aircut?" So Haman went looking for a barber, but could not find one. What id he do? He went to his house and brought barber's instruments, and as he at down to cut Mordecai's hair, he began to sigh. Mordecai asked: "Why re you sighing?" He replied: "Alas for the father of a man who once had he power to appoint the superintendent of the palace[42] and to appoint the fficer who arranged the king's appointments, but now has become bath ttendant and barber!" Mordecai said: "What cause for wonder is this? Did I ot see him, the father of this man, work as bath attendant and barber at the illage of Karnaim?[43] Indeed, you found, and are using on me, the barber's nstruments that belonged to him." Haman said: "Rise up, ride on this orse." Mordecai replied: "I have no strength, for I am an old man." Haman sked: "Am I not also an old man?" Mordecai replied: "But did you not ring this waiting on me upon yourself?" Haman said: "Rise. I will lower my eck, so that you can step on it, and then get up and ride, thus fulfilling the promise made to your people, *And thou shalt step upon the backs of their necks*[44] (Deut. 33:29)." As Mordecai was riding upon the horse, he pro- ceeded to praise the Holy One: *I will extol Thee, O Lord, for Thou hast raised me up, and hast not suffered mine enemies to rejoice over me. O Lord my God, I cried unto Thee, and Thou didst heal me; O Lord, Thou brought- est up my soul from the nether world; Thou didst keep me alive, that I should not go down to the pit* (Ps. 30:2–4). And his disciples, what did they say? *Sing praise unto the Lord, O ye His godly ones, and give thanks to His holy name. For His anger is but for a moment, His favor is for a lifetime; weeping may tarry for the night, but joy cometh in the morning* (Ps.

39. "Twenty talents"—O_1. A talent = 3,000 shekels = 100,000 sesterces.
40. Which Haman paid to the king's treasury as the price of the Jews. See Esther 3:9.
41. For three days Mordecai had been fasting and so was too weak to bathe without an attendant's aid.
42. See Krauss, *Lehnwörter*, p. 509b.
43. See Piska 7.10, and PR 17:6.
44. JV: *upon their high places.*

30:5–6). And that wicked Haman, what did he say? *I had said in m security: "I shall never be moved." Thou hadst established, O Lord, in Th favor my mountain as a stronghold—Thou didst hide Thy face; I was a frighted* (Ps. 30:7–8). And Esther, what did she say? *Unto Thee, O Lor did I call, and unto the Lord I made supplication: What profit is there in m blood when I go down to the pit? Shall the dust praise Thee? Shall it declar Thy truth?* (Ps. 30:9–10). And Israel, what did they say? *Hear, O Lor and be gracious unto me; Lord, be Thou my helper. Only Thou canst tur for me my mourning into dancing, only Thou canst loose my sackcloth, an gird me with gladness* (Ps. 30:11–12).

R. Phinehas said: [When Haman came with the royal steed], Mordeca was engaged in uttering the Shĕma‘ and he did not stop, as is said *So tha [my spirit, which is] my glory, may sing unto Thee, and not become silen O Lord my God, let me continue to utter praise of Thee for ever* (Ps. 30:13)

PISKA 9

SUMMARY

The infinite range of God's mercy

Discussion of the verse *Thy righteousness is like the mighty mountains; Thy judgments are like the great deep: man and cattle Thou preservest, O Lord* (Ps. 36:7) leads to the conclusion that God's execution of justice—His reward of the righteous and His punishment of the wicked whether in this world or in the world-to-come—points to His mercy as exceeding His justice. Indeed, were it not for His mercy, man's wickedness, unrestrained by fear of His justice, would bring about God's destruction of the entire world. The deeds of the righteous, however, or possibly His concern for other living creatures leads Him to withhold such dire punishment. In particular, the righteousness of the people of Israel will ultimately earn for each one of them an Eden of his own making, for Israel, with the innocence of cattle is drawn after God's commandments: that God's decrees for both men and cattle are prompted by mercy is shown by such facts as that He does not require circumcision of an infant until it is eight days old and strong enough to endure it, and that He does not require the offering up of a new-born animal until it is eight days old, so that its dam may not suffer its loss too soon. It must be concluded, therefore, that even when God administers justice, His decrees are rooted in mercy (Sec. 1). Indeed His mercy is such that when a man of his own accord does good deeds, God deems them to be equivalent to an act of creation. As for the man who gives no more than what he is supposed to or commanded to, let him remember that what he gives, he has, in fact, received from God (Sec. 2).

When God suggests that gifts be given to Him, He makes certain so to phrase His request as to give no offense. Thus He asks for *a bullock* (Lev. 22:27) as an offering, not a calf, in order to avoid reminding Israel of their iniquity in making the golden calf (Sec. 3). His mercy extends even further in that He asks that only such animals as are hunted—not those who hunt—be offered to Him (Sec. 4). As for Israel, even when He is about to prefer charges against them, He unexpectedly turns His case into a promise of redemption, or a reproach of their forgetting His past kindnesses, or He even goes so far as to make light of the offense they are charged with. Moreover, God does not expect Israel's prayers to be uttered in a formal way or spoken in abject submission. Nor does God expect Israel to weary themselves in seeking out animals for offerings. He asks only for animals that are near at hand, animals which are reared at Israel's trough (Sec. 5).

In reward for Israel's cry at Sinai, "All that the Lord hath spoken we will do, and obey" (Exod. 24:7), God is ready to accept and hallow even th bullock, symbol of Israel's degradation when they made the molten calf (Sec 6). The fact is, however, that when Israel fashioned the calf, they meant n rebellion against God; they intended only to give visual representation to bullock—one of the four "faces" or creatures of God's chariot (Sec. 7).

According to some authorities, it was non-Israelites who made the molte calf. And still other authorities maintain that though Israelites did make th calf, they made it not because they were rebels against God, but because the had come to take Him for granted (Sec. 8). Israel's three offerings—th bullock, the ram, the goat—are construed as symbolic of significant events in the lives of Abraham, Isaac, and Jacob (Sec. 9). The requirement that th offering *be seven days under the dam* (Lev. 22:27) is taken to mean that Sabbath, the queen of days, must intervene between the birth of the anima and its being offered, so that, in a manner of speaking, the offering is crowned by the Sabbath (Sec. 10). God further ordained that the dam and its young must not be slain on the same day—an ordinance of mercy which the wicked heathen in their onslaughts on Israel have consistently ignored over the generations. Hence, in the days of Gog and Magog, God Himself will fight in Israel's behalf (Sec. 11). Hence, too, even in the time-to-come neither the thank offering nor the prayer of thanksgiving will cease (Sec. 12).

PISKA 9

A bullock, or a sheep (Lev. 22:27)[1]

1. *Thy righteousness is like the mighty mountains; Thy judgments are like* *e great deep; man and cattle Thou preservest, O Lord* (Ps. 36:7). R. hmael and R. 'Aḳiḇa differed in their interpretations of the first part of this erse.[1a] R. Ishmael said: To the righteous who obey the Torah which was ven on the mighty mountains, the Holy One accords love in such abun-

1. Lev. 22:26–23:44 is the lesson for Passover. See B. Meḡ 30b and Rashi.

1a. Each of the ensuing comments on the verse's comparison of God's mercy ith mighty mountains and His judgments with the great deep seems to be distinct nd separate from the others, so that at first glance the *pĕṯiḥah* as a whole seems to ck coherence and climax.

Beneath the seemingly disparate comments, however, a close discussion is going n of the apparent discrepancies between rewards and punishments that God etes out to the righteous and the wicked and how these discrepancies are to be xplained and justified in relation to His justice and His mercy.

The discussion begins with 1) R. Ishmael's maintaining that in this world the ghteous receive their full reward and the wicked their full punishment. To account, owever, for the fact that the righteous sometimes suffer and the wicked sometimes rosper, the *pĕṯiḥah*'s author cites 2) R. 'Aḳiḇa's declaration that in this world the ighteous are also punished for their few wicked deeds and the wicked are re-varded for their few good deeds. Nevertheless, the discourse goes on, despite the nfrequent lapse of the righteous into wickedness and infrequent ascent of the vicked to righteousness, the righteous, according to 3) R. Judah, are creatures of ight and the wicked are creatures of darkness. In answer, next, to the inevitable uestion of how it is that such radiant beings as the righteous are so often without oy, the *pĕṯiḥah* cites 4) Rabbi Jonathan's assertion that the righteous are joyless ecause theirs is the arduous task of having to hold back the punishment that the vickedness of the world deserves. For their efforts, the righteous will receive com-ensation in full in the world-to-come. In the meantime, 5) in this world they have he satisfaction of knowing that everything they do, they can do openly. To this leclaration comes the reply that what the wicked do, they also do openly—*They leclare their sin as Sodom, they hide it not* (Isa. 3:9). 6) Even so, the *pĕṯiḥah* continues, the doings of the wicked are fruitless while the righteous know that heir doings are fruitful. However, to this expression of faith in the efforts of the righteous is opposed the doubt of R. Judah bar Simon who sees the wickedness of men as so great that God would destroy the world were it not for the fact that His concern is not for mankind alone but for all the living beings of His creation. Hence the seeming *non sequitur* of the verse, *Man and cattle Thou preservest* is, according to the *pĕṯiḥah*, the natural and logical conclusion to the first part of the verse, *Thy righteousness is like the mighty mountains; Thy judgments are like the great deep.*

dance that it towers up like His mighty mountains: hence *Thy righteousness is like the mighty mountains*. But to the wicked, to those who do not obe the Torah which was given on the mighty mountains, the Holy One, search ing out the very depths of their beings, accords the strictness of His judg ment: hence *Thy judgments are like the great deep*. R. 'Aḳiḇa, on the othe hand, interpreted the verse as follows: God accords His justice as strictly t the righteous as to the wicked. He is strict with the righteous, [searching ou the very depths of their being] and holding them to account for the fev wrongs they commit in this world, so that in the world-to-come He can eve the balance with full reward for their righteousness, [a reward so abundan that it will tower up like His mighty mountains]; upon the wicked, however He bestows ease in this world in an abundance [as great as His mighty mountains], rewarding them thus for their few good deeds in this world, sc that in the world-to-come He can even the balance with entire requital fo their wickedness, [a requital as profound as His great deeps].

R. [Judah had a different idea of the verse's meaning, for he] maintained that the verse in the Psalm likens the righteous to the loftiness of the abode where they are to dwell and likens the wicked to the abyss where they are tc dwell. Thus, likening the righteous to the abiding place which is to be theirs, Scripture says [of Israel returning from the exile's world of darkness], *I will feed them in a green pasture, and upon the mountains of the lofty One of Israel shall be their fold* (Ezek. 34:14). Then likening the wicked to the abiding place which is to be theirs, another verse says, *Thus saith the Lord God: In the day when [the wicked king] went down to the grave I caused to mourn (he'ĕḇalti), I covered him with the abyss*[3] (Ezek. 31:15). However, as R. Judah Berabbi noted, the *kĕṯiḇ* of *he'ĕḇalti*, "caused to mourn," is *heyḇalti*, "caused to go down," [so that the latter part of the verse is to be read "I had him go down even deeper, I used him to cover over the abyss]." A parable to explain the verse's intent: A cover for a wine vessel is not made of silver, nor of gold, nor of copper, nor of iron, nor of tin, nor of lead (see Num. 31:22): it is made of clay, which is of the same material as the earthenware vessel itself. So, too, the Holy One said: Gehenna is darkness, the abyss is darkness, and the wicked are darkness. Let darkness come and

2. In the comments that follow, the word for "righteousness," *ṣĕḏaḳah*, takes on as in later Hebrew the meanings of "love" and "charity."

And in R. [Judah's] comment, *righteousness* will be taken to mean those who are righteous, that is, those who act in love and charity, ['*ośay*] *ṣiḏḳaṯḵa*; and *judgments* will be taken to mean those who suffer God's judgments. By a slight change of vowels, *mišpaṭeḵa*, "Thy judgments," may be read *mušpaṭeḵa*, "they who are judged by Thee."

3. JV: *I caused the deep to mourn and cover itself for him.* The commentator is concerned here with working out what God means by saying that He would have the grave mourn for a wicked man and cover itself for him as though in

cover darkness: [*The wicked*] *cometh in* [*the darkness of*] *a thick fog, he departeth in darkness, his body serves as a cover for the darkness* [*of the abyss*] (Eccles. 6:4).[4]

R. Jonathan, citing R. Josiah, transposed the verse of the Psalm, reading it: Thy righteousness—that is, Thy mercy—towers above Thy judgments as the mountains of God tower above the great deep. As the mountains hold back the deep so that it cannot come up and overwhelm the world,[5] so the deeds of the righteous hold back punishment so that it cannot come and overwhelm the world.

Then [reading the verse without transposing its words, R. Jonathan, citing R. Josiah, said] in further comment on *Thy righteousness is like the mighty mountains* (Ps. 36:7): As the mountains are without end, so [if not in this world, then surely] in the world-to-come, the bestowal of reward upon the righteous will be without end; and in comment on *Thy judgments are like the great deep* continued: As the deep is without end, so [if not in this world, then surely] in the world-to-come, the infliction of punishment upon the wicked will be without end.

Another comment: *Thy righteousness is like the mighty mountains* (*ibid.*). As the mountains are clearly visible, so the deeds of the righteous are clearly visible: "Because they fear Thee, [their deeds are always visible], are always done in the full light of day or in the radiance of the moon by night"[6] (Ps. 72:5). But [*deeds which bring on*] *Thy judgments are like the great deep.* As the deep is hidden, so are the deeds of the wicked hidden: "Their works are in the dark" (Isa. 29:15).

Another comment: *Thy righteousness is like the mighty mountains* (Ps. 36:7). As the mountains are sown and yield fruit, so the deeds of the righteous yield fruit: "Say ye of the righteous, that it shall be well with them;

---

mourning for him. And so the commentator takes *caused . . to mourn* to have two meanings: (1) the grave's black pit, made blacker by the presence of the wicked, mourns his presence; and (2) from the grave's black pit being considered not black enough for the wicked, he is made to go down into a greater depth where his remains are used to cover the abyss whose blackness equals his. Cf. Num. Rabbah 1:1.

4. JV: *For it cometh in vanity, and departeth in darkness, and the name thereof is covered with darkness.* However, the alteration of one vowel changes *yĕḵusseh*, "is covered," to *yĕḵasseh*, "serves as a cover." Presumably the commentator resorts to this reading in order to explain the assertion in the preceding verse, Eccles. 6:3, that the wicked man will have no burial, for burial is rarely denied to a man of means no matter how great his wickedness.

5. See MTeh 93:5, and 104:8.

6. JV: *They fear Thee, while the sun endureth, and so long as the moon, throughout all generations.* But the Hebrew lends itself also to the translation supporting the commentator's statement.

for men shall eat the fruit of their doings"[7] (Isa. 3:10). *Thy judgments are like the great deep* (Ps. 36:7): as the deep cannot be sown to yield fruit, so the deeds of the wicked cannot produce fruit:[8] "Woe unto the wicked! it shall be ill with him; for the work of his hands"—[note that the text does not speak of the fruit of his deeds but of the work of his hands, which, as the verse concludes]—"shall be done to him" (Isa. 3:11).

Another comment on *Thy righteousness is like the mighty mountains* (Ps. 36:7). R. Judah bar R. Simon read the verse: Thy righteousness—Thy mercy—is as lofty as Thy mountains, which Thou didst accord to Noah in the ark for a landing place: "The ark rested upon the mountains of Ararat" (Gen. 8:4). And the judgments which Thou didst pass upon Noah's generation, Thou didst carry out with such thoroughness that they reached down to the great deep [whose waters surged up from below to mingle with the waters that fell from above]: "On the same day all the fountains of the great deep were broken up" (Gen. 7:11). Nay more, when Thou didst remember Noah, Thou didst remember not him alone—no, but him and all who were with him in the ark, as it is written "God remembered Noah, as well as every living thing," etc. (Gen. 8:1).[9] [The stress upon God's concern for every living thing besides Noah and his family will be understood when you reflect that the men of our generation are just as sinful as the men of Noah's generation were. For an example of the sinfulness of the men of our generation, consider that] when R. Joshua ben Levi went to Rome, he saw marble pillars there which had been carefully covered with wrappings to keep them from cracking during the heat and from freezing during the cold. By contrast he saw there a poor wretch who had no more than a reed mat under him and a reed mat over him [to protect him from the heat and cold]. In regard to the pillars R. Joshua cited the words *Thy care is like the mighty mountains* (Ps. 36:7): where Thou dost allow care to be given, Thou allowest men to give it like the rush of streams from the mountains; and in regard to the poor wretch he cited the words *Thy judgments are like the great deep* (*ibid.*): where Thou dost allow

7. JV: *Say ye of the righteous, that it shall be well with him; for they shall eat the fruit of their doings.*

8. For if they would produce fruit, it would be evil and would destroy the world.

9. A conclusion taken to be implied in the end of Ps. 36:7: *Man and beast Thou deliverest, O Lord.*

Righteous men whose deeds are visible and fruitful have a kind of innocence like that of creatures of the field. Because of this likeness, the two preceding paragraphs setting out the characteristics of the righteous are followed by a paragraph declaring that God remembered not only Noah, a righteous man, but every creature of the field. Accordingly, when people exercised by the wickedness of mankind go so far as to demand the world's destruction, let them remember that human beings are not the sole inhabitants of the world, but that there also dwell upon it the creatures of the field with whose well-being God is equally concerned.

punishment to be inflicted, Thou allowest men to inflict it upon others down to the uttermost depths.

[Since men are still as wicked as they were in Noah's time, why then does God permit the world to continue to exist? Because, as two stories in connection with the verse *Man and cattle*, etc. (*ibid.*) show, the continued existence of the world depends on humbler creatures—women, for example—than men: The first story tells us that] Alexander of Macedon paid a visit to a king at the end of the world[10] beyond the Mountains of Darkness and eventually came to a principality called Ḳarṭigna, inhabited entirely by women.[11] These came out to meet him and said: "If you make war against us and defeat us, your name will go forth in the world as of one who laid waste a province of women; while if we make war upon you and defeat you, your name will go forth in the world as of one whom women made war against and defeated, so that you will always be ashamed to face any king." When he left, he wrote upon the city gate: I, Alexander of Macedon, was a fool until I came to the principality of Ḳarṭigna and learned wisdom from women.

[The other story tells us that] Alexander also went to another principality called "Africa [Propria]."[12] The people came out to meet him with golden apples, golden pomegranates, and golden bread. "[What is the meaning of this]"? he asked. "Do you eat gold bread in your country?" They replied: "Do you not have it in your own country that you must come to us for it?" He replied: "I have not come to see your wealth—it is your customs I have come to observe." As Alexander and his questioners were thus engaged in discourse, two men came before the king for judgment. One said: I bought a ruin from this man and while digging in it found a treasure, and so I said to him "Take your treasure—I bought a ruin—a treasure I did not buy." The other said to the king: "Sire! For my part, when I sold that man the ruin, I sold him everything that was in it."

The king addressed one of them and asked him: "Have you a son?" He replied: "Yes." The king asked the other: "Have you a daughter?" He replied: "Yes." "Go, then," said the king, "wed one to the other, and let the two make use of the treasure." Thereupon Alexander showed his amazement. The king asked: "Why are you amazed? Have I not judged well?" Alexander replied: "Yes." The king asked: "If such a case had come up in your country, how would you have handled it?" Alexander replied: "We would have removed the head of the one and the head of the other, and the

10. Believed to have been Africa, where, according to authors of antiquity, men led ideal lives. The Aramaic *Ḳaṣia* is taken to mean "end of the world." See Saul Lieberman's note in PRKM, 274.

11. Ḳarṭigna is taken to be made up of the Aramaic *ḳarta*, "city," and the Greek *gyné*, "woman."

12. The name given by the Romans to North Africa.

treasure would have gone to the royal treasury." The king asked Alexander: "Does the sun shine where you dwell?" Alexander replied: "Yes." "Does rain fall where you dwell?" Alexander said: "Yes." The king asked: "Perhaps there are small cattle in your country?" Alexander replied: "Yes." The king said: "May the breath of life in such a man as you be blasted out![13] It is for the sake of the small cattle that the sun shines where you dwell, that the rain falls where you dwell: on account of the small cattle you are preserved alive." Such is the meaning of *Man and cattle Thou preservest, O Lord* (Ps. 36:7)—on account of the cattle Thou preservest man, O Lord.

[In further comment the verse is read *Men who are like cattle Thou preservest, O Lord* (ibid.)]. Hence Israel said: Master of universes, though we be men inclined to sin, save us, [should we sin], from punishment as Thou dost spare cattle from punishment, for, in truth, [the innocence of our faith in Thee is like the innocence of cattle]: like them we are drawn after Thee, saying to Thee, *Draw me after Thee, [for in following Thee], I shall be satisfied*[14] (Song 1:4). And because, like cattle, we let ourselves be drawn after Thee, whither [do we find ourselves drawn? Each one of us] to his own Garden of Eden, declares the School of Rabbi, for, the Psalm goes on to say, *They will be abundantly satisfied with the fatness of Thy house; and Thou permittest them to drink from the river of Thine Edens*[15] (Ps. 36:9). The text does not say "Thine Eden" but *Thine Edens*, indicating, as R. Eleazar bar R. Menahem pointed out, that each and every righteous man has his own Garden of Eden[16], [for both in God's judgments or in lack of them, he sees evidences of mercy]. As R. Isaac taught: [When examined in depth], God's judicial decree for mankind like[17] His judicial decree for cattle [is prompted by mercy]. His decree for mankind: *In the eighth day the flesh of his foreskin shall be circumcised* (Lev. 12:3); His decree for

13. The Aramaic is careful to preserve the rules of polite discourse: "in that man be blasted out"—a courteous circumlocution for the direct "be blasted out of you." Leon Nemoy provided the comment.

Or, as my friend Fr. David McCarthy suggests, "May your heart beat you to the grave."

14. JV: *Draw me, we will run after Thee*. But apparently by a slight change in vocalization the commentator takes *naruṣah*, "we will run," as a form of *rṣh*, "be pleased, be satisfied." Then, too, the *na* in *naruṣah*, may be taken to represent *'n'*, "I."

15. JV: *the river of Thy pleasures.*

16. Thus Eden is not an abode (as, for example, in B.Shab 152a and BM 53b) but a state of mind. At times the term Gehenna also designates a state of mind. For example: "R. Samuel bar Naḥmani . . . said, 'Whenever a man gets angry, all kinds of Gehenna possess him' " (B.Neḏ 22a).

17. The conjunction *u*, "and," is construed as though it were the pronoun *hu'*, "like." See Saul Lieberman, *Tarbiṣ, 4* (1933), 377.

cattle: *From the eighth day and thenceforth it may be accepted for an offering* (Lev. 22:27).[18]

2. R. Tanḥuma began his discourse with the verse *Whosoever without being required to bestirs himself [to help provide instruction in Torah which] under the whole heaven was [first]*[18a] *Mine—I will repay by not turning a deaf ear to his prayer for male children*[19] (Job 41:3–4a). To start with, R. Tanḥuma applied the verse to an unmarried man who lives in an outlying place [without schools][20] yet pays the fee for teachers of Scripture and teachers of Mishnah [elsewhere]. Of such a man, the Holy One says: It is for Me to pay him [when he marries] by not turning a deaf ear to his prayer for male children.

[Then R. Tanḥuma quoted] R. Jeremiah bar R. Eleazar [who read Job 41:3 as also asserting *Whosoever without being required to bestirs himself (to help provide instruction in Torah which) under the whole heaven was (first) Mine—I will repay (by having a Voice proclaim) under the entire heaven that such a man has wrought as I have wrought.* And R. Tanḥuma went on to quote R. Jeremiah's comment on the verse]: Some day in the future a Divine Voice[21] reverberating on the mountain tops will declare, Whosoever wrought with God [as the unmarried man wrought],[22] let him come and receive the reward due him. Of this it is said *At the due season shall it be told to Jacob and to Israel: "Who hath wrought with God"*[23]

18. God does not require that circumcision be performed until the eighth day after birth when the infant is strong enough to endure it, and He does not accept an animal for sacrifice until it is at least eight days old, so that its dam may not suffer its loss too soon.

Hence, concludes the *pĕṯiḥah*'s author, whether God bestows mercy or administers justice, His governance of the world is grounded in considerations of mercy.

18a. Of the seven things which by two thousand years preceded the creation of the world, the Torah came first. See MTeh 90:12 (YJS, *13*, 2, 94).

19. *Who hath given Me anything beforehand that I should repay him? Whatsoever is under the whole heaven is Mine. Would I keep silence concerning his boastings.* But *baddaw*, "his boastings," may be rendered "his branches," hence "his male children" or "his prayer for male children." See Rashi.

Professor Morton Smith suggests that R. Tanḥuma read Job 41:3a thus: "Whosoever carries My cause forward, he under the whole heaven is My very own."

20. Though organized schools existed only in larger cities and though this man had no children of his own, he still deemed it his duty to provide for other men's children the wherewithal to be instructed in Torah.

21. Literally "Daughter of a Voice." See B.Yoma 9b, and Song Rabbah 8:9.

22. The fact that the unmarried man of his own accord, without being required to or specifically commanded, made it possible for children to study God's commands is deemed by God to be equivalent to an act of creation.

23. Cf. Isa. 40:9–10 which may be read, "His reward is with the one whose work anticipates His own." In JV, Num. 23:23 reads: *Now it is said of Jacob and*

(Num. 23:23): whosoever wrought with God, let him come and receive th reward due him.

In another comment[24] the verse is read to mean that the holy spirit i asking *Who hath given Me anything beforehand that I should repay him* (Job. 41:3). Who sang out in praise of Me before I put breath into him Who could circumcise in My name before I gave him a male child? Who, a My request, made fringes before I gave him a garment? Who, at My request made a mezuzah before I gave him a house? Who, at My request, built a parapet[25] before I gave him a roof? Who, at my request, built a sukkah before I gave him a courtyard? Who, at My request, set aside the corners o the crop before I gave him a field? Who, at My request, set aside heave offering for priests and tithes for Levites before I gave him a threshing floor? Who, at My request, set aside an offering before I gave him cattle? *When a bullock, or a sheep, or a goat is brought forth,* etc. (Lev. 22:27).[26]

3. [In further reference to the verse just above], R. Jacob bar Zabdi, citing R. Abbahu, began his discourse with the verse *Bringing* THE *iniquity*—the making of the golden calf—*to remembrance against the House of Israel will not continue to be a source of reassurance* [*for heathen nations*][27] (Ezek. 29:16), and went on to quote the following: "Above Him stood the seraphim; each one had six wings," etc. (Isa. 6:2). "With two he did fly" (*ibid.*), singing out God's praise as he flew;[28] "with two he covered his face" (*ibid.*), so as not to gaze upon the Presence; "and with two he covered his feet" (*ibid.*), that his feet should not be exposed to the Presence. Since "the sole of the [seraphim's] feet was like the sole of a calf's foot" (Ezek. 1:7), [the seraphim covered their feet] so that *Bringing* THE *iniquity to remembrance against the House of Israel will not continue to be a source of reassurance* [*for heathen nations*] (Ezek. 29:16).

Elsewhere we are told in a Mishnah "All horns are proper for blowing except that of the cow" (RH 3:2). Because a cow is of the same breed as a calf, therefore the horn may not be used, in order that *Bringing* THE *iniquity to remembrance against Israel will not continue to be a source of reassurance* [*for heathen nations*][29] (Ezek. 29:16).

In still another place we are told: "If a woman approach unto any beast,

---

of Israel: "*What God hath wrought.*" But the commentator takes *mh,* "what," for a variant spelling of *my,* "who, whosoever."

24. "In another comment"—Mah on Lev. Rabbah 27:2.

25. See Deut. 22:8.

26. Still God rewards man for obeying His commands.

27. The nations of the earth gloated when Israel made the golden calf (Piska 2.1; and PR 10:10). JV: *And it shall be no more the confidence of the house of Israel, bringing iniquity to remembrance.*

28. See B.Ḥag̅ 13b; and PRE, chap. 4, end.

29. See B.RH 26a.

nd lie down thereto, thou shalt kill the woman and the beast" (Lev. 0:16). In such a case, the human being commits a sin, but what sin does he animal commit? None. However, because the animal is a stumbling block whereby a human being falls into sin, Scripture orders that the animal be stoned to death. Another reason for killing the animal is that if it were allowed to live, people seeing it pass through the streets [would be reminded of the sin] and would be tempted to say: "There's the one on account of whom So-and-so was stoned to death."[30] The animal is therefore put to death in order that *Bringing an iniquity to remembrance against the House of Israel will not continue to be a source of satisfaction* [*for malicious people*] (Ezek. 29:16).

We are also told in a Baraita that a woman suspected of infidelity is not to drink from the cup of a woman who was also suspected of infidelity [and who, having drunk from the cup, died.[31] The woman under suspicion is not to drink from the same cup] in order to keep people from saying "A woman like her, also suspected of infidelity, drank from this cup and died," and thus bringing up a reminder of the former guilty woman's iniquity: *Bringing iniquity to remembrance should not continue to be a source of satisfaction* [*for malicious people*] (Ezek. 29:16).

Consider finally another instance [of how Scripture avoids *Bringing iniquity to remembrance*]. In the verse *When a bullock, or a sheep, or a goat is brought forth* (Lev. 22:27), is it precise to speak of a bullock as "brought forth?" Is it not termed a "calf" when it is brought forth? However, because Scripture says in Exodus 32:8 "They have made them a molten calf," Leviticus in speaking of the young of animals to be used for offerings —*when a bullock, or a sheep, or a goat is brought forth* (Lev. 22:27)— chooses deliberately to use "bullock," not "calf," [so as to avoid *Bringing iniquity to remembrance*].

4. [*God brings to pass that men should revere Him* (Eccles 3:14b). These words are to be understood in the light of the verse that follows them]: *That which hath been is now; and that which is to be hath already been* (Eccles. 3:15). R. Judah and R. Nehemiah differ in interpreting the verse. R. Judah said: If any one says to you, "Had Adam not sinned, can we believe that he would have lived—endured—till now?" say in reply *That which hath been is now,* for Elijah, ever remembered on good occasions, who never sinned—is he not alive, does he not endure even now? *And that which is to be hath already been.* If a man says to you, "Can we believe that the Holy One is capable of bringing the dead back to life?" say in reply, *That*

30. See Śem 8:16 (YJS, *17*, 66); and Sanh 7:4.

31. Apparently the regulation that a new cup was to be used each time for the ordeal of bitter water (Soṭ 2:2) is construed as meaning a cup which had not been used by another woman similarly charged.

which is to be hath already been. Has He not already, by the hand of Elijah, then by the hand of Elisha, then by the hand of Ezekiel brought back the dead?"[32]

R. Nehemiah said: If a man says to you, "Can we believe that the earth was covered with waters upon waters?" say in reply, *That which hath been is now:* is not the Ocean, all of it, waters upon waters? *That which is to be hath already been.* If a man says to you, "Can we believe that the Holy One will make the sea dry land?"[33] say in reply, Has He not already done so by the hand of Moses? *The children of Israel walked upon dry land in the midst of the sea* (Exod. 14:29).

R. Aḥa, citing R. Simeon bar Ḥilfa, said: All that the Holy One will do in the time-to-come, He has already anticipated and done in part by the hand of the righteous in this world. The Holy One says: I shall quicken the dead. He has already done so by the hand of Elijah, by the hand of Elisha, by the hand of Ezekiel. The Holy One says: I shall make the sea dry land. Has He not already done so by the hand of Moses? *The children of Israel walked upon dry land in the midst of the sea* (Exod. 14:29). The Holy One says: I will open the eyes of the blind.[34] Has He not already done so—*The Lord opened the eyes of the young man* (2 Kings 6:17)? The Holy One says: I shall remember barren women.[35] Has He not already done so—*The Lord remembered Sarah* (Gen. 21:1)? The Holy One says: *Kings shall be thy foster-fathers, and their queens thy nursing mothers; they shall bow down to thee with their face to the earth* (Isa. 49:23). Has He not already brought about these things? Was not Nebuchadnezzar a king, and to whom did he bow down? To Daniel, as Scripture says, *The king Nebuchadnezzar fell upon his face, and worshiped Daniel* (Dan. 2:46).

[As between pursuers and the pursued, such as "a bullock, or a sheep, or a goat"], *God seeketh the pursued* (Eccles. 3:15). R. Huna said in the name of R. Joseph: The Holy One will demand the blood of the pursued from the hand of those who pursued them. When a righteous man pursues a righteous man, "God seeks the one pursued." When a wicked man pursues a wicked one, "God seeks the one pursued." When a wicked man pursues a righteous man, "God seeks the one pursued." Even if you were to turn the matter about and speak of a righteous man pursuing a wicked one, nonetheless "God seeks the one pursued." You can see for yourself that He does so in this world, for Abel was pursued by Cain.[36] "And in His seeking the one

32. 1 Kings 17:22; 2 Kings 4:35; Ezek. 37.

R. Judah applies Eccles. 3:15 to miraculous events in the life of man; R. Nehemiah will apply the verse to such events in the realm of nature.

33. Isa. 11:15.

34. Isa. 35:5.

35. Isa. 54:1.

36. He sought to drive him off the earth's face. See Exod. Rabbah 31:17.

pursued," *The Lord looked for Abel and his offering* (Gen. 4:4). Noah was pursued by his generation.[37] Therefore, since "God seeks the one pursued," *Noah found grace in the eyes of the Lord* (Gen. 6:8). Abraham was pursued by Nimrod.[38] Therefore, since "God seeks the one pursued," Scripture says, *Thou art the Lord, the God, who didst choose Abram* (Neh. 9:7). Isaac was pursued by the Philistines.[39] Therefore, since "God seeks the one pursued," the Philistines were forced to say, *We saw plainly that the Lord was with thee* (Gen. 26:28). Jacob was pursued by Esau. Therefore, since "God seeks the one pursued," *The Lord hath chosen Jacob unto Himself* (Ps. 135:4). Joseph was pursued by his brothers. Therefore, since "God seeks the one pursued," *The Lord was with Joseph, and made all that he did to prosper* (Gen. 39:2). Moses was pursued by Pharaoh. Therefore, since "God seeks the one pursued," *He said that He would destroy them, but for Moses His chosen* (Ps. 106:23). Israel are pursued by the nations of the earth. Therefore, since "God seeks the one pursued," *The Lord hath chosen thee to be His own treasure* (Deut. 14:2).

R. Judah bar R. Simon said in the name of R. Jose bar Nehorai: Since the bullock is pursued by the lion, the sheep by the wolf, the goat by the leopard,[39a] the Holy One said: Bring no offering before Me of those that pursue—only of those that are pursued:[40] *When a bullock, or a sheep, or a goat is brought forth,* etc. (Lev. 22:27).

5. [For an offering to Me, I have not wearied thee by asking for other than "a bullock, or a sheep, or a goat." Hence], *O My people, what have I done for thee? And wherein* [*by contrast*] *have I wearied thee? Testify* [*truthfully*] *concerning Me* (Micah 6:3)—that is, according to R. Aḥa, Testify truthfully concerning Me[41] and receive the reward [of vindication]. Do not testify against [Me], your Friend, and thus bring yourselves to scrutiny and account. Then, to prove that God finds ways of vindicating Israel, R. Aḥa, citing R. Samuel bar Naḥman, continued: On the three occasions that the Holy One came to argue with Israel, the nations of the earth were glad. When the Holy One said: *Come now, and let us argue it out, saith the Lord* (Isa. 1:18), the nations of the earth rejoiced, saying, How can these people argue successfully against their Creator? He will now obliterate them from the world. But when the Holy One saw that the nations were

37. They called him a contemptible old man (Gen. Rabbah 30:7).

38. Nimrod, identified as Amraphel, sought to burn Abraham (Gen. Rabbah 42:4).

39. Gen. 26:16.

39a. See Isa. 11:6.

40. Since animals, in any event, are meant to be slaughtered, the ones that are pursued, in being offered to Him on high, are thus singled out for honor. *Yĕfeh to'ar.*

41. Meaning, Say the Shĕma'. B.Ber 14b.

glad, He turned His case against Israel into an expression of favor: *Though your sins be as scarlet, they shall be white as snow* (*ibid.*). Thereupon the nations of the earth were astonished, saying: Is God's statement of His case a proper reproach of Israel? He has come merely to be indulgent with His children.[42] Then again when the Holy One said: *Hear, O ye mountains, the Lord's controversy,* etc. (Micah 6:2), the nations of the earth rejoiced, saying: How can these people contend with their Creator? Now He will indeed obliterate them from the world. But when the Holy one saw that the nations of the earth were glad, He turned His case against Israel into [a reproachful reminder of His past] kindnesses to them: *O My people, what have I done for thee, and wherein* [*by contrast*] *have I wearied thee? Testify about Me,* etc. *Remember now what Balak king of Moab devised,* etc. (Micah 6:3, 5). Then again when God said: *The Lord hath also a controversy with Judah,* etc. (Hos. 12:3), the nations of the earth were glad, saying: Now He is certain to obliterate them from the world. But when the Holy One saw that the nations of the earth were glad, He turned His case against Israel into a reminder of His having made light [of their past offenses such as the offense committed by Jacob in his mother's womb]: *In the womb he took his brother by the heel,* etc. (Micah 12:4).

[That God is Israel's Friend is plain from] a parable of a woman who was about to bring charges against her son because he had kicked her when he was in her womb. When the woman saw the judge sitting in judgment and heard him sentencing people to death, she said: If I make known the misconduct of my son to the judge, he will forthwith sentence him also to death. What did she do? She waited until the judge had finished trying the cases before him. After he settled the cases before him, he asked her: What was the misconduct of your son against you? She replied: He kicked me when he was in my womb. He asked her: Has he done anything to you since? She replied: No. He said to her: Then there is no offense in what he did. The nations of the earth were astonished: Is God's judgment in the case of Israel an appropriate one? No! It is a *non sequitur*! He has come merely to be indulgent with His children.[43]

With reference to God's saying to Israel, *Wherein have I wearied thee?* (Micah 6:3), R. Berechiah told the parable of a king who sent a proclamation of his to a province. What did all the people of the province do? When they received it, they rose to their feet, uncovered their heads, and read it

42. [The Hebrew is much more expressive: "What kind of a rejoinder or contest is this?" The same applies to the following where *lo'* . . . *'ella'* is meant as emphasis: "(Evidently) He has come to do nothing but play with His children." L.N.]

43. [Are you sure that *zo 'aḥar zo* means "It is a *non sequitur*?" I would say: "What kind of a rejoinder or contest is this, time and time again? (Evidently) He has come to do nothing but play with His children." L.N.]

with fear and reverence, with trepidation and awe. Like the king, the Holy One said to Israel: The reading of the Shĕma' is My proclamation. With regard to it, however, I do not put you to any trouble. I do not tell you that you are to read it [in a formal way], standing on your feet and uncovering your heads [in submission to Me], but simply *When thou sittest in thy house, and when thou walkest by the way*, etc. (Deut. 6:7).

Another comment: *Wherein have I wearied thee?* (Micah 6:3). According to R. Judah bar R. Simon, the Holy One said: I have made available ten clean beasts as food for you—three of these subject to your control, and seven not subject to your control. Subject to your control: *The ox, the sheep, and the goat* (Deut. 14:4); not subject to your control: *The hart, the gazelle, the roebuck, the wild goat, and the ibex*, etc. (Deut. 14:5). I have not burdened you. I have not told you to chase over mountains or weary yourselves in fields to fetch Me an offering out of those that are not subject to your control—only such as are subject to your control, such as are reared at your trough: *When a bullock, a sheep, or a goat is brought forth*, etc. (Lev. 22:27).

6. [In further comment on the foregoing verse, Isaiah's words are cited]. *Behold (Hen), ye are me'ayin, and the making of you me'afa'*[44] (Isa. 41:24): behold, you are from nothing (*me'ayin*), from a foul fluid, and the making of you is no more than haphazard chance: the hundred cries[45] that a woman gives voice to when she sits upon the birthstool intimate that your chances of death are ninety-nine, your chance of life only one. Yet even when you are *An abomination, one takes you up*[46] (*ibid.*). Even though the new-born child issues foul and soiled, covered with fluids and blood from the

44. JV: *Behold, ye are nothing, and your work a thing of nought.* Apparently the commentator regarding the *me*, "from," in *me'ayin* and in *me'afa'* as superfluous—and the entire verse as unnecessary, indeed anticlimactic for Isaiah's argument against idolatry—proceeds to develop it as follows: In the first comment (which in the parallel in Lev. Rabbah M, 640 is attributed to R. Levi), Isaiah, understood to be addressing not the idols but the people Israel, says to them: "You so wondrously made, how can you demean yourselves by the worship of deities which are inanimate?"

In R. Levi's second comment, Isa. 41:24 is construed not as the last verse of Isaiah's utterance concerning idolatry, but as the first verse of the ensuing passage in which Isaiah foretells the coming of Cyrus who is to initiate Israel's return to the Land. Wrestling with the question of whether in view of Israel's adoration of idols, Israel deserves redemption, the commentator concludes that Israel's wholehearted acceptance of God's commands at Sinai outweighs all Israel's subsequent derelictions. Indeed, God Himself so indicated in that He asked that a bullock—the symbol of Israel's abominable straying—be brought as an offering.

45. *Me'afa'* is here regarded as a contraction of *me'ah pĕ'iyyoṯ*, "one hundred cries."

46. JV: *An abomination is he that chooseth you.*

womb of its mother, it is taken up, and all caress it, all kiss it, particularly if it is a male child, [for it is no botched-up idol of wood or stone, but flesh-and-blood wondrously made].

Another comment: *Hen ye are me'ayin* (Isa. 41:24). According to R. Berechiah, the word *Hen*, [usually translated "behold"], is a Greek word *ena*[47], meaning "one," so that God is saying in the verse "For Me you are the one, the only one of all the nations of the earth," the others in My sight being nothing (*me'ayin*). Of them Scripture says, "All the nations are as nothing (*'ayin*) before Him" (Isa. 40:17). The words *And your reward me'afa'* (Isa. 41:24) mean, according to R. Levi, that all the kindnesses and consolations which I, the Lord, extend to you are your reward for the one cry (*pĕ'iyyah*) you voiced before Me at Sinai when you said: "All that the Lord hath spoken, we will do, and obey" (Exod. 24:7). *An abomination He takes up from among you* (Isa. 41:24) refers to that abomination of which it is written "They have made them a molten bullock" (Exod. 32:4). It is of that very abomination that I say, Bring an offering unto Me: *A bullock,* etc. (Lev. 22:27). [That which was an abomination, I thus take up and hallow].

7. *With their "wickedness" they make glad the King, for even in their act of denial* [*such as the making of the calf they intended no more than the representation of one of God's heavenly*] *princes*[48] (Hos. 7:3). Why did Scripture deem it necessary to set the bullock as first among all the offerings? R. Levi answered this question with a parable of a noble lady. An evil rumor had gone forth, linking her with one of the notables in the kingdom, but when the king investigated the reports, he found no substance in them. What did he do? He prepared a great feast and put the notable at the head of the guests at the table.[49] All this for what reason? To make it known that the king had investigated the reports and found no substance in them. So, too, because the nations of the earth were taunting Israel, saying to them: "You made the calf," the Holy One investigated the reports and found no sub-

47. [The Greek has a hard breathing at the beginning—*hena*—and the reason R. Berechiah drops it is, I suppose, because he came from a region where the spoken Aramaic did not voice the gutturals. L.N.]

48. Accordingly, when they made the bullock or calf, the children of Israel did not intend to deny God; they only meant to give visual representation to one of the four "faces" or creatures in Ezekiel's account of the chariot (Ezek. 1:10; Ps. 106:20; and Exod. Rabbah 3:2, 49:2). In R. Levi's view, Hosea's denunciation of his people is thus considerably softened, since R. Levi construes Hos. 7:3 as saying that Israel's intent in making the heinous bullock or calf was, in a misguided way, honorable.

49. Literally "at the head of the reclining guests." At Roman feasts guests were not seated but reclined on couches.

stance in them. Therefore, the bullock was put at the head of the list of offerings: *A bullock, a sheep, or a goat,* etc. (Lev. 22:27).

8. [Because of the Holy One's investigation], said R. Huna and R. Idi in the name of R. Samuel bar Naḥman, the children of Israel were exonerated from blame for that unspeakable deed. Had Israel made the calf, one would have expected them to say, "This is OUR God, O Israel." It was, however, the [insincere] proselytes who had come up from Egypt with them—it was they who made the calf and mocked Israel, *This is thy God, O Israel* (Exod. 32:4). R. Judah bar R. Simon said: It is written *The ox knoweth his owner, and the ass his master's crib, but Israel doth not know* (Isa. 1:3). Did they not know their Master? Of course they did. But they came to take God for granted. Likewise, *My people is foolish, they know Me not* (Jer. 4:22). Did they not know who their Master was? Of course, they did. But they came to take Me for granted. Likewise, *She did not know that it was I that gave her the corn,* etc. (Hos. 2:10). Did she not know that it was I? Of course, she did. But she came to take Me for granted.[50]

9. [Why *A bullock, or a sheep, or a goat for offerings*]*? A bullock* (Lev. 22:27) through the merit of Abraham: "Abraham ran unto the herd, and fetched a young bull" (Gen. 18:7). *A ram*—a sheep, through the merit of Isaac: "Abraham . . . looked, and behold behind him a ram caught in the thicket by his horns," etc. (Gen. 22:13). *A goat,* through the merit of Jacob: "Go now to the flock, and fetch me from thence two good kids of the goats" (Gen. 27:9). Why did Rebekah say "good?"[51] Because she meant, explained R. Berechiah in the name of R. Ḥelbo, they will be good for you, [O Jacob], and good for your children—good for you since through them you will receive [your father's] blessings; and good for your children, for, because of the offering of he-goats, atonement will be made for your children on Atonement Day: *On this day shall atonement be made for you,* etc. (Lev. 16:30).

10. In comment on the verse *It shall be seven days under the dam* (Lev. 22:27), R. Joshua of Siḵnin told, in the name of R. Levi, the parable of a king who entered a province and issued a decree, saying: "Let no visitors here attend upon me until they shall have first attended upon my queen." So, too, the Holy One said to Israel: My children, you shall not bring an offering unto Me until a Sabbath day, [the queen of days], shall have passed over it. And since it is required that the youngling be a period of seven days under its dam, a Sabbath must fall within this period, just as a Sabbath must intervene in the period before a circumcision can take place. As R. Isaac observed:

50. Literally "they stepped on it with their heels."

51. Apparently in this instance the author takes "good" to mean not "good in flavor" but "good in purpose."

The ordinance with regard to man and the ordinance with regard to beast are alike [in the time intervals they specify]. The ordinance with regard to man: *In the eighth day the flesh of his foreskin shall be circumcised* (Lev 12:3); and the ordinance with regard to beast: *From the eighth day and thenceforth it may be accepted for an offering made by fire unto the Lord* (Lev. 22:27).

11. *And whether it be cow or ewe, ye shall not kill it and its young both in one day* (Lev. 22:28). R. Berechiah said in the name of R. Levi: *The righteous regardeth the life of his beast* (Prov. 12:10), the righteous being the Holy One who wrote in His Torah "Thou shalt not take the dam with the young"[52] (Deut. 22:6). [The wicked, however, kill mothers and their children on the same day, as is said] *But mothers*[53] *also—the wicked being cruel* (Prov. 12:10). Such a wicked one was Sennacherib,[54] at whose orders "The mother was dashed in pieces with her children" (Hos. 10:14).

Another comment: *The righteous regardeth the life of his beast* (Prov. 12:10), the righteous being the Holy One who wrote in His Torah "Whether it be cow or ewe, ye shall not kill it and its young both in one day" (Lev. 22:28). *But the tender mercies*[55] *of the wicked are cruel* (Prov. 12:10): such was the wicked Haman, at whose orders "Letters . . . were sent . . . to destroy, to slay, and to cause to perish all Jews, both young and old, little children and women, in one day" (Esther 3:13).

R. Levi said: Woe to the wicked who busy themselves with evil counsel against Israel, each one boasting "My counsel is better than your counsel." Esau said: Cain was a fool, for he slew his brother while his father was still alive. Did not Cain know that his father would be fruitful and multiply? I shall not act so unknowingly: *Let the days of mourning for my father be at hand, and then I will slay my brother Jacob* (Gen. 27:41). Pharaoh said: Esau was a fool in saying, *Let the days of mourning for my father be at hand*, etc. Did he not know that while his father was still alive, his brother [Jacob] would be fruitful and would multiply? I shall not act as unknowingly as Esau. Under the very birth-stools of Israelites' mothers, while the male infants are still tiny things, I shall strangle them. At once Pharaoh charged his people: [*Ye shall look upon the birth-stool: if it be a son, ye*

52. In order to teach kindness to animals.

53. JV: *But the tender mercies of the wicked are cruel.* The word *rḥm*, "tender mercy," is here construed literally as "womb" (cf. Judg. 5:30). Hence, "mother."

54. Sennacherib is said to have had eight names, one of which was Shalmaneser (B.Sanh 94a).

55. Ostensibly he was eager to protect the nations of Persia from *a certain people who . . . do not keep the king's laws* (Esther 3:8). In the last two comments, the explanations of Mošeh Pfefferberg are followed. See his *Dib̠re Mošeh* (Warsaw, 1914), *3*, 156.

shall kill him, and then charged his people]: *Every son that is born ye shall cast into the river* (Exod. 1:16, 22). Haman said: Pharaoh was a fool when he charged his people: *Every son that is born ye shall cast into the river, and every daughter ye shall save alive* (*ibid.*). Did he not know that the daughters would marry, would be fruitful, and would multiply? I shall not act as unknowingly as Pharaoh. I shall *destroy, slay, and cause to perish all Jews, both young and old, little children and women* (Esther 3:13). R. Levi went on: At the time of the Messiah's coming Gog and Magog will likewise say: Fools were all the former who busied themselves with evil counsel against Israel. Did they not know that Israel have their Partisan in heaven? We shall not act as unknowingly as all the other enemies of Israel—first, we will make war against their Partisan, and then we shall turn upon Israel. Hence it is said *The kings of the earth set themselves, and the rulers take counsel together against the Lord and against His anointed* (Ps. 2:2). But the Holy One will say to Gog and Magog: Oh ye wicked, do you set yourselves to make war against Me? As ye live, I Myself will wage war against you. Accordingly, Scripture: [*At first,*] *the Lord will go forth merely as a mighty man, a man of war, even as He stirs up envy* [*of Israel in Gog and Magog*], *whilst,* [*like a mortal*], *He cries and shouts aloud*[56] (Isa. 42:13). But then *As the Lord, He will go forth and fight against the nations, even as He fought in the day of battle* [at the Red Sea][56a] (Zech. 14:3).

12. *And when ye sacrifice a sacrifice of thanksgiving unto the Lord—you will continue to offer it* [*even in the time-to-come*] *when you have all that delights you*[57] (Lev. 22:29). R. Phinehas, R. Levi, and R. Johanan citing R. Menahem of Gallia[58] said: In the time-to-come all offerings will cease,[59] except the thank offering which will never cease. All prayers will cease, except the prayer of thanksgiving which will never cease. Hence it is written of the time-to-come *The voice of joy and the voice of gladness, the voice of*

56. JV: *The Lord will go forth as a mighty man, He will stir up zeal like a man of war, He will cry, yea, He will shout aloud*, etc.

56a. "[at the Red Sea]"—Targum Jonathan, Rashi, and Ibn Ezra. Cf. S2.2. Exod. 14:25 reads *The Lord fighteth for them against the Egyptians*.

57. JV: *Ye shall sacrifice it that ye may be accepted*. But *lirĕṣonḵem*, "that ye may be accepted," may also be rendered "when you have all that delights you." Inasmuch as the sacrifice of thanksgiving had already been ordained in Lev. 7:12, the commentator construes its repetition in Lev. 22:29 as intimating that the sacrifice of thanksgiving will continue in the time-to-come. See also *Yĕfeh to'ar* on Lev. Rabbah 9:7.

58. Gallia may be a place in Judea or Philistia (Levy, *Wörterbuch*, *1*, 344). In his edition of Leviticus Rabbah, Mošeh Mirkin identifies Gallia with Eglaim, a city in Moab, mentioned in Isa. 15:8 (*Way-yiḵra' rabbah* [Tel Aviv, 1961], *1*, 95).

59. Offerings to atone for sins, which in time-to-come will not be committed.

the bridegroom and the voice of the bride, the voice of them that say: "Give thanks to the Lord of hosts, for He[60] *is good, for His mercy endureth for ever"* (Jer. 33:11): these are prayers of thanksgiving; *and of them that bring offerings of thanksgiving into the house of the Lord* (*ibid.*): these are thank offerings. So, too, David said: *Thy vows are upon me, O God* (Ps. 56:13). He did not go on to say, "I will render a thank offering" but *I will render thank offerings unto Thee* (*ibid.*), a statement which intimates that both thanksgiving and thank offering will be rendered [in the time-to-come].

60. MT: *for the Lord.*

PISKA 10

SUMMARY

Tithe that you may be blithe

Niggardliness in one's household, in lending, and more especially in tithing leads eventually to a decrease of one's possessions (Sec. 1). But faithfulness in tithing increases them (Sec. 2). Whatever exceptional gifts are given to a man—looks, voice, or produce—he should therewith honor the Lord (Sec. 3). Thus Israel are saved from Gehenna because again and again, in every activity in life, they are determined to honor those commandments which require giving up a portion of one's possessions (Sec. 4). When men scheme to act deceitfully with regard to tithes and offerings due from the Land's produce, the Land, in return, leads such men to believe that they will reap a good harvest, but then denies it to them (Sec. 5). The regulations concerning tithes and offerings from crops were observed by David and practiced by the Patriarchs (Sec. 6) and by Job (Sec. 7). When one considers all that God does to make a crop grow, His demand for a tithe is modest (Sec. 8). A man who eats his produce untithed is as one who eats the forbidden flesh of animals that die a natural death or are torn by beasts of prey; such a man causes the corn to be blasted before it ripens (Sec. 9). Tithes do not make you poor. On the contrary: tithe and be blithe, for God will make you blithe by making you prosperous (Sec. 10).

PISKA 10

Tithe, and then thou shalt again tithe (Deut. 14:22).[1]

1. *He that hath an evil eye hasteneth after riches, and knoweth not that want shall come upon him* (Prov. 28:22). R. Ḥanina interpreted the verse as applying to Ephron. According to R. Ḥanina, [even though] the word "shekel" [when used without qualification] in the Pentateuch means a *sela'*, when used in the Prophets means a *liṭra*, and in the Writings means a centenary,[2] [nevertheless, he had in mind as an exception to his observation, Ephron's demand, as noted in the Pentateuch, for shekels valued not as *sela'*s, but as centenaries]. Proof of the exception, as R. Judah ben R. Pazzi pointed out, is found in the verse in which Abraham says in regard to Ephron: *With silver [shekels] at their highest value let him give [the field] to me,*[3] etc. (Gen. 23:9). Because Ephron cast a covetous eye upon our father Abraham's money, Scripture saw to it that one letter, the *waw*, was wanting in his name. For, according to Scripture, Ephron said to Abraham, *My lord, hearken unto me: a piece of land worth four hundred shekels of silver, what is that betwixt me and thee?* (Gen. 23:15)—if you had a mind to give me, say, four hundred centenaries worth of silver you could easily give it to me [out of the income] from your estate's manure. And thus because he cast a covetous eye upon our father Abraham's possessions, Scripture saw to it that the *waw* previously part of his name, was wanting: *And Abraham weighed to Ephrn* (Gen. 23:16)—this time spelled "Ephrn," wanting the *waw*.[4]

R. Ammi applied the verse in Proverbs to a borrower too niggardly to hire two heifers at one time. So he borrows one and hires one, and *knoweth not that want shall come upon him* (Prov. 28:22), [since if the borrowed animal gets hurt or dies], "The owner thereof not being with it, the borrower shall surely make restitution"[5] (Exod. 22:13).

1. EV: *Thou shalt surely tithe.* But such a translation glides over a redundancy in verbs, a redundancy which the commentator will presently exploit.

In the Land of Israel, Deut. 14:22–16:17 was read on the Sabbath during Passover as well as on the Sabbath during Sukkot. See Ezra Fleischer in *Tarbiṣ, 36* (5727/1966), 155. Outside the Land of Israel, Deut. 14:22–16:17 is read on the eighth day of Passover as well as on the second day of Pentecost when the day falls on the Sabbath.

2. A *liṭra* equals 25 *sela'*; a centenary equals 100 *sela'*. Cf. B.Beḳ 50a. Shekel is bullion, and *sela'* is currency; the latter, through the years, has depreciated in value.

3. JV: *For the full price let him give it to me.*

4. In other places in this account Ephron's name is spelled *plene*, with a *waw*.

5. See Exod. 22:13–14. Had he not been so mean of eye and had paid for the hire of both heifers, he would not have been called upon to pay if both had died.

R. Isaac applied the verse in Proverbs to the Jew who lends on interest to another Jew. Being too niggardly to let the other have the money without interest, he lends it on interest, and *knoweth not that want shall come upon him* (Prov. 28:22). [For, what he wrings out in interest from his fellow Jew, Esau will in return wring out of him and "graciously" give it to the poor, leaving the lender in want], as it is written "He that augmenteth his substance by interest or increase, gathereth it for him that is gracious to the poor" (Prov. 28:8). Esau "gracious to the poor"? Wicked Esau? Is not wicked Esau an oppressor of the poor? Yes, he is like those administrators who go into villages where they wring out all they can from their tenants and then come back into the city and ["graciously"] announce, "Gather the poor folk, we wish to give them charity." It is Esau's kind that the proverb refers to: The harlot who sells herself for apples thinks to make a good name for herself by giving them to the sick.[6]

R. Levi applied the verse in Proverbs to one who is not scrupulous about paying his tithes, and R. Levi told the story of a man who was scrupulous about paying his tithes. He had a field which yielded a thousand measures, from which he would pay a hundred measures in tithe—from this field he sustained himself all his life, indeed provided for all his various needs throughout his life. When he was about to die, he called his son and said to him: My son, give heed to this field which produces such-and-such, and from which I have been paying such-and-such in tithes. From this field I sustained myself all my life, indeed provided for all my various needs throughout my life.

The first year the son sowed the field, it produced a thousand measures from which he gave a hundred measures in tithe. The second year, however, having decided to reduce his tithe by ten, he brought niggardliness into the field, and the field, in turn, produced a hundred measures less. As he continued to reduce the tithe by ten, the field produced less by the hundred, until finally it produced only the amount of its original tithe.[7] When his kin observed what had happened, they put on [festive] undergarments of white, wrapped themselves in [festive] outergarments of white, and went to his house. When he asked, "What! Have you come to rejoice over one who is afflicted?" They replied: "God's mercy, no! We came only to rejoice with you. In the past you were the owner, and the Holy One was the priest. Now you have become the priest,[8] and the Holy One is the owner." R. Levi concluded: As year after year he reduced the tithe from the field, year after

6. [I would translate . . . literally: "She fornicates for apples and then distributes them to the sick." L.N.]

7. Only 100 measures of corn. God had now become the owner, as it were, because He gave the man only a tenth of what the field used to produce.

8. The point is that the son who at the end gets only one hundred measures from the field is getting from it only the amount of the original tithe. And since

year the field reduced its yield. Therefore, Moses enjoins Israel, saying *Tithe scrupulously all the increase of thy seed* (Deut. 14:22).

2. *Trust in the Lord, and do what is right; dwell in the Land, and cherish faithfulness* (Ps. 37:3). R. Haggai cited R. Isaac who transposed the words in the first half of the verse to read "Do what is right, and trust in the Lord," and illustrated their meaning by the story of an inspector of measures. When he went out to inspect the measuring vessels belonging to a certain man, the man saw him and proceeded to hide himself from the inspector. The inspector said: "Why do you hide yourself? Make sure your measures are honest, and you will have no reason to be afraid." Hence, "Do what is right, and trust in the Lord." *Dwell in the Land* (*ibid.*)—Make it possible for the children of Israel to dwell in the Land, to sow and to plant by their being sure to *cherish faithfulness*—cherishing, that is, the Fathers' faithfulness [in scrupulous payment of tithes]—*Mine eyes being upon those faithful with regard to the Land* (Ps. 101:6).

R. Joshua of Sikhnin said in the name of R. Levi: By virtue of two merits—the merit of the Sabbath and the merit of tithes—Israel can live in delight in the very presence of Him who is everywhere. The proof for the merit of the Sabbath? The verse *If thou turn away thy foot because of the Sabbath* (Isa. 58:13). What follows? [Because of thy observance of the Sabbath] *thou shalt delight thyself in the Lord, and I will make thee to ride upon the high places of the Land* (Isa. 58:14). And the proof for the merit of the tithes? [Because of thy payment of the tithes] *Thou shalt rejoice in all the good which the Lord thy God hath given unto thee and unto thy house, thou, and the Levite, and the stranger that is in the midst of thee*[9] (Deut. 26:11).

Another comment: *And thou shalt rejoice in all the good* (*ibid.*). *Good* here refers to study of Torah, of which it is written "I give you doctrine which is good, forsake ye not My teaching" (Prov. 4:2). Therefore Moses enjoined Israel, saying: *Tithe, and then thou shalt again tithe, all the increase of thy seed . . . that thou mayest study . . .* [*Torah*] *always* (Deut. 14:22, 23).

3. *Honor the Lord with thy substance,* [*with whatever exceptional quality He hath bestowed upon thee*],[10] *and with the first fruits of all thy increase* (Prov. 3:9). If you are a man with exceptional good looks, be not loose in pursuit of women, so that people will not say, So-and-so has good looks but cannot keep away from women as he should: comply with the

---

this amount is what the priest got, the relatives sarcastically designate him a "priest." See Num. 5:10 and Rashi.

9. Rejoicing in the Land is contingent upon the tithe to the Levite, the stranger, the orphan, and the widow, the tithe which is commanded in the next verse.

10. A play on *ḥnnk*, "bestowed upon thee," and *hwnk*, "the substance given thee."

teaching *Honor the Lord with whatever exceptional quality He hath bestowed upon thee* (*ibid.*). Then again, if you have an exceptionally good voice, [instead of reciting the Shĕma' in the customary whisper] when standing before the reader's desk, recite it in a ringing voice[11] so as to comply with the teaching *Honor the Lord with whatever exceptional quality He hath bestowed upon thee.* [You will recall that] R. Ḥiyya bar Adda, the son of Bar Ḳappara's sister, had a good voice, and that Bar Ḳappara used to say to him: My son, when you take your stand before the reader's desk recite the Shĕma' in a ringing voice, so as to comply with the teaching *Honor the Lord with thy substance,* [*with whatever exceptional quality He hath bestowed upon thee*].

Another comment: *Honor the Lord with thy substance* (*ibid.*). Honor Him while you have your wits, before you are led to do foolish things after you have lost your wits.[12] [Give heed to] the story of a man who kept adding to his store of wine and oil, but never once paid the tithes due from him. What did the Holy One do? He caused a spirit of madness to enter into the man, so that he took a stick and began breaking his jars of wine and oil. When his steward rebuked him, what did the man do? He took the stick and cut the steward's head with it, saying: "Instead of helping me, you rebuke me." Then the steward said: "Give me a stick, too, and I, too, shall break the jars." So the man gave a stick to his steward, and while he was breaking one jar, the steward was breaking two. What brought on such witless waste? The fact that the man had never once given the tithes due from him.

R. Levi, however, told a story of a man who always used to pay out the tithes due from him. The man owned a field, and the Holy One put it into his mind that he use half of the field for crops and the other half for storing water. Then came a year of drought when people were sending out criers to offer a *sela'*[13] for a *sĕ'ah*[14] of wheat and three *sela'* for a *sĕ'ah* of water. And so as the man went about calling out "Who wants to buy a *sĕ'ah* of water?" it brought him as much money as three *sĕ'ah* of wheat. What brought on such an exceptional return to the man? The fact that he scrupulously paid out the tithes due from him. Therefore Moses enjoined Israel, saying *Tithe scrupulously all the increase of thy seed* (Deut. 14:22).

4. [*Israel*] *is not afraid of* [*Gehenna's*] *snow for her household, for all her household are protected by their carrying out of the precepts of Scripture*

11. See L. Finkelstein, *JQR*, *32* (1941–42), 387–406.

12. Since the latter part of the verse commands honoring the Lord with the first fruits of one's increase, the command to honor Him with one's substance is regarded as superfluous: hence in this comment the word *hwn*, "substance," is taken to mean "wits."

13. 1 *sela'* = 4 denar.

14. A *sĕ'ah* equals 6 *ḳab̲*; a *ḳab̲* equals 4 *log*; a *lōg* equals contents of 6 eggs.

[*not once*], *but again and again*[15] (Prov. 31:21). Hizkiah said: "The punishment of the wicked in Gehenna lasts twelve months"[16]—a total of six months in the heat and a total of six months in the cold. At first the Holy One inflicts an itch upon the wicked as He brings them into Gehenna, into the region whose heat eases the itch. Whereupon the wicked say, Is this all there is to the Holy One's Gehenna? [When the heat becomes unbearable, however], He brings them out into the snow-cold region. And [at first, as they enjoy the relief from the heat], they say, Is this all there is to the cold region of the Holy One's Gehenna? [Later on, however, when the cold becomes unbearable, He takes them back to the hot region].[17] Thus at the beginning [of their stay in each region of Gehenna], they say, "Wow, how pleasant!" And at the end they say "Woe, how painful!" It is to these two regions of Gehenna that David referred when he said *He brought me up out of the horrible pit, out of the hywn bog*[18] (Ps. 40:2). What does *out of the hywn bog* mean? Out of the treacherous bog where people first say "Wow, how pleasant!" but end up by saying "Woe, how painful!" And in what region of Gehenna do the wicked surrender their souls?[19] According to R. Judah Berabbi, in the snowy region, of which it is written *When men separate themselves from the Almighty, and from* [*the Torah*] *whereby kings reign,*[20]

15. JV: *She is not afraid of the snow for her household, for all her household are clothed with scarlet*. As the verse is usually translated, however, the woman of valor—Israel—deserves no particular credit for the preceding verse's testimony that on one occasion *she stretched out her hand to the poor*, or on another occasion *reached forth her hands to the needy*. Consequently, verse 21 is construed not as an account of Israel's being well clothed, but rather as an account of the reward given to people of Israel after they die because while alive they tirelessly persist in carrying out the precepts of Scripture. The word *šanim*, "scarlet," is read *šĕnayim*, "twice"—that is, again and again.

16. Ed 2:10.

17. The idea of alternation from heat to cold and back again in Gehenna may be derived from Gen. 3:24 which can be rendered "the heat of the flame that alternates [with the cold of ice]." See Tanḥuma B, p. 18; and Tanna dĕḇe Eliyyahu, ed. Fr., p. 1.

John Milton makes use of this conception of Gehenna in his *Paradise Lost*, Book 2, lines 593–603.

18. EV: *the miry clay*. But R. Abba takes *hywn*, a *hapax legomenon*, to be a combination by metathesis of the cries *wh* (wow!) and *wy* (woe!), with the letter "n" (mark of the plural) indicating that there will be many such cries. To R. Abba *hywn bog* thus means "the treacherous bog of 'wows' and 'woes'."

While "wow" is a colloquial, even slangy expression of joy, it is used because it comes close to reproducing the play on words in the comment on Ps. 40:2.

19. That is, come to the end of their term in Gehenna and rest in peace.

20. See Prov. 8:15.

it will be snowing at death's darkness[21] (Ps. 68:15)—that is, death's final darkness will befall them in the snowy region of Gehenna. One may suppose that the same fate will befall Israel, but it is not so, for Scripture says, [*Israel*] *is not afraid of* [*Gehenna's*] *snow: all her household are protected by their carrying out of the precepts of Scripture* [*not once*], *but again and again* (Prov. 31:21). Scripture commands *again and again—milah* followed by *pĕri'ah*[22]—in the rite of circumcision; *again and again* in the signs—fringes and then tefillin—that identify the Jew. Scripture further commands: *Again and again furnish liberally* [the Hebrew slave who is being released from bondage] (Deut. 15:14); *again and again give* [to thy needy brother] (Deut. 15:10); *again and again open thy hand* [unto thy poor brother] (Deut. 15:11); *Tithe, and then thou shalt again tithe* (Deut. 14:22). Moses has all the foregoing in mind when he enjoins Israel, saying *Tithe, and then thou shalt again tithe,* etc. (*ibid.*).

5. *The Land, in return, acts deceitfully under*[23] [*the feet of*] *the inhabitants thereof,* etc. (Isa. 24:5). R. Isaac said: If you scheme to act deceitfully with regard to [tithes and offerings due from] the Land's produce, the Land, in return, acts deceitfully[24]: it shows you standing grain, but then will not show you the harvested sheaf; and even if it shows you the harvested sheaf, it will not show you the threshed grain; and even if it shows you the threshed grain, it will not show you the winnowed heap. Why not? *Because* [*the children of Israel*] *will have transgressed the Torah* (*ibid.*)—the Written Torah as well as the Oral Torah. *Violated the statute* (*ibid.*)—they will have violated the statute concerning tithes. *Broken the covenant of the world* (*ibid.*)—broken the covenant made with the Fathers [who are the pillars of the world].[25] Therefore Moses enjoins Israel, saying *Tithe, and then thou shalt again tithe*, etc. (Deut. 14:22).

21. JV: *When the almighty scattereth kings therein, it snoweth in Zalmon.* But *prś* can mean "separate" as well as "scatter."

22. The cutting off of the foreskin and the rolling back of the inner lining of the prepuce. See *JE, s.v.* "Circumcision."

Intimations for the precepts that ensue are found as follows: *Strength and dignity are her clothing* (Prov. 31:25) intimates fringes and tefillin; *she openeth her mouth with wisdom* (Prov. 31:26) intimates "Again and again furnish liberally [the Hebrew slave, etc.]" (Deut. 15:14); *the law of kindness is on her tongue* (Prov. 31:26) intimates "Again and again give [to thy needy brother]" (Deut. 15:10); *she looketh well to the ways of her household* (Prov. 31:27) intimates "Again and again open thy hand [unto thy poor brother]" (Deut. 15:11); finally *she eateth not the bread of idleness* [= wickedness] (Deut. 31:27) intimates "Tithe and then thou shalt again tithe" (Deut. 14:22).

23. JV: *The earth also is defiled under.*

24. Cf. PR 26:3.

25. The Fathers set aside heave offerings and tithes.

6. *My son, keep the commandment of thy father, and forsake not the teaching of thy mother* (Prov. 6:20). R. Huna said: The Patriarchs set aside not only the first portion of the harvest due to priests but also the tithes, [the first tithe going to the Levites, the second tithe going to the poor]. Thus Abraham set aside the first or great heave offering,[26] for he said to the Priest Melchizedek: *I have lifted up my hand unto the Lord* (Gen. 14:22), "lifting up" here connoting heave offering as in the verse "ye shall lift a heave offering of it for the Lord" (Num. 18:26). Isaac set aside the second tithe [for the poor]: *Isaac sowed in that land, and found in the same year a hundredfold* (Gen. 26:12). Since we know, as R. Abba bar Kahana pointed out, that God's blessing is not bestowed upon that which is measured, weighed, or counted, why did Isaac measure his crops? In order to tithe them [a second time, the second tithe being indicated in the verse's conclusion] *And the Lord blessed him*[27] (*ibid.*). In his turn, Jacob set aside the first tithe, for it is written *Of all that Thou shalt give me, I will surely give a tenth unto Thee* (Gen. 28:22).

A Cuthean came and challenged R. Meir with the question: "Do you not keep saying that Jacob the father of your people was truthful?" R. Meir replied: "Yes! It is written *Thou givest truthfulness to Jacob"* (Micah 7:20). The Cuthean declared: "Did Jacob set aside the Tribe of Levi for a tithe as if his Tribe were one of only ten Tribes? Should he not, however, have set aside a larger tithe because there were actually two more Tribes to reckon?" R. Meir replied: "You say there were actually twelve; I say there were actually fourteen!—*Ephraim and Manasseh, even as Reuben and Simeon shall be mine"* (Gen. 48:5). The Cuthean said: "That's exactly right! Do you not, in fact, support what I say? Whenever you add more flour, you should also add more water." R. Meir replied: "Will you not admit that there were four Matriarchs?" The Cuthean said: "Yes." R. Meir said: "Subtract from the fourteen the four first-born of the four Matriarchs, for a first-born is not reckoned in tithing." "Why not?" "Because a first-born is himself holy, and it is not required that something which is holy should free for use something else that is holy." The Cuthean said: "Happy is your people to have such people as you!" In comment, one may quote Scripture here: *Forsake not the teaching of thy mother* (*'immeḵa*) (Prov. 6:20), *'immeḵa* here being read as though spelled *'ummaṯeḵa*, "thy people."

With reference to such teaching, David said: "I delight to do Thy will, O my God; yea, Thy Teaching is in my belly" (Ps. 40:9). Rightly did R. Aḥa bar 'Ulla ask, Is Torah's teaching within a man's belly? Does not Scripture say "In their heart will I write it" (Jer. 31:33)? What David meant, how-

26. One fiftieth of the crop.

27. And in connection with the second tithe, blessing is mentioned. See Deut. 14:24.

ver, was: "May evil befall me if any food which I have not tithed come into my belly!" David's care for tithing was such [that he sent overseers all over the Land to collect the tithes]: *Over the king's treasuries was Azmaveth the son of Adiel; and over the treasuries in the fields, in the cities, and in the villages . . .* (1 Chron. 27:25). Thus *Tithe*, as Moses enjoins Israel, *and then thou shalt again tithe* (Deut. 14:22).

7. *If my earth cry out against me, and the furrows thereof weep together* (Job 31:38). The verse intimates that God was asking Job, Will you own more than three cubits of the earth when you die? How, then, do you presume to say *If* MY *earth cry out against me* as though the earth were all yours? The elder R. Ḥiyya explained God's question to Job by the story of a man selling a cloak in a market. Someone passed by, saw the cloak, and said "It is mine." The man selling the cloak replied: "Wrap yourself in it. If it fits you, it is yours. Otherwise, it is not yours." Likewise the Holy One said to Job: Am I not the One of whom it is written *Do not I fill heaven and earth,* etc. (Jer. 23:24)? And yet you say *If* MY *earth cry out against me* (Job 31:38) as though the earth were your property. R. Simeon ben Ḥalafta explained God's question to Job by the story of a man selling a maidservant in a market. Someone passed by, saw her, and said "She is mine." The man selling her replied: "Look commandingly at her. If she trembles, she is yours. If not, she is not yours." Likewise the Holy One said to Job: Am I not the one of whom it is written *Who looketh on the earth, and it trembleth; He toucheth the mountains, and they smoke* (Ps. 104:32). And yet you say *If* MY *earth cry out against me* (Job. 31:38) as though the earth were your property.

Thereupon Job spoke up to the Holy One: Master of universes, that is not what I meant. What I meant by the words *If my earth cry out against me* (Job 31:38) was "If my earth cry out against me because I did not pay the tithes due from my fields"; and further, what I meant by the words *if the furrows thereof weep together* (*ibid.*) was "If the furrows of my fields weep because I sowed them with a mixture of plants that is forbidden."[28] What I was referring to by the word *money*, in *If I have eaten the fruits thereof without money* (Job 31:39), was the second tithe of the fruits I had grown: [whenever I could not take this tithe to Jersualem, as is required, then, as is also required, I sold it and took the money to Jerusalem to spend there]. As Scripture says, "Then thou shalt turn it into money, and bind up the money in thy hand, and shalt go unto the place which the Lord thy God shall choose" (Deut. 14:25). What I was referring to by the word *disappointed* in *Or have caused the tillers thereof to be disappointed* (Job 31:39) was the disappointment of my poor tillers because they had not received from me the tithe due them. If I have not heeded any of the aforementioned precepts, *Let*

28. *Kil'ayim.* See Lev. 19:19; Deut. 22:9.

thistles grow instead of wheat, and cockle instead of barley. The words of Job are ended (Job 31:40). R. Hoshaia taught that here, incidentally, the Torah is giving you sound agricultural advice: A field that grows thistles, if sown to wheat, will produce a good crop; and a field that grows cockles, if sown to barley, will produce a good crop. And the proof? *Let thistles grow instead of wheat, and cockle instead of barley.*

It is a fact that Job continued to utter any number of prophecies, yet Scripture says at the conclusion of the verse *The words of Job are ended* (*ibid.*). What Job meant by the statement, however, was: If I have not heeded any of the aforementioned precepts, may my words of avowal come to an end, may I have no opportunity ever again to say before Thee *I have put away the hallowed things out of my house, in that I have given them unto the Levite, to the stranger, to the fatherless, and to the widow* (Deut. 26:13).[29] Thus Job spoke in the spirit of the verse *Tithe*, as Moses enjoins Israel, *and then thou shalt again tithe* (Deut. 14:22).

8. *O Lord, charity belongeth unto Thee, but unto us confusion of face, as at this day* (Dan. 9:7). R. Judah bar R. Il'a'i said: A graven image passed with Israel over the Red Sea. And the proof? "Over the sea a rival did pass" (Zech. 10:11), the term "rival" here referring to an idol, as in the verse "the molten thing was a rival to Him who caused the gathering [of waters as in a heap]" (Isa. 28:20).[30]

R. Yudan, quoting the verse *The house of Joseph, they also went up to Beth-el; yet the Lord was with them* (Judg. 1:22), said: Though they were heading for worship of an idol,[31] still Scripture says, *the Lord was with them.* Can you think of an instance of charity greater than this? Hence, *O Lord, charity belongeth unto Thee, but unto us confusion of face, as at this day* (Dan. 9:7). R. Judah bar R. Simon, citing the verse *They took that which Micah had made, and the priest whom he had, and came unto Laish, unto a people quiet and secure, and smote them with the edge of the sword* (Judg. 18:27), commented: *They took that which Micah had made,* the idol's image; *and the priest whom he had* (*ibid.*), the priest who tended to the idol; *and they came unto Laish* (*ibid.*), to Paneas;[32] *unto a people quiet and secure, and smote them with the edge of the sword.* Note that the Danites served an idol which brought them luck, for Scripture says of the Danites that they came *unto a people quiet and secure, and smote them.* Can you think of an instance of charity greater than God's allowing the Danites to

29. See MSh 5:10.

30. See Lev. Rabbah 17:7, and Ps. 33:7; and MTeh 101:2. JV: *The covering too narrow when he gathered himself up.* But *mskh*, "covering," can also mean "molten thing," and *ṣrh*, "narrow," can also mean "rival."

31. Micah, who owned the idol, was of the Tribe of Ephraim, hence of the house of Joseph.

32. City in southern Syria, the modern Baniyas.

be successful? Hence, *O Lord, charity belongeth unto Thee, but unto us confusion of face* (Dan. 9:7). R. Samuel bar Naḥman said: You find that on the day that manna came down for Israel, on that very day children of Israel paid homage to idols. Nay more, they took some of the manna and offered it to their idols. Of such offerings it is written *My bread also which I gave thee—tasting like fine flour, and oil, and honey—wherewith I fed thee, thou didst even set it before them for a sweet savor, and thus it was* (Ezek. 16:19). What is meant by *and thus it was*? R. Judah explained: And thus the manna was to continue to fall even on the next day—despite their having set it before idols, Thou didst not withhold Thy manna from them.[33] Can you think of an instance of charity greater than this? Hence, *O Lord, charity belongeth unto Thee, but unto us confusion of face* (Dan. 9:7). R. Eleazar said: This was the verse that Hananiah, Mishael, and Azariah recited when they left the fiery furnace. You find that after Hananiah, Mishael, and Azariah came up out of the fiery furnace, all the kings of the nations of the world gathered themselves over against the three, for it is written *The satraps, the prefects, the governors, and the king's ministers, being gathered together, saw these men, that the fire had no power upon their bodies* (Dan. 3:27). And so all the nations of the world said to the three: You know that with your God there rests the power to perform all such miracles for you, yet you Jews brought it about that He destroyed His house and exiled His children! Thereupon all the nations of the world spit into the faces of the three until they seemed to be a mass of spittle, whereupon Hananiah, Mishael, and Azariah, lifting their faces to heaven above, cried out: *O Lord, charity belongeth unto Thee, but unto us disgrace of face* (Dan. 9:7). R. Joshua bar R. Nehemiah said the words *O Lord, righteousness belongeth unto Thee* were the three martyrs' acknowledgment of the righteousness of God's judgment, as though they were saying, "No matter how much we provoke Thee, Thou bearest with us and bearest us up." Thus it is taught in the name of R. Nehemiah that in the world's practice, when a man has a field, he may lease it for a half, for a third, or for a fourth of its yield. But it is not so with the Holy One: He causes winds to blow, clouds to rise, rains to come down, dews to bespangle plants, plants to spring up, fruits to grow plump, and yet tells us to set aside no more than a tithe—a mere tenth of the yield. Hence Moses enjoins Israel, saying *Tithe, and then thou shalt again tithe* (Deut. 14:22).

9. What verse in the lesson precedes the one just above? *Ye shall not eat of anything that dieth of itself; thou mayest give it unto the stranger that is within thy gates* (Deut. 14:21). R. Azariah, R. Jonathan ben Haggai, and R. Isaac bar Marion, citing R. Jose bar R. Ḥanina, said: He who eats his produce untithed is as one who eats the forbidden flesh of animals that die a natural death or are torn by beasts of prey. And the proof? The verse just

33. Cf. MTeh 3:3.

cited *Ye shall not eat of anything that dieth of itself*. R. Abba bar Huna sai in the name of Rab: He who eats his produce without having set aside th tithe for the poor deserves death.

R. Isaac said: In three places it is written "Thou shalt not seethe a kid i its mother's milk." Once for its own sake—[to prohibit the mixing of mea and milk]; once in connection with the giving of Torah; and once again wit regard to tithes. The prohibition for its own sake—how does Scripture put it Right after the verse *The choicest fruits of thy Land thou shalt bring into th house of the Lord thy God* (Exod. 23:19) comes the prohibition *Thou sha not seethe a kid in its mother's milk* (*ibid.*), followed by the verse tellin Israel that if they heed the prohibition, an angel will keep them on their way *Behold, I send an angel before thee, to keep thee by the way* (Exod. 23:20)

The prohibition *Thou shalt not seethe a kid in its mother's milk* is agai stated in connection with the giving of Torah. How does Scripture put it Right after the verse *The choicest first fruits of thy Land thou shalt brin into the house of the Lord thy God* (Exod. 34:26) comes the prohibitio *Thou shalt not seethe a kid in its mother's milk* (*ibid.*), and these words ar at once followed by God's telling Moses that the right moment had come fo him to take down the Ten Commandments—*The Lord said unto Moses Write thou these words* (Exod. 34:27)—and His going on to say: Moses [the angels at this moment are confounded by My reminder to them] *Thou shalt not seethe a kid in its mother's milk*,[34] so while the sandal is on you foot, crush the thorn [of their opposition to My giving the Torah to mortals. Take advantage of the angels' confusion and] write down the Ten Commandments.

The prohibition *Thou shalt not seethe a kid in its mother's milk* is stated a third time in regard to the payment of tithes. How does Scripture put it? The beginning of the verse *Ye shall not eat of anything that dieth of itself; thou mayest give it to the stranger that is within thy gates* (Deut. 14:21) [intimates that the non-payment of tithes is as much of a sin as is the eating of meat not ritually slaughtered], and the conclusion of the verse *Thou shalt not seethe a kid in its mother's milk* (*ibid.*) [goes on to intimate that the non-payment of tithes is as much of a sin as the seething of a kid in its mother's milk]. That these are the intimations of the verse is proved by the command given in the very next verse *Tithe, and then thou shalt again tithe* (Deut. 14:22). By your sin in not tithing, the Holy One said, do not bring Me to have the kernels of your crops ripen prematurely in their mothers' wombs, [in their seedpods].[35] For if you do not pay the proper tithes from

34. A pointed reminder that while visiting Abraham, the angels in all too human fashion violated the law when they ate meat and milk together. See PR 25:3.

35. In the original, the analogy of the kid in the womb and the kernel in the seedpod is all the more forceful because the Hebrew word for "kid" and "kernel" is the same.

your produce, I will dispatch a searing blast from the east wind to wither up the seedpods. "The corn will thus be blasted before it is grown up" (2 Kings 9:26).

10. *Tithe, that thou mayest tithe again* (Deut. 14:22)—that is, tithe that you may not be in want. Tithe, that you may be blithe,[36] by which the Holy One meant: Tithe that which is Mine, and I will make you blithe by making prosper that which is yours.[37]

The words *Tithe all*[38] (Deut. 14:22), according to R. Abba bar Kahana, are a hint to merchants and seafarers that they are to set aside a tithe of their earnings for men who labor in the Torah.

The increase of thy seed, that which goeth forth in the field (*ibid.*). If you merit such reward by tithing, you will continue to go forth to sow in the field. But if you do not merit it, the hunter who is notorious for going forth into the field will in the end wage war against you. And who is that? The wicked Esau, of whom it is written "Esau was a cunning hunter, a man of the field"[39] (Gen. 25:27).

Another comment: *The increase of thy seed, the going out into the field* (Deut. 14:22). If you merit such reward by tithing, then, upon going out into the field and seeing the world in need of rain, when you pray for rain, your prayer will, in the end, be granted.[40] But if you do not merit it by tithing, in the end [Israel—let it be said of] Israel's enemies[41]—will be going out into the field to bury their sons.

Year by year! (Deut. 14:22): This year's produce is not to be tithed in lieu of the tithe of last year's produce—so taught R. 'Akiba.[42] *And thou shalt eat before the Lord thy God . . . the tithe of thy corn, of thy wine* (Deut. 14:23): If you merit such reward by tithing, the corn will be yours; if not, the corn will be Mine, as Scripture says, "Therefore will I take back MY corn in the time thereof" (Hos. 2:11). If you merit such reward by tithing, the wine will be yours; if not, the wine will be Mine, as Scripture goes on to say "and MY wine in the season thereof" (*ibid.*).

According to R. Simeon ben Lakish, the Holy One said: I told you that

36. Here there is a play on *'aśśer*, "tithe"; and *'aššer*, "[be blithe through] prosperity."

37. Cf. PR 25:2, end.

38. R. Abba reads *all* as a collective noun rather than as an adjective qualifying *the increase of thy seed.*

39. See PR 12:4.

40. Rains come down as a reward for the giving of tithes. See Mal. 3:10; and Piska 1.4.

41. The text really says, "Israel's enemies will be going out into the field to bury Israel's sons": the commentator cannot bring himself to predict such a sad outcome for Israel.

42. See Sif, *Běhukkotai*, chap. 12, end (ed. Weiss, 115b).

you were to pay your tithes from the finest part of the crop. How get a fine crop? When a Levite comes to you, if you give him the finest, I have the power as well to give you of the finest: "The Lord will open unto thee His good treasure, the heaven," etc. (Deut. 28:12). But if you give him of the blemished and inferior part of the crop, I have the power as well to give you of the blemished and inferior part: "The Lord will make the rain of thy Land powder and dust" (Deut. 28:24). *And the Levite, because he hath no portion nor inheritance with thee, and the stranger . . . shall come* (Deut. 14:29). According to R. Luliani of Daroma who cited R. Judah bar R. Simon, the Holy One said: You have four persons in your household, and I, too, have four persons in My household. The four persons in your household are your son, your daughter, your manservant, and your maidservant. The four persons in My household are the Levite, the stranger, the fatherless, and the widow. Scripture refers to all the persons, yours and mine, in a single verse: *And thou shalt rejoice in thy feast, thou, and thy son, and thy daughter, and thy manservant, and thy maidservant, and the Levite, and the stranger, and the widow, that are within thy gates* (Deut. 16:14). By these words the Holy One meant: I told you that you were to bring joy to the persons in My household and to those in yours on the festal days I gave you. If you do so, I, for My part, will bring joy to yours and to Mine. To these as well as to those I shall bring joy in the Temple in Jerusalem: *Even then will I bring to My holy mountain, and make them joyful in My house of prayer* (Isa. 56:7).

PISKA 11

SUMMARY

The awesome doings of God and the radiance of certain personages in Israel

When a man's ways please the Lord, He may cause even the man's enemies to give up life for his sake, or may have them make peace with him, as God did in Israel's behalf when Pharaoh let them go out of Egypt (Sec. 1). After Israel's departure, the Egyptians, who at one time ordered that every son of Israel be cast into the Nile River, were themselves drowned in the Red Sea—an awesome reversal which only God is capable of bringing about (Sec. 2). The Egyptians, at first foolishly unwilling to let Israel go, were to discover that they should have done so at once. As matters turned out, the Egyptians, unwilling to be admonished, were afflicted by plagues, were compelled to part with their wealth, and were forced to let Israel go (Sec. 3)—indeed were to receive measure for measure (Sec. 4): the stew which they cooked for others they were to stew in themselves (Sec. 5).

Israel were redeemed from Egypt for four reasons: they did not change their names; they did not change their language; they did not inform on one another; they were not wanton. According to one authority, it was solely because they hedged themselves in against Egypt's unchastity that Israel were redeemed (Sec. 6).

Exposition of several ensuing verses in Exodus 13 follows:

1. At sight of the well-disciplined people of Israel whom the Egyptians had had to let go, they cried woe (Sec. 7).

2. God led Israel not *in the way of the earth* (Exod. 13:17)—that is, not in the usual manner, but in ways that were miraculous, eight examples of which are given (Sec. 8).

3. The meaning of *Because it was near* (Exod. 13:17) is construed variously as referring to the place and time of the Egyptians' punishment; to the recent respect which the Canaanites had shown to the deceased Jacob; and to the recency of the oath which Abraham had sworn to Abimelech, king of Philistia (Sec. 9).

4. God did not lead Israel through the land of the Philistines, the shortest route to the Land, because He did not want Israel to be disheartened at sight of the bones of those Israelites who had died during a premature attempt to leave Egypt (Sec. 10).

5. Only a small number of the children of Israel—possibly as few as one out of five hundred—actually left Egypt (Sec. 11).

6. Moses recovered Joseph's coffin from the Nile, and Joseph's bones were reverently carried through the wilderness (Sec. 12).

7. The waters of the Red Sea, which became a wall for Israel, shone because of the radiance of such personages as Moses and Aaron who had drunk deep of Torah's waters. Small wonder that because of such men in Israel, that God had Himself counted as the seventieth among the souls of the house of Jacob that came into Egypt (Sec. 13).

The radiance of Israel's personages is derived also from a willingness to hallow the Name (Sec. 14). One such personage, R. Simeon ben Yoḥai, was said to have been as radiant as the rainbow, token of the covenant between God and earth—indeed all generations until the resurrection of the dead will be illumined by his radiance (Sec. 15). In part, at least, the radiance which was R. Simeon's came from his having endured privation in a cave for thirteen years because he had dared speak harshly of Rome's iniquitous rule. Upon emerging from the cave he bestowed boons upon the people of Tiberias, punished mockers severely, and was stern with the supercritical (Sec. 16) and with those who would disobey the dicta of the Sages (Sec. 17).

R. Simeon's son, Eleazar, when young, was a man whose strength was extraordinary, whose appetite for food and drink was huge, and who, as servant of Rome, acted in person as executioner (Secs. 18–20). But the clouds of glory which enveloped Israel in the wilderness (Sec. 21) were also to envelop Eleazar. For Elijah the prophet undertook to have Eleazar take up the study of Torah, the vocation of his fathers. So much of his strength then went into learning that he could not even carry his own cloak (Sec. 22). But because on one occasion R. Eleazar took no legal action against a man uttering blasphemy, he was denied for years the privilege of being put to rest next to his father in Meron (Sec. 23). Like R. Simeon his father, R. Eleazar was willing to suffer afflictions for Israel's sake. Such was the degree of his saintliness that after he died, his widow felt that marrying R. Judah would have been a come-down in holiness for her (Sec. 24).

Returning to the subject of the bones of Joseph, the text states that the people of each Tribe took the bones of their own Tribe Father with them (Sec. 25).

PISKA 11

And it came to pass that Pharaoh let the people go (Exod. 13:17).[1]

1. *When a man's ways please the Lord, He maketh even his enemies eager to give up life*[2] *for him* (Prov. 16:7). By "enemy" here, according to R. Meir, is meant a [wild] dog; according to R. Joshua ben Levi, a snake. R. Meir, who said a dog is meant, told the story of herdsmen who had just milked a cow. A snake came and drank of the milk, and a dog saw it drinking. When the herdsmen sat down to eat, the dog began to bark warningly at them, but they did not understand what his barking meant. Whereupon the dog sprang forward, drank of the venom-tainted milk, and died. When the herdsmen buried him, they set a monument over him, which to this day is called "The Dog's Monument."[3] R. Joshua ben Levi, who said that by "enemy" a snake is meant, told the story of a man who had ground up some garlic. A wild snake[4] came and ate of it, and a tame snake saw it eating. When the people sat down to eat, the tame snake began stirring up dust towards them, but they did not understand what the snake meant. Whereupon it threw itself into the venom-smeared garlic and died.

R. Abbahu went to Caesarea and happened to visit a certain man who seated a dog next to R. Abbahu. When he asked his host, "Do I deserve such humiliation?" the host replied: My master, I happen to be one who owes the dog much gratitude: slavers once came into the city, and when one of them sought to rape my wife, the dog saved her by springing upon him and biting off his testes.

R. Johanan construed the word *enemies* in the verse *When a man's ways please the Lord, He maketh even his enemies to be at peace with him* (Prov. 16:7) as referring to a man's wife. In proof he cited the verse "A man's enemies are the people in his household" (Micah 7:6), "his household" designating his wife.[5] R. Johanan went on: A brigand's wife, for example, is apt to act like a brigand herself; in fact, it happened that a certain brigand's wife falsely accused her husband before a judge who thereupon sentenced

1. Exod. 13:17–15:26 is the lesson of the Seventh Day of Passover.
In the several comments that follow, the clause *And it came to pass*, etc. (Exod. 13:17) will be construed not as subordinate, as JV construes it, but as coordinate.
2. *Yĕšallem* can mean "make peace," or "give up one's life."
3. "On monuments to dogs in antiquity, see F. Cumont, *Recherches sur le Symbolisme Funéraire des Romains*, p. 509." Saul Lieberman, HJP, p. 213.
4. Literally "mountain snake."
5. [It is customary throughout the Near East to refer to another man's wife as his household, the use of the word "wife" in direct conversation being regarded as unmannerly. It is so in Arabic. L.N.]

him to be beheaded. Later, the same judge, on a trumped up charge, found against her also and had her executed.

R. Samuel bar Naḥman construed the words *When a man's ways please the Lord* (Prov. 16:7) to refer to the Impulse to good, and the words *He maketh even his enemies to be at peace with him* (*ibid.*) to the Impulse to evil. Generally, if a man is brought up with another in the same city, if only for two or three years, he binds himself in friendship to the other. But as to this side of man—the Impulse to evil—though it grow up with a man from his youth to his old age, its enmity is such that if it finds occasion to bring him down when he is twenty, it will bring him down; when he is sixty, it will bring him down; even when he is eighty, it will bring him down. Thus it is said of Johanan the High Priest that he served as High Priest for eighty years, and in the end the Impulse to evil led him to become a Sadducean. With regard to the Impulse to evil, David said: *All my bones shall say, Lord, who is like unto Thee, who deliverest the poor from him that is too strong for him* (Ps. 35:10)—deliverest the weak Impulse to good from the strong Impulse to evil. David went on: *Deliverest . . . the poor and the needy from him that spoileth him* (*ibid.*): what despoiler is there stronger than the Impulse to evil?

R. Berechiah applied to the Impulse to evil the verse *If thine enemy be hungry, give him bread to eat* (Prov. 25:21)—that is, if your enemy be hungry, have him eat the bread of Torah; *if he be thirsty, give him water to drink* (*ibid.*), the water[6] of Torah. Why? Because *Thou wilt heap coals of fire upon his head, and the Lord will reward* (*yĕšallem*) *thee* (Prov. 25:22), by which is meant that "the Lord will make the Impulse to evil be at peace[7] with you."

R. Berechiah, commenting on *even* in the phrase *even his enemies* (Prov. 16:7), took it to suggest that even such pests as flies, hornets, gnats, and fleas [are at peace with a man whose *ways please the Lord* (*ibid.*)].

But the Rabbis construed the words *When a man's ways please the Lord* (Prov. 16:7) as designating Israel, so referred to in the verse "every man of Israel" (1 Sam. 17:24); and the words *He maketh even his enemies to be at peace with him* (Prov. 16:7) as referring to Pharaoh: "The enemy said, 'I will pursue, I will overtake, I will divide the spoil' " (Exod. 15:9). You find that when Moses came to Pharaoh and said: *Thus saith the Lord, Let My people go, that they may serve Me* (Exod. 8:16), the wicked one replied: *Who is the Lord, that I should hearken unto His voice? I know not the Lord, and moreover I will not let Israel go* (Exod. 5:2). But the same mouth which said, *Who is the Lord that I should hearken unto His voice*, exclaimed

6. "water"—O_1; O: "wine."

7. *Yĕšallem* may mean "reward," or "make peace." [O_1 and C read *yšlymnu*, "God will deliver him into your hands." L.N.]

in repentance *The Lord is righteous, and I and my people are wicked* (Exod. 9:27). The same mouth which said, *I know not the Lord, and moreover I will not let Israel go,* ended up making the rounds of Israel's dwellings and saying "Go forth in peace, go in peace." Hence it is said *And it came to pass that* PHARAOH *let the people go* (Exod. 13:17).

2. *Say unto God: "How awesome are Thy doings! Through the greatness of Thy power shall Thine enemies crumble away before Thee"* (Ps. 66:3). R. Johanan said: As we say to a good workman, "Well done, well done, indeed!" so we say to God "How awesome are Thy doings!" For they that were to be slain, slew those that would have slain them. They that were to be hanged, hanged those that would have hanged them. They that were to be drowned, drowned those that would have drowned them. The very mouth that said, *Every son that is born ye shall cast into the river* (Exod. 1:22), was cast into the sea: *Pharaoh's chariots and his host hath He cast into the sea* (Exod. 15:4). The rest as above, in Piska 11.1.

3. *A rebuke entereth deeper into a man of understanding than a hundred stripes into a fool* (Prov. 17:10). R. Ishmael taught: The hundred stripes for a fool may be understood by the parable of a king who said to his servant: "Go get me a fish from the market." The servant went and brought him a fish which stank. The king said, "As you live, you will not escape one of three punishments: You will eat the stinking fish, or you will receive a hundred stripes, or you will pay a fine." The servant said: "I will eat the stinking fish." But no sooner had he begun to eat the stinking flesh than it nauseated him, and he said: "I would rather receive stripes." He had absorbed no more than fifty stripes when he said, "I will pay the fine." Thus he ate stinking flesh, *and* got stripes, *and* paid a fine. So, too, the Holy One said to the wicked Pharaoh: As you live, you will receive ten stripes, or you will pay a fine out of your wealth, or you will let Israel go. You will receive ten stripes—the ten plagues; you will pay a fine out of your wealth—AND *they despoiled the Egyptians* (Exod. 12:36); *and* you will yet Israel go—AND *it came to pass, that Pharaoh let the people go* (Exod. 13:17).

4. *Did He not indeed smite him with the smiting whereby he smote* [*Israel*]*? Was he not in fact slain with the weapon wherewith he slew his slain?*[8] (Isa. 27:7). R. Judah and R. Nehemiah differ in the interpretation of this verse. R. Judah, emphasizing the first part of the verse, said that with the stick whereby the Egyptians smote Israel, therewith they were smitten. R. Nehemiah, emphasizing the second part of the verse, said that with the sword whereby the Egyptians slew Israel, therewith they were slain. And such was

8. JV: *Hath He smitten him as He smote those that smote him? Or is he slain according to the slaughter of them that were slain by him?* The letter *he'* at the beginning of the verse may be taken as an interrogative or as a declarative particle. See Rashi.

the outcome, as the next verse goes on to say, *When in full measure (sĕ'assĕ'ah) ere thou,* [*O Pharaoh*], *wouldst let* [*Israel*] *go, Thou didst contend* [*with Egypt*] (Isa. 27:8): *sĕ'assĕ'ah* is read "*sĕ'ah* for *sĕ'ah*," measure for measure—that is, as is taught in the name of R. Meir, in the measure a man measures out, so it is measured out to him. *Ere thou,* [*O Pharaoh*], *wouldst let* [*Israel*] *go, Thou,* [*God*], *didst contend* [*with Egypt*]. For Pharaoh had to be smitten before he would let Israel go. Hence *And it came to pass that Pharaoh,* [*after being smitten*], *let the people go* (Exod. 13:17).

5. *Now I know*—said Jethro—*that the Lord is greater than all gods; in the thing wherein* [*the Egyptians*] *dealt mischievously* (*zaddu*), *He was above them* (Exod. 18:11).[9] R. Eleazar, R. Joshua ben Levi, and the Rabbis differ in their comments on this verse. According to the first, in the manner the Egyptians desired others to fall, they themselves fell; in the manner they sought to shortweight others, they were themselves shortweighted. According to the second, the stew the Egyptians cooked up for others was cooked up for them, the word *zaddu* being understood as in the verse *Jacob was cooking* (*way-yazeḏ*) *a stew* (Gen. 25:29). And according to the Rabbis, the scheme the Egyptians schemed for others was schemed against them, *zaddu* being understood as in the verse *When a man schemes* (*yaziḏ*) *against another and kills him treacherously* (Exod. 21:14).

In the verse *Who executeth justice for the oppressed; who giveth bread to the hungry*, etc. (Ps. 146:7), the words *Who executeth justice for the oppressed* apply to Israel, of whom it is said "Thus saith the Lord of hosts: The children of Israel and the children of Judah are oppressed together," etc. (Jer. 50:33); "Their Redeemer is strong, the Lord of hosts is His name, He will thoroughly plead their cause" (Jer. 50:34). Thus the very mouth that said, *Every son that is born ye shall cast into the river* (Exod. 1:22). The rest as above, in Piska 11.1.

6. *A garden shut up is My sister, My bride; a spring shut up, a fountain sealed* (Song 4:12). R. Judah bar R. Simon, citing R. Joshua ben Levi, told a parable of a king who had marriageable daughters whom he neglected to marry off. So when he went away to a far city by the sea, the daughters bestirred themselves and arranged to be wed to certain men of their choosing, each of the daughters making certain to get hold of her husband's ring and seal. At length the king returned from the far city by the sea and heard people gossip about his daughters, saying that the king's daughters had been wanton. What did the king do? Into the streets he sent a herald who cried

9. "*Now I know that the Lord is greater than all gods; in the thing wherein they dealt proudly (zaddu), He was above them* (Exod. 18:11)"—C. The word *zaddu* will successively be construed "acted mischievously," weighed out," "cooked up," "schemed." O inappropriately cites 1 Sam. 2:3.

out: "All people to the forum!" Then the king summoned his first son-in-law and publicly asked him, "Who are you?" The other replied, "I am your son-in-law." Thereupon producing the other's ring, the king asked, "To whom does this ring belong?" "It is mine." Then producing the other's seal, he asked, "To whom does this seal belong?" "It is mine." The king having done likewise with the second son-in-law and with the third one also, said finally: My daughters on their own bestirred themselves and got themselves wed: how dare anyone say that the king's daughters have been wanton!

So, too, the nations of the earth taunted Israel by saying to them that Israel were children of the Egyptians who, because they were masters of the Israelites' persons, must surely have been masters of the Israelites' wives. Thereupon—so taught R. Hoshaia—the Holy One summoned the angel in charge of conception and said: "Go and shape for Me the embryos of Israelites with the unmistakable features of their fathers." With regard to this decree of God's it is written *Reuben . . . the families of the Reubenites . . . Simeon . . . the families of the Simeonites* (Num. 26:7, 14). Though R. Marinus bar R. Hoshaia said: These verses merely identify Israelites, even as people say, "Varonians, Severians, Saconians," R. Addi insisted: The *he'* as the initial letter and the *yoḏ* as the concluding letter in the Tribal family names,[10] spell the name YH, "Lord," and thus bear witness concerning Israelites that they were indeed their Tribe Fathers' sons. And the Scriptural proof? The verse *Jerusalem . . . whither the Tribes went up, the Tribes concerning whom the letters yoḏ and he' bear witness that they are of Israel*[11] (Ps. 122:4) and are true descendants of Israelite fathers.

Another comment: *A garden barred is My sister, My bride, a spring shut up* (Song 4:12). [*A garden barred*] applies to virgins; *a spring shut up*, to married women; *a fountain sealed* (*ibid.*), to males. R. Nathan taught: The conjunction of the two phrases *a garden barred* and *a spring shut up* signifies [that Israelite virgins in Egypt refrained from cohabitation], natural or unnatural. [It was Sarah who set an example for them], for, according to R. Ḥunya, citing R. Ḥiyya bar Abba, when she went down to Egypt, she took pains to hedge herself in against unchaste conduct of any kind; thereafter, all Israelite women, inspired by her example, also took pains to hedge themselves in against unchaste conduct of any kind. According to R. Ḥiyya bar Abba, such hedging in against unchastity was in itself of sufficient merit to bring about the redemption of Israel.

R. Huna taught in the name of Bar Ḳappara that Israel were redeemed from Egypt for four reasons: they did not change their names; they did not change their language; they did not inform on one another; and they were not

10. E.g. *Hr'wbny*, "the Tribe of Reuben." See Num. 26:7, 14, 27.

11. JV: *Whither the tribes went up, even the tribes of the Lord* (YH), *as a testimony unto Israel.*

wanton. They did not change their names: they went down [to Egypt] as Reuben and Simeon and came up as Reuben and Simeon. They did not change their language: *It is my mouth*—said Joseph—*that speaketh unto you* (Gen. 45:12), and he spoke his own language, the sacred language. They did not inform on one another [while they were preparing for their exodus and, as Moses was enjoined to tell them, laying up Egyptian treasures to take with them]: *Speak now in the ears of the people, and let them ask every man of his neighbor, and every woman of her neighbor, jewels of silver, and jewels of gold* (Exod. 11:2). [Upon examining the account in Scripture], you find that the purpose of borrowing treasure from the Egyptians had been confided to Israel for twelve months[12] previously, and yet not one Israelite had informed on another. Finally, they were not wanton: You can see for yourself that this was so. There was only one Israelite woman guilty of wantonness, and Scripture makes her name known: *His mother's name*[13] *was Shelomith, the daughter of Dibri, of the Tribe of Dan* (Lev. 24:11).

R. Phinehas, citing R. Ḥiyya bar Abba, insisted, however: It was solely on account of Israel's chastity—for, even though Israel had gone down into Egypt, they [had not gone down into Egypt's unchastity, but] had taken pains to hedge themselves in against it—solely on this account had God enabled them to go forth from Egypt, the going forth being intimated in *Therefore thy shoots* (Song 4:13). [Note that the words *a garden barred* (Song 4:12), alluding to virgins and the words *a fountain sealed* (*ibid.*), alluding to males, are followed directly by *Therefore thy shoots* (*šlḥyk*) (Song 4:13). This word is] here construed, however, as *šllwḥyk*, "thy goings forth," [so that the sense of the entire verse is "Therefore thy people, O Israel, in their goings forth from Egypt are to be an orchard of pomegranates" (*ibid.*)—that is, they are to be as full of obedience to commandments as a pomegranate is full of seeds].[14] The foregoing is all implied in the verse *And it came to pass that Pharaoh let the people* GO FORTH (Exod. 13:17).

7. [In another comment, the word *wayĕhi* is read not *And it came to pass* (Exod. 13:17), but] "There was woe."[15] Who was the one crying woe? Egypt cried woe. R. Simeon ben Yoḥai illustrated the Egyptians' plight after Israel went forth by a parable of a man to whom there had fallen an

12. In Exod. 3:21–22, God told Moses that when the children of Israel left Egypt, they would not go forth empty-handed. From the time of God's promise to Moses to the redemption from Egypt twelve months were to elapse, "the judgment of the Egyptians enduring twelve months" (Ed̲ 2:10).

13. Throughout Scripture, the father's name is invariably specified, implying that in this case the child was the issue of an adulterous union.

14. See Song Rabbah 4:4 for the part interpolated.

15. Play on the syllable *way* in *wayĕhi*, *way* in Aramaic meaning "woe."

inheritance in a far city by the sea. The heir, being slothful however, proceeded to let his inheritance go for a trifle. On the other hand, the purchaser went to the property, dug in the earth, and found therein a treasure with which he built a palace; he was so rich that whenever he passed through the market, there were footmen before him and footmen behind him. Thereupon the seller, choking with grief, said, "Woe, what wealth have I let slip through my fingers!" So, too, when Israel were encamped on the seashore, they looked like such a well-disciplined military force that the Egyptians, choking with grief, said: "Woe, what a people have we let slip out of our land!"

R. Jose illustrated the Egyptians' plight by a parable of a man who inherited so large a field that it would require a *kor* of seed for sowing,[16] but would have to be broken up for cultivating. Consequently the slothful heir let it go for a trifle. The purchaser, on the other hand, went to the field, dug in the earth, discovered a well in it, and then turned the field into gardens and orchards. Thereupon the seller began choking with grief, saying "Woe, what wealth have I let slip through my fingers!" So, too, when Israel were encamped on the seashore, they looked like such a well-disciplined military force that the Egyptians, choking with grief, said: "Woe, what a people have we let slip out of our land!"

R. Nathan illustrated the Egyptians' plight by a parable of a man who inherited the trunk of a cedar tree. The heir, being slothful, let it go for a trifle. The purchaser, however, went and turned the trunk into tables, chairs, and benches. Thereupon the seller, choking with grief, said, "Woe, what wealth I let slip through my fingers!" So, too, when Israel were encamped on the seashore, they looked like such a well-disciplined military force, etc.

8. *God led them not in the way of the earth,*[17] *nor in the way of the Philistines*[17a] (Exod. 13:17), *in the way of the earth* signifying "in the usual manner." Of this way, R. Levi, citing R. Ḥama bar Ḥanina, gave eight examples, saying: It is the way of the earth, the usual thing, for water to come from above and bread from below. But on Israel's way from Egypt, bread came from above and water from below. Bread from above: *Behold, I*

16. Measurements of fields are generally indicated by the amount of seed that can be sowed in them. See Jastrow, p. 625. A *kor* is approximately eleven bushels.

17. The phrase *by way of the land of* occurs nowhere else in Scripture. Hence the commentator takes *the land* to have both geographical and "meta-geographical" meaning, and construes the verse as "God led them not in the way of the earth, nor in the way of the Philistines." JV: *God led them not by way of the land of the Philistines.*

The word *dere<u>k</u>*, followed by a locality, means—so Professor Jacob Milgrom says—not "the way of" but "the way to."

17a. Or: *God led them not to the Philistines*—here identified as Amorites—*in the way of the earth, because it*—Israel—*was near to Him.* Cf. *'Aruḡa<u>t</u> habbośem*, ed. E. E. Urbach, 4 vols., Jerusalem, 5699–5723 [1939–63], 2, 165.

will cause to rain bread from heaven for you (Exod. 16:4); and water from below: *Then sang Israel this song: Spring up, O well—sing ye unto it* (Num. 21:17). It is the way of the earth, the usual thing, for a disciple to carry the lantern as he walks ahead of his master. On Israel's way from Egypt, however, *The pillar of cloud by day, and the pillar of fire by night departed not from before the people* (Exod. 13:22). It is the way of the earth, the usual thing, for a disciple to walk first with his master behind him. But on Israel's way from Egypt, *The Lord went before them* (Exod. 13:21). It is the way of the earth, the usual thing, for a disciple to wash his master. But on Israel's way from Egypt, God said: *Then washed I thee with water* (Ezek. 16:9). It is the way of the earth, the usual thing, for a disciple to clothe his master. But on Israel's way from Egypt, *I clothed thee with richly woven work* (Ezek. 16:10)—purple in color, according to R. Simai; many-colored, according to Aquila's translation.[18] It is the way of the earth, the usual thing, for a disciple to provide shoes for his master. But on Israel's way from Egypt, *I shod thee with sealskin* (*ibid.*). It is the way of the earth, the usual thing, for a disciple to carry his master. But on Israel's way from Egypt, *I bore you on eagles' wings* (Exod. 19:4). It is the way of the earth, the usual thing, for the master to sleep while the disciple stands watch over him. But on Israel's way from Egypt, *He that standeth watch over Israel doth neither slumber nor sleep* (Ps. 121:4).

9. The words *Because*[18a] *it was near* (Exod. 13:17) refer to the nearness of the place of wicked Pharaoh's punishment, [the Red Sea], where the Holy One would punish him.[19]

Another comment on *Because it was near*: the time of the Egyptians' punishment, when the Holy One would afflict them, was near.

Another comment on *Because it was near*: the respect which the Canaanites showed our father Jacob had occurred too recently [for the Israelites to take their land away from them].[20] With regard to the Canaanites' show of respect Scripture says, *The inhabitants of the Land, the Canaanites, made a show*[21] *of mourning* (Gen. 50:11) for Jacob, by undoing the girdles on

18. Aquila (flourished 130 C.E.) is best known for his literal translation of the Hebrew Bible into Greek, a translation extant only in fragments.

18a. The usual translation is "although it was near." But since Philistia's proximity to Egypt is both obvious and well-known the commentator prefers to take *ki* as meaning "because," which, as it happens, is the conjunction's more common meaning.

19. Hence God led Israel by the way of the wilderness, by the Red Sea. "him"—O_1, S, and Yalḳuṭ; O: "them."

20. God, therefore, led Israel in a roundabout way for forty years.

21. JV: *saw the mourning*. But the commentator apparently reads the verb as passive, a reading made possible through a slight change in vowels.

On God's willingness to accept a show of repentance, see Piska 24.11.

their loins, according to R. Eleazar; by undoing their shoulder knots, according to R. Simeon ben Laḳish; by [laying down their burdens and] standing upright, according to the Rabbis; by poking their fellows to compel their attention to the funeral procession, according to R. Yudan. The matter may be argued *a fortiori*: Neither with their hands nor with their feet had the Canaanites unequivocally shown respect [for the deceased Jacob]. But for no reason other than that they poked their fellows to compel their attention to the funeral procession, they were spared immediate invasion by Israel. How much more and more is to be done for our Jewish brothers who show all manner of respect to their elderly people and to their little ones and, of course, to their Sages!

Another comment on *Because it was near* (Exod. 13:17): the oath Abimelech made our father Abraham swear had been sworn too recently [for the Israelites to take the land of the Philistines away from them]. This is the oath spoken of in the verse *Now therefore swear unto me here by God that thou wilt not deal falsely with me, nor with my son, nor with my son's son* (Gen. 21:23). In regard to how many generations did Abimelech have Abraham swear? He had him swear in regard to three generations: *that thou wilt not deal falsely with me, nor with my son, nor with my son's son:* not while I, or my son, or my son's son is alive.[22]

And Abraham set seven ewe lambs of the flock by themselves (Gen. 21:28). According to R. Joshua of Sikn̲in, citing R. Levi, the Holy One said to Abraham: Thou gavest seven ewe lambs to the Philistines.[23] Hence, as thou livest, the Ark of the Covenant will abide captive among the Philistines for seven months. That the Ark so abode is intimated in the verse *He . . . delivered His strength into captivity, and His beauty into the adversary's hand* (Ps. 78:61), the word *strength* referring to the Ark of the Covenant—"The Ark of the Lord was in the country of the Philistines seven months" (1 Sam. 6:1), and the word *beauty* referring to the garments of the High Priest[24]—"Thou shalt make holy garments for Aaron thy brother, for splendor and for beauty" (Exod. 28:2).

According to R. Joshua of Sikn̲in who cited R. Levi, the Holy One said to

22. At that time, accordingly, the people of heathen nations lived longer than the Israelites. God's oath to Abraham "to thy seed I will give this Land" was fulfilled in Moses' generation, the seventh after Abraham's, whereas in the same period there were only three generations of Abimelech's dynasty: thus, at the exodus, Abimelech's grandson being still alive, *God led them not by way of the Philistines* (Exod. 13:17).

23. The commentator frowns on the idea of a covenant with a heathen people; the Prophets likewise denounced such alliances. See Isa. 30:2, Jer. 2:18, and 2 Chron. 20:37.

24. When Hophni and Phinehas who were priests—not High Priests—were slain (1 Sam. 4:11).

Abraham: Thou gavest the Philistines seven ewe lambs. [Because thou didst make a covenant with heathen], as thou livest, they will slay seven righteous of thy descendants, namely, Saul and his three sons,[25] Eli,[26] Hophni, and Phinehas—(according to some, Samson, not Eli).[27]

Again according to R. Joshua of Sik̲nin, citing R. Levi, the Holy One said to Abraham: Thou gavest seven ewe lambs to the heathen Philistines. As thou livest, the heathen will be responsible for the destruction and loss of seven shrines to thy children: the Tent of Meeting, Gilgal, Shiloh, Nob, Gibeon, and [Jerusalem's] Temple twice, shrines which otherwise would have endured throughout eternity.

10. [Concerning Israel's avoidance of the land of the Philistines, the shortest route to the Land, it is written] *God said: "Lest peradventure the people repent when they see* [*the results of a preceding*] *war"* (Exod. 13:17). Who were involved in that war? Descendants of Ephraim, specifically sons of Shuthelah[28] who, according to the Rabbis, erred by eighty years[29] too soon with regard to the time set for redemption from Egypt, and from whose number 180,000 men fell in battle with the Egyptians. Of these it is written *The descendants of Ephraim, though armed and carrying bows, were turned back in the day of battle*[30] (Ps. 78:9).

11. *But God led the people about, by the way of the wilderness by the Red Sea* (Exod. 13:18): that is, not only *led them about*, but encompassed them about [with His protection][31] while Israel were going through the wilderness.

And the children of Israel went up ḥămuššim[32] *out of the land of Egypt* (Exod. 13:18), *ḥămuššim* indicating that they were provided with five (*ḥămiššah*) kinds of weapons.

Another comment on *Israel went up ḥămuššim:* only one out of five (*ḥămiššah*) succeeded in going up out of Egypt. Only one out of fifty (*ḥămiššim*), according to other authorities; only one out of five hundred,

25. See 1 Sam. 31:6.

26. Eli died when he heard that his sons were slain by the Philistines (1 Sam. 4:17–18).

27. Since, after all, the Philistines had not actually killed him.

28. See 1 Chron. 7:20–21.

29. They believed that the year of Moses' birth was the year of redemption.

30. An old tradition speaks of an exodus from Egypt sometime before the one under the leadership of Moses took place. The first exodus, that of the Ephraimites, failed, and the bones of the dead remained strewn in the land of the Philistines into which, accordingly, God was reluctant to have the children of Israel enter. See Mek̲, *1*, 172–73; Exod. Rabbah 20:11; and PRE, chap. 48.

31. *Way-yasseb̲* is thus construed as both "led them about" and "encompassed them about." See Deut. 32:10.

32. JV: *armed.*

according to still other authorities. R. Nehorai declared: I avow by the Temple worship that not even one out of five hundred succeeded in going up out of Egypt. And R. Jose said: *Israel went up ḥămuššim* means that in the fifth generation [from Jacob] they went up out of Egypt.[33]

And the children of Israel were fruitful, and increased abundantly, and multiplied, and waxed exceeding mighty (Exod. 1:7). Two Amoraim [taking the word *wayyišrĕṣu*,[34] "increased abundantly," to be a verbal form of *šereṣ*, "small animal," read the verse as follows, "The children of Israel, being as fertile as small animals, multiplied and increased very greatly," and then commented: The verse gives us an idea of just how fertile the Israelites were: for] if by "small animal" is meant the largest of small animals, the mouse, it bears six young at a time; if the smallest of small animals, the scorpion, is meant, it bears sixty at a time.[35]

12. *And Moses took the bones of Joseph with him* (Exod. 13:19). Scripture makes known the excellence of Moses: While all Israel were busy taking up Egypt's booty, Moses busied himself taking up the bones of Joseph. Thus Scripture: *Moses took the bones of Joseph with him.* Why is it necessary to say *with him*? Because he took them with him into the camp of the Levites.[36] Who made it known to Moses where Joseph was buried? People say that it was Serah, daughter of Asher, who was still alive in that generation and told Moses, "Moses, Joseph is buried in the Nile River." Thereupon Moses went and stood by the Nile River, calling out: Joseph, Joseph, the time has come when the Holy One is redeeming His children. The Presence is awaiting you. Israel are awaiting you. The clouds of glory are awaiting you. If you make yourself visible, well and good. If not, we shall be innocent of violation of the oath you made our forebears swear.[37] Immediately, at these words, Joseph's coffin floated up to the surface of the river. According to another account, however, Moses took a shard, wrote God's Ineffable Name upon it, and threw the shard into the river. At once Joseph's coffin floated up to the surface. Two watchdogs were close by, dogs contrived by magicians to guard the coffin, and they began to snarl at Moses. Thereupon Moses said: O

33. Jacob, Levi, Kohath, Amram, Moses.

34. The verb *šrṣ* with regard to human fertility occurs elsewhere only in Gen. 9:7.

35. The number of Israelites at the exodus should, accordingly, have been at least 500 times 600,000. That the number was only 600,000, however, is further explained by parallel passages which say that many Israelites who spurned redemption died during the three days of darkness (Exod. 10:22). See Mek, *1*, 95, 175; and PR 15:11.

36. Thus teaching that the bones of a dead man or a full-fleshed corpse may be brought into the camp of the Levites but not into the camp of the priests (see B.Pes 67a).

37. See Gen. 50:25.

people, come and see! Real dogs would not be snarling now: only make-believe dogs would be snarling. Moses could tell that they were make-believe dogs—so said R. Yudan—because each of them was snarling, and Moses knew of God's promise that at the time of Israel's departure from Egypt, *against any of the children of Israel shall not a dog snarl*[38] (Exod. 11:7).

Two arks accompanied Israel in the wilderness, the ark containing Joseph's remains and the Ark of Him who lives for ever. The nations of the world kept asking Israel: What is the significance of these two arks? And Israel replied: This is the ark of Joseph who was mortal, and this is the Ark of Him who is immortal. Then the nations of the earth began to taunt Israel, saying "Is it proper that God's Ark should accompany an ark with a dead man in it?" And Israel replied: The dead man who was put into this ark fulfilled all the commandments that God had set down in the other Ark.[39]

13. From the teacher's seat R. Johanan sought to explain just how the waters of the Red Sea became a wall for Israel.[40] Even as R. Johanan was explaining that the wall of water looked like a lattice, Serah, daughter of Asher, looked down and said:[41] I was there. The waters rising up like a wall for Israel were shining because the radiance [of such personages as Moses and Aaron, who had drunk deep of Torah's waters], made the waters shine.[42]

Again R. Johanan from the teacher's seat sought to explain how the number seventy in the following verses was arrived at: *All the souls belonging to Jacob that came into Egypt, that came out of his loins . . . were threescore and six . . . All the souls of the house of Jacob, that came into Egypt were threescore and ten* (Gen. 46:26, 27). Even counting Joseph and his two sons, [said R. Johanan], the souls of the house of Jacob were still

38. So New Jewish Version; JV: *shall not a dog whet his tongue.*

39. Joseph is said to have kept each of the Ten Commandments. See Meḵ *1*, 179–81.

40. See Exod. 14:22.

41. Serah is said not to have died, but to have entered the Garden of Eden alive (see Targum Jonathan on Gen. 46:17). Hence, unlike those who were dead, she could speak to R. Johanan, just as Elijah could speak to mortals (Piska 11.15).

42. The Greek *emphōmata* is thus read *phasmata*, "something resembling [water]" (see Levy, *Wörterbuch*, p. 137). The proposed translation is supported by a lost Midrash which Baḥya ben Asher (13th century), in his comment on Exod. 14:22, cites as follows: "*The waters were a wall unto them.* Likened to water, Torah, which Israel were to receive, protected them like a wall and made the Egyptians perish." See *Rabbenu Baḥye*, ed. Ḥayyim Doḇ Šewel (Jerusalem, 5727/1967), 2, 118.

If the reading *emphōmata* is retained, Serah's words would read: "I was there. The openwork of the lattice looked like shining windows."

one short of seventy.[43] R. Levi, citing R. Ḥama bar R. Ḥanina said: The seventieth person was Jochebed, born within the gates of Egypt.[44] And some say it was Serah, daughter of Asher, who brought the count up to seventy.[45] For [Serah, identified in Scripture as the wise woman of the city of Abel, spoke of herself as] *I am šělume 'ěmune of Israel*[46] (2 Sam. 20:19): [when Jacob and his sons came into Egypt], I was the one who brought Israel's count up [to seventy]; I was the one who in faithful accounting turned the body of a faithful one over to a faithful one.[47]

R. Tanḥum bar Ḥanila'i said: The Holy One in His glory came in with them [as the seventieth]. And the proof? The verse *He is thy glory, and He is thy God* (Deut. 10:21). What follows directly? *Thy fathers went down into Egypt with threescore and ten* (Deut. 10:22).[48]

14. *A Psalm of David: Unto Thee, O Lord, do I lift up ('eśśa') my soul* (Ps. 25:1). The *kĕṯiḇ*, however, is *'eššа'*,[49] [which may be read *'eššaḥ*, "bent low"], so that David can be considered as saying sadly to the Holy One: Master of universes, my soul is bent low in distress for those who will give up their lives for the hallowing of the Name. Who, for example? Such a generation as will suffer [Hadrian's] persecution. The Holy One asked: David, will such men have really suffered any loss? Is it not true, as Scripture

43. Note that Gen. 46:26, which does not include Joseph and his two sons, gives the total of all the souls of the house of Jacob as threescore and six.

44. *The name of Amram's wife was Jochebed, the daughter of Levi, who was born to Levi in Egypt* (Num. 26:59). The purpose of the qualifying *born . . . in Egypt* is somewhat difficult to explain, since not only Jochebed, but also others were born in Egypt. The phrase *born . . . in Egypt* is taken to imply, therefore, that Jochebed had already been conceived in her mother's womb at the time of the reckoning and therefore counted as the seventieth among *the souls of the house of Jacob* (Gen. 46:27).

45. She is mentioned by name among the sixty-six souls of the house of Jacob (Gen. 46:17) and also among those who left Egypt and went into the wilderness (Num. 26:46); because of her longevity she is reckoned as though she were two people.

The name Serah, associated with the stem *srḥ*, "stretch, overhang," is taken to mean "one whose years stretched out in time." See *Śeḵel ṭoḇ*, ed. Buber (Berlin, 1900), *1*, 291, on Gen. 46:17.

46. ERV: *I am of them that are peaceable and faithful in Israel.* But in the comments that follow *šělume*, "peaceable," will be construed as a form of *hišlamti*, "completed, turned over"; and *'emune*, "faithful," will be construed as a form of *minyan*, "count," and of *ne'eman*, "faithful."

47. *Joseph was faithful* (Gen. 39:4), and so was Moses (Num. 12:7).

48. Cf. PRE, chap. 39.

49. In unpointed Hebrew there is no mark to distinguish the letter *śin* from the letter *šin*.

says, that their portion is in life [eternal]? *Their portion is in life [eternal]; that which is laid up for thee will fill their belly* (Ps. 17:14). David queried the Holy One: Master of universes, am I to gather, then, that my portion is to be with them? The Holy One replied: Yes, Scripture does not say here, "That which is laid up for *them* will fill their belly," but says, *That which is laid up for thee will fill their belly.* Accordingly, thy portion will be with theirs. Thereupon David said to the Holy One: Master of universes, such men, and others like them, come into Thy presence through the strength of their faith in Torah and their unquestioning giving of themselves to the hallowing of Thy name.[50] As for me, [not through hallowing Thy name, but] only *through charity may I see Thy face* (Ps. 17:15). [The physical anguish that hallowing the Name can entail led] R. Ḥiyya bar Abba to declare: If a man say to you, "Give up your life to hallow the Name," you could reply, "I am ready to give it up, provided my head be removed at once [and my suffering be brief]." But you would not say "yes" so readily if you were living in the generation that suffered [Hadrian's] persecution when those who hallowed the Name were tortured with white-hot iron balls wedged into their armpits and with sharpened reeds pushed in under their nails.

15. A story: R. Judah bar Giyoraya, R. Isaac, and R. Nathan went to hear the passage on libations[51] expounded by R. Simeon ben Yoḥai and stayed with him three days. Then they said: We ought to ask permission to depart.[52] Thereupon, [according to custom on such occasions], one of the three came into R. Simeon ben Yoḥai's presence and, expounding the verse *I have set My bow in the cloud* (Gen. 9:13), said: R. Simeon ben Yoḥai—he is indeed [the rainbow], a token of the covenant between God and earth.

50. Literally "good works." [Two things trouble me here: (1) *Torah u-ma'aśim ṭoḇim* usually means study of Torah and practice of its teaching; *Torah* does not usually mean "faith in Torah"; nor is *ma'asim ṭoḇim* usually a synonym of *ḳidduš haš-šem*, "hallowing the name." (2) JV translates *bĕṣeḏeḳ in righteousness* and not as the equivalent of *ṣĕḏaḳah*. And so I suggest: ". . . come into Thy presence on the strength of their (lifelong) study of Torah and their good works. But I, who am master neither of Torah nor of an unblemished record of deeds, *shall I behold Thy face in righteousness?* (Ps. 17:15)." In other words, the martyrs who died during Hadrian's persecution were men of profound learning and goodness, whereas I am but an indifferent scholar, and my record is blemished by grievous sins. L.N.]

51. The requirement that as part of a sacrifice or a festive occasion, liquids such as oil, wine, or water be poured upon the altar. See Exod. 29:40, Lev. 23:37, Num. 28:9, and 28:12; and Piska 28.8. Since such liquids have a characteristic shine, radiance is naturally associated with them.

52. Before leaving his master, a disciple must wait for the master to take the lead in bringing their meeting to a close. Then, too, the usual goodbyes are not

Then another of the three came in and, expounding the verse *the bow is seen in the cloud* (Gen. 9:14), said: R. Simeon ben Yoḥai—he is indeed [the rainbow], a token of the covenant between God and earth.

R. Hizkiah in the name of R. Jeremiah testified to the supernatural power of R. Simeon. R. Simeon ben Yoḥai had only to command "O valley, valley, fill up with golden denar," and the valley would fill up with them.[53]

R. Hizkiah said further in the name of R. Jeremiah: Elijah, ever remembered on good occasions, and R. Joshua ben Levi sat together[54] expounding Torah. When they came to a certain traditional interpretation transmitted in the name of R. Simeon ben Yoḥai, R. Simeon ben Yoḥai himself happened to pass by. So they said: Here comes in person the transmitter of the interpretation. Let us rise and ask him to state it. When they proceeded to ask him, R. Simeon ben Yoḥai inquired of Elijah: "Who is this with you?" Elijah replied: It is Joshua ben Levi, and he is the greatest man of his generation. R. Simeon ben Yoḥai asked: "Is the rainbow seen in his days?" Elijah answered: "Yes." Then R. Simeon ben Yoḥai remarked: If the radiance of the rainbow is seen in his days, he is not up to beholding the radiance of my countenance.[55]

Again in the name of R. Jeremiah, R. Hizkiah said: According to R. Simeon ben Yoḥai, the Holy One swore to our father Abraham that the world would never be without thirty righteous men like him. And the proof? The verse *Abraham shall surely become* (*yhyh*) *a great nation* (Gen. 18:18), the numerical value of the letters in *yhyh*—*yoḏ* ten, *he'* five, *yoḏ* ten, *he'* five—adding up to thirty. But, R. Simeon concluded, if there be only one righteous man in my generation, I am the one.

Again in the name of R. Jeremiah, R. Hizkiah said: R. Simeon ben Yoḥai used to say, Let Abraham bring close to God the people from his generation to my generation, and I will bring close to Him the people from my generation to the generation of the time when the king Messiah comes. And if

---

to be uttered when departing from one's master (Šulḥan 'aruḵ, *Yoreh de'ah*, 242:15). Hence disciples resorted to expounding a verse in such a way as to itimate a request to depart and simultaneously to express indirectly the words of leave-taking.

53. See MTeh 92:8.

54. Elijah the prophet is believed never to have died and hence could appear at will to distinguished Rabbis. Cf. B.Ta 22a.

55. The rainbow in the sky, the token of God's pledge never again to bring a flood, does not, according to R. Simeon ben Yoḥai, appear in the sky during the lifetime of one like himself who in his own person is "a rainbow." Since R. Joshua ben Levi, who lived a hundred years later, was not such a "rainbow," R. Simeon, deeming him incapable of spanning the gulf between the living and the dead, as R. Simeon was capable of doing, said that R. Joshua could not hold converse with him.

Abraham is unwilling, let Ahijah the Shilonite[56] join me, and he and I will bring close to God all the world's inhabitants—[not only all the living, but all who have ever lived and all who are yet to be born].

[In concluding the story of the three Rabbis—R. Judah, R. Isaac, and R. Nathan—who came and studied for three days with R. Simeon ben Yoḥai] the third one of the Rabbis came into his presence and in praise of him[57] expounded the verse *Go, sell the oil and pay thy debt, and live thou and thy sons of the rest* (2 Kings 4:7).[58]

16. A story: R. Simeon ben Yoḥai and his son R. Eleazar hid themselves [from Roman persecution] in a cave in a valley for thirteen years. All they had to eat was Teruman[59] carobs, so that their bodies came to be covered with sores. At the end of the thirteen years, R. Simeon ben Yoḥai went out and sat at the entrance to the cave whence he saw a man spread a net to catch birds. When the man spread it the first time, R. Simeon heard a heavenly voice say "Mercy," and thereupon the bird went free; when the man spread it a second time, R. Simeon heard the heavenly voice say "Death," and thereupon the bird stayed caught. R. Simeon then said: Without the will of heaven, even a bird does not perish, so why should we remain

56. See MTeh 5:8.

57. ["In praise of him" seems inconsistent with the story of the three disciples. Their purpose was not to praise R. Simeon, but to hint at their wish to depart. The first two brought up the significance of the rainbow, which wrote finis to floods—in other words, they meant, "Thank you for your instruction, Rabbi. May we regard it as completed and bid you adieu?" The third disciple quoted a verse which contained the more direct and blunt *lĕḵi*, "go"—in other words, "May we go now, Rabbi?" I would cross out "in praise of him." L.N.]

58. Here only the verse upon which the comment is based is given. The comment in full is found in Gen. Rabbah 35:3: "The third expounded: It is already written *Thereupon she* [the woman whom Elisha had saved from slavery by the miracle of the increasing oil] *went from Elisha* (2 Kings 4:5). Why then is it stated further, *Then she came and told the man of God* (2 Kings 4:7) [that the miracle had taken place]? The reason, as the verse goes on to say, is that *the oil stayed* (2 Kings 4:6)—stood up. That is, the market price of the oil advanced, and so she came to ask him whether to sell then, or wait for a further increase. His second blessing was greater than the first, viz. *And live on thou and thy sons of the rest* (2 Kings 4:7). [The first blessing had merely been to the effect that the oil would suffice to pay her debts]. But the second blessing seemed to imply that she and her sons would live on until the resurrection of the dead."

According to Julius Theodor, Elisha's blessing was that the oil would be so plentiful as to sustain the woman and her children even if they were to live until the resurrection (see Gen. Rabbah TA 332-33).

Thus the third Rabbi's parting salutation to R. Simeon was that all generations until the resurrection of the dead would be illumined by his radiance.

59. Perhaps the name of a place.

a cave? [Thereupon he and his son left the cave], and after a while, having heard that the execution of [Rome's] decrees had been relaxed, R. Simeon said: Let's go down to the springs of Tiberias, bathe in them, and be healed. Later, R. Simeon and his son said, We ought to show our gratitude as our forebears used to do: they set up markets where they sold produce at low prices.[60] So R. Simeon set up a market where he sold at low prices. [To show their gratitude further], he and his son said: We ought to remove the impurity caused by the bones of the dead strewn about Tiberias.[61] R. Simeon then gathered lupines, cut them up, and scattered the pieces around the public thoroughfares: thereupon, wherever a corpse was buried, it rose up and came to the surface.[62] A Cuthean saw what R. Simeon was doing, and said: Shall I not make sport of this elder of the Jews? What did he do? He got hold of a corpse and buried it in a thoroughfare which R. Simeon ben Yoḥai had purified. The Cuthean then went to him and said: Do you claim to have purified such-and-such a thoroughfare? He replied: Yes. The Cuthean said: Suppose from that very place I produce a corpse for you? He replied: "Say no more: show me." R. Simeon ben Yoḥai, having perceived by the power of the holy spirit that the Cuthean had placed it there, declared: I decree that they who are above shall descend and they who are below shall ascend. And thus it befell that the Cuthean descended.

As R. Simeon was departing, he passed by the Synagogue of Magdala[63] and heard the voice of [Naḳai],[64] Magdala's schoolmaster, call out: Here is bar Yoḥai who is supposed to have purified Tiberias. R. Simeon said to Naḳai: Were you not counted among those who officially declared that Tiberias was purified? Thereupon he lifted his eyes and looked at the schoolmaster—in that instant the man became a heap of bones.

17. In a Sabbatical year R. Simeon ben Yoḥai was passing [through the valley of Beth Neṭufa][65] and saw the owner of a field of vegetables greedily gathering aftergrowths of the seventh year [to store up for his own use]. He said to him: My son, is it not the seventh year, when such an act is prohibited? The man replied: Are you not the one who said that such an act is permitted?[66] R. Simeon said: Yes, but did not my colleagues disagree with

60. See Gen. Rabbah 79:6.

61. Num. 19:11–16. Herod Antipas built Tiberias on the site of tombs which had been obliterated. See Josephus, *Antiquities*, *18*, 2, 3.

62. The corpses were then buried outside of Tiberias, which was thus cleansed of defilement.

63. Magdala lay nearby, southeast of Tiberias.

64. Naḳai, "clean," may here be used in the sense of "super-critical." Hence, Naḳai = the knocker.

65. "The valley of Beth Neṭufa"—Gen. Rabbah 79:6; in lower Galilee in the vicinity of Tiberias.

66. Shebi 9:1.

me? And thereupon he applied to the man the verse *Whoso breaketh through a fence,*[67] *a serpent shall bite him* (Eccles. 10:8). And thus it befell the man.

18. Wishing to buy corn, some donkey-drivers came to the city where dwelt[68] Eleazar, son of R. Simeon [ben Yoḥai]. They saw him seated near the oven from which his mother kept bringing him loaves of bread, and he ate and ate until he had consumed the entire troughful of bread. They said: Alas, a pernicious snake is lodged in this young man's belly. Hearing what they said, what did he do to them? He took their donkeys and lifted them up onto the roof. They went and reported his conduct to R. Simeon, father of Eleazar. He asked: Perhaps you said something to offend him? They replied: We saw him seated near the oven while his mother was bringing him loaves of bread which he ate until he had consumed the whole troughful of bread. So we said: Alas, a pernicious snake is lodged in this young man's belly. R. Simeon asked them: Was it perhaps your bread he ate? He who created him created food for him. All the same, go and speak to him in my name, and he will fetch the donkeys down for you.

They went and said to R. Eleazar what his father had told them to say. The second feat was more striking than the first. In taking up the donkeys, Eleazar had taken them up one by one; in bringing them down, he brought them down two by two.

19. Appointed chief of customs, Eleazar bar R. Simeon had to act in person as executioner of people who were sentenced to die. R. Joshua ben Ḳorḥa then began to call him, "Vinegar, son of wine!" Eleazar replied: "Whom are you calling 'Vinegar, son of wine'? Have I not cut down thorns which should have been cut down? Have I not executed men who have been sentenced to death?" R. Joshua replied: "I know indeed that you did not even want the appointment and that you fled away to Laodicea[69] to avoid it: just the same you should have fled to the end of the world and let the Owner of the garden come Himself and weed out His thorns."[70]

67. By *fence* R. Simeon meant the injunction by which his colleagues forbade the eating of aftergrowths during a Sabbatical year, an act which Scripture permits, as R. Simeon pointed out. R. Simeon's colleagues feared, however, that during a Sabbatical year farmers might be tempted to plant produce surreptitiously, store it, and then sell it as aftergrowth. Consequently, the *fence*. See Ab̲ 1:1, and Maimonides' Code, VII, v, iv, 1.

68. Since R. Eleazar had not yet become a scholar, the title "Rabbi" is deleted in the translation here and further on.

69. The emendation suggested *ad loc.* by Saul Lieberman is followed.

70. Cf. Matthew 13:24 ff.

L.N. suggests that R. Joshua's reply be translated as follows: "[Is that so]? Did you, for example, flee and go [even as short a distance as] to Laodicea? Don't you realize that you were duty-bound to flee even to the end of the world, and let the Owner," etc.?

20. Eleazar bar R. Simeon went to visit his father-in-law R. Simeon bar Jose bar Laḳonya who slaughtered an ox for him, baked a troughful of bread for him, and opened a cask of wine for him. As rapidly as R. Simeon mixed the wine, Eleazar drank it down. R. Simeon then asked Eleazar: Perhaps you were informed by your father how many draughts a man takes to down a cup of wine? Eleazar replied: A cup of [unmixed] wine, in a single draught; [mixed wine], when cold, in two draughts; [mixed wine], when hot, in three. But the Sages give no estimates for your cup which is small, for your wine which is good, and for my stomach which is big.

21. Eleazar bar R. Simeon asked his father-in-law R. Simeon bar R. Jose bar Leḳonya: "What is meant by *Thy clothes upon thee did not wear out* (Deut. 8:4)? Did weavers' gear go with Israel in the wilderness?" R. Simeon replied: "[There was no need for weavers' gear, for] clouds of glory clothed them." "But did not even these wear out?" "No, for, as Moses said, *Thy clothes upon thee did not wear out.*" "But did not the little ones in Israel grow up?" R. Simeon replied: "Consider the snail—all the time that he is growing, his shell grows with him." "But did not the garments require washing?" R. Simeon replied: "Other clouds of glory, [fiery ones], cleansed their garments. And do not be astonished at this. For their garments were made of asbestos linen[71]—and such are cleansed only by fire." "But did not the garments reek with sweat?" R. Simeon replied: They used to sweeten their garments with the grasses around [Miriam's] well, so that it was said to Israel *The smell of thy garments is like the smell of Lebanon* (Song 4:11). [How do we know that the grasses had such fragrance? Because they were moistened *Out of the fountain of gardens, the well of living waters*[72] (Song 4:15)].

22. Eleazar bar R. Simeon was put in charge of pressing men and animals into forced labor. Elijah, ever remembered on good occasions, in the guise of an old man came to him one time and said to him: Get a beast of burden ready for me. Eleazar asked: And what do you have to load on the animal? Elijah replied: This worn skin bottle, my cloak, and my own person as rider. Eleazar said: Take a look at this old man whom I can pick up with one hand

71. Literally "amiantus," a variety of fine asbestos from which asbestos linen was spun.

72. "How do we know . . . *living waters*"—Deut. Rabbah 7:11. The well was said to have been created at twilight on the eve of the first Sabbath (Ab̲ 5:8); it was this well, dug by the Patriarchs, which Hagar had come upon (Gen. 16:14); it was the well seen at Marah (Exod. 15:25); the well whose water sprang from the rock at Rephidim (Exod. 17:6); the well whose waters sprang from the rock at Kadesh (Num. 20:8). On account of Miriam's merit this same well accompanied Israel through the wilderness, and Israel drank from its waters. In the days of the Messiah the waters of this well will issue from under the Temple's threshold (Ezek. 47:8). See Lieberman, TKF, Mo'ed̲, *4*, 876–77.

and carry to the end of the world; and he says to me as if he weighed a ton: Get a beast of burden ready for me! So what did Eleazar do? He put Elijah on his own back, took him up mountainsides, and brought him down into valleys, across fields of thorns and fields of thistles. Finally, Elijah began to bear down with his weight upon Eleazar. Thereupon Eleazar said: Old man, old man, ride more lightly. If not, I shall throw you off. Elijah asked: Would you like to rest a bit? Eleazar replied: Yes. What did he do then? He took Elijah to a field where he set him down under a tree and gave him something to eat and drink. After Elijah ate and drank, he asked Eleazar: What will all this wandering around get you? Would it not be better for you to settle down and take up the vocation of your forebears? Eleazar asked: Can you teach me their vocation? Elijah replied: Yes. Then, according to some, Elijah, ever remembered on good occasions, taught Eleazar for thirteen years until he was able to recite the Sifra.[73] [So much of his strength went into learning that] once he was able to recite the Sifra he could not even carry his own cloak.

In Rabban Gamaliel's household they had a steward who could carry as much as forty *sĕ'ah* of corn to the baker. Some one said to him: You have such great strength and yet you do not give yourself to the study of the Sifra. As soon as he heard the words "study of the Sifra," he could no longer carry even one *sĕ'ah*—[that is, the idea of study of the Sifra came upon him so strongly that it drew off all his strength]. Even his garment—some say, had not another taken it off him, he would not have been able to take it off by himself.

23. As R.[74] Eleazar bar R. Simeon was wasting away [in his last illness], his arm once happened to get exposed, and he saw his wife both laughing and weeping. He said to her: As you live, I know why you are laughing and why you are weeping. You laugh because you said to yourself, "How happy am I with what has been my lot in this world! How happy am I that I have been able to cleave to the body of so righteous a man!" And you weep because you said, "Alas that such a body is going to the worms!" True, I am about to die, but worms, God forbid, will have no power over me. I shall not lie entirely unmolested, however, for once, as I entered a synagogue, I heard a man uttering blasphemy and I should have taken legal action against him, but I kept silent, and therefore for punishment, in the grave I shall have to put up with a moth's nibbling away behind my ear.

After R. Eleazar died, he was buried in Giscala, a place not worthy of him. Thereupon R. Simeon ben Yoḥai began revealing himself in dreams to the people of Meron, saying to them: I was not privileged to have my son,

73. The Tannaitic Midrash on Leviticus, a particularly difficult treatise.

74. Eleazar, having become a scholar, the title "Rabbi" is given him henceforth in the translation.

who was my right eye, put to rest next to me? Thereupon the people of Meron went out to try to bring R. Eleazar's body to be put beside R. Simeon's. But the people of Giscala came out and fought them off with sticks and spears. Some time later, on the eve of the Great Fast, the people of Meron said: This is the time, while they of Giscala are stuffing themselves, we can go get R. Eleazar's body. As soon as the people of Meron got outside of the city, two snakes of fire came to walk before them. So they said: It is evident that this is the right time for us to go fetch R. Eleazar's body. When they got to the cave, the two snakes of fire stationed themselves on either side of the entrance. The people of Meron then said: Who will go into the cave to bring him out? R. Eleazar's wife said: I will go in and bring him out, since I know a way of recognizing his body. She went in and, seeing the moth nibbling behind her husband's ear, was about to bring out his body. But when she started to remove the moth, she heard a Divine Voice say, Let the Creditor continue to collect the debt due Him. Finally, however, they brought out R. Eleazar's body and placed it next to his father's. Thereafter, it is said, R. Simeon ben Yoḥai did not reveal himself in dreams to the people of Meron.

24. Whenever R. Eleazar bar R. Simeon entered the chamber where scholars were wont to study, the face of R. Judah darkened.[75] Thereupon R. Judah's father said to his son: Try to accept the fact that he is a lion and son of a lion while you, it is true, are yourself a lion, but only son of a fox. After R. Eleazar bar R. Simeon died, R. Judah sent an offer to marriage to his widow. In reply she sent this message: Shall a vessel which has been used for a sacred purpose be used for a profane one? R. Judah asked: What did he do that I have not also done? She told him: After he had labored in the Torah as much as he could and was about to lie down to sleep, he would say, "Let all of Israel's afflictions come upon me," and they would, indeed, come upon him. And when the time came for him to labor in the Torah, he would say, "Let each of the afflictions go back where it came from," and they would all go away. R. Judah said: I will do the same as R. Eleazar did. When he summoned the afflictions, they came. But when he told them to go away, they would not go. Some say he was afflicted with toothache for thirteen years.

The widow's last word to R. Judah was: It is well said that we may go up in holiness, but that we may not go down.

25. *For Joseph . . . had made the children of Israel swear again and again*[76] (Exod. 13:19). Why swear an oath again and again? Scripture intimates that Joseph made his brothers swear in their own behalf and made

75. R. Eleazar used to criticize his opinions. See B.BM 84b.

76. The added infinitive absolute of "swear" is interpreted in this comment as referring to another act of swearing besides the one indicated in the finite verb. JV: *For Joseph . . . had straitly sworn the children of Israel.*

sure his brothers would have their children and the children of the next generation likewise swear in their own behalf.

God will remember you again and again[77] (*ibid.*). Why does Scripture refer to successive acts of remembering? Because there will be a remembering in Egypt and a remembering at Sinai, a remembering in Nisan and a remembering in Tishri,[78] a remembering in this world and a remembering in the world-to-come.

And ye shall carry up my bones away hence (*ibid.*). Lest one might take this verse to mean that Joseph's bones were to be carried up from Egypt immediately after his death, the verse goes on to say *with you*—that is, his bones are to be carried away when you, the children of Israel, go up from Egypt. *With you*, says R. Meir, further suggests that the people of each and every Tribe were to take the bones of their own Tribe Father with them.

77. Here, too, Scripture uses both the finite and the infinitive forms of the verb.

78. The month in which Israel's servitude in Egypt came to an end. See MhG Gen., 884.

PISKA 12

SUMMARY

Torah and its range of eternal meaning

In earlier ages, before the revelation on Sinai, a number of commandments had been given to certain illustrious men: six commandments to Adam, one to Noah, one to Abraham, one to Jacob, and one to Judah. But only to Israel were given all 613 commandments.

Even as Israel was thus distinguished, so was Moses distinguished among the Prophets, every one of whom bluntly demanded that the Holy One meet Israel's needs (Sec. 1). God's willingness to meet Israel's needs is so strong, that as a mother draws out her breast to suckle her child He drew out the Torah for Israel (Sec. 2). Still He had to delay giving the Torah to Israel, so that with the waters of the well, with the manna, and with the quail, He might nurse them back to good health after their years of servitude (Sec. 3).

The day God gave the Torah was the sixth of Sivan (Sec. 4). Though given long ago, matters of Torah should be looked upon not as antiquated decrees, but as decrees freshly issued, as recently as the day before yesterday (*šlšm*) (Prov. 22:20). In further explication, the word *šlšm* is taken to mean weapons: as weapons stand up in battle for their owners, so, too, do words of Torah stand up for him who valorously gives them the labor they require to be understood. The words of both Torahs are meant—the Torah given by the written word and the Torah given by word of mouth. Preoccupation with Torah assures life in this world as well as in the world-to-come, and like wine, honey, and pepper, gives zest to the daily round of life (Sec. 5). To be God, God requires that the people of Israel witness His presence (Sec. 6). Hence Torah, the most desirable thing in heaven above, was given to Moses dwelling on the earth below (Sec. 7). The Ten Commandments alone are not sufficient, however, for the guidance of Israel. Innumerable laws precede and follow the Ten Commandments to give them validity and force (Sec. 8). No stranger, not even Moses' father-in-law, was allowed to be present at the revelation (Sec. 9), because it is only the children of Israel who under no circumstances shun the Holy One. Other nations, however, are apt to say of Him that He is too severe in His demands upon mankind (Sec. 10).

Several parables speak of the giving of Torah as coinciding with the beginning of a new era; of certain events preceding the giving of Torah as stages in God's wooing of Israel; and of the revelation itself as marking the time when heaven and earth were no longer apart (Sec. 11). The words *šališi* and *šališim* which describe Torah are construed consecutively as "trustworthy and as "day before yesterday," the latter meaning indicating that one is regard the Torah as having been given "the day before yesterday"—hence i decrees are never antiquated (Sec. 12). *Sališi* in the sense of "third" an "three" points to the many triads associated with Torah and with the da when it was given (Sec. 13). To receive the Torah, however, and to hold o to it, Israel had to become one brotherhood (Sec. 14) and to resolve upo "slothfulness" in the committing of transgressions (Sec. 15). No wonder th in the moment of union between God and Israel no stranger was permitted be present (Sec. 16). To make doubly certain that strangers were not to tak part in the union between God and Israel, it was decreed that three month were to elapse between redemption and revelation, three months being th length of time which a female convert, a female captive, or an emancipate female slave had to wait before marrying in order to prove that she had bee chaste (Sec. 17).

Moses knew the site of the mountain where Israel were to serve God, bu not until God said, "The month is come" did he know the particular time th revelation was to occur (Sec. 18). God had delayed the revelation in orde to have time for the renewal of Israel so that the blind could see, the dea could hear, the lame could stand upright, and the mute could sing out (Sec 19). He had also delayed it so that the Torah would be given in the thir month under the zodiacal sign of Twins, by way of indicating that the de scendants of Jacob's twin brother were also asked to come and accept th Torah.

The Torah was given in the wilderness to make men aware that unless man makes himself ownerless like a wilderness, he will not be able to acquir Torah (Sec. 20). Its words must seem as fresh as though they were given thi very day (Sec. 21).

The words *I am the Lord* are considered in the light of Ps. 68, where it i stated that myriads came down with God upon Sinai. According to on opinion, the myriads were angels whose number corresponded to the numbe of Levite males who retained their integrity in the matter of the golden calf According to another opinion, the myriads were chariots, each and every on like the chariot which Ezekiel was to see. Their number, another commen tator adds, could not be reckoned.

Other commentators maintain that the myriads of angels came down int the world sharply intent upon destroying it had Israel refused the Torah; bu this view is rejected in several comments which follow. To hold these myr iads, Sinai extended its boundaries, even as in the time-to-come Jerusalem will extend her boundaries to accommodate all the children of Israel.

The angels, being God's couriers, have His name engraved upon thei hearts. As God's lordship is upon and among the angels, so it is upon and among the children of Israel (Sec. 22). As Israel's patron, God favors Israel ıder all circumstances. No judge, not even Moses, is accorded such outright vor. According to another opinion, however much He favors Israel, He still aintains His sovereignty over His people (Sec. 23).

Various significances are attached to the word *'nky* and to the letters of hich it is composed. We are told, for example, that God began the Ten ommandments with *'nky*, whose first letter *'ale*f is the first letter in the phabet, to assuage the hurt feelings of the *'alef* at the fact that the creation the world began with the letter *beṯ*, the first letter of the word *br'šyt*, the st word of Torah.

According to one commentator, the word *'nky* is an Egyptian word, for od had to address His people in the language they had acquired during eir stay in Egypt.

Though the Holy One may appear to Israel in many guises—as a pedagogue, as a mighty man waging war, as an elder teaching Torah—still He is ne and the same (Sec. 24). Though for different purposes He appeared to rael with a stern face, with a joyous face, He is unchangingly one and the me. Moreover, the one and the same God appears to every human according to his particular capacity to respond to Him, saying to every individual, *I n the Lord thy God*—thy very own God (Sec. 25).

PISKA 12

In the third month (Exod. 19:1).[1]

1. R. Judah bar R. Simon began his discourse with the verse "Man illustrious sons of mankind have acquired some of the ways of attainin virtue, but [in the number of such ways] thou, [O Israel], hast exceede them all"[2] (Prov. 31:29). Adam, to begin with, was given six commands to refrain from idolatry, to refrain from blasphemy, to institute civil courts to refrain from shedding blood, to refrain from unchastity, and to refrai from seizing what belongs to another. All six of these commands are implie in the verse whose every element is explicated by relevant parallels in Scripture: [God commanded Adam (1) to refrain from obedience] *to the command,* (2) *with regard to the Lord,* (3) [*with regard*] *to God,* (4 *concerning man,* (5) *saying,* (6) *of every tree in the garden thou mayes freely eat*[3] (Gen. 2:16). Thus the words [God commanded Adam to refrai from obedience] *to the command* [of a mortal] are taken as enjoinin Adam from idolatry, and are so taken because of the meaning of "command" in a verse which derides idolatry, "Ephraim . . . was content to wall after the command [of Jeroboam who set up calves to be worshiped]" (Hos. 5:11); the words *with regard to the Lord* are taken to enjoin Adan from blasphemy and are so taken because of the context of the words *the Lord* in a verse which enjoins against blasphemy, "He that blasphemeth the

1. Exod. 19:1–20:26 is the lesson for Pentecost. See B.Meḡ 30b.

2. JV: *Many daughters have done valiantly, but thou excellest them all.* R. Judah takes *banot*, "daughters," however, to have the general meaning of "builders" (from *bnh*, "build")—hence, "illustrious sons of mankind" (see B.Sanh 20a) The word *'aśu* may mean "done" or "acquired" even as *ḥayil* may mean "valiantly valor, virtue"—hence "ways of attaining virtue."

3. JV: *And the Lord God commanded the man, saying: Of every tree of the garden thou mayest freely eat.* But for the commentator, the term *commanded* seems to be out of place, since God does not command Adam, but only tells him that out of the trees of the Garden of Eden he may freely eat. Moreover, the verse seems to use more words than necessary. Hence the conclusion that the six commands given to Adam are here intimated.

Close reading of Scripture is responsible for the preceding exegesis. Cain's having said *My sin is too great to be forgiven* (Gen. 4:13) is taken to imply his awareness that murder was a sin. Of the generation of the flood, Scripture says *The earth was filled with violence* (Gen. 6:11) and that *all flesh had corrupted its way* (Gen. 6:12), indicating awareness of wrongdoing in acts of violence as well as in acts of unchastity. Moreover, the fact that of Enoch it is said *He walked with God* (Gen. 5:24) is taken to imply awareness of the command to refrain from idolatry, and the statement *Cain be avenged sevenfold*, etc. (Gen. 4:15) is taken to suggest the existence of civil courts. Cain would not have spoken of his deed as a sin,

ame of the Lord, he shall surely be put to death" (Lev. 24:16); the words) *God* (Elohim) are taken to enjoin Adam to institute a judiciary, and are) taken because of the meaning of *God* (Elohim) in a verse which enjoins srael to respect the judges, "Thou shalt not revile Elohim—the judges" Exod. 22:27); the words *concerning man* are taken to enjoin Adam from hedding blood and are so taken because of the context of *man* in a verse vhich, in the words "Whoso sheddeth man's blood" (Gen. 9:6), forbids the hedding of blood; the term *saying* [words loose and libidinous] is taken to njoin Adam from unchaste conduct, and is so taken because of the sense of *aying* in a verse which, in the words ". . . saying, if a man put away his vife,"[4] etc. (Jer. 3:1), enjoins against unchastity; the words *of every tree of he garden thou mayest freely eat* are taken to enjoin Adam from seizing what elongs to another, and are so taken because of the next verse, "But of the ree of the knowledge of good and evil thou shalt not eat of it" (Gen. 2:17).

Noah was enjoined from eating flesh cut from a living animal, "Only flesh vith the life thereof, which is the blood thereof, shall ye not eat" (Gen.):4). Abraham was commanded to observe the practice of circumcision, for ne was told "Thou shalt keep My covenant . . . every male . . . shall be ircumcised" (Gen. 17:9). Circumcision was inaugurated with Isaac, for vhen he was eight days old, he was the first to be circumcised, as is said 'Abraham circumcised his son Isaac when he was eight days old" (Gen. 21:4). Jacob was commanded to refrain from eating the sinew of the thigh-vein, as is said "Therefore the children of Israel eat not the sinew of the thigh-vein" (Gen. 32:33). Judah was commanded to meet the obligation of marry-ng a brother's wife who is widowed and childless, as in the verse "Judah said unto Onan: 'Go in unto thy brother's wife, and perform the duty of a husband's brother unto her,' " etc. (Gen. 38:8). But at Sinai, [*in the number of such ways of attaining virtue*] *thou hast exceeded them all*[5] (Prov. 31:29), for there, O Israel, you were given six hundred and thirteen commandments, of which two hundred and forty-eight are positive commands and three hundred and sixty-five are negative ones. Two hundred and forty-

---

proceedings against those who might harm him could not have been instituted, the generation of the flood could not have been punished, according to Jewish law, unless the several injunctions of the kind mentioned in R. Judah b. R. Simon's comment on Gen. 2:16 had been previously given. See Menahem Reubeni, *Darke ham-Midraš* (Tel Aviv, 1967/5727), 59, where he quotes Jehiel Michael Guttmann, *'Asmaḵta*, p. 36.

4. The actions of a woman who upon being divorced marries another from whom she is also divorced, and thereupon wishes to remarry her first husband, and the actions of a woman suspected or actually guilty of infidelity are seen to be somewhat analogous. See Naḥmanides on Deut. 24:4, and B.Yeb 11b.

On the overtones of *saying*, see Rashi Lev. 24:11.

5. "[*in the number . . . thou hast exceeded them all*"—Yalḳuṭ.

eight positive commands were given to correspond to the two hundred a forty-eight parts of the body, each and every one of these parts saying to man, "I beg you, perform through me the commandment that applies to me Three hundred and sixty-five negative commandments were given to co respond to the three hundred and sixty-five days in the solar year, each which says to a man, "I beg you, do not perform a transgression during m span of hours." Thus *Grace is deceitful, and beauty is vain; but a woman th feareth the Lord, she shall be praised* (Prov. 31:30). *Grace is deceitf* Noah's grace—"Noah found grace in the eyes of the Lord" (Gen. 6:8)- proved deceitful. *And beauty is vain:* Adam's beauty proved vain.[6] Even th round of Adam's heel outshone the globe of the sun. And do not wonder this! Human nature is such that when a man has two salvers made for hi one for himself, and one for his steward, whose salver does he have made th more beautiful? Not his own? So Adam was created for the service of th Holy One, and the globe of the sun was created for the service of morta Does it not follow, then, that the round of Adam's heel outshone the globe the sun? And if the round of Adam's heel outshone the globe of the sun, ho much more brightly shone the countenance of his face? [Still his beau proved vain].

The words *But a woman that feareth the Lord, she shall be praised* (Pro 31:30) apply to Moses more than to any of the other illustrious sons mankind: *Give her of the fruit of her hands, and let her works praise her the gates* (Prov. 31:31). R. Jose bar Jeremiah asked: Why does Scriptu liken Prophets to women? To show that just as a woman is not ashamed demand from her husband the requirements of her household, so Prophe are not ashamed to bluntly demand the requirements of Israel from the Ho One.

The Holy One said to Israel: My children, be sure to read every year th passage in Scripture beginning *In the third month*, and I will deem you reading it as being the same as your standing before Mount Sinai and accep ing the Torah. And when did this event take place? *In the third month afte the children of Israel were gone forth out of the land of Egypt* (Exod 19:1).

2. R. Johanan began his discourse with the verse *He delivered me fro mine enemy most strong, and from them that hated me, for they were to mighty for me* (Ps. 18:18). The words *He delivered me from mine enem most strong* apply to Pharaoh: "The enemy said, 'I will pursue'" (Exod 15:9). The words *and from them that hated me, for they were too mighty fo me* apply to the Egyptians. The words *They confronted me in the day of m calamity* (Ps. 18:19) apply, according to some, to Pharaoh; and, accordin to others, to Amalek. *But the Lord was a stay unto me* (*ibid.*) against all o

6. Noah became drunk, and Adam fell from grace and was expelled from th Garden of Eden.

y enemies. *He brought me forth into a large place* (Ps. 18:20) in that He ive me the Torah [whose measure is longer than the earth and wider than e sea].[7] *He drew out*[8] *for me, because He delighted in me* (*ibid.*). That said R. Johanan, His delight and trust in me rose up so strongly in Him[9] at He drew out the Torah for me [as a mother draws out her breast for er child]. When? *In the third month* (Exod. 19:1).

3. R. Isaac began his discourse with the verse, [usually read *Stay ye me ith dainties* (*'ăšišot̲*) (Song 2:5)], by reading "Stay ye me with *'ăšišot̲*"—ith the two fires (*'iššot̲*)—the fire of Abraham[10] and the fire of Hananiah, lishael, and Azariah.[11]

Another comment: "Stay ye me with *'ăšišot̲*"—with the two fires—the fire f Moriah[12] and the fire of the bush.[13]

Another comment: "Stay ye me with *'ăšišot̲*"—that is, with laws which are losely reasoned and precisely expressed (*mĕ'uššašot̲*); *comfort me with pples* (*ibid.*)—with words of Torah whose fragrance is as goodly as the agrance of apples.

But I yearn for love[14] (*ibid.*). R. Isaac said: Formerly, when there was nough money around for one to do with, people were strong for studying a opic in Mishnah or a topic in Talmud; but now that there is not enough ioney to do with, and at the same time we are made to suffer ill from the ingdoms,[15] every man yearns to be consoled by hearing set forth a passage n Scripture or a theme in *'Ăg̲ad̲ah*.

In another comment, the verse, [usually read *For I am love-sick* (Song :5)], is read "Because I am still sickly, I require love," which R. Levi llustrated by the parable of a king's son who had just got up from a sick bed. His tutor said: Let him go back to school. The king replied: My son's look f good health has not come back since his illness—should he be returning

7. The parallel in MTeh 18:21 continues: "which is called a large place because The measure thereof is longer than the earth, and larger than the sea' (Job 11:9)."

8. Cf. Lam. 4:3. JV: *He delivered me.*

9. S and C are followed here.

10. The reference is probably to the legend that after Abraham had rejected idolatry, Nimrod cast him into a fiery furnace (Gen. Rabbah 42:4).

11. See Dan. 3:19. R. Isaac thus construes "Stay ye me with the two fires" as Israel's prayer for strength to face the fire of martyrdom.

12. Fire came down from heaven and burnt the ram instead of Isaac. So Yalkuṭ.

13. See Exod. 3:2. R. Isaac now construes "Stay ye me with the two fires" as Israel's prayer to be capable of ever seeing in Torah the fire of revelation.

14. JV: *For I am love-sick.* But *ḥlh*, "to be sick," can also mean "yearn."

15. During the military anarchy in Palestine in the third century, the famine was so great that people fell to eating unripe grain in the fields (Gen. Rabbah 20:10).

so soon to school? My son ought to be indulged for two or three months wit good food and drink—then he can go back to school. So, too, after Isra went forth out of Egypt, it was intended that they receive the Torah at onc but among them there were men who had been crippled by servitude in cla and bricks. Therefore the Holy One said: Because of their servitude in cla and bricks, my sons' look of good health has not yet come back. Should the now receive the Torah? Let My sons be indulged for two or three months wit the waters of the well,[16] with the manna, and with the quail—then let ther receive the Torah. When? *In the third month* (Exod. 19:1).

4. R. Johanan began his discourse with the verse *So,* [*precious to Me o account of her*] *sterling men,*[17] *I bought Me on the fifteenth,*[18] etc. (Hos 3:2). R. Johanan [then construed the entire verse, and the one that follows as intimating the day when the redemption from Egypt took place; as intimating the number of days between the day of redemption and the day th Torah was given; and as intimating the first two of the Ten Commandments the only ones God uttered directly to the people of Israel. Thus he] read th verse *So,* [*precious to Me on account of her*] *sterling men, I bought Me o the fifteenth,* etc. to mean *So,* [*precious to Me on account of her*] *sterlin men, I declared her to be Mine*—[that is, covenanted with Israel]—*on th fifteenth*—that is, on the fifteenth day of Nisan [the day of redemption] *with a homer of barley* (*ibid.*) whose thirty *sĕ'ah* symbolize thirty days,[19] *and with a half-homer of barley* (*ibid.*) [whose fifteen *sĕ'ah* symbolize fifteen days], the forty-five together [standing for the number of days beyond the fifteenth of Nisan]. But where in the passage are the five additiona days [which make up the fifty that passed between the day of Israel's redemption and the day of Israel's receiving the Torah]? In the verse that follows, namely, *Thou shalt abide for Me many days* (Hos. 3:3)—here *days*, as R. Ḥiyya taught in a Baraita, signifies two days, and *many* signifies

16. The well which accompanied the children of Israel through the wilderness and is said to have been created on the eve of the sixth day of creation. See Piska 11, n. 72, and Ginzberg, *Legends*, *1*, 265.

17. Literally *silver*, which in this comment is taken in the sense of "sterling men," or "righteous men." See Piska 5.10, B.Sanh 96b, and Ḥul 92a.

18. JV: *So I bought her to me for fifteen pieces of silver.* In his comment, however, R. Johanan takes not the prophet, but God to be the speaker.

19. Presumably R. Johanan takes the number thirty to represent the thirty days between the fifteenth of Nisan and the fifteenth of Iyar; on the latter day, Israel, having concluded at Elim its meditation upon the commandments concerning Sabbath and honoring parents which had been given earlier at Marah (see Rashi and U. Cassuto's Commentary on Exod. 15:25–16:1; and Meḳ, *1*, 98), arrived at the wilderness of Sin. R. Johanan further takes the number fifteen to represent the days from the fifteenth of Iyar to the first of Sivan when Israel encamped at the foot of the Mount ready to receive the revelation. See Rashi on Exod. 19:2. As for the meaning of "barley" in this context, see Piska 5.10, n. 90.

three more.[20] Thus we have the fifty days of *'Omer* [between redemption and Torah], the giving of the Ten Commandments. [The first two of these God uttered directly to Israel]: *Thou shalt not play the harlot* (*ibid.*), implying the Commandment "Ye shall make you no idols" (Lev. 26:1); *Thou shalt not be any man's wife* (Hos. 3:3), implying "Thou shalt have no other gods before Me" (Exod. 20:3). If you are heedful of these Commandments, *So will I also be toward thee* (Hos. 3:3)—[that is, heedful of thee]. When? *In the third month*[21] (Exod. 19:1).

5. R. Abun began his discourse with the verse *Was it not šlyšwm that I have written for thee of counsels and knowledge?* (Prov. 22:20). The word that we read *šlyšym* in the phrase *šlyšwm . . . of counsels and knowledge* is actually written *šlšwm*, meaning—so Bar Ḥuṭa pointed out—"as though it were only the day before yesterday." That is to say, according to R. Eleazar, matters of Torah should not look to you like an antiquated decree, but[22] like a decree freshly issued which all rush to read. With regard to looking upon matters of Torah as though they had just been decreed, Scripture says, "This day the Lord thy God commandeth thee to do" (Deut. 26:16).

R. Samuel bar R. Naḥman read the word *šlyšym*[23] to mean "captains," as in the verse "and captains (*šlyšym*) over all of them" (Exod. 14:7), for, as R. Samuel bar Naḥman used to say, words of Torah are like [captains'] weapons. Even as such weapons stand up in battle for their owners, so do words of Torah stand up for him who valorously gives them the labor they require to be understood. And the proof? The verse *The glories*[24] *of God in their throat are like a sword pifiyyoṯ in their hand* (Ps. 149:5). R. Judah, R.

20. The original reads *days many*, which, being a vague and indefinite number, the commentator rejects, because according to Rabbinic tradition, Scripture always intends to give precise information. Hence the commentator assumes *days* to mean "two days," the minimum plural, and *many* to mean "three days," one more than the minimum plural.

21. Since Exodus 19 does not fix the day on which the Ten Commandments were given, Sadducees reckoned the day as the fiftieth from *the morrow after the Sabbath* (Lev. 23:11) during the week of Passover. See PR 18:2 (YJS, *18*, 382). According to Jubilees 1:1, the Ten Commandments were given on the twenty-third of Sivan. As a matter of fact, even Rabbis differed among themselves as to whether the Ten Commandments were given on the sixth or the seventh of Sivan. And so, by a kind of "radical surgery," R. Johanan finds in Hosea (3:2–3) proof that the giving of the Ten Commandments took place on the sixth of Sivan, fifty days after the fifteenth of Nisan.

22. The words "rather look to you" in O are omitted, as in S, O_2, and G.

23. JV: *excellent things*. But the word is difficult. R. Samuel will apparently read Prov. 22:20: "Have I not written unto thee that [through valor associated with] captains [thou wilt come to excel] in [God's] counsels and knowledge?"

24. *The glories of God* are taken to stand for words of Torah which reflect so many facets of God's being. JV: *The high praises of God.*

Nehemiah, and the Rabbis differ on the interpretation of this verse. R. Judah taking the word *pifiyyoṯ* as meaning "a mouth that is two mouths"—*peh* signifying "mouth," and *fiyyoṯ* signifying "two mouths"[25]—applied it to the two Torahs, the Torah given by the written word and the Torah given by word of mouth. R. Nehemiah, considering the word *pifiyyoṯ* as meaning "an edge that is two edges"—*peh* signifying "edge," and *fiyyoṯ* signifying "two edges"—took it to be depicting the Torah as a blade which cuts with both edges and is therefore capable of assuring life in this world as well as in the world-to-come. The Rabbis, however, took "mouths" to be referring to priests whose utterances showed them to be Sages, "princes of holiness and princes of godlike beings" (1 Chron. 24:5), as Scripture describes them, who issue decrees for angels in heaven, which the angels obey, and decrees for Israel on earth, which Israel obey.[26]

R. Aḥa said: Words of Torah are mighty to retaliate against him who does not give them the labor they require to be understood.[27]

R. Abun, [taking the word *šlyšym* as meaning "made up of three ingredients"], said that words of Torah are like spiced wine: as spiced wine contains wine, contains honey, and contains pepper, so words of Torah contain wine, "Thy love is good because of wine" (Song 1:2); contain honey, "sweet because of honey" (Ps. 19:11); and contain pepper, "Thy word is very sharp" (Ps. 119:140).

[Hence the three foregoing meanings—"only day before yesterday," "captains' weapons," and "made up of three ingredients"—are implied in the phrase *In the šeliši month* (Exod. 19:1)].

6. *I have declared, and I have saved, I have caused to be heard, and there was no stranger in your midst; ye are My witnesses, I am God* (Isa. 43:12). *I have declared* in Egypt—"Moses declared to Aaron all the words of the Lord" (Exod. 4:28); *I have saved* at the Red Sea—"Thus the Lord saved Israel that day" (Exod. 14:30); *I have caused to be heard* at Sinai—"Thou didst cause the Law to be heard from heaven" (Ps. 76:9); *And there was no stranger in your midst*—a stranger such as Jethro;[28] *ye are My witnesses, I am God*—that is, so taught R. Simeon ben Yoḥai, "only when ye are My

25. The minimum plural being two. See Piska 12, n. 20.

26. In the parallel (Song Rabbah 1:2), the verse in which God says to Israel, *Ye are godlike beings* (Ps. 82:6), is cited.

27. The editor thus rounds out the matter. Words of Torah, according to R. Samuel b. Naḥman, stand up for him who valorously gives them the labor they require to be understood; and, according to R. Aḥa, these words retaliate when a man refuses to give them the labor they require. The sword is thus two-edged.

28. The comment endeavors to explain why directly before the revelation on Sinai Moses decided to send his father-in-law back to his own country. See Exod. 18:27.

witnesses, am I God, but when ye are not My witnesses, I"—if one dare speak thus—"am not God."

7. *To everything there is a time* (Eccles. 3:1). There was a set time for Adam to enter the Garden of Eden, "The Lord God took Adam and put him into the Garden of Eden" (Gen. 2:15), and a set time for him to go out of the Garden, "So He drove out Adam" (Gen. 3:24). There was a set time for Noah and his sons to enter the ark, "Come thou and all thy house into the ark" (Gen. 7:1), and a set time for him to go out, "Go forth from the ark" (Gen. 8:16). There was a set time for our father Abraham to have the practice of circumcision ordained through him, "God said unto Abraham: . . . thou shalt keep My covenant" (Gen. 17:9), and there was a set time for the practice of circumcision to lapse twice among his children, once in Egypt and again in the wilderness.[29] *There was also a set time for the supremely desirable thing [to come] under heaven*[30] (Eccles. 3:1): R. Bebai took this verse to be referring to the time when the most desirable thing in heaven above was given from heaven to Moses under heaven. And what thing was that? Torah. What was the time set for it to be given? *In the third month* (Exod. 19:1).

8. *I walk in the way of mercy, yes—but also in the midst of paths prescribed by ordinances* (Prov. 8:20). Here the Torah is saying: On which road am I to be found [first and foremost]? On the road of those who do acts of mercy, [God replies but then warns: Take care, however, for the mercy which is Mine is set] *in the very midst of paths [which prescribe] ordinances.* R. Huna illustrated the verse by analogy with the way the carriage of a queen as it goes along the thoroughfare is set between a sword and other weapons preceding it and a sword and other weapons following it. So, too, with [the setting of the Decalogue in] the Torah: ordinances with penalties for their infraction precede it, ordinances with penalties for their infraction follow it. Of the ordinances preceding it, we are told "There He made for them a statute and an ordinance" (Exod. 15:25), and of the ordinances following it, we are told "Now these are the ordinances which thou shalt set before them" (Exod. 21:1).[31]

29. Neither in Egypt nor in the wilderness did the children of Israel perform the rite of circumcision. See Piska 5.9; Exod. Rabbah 19:4; and PR 52:4 (YJS, *18*, 878, n. 22).

30. JV: *A time to every purpose under the sun.* But since this clause states no more than what is said in subsequent verses, the commentator gives it special meaning.

31. The intention of the passage seems to be a reconciling of the concepts of divine mercy and divine justice as they are represented in the Torah by the Ten Commandments on the one hand, and on the other, by the various statutes and ordinances that come both before (at Marah, see Piska 12, n. 19) and after the

9. *The heart knoweth its own bitterness, and with its joy no stranger can intermeddle* (Prov. 14:10). Whenever a man smells the odor of brimstone, R. Jonathan said, his soul recoils in terror, for the soul knows that it will be punished with brimstone. And the proof? The verse "Upon the wicked He will pour coals, fire, and brimstone" (Ps. 11:6), and "afterwards a double cup of scalding wind[32] will be their drink" (*ibid.*), this being the counterpart, said R. Samuel bar Naḥman, citing R. Jonathan, of the double cup [of wine] served after a bath.[33]

In another comment the verse is read: *The heart*—Israel's—*knoweth the bitterness in* [*a heathen's*] *soul* (Prov. 14:10). Hence *with* [*the heart's*] *joy no stranger*—such as Jethro—*can intermeddle* (*ibid.*). "Then Moses sent his father-in-law away; and he went back to his own land" (Exod. 18:27). What follows directly? *In the third month* (Exod. 19:1).

10. *As an apple tree among the trees of the wood, so is my Beloved among the sons* [*of mankind*] (Song 2:3). R. Huna and R. Aḥa, citing R. Jose ben Zimra, said: The apple tree—as all shun it because it gives no shade,[34] so the nations of the world shunned the Holy One on the day of the giving of Torah.[35] Should you imagine that Israel also shunned the Holy

---

Ten Commandments. The Ten Commandments as the sovereign rule of Torah are likened to a queen in her carriage going along the high road with armed men preceding and following her. Because the queen herself is not armed and so does not, in her own person, punish those who disobey her rule—indeed, like the Ten Commandments, does not even specify any punishment for such disobedience—she represents God's mercy. At the same time, however, as the drawn sword and other weapons that precede and follow the queen represent the means of punishment for infractions of her sovereign rule, so the penalties prescribed for infractions of the statutes and ordinances that preceded and followed the giving of the Ten Commandments at Sinai represent the exercise of God's justice. As the carriage of the merciful queen goes along with the weapons that maintain her sovereignty, so the weapons that maintain her sovereignty go along with the carriage of the merciful queen; as God's mercy goes along with His justice, so His justice goes along with His mercy.

32. JV: *a burning wind*. But the precise meaning of the term *zl'fwt*, here construed as "*zĕlu'a* (cup) *fwt* (double)," is not known. For R. Samuel bar Naḥman's construing of *fwt*, see Rashi on Exod. 13:16.

33. For R. Samuel bar Naḥman the verse evidently evokes an image of the procedure in a Roman bath. But instead of the hot water poured over the bathers, "coals, fire and brimstone" are poured over the wicked occupants of Gehenna's "bath." Then, when parched with thirst, they expect the refreshing double cup of wine customarily served after a bath, they must drink instead a double cup of scalding wind. See MTeh 5:8 (YJS, *13*, 88–89).

34. "Certain varieties of the apple tree shed their leaves in the summer, and thus give very little shade": Professor Yehuda Feliks of Bar-Ilan University in a letter.

35. See Sif Deut. 343 (ed. Finkelstein, p. 396); and PR 21:2/3 (YJS, *18*, 417).

One as giving no shade, the verse goes on to say *under His shadow I delighted to sit* (*ibid.*).

R. Aḥawa bar Zĕʿira said: Even as the apple tree puts outs its blossoms before its leaves,[36] so Israel at Sinai put "doing" before "hearing."[37]

R. Azariah said: Like the apple tree whose fruit does not ripen until Sivan, so Israel was not to give forth good fragrance to the entire world until Sivan. When? *In the third month* (Num. 19:1).

11. [The words usually read *In the third month* are read] "The third month is come"[38] (Exod. 19:1). In regard to this reading consider an analogy with a king who betrothed a noblewoman and set a time [for the wedding]. When the time came, he was told, "The hour has come for the bride to enter the nuptial chamber." So, too, when the time came for the Torah to be given, the announcement was made, "The time has come for the Torah to be given to Israel."

R. Levi, in the name of R. Samuel ben Ḥalafta, told a parable of a king whose son was captured. The king, putting on the cloak of requital, went forth and freed his son. Thereupon he said: Count the years of this era as beginning with the month of the freeing of my son. So, too, the Holy One said: Count the years of this era as beginning with the month of the exodus from Egypt.

But R. Ḥama bar Ḥanina told a parable of a king who, as he was about to give his daughter in marriage, said: Count the years of this era as beginning with the month of the wedding of my daughter. So, too, the Holy One said: Count the years of this era as beginning with the month of the giving of Torah.[39]

[Immediately after Jethro's departure, Scripture declares]: *The same day came they into the wilderness of Sinai* (Exod. 19:1). R. Joshua ben Levi said: Consider the parable of a prince who was walking in the marketplace where a friend of the king met him and filled his bosom with precious stones and pearls. Thereupon the king, [who had long been amassing great riches for his son], said: For my son's sake open up my treasuries right away, lest he say, "But for the example of my father's friend, my father would have

36. See Rashi on B.Shab 88a. "There may have been such varieties of the apple tree. Occasionally at the end of the summer after the leaves have fallen, we find that after a tree has been irrigated, there appears on it a fresh bloom, and even a blossoming." Yehuda Feliks, *ibid.*

37. They said, *We will do, and we will hear* (Exod. 24:7). See B.Shab 88a.

38. The particle *ba*, "in," is read as though spelled *ba'*, "is come."

39. "*In the day of His espousals* (Song 3:11), that is, the day of His giving of Torah" (Ta 4:8).

In his parable, R. Samuel ben Ḥalafta implies that a New Year is to begin on the fifteenth of Nisan; whereas R. Ḥama ben Ḥanina maintains that it is to begin on the sixth of Sivan.

given me nothing." Likewise the Holy One, [who had long been treasuring the Torah against the day He would give it to Israel], said to Moses: Lest Israel say to you, "Had not Jethro come and taught you laws, God would not have given us the Torah," I herewith open for Israel the treasury of Torah with its entire riches of law: "These are the laws which thou shalt set before them" (Exod. 21:1).

R. Levi said: Listen to the story of a king who wanted to marry a woman of goodly stock, yea, of noble lineage. So he said: Without doing something in her behalf, I shall not ask her hand in marriage. Only after I do a great many good things in her behalf, will I ask for her hand. Accordingly, when he saw her without fine garments, he clothed her [as God clothed Israel]: "I clothed thee with richly woven work"[40] (Ezek. 16:10). At the sea, he brought her safely across [as God brought Israel across the Red Sea]: "The children of Israel walked upon dry land in the midst of the sea" (Exod. 14:29). When slavers, such as the Amalekites, would have seized her, he saved her [as God saved Israel from those who would have enslaved them].

For his part, R. Eleazar said: Listen to the story of a king who wanted to marry a woman of goodly stock, yea, of noble lineage. So he said: Without doing something in her behalf, I shall not ask her hand in marriage. Only after I do a great many good things in her behalf, will I ask for her hand. Accordingly, when he saw her at the baker's, he filled her arms with loaves of white bread; at the tavern keeper's, he gave her spiced wine to drink; at the shop of one who force-feeds birds, he filled her arms with force-fed birds; at the shop of one dispensing dried figs,[41] he filled her arms with dried figs. So, as at a baker's, God filled Israel's arms with loaves of white bread: "Behold, I will cause to rain bread from heaven for you" (Exod. 16:4); as at a tavern keeper's, He gave her spiced wine to drink: "Then sang Israel this song: Spring up, O well—sing ye unto it"[42] (Num. 21:17); as at a shop of one who force-feeds birds, He filled Israel's arms with force-fed birds: "A wind from the Lord . . . brought across quails from the sea" (Num. 11:31); as at a shop of one dispensing dried figs, He filled Israel's arms with dried figs: "He made him to suck honey out of the crag" (Deut. 32:13).

Finally, R. Abba bar Yudan said: Listen to a story of a king who was about to give his daughter in marriage. Now this king had issued a decree forbidding marriages with people from across the sea, specifying that Romans should not go down to Syria [to get wives] and that Syrians should not go up to Rome [to get wives]. But then he himself gave his daughter in

40. See PR 47:2 (YJS, *18*, 799); and Deut. Rabbah, ed. Lieberman, p. 14.

41. See J. Fürst (MGWF *37* [1893], 501) who takes *prḳdys* to be a corruption of the Greek *prochnis* or *prochris*. Or, as suggested in Krauss, *Lehnwörter*, 467–68, *prḳdys* may mean "tidbits."

42. See Piska 11.21, and n. 72; and MTeh 23:4.

marriage [to one beyond the sea], and he withdrew the decree.[43] So, too, before the Torah was given, as Scripture tells us, [God had decreed the separation of heaven and earth]: "The heavens are the heavens of the Lord, but the earth hath He given to the children of men" (Ps. 115:16). But after the Torah was given from heaven, [God withdrew His decree]: *Moses went up unto God* (Exod. 19:3), *And the Lord came down upon Mount Sinai* (Exod. 19:20).

[44]12. [In another comment the verse, previously read *In the third* (*šĕliši*) *month*, is read] "In the month when that which is to be trusted (*šališi*) [was given]" (Exod. 19:1). The verse is so read in the light of *In* [*the Books of*] *counsels and knowledge have I not written unto thee things which are to be trusted* (*šališim*)? (Prov. 22:20). Whenever you seek to find counsel, it is in the Torah you should seek to find it. As David said: When I sought to find counsel, I would look into the Torah and there find counsel: "I will meditate in Thy precepts, and look into Thy ways" (Ps. 119:15), and again "From Thy precepts I get understanding" (Ps. 119:104).

Even if you wish to put up a building, said Ben Ḥuṭa, and do not know how to manage its height, look into the Torah and you will learn how. How does Scripture put it? "With lower, second, and third (*šališim*) decks shalt thou make [the ark]" (Gen. 6:16). Hence *In* [*the Books*] *of counsels and knowledge* (Prov. 22:20).

In another comment the verse is read "Did I not write unto Thee *šlyšym?*"[45] (*ibid.*), which Rabbi took to mean: Let the Torah never be for you an antiquated decree, but rather like a decree freshly issued, no more than two or three days old, for the *kĕṯiḇ* in "Did I not write unto thee *šlyšym*?" is *šlšm*, a word, which read *šilšom*, means "day before yesterday." But Ben Azzai said: Not even as old as a decree issued two or three days ago, but as a decree issued this very day. You can see for yourself that this is the way to regard the Torah. For the verse beginning *In the third month*, etc. (Exod. 19:1) does not go on, as one might expect, "on *that* day came they," but instead *on* THIS *day came they into the wilderness of Sinai* (*ibid.*). *This day*, says Scripture elsewhere, *the Lord thy God commandeth thee to do these statutes and ordinances* (Judg. 26:16).

13. Further explication of *In the third month* (Exod. 19:1) [evokes comments on the word "third" and the word "three"]. Torah is likened to three things. The Patriarchs are three. The name of the Tribe through whom Torah was given is made up of three letters. The month [in which Torah was given] is the third month. Whence do we know that Torah is likened to

43. There is an allusion here to the Emperor Lucius Septimius Severus (reigned 193–211) who married a Syrian woman. See Lieberman, GJP, 10–12.

44. Secs. 12–25 are found only in O and in S.

45. JV: *excellent things.*

three things? R. Abun the Levite Berabbi asked this very question: Why should Torah be likened to three things? It is so likened because in some particulars it resembles three things—wine, honey, and peppers. Proof that Torah is like wine? The verse "Come eat of My bread, and drink of the wine which I have mingled" (Prov. 9:5). Like honey? The verse "[The ordinances of the Lord] . . . are sweeter than honey" (Ps. 19:11). Like peppers? "Every word of God is zestful" (Prov. 30:5), which R. Abun the Levite Berabbi took to mean, "as zestful as pepper." Now you see why Torah is likened to three things.

All things that are associated with that day in the wilderness when the Torah was given came in threes. The Torah itself comes in three parts—Torah, Prophets, and Writings. The total number of the letters in the Hebrew alphabet is divisible by three.[46] Israel is made up of three groups: Priests, Levites, and Israelites. The Patriarchs were three: Abraham, Isaac, and Jacob. [In the triad of God, Israel, and Moses], Moses was the intermediary between God and Israel: "I stood between the Lord and you" (Deut. 5:5). The letters in Moses' name, *Mšh*, are three, and he was a scion of the third Tribe, Levi, Reuben and Simeon being first and second respectively; the letters *Lwy*, in Levi's name are also three. There were three children in the family of Moses: Moses, Aaron, and Miriam. Moses was hidden for three months: "She hid him three months" (Exod. 2:2). The revelation of Torah took place on the third of the three days [during which the men of Israel were enjoined to keep apart from their wives][47]—"The third day the Lord will come down in the sight of all the people" (Exod. 19:11). And the month was the third: *In the third month* (Exod. 19:1).

14. The words just cited are to be considered in the light of the verse *Her ways are ways of pleasantness, and all her paths are peace* (Prov. 3:17). *Torah's ways are ways of pleasantness* [and are made known only to those who live at peace with one another]. The Holy One wanted to give the Torah to Israel as soon as Israel left Egypt, [but He did not do so] because the children of Israel were at cross purposes with one another, some even saying, "Let us make a captain, and let us return unto Egypt" (Num. 14:4). Note that Scripture says, "*They* took their journey from Succoth, and *they* encamped in Etham" (Exod. 13:20), that is, they journeyed in dissension and they encamped in dissension. But no sooner had they come to Rephidim

46. Twenty-two, together with the five final forms of *mem, nun, ṣade, pe, kaf*, add up to 27. Or: In each group of three letters, beginning with *'alef, bet, gimmel*, the numerical value of the middle one is one-third the sum of the numerical values of the three. Thus *bet* is one-third of the sum of *'alef* which is 1, of *bet* which is 2, and of *gimmel* which is 3; the sum of the three letters is 6; and one-third of six = 2, the value of the middle letter, *bet*. There are other explanations of this rather obscure statement.

47. See Exod. 19:15.

than they made peace with one another and became one brotherhood. Note how Scripture describes Israel's journeys and encampments at this point: "They journeyed from Rephidim, and they came to the wilderness of Sinai" (Exod. 19:2). But what is the proof that they made peace with one another and became one brotherhood? The proof is that the verse does not go on to say "and Israel—there *they* encamped," but says, "and Israel—there *it* encamped before the Mount" (*ibid.*). Then and there the Holy One said: The Torah, all of it, is peace. To whom shall I give it? To a people that holds on to peace. Hence *and all her paths are peace.*

15. The passage containing the words *In the third month* (Exod. 19:1) is to be considered in the light of the verse *By slothfulness the rafters* (*mĕḳareh*) *sink in; and through idleness of the hands, the house leaketh* (Eccles. 10:18). [The verse is first construed as referring to a woman whose menstrual flow is excessive]. What causes a woman to have an excessive menstrual flow? It is punishment for her slothfulness in examining herself[48] to find out whether or not she is ritually unclean. Why should she keep examining herself? For the reason taught by our Masters in a Mishnah: "The hand that oftentimes makes examination is, among women, praiseworthy; but among men—let it be cut off"[49] (Nid 2:1). A story of Rabban Gamaliel's maidservant: While removing ritually clean jars and jugs from one house to another, she examined herself before touching each vessel [to make sure her menstrual flow had not begun]. When she came to the last vessel and examined herself, she found that she was ritually unclean. Rabban Gamaliel, distraught, wondered: Perhaps all the ritually clean vessels are now unclean. Thereupon Rabban Gamaliel summoned her and asked her: Am I right in thinking that you have not been examining yourself? She replied: As you live, my lord, I examined myself before I touched each vessel and found myself unclean only when I came to the last one. Said Rabban Gamaliel thankfully: Had this maidservant been slothful, all kinds of ritually pure things in my household would now be unclean.

Taken in a special sense, the word *rafters, mĕḳareh,* in *By slothfulness the rafters sink in,* provides additional proof that by a woman's slothfulness, the well of her blood sinks in—that is, because she is slothful in examining herself, her menstrual flow is excessive. For in *the rafters* (*mĕḳareh*) *sink in, mĕḳareh* is taken as a cognate of *mĕḳorah,* "the well of her menstrual blood," as in the verse "he hath made naked her well (*mĕḳorah*)" (Lev. 20:18); *and* [*so*] *through idleness of the hands the house*[50] *leaketh*

48. Presumably the commentator regards the plain meaning of Eccles. 10:18 as somewhat obvious. So in *'aṣaltayim*, the dual form of "slothfulness," he finds an intimation of "two-handed" slothfulness; and the word *house* he sees as a metaphor for a woman's body.

49. Since such action leads to the discharge of semen.

50. *The house* is taken to mean the female body.

(Eccles. 10:18)—that is, "a woman [who is so idle as not to check upon herself] will have an issue of her blood many days" (Lev. 15:25).

In another comment the verse is read *Because of slothfulness,* [*God*] *the Rafter-maker* (*mĕḳareh*)[51] *came down low* (Eccles. 10:18), and the verse is taken to be alluding to Israel at the time they came to Rephidim. How does the text put it? "They journeyed from Rephidim and came to the wilderness of Sinai" (Exod. 19:2). Here the name of the place Rephidim is read as a combination of *rippu* and *yaḏayim*? Why? Because there Israel's hands (*yaḏayim*) grew slothful (*rippu*) in the committing of transgressions.[52] *Because of* [*such*] *slothfulness,* [*God*] *the Rafter-maker* (*mĕḳareh*) *came down low* (Eccles. 10:18)—"The Lord came down upon Mount Sinai, to the top of the Mount" (Exod. 19:20). *And through idleness of the hands, the house leaketh* (Eccles. 10:18)—that is because Israel's hands were idle in the committing of transgressions, "the house leaketh." How does Scripture make clear elsewhere what these words signify? "The earth trembled, the heavens dropped [the dew of Torah upon me], yea, [in the night] the clouds dropped water"[53] (Judg. 5:4). When did these things happen? On the day of the giving of Torah, *In the third month,* etc. (Exod. 19:1).

16. What comes directly before the phrase just cited? The passage concerning Jethro, wherein he instructs Moses, "Thou shalt provide out of all the people able men," etc. (Exod. 18:21), after which *In the third month* (Exod. 19:1) follows. [In connection with Jethro and the giving of Torah in the third month] a verse of Solomon's is cited: "The heart knoweth its own bitterness" (Prov. 14:10); therefore "with its joy no stranger is to intermeddle" (*ibid.*). The Holy One said: While Israel were in servitude to clay and bricks in Egypt, Jethro dwelt in quietness and security in his own home, and now he has come, [a stranger], to behold the joy of Torah with My children. Therefore *Moses sent his father-in-law away* (Exod. 18:27). And after these words: *In the third month,* etc. (Exod. 19:1).

Another comment: What reasoning led Moses to send Jethro away? Drawing an inference *a fortiori*, Moses reasoned: If, when only one commandment was involved at the time the Holy One was about to give the commandment concerning the Passover lamb, He decreed that "no alien shall eat thereof" (Exod. 12:43), now that He is about to give the entire Torah to Israel, shall Jethro, an alien, be present and watch us? Therefore *Moses sent his father-in-law away,* etc. (Exod. 18:27). And after that *In the third month* (Exod. 19:1).

51. Here *mĕḳareh* means the Holy One, of whom it is said "who layest the beams of Thine upper chambers (*mĕḳareh*) in the waters" (Ps. 104:3). See B.Meḡ 11a.

52. Cf. Piska 3.a.

53. See Piska 5.6; and PR 15:6, 20:1.

17. Why in the third month, and not in the second month or in the fourth? Because, said R. Hoshaia, R. Ḥiyya the elder taught me that a female convert, a female captive, or an emancipated female slave may neither marry nor be betrothed for three months.[54] Analogously, Israel were called converts, as is said "Ye became converts in the land of Egypt" (Lev. 19:34); they were called captives, as is said "they shall take them captives whose captives they were" (Isa. 14:2); they were called emancipated bondmen, as is said "I am the Lord your God, who brought you forth out of the land of Egypt that ye should not be their bondmen" (Lev. 26:13). Therefore the Holy One declared: I will have them wait for three months, and then I shall give them the Torah. *In the third month* (Exod. 19:1).

18. R. Aibu [construed *baḥodeš*, "in the month," as though it read] *ba' ḥodeš*, "the month is come." At the time the Holy One from on high revealed Himself to Moses, He seemed to have made an agreement with Moses [as to what was to happen immediately after Moses had liberated Israel]: "When thou hast brought forth the people out of Egypt, ye will serve God upon this mountain" (Exod. 3:12). Moses, looking forward eagerly, kept saying, "When will the time come?" But God did not set the time at once. Not until the time for serving Him was right, did the Holy One say to Moses: The month to which thou hast been looking forward is come: *The third month is come* (Exod. 19:1).

19. [Why did God wait so long to have the people serve Him? The first reason is suggested by the term which Scripture uses here to designate the time]. It does not say "the third moon" (*yeraḥ*) as it generally does when referring elsewhere to a particular month, as "in the moon (*yeraḥ*) Ziv" (1 Kings 6:37), "in the moon (*yeraḥ*) Bul" (1 Kings 6:38), or "in the moon (*yeraḥ*) Ethanim" (1 Kings 8:2). Instead it says, *In the third month* (*ḥodeš*) (Exod. 19:1)—[that is, after a time long enough to make renewal possible, *ḥdš*], implying, according to R. Judah bar R. Simon, that the Holy One said to Israel "I am about to do new and unprecedented things in My renewal of you." Consider here a parable of a king who had a son. When the son reached marriageable age, the father wished to have him get married. But since the son did not have a marriage chest containing new table appointments, the king said: "Such a lack is not becoming for my son. On the other hand, if I wait until I can provide new table appointments, I shall have to delay the nuptials of my son." What did the king do? He brought smiths and artisans who polished the copper vessels he already had, and he brought woodworkers who carved new designs in the wooden vessels he already had; thus the king was able to get his son married, having provided him with a marriage chest of table appointments which, though old, appeared new. So, too, when Israel went forth out of Egypt, the Holy One wished to give them

54. To make certain that she is not with child.

the Torah. But there were blind, lame, and deaf among them, so that the Holy One, saying "The Torah, all of it, is whole and unblemished"—'The Lord's Torah is perfect' (Ps. 19:8)—declared: Shall I give it to this generation among whom are men with physical blemishes? On the other hand, if I wait until a new generation, their children, rise up, I shall have to delay [for a generation] Israel's joyous nuptials with the Torah. What did the Holy One do? He healed those who were blemished and after that gave Israel the Torah. And the proof that He healed them? He who had been blind was made to see, as is said "*All* the people *saw* the thunderings" (Exod. 20:18). He who had been deaf was made to hear, as is said "All that the Lord hath spoken we will do and hear" (Exod. 24:7). He who had been lame became whole, as is said "They, [even the lame], *stood* at the nether part of the Mount" (Exod. 19:7). Now, [said God], there is to be a renewal: as I make you new again, I show you a kind of earnest of the world-to-come. As in the time-to-come "The eyes of the blind shall be opened" (Isa. 35:5), so at Sinai, "*All* the people *saw*" (Exod. 20:18). As in the time-to-come "The ears of the deaf shall be unstopped" (Isa. 35:5), so at Sinai, "They said: 'All that the Lord hath spoken we will do and hear'" (Exod. 24:7). As in the time-to-come "The lame man shall leap as a hart" (Isa. 35:6), so at Sinai, "Moses brought forth the people out of the camp to meet God; and they, [even the lame], *stood* at the nether part" (Exod. 19:7). As in the time-to-come "The tongue of the dumb shall sing" (Isa. 35:6), so at Sinai "All the people *sang out* together" (Exod. 19:8).

20. [The second reason for God's delay in having the people serve Him is suggested by the phrase] *In the third month* (Exod. 19:1). Why the delay to the third month? In order not to give to the nations of the earth a chance to claim falsely: Had He given the Torah to us [as well as to Israel], we would have kept it. The Holy One replied: [When I offered it to you, you refused it.[55] But you are still free to accept it, for] take note in what month I gave the Torah—in the third month, under the zodiacal sign of Twins—by way of indicating thereby that if any one of you descended from the wicked Esau—[after all, he was Jacob's twin]—wishes to become a proselyte, wishes to repent and to come study Torah, let him come and study, and I will accept him. Thus, for the sake of the nations, the Torah was given in the third month.

Why was the Torah given in the wilderness of Sinai? To teach that if a man does not make himself ownerless like a wilderness, he will not be able to acquire words of Torah. Even as the wilderness has no end, so the Torah has no end, as is said "The measure thereof is longer than the earth, and wider than the sea" (Job 11:9); and even as the Torah has no end, so there is no

55. See Piska 12.10; PR 21:2/3 (YJS, *18*, 417).

end to the reward for it, as is said "Oh how abundant is Thy goodness, which Thou hast laid up for them that fear Thee!" (Ps. 31:20).

21. *On this day they came to the wilderness of Sinai* (Exod. 19:1). By *on this day* can Scripture possibly mean that the children of Israel arrived in the wilderness today? No—what God is saying in the verse is this: When you study My words of Torah, they are not to seem antiquated to you, but as fresh as though the Torah were given this day. Note that the text does not say "on that day," but *on this day*—[that is, on this day, freshly given]. But though I gave you the Torah to study in this world, all too few labor in it. In the world-to-come, however, I Myself shall be teaching it to all Israel, and they will study it and not forget it, as is said "This is the covenant that I will make with the house of Israel after those days, saith the Lord, I will put My law in their inward parts, and in their heart will I write it; and I will be their God, and they shall be My people" (Jer. 31:33). Nay more, I shall make peace abundant among them, as Isaiah said: "When all thy children shall be taught by the Lord, abundant shall be the peace of thy children" (Isa. 54:13).

22. *I am the Lord thy God, who brought thee out of the land of Egypt* (Exod. 20:2). These words are to be considered in the light of the verse "The chariots of God: two myriads and two thousand angels; the Lord is among them: it is Sinai in holiness"[56] (Ps. 68:18). R. Abdimi of Haifa said: In the study of a Mishnah which is in my possession, I learned that twenty-two thousand ministering angels came down with the Holy One on Mount Sinai, as many, so said R. Berechiah the Priest Berabbi, as there were males in the camp of the Levites.[57] For the Holy One foresaw that [in the matter of the golden calf], only the Tribe of Levi would retain its water-clear integrity. Therefore, [in honor of the Levites], twenty-two thousand angels, as many as there were males in the camp of the Levites, came down: "The chariots of God: two myriads, and two thousand angels."

Another comment: "The chariots of God: two myriads and two thousand angels." With the Holy One there came down twenty-two thousand chariots, and each and every chariot was like the chariot which Ezekiel saw. Proof of this statement comes out of a text[58] that was brought from Babylonia in which it is asserted that twenty-two thousand chariots—so Elijah, ever remembered on good occasions, taught—came down with the Holy One.

56. JV: *The chariots of God are myriads, even thousands upon thousands.* But the word for myriads carries a dual suffix, which the author interprets as "two myriads," while the word for "thousands" carries a construct suffix common to both dual and plural which the author prefers to take for a dual.

57. See Num. 3:39.

58. Reading, with David Luria (PRF 21:7), *mskt*, "text," instead of *mkt*. The "text" referred to may have been Seder Eliyyahu (see Meir Friedmann's introduction to Seder Eliyyahu, Vienna, 1902, pp. 77–78).

Reading the verse "The chariots of God—myriads, thousands multiplied"[59] (Ps. 68:18), R. Tanḥum bar R. Ḥanilai said: There were thousands multipied by thousands, myriads multiplied by myriads, to a number which only a mathematician can calculate.[60]

[Differing with those who teach that the angels came down with good intentions], R. Eleazar ben Pedaṯ in another comment on *The chariots of god are myriads, thousands of angels* (*šinĕ'an*) (Ps. 68:18) said: All these angels came sharply intent[61] on destroying the children of Israel,[62] and indeed, had they not accepted the Torah, the angels would have tried to destroy them. Israel had seen the face of the Holy One, however, as R. Levi said, and he who has seen the face of the King cannot die, as is said "In the light of the King's countenance is life" (Prov. 16:15).[63]

In further comment, R. Eleazar ben Pedaṯ read the verse in hand differently: "The chariots of God are myriads, *alfe šinĕ'an*." How, he asks, is *alfe šinĕ'an* to be understood except as "the most beautiful (*šenna'in*) and most radiant (alpha)[64] of the angels?" Nevertheless, [radiant as the angels are], "among them is the Lord" (Ps. 68:18), outshining them all, so that the congregation of Israel exclaimed: "My Beloved is white and ruddy, the chiefest among myriads [of angels]!" (Song 5:10). When a king of flesh-and-blood strides forth into the field, there are many as striking as he, and many as mighty as he, and many have their locks curled as beautifully as his—indeed, many are more beautiful than he. This was not so, however, of the Holy One among the angels: even though, when He came to Sinai, He brought with Him the most beautiful and most radiant ministering angels, [He outshone them all].[65] As R. Judah bar R. Simon pointed out in answer to the question, How does Scripture describe him at Sinai? "He

59. Taking *šn'n*, previously rendered "angels," to be a nominal form of *šnh*, "to repeat."

60. Or: "which not even a mathematician can calculate" as in parallel in Yalḳuṭ Ps. 776, and in PR 21:8.

61. Play on the words *šinĕ'an*, "angels, sharp-visaged ones," and *šĕnunim*, "sharply intent."

62. Literally "Israel's enemies," a euphemism for Israel.

63. Even though Israel does not obey the Torah which it accepted, the destroying angels cannot work their will upon Israel, because having seen the King's countenance, Israel enjoys immortality.

64. Here R. Eleazar takes *alfe* in the sense of *alpha*, "A1." Cf. "As regards oil, Tekoa in *alpha*" (Men 8:3).

65. Song 5:10–11 reads: *My Beloved is white and ruddy . . . His locks most beautifully curled.*

The presence of hosts of angels on Mount Sinai serves to explain *The Lord talked with you*—the people of Israel—*face to face on the Mount* (Deut. 5:4), a verse which seems to contradict the assurance that only Moses beheld *the similitude of the Lord* (Num. 12:8). However, since the word *panim* may be construed as

shined forth from Mount Paran,[66] He *'aṯa* among[67] the myriads holy" (Deut. 33:2). By *'aṯa* is meant that He was *'oṯ*—He stood out among the holy myriads when He came to Sinai.

In still another comment on "The chariots of God: myriads," etc. (Ps. 68:18), R. Eleazar ben Pedaṯ said: Wherever there are crowds of people, they feel the discomfort of their pressure upon one another. But when the Holy One came down to Sinai bringing with Him thousands of thousands and myriads of myriads of angels, these "myriads and thousands [were] *šině'an*" (*ibid.*) as Scripture tells us—that is, they were comfortable, *šině'an* being understood here as in the verse "Moab hath been comfortable (*ša'anan*) from his youth"[68] (Jer. 48:11). [That the angels were comfortable was due to the enlargement of Sinai to accommodate them, says R. Eleazar ben Pedaṯ following a Tannaitic tradition as set forth in] the comments of R. Eleazar ben Azariah and R. Eliezer the Modiite. One asked, "But could Mount Sinai hold all of Israel?" and answered the question himself saying that the Holy One told Mount Sinai: "Extend thyself, enlarge thyself,[69] and receive thy Lord's children." The other, with Jerusalem in mind, citing the verse "Behold, these shall come from far; and lo, these from the north," etc. (Isa. 49:12), asked: "But could Jerusalem hold all those who would return?" and answered the question himself, asserting that the Holy One would say to Jerusalem: "Enlarge the place of thy tent," etc. (Isa. 54:2).[70]

[Differing with R. Eleazar ben Pedaṯ], Resh Laḳish maintained that the verse [*The chariots of God . . .*] *the Lord is in them* (Ps. 68:18) [is not so much intimating the enlargement of Sinai as asserting that God is the angels' source of vitality]:[71] Upon the heart of each and every angel there is a tablet with the name of the Holy One as a part of the name of the angel: Micha-El,[72] Gabri-El, Rapha-El.

[Another comment on] *The Lord* (*'Adonay*) *is among them* (Ps. 68:18) [stresses the idea of God's authority over the angels and Israel rather than His vitalizing power]. Note that the verse does not refer to God as YHWH but as *'Adonay*, meaning "lordship," so that the verse as a whole is

---

"face" as well as "[an angel's] presence," Deut. 5:4 is read "On the Mount the Lord talked with you in the presence of innumerable angels."

66. Regarded as one of Sinai's names. See Ginzberg, *Legends*, *3*, 80.

67. Usually rendered "came from."

68. Since angels, according to R. Abin, are half fire, half water (PRK 1.3, and P.RH 2.5, 58a), they take up space, space miraculously provided for them on Sinai.

69. The Tanna apparently construes *ribboṯayim*, "myriads," a form of *rbh*, "extend, enlarge" as referring not to the number of angels, but to the area of Sinai.

70. Thus the people of Israel who have been and will be miraculously provided for are likened to angels.

71. See David Luria's Novellae on Exod. Rabbah 29:2.

72. *'El* = God.

to be read "My lordship is among them." And do not suppose that by "among them" is meant that His lordship is only over the ministering angels. [It is over Israel as well]. For at the time that He came to give His Torah, in giving it to Israel, He used the name *'Adonay* of Himself, beginning His utterance with the words, "I am the Lord (*'Adonay*)[73] thy God."

23. *Hear, O My people, and*[74] *I will speak; O Israel, and I will warn thee: God, thy God, am I* (Ps. 50:7). R. Phinehas ben Ḥama took these words to mean: "Obey [the Torah], O My people, in order that I may speak," that is, that [at the last judgment] I may have the right to speak in your defence to the princes of the nations of the earth.[75] *Hear, O My people, that I may speak.*

In the name of R. Judah bar R. Simon who cited R. Joshua ben Levi, [R. Phinehas went on to explain God's intention in addressing His people as Israel. He understood God to be saying]: "Formerly your name was Israel. Before you accepted the Torah, your name, Israel, was a name much like the names of other nations of the earth, such as 'Sheba, Havilah, Sabta, and Raamah' (Gen. 10:7). But after you accepted the Torah, your name became 'My people,' [and that is the name I have usually addressed you by]: *Hear, O My people, and I will speak.*" [Why, then, do I go on in the Psalm verse to address you not as "My people," but as "Israel"]? Since legal warning may be given only to one who is willing to heed [and you are unwilling to heed, therefore I address you by name as I do the other nations of the earth]—*O Israel, and I will warn thee* (Ps. 50:7). [Thus addressed as though you are a people who had not received the Torah, you will not be held guilty by Me. I resort to such a device] Because *God thy God am I* (*ibid.*). As to what is meant by this part of the verse, R. Johanan and Resh Laḳish by different ways came to much the same conclusion. R. Johanan took this part of the verse to be saying: "I am God— I am the judge of all. But I am also *thy* God so that as thy patron I maintain thy cause." Resh Laḳish responded: You say that *God, thy God, am I* means "I am both judge and patron." In the exercise of justice, however, a patron has no say. Hence *God, thy God am I* must mean "A patron, thy patron, who favors thee, am I."

Continuing his discourse, R. Phinehas the Priest ben Ḥama read the words *God, thy God am I,* as *god, thy God am I,* and asking "Whom did the Lord address as 'god'?" replied: "Moses, to whom He said: Even though I address

73. MT: YHWH.

74. The copula *and* will be construed as meaning "in order that."

75. For the nations of the earth, who declined the Torah, might well argue that they were more honest than Israel who accepted the Torah and then proceeded to disobey it. See Rashi on Deut. 33:3. See also Bacher, W., *Die Agada der Palästinensischen Amoräer* (Salzburg, 1899), *3*, 229. Professor Jakob J. Petuchowski has provided the latter reference and the explanation.

thee as god—'See, I have made thee god to Pharaoh' (Exod. 7:1)—still *God am I* over thee."

In further comment on *god, thy God am I*, [R. Phinehas the Priest ben Ḥama quoting] the Rabbis said that the Lord was addressing judges as "gods" and declaring to them: Make not much of the fact that I ascribed divinity to you when I said "Thou shalt not revile Elohim (judges)" (Exod. 22:27), for *God am I* over you, nevertheless.

[Disagreeing with R. Phinehas the Priest ben Ḥama], R. Judah the Levite bar R. Shallum asserted that the Lord was addressing Israel as "god," saying: Make not much of the fact that I addressed you as gods when I declared: "I said, ye are gods" (Ps. 82:6), for *God am I* over you, nevertheless—[not merely your patron but your sovereign].

24. *I ('nky) am the Lord thy God* (Exod. 20:2). What is implied by the letters making up the word *'nky*?[76] That you are not—so said Rab—to make light of the Torah which I gave you, for *'nky* is an acronym which is to be read "I Myself wrote and gave it."[77]

Or *'nky* read as a reverse acronym signifies: "What was given in writing, pleasant are its words."[78]

According to R. Berechiah the Priest, *'nky* is an acronym by which the Holy One said: "I will be thy light, thy crown, thy grace."[79] When? When you accept the Ten Commandments, *I will be the Lord thy God* (Exod. 20:2).

R. Aḥa said: During the twenty-six generations [between the creation and the giving of Torah],[80] the *'alef* kept raising a cry before the Holy One, saying: Even though I am first of all the letters, Thou didst not create the world with me, but with the *beṯ*, the second letter of the alphabet, which begins *Br'šyt*, the first word of Torah: "In the beginning God created" (Gen. 1:1). The Holy One replied: As thou livest, I will make it up to thee. For two

76. The word *'nky* for "I" is found only in the older parts of Scripture. In Rabbinic times *'nky* was not used at all. Hence follow attempts to discern the word's special significance in this verse.

77. Each of the letters in the pronoun *'nky*, is taken in the following comments as the initial letter and abbreviation of a word that the letter stands for. Thus in the first comment the *'alef* is taken to represent *'n'*, "I"; the *nun, nfšy*, "Myself"; the *kaf, ktbyt*, "I wrote"; the *yoḏ, yhbyt*, "I gave."

78. The *yoḏ* is taken to represent *yhyḇh*, "given"; the *kaf, ktybh*, "writing"; the *nun, n'ymym*, "pleasant"; the *'alef, 'mryh*, "its words." Cf. B.Shab 104a, and Saul Lieberman, Sinai, *38*, ½, 1–3.

79. The *'alef* is taken to represent *'n'*, "I"; the *nun, nhwrk*, "thy light"; the *kaf, klylk*, "thy crown"; the *yoḏ, y'wwtk*, "thy grace."

The three prceding acronyms set forth respectively Torah's divine authority, the delight which involvement in Torah brings, and the glory it confers.

80. Ten generations from Adam to Noah; ten from Noah to Abraham; and six from Abraham to Moses: Isaac, Jacob, Levi, Kohath, Amram, Moses.

thousand years, while the world was still uncreated, the Torah dwelt as a creation in My presence only.[81] Now as I come to give the Torah to Israel, I inaugurate My giving it with thee, the *'alef* [of *'nky*]: *I ('nky) am the Lord thy God.*[82]

R. Nehemiah said: What is *'nky*? It is an Egyptian word. Why did God find it necessary to use an Egyptian word? For answer, consider the story of a mortal king whose son had been captured. The son spent many years among his captors, until the king, cloaked in vengeance, went to free his son, brought him back, and then found he had to talk with him in the captors' speech. So it was with the Holy One, [the eternal King]. Israel had spent all the years of their servitude in Egypt where they learned the Egyptian speech. Finally, when the Holy One redeemed them and came to give them the Torah, they could not understand it. So the Holy One said: I will speak to them in their captors' speech.[83] Thereupon the Holy One used the word *'nky* which is a form of the Egyptian *'nwk*, so that the Holy One began His inauguration of the giving of Torah with Israel's acquired way of speaking: *I ('nky) am the Lord thy God.*

Because the Holy One appeared to Israel at the Red Sea as a mighty man waging war,[84] and appeared to them at Sinai as a pedagogue who teaches the day's lesson and then again and again goes over with his pupils what they have been taught,[85] and appeared to them in the days of Daniel as an elder teaching Torah, and in the days of Solomon appeared to them as a young man, the Holy One said to Israel: Come to no false conclusions because you see Me in many guises, for I am He who was with you at the Red Sea and I am He who is with you at Sinai: *I am the Lord thy God.* The fact is, R. Ḥiyya bar Abba said, that He appeared to them in a guise appropriate to each and every place and time. At the Red Sea He appeared to them as a mighty man waging their wars,[84] at Sinai He appeared to them as a pedagogue, as one who stands upright in awe when teaching Torah; in the days of Daniel, He appeared to them as an elder teaching Torah,[86] for the Torah is at its best when it comes from the mouths of old men; in the days of

81. Wisdom—Torah, that is—says of itself: *When He appointed the foundations of the earth, I was already by Him . . . all delight a day and a day* (Prov. 8:30), and God's day is a thousand years. See Ps. 90:4.

82. Presumably, according to R. Aḥa, the unusual *'nky* is meant to call attention to the *'alef*'s being first at the revelation. Since the revelation consisted of commands, one would have expected it to begin not with an *'alef* but with a letter of the alphabet which introduces positive or negative commands.

83. Cf. Piska 11.6; and Acts 2:5–12.

84. Exod. 15:3.

85. See B.Er 54b, and Meḵ, *3*, 1. Thanks are due to Professor Jakob J. Petuchowski for his comment and the references.

86. Dan. 7:9.

Solomon He appeared to them as a young man in keeping with the youthful spirit of Solomon's generation—"His aspect is like Lebanon, young as the cedars" (Song 5:15). At Sinai, then, when he said, *I am the Lord thy God*, appropriately He appeared to them as a pedagogue teaching Torah.

25. Another comment on *I am the Lord thy God*. R. Ḥanina bar Papa said: The Holy One appeared to Israel with a stern face, with an equanimous[87] face, with a friendly face, with a joyous face: with a severe face appropriate for the teaching of Scripture—when a man teaches Torah to his son, he must impress upon him his own awe of Torah; with an equanimous face appropriate for the teaching of Mishnah; with a friendly face appropriate for the teaching of Talmud; with a joyous face appropriate for the teaching of 'Āḡaḏah.[88] Therefore the Holy One said to them: Though you see Me in all these guises, [I am still One]—*I am the Lord thy God*.

R. Levi said: The Holy One appeared to them as though He were a statue with faces on every side, so that though a thousand men might be looking at the statue, they would be led to believe that it was looking at each one of them. So, too, when the Holy One spoke, each and every person in Israel could say, "The Divine Word is addressing me." Note that Scripture does not say, "I am the Lord *your* God," but *I am the Lord* THY *God*, [thy very own God]. Moreover, said R. Jose bar R. Ḥanina, the Divine Word spoke to each and every person according to his particular capacity. And do not wonder at this. For when manna came down for Israel, each and every person tasted it in keeping with his own capacity—infants in keeping with their capacity, young men in keeping with their capacity, and old men in keeping with their capacity. Infants in keeping with their capacity: like the taste of the milk that an infant sucks from his mother's breast, so was the taste of manna to every infant, for it is said "Its taste was like the taste of rich cream" (Num. 11:8); young men according to their capacity, for of the manna they ate it is said "My bread also which I gave thee, bread,[89] and oil, and honey" (Ezek. 16:19); and old men according to their capacity, as is said of the manna they ate "the taste of it was like wafers made with honey" (Exod. 16:31). Now if each and every person was enabled to taste the manna according to his particular capacity, how much more and more was each and every person enabled according to his particular capacity to hear the Divine Word. Thus David said: "The voice of the Lord is in its strength"[90] (Ps. 29:4)—not "The voice of the Lord in His strength" but "The voice of the Lord in its strength"—that is, in its strength to make itself

87. "Equanimous," a rare word, is deliberately chosen to match the rarity and obscurity of the word it stands for in Hebrew.

88. Cf. PR 21:6.

89. MT: *fine flour*.

90. Literally *The voice of the Lord is in strength*, a deviation from normal syntax which requires suffixing the appropriate personal pronoun—e.g. *Jacob lifted*

heard and understood according to the capacity of each and every person who listens to the Divine Word. Therefore the Holy One said: Do not be misled because you hear many voices. Know ye that I am He who is one and the same: *I am the Lord thy God.*

Up to this time, Israel were redeemed from Egypt and then enslaved in Babylon; redeemed from Babylon, enslaved in Media; redeemed from Media, enslaved in Greece; redeemed from Greece, enslaved in Edom (Rome). But from Edom the Holy One will redeem them, and they will not again be enslaved, as is said "O Israel that art saved by the Lord with an everlasting salvation: ye shall not be ashamed nor confounded, world without end" (Isa. 45:17).

---

his feet (Gen. 29:1), not simply "lifted feet"—whenever a part or an attribute of the body is mentioned. Cf. Tanḥuma, *Šĕmoṯ*, 25.

PISKA 13

SUMMARY

Israel are to occupy themselves with matters right and proper for them, or else become wanderers

Cry aloud with thy voice, etc. (Isa. 10:30) is construed as an appeal to Israel: Instead of occupying yourselves with songs and chants to idols, cry aloud in words of Torah, words that are right and proper in your mouth. Else you will be forced to be wanderers (Sec. 1). Give up your obsession with idols, an obsession which may lead to your extermination (Sec. 2). Say not disdainfully, "The Prophets do not live for ever." Their prophecies do endure (Sec. 3). Rahab, the harlot of Jericho, mended her ways, but you refuse to do so. It is right then that Jeremiah, a descendant of Rahab, come and remind you, O Israel, again and again of the shamelessness of your ways (Sec. 4).

Had you driven out all of Jericho's inhabitants in Rahab's days, who knows, a commentator says ironically, but what Jeremiah might not have come into being and would not now be thrusting words into you that are thorns in your sides (Sec. 5)? Whatever you may say of Jeremiah's lowly origins, remember that in many ways he resembles no less a prophet than Moses (Sec. 6). Heed, then, his words of ill-omen (Sec. 7), words bespeaking lamentations and pestilences that lead to death. You, who have violated all of the Ten Commandments, have no right to feel aggrieved at his words (Sec. 8). Nevertheless, despite your transgressions, God cannot utterly reject you. He will—if one dare say such a thing—go into exile with you and ultimately redeem you (Sec. 9). In the meantime, after the Temple's destruction not a bird will be seen flying over the Land of Israel (Sec. 10). But remember, O Israel, that the Presence is so reluctant to leave the Temple in Jerusalem that when It does leave, It will do so in ten slow stages. Even after departing from the Temple, It will linger for three and a half years on the Mount of Olives, crying three times a day, "Return, ye backsliding children, and I will heal your backslidings" (Sec. 11).

As for Jeremiah's lowly origin to which another commentator returns, Phinehas, Uriah, and Ezekiel also came from blemished stock and like Jeremiah were also belittled. But God chose to ascribe lofty pedigree to them (Sec. 12).

Jeremiah, who sprang of priestly stock on his paternal side, lamented that unlike his kin who were asked to bless Israel, he was called upon to curse them (Sec. 13). Jeremiah's living in the land of Benjamin—Benjamin, whose very birth confirmed prophecy—is taken to denote the certainty of

Jeremiah's prophecy; to denote also that as long as he remains in Jerusalem, Jerusalem will not be destroyed; and finally to denote that even as Benjamin was the last of all the Tribe Fathers, so Jeremiah was the last of all the Prophets.

Despite the somberness of Jeremiah's words, he, too, like all the other Prophets, concluded with words of comfort for Israel (Sec. 14).

That Jerusalem was destroyed in the month of Ab, in the zodiacal sign of the Lion, intimates that God the Lion will come back in the same month and rebuild the Temple, the Lion of God (Sec. 15).

PISKA 13

The words of Jeremiah (Jer. 1:1).[1]

1. Beginning his discourse with the verse *Cry aloud with* THY *voice, O daughter of Gallim! Hearken, O Laishah, O thou poor, Anathoth!* (Isa. 10:30), R. Abba bar Kahana took Isaiah to be saying to Israel: Instead of occupying yourselves with songs and chants to idols, cry aloud in words of Torah,[2] [words that are right and proper in the mouth of Israel]. *O daughter of Gallim,*[3] as the waves (*gallim*) stand out in the sea, so your Fathers stood out in the world. On the other hand, *O daughter of Gallim* may also be read "O daughter of *golim*"—daughter of those who were forced to be wanderers. [O Israel], daughter of Abraham, remember what is written of him? "The Lord said unto Abram, 'Get thee out of thy country,' " etc. (Gen. 12:1). O daughter of Isaac, remember what is written of him? "Isaac was forced to go unto Abimelech king of the Philistines, unto Gerar" (Gen. 26:1). O daughter of Jacob, remember what is written of him? "Jacob hearkened to his father and his mother, and was forced to go to Paddan-aram" (Gen. 28:7).

Hearken (Isa. 10:30): hearken to My commands, hearken to words of Torah, hearken to words of prophecy. If you do not, *Laishah* (*ibid.*), the "lion" (*layiš*) will come upon you, the wicked Nebuchadnezzar, of whom it is written "The lion is gone up from his thicket" (Jer. 4:7). *O thou* [*who at this time art*] *poor* (Isa. 10:30) in righteous men, poor in words of Torah, poor in obedience to divine commandments, and poor in deeds in behalf of your fellow men! If you do not hearken, *Anathoth* (Isa. 10:30), the man of Anathoth, [Jeremiah], will come and will prophecy dire things as punishment for you.

But because Israel disregarded Isaiah's warning, it became necessary for Scripture to set down *The* [*direful*] *words of Jeremiah the son of Hilkiah* (Jer. 1:1).

2. R. Aḥa began his discourse with the verse *How long, ye thoughtless, will ye love thoughtlessness? And how long will scorners delight them in*

1. Jer. 1:1–2:3 is the haftarah of rebuke for *Maṭṭoṯ*, the first of the three Sabbaths preceding the Fast of the Ninth of Ab.

2. "Isaiah . . . words of Torah"—S. No such place as Bath-gallim is otherwise known, and Laish is not in Jerusalem's environs. Hence the comments that follow.

3. Before and after the reference to Gallim, Isaiah mentions ten places which Sennacherib passed through on his way to Jerusalem. Only in the verse in hand does Isaiah shift from the perfect to the imperative, implying that in this particular verse he does not give an account of Sennacherib's advance, but instead addresses himself to Israel.

scorning? (Prov. 1:22). The latter part of this verse—so said R. Simeon ben Nezira—implies that human nature being what it is, a man may partake of rotting food for two or three days, but then will draw away from it with loathing. But you, how many years have you been in service to idolatry, of which it is written "Thou shalt speak of it as 'That which is discharged' "[4] (Isa. 30:22)? In short, you are to name it excrement—yet you have no aversion to it. Two men, Solomon and Isaiah—said R. Yudan—prophesied against scorn of God. Solomon said: *Scorners delight them in scorning* (Prov. 1:22).[5] Isaiah said: *Now therefore be ye not scoffers, lest your bands be made strong* (Isa. 28:22). Of the latter verse, R. Phinehas and R. Jeremiah, citing R. Samuel bar R. Isaac, said: Grievous is the requital for scoffing. It begins with [bands of] suffering and ends with extermination—begins with [bands of] suffering: *lest your bands be made strong*; and ends with extermination: *extermination wholly determined have I heard from the Lord, the God of hosts* (*ibid.*).

[*Wisdom crieth aloud*]*: Turn you at my reproof; behold, I will pour out my spirit unto you, else I will make known my* [*direful*] *words unto you* (Prov. 1:23): If you turn at my reproof, cries wisdom, I will pour out my spirit through Ezekiel—"The word of the Lord came expressly unto Ezekiel[6] the priest, the son of Buzi" (Ezek. 1:3). If you do not turn, *I will make known my direful words unto you* (Prov. 1:23) through Jeremiah. But because Israel disregarded wisdom's warning, Scripture deemed it necessary to set down *The* [*direful*] *words of Jeremiah the son of Hilkiah* (Jer. 1:1).

3. R. Aḥa began his discourse by citing the verse *Your fathers, where are they? And the Prophets, do they live for ever?* (Zech. 1:5). And R. Aḥa went on: When the Holy One asked Israel, "My children, your fathers who sinned brazenly, where are they now?" Israel replied impudently: "Master of universes, what of the Prophets? Do they live for ever?" God said to them: "They died, to be sure, but does not their prophecy endure? Moses is dead,

4. A play on the words *ṣe'*, "get thee hence," and *ṣe'ah*, "excrement." JV: *Thou shalt say unto it: "Get thee hence."* But see Ḳimḥi.

5. The second verse after the one with which R. Aḥa begins his discourse reads *I have stretched out my hand, and no one hearkened* (Prov. 1:24). So, too, below in Section 3, the verse directly preceding the one with which R. Aḥa begins his other discourse reads *But they did not attend, nor hearken unto Me* (Zech. 1:4). Finally, in Section 4 the second verse after the one with which R. Joshua begins his discourse reads, *An evil-doer hearkeneth to wicked lips* (Prov. 17:4). Accordingly, all who prefer to hearken to "wicked lips" instead of hearkening to God or to wisdom, are included among those who spurn Isaiah's plea, "Hearken to My commands, hearken to words of Torah" (Piska 13.1).

6. Ezekiel says elsewhere, *The hand of the Lord was upon me, and the Lord carried me out in a spirit* (Ezek. 37:1).

ut does not his prophecy endure? And Jeremiah who is now alive, his words, too, will endure [long after his death]." And because Israel disregarded Zechariah's admonition [to hearken unto the Lord], Scripture deemed it necessary to set down *The [direful] words of Jeremiah the son of Hilkiah* (Jer. 1:1).

4. R. Joshua of Siḵnin, citing R. Levi, began his discourse with the verse *A servant that dealeth wisely shall have rule over a son that doeth shamefully; and shall have part of the inheritance among the brethren* (Prov. 17:2). The words *A servant that dealeth wisely* apply to Jeremiah;[7] the words *shall speak in prophetic parable*[8] *of a son that doeth shamefully* mean that Jeremiah had in mind Israel who brought shame on themselves through service to idolatry. R. Abba bar Kahana applied to Israel the verse "You are not as the harlot who made her deeds comely"[9] (Ezek. 16:31), and then said: Let the descendant of a shameless woman who made her deeds comely, present himself and reprimand the son of a comely woman who made her deeds shameless. You find that all those words of Scripture which are used in tribute to Rahab contain a reproach of Israel. Thus Rahab is quoted as saying "Now therefore, I pray unto you, swear unto me by the Lord, since I have dealt kindly with you" (Josh. 2:12); and of Israel it is said, "Surely they swear falsely" (Jer. 5:2). Rahab is quoted as saying "Save alive my father and my mother" (Josh. 2:13); but to Israel it is said "In thee have they made light of father and mother" (Ezek. 22:7). Of Rahab it is said, "She had brought them up to the roof" (Josh. 2:6); but of Israel it is said, "They that worship the host of heaven upon the housetops" (Zeph. 1:5). Of Rahab it is said that she "hid them with the stalks of flax" (Josh. 2:6); but of Israel it is said, "Who say to a stock: 'Thou art my father' " (Jer. 2:27). Rahab is quoted as saying "Get you to the mountain" (Josh. 2:16); but of Israel it is said, "They sacrifice upon the tops of the mountains" (Hos. 4:13). Rahab is quoted as saying "Give me a true token" (Josh. 2:12); but of Israel it is said, "Truth they speak not" (Jer. 9:4). You thus see that all

7. A descendant of Rahab, a woman of Canaan, and thus a servant. See Piska 13.5.

8. JV: *shall have rule.* But *mšl*, "rule," can also mean "utter a parable," and by extension "a reprimand."

9. JV: *and hast not been as a harlot that enhanceth her hire.* But apparently in this comment *'tnn*, "hire," is derived from *'t'*, "come," and by extension "deeds"; and *ḳls*, "enhance," is construed in its other meaning "make beautiful, comely."

[You can use JV here as it stands, by substituting the modern equivalent of *enhanceth her hire*, "boasts of her (high) fee." The point is not that Israel think idolatry comely, but that they brazenly boast of their disobedience.

Accordingly, the next sentence would be translated: "Let the son of the wanton woman who had mended her ways present himself and reprimand the son of the virtuous woman who had turned to wantonness." L.N.]

those words in Scripture which are used in tribute to Rahab contain a reproach of Israel.

The words *And shall have part of the inheritance among the brethren* (Prov. 17:2) apply to Jeremiah, of whom it is written "Then Jeremiah went forth out of Jerusalem to go into the land of Benjamin [which included Jericho, Rahab's city], to receive his portion (*laḥălik*) there in the midst of his brethren" (Jer. 37:12)—that is, said Rab, Jeremiah went forth to take possession of the portion of land which was his. But R. Benjamin ben Levi said: Jeremiah [did not go forth to receive his portion there, but] to portion out (*lĕḥallek*) many direful prophecies there.[10] The text does not say "the *word* of Jeremiah" but *the* WORDS *of Jeremiah.* Therefore Scripture deems it necessary for the Book to begin with *The* [*direful*] WORDS *of Jeremiah* (Jer. 1:1).

5. R. Samuel bar Naḥman began his discourse with the verse *But if ye will not drive out the inhabitants of the Land before you, then shall those that remain of them be as thorns in your eyes, and as pricks in your sides* (Num. 33:55). The Holy One reminded Israel: I said to you, "Thou shalt utterly destroy them: the Hittite and the Amorite" (Deut. 20:17). But you did not do so; for "Rahab the harlot, and her father's household, and all that she had, did Joshua save alive"[11] (Josh. 6:25). Behold, Jeremiah will spring from the children's children of Rahab the harlot and will thrust such words into you as will be thorns in your eyes and pricks in your sides. Hence Scripture deems it necessary for the Book to begin with *The* [*sharp*] *words of Jeremiah* (Jer. 1:1).

6. R. Judah bar R. Simon began his discourse with the verse *I will raise them up a prophet from among their brethren, like unto thee* (Deut. 18:18). But a little farther on, Scripture says, "And there hath not arisen a prophet since in Israel like unto Moses" (Deut. 34:10), even though the first verse speaks of *a prophet . . . like unto thee.* The point, however, is that there will be, God promised, "a prophet like unto thee" in the uttering of reproofs. As a matter of fact, you find that much of what is written of the one, Moses, is written of the other, Jeremiah: the one prophesied forty years, and the other prophesied forty years; the one prophesied concerning Judah and Israel, and the other prophesied concerning Judah and Israel; the one—people of his own Tribe rose against him, and the other—people of his own Tribe rose

10. Presumably being afraid to utter his direful words in Jerusalem, Jeremiah went to Anathoth, where, as R. Benjamin construes Prov. 17:2, Jeremiah "portioned out the inheritance [of prophetic inspiration] among [his own] brethren."

11. Disapproval of the extent of mercy shown to Rahab is based on the verse "The young men . . . went in and brought out Rahab . . . and her brethren . . . all her kindred also" (Josh. 6:23), words taken to refer to Rahab herself, her immediate relatives, and also their relatives, in ever-widening circles, all of them totaling many hundreds. See Ruth Rabbah 2:1.

against him;[12] the one was cast into a river and the other was cast into a pit; the one was saved by a maidservant, the other was saved by a manservant;[13] finally, the one came with words of reproof, and the other came with words of reproof. Therefore the Book begins *The* [*reproving*] *words of Jeremiah* (Jer. 1:1).

7. R. Tanḥuma in the name of R. Eleazar who cited R. Berechiah,[14] and R. Mĕnaḥĕma and R. Beba, in the name of R. Eleazar, citing R. Meir, agreed in saying: In Scripture, whenever a word or words from the stem *dbr*, denoting "stern word,"[15] is used, the connotation [is one of ill-omen and] intimates that curses and denunciations from heaven are to follow. Thus we find "These are the *words* which Moses spoke unto all Israel" (Deut. 1:1). What follows? "The wasting of hunger, and the devouring of the fiery bolt" (Deut. 32:24). We find "The *word* of the Lord that came unto Hosea the son of Beeri" (Hos. 1:1). And what follows? God's saying "Ye are not My people" (Hos. 1:9). We find *The* WORDS *of Jeremiah the son of Hilkiah* (Jer. 1:1). And what follows? "Such as are for death to death, and such as are for captivity to captivity" (Jer. 43:11).

8. R. Tanḥum bar Ḥanila'i said: In three places—in the Book of Jeremiah, in the Book of Kings, and in the Book of Chronicles—the Holy One complains about the wicked Nebuchadnezzar. Like a man who says to his fellow, "See what So-and-So, may his bones be ground up, has done to me!" so, too, the Holy One says: See what the dwarf of Babylon[16] has done to Me!

In another comment, the name *Jeremiah* is construed as derived from the Greek *erēmos*, "void, destitute,"[17] and is taken to bespeak the lamentations of Jeremiah in such verses as "How doth the city sit solitary!" (Lam. 1:1), "How in His anger hath He covered Himself with a cloud!" (Lam. 2:1), "How is the gold become dim!" (Lam. 4:1).

In another comment, the word *dib̲re* in the phrase *The words* (*dib̲re*) *of Jeremiah* (Jer. 1:1), usually derived from *dab̲ar*, "word," is derived instead *from* *d̲eb̲er*, "pestilence leading to death," so that the entire phrase is construed as "The death-dealing words of Jeremiah" (*ibid.*): *Such as are for death to death* (Jer. 43:11).

Another comment reads the phrase [not *The words* (*dib̲re*) *of Jeremiah*,

12. Korah, who was of the Tribe of Levi, against Moses, and the people of Anathoth against Jeremiah. See Jer. 11:21.

13. See Exod. 2:5, and Jer. 38:10.

14. "R. Berechiah"—S; O: "R. Meir."

15. See Rashi on Num. 12:1.

16. The words *the lowest of men* in the clause *and setteth up over it the lowest of men* (Dan. 4:14) refer to Nebuchadnezzar, who is said to have been very short in stature.

17. Literally "the name Jeremiah is a warning of [the coming] devastation."

but] "My word (*dĕḇari*) through Jeremiah."[18] The Holy One said to Jer miah: Go, say to Israel, "Turn in repentance, else I will destroy My Ten ple." Thereupon the children of Israel said [to one another]: And if H does destroy His Temple, will He not have destroyed what is His, [not wh is ours]? To this the Holy One replied: Just as surely as I shall hav destroyed My Temple, even as surely shall My word through Jeremia [concerning the destruction of what is yours] also be fulfilled.

Another comment on *The words of Jeremiah* (Jer. 1:1), *diḇre*, "words, being construed as *dĕḇaray*, "My words" (i.e. the Ten Commandments) The Holy One said to Jeremiah: I have been demanding from Israel heeding of My words, O Jeremiah. My word to them was *I am the Lord th God* (Exod. 20:2), which they did not heed, "saying to a stock: 'Thou a my father'" (Jer. 2:27). My word to them was *Thou shalt have no othe gods before Me* (Exod. 20:3), which they did not heed, instead "worshipin the host of heaven upon the housetops" (Zeph. 1:5). My word to them wa *Thou shalt not take the name of the Lord thy God in vain* (Exod. 20:7) which they did not heed—"surely they swear falsely" (Jer. 5:2). My word t them was *Remember the Sabbath day to keep it holy* (Exod. 20:8), whic they did not heed: "Thou hast despised My holy things, and hast profane My Sabbaths" (Ezek. 22:8). My word to them was *Honor thy father and th mother* (Exod. 20:12), which they did not heed: "In thee have they made light of father and mother" (Ezek. 22:7). My word to them was *Thou shal not murder, thou shalt not commit adultery, thou shalt not steal* (Exod. 20:13), which they did not heed: "Ye steal, murder, and commit adultery" (Jer. 7:9). My word to them was *Thou shalt not bear false witness against thy neighbor* (Exod. 20:13), which they did not heed: "They bend their tongue, their bow of falsehood" (Jer. 9:2). My word to them was *Thou shalt not covet* (Exod. 20:14), which they did not heed: "They covet fields, and seize them; and houses, and take them away" (Micah 2:2).

9. Another comment on *The words of Jeremiah* (Jer. 1:1)[19] *diḇre* "words," being construed as *dabray*, "as to leading." The Holy One said to Jeremiah: Either thou go lead them down to Babylon and I will remain here, or thou remain here and I will go lead them down. Jeremiah replied bluntly to the Holy One: Master of universes, if I lead them down, what good can I do for them? Let their Creator lead them down—He can do them good.[20]

Nebuchadnezzar gave Nebuzaradan three orders concerning Jeremiah:

18. "My word (*dĕḇari*) through Jeremiah"—O_1; O: "Jeremiah."

19. "*The words of Jeremiah*"—O_1; O: "*Jeremiah.*"

20. [I can see no implication of leadership, either by Jeremiah or by the Almighty here or in the rest of the story. Hence the *dabray* does not seem relevant. Since Jeremiah's reply invites the Almighty to accompany the exiles, I wonder if the *derush* here, based on *brywhwn* in line 8, is *dibbri'*, "He who had created them." L.N.]

Take him, look well to him, and do him no harm" (Jer. 39:12). But when remiah saw a band of young men tied by neck chains one to the other, he ent and cast in his lot with theirs. Then again when he saw a band of old en tied together by neck chains, he went and cast in his lot with theirs. hereupon Nebuzaradan said, "I see that you are one of three things: a rophet who thought he was telling lies, or a protester against the justice of e punishment that God inflicts, or a murderer. You are a prophet who ought he was telling lies—for many many years you have been prophesying oncerning this insignificant Temple of yours that it would be destroyed, and ow that I have destroyed it, you are distraught. Or, secondly, you are a rotester against the justice of the punishment that God inflicts—I do not ish to tie you up in chains, and, [when you choose to cast your lot in with he others], the just apportioning of God's punishment appears to have no neaning for you. Or, thirdly, you are a murderer. For if the king hears of what you have done on your own while I did nothing to stop you, he will end word to have the head of a certain person[21] removed. In other words "If it seem good unto thee to come with me into Babylon, come, and I will ook well unto thee; but if it seem ill unto thee to come with me into Babylon, forbear" (Jer. 40:4). "Yet Jeremiah would not go back" (Jer. 40:5), until the Holy One disclosed to him what he was to do, whereof it is written "The word which came to Jeremiah from the Lord, after Nebuzaradan . . . let him go" (Jer. 40:1). The verse goes on to say "When [Nebuzaradan] had taken him—and he was bound in chains" (*ibid.*). [Should not the text have read "he," not "and he?"] What, then, is implied by the phrase "and he"? R. Aḥa's answer was that Jeremiah "and He,"[22] if one dare say such a thing, were bound in chains.[23]

What was "the word which came to Jeremiah from the Lord?" On this point, R. Eleazar and R. Johanan differ. According to R. Eleazar, the word was "He that scattered Israel will gather him, and keep him, as a shepherd doth his flock" (Jer. 31:10). According to R. Johanan, it was "The Lord will ransom Jacob, and redeem him from the hand of him that is stronger than he" (Jer. 31:11). [Having been released by Nebuzaradan] and on his way back [to Jerusalem], Jeremiah saw fingers and toes [of captive Israel] that had been cut off and flung on the roadways. He picked them up, clasped them close, kissed them, and put them in his cloak, saying to them: O my children, did I not say to you, "Give glory to the Lord your God, before it grow dark, and before your feet stumble," etc. (Jer. 13:16)—before words of Torah grow dark for you, before words of prophecy grow dark, [and you are brought to the fate that has now befallen you].

21. ["a certain person"—euphemism for "me." L.N.]
22. One of God's names. See B.Suk 45a.
23. In keeping with God's promise *I will be with him in trouble* (Ps. 91:15).

10. *For the mountains will I take up a weeping and wailing, and for th pastures turned into wilderness a lamentation* (Jer. 9:9). I take up a lamen tation for the high mountains which have become a wilderness. *Because the are burned up, so that none passeth through—because they hearkened not t the Voice, nay miḳneh*[24] (*ibid.*). It was not enough for you, O Israel [tha you were like a thoughtless wife who] hearkens not to her husband's voice you even went so far as to make God warn you, *miḳneh* [as a husband ma formally warn his wife] to desist or face the consequences[25] of your whor ish seeking after idols. And so *Both the fowl of the heavens and the beast ar fled, and gone* (*ibid.*). As R. Jose bar Ḥalafta said: For fifty-two year [after the Temple's destruction], not a bird was seen flying over the Lan of Israel, thus fulfilling the prophecy *Both the fowl of the heavens and the beast are fled, and gone*. Nevertheless, said R. Ḥanina, [God saw to it that] forty years before Israel were exiled into Babylon, palm trees were planted in Babylon, because Israel crave sweet kinds of fruit which accustom the tongue to the sweetness of Torah. As taught in the name of R. Judah: [Not only were the birds and the beasts fled, but] for seven years in the Land there was fulfilled the prophecy "The whole Land thereof is brimstone, and salt, and a burning" (Deut. 29:22), because, as Scripture says, "The [consequences of the forsaken] covenant shall cause the many enemies [of Israel] to prevail for a week of years"[26] (Dan. 9:27).

[With such burning in the Land], how did the Cutheans manage to survive in it? Since the Land caught fire in strips here and there, they used to cultivate in one spot until it caught fire and then cultivate in another spot until it, too, caught fire. R. Ze'era said: Come and see how brazen [in its plenty] is the Land of Israel! [Even as it burned], it produced fruits. Two Amoraim differ in their answers as to why the Land grew fruits despite its burning. One said: Because the Cutheans manured it.[27] The other said: Because they turned over its soil the way one turns over a measure of seed, so that what is on top goes to the bottom, and what is at the bottom comes to

24. JV: *And they hear not the voice of the cattle:* of course they could not do so, for the verse goes on to say that fowl and beast had fled. Hence the comment which follows.

25. Of conviction on testimony of eyewitnesses, or the awesome ordeal of bitter water.

The word *miḳneh*, taken to be a form of *ḳinĕ'ah*, is thus given two meanings: the older one, signifying the emotion of jealousy, and the later, legal one, signifying the formal warning to the wife to cease and desist from reprehensible behavior. Leon Nemoy provided the comment and the explanation.

26. JV: *He shall make a firm covenant with many for one week.* But see B.Yoma 54a, and PR 1:5.

27. [Thus quenching the fire on that particular piece of ground. L.N.]

the top.[28] [So hot was the burning Land that] when a man who was busy plowing in the valley of Arbel let his ploughshare cut deep, the fiery soil that was turned up burned the seed.

R. Ḥanina bar R. Abbahu said: There are seven hundred species of kosher fish, eight hundred kinds of kosher grasshoppers, and birds beyond number; and they all went into exile with the children of Israel to Babylon, and when the children of Israel came back, all returned with them except for the fish known as *šibbuṭa*.[29] But how did the fish go into exile? R. Huna said in the name of R. Jose: They went into exile by way of the subterranean abyss [on which the earth floats] and they returned by way of the subterranean abyss.

11. In another comment, the letters in the name Jeremiah (*yrmyh*) are construed as follows: *yoḏ*, "ten"; *rm*, "journeyed up and away"; *yh*, "the Presence"—that is, in ten stages the Presence journeyed up and away [from the Temple in Jerusalem]: (1) From the one cherub over the Ark to the other cherub over the Ark; (2) from the cherub to the Temple's threshold; (3) from the Temple's threshold back to the two cherubim; (4) from the two cherubim to the east gate; (5) from the east gate to the Temple's court; (6) from the Temple's court to the altar; (7) from the altar to the roof; (8) from the roof to the wall [surrounding the Temple]; (9) from the wall to the city [of Jerusalem]; (10) from the city to the Mount of Olives.

From the one cherub to the other cherub: "The glory of the God of Israel was gone up from the cherub, whereupon it was" (Ezek. 9:3) to the other cherub. From the other cherub to the Temple's threshold: "The glory of the Lord mounted up from the cherub to the threshold of the House" (Ezek. 10:3). From the Temple's threshold [back] to the cherubim: "The glory of the Lord went forth from off the threshold of the House, and stood over the cherubim" (Ezek. 10:18). Is it not strange that the text reads "The glory of the Lord went forth from off the threshold" [as if to leave the House]? Should it not have read "The glory of the Lord came [in from the threshold and stood over the cherubim]"? The verse's peculiar phrasing may be explained by a parable. A king who was departing from his palace, kissed its walls, embraced its pillars, and said, "Farewell, my home! Farewell, my palace!" Even so, the Presence kissed the Temple's walls and embraced its pillars, saying, "Farewell, My home! Farewell, My palace!"[30] After returning to the cherubim, the Presence then went from them to the east gate: "The

28. [Thus again quenching the fire. L.N.]

29. [Variously identified as mullet, carp, etc. The Arabic equivalent *shabbūṭ* is now used for carp. L.N.]

30. Thus on its way hence from the Temple's threshold, the Presence returned for a while to the cherubim.

cherubim lifted up their wings, and mounted up from the earth in m sight"[31] (Ezek. 10:19). From the east gate to the court: "The court wa full of the brightness of the Lord's glory" (Ezek. 10:4). From the court t the altar: "I saw the Lord standing beside the altar" (Amos 9:1). From th altar to the roof: "It is better to dwell in a corner of the housetop"[32] (Prov 21:9). From the roof to the wall: "Thus He showed me; and, behold th Lord stood beside the wall made by a plumb line[33] (Amos 7:7). From th wall to the city: "A voice crieth, 'The Lord into the city' "[34] (Micah 6:9) From the city to the Mount of Olives: "The glory of the Lord went up fron the midst of the city, and stood upon the mountain which is on the east sid of the city" (Ezek. 11:23). There, on the Mount of Olives, for three and a half years—so said R. Jonathan—the Presence lingered, crying three times a day: "Return, ye backsliding children, I will heal your backslidings" (Jer. 3:22). But when they did not repent and return, the Presence proceeded to soar up into the empyrean, exclaiming, as Scripture tells us, "I will go and return to My place, till they acknowledge their guilt, and seek My face; in their trouble they will seek Me earnestly" (Hos. 5:15).

12. In another comment, the name "Jeremiah" is taken as related to the Greek word *erēmos*, for in his days the Temple became a desolation (*erēmon*).

In still another comment, the name "Jeremiah," translated as "The Lord rises," is taken to mean that in Jeremiah's days the measure of justice rose to its full height.

The son of Hilkiah, "the Lord is the portion" (Jer. 1:1)—that is, said R. Judah bar R. Simon, Jeremiah was of that Tribe to whom God said: "I am thy portion (*ḥeleḳ*) and thine inheritance"[35] (Num. 18:20). [God deemed it necessary to speak thus of Jeremiah, for] he, according to R. Samuel bar Naḥman, was one of four men—Phinehas, Uriah, Ezekiel, and Jeremiah—who were reputed to have come from blemished stock. Of Phinehas, you find that when he was about to trace the pedigree of the children of Israel, they said to him: "You would trace our pedigree? Eleazar [your father]—to whom was he wed? Was it not to the daughter of Putiel, [a man who

31. The verse goes on: "and they stood at the door of the east gate of the Lord's House."

32. The verse goes on: "than a house in common with a contentious woman"—that is, with an idol, which the Presence avoided by going to a rooftop. Cf. "Like a sparrow that is alone upon the housetop" (Ps. 102:8).

33. The numerical value of *'nk*, "plumb line," is 71, corresponding to the number of judges in the Sanhedrin whose decisions went as precisely to the point as a plumbline.

34. JV: *Hark! the Lord crieth unto the city.*

35. Jeremiah, a priest, was thus a descendant of Aaron. Hilkiah is taken to mean *ḥeleḳ*, "portion," *yah*, "of the Lord."

fattened (*pittem*) calves for idolatry]?[36] Does not Scripture say, 'Eleazar, Aaron's son, took for wife one of the daughters of Putiel' (Exod. 6:25)? And you would presume to trace our pedigree!" When the Holy One saw that Israel were running Phinehas down, He proceeded to trace his lofty pedigree: "Phinehas, the son of Eleazar, the son of Aaron the priest" (Num. 25:11)—priest and son of a priest, zealous man and son of a zealous man. Uriah, too—Israel were running him down, saying, "Is he not a Gibeonite, [and should he not, therefore, have remained a hewer of wood and drawer of water]? Does not Scripture rightly tag him in the verse 'There was also a man that prophesied in the name of the Lord, Uriah the son of Shemaiah of Kirjath-jearim' (Jer. 26:20), a Gibeonite city along with 'Gibeon and Chephirah' (Josh. 9:17)?" To set the record straight, however, Scripture finds it necessary to indicate his lofty pedigree: "I will take unto Me faithful witnesses to record, [one of them being] Uriah the priest" (Isa. 8:2). Ezekiel also—Israel were running him down, saying, "Is he not of the descendants of Rahab the harlot?" To set the record straight, however, Scripture finds it necessary to indicate his lofty pedigree: "The word of the Lord came expressly unto Ezekiel the priest, the son of Buzi" (Ezek. 1:3). Jeremiah as well—Israel were running him down, saying, "Is he not of the descendants of Rahab the harlot?" To set the record straight, however, Scripture finds it necessary to indicate his lofty pedigree: *The words of Jeremiah the son of Hilkiah, of the priests* (Jer. 1:1).

13. *Of (min) the priests that were in Anathoth* (Jer. 1:1). By *min*, "of," in the phrase *Of the priests that were in Anathoth,* Jeremiah meant, according to R. Berechiah: Among the priests my name is deprived of the respect due it. In the days of Moses, priests were told to say, "The Lord bless thee" (Num. 6:24); but in my days, said Jeremiah, I am told "Of them shall be taken up a curse" (Jer. 29:22). In the days of Moses, priests were told to say, "and keep thee" (Num. 6:24); but in my days, said Jeremiah, I am told "Such as are for death, to death" (Jer. 15:2). In the days of Moses, "The Lord make His face to shine upon thee" (Num. 6:25); but in my days, "He hath made me to dwell in dark places as those do that have been long dead" (Lam. 3:6). In the days of Moses, "and be gracious unto thee" (Num. 6:25); but in my days, "I will show you no favor" (Jer. 16:13), [said God]. In the days of Moses, "The Lord lift up His countenance upon Thee" (Num. 6:26); but in my days, "A nation of fierce countenance, that shall not regard the person of the old, nor show favor to the young" (Deut. 28:50). In the days of Moses, "and give thee peace" (Num. 6:26); but in my days, "I have taken away My peace from this people, saith the Lord, even mercy and compassion" (Jer. 16:5).

36. Putiel was one of the names by which Jethro was known. See B.BB 109b.

14. *In the land of Benjamin* (Jer. 1:1). Jeremiah's portion was set in the land of Benjamin. Why Benjamin? Because until Benjamin was born, it was not certain,[37] [despite the prophecy that a twelfth son would be born to Jacob],[38] that our Father Jacob would, in fact, raise up Twelve Tribes; so too, despite all the Prophets who prophesied against Jerusalem, their prophecy did not become a certainty until Jeremiah rose up.

Another explanation of why Jeremiah's portion was set in the land of Benjamin: as long as Benjamin was in his mother's womb, she did not die, but as soon as he went forth from it, she died, as is written "and it came to pass as he went forth, her soul—it expired"[39] (Gen. 35:18). So, too, during all the days that Jeremiah was in Jerusalem, it was not destroyed, but when he went forth from it, it was destroyed. It was of this going forth that Jeremiah said: "O Lord, Thou hast enticed me, and I was enticed" (Jer. 20:7)—Thou didst set out to entice me, and I let myself be enticed. Thou didst have me go forth out of Jerusalem, and then Thou didst destroy it. Yesterday, Thou didst tell me, "Behold, Hanamel, the son of Shallum thine uncle, shall come unto thee, saying: Buy thee my field" (Jer. 32:7), and it was "thus [that] Thou didst overcome me, and didst prevail over me" (Jer. 20:7).

Another explanation of why Jeremiah's portion was set in the land of Benjamin: as Benjamin was the last of all the Tribe Fathers, so Jeremiah was the last of all the Prophets. But did not Haggai, Zechariah, and Malachi prophesy after him? On this question R. Eleazar and R. Samuel bar Naḥman differ. R. Eleazar said: Yes, but their periods of prophecy were brief. R. Samuel bar Naḥman said: [Though they did not utter their prophecies until after Jeremiah's time], the prophecy they were to utter had already been entrusted [in his days] to the three—entrusted to Haggai, Zechariah, and Malachi.

R. Eleazar and R. Johanan differ [on the way in which Prophets conclude their prophecies]. R. Eleazar said: All Prophets begin with words of reproof, but all conclude with words of comfort, except Jeremiah who concludes with words of reproof, saying "Thus shall Babylon sink, and shall not rise again" (Jer. 51:64). R. Johanan said: But Jeremiah also concludes with words of comfort, for since he keeps prophesying the Temple's destruction, you might suppose that he would conclude with the Temple's destruction. Not at all. Scripture brings his prophecy to a close with the verse "Thus far are the words of Jeremiah" (*ibid.*), so that he concludes with prophecy of the downfall of those who destroyed the Temple. On the other hand, does

37. "it was not certain"—Yalḳuṭ; O: "the blessing was not fulfilled."
38. See PR 3:4 (YJS, 18, 71–73).
39. JV: *And it came to pass, as her soul was in departing—for she died.* But the subject of *was in departing* may be construed to be Benjamin.

not Isaiah, too, conclude with words of reproof, saying "They shall be an abhorring unto all flesh" (Isa. 66:24)? Yes, but in this verse Isaiah is talking of heathen nations, [not of Israel].

[Returning to Jeremiah's concluding prophecy], is it not a fact that he says therein "But Thou hast utterly rejected us" (Lam. 5:22)? Yes, but directly after he says "Thou hast utterly rejected us," he goes on to say comfortingly, "Turn Thou us unto Thee"[40] (Lam. 5:21).

15. *To whom the word of the Lord came in the days of Josiah . . . unto the end of the tenth*[41] *year of Zedekiah the son of Josiah, king of Judah, unto the carrying away of Jerusalem captive in the fifth month* (Jer. 1:1–3). R. Abun said: A lion came up in the sign of the Lion and destroyed the Lion of God. A lion came up—the wicked Nebuchadnezzar, of whom it is written "A lion is gone up from his thicket" (Jer. 4:7); in the sign of the Lion—*the carrying away of Jerusalem captive in the fifth month;*[42] and destroyed the [Temple], the Lion of God:[43] "Woe to Ariel, Ariel, the lion of God; the city where David encamped" (Isa. 29:1). [All of these events took place], but the expectation is sure that the Lion will come back in the sign of the Lion and rebuild the Lion of God: It is certain that the Lion will come back—the Holy One, of whom it is written "The Lion hath roared, who will not fear?" (Amos 3:8); He will come back in the sign of the Lion—"I will turn their [month of] mourning[44] into joy" (Jer. 31:13); and when "The Lord rebuilds Jerusalem, and gathers together the dispersed of Israel" (Ps. 147:2), He will also rebuild the Lion of God.

40. The Masorah, in line with its usual custom, prescribes the repetition of Lam. 5:21 after the concluding verse 22, in order to end the book on a note of consolation.

An alternative translation: "Yes, but Jeremiah's concluding prophecy is to be understood: 'Turn us unto Thee, because long enough hast Thou rejected us' " or 'Turn us unto Thee, because Thou canst not have utterly rejected us.' See Ginzberg, CPT, *4*, 60; and Šĕlomoh Goren, *Hay-Yĕrušalmi ham-mĕforaš* (Jerusalem 5721/1961), 189.

41. MT: "*eleventh* year."

42. Ab, whose sign is the Lion.

43. See PR 2:5 (YJS, *18*, 55, n. 24); and B.Yoma 21b and Rashi.

44. The month of Ab.

PISKA 14

SUMMARY

God's mild reproach of Israel, and the happy consequences of hearkening to Him

In His reproach of Israel, God's manner is mild and conciliatory (Sec. 1). If Israel were only to hearken to Him, their entire being would soon be saturated with God's teaching (Sec. 2). Israel's poverty is God's means of getting Israel to repent. Indeed, God chose Jeremiah, a poor man from the country, knowing that he would reprimand Israel not sharply but gently (Sec. 3).

At Sinai, Israel had promised to do God's will and to hearken to His words. When they made the golden calf, they violated their promise to do His will, but they will still have to hearken—indeed God will have them hearken in the Land or outside the Land. Even after Israel die, their dead bodies and dry bones will be made to hearken.

Even if Israel refuse to hearken, yet become one as they were in Egypt, God may still save them as He did in Egypt where they stood shoulder to shoulder as one.

For their failure to hearken, however, Israel in exile are now doing for others what they used to do for themselves in the Land, and they find further that in exile obedience to Torah is not as rewarding as it was in the Land (Sec. 4).

God's conduct, however, toward Adam, Pharaoh, and Moses—indeed toward the people of Israel—is cited by way of demonstrating that God does not lack consideration for His people (Sec. 5).

In their refusal to hearken, Israel, not content to have gone far from God, even chased away others who would have returned to Him (Sec. 6). Still God chose to overlook Israel's dereliction, regarding the idols that Israel worshiped as nought, as things that have no substance (Sec. 7).

PISKA 14

Hearken (Jer. 2:4).[1]

1. [Elihu said harshly], *Therefore, hearken unto me, ye men of understanding: It would be a profanation for God, that He should do wickedness; and for the Almighty, that He should commit iniquity* (Job. 34:10). R. Azariah and R. Jonathan bar Haggai, citing R. Samuel bar R. Isaac, said: Rather the "wrathful" speech of the Fathers than the "gentle" speech of their descendants [such as Elihu]. That the "wrathful" speech of the Fathers is endurable, we learn from our Father Jacob: "And Jacob was wroth, and strove with Laban. And Jacob answered and said to Laban: 'What is my trespass, and what is my sin?' " (Gen. 31:36). You might suppose that threats of blows or wounds entered into the argument. In fact, with soothing words Jacob sought to conciliate his father-in-law.[2] On the other hand, that the "gentle" speech of the descendants of the Fathers is not endurable, we may learn from David: "David fled from Naioth in Ramah, and came before Jonathan: 'What have I done? What is my guilt? And what is my sin before thy father, that he seeketh my life?' " (1 Sam. 20:1). Thus, though speaking of possible conciliation, David mentioned Saul's murderous intent. R. Simon pointed out: Usually, when a son-in-law has been living with his father-in-law and then is about to leave his father-in-law's house, is it not likely at the very least that there will be found in his possession some trifling thing [belonging to his father-in-law]? But in regard to this particular son-in-law—Jacob—not even a needle, not even a pin or two were found in his possession. As Jacob is quoted in Scripture: "Though thou hast rummaged through all my stuff, what single one of all thy household things hast thou found?" (Gen. 31:37). Thereupon the Holy One said to Jacob: As thou livest, with the same mild words of reproach that thou didst speak to thy father-in-law, with those words I shall reproach thy descendants: *Thus saith the Lord: What [single] iniquity have your fathers found in Me, that they are gone far from Me?* (Jer. 2:8).

2. *But whoso hearkeneth unto me shall dwell securely, and shall be quiet without fear of evil* (Prov. 1:33). In connection with hearkening, four kinds of hearkeners are spoken of in Scripture: one who hearkened and suffered loss therefor; one who hearkened and gained reward therefor; one who did not hearken and suffered loss therefor; and one who did not hearken and won reward therefor. The one who hearkened and suffered loss therefor was

1. Jer. 2:4–28, etc., is the haftarah of rebuke for *Mas'e*, the second of the three Sabbaths preceding the Fast of the Ninth of Ab.

2. "You might suppose that threats . . . father-in-law"—Gen. Rabbah 74:10.

Adam: "Unto Adam He said: 'Because thou hast hearkened unto the voice of thy wife'" (Gen. 3:17). And what loss did he suffer? [Nothing less than eternal life]: "Dust thou art, and unto dust shalt thou return" (Gen. 3:19). Then there was the one who hearkened and gained reward therefor. This one was our Father Abraham: "God said: . . . 'All that Sarah saith unto thee, hearken unto her voice'" (Gen. 21:12). And what reward did he win? [The continuation of his line through an exemplary son]: "In Isaac shall seed be called to thee" (*ibid.*). Then there was the one who did not hearken and won reward therefor—Joseph: "He hearkened not unto Potiphar's wife, to lie by her, or even to be with her" (Gen. 39:11). What reward did he gain? God told Jacob: [Because Joseph's hand was not guilty of touching her], "Joseph shall put his hand upon thine eyes [at the moment of thy dying]" (Gen. 46:4). Finally, there were those who did not hearken and who suffered loss therefor—Israel themselves: "Yet they hearkened not unto Me, nor inclined their ear" (Jer. 7:26). And what loss did they suffer? [Nothing less than life itself]: "Such as are for death, to death; and such as are for the sword, to the sword," etc. (Jer. 15:2). R. Levi said: To the body, the ear is like a vessel that is used for fumigating garments. When such a vessel is filled with garments, and one gets the purifying smoke going underneath it, all the garments become saturated with the smoke;[3] so, too, [by way of the ear that hearkens, all of your being will become saturated with God's teaching]: *Incline your ear, and come unto Me; hearken, and all of you, body and soul, shall live* (Isa. 55:3).

3. *If ye be willing and obedient, ye shall eat the good of the Land; but if ye refuse and rebel, ye shall eat carobs*[4] (Isa. 1:19–20). The reason Isaiah said *Ye shall eat carobs,* R. Aḥa explained, was that [carobs are poor eating, and] poor eating is what Israel require to get them on the road to repentance. Indeed, said R. 'Aḳiḇa, poverty is as becoming to the daughter of Jacob as a red ribbon on the neck of a white horse.

R. Samuel bar Naḥman said: When a palace falls into ruin, people still call it a palace; but when a dungheap is raised to eminence, people keep on calling it a dungheap. When a palace falls into ruin, people still call it a palace: *Hear ye the word of the Lord, O house of Jacob, and all the families of the house of Israel* (Jer. 2:4). Even as Israel are falling into ruin, God

3. See Kel 22:10. "If a man put out [another's] eye he must pay him for the value of his eye . . . but if he made [the other] deaf, he must pay for the value of the whole of him" (B.BḴ 85b) because by having made him deaf he has made the other unfit to do anything, whereas a person blinded in one eye can still see well with his remaining good eye.

4. JV: *Ye shall be devoured with the sword,* a reading which does not provide as sharp a contrast as the commentator's rendition. The word *ḥrb*, if read *ḥereḇ*, means "sword", and if read *ḥaruḇ*, means "carob"; and, by a slight change in vowels, "be devoured" (passive) may be read "eat" (active).

still calls them "house of Israel." But when a dungheap is raised to eminence, people keep on calling it a dungheap: "Behold, the land of the Chaldeans—this is the nation that was nothing" (Isa. 23:13). [Despite its present eminence], let it still be called a nothing!

[In accounting for the kindly tone of Jeremiah's reprimand of Israel], R. Levi told the parable of a Roman lady who had in her household two representatives of her family, one from the countryside and the other from the city. When the countryman had occasion to reprimand her, he would do so in a kindly way, "Are you not a daughter of goodly stock, are you not the daughter of noblemen?" But the one who was the city man would reprimand her in a sharp way, "Are you not a daughter of the lowly poor, are you not a daughter of humble origins?" Jeremiah, too, because he was a countryman, from Anathoth, would come into Jerusalem and likewise reprimand Israel in a kindly way: *Hear ye the word of the Lord, O house of Jacob* (Jer. 2:5). After all, did your fathers[5] ever do the uncomely things you do? Isaiah, however, who was a city man, from Jerusalem, would reprimand Israel in a sharp way: "Hear ye the word of the Lord, ye refuse[6] of Sodom" (Isa. 1:10)—are you not, in fact, of the refuse of the people of Sodom?

Moreover, said R. Levi, Amoz, [Isaiah's father], and Amaziah, [king of Judah], were brothers; thus Isaiah as nephew of a king could presume to reprimand Israel in a sharp way, in keeping with the verse "The rich man speaketh up roughly" (Prov. 18:23).

4. R. Levi told another parable of a noblewoman who [in her dowry] brought two myrtles to the king, but then lost one of them and was distressed at the loss. Thereupon the king said to her: Take care of the remaining one as though you were taking care of both of them. Likewise when Israel stood at Mount Sinai, the children of Israel said, *All that the lord hath spoken we will do, and hearken* (Exod. 24:7). However they lost the [myrtle of] *we will do* when "they made them a molten calf" (Exod. 32:8). Thereupon the Holy One said to them: Take care of [the myrtle of] *we will hearken* as though you were taking care of both [myrtles]. When Israel did not hearken, the Holy One said to them, If you were to *Hearken to the word of the Lord* (Jer. 2:4), you would not be made to hearken to the words of Jeremiah; if you were to hearken to words of Torah, you would not be made to hearken to words of prophecy; if you were to hearken to words of prophecy, you would not be made to hearken to words of reproach; if you were to hearken to words of reproach, you would not be made to hearken to words of rebuke; if you were to hearken to words of rebuke, you would not be made to hearken "to the sound of the horn and pipe" (Dan. 3:15) [sum-

5. "your fathers"—O_1, Pa; O: "their fathers."

6. JV: *rulers*. But the commentator associates *ḳṣyn*, "ruler," with *ḳṣh*, "end, refuse," or [*ḳwṣ*, "to loathe, despise." L.N.].

moning you to worship the golden image which Nebuchadnezzar set up]; if you were to hearken in the Land, you would not be made to hearken outside the Land; if you were to hearken while you are alive, you would not be made to hearken after you are dead. Let your ears hearken so that your dead bodies will not be made to hearken; let your bodies hearken so that your bones will not be made to hearken: "O ye dry bones hearken to the word of the Lord" (Ezek. 37:4).

[Even if Israel do not hearken, at least let them become one as they were in Egypt, so that God may still save them].[7] Thus R. Aḥa, citing R. Joshua ben Levi, said [of God's saving of Israel in Egypt]: Some eight times[8] it was admitted by the Egyptians that the men and women of Israel stood shoulder to shoulder as one. And the proof? The verse "Come, let us deal wisely with Israel, lest *he* multiply," etc. (Exod. 1:10). Because Israel was then one, God leaped forth to save Israel: "I am come down to deliver *him* out of the hand of the Egyptians," etc. (Exod. 3:8).

[In comment on Israel in exile], R. Abin and R. Ḥiyya, in the name of R. Johanan, cited the verse "The descendants of my mother [Rebekah, the children of Esau], were incensed against me, they made me keeper of the vineyards" (Song 1:6). What forced me—asked Israel—to become keeper of the vineyards of heathen nations? The fact that "mine own vineyard have I not kept" (*ibid.*). What forced me in Syria to set aside two offerings of dough?[9] The fact that in the Land of Israel I failed to set aside one offering of dough as I was ordained to do. When I had to set aside two offerings of dough, I supposed that I would receive reward for both, but it was only for one that I received reward. What forced me in Syria to observe two days of the festivals? The fact that in Israel I had not observed the festival for the one day it was ordained to be observed on. When I was made to observe the two, I supposed that I would receive reward for both, but it was only for one that I received reward. [Of such enforced observances outside the Land], R. Johanan cited the verse "Wherefore I gave them also statutes that were not rewarding" (Ezek. 20:25).

5. It is written *Thus saith the Lord: What iniquity have your fathers found in Me, that they are gone far from Me, and have walked after things of nought, and are become nought?* (Jer. 2:5). R. Isaac said: Of one who forsakes an open Scroll of Torah and goes away, Scripture says, *What iniquity have your fathers found in Me, that they are gone far from Me?* The

7. Cf. Piska 12.14.

8. R. Aḥa is somewhat indefinite as to the number because in one instance, *He will go up from the land* (Exod. 1:10), the subject may be not Israel but Egypt, which feared that it would be forced out of the land; and in the other instance, *Nevertheless [Israel] will multiply, nevertheless will grow* (Exod. 1:12), the speaker is the holy spirit.

9. One to be burnt, and one to be given to the priest. See Ḥal 4:8.

Holy One said to Israel: My children, your fathers found no iniquity in Me, but you found iniquity in Me. Adam found no iniquity in Me, but you found iniquity in Me. With whom may Adam be compared? With a sick man whom a physician was attending. The physician said: "Such-and-such you may eat and such-and-such you are not to eat." But the sick man disregarded the physician's instructions and so found himself on his deathbed. When his kin came in to him and asked him: "Would you say that the physician used bad judgment in his treatment of you?" he replied: "Certainly not. I am the one who brought death upon myself. The physician gave me specific instructions, saying, 'Such-and-such you may eat and such-and-such you may not eat:' But when I disregarded his instructions, I brought death upon myself." Likewise all the generations of mankind came in to Adam and asked him: Would you say that the Holy One showed a lack of consideration in his treatment of you? Adam replied: "Certainly not. I am the one who brought death upon myself. He had given me specific instructions, saying 'Of every tree in the garden thou mayest freely eat; but of the tree of the knowledge of good and evil, thou shalt not eat of it' (Gen. 2:17). But when I disregarded his instructions, I brought death upon myself, for He said, 'In the day thou eatest thereof, thou shalt surely die' (*ibid.*)."

Pharaoh found no iniquity in Me, but you found iniquity in Me. With whom may Pharaoh be compared? With [the steward of] a king who, before going to a far city by the sea, proceeded to deposit with the steward all that he possessed. After a while, the king returned from the far city by the sea and said to his steward, "Return to me what I deposited with you." The steward lied: "I am not your servant, nor did you deposit anything with me." What did the king do to the steward? He had him seized and suspended from a torturer's scaffold.[10] Thereupon the steward said: "I acknowledge that I am your servant and I am ready to return all you deposited with me." Likewise, [when Israel was in Egypt], the Holy One began by saying to Moses, "Come now, therefore, and I will send thee unto Pharaoh, that thou mayest bring forth My people" (Exod. 3:10). In reply to God's messenger, wicked [Pharaoh] said: "Who is the Lord, that I should hearken unto His voice? . . . I know not the Lord," etc. (Exod. 5:2). But after the Lord brought ten plagues upon him, he acknowledged Him, saying "The Lord is just, and I and my people are wicked" (Exod. 9:27).

Moses found no iniquity in Me, but you found iniquity in Me. With whom may Moses be compared? With [a tutor in the employ of] a king. When the king turned his son over to the tutor, the king said: "Whatever you do, do not call my son *moreh*." What is meant by the term *moreh*? It is the same, said R. Reuben, as *moros*, the epithet that the Greeks use for a moron. Once, however, when the son angered the tutor, the tutor called him *moreh*. There-

10. The *gradus* or *catasta*. See Saul Lieberman in JQR, *35* (1944), 13–15.

upon the king said: "With all the authority that I possess I gave you the explicit command, 'Do not call my son *moreh*,' yet you called him *moreh*. A man as clever as you should be spared further business with a moron." Likewise it is written of God's command "The Lord spoke unto Moses and unto Aaron, and gave them a charge concerning the children of Israel" (Exod. 6:13). And what was the charge He gave them? He told them, "Do not call My children morons." But when they angered him at the waters of Meribah, Moses said to them, "Hear now, ye morons"[11] (Num. 20:10). Thereupon the Holy One said: "With all the authority that I possess I charged you, saying 'Do not call My children morons,' yet you called them morons. Men as clever as you should be spared further business with morons." Therefore Scripture tells us that God did not punish Moses alone, by saying "Thou shalt not bring," but punished his kin as well, for He said, "Ye shall not bring" (Num. 20:12): neither thou, nor thy brother, nor thy sister shall enter the Land of Israel.

The Holy One said to Israel: Your fathers in the wilderness found no lack of consideration in Me, but you found lack of consideration in Me. I said to them "He that sacrificeth unto the gods shall be utterly destroyed" (Exod. 22:19), but they, not mindful, "worshiped [a golden calf] and sacrificed unto it" (Exod. 32:8). Yet even after all the wicked things they did [in their worship of the golden calf], "The Lord repented of the evil which He said He would do unto His people" (Exod. 32:14).

According to R. Judah bar Simon, the Holy One said to Israel: Your fathers found no lack of consideration in Me, but ye found lack of consideration in Me. I said to them: "Six days ye shall gather manna; but on the seventh day is the Sabbath, in it there shall be no gathering" (Exod. 16:26). But they were not mindful, "And it came to pass on the seventh day, that there went out some of the people to gather, and they found none" (Exod. 16:27). Had they found manna, they would have gathered it.[12]

6. R. Phinehas, citing R. Hoshaia, read the words "They have made others go far[13] from Me" (Jer. 2:5)—that is, in the sense in which Scripture says, "Therefore I chased him from me" (Neh. 13:28), they chased away [and made go far from Me] those who would have returned to Me.

7. *And have walked after things of nought, and are become nought* (Jer. 2:5). In comment on this verse, R. Isaac told the parable of a banker's son against whom a due bill was issued. The banker's son was terrified, saying, "This due bill may be for a hundred gold pieces or even two hundred gold pieces." Thereupon the creditor said to him: Do not be afraid: it is a due bill

11. In Hebrew, *morim* plural of *moreh*, "fool, moron." JV: *ye rebels*.

12. Out of His consideration for the children of Israel, He did not put temptation in their way.

13. A reading made possible by a slight change in vowels.

for no more than a measure of bran or of barley, and anyway, whatever it is, it has already been paid [and amounts to nothing]. So, too, the Holy One said to Israel: My children, whatever idols you passionately follow are not things of substance. "They are nought, a work of delusion," etc. (Jer. 10:15). *Not like these is the portion of Jacob; for He is the former of all things, and Israel is the Tribes*[14] *of His inheritance; the Lord of hosts is His name* (Jer. 10:16).

14. MT: *Tribe.*

PISKA 15

SUMMARY

Lament for Jerusalem

Even as God lamented the fall of Adam, so He lamented the fall of Jerusalem (Sec. 1), the city which, when touched by God's hand, was left sitting solitary (Sec. 2). Like a king of flesh-and-blood in mourning, God hung sackcloth over the entrance of His house, extinguished the lamps, kept silent, turned the couches upside down, rent His purple garment, and sat down to lament (Sec. 3). Blaming Himself for Jerusalem's fall, He refused to be comforted (Sec. 4).

Neglect of study of Torah was the ultimate cause for God's destruction of Jerusalem. Though God tends to be lenient with regard to idolatry, unchastity, or even bloodshed, He refuses to be lenient when Jews forsake the study of Torah because its inner force is such as to bring Jews back to Him. Indeed, when Jewish children study Torah, it provides such strength that no nation is able to take on the Jewish people in battle (Sec. 5).

The word *How*, taken as an outcry, in *How is the faithful city become a harlot* (Isa. 1:21), is construed by one commentator as a sharp reproach and by another as a lament (Sec. 6).

As proof of Jerusalem's degradation, incidents of murder, dishonesty, and venal behavior of princes and judges are set forth (Secs. 7–9). God promises nevertheless to remain *The mighty one of Israel* (Isa. 1:24) to deal with Israel's adversaries, and even to restore to life Moses, Aaron, and David when Zion is redeemed (Secs. 10–11).

PISKA 15

'Eykah, "How" (Lam. 1:1).[1]

1. R. Abbahu, citing R. Jose bar Ḥanina, began his discourse with the verse *But they like man*[2] *have transgressed the covenant; there they have dealt treacherously against Me* (Hos. 6:7). *They like man*—that is, the children of Israel are like the first man of whom the Holy One said: The first man—I brought him into the Garden of Eden, I gave him a command, but he transgressed My command. Thereupon I condemned him to separation, condemned him to banishment, and cried out *'Eykah* in lament over him. I had brought him into the Garden of Eden: "The Lord God took the man, and put him into the Garden of Eden" (Gen. 2:15). And I had commanded him: "The Lord God commanded the man," etc. (Gen. 2:16). But he transgressed my command: "Hast thou eaten of the tree whereof I commanded thee that thou shouldst not eat?" (Gen. 3:11). And so I condemned him to separation: "So He separated the man," etc. (Gen. 3:24). And condemned him to banishment: "Therefore the Lord God banished him from the Garden of Eden" (Gen. 3:23). And uttered a lament over him, as indicated in the verse "The Lord God called unto the man, and said unto him, *'Aykah* ('Where art thou?')" (Gen. 3:9). *'Aykah,* usually spelled *'ayka,* is here spelled with the letter *he'* added at the end,[3] so that the word has the further significance of "How," [a howl, if one dare speak thus of God, expressing the ache of His grief, as in Lamentations 1:1]: "How [solitary He has become]!"

As with Adam, said God, so with his children: I brought them into the Land of Israel, I gave them commands, but they transgressed My commands. Thereupon I condemned them to separation, condemned them to banishment, and uttered a lament over them. I brought them into the Land of Israel: "I brought you into the Land of fruitful fields" (Jer. 2:7); and gave

1. Isa. 1:1–27 is the haftarah of rebuke for *Dĕḇarim,* the third of the three Sabbaths preceding the Fast of the Ninth of Ab. Isa. 1:21 reads *How ('Eykah) is the faithful city become a harlot.*

The transliteration of 'Eḵah as *'Eykah,* here and below, departs from the norm to provide the English reader grasp of the play on words in the Hebrew.

2. JV: *men.* The Hebrew *'Adam,* "man," may be construed as a singular (that is, Adam the first man) or a collective noun.

3. To preserve the norm in transliterating *'ayyekkah,* Leon Nemoy suggests the following rendition: "and said unto him ('where art thou?') (Gen. 3:9). Note that *'ayyekkah* is spelled here with an added *h* at the end, *'ykh,* [in which form it is indistinguishable from *'Eḵah*], showing that God was grieving when He spoke thus to Adam."

them commands: "Command the children of Israel" (Lev. 24:2); but they transgressed My command: "Yea, all Israel have transgressed Thy Torah" (Dan. 9:11). And so having condemned them to separation—"I will separate them out of My house" (Hos. 9:15)—and condemned them to banishment—"Banish them from My sight, and let them go forth" (Jer. 15:1) —God exclaimed, *'Eyḵah,* "How," a howl, [if one dare speak thus of God, expressing the ache of His grief]: "How the city has become solitary" (Lam. 1:1)!

2. R. Abba bar Kahana began his discourse with the verse *I sat not in the assembly of them that make merry, nor rejoiced; I sat solitary because of Thy hand* (Jer. 15:17). The congregation of Israel said to the Holy One: Master of universes, [in obedience to Thee] never have I gone into the theatres and circuses of the nations of the earth, nor have I made merry and rejoiced with them.

[In another interpretation, the words] *I sat solitary because of Thy hand* [are taken to refer to God's punishment of Israel]: When Pharaoh's hand touched me, I was not left sitting solitary. When Sennacherib's hand touched me, I was not left sitting solitary. But when Thy hand touched me, I was left sitting solitary: *How doth the city sit solitary* (Lam. 1:1).

3. Bar Ḳappara began his discourse with the verse *In that day did the Lord, the God of hosts, call to weeping, and to lamentation, and to girding with sackcloth* (Isa. 22:12). The Holy One said to the ministering angels: A king of flesh-and-blood, when in mourning, what does he do? They replied: He hangs sackcloth over the entrance of his house. God said: I will do likewise; "I will clothe the heavens with blackness, and make sackcloth their covering" (Isa. 50:3). Then He asked the angels: A king of flesh-and-blood, when in mourning what else does he do? They replied: He extinguishes the lamps. God said: I will do likewise; "The sun and the moon will become black, and the stars withdraw their shining" (Joel 4:15). Then He asked them: A king of flesh-and-blood when in mourning, what else does he do? They replied: He goes barefoot. God said: I will do likewise; "The Lord in the whirlwind and in the storm will be His way, and the clouds the dust of His feet" (Nahum 1:3). Then He asked them: A king of flesh-and-blood, when in mourning, what else does he do? They replied: He sits and keeps silent. God said: I will do likewise; "He will sit alone and keep silence, because He hath laid it upon Himself" (Lam. 3:28). Then He asked them: A king of flesh-and-blood, when in mourning, what else does he do? They replied: He turns the couches upside down. God said: I will do likewise; "I beheld till [the seats of] thrones were placed right side up"[4] (Dan. 7:9). Then He asked them: A king of flesh-and-blood, when in mourning, what else does he do? They replied: He rends his purple garment. God said: I will

4. Thus implying that previously they had been upside down.

do likewise; "The Lord hath done that which He devised, He rent His wool"[5] (Lam. 2:17). What is meant by "He rent His wool?" That He rent, so said R. Jacob of Kefar Ḥanan, His imperial purple garment. Finally He asked them: A king of flesh-and-blood, when in mourning, what else does he do? They replied: He sits and laments. God said: I will do likewise, *How doth [the Presence] sit solitary*[6] (Lam. 1:1).

4. *Thus saith the Lord of hosts: Consider ye, and call for the mourning women, that they may come*, etc. (Jer. 9:16). R. Johanan, R. Simeon ben Laḳish, and the Rabbis differ in their comments on this verse. R. Johanan told a parable of a king who had two sons. When he became angry at the first, he seized a stick, struck him, and banished him, saying, "Woe to this boy! What a good life is he banished from!" But when he became angry at the second one, he seized a stick, struck him, and likewise banished him: this time, however, the king said, "I am to blame; the upbringing he had from me was bad." So, too, when the Ten Tribes were banished, the Holy One began to recite the verse "Woe unto them! for they have strayed from Me" (Hos. 7:13). But when the Tribes of Judah and Benjamin were banished, the Holy One—if one dare say such a thing—cried out "Woe is Me—the hurt is come from Me" (Jer. 10:19).

R. Simeon ben Laḳish also told a parable of a king who had two sons. When he grew angry at the first, he seized a stick and struck him, and the son shuddered and died. His father went into mourning for him. When the king became angry at the second son, he seized a stick and struck him, and the son shuddered and died. The king then said: I have no strength left to mourn for this one. Call the professional mourning women, and let them mourn for him. So, too, when the Ten Tribes were banished, the Holy One began mourning for them with the verse "Hear ye this word which I take up for a lamentation over you" (Amos 5:1). But when the Tribes of Judah and Benjamin were banished, the Holy One—if one dare say such a thing of Him—cried out: I have no strength left to mourn for these two. Call the professional mourning women, and let them mourn for them. Hence it is written *Call for the mourning women, that they may come*, etc. (Jer. 9:16).

5. JV: *His word*. But Bar Ḳappara takes the Hebrew *'mrh*, "word," to be a variant of the Aramaic *'mr*, "wool."

6. The symbolic meanings of the different forms of God's mourning are explained as follows: (1) The hanging of sackcloth over the door shows that the Temple's destruction keeps converts away; (2) the extinguishing of the lamps shows the diminution of prosperity; (3) the going barefoot shows the weariness of exile and wandering; (4) the sitting in silence shows the cutting off of prophecy; (5) the turning upside down of the couches shows the profanation of God's name; (6) the rending of the purple shows the diminution of wisdom; (7) the sitting solitary shows the loss of Jewish lives as a result of massacre and exile. See *Yĕfeh 'anaf* on Lam. Rabbah 1:1.

The verse does not go on to say, "let them make haste and take up a wailing for them," but says, *take up a wailing for us* (*ibid.*)—for Me, says God, and for them. The verse does not go on further to say, "that their eyes may run down with tears," but says, *that our eyes*—Mine, says God, and theirs—*may run down with tears* (*ibid.*). Nor does the verse go on to say, "and their eyelids gush out with waters," but says, *and our eyelids*— Mine, says God, and theirs—*gush out with waters* (*ibid.*).

The Rabbis told a parable of a king who had twelve sons. When two died, he proceeded to comfort himself with the ten left. When two more died, he comforted himself with the eight left. When two more died, he comforted himself with the six left. When two more died, he comforted himself with the four left. When two more died, he comforted himself with the two left.[7] But when all of them were dead, it was then he began mourning for them all: *How doth* [*the Presence*] *sit solitary* (Lam. 1:1).

5. R. Abba bar Kahana began his discourse with the verse *Who is the wise man, that may understand this? And who is he to whom the mouth of the Lord hath spoken, that he may declare it? Wherefore is the Land perished*, etc. (Jer. 9:11). R. Simeon ben Yoḥai taught in a Baraita: When you see whole villages of people plucked up and removed from their place in the Land of Israel, know that this fate befell them because they failed to provide fees for teachers of Scripture and teachers of Mishnah. And the proof? The verse *Wherefore is the Land perished, and laid waste like a wilderness?* (*ibid.*), words which are followed directly by *The Lord said: Because they have forsaken My Torah*[8] (Jer. 9:12).

R. [Judah II the Patriarch] sent R. Asi and R. Ammi to go and check up on [the teaching of Torah in] the villages of the Land of Israel. On coming into a settlement, they would say, "Bring us the guardians of the settlement." When the commander of the watch or his lieutenant was brought, R. Asi and R. Ammi would say: Are soldiers the guardians of the settlement? Such may well turn out to be the destroyers of the settlement. Who, then, are the true guardians of the settlement? They are the teachers, the teachers of Scripture and teachers of Mishnah who guard the settlement day and night, imparting knowledge of that "Wherein thou art to meditate day and night" (Josh. 1:8). As Scripture says, "Except the Lord build the house, they labor in vain that build it; except the Lord keep the city, the watchman waketh but in vain" (Ps. 127:1).

7. "When two more . . . with the two left"—S.

8. In going on to say *which I have set before them* (*ibid.*) the verse refers to children before whom the Torah was to have been set; in *and have not hearkened to My voice* (*ibid.*) the verse refers to women who should have hearkened; in *and neither walked therein* the verse refers to men who should have both studied and practiced the Torah. So Solomon Jaffe, as cited by David Frankel in his *Šiyyure haḳ-ḳorban*, on P.Ḥag 1:7.

R. Huna and R. Jeremiah, citing R. Samuel bar R. Isaac, said: We find that the Holy One tends to be lenient with regard to idolatry, unchastity, or even bloodshed, but refuses to be lenient when study of Torah is forsaken. Thus when Scripture asks, *Wherefore is the Land perished?* the text does not go on to answer, "Because of idolatry, unchastity, or bloodshed," but, as *The Lord saith, Because they have forsaken My Torah* (Jer. 9:12).

R. Huna and R. Jeremiah, citing R. Ḥiyya bar Abba, said: It is written "Your fathers . . . have forsaken Me and have not kept My Torah" (Jer. 16:11). If only they had kept studying My Torah! Indeed, if they forsook even me, all would turn out well, provided they kept studying My Torah. If they did forsake Me, yet kept on studying My Torah, its inner force, through their engagement with it, would be such as to bring them back to Me.

R. Huna said: Study Torah, even if you do not do so for its own sake. For when you study it, even though not for its own sake, finally, because you are engaged with it, you will have a change of heart and study it for its own sake.

[Of those who do not take up the study of Torah], "R. Joshua ben Levi said: Each and every day a Divine Voice goes forth from Mount Horeb[9] and says, 'Woe unto you, O creatures of God, because of the humiliation Torah suffers from your neglect' " (Ab̲ 6:2).

R. Abba bar Kahana said: Among the nations of the world there had risen no philosophers equal to Balaam son of Beor and Oenomaus of Gadarah.[10] Now when the nations of the earth came to see Oenomaus of Gadarah and asked him, "Can we take on this nation of Israel in battle?" he replied: Go make the round of their synagogues and schools. If you come upon young children singing away within them, you will be unable to take on this people in battle; but if you do not find children singing away, you will be able to take on this people in battle. For what Isaac, one of the Fathers of Israel, declared to his children was this: "Either the voice is the voice of Jacob, or else the hands will be the hands of Esau."[11] (Gen. 27:22). As long as the voice of Jacob sings away in synagogues and in schools, the hands will not be the hands of Esau. But when the voice of Jacob does not sing away in synagogues and in schools, the hands will be the hands of Esau.

[In further comment on the study of Torah], Samuel cited the verse "The host will be set [upon Israel] because of transgression against that which is [to be studied] continually"[12] (Dan. 8:12)—that is, transgression against the Torah. As long as Israel fling words of Torah to the ground,

9. That is, Mount Sinai, the place which had witnessed the revelation.

10. A cynic philosopher of Gadarah, in Palestine, who lived during the reign of the emperor Hadrian (117–38).

11. JV: *The voice is the voice of Jacob, but the hands are the hands of Esau.*

12. JV: *The host was given over to it together with the continual burnt offering through transgression.*

the wicked kingdom [of Rome] will issue decrees and succeed in enforcing its decrees.[13] And the proof? The words "When thou didst fling down truth to the ground, [Rome's host] wrought and prospered" (*ibid.*): here "truth" stands for words of Torah, as in the verse "Buy the truth, and sell it not" (Prov. 23:23).

R. Judah bar Pazzi cited the verse "Israel hath cast off that which is good; the enemy shall pursue him" (Hos. 8:3). By "good," Torah is meant, as in the verse "I give you good doctrine; forsake ye not my teaching" (Prov. 4:2). In this regard, Scripture says, *As stubble devoureth the tongue of fire*[14] (Isa. 5:24). But does stubble devour fire? Is it not the way of fire to devour stubble? How can you say *As stubble devoureth the tongue of fire*? Here, however, *stubble* stands for the house of Esau, which, as in the verse "The house of Esau for stubble" (Ob. 1:18), is likened to stubble. *The tongue of fire* stands for the house of Jacob which, as in the verse "The house of Jacob shall be a fire" (*ibid.*), is likened to fire. The *flame* in the words *And as the chaff consumes the flame*[15] (Isa. 5:24), stands for the house of Joseph, likened to a flame in the verse "And the house of Joseph shall be a flame" (Ob. 1:18). *Their root* in the words *Their root shall be as rottenness* (Isa. 5:24) stands for the Patriarchs, who are Israel's root. *And their blossom shall go up as dust* (Isa. 5:24) stands for the Tribes who are Israel's blossoms. Wherefore such calamities of rottenness and dust upon all Israel? *Because they have rejected the Torah of the Lord of hosts* (Isa. 5:24)—[all of His Torah]. The verse's beginning *Because they have rejected the Torah of the Lord of hosts*—said R. Yudan—refers to the Written Torah; and the verse's conclusion, *and contemned the word of the Holy One of Israel* (*ibid.*), refers to the Oral Torah.

6. *How is the faithful city become a harlot* (Isa. 1:21). R. Judah and R. Nehemiah differ in their comments on this verse. R. Judah said: The word *How* in this verse implies sharp reproach, as in the verse "How dare you say: 'We are wise'?" (Jer. 8:8). But R. Nehemiah said: *How* here, too, implies lamentation, as in "How doth the city sit solitary" (Lam. 1:1), "How in His anger hath He covered Himself with a cloud" (Lam. 2:1), and "How is the gold become dim" (Lam. 4:1).

[Though R. Judah takes Isaiah's exclamation to be a reproach and R. Nehemiah takes it to be a lament, they agree, as the following parable indicates, on what is intimated not only by the verse in hand but also by two

13. The verse goes on to say, *it*—the host set upon Israel—*wrought, and prospered.*

14. JV: *As the tongue of fire devoureth the stubble.* However, the sentence may also be understood as R. Judah suggests, since in the Hebrew text *stubble* precedes *tongue of fire* without the usual article *'et* indicating which is the subject and which is the object.

15. JV: *And as the chaff is consumed in the flame.* Here, too, R. Judah's rendition is possible.

other verses, all three beginning with the word "How" and each one addressed to the people who were to dwell in Jerusalem]: A noblewoman [at three successive times in her life] was observed by three representatives of her family. One of them beheld her during the time of her prosperity, another beheld her during the time of her harlotry, and a third beheld her during the time of her degradation. Likewise, Moses saw Israel during the time of her prosperity: "How can I myself bear up under the weight of your prosperity?" (Deut. 1:12). Isaiah saw her during the time of her harlotry: "How is the faithful city become a harlot" (Isa. 1:21). Jeremiah saw her in the time of her degradation: "How doth the city sit solitary" (Lam. 1:1).

7. *How is the faithful city become a harlot!* (Isa. 1:21)—become a city of lewd revelry, brazen and strident. R. Phinehas, citing R. Hoshaia, said sadly: In Jerusalem in times past there were 480[16] synagogues, and each and every one of them had a school for younger students and a school for older students—a school for younger students learning Scripture, and a school for older students studying Mishnah; all of these schools, when Vespasian came up [into Jerusalem], he destroyed. Of this destruction of the synagogues and schools, it is written: "He took away the covering of Judah, and thou didst look [in vain] that day to the armor shielding the house of the forest"[17] (Isa. 22:8), [the "house of the forest," meaning the Temple which was made of cedar of the forests of Lebanon].

[*How is the faithful city become a harlot*], *she that was full* [*of the study*] *of law!* (Isa. 1:21) such as the Mishnah of R. Ḥiyya, the Mishnah of R. Hoshaia, and the Mishnah of Bar Ḳappara.[18]

Righteousness lodged in her (Isa. 1:21). R. Yudan bar R. Simon said: No man who lodged in Jerusalem for a full day could stay possessed of sin. How so? The morning offering made expiation for transgressions committed in the nighttime; and the offering at dusk made expiation for transgressions committed in the daytime. No matter what, no man who lodged in Jerusalem for a full day could stay in possession of sin. And why not? Because *Righteousness lodged in her.*

But now murderers (Isa. 1:21) are abroad in her, murderers who slew Uriah,[19] who slew Zechariah.[20] R. Yudan asked R. Aḥa: In what part of the Temple's Court did they slay Zechariah—in the Court of Israelites or in the Court of Women? R. Aḥa replied: Neither in the Court of Israelites nor

16. R. Phinehas apparently derives the number from the numerical value of *mlty*, "full" in Isaiah's assertion that Jerusalem *was full* [*of the study*] *of the Law* (Isa. 1:21). See *Minḥat̠ šay* and Lam. Rabbah *Pĕt̠iḥta* 12.

17. See Piska 15.5.

18. All these are collections of Baraitas and Toseftas.

19. "Uriah"—O_1, Pa; O: "Uriah the Priest." See Jer. 26:23.

20. "Zechariah, the son of Jehoiada, was a priest who flourished during the reign of Joash, king of Judah. On account of his stern denunciation of idolaters a

in the Court of Women, but in the Court of Priests. Nay more: they did not do with his blood what one does with the blood of a slain hind, the blood of a slain stag, or the blood of a slain bird. With regard to the blood of such animals, it is written "Whatsoever man there be of the children of Israel, or of the strangers that sojourn among them, that taketh in hunting any beast or fowl that may be eaten, he shall pour out the blood thereof, and cover it with dust" (Lev. 17:13). In Jerusalem, however, "The blood she has shed remains in the midst of her: it is set upon the bare rock; it is not poured upon the ground, to cover it with dust" (Ezek. 24:7). And why was the blood left uncovered? "That it might cause fury to come up, that vengeance might be taken: on this account, I have set the blood upon the bare rock, that it should not be covered" (Ezek. 24:8).

On that day Israel—[through the one act of slaying Zechariah]—committed seven transgressions: they slew a man who was priest, prophet, and judge; they shed innocent blood; they profaned God's name; they polluted the Temple Court, all of these transgressions on the Day of Atonement, a Sabbath at that. When Nebuzaradan came up [to the Temple], the blood [on the Temple rock] began to seethe, and he asked: "What sort of blood is this that seethes?" The priests replied: "The blood of bullocks, lambs, and rams which we offered upon the altar." At once he had men fetch bullocks, rams, and lambs which he slaughtered beside Zechariah's blood. [The animals' blood did not seethe, but] Zechariah's kept on seething. Since the priests had not disclosed the truth to Nebuzaradan, he suspended them from a torturer's scaffold. Then they said to him: Since God is determined to demand punishment from us for this blood, know that it is the blood of a priest, prophet, and judge. It was he who predicted to us all the evil things that you are doing: nevertheless, we rose up and slew him.

At once Nebuzaradan took eighty thousand young priests and slew them one by one over Zechariah's blood until the stream of their blood reached Zechariah's grave. And the proof? The verse "[The foes] broke all bounds, as blood touched blood"[21] (Hos. 4:2). And still Zechariah's blood kept seething. Thereupon Nebuzaradan rebuked it, saying, "What can make you stop seething?[22] What do you want? Shall I, on your account, cause all your

---

conspiracy was formed against him, and he was stoned in the Temple Court at the king's command—2 Chron. 24:20–22. In his dying words he called for vengeance." See B.Sanh 96 b, Soncino tr., p. 651, n. 9; and Rashi on Jer. 2:30.

21. Apparently, since killing—"swearing and killing" (Hos. 4:2a)—is already mentioned in the first part of the verse, the latter part is considered as "available" for allusion to Nebuzaradan.

22. At the suggestion of Leon Nemoy the word *sb* is taken as the imperative of *nsb*, "take, withdraw, stop [seething]."

people to perish?" At that moment, the Holy One, filled with compassion, said: If this man, a cruel being of flesh-and-blood, here today and tomorrow no more, is filled with compassion for My children, all the more so should I be, I, of whom it is written "The Lord thy God is a merciful God; He will not fail thee, neither destroy thee" (Deut. 4:31). Thereupon the Holy One signaled to Zechariah's blood, and then and there it was absorbed into the earth.

8. *Thy silver is become dross, thy wine mixed with water* (Isa. 1:22). At one time coins made of silver were current. As tricksters grew numerous, however, coins made of copper but silvered over were put into use, so that when a man went to a silversmith [for currency], he was apt to hear him mutter to his apprentice, "Copper it for him." So, too, when a man would go to buy a pint of wine at a wine dealer's, he was apt to hear him mutter to his clerk, "Water it for him." Hence it is written *Thy silver is become dross* just as *thy wine is mixed with water.*

9. *Thy princes are rebels* [*against the order they are presumed to represent*], *and companions of thieves* (Isa. 1:23). Bar Ḳappara said: As chiefs of bands of brigands, the princes provided arms for lawless men. *Thy princes are rebels* against the law: every one of them loved stolen goods. *And companions of thieves*: every one of them associated with thieves. R. Berechiah told the story of a woman whose kettle was stolen. When she went to a judge to report the matter, she found her kettle sitting on the judge's stove. Another story is told of a man whose cloak was stolen. When he went to report the matter to a judge, he found his cloak spread out on the judge's couch.

R. Levi told the story of a woman who presented a silver lamp to a judge. Thereupon her opponent in the suit went and presented him with a foal made of gold. The next day the woman found that the judgment which had been issued in her favor was reversed. She said: "My lord, should not the previous judgment in my favor shine before you like a silver lamp." He replied: "What's to be done? The foal has overturned the lamp." Of such it is written *Every one loveth bribes* (Isa. 1:23)—every one of them has larceny in his heart. *And followeth after payments* (*ibid.*)—you scratch my back and I'll scratch yours.[23] *They judge not the fatherless, neither doth the cause of the widow come unto them* (*ibid.*). R. Eleazar and R. Johanan comment on this verse. R. Eleazar said: In Jerusalem in Isaiah's days it was customary for a man to appoint guardians to take care of his children after his death. When the man died, his widow would demand from the children her due according to the terms of her marriage contract. Then, if the widow and the children had to go to a judge about the matter, the judge was usually suspect of being

23. Literally "you pay me and I'll pay you."

in collusion with the guardians of the estate. R. Johanan said: In times past when a man would go up to Jerusalem to plead a lawsuit, the judge would say, "Split a couple of logs for me," "Fill a couple of casks of water for me," [and so on]. While the man was doing such chores, his money ran out, and he would have to leave Jerusalem with a broken spirit. When a widow happened to meet him on the way and asked him, "How did your lawsuit come out?" he would reply, "My money ran out, and I got nowhere at all." The widow would then say, "If this person, who is a man, got nowhere at all with his case, all the more certain will I, who am a widow, get nowhere with mine." Thus were fulfilled literally the words *They judged not the fatherless, nor doth the cause of the widow come unto them* (*ibid.*).

10. *Therefore saith the Lord ('aḏon), the Lord of hosts, the Mighty One of Israel* (Isa. 1:24). R. Samuel bar Naḥman declared: Wherever Scripture says "[24]the Lord (*'aḏon*)," the implication of *'aḏon* in the context is that God is about to uproot the inhabitants of a place and bring in other inhabitants in their stead. The general principle is established by the verse "Behold, the Ark of the covenant of the Lord (*'aḏon*) of all the earth passeth on before you over the Jordan" (Josh. 3:11). Thereupon, as the narrative goes on, God uprooted the Canaanites and brought in the Israelites.

Nevertheless, [though the Lord was to uproot Israel], God remained *The Mighty One of Israel* (Isa. 1:24). R. Tanḥum bar Ḥanil'ai explained: [Once He had spent His wrath against Israel], the Mighty One remained Israel's. The Rabbis said, however: [Though He had uprooted Israel, He continued to declare them His own] to the very faces of the nations of the earth; thus He remained the Mighty One of Israel.

11. *Ah, I will ease Me of Mine adversaries, and avenge Me of Mine enemies* (Isa. 1:24). R. Judah and R. Nehemiah differ in their comments on this verse, [both agreeing, however, that by *adversaries* and *enemies* not the children of Israel but the nations of the earth are meant]. R. Judah said of God and His adversaries: Say a man had ten gold coins, and an adversary of his came[25] and got around him and made off with the coins, so, [as the former would be inclined to do], the Holy One pledges, "I must requite the man who took them,[26] and wreak vengeance upon him."

R. Nehemiah, [identifying the adversaries as the four kingdoms], said: The words *I will ease Me of My adversaries* imply two enemies; and the words *and avenge Me of Mine enemies* imply two more enemies—hence the four kingdoms.[27]

24. The word "Saith" is omitted as in S and Yalḳuṭ.

25. O_1 reads *'th* which, in the translation, is taken to be a variant spelling of *'t'*, "came."

26. The Ten Tribes.

27. Babylonia, Media, Greece, and Rome. See Dan. 7:17 ff.

And I will restore [*to life*] *thy judges as at the first, and thy counselors as at the beginning*, etc. (Isa. 1:26). The words *I will restore* [*to life*] *thy judges as at the first* refer to Moses and Aaron; and the words *thy counselors as at the beginning* to David and Solomon. *Afterward thou shalt be called the city of righteousness*, etc. (*ibid.*). *Zion shall be redeemed with justice, and they that return of her with righteousness* (Isa. 1:27).

PISKA 16

SUMMARY

The certainty of God's comforting

If Boaz' words succeeded in comforting Ruth, then when God comes to comfort Jerusalem, saying *Comfort ye, comfort ye, My people* (Isa. 40:1), He will surely succeed (Sec. 1). He will speak to the heart of Jerusalem because the heart is the seat of all action (Sec. 2). Indeed, it was Jerusalem's heart which inspired her misdeeds—misdeeds which God sought to prevent by sending Prophets to warn Israel; by having myriads of angels with crowns to crown Israel descend with Him on Sinai; by giving Israel the booty of nations; by providing six meeting places with Israel; by miracles performed in Israel's behalf; by giving the name Zion to Israel, a name which, meaning "sign," sets her apart from all other peoples. Accordingly, since the breach caused by Israel's misdeeds is so great, only God will be able to heal it and bring comfort to Jerusalem (Sec. 3).

God will comfort Jerusalem through a great prophet, Isaiah, to whom the words *Thou hast loved righteousness* (Ps. 45:8) apply. Isaiah will prophesy as from the mouth of the Divine Power, with a double portion of the Divine Power (Sec. 4). God will speak kind and comforting words to Israel as Joseph spoke to the hearts of his brothers, and, like Joseph, He will succeed in comforting Jerusalem (Sec. 5). And if Job who sinned was eventually given a double recompense, so Jerusalem will eventually be given a double recompense of comfort: *Comfort ye, comfort ye, My people* (Sec. 6).

The disasters that befell Israel were of such a kind as to invite comfort from others who have suffered disaster, so that the Ten Tribes, banished first, and the Tribe of Judah, banished next, comforted each other (Sec. 7).

When God sent the Prophets to comfort Israel, the words they uttered turned out to be contradictory, so that Zion retorted to each of the Prophets, "Keep your comforting to yourself." When the Prophets told God: "We sought to comfort Zion, but she would not heed," God replied: "Come with Me. You and I shall go to her and comfort her" (Sec. 8). According to another comment, God Himself required comforting.

Moses' mode of arguing with God after the incident of the golden calf is cited by way of emphasizing the idea that Israel are for ever God's people and that He is to be their comforter (Sec. 9). Through Isaiah He came to comfort all the generations (Sec. 10): He will comfort them by the very parts of the body with which they sinned and by the very words which Israel used at the time they sinned and were smitten (Sec. 11).

PISKA 16

Comfort ye, comfort ye My people (Isa. 40:1).[1]

1. *Shall mortal man act more justly than God? Shall a man outshine his Maker?*[2] (Job 4:17)—can mere man be more just than his Creator? Shall a man's comforting outshine his Maker's? By these words the Holy One meant: Boaz comforted, and shall I not—shall I not, at the very least—comfort as effectively? Boaz began to comfort Ruth by saying *It hath been told and told me* (Ruth 2:11). Why did he use *told* twice? Because he meant: Your good conduct in the house has been told me, and your good conduct in the field has been told me. And Boaz continued: It has been told *what*[3] *thou didst for thy mother-in-law even after the death of thy husband* (*ibid.*)—and need I speak of what you did for her while your husband was still alive? It has been told *how thou didst leave thy father and thy mother* (*ibid.*), your own flesh and blood; and how you did leave the *land of thy nativity* (*ibid.*), your own home. On the other hand, by the words *thy father and thy mother* Boaz may have meant that Ruth forsook idolatry, the words being thus understood as in the verse "Who say to a stock: 'Thou art my father,' and to a stone: 'Thou hast brought us forth' " (Jer. 2:27). By the words *the land of thy native ways* (Ruth 2:11) Boaz meant further that Ruth forsook the ways to which she was accustomed.[4] And in saying *thou art come unto a people which a short time ago thou wouldst not have been permitted to know*[5] (*ibid.*), Boaz meant: Had you come a short time ago, we could not have accepted you as a proselyte because the new interpretation of the law concerning proselytes had not yet been established, the new interpretation being as follows: "An Ammonite man may not marry an Israelite woman, but an Ammonite woman [who has been converted] may marry an Israelite. A Moabite man may not marry an Israelite woman, but a Moabite woman [who has been converted] may marry an Israelite."[6] [And Boaz said further to Ruth]: *The Lord recompense thy work* (Ruth 2:12), by which he meant, "He who gives recompense to the righteous will give you your recompense." *And thy reward will be complete* (*šlmh*) (*ibid.*), the

1. In the seven-Sabbath cycle of consolation, Isa. 40:1–26 is the haftarah for *Wa'ethannan*, the first Sabbath following the Ninth of Ab.
2. JV: *Shall mortal man be just before God? Shall a man be pure before his Maker?* Apparently the commentator construes *ṭhr*, "pure," as though written *zhr*, "outshine."
3. MT: *All.*
4. Pa: *pmly'*; O: *'prkyh.*
5. JV: *and art come unto a people that thou knewest not heretofore.*
6. See Yeb 8:3; and MTeh 1:1. Ruth came from Moab.

word *šlmh* hinting, so taught R. Jose, that Solomon (Šlmh)[7] will descend from you. Boaz went on to say to Ruth: [Your reward will come] *from the Lord, the God of Israel, under whose wings thou art come to take refuge* (*ibid.*). According to Scripture, taught R. Abin, the earth has wings, the morning star has wings, the sun has wings, the cherubim have wings, the creatures of the chariot have wings, the seraphim have wings. And the proof that the earth has wings? The verse *From under the wing of the earth have we heard songs* (Isa. 24:16). Proof that the morning star has wings? The verse *If I take the wings of the morning* (Ps. 139:9). Proof that the sun has wings? The verse *But unto you that fear My name shall the sun of righteousness arise with healing in its wings* (Mal. 3:20). Proof that the cherubim have wings? The verse *And the sound of the wings of the cherubim* (Ezek. 10:5). Proof that the creatures of the chariot have wings? The verse *The noise of the wings of the living creatures* (Ezek. 3:13). Proof that the seraphim have wings? The verse *Above Him stood the seraphim; each one had six wings* (Isa. 6:2). Great is the power of those who do deeds of kindness—R. Abin went on to say—for they are given refuge not merely under the wings of the earth, not merely under the wings of the morning star, not merely under the wings of the sun, not merely under the wings of the cherubim, not merely under the wings of the creatures of the chariot, not merely under the wings of the seraphim. In the shadow of whose wings, then, are they given their greatest refuge? In the shadow of the wings of the Holy One: *The God of Israel under whose wings thou art come to take refuge*[8] (Ruth 2:12). Of this refuge, Scripture says, *Precious is the lovingkindness ordained by Thee, O God! Because of it, the children of men take refuge in the shadow of Thy wings* (Ps. 36:8).

Then Ruth answered Boaz: *I have surely found favor in thy sight, my lord: for that thou hast comforted me, and for that thou has spoken to the heart of thy maidservant* (Ruth 2:13). "Heaven forbid! *No,*"[9] *said Boaz* (Ruth 2:14), "speak not of yourself as a maidservant—you are counted among the Maidriarchs."[10]

Now does it not follow that if Boaz, speaking kind words, comforting

7. Since the text had already stated *The Lord recompense thy work*, why add *and thy reward will be complete?* The commentator concludes that the added words intimate an additional and extraordinary gift to Ruth, namely, that among her descendants was to be Solomon ("the complete one") in whose days Israel's glory was "complete." See PR 15, Preamble (YJS, *18*, 302).

8. "*The God of Israel . . . take refuge*"—Pa.

9. Since the word *lh*, "to her," is spelled exceptionally without the *mappiḳ*, it is construed as though spelled *l'*, "no." Cf. Rashi on Num. 32:42; and Ruth Rabbah 2:13.

10. In the Hebrew there is a play on *'amahot*, "maidservants," and *'immahot*, "Matriarchs."

words, to the heart of Ruth succeeded in comforting her, surely when the Holy One comes to comfort Jerusalem, and says *Comfort ye, comfort ye, My people* (Isa. 40:1), He will succeed in comforting her?

2. *I spoke with my own heart, saying: Lo, I have gotten great wisdom, more also than all that were before me,* etc. (Eccles. 1:16). According to Scripture, the heart can see, the heart can hear, the heart can speak, the heart can know, the heart can stand, the heart can fall, the heart can walk, the heart can cry out, the heart can be glad, and the heart can be comforted. The proof that the heart can see? The verse *Yea, my heart had seen much experience* (*ibid.*). Proof that the heart can speak? The verse *I spoke with my own heart* (*ibid.*). Proof that the heart can know? The verse *The heart knoweth its own bitterness* (Prov. 14:10). Proof that the heart can hear? The verse *Give thy servant therefore a heart that hears* (1 Kings 3:9). Proof that the heart can stand? The verse *Can thy heart stand and endure, or can thy hands be strong?* (Ezek. 22:14). Proof that the heart can fall? The verse *Let no man's heart fall*[11] *within him* (1 Sam. 17:32). Proof that the heart can walk? The verse *And he said unto him: "Went not my heart* [*with thee*]*?"* (2 Kings 5:26). Proof that the heart can cry out? The verse *Their heart cried unto the Lord* (Lam. 2:18). Proof that the heart can be glad? The verse *Therefore my heart is glad, and my glory rejoiceth* (Ps. 16:9). Proof that the heart can be comforted? The verse *Comfort ye, comfort ye My people. Speak ye comfortably to the heart of Jerusalem* (Isa. 40:1, 2).

3. *By what means* [*other than those I employed*] *could I have forewarned thee* [*of the coming of a time when thou wouldst be in dire need of comforting*]*? What other circumstances favoring thee over other nations could I have brought about* [*for thy comforting*]*?*[12] (Lam. 2:13). By what additional means might I have given thee warning? By how many more Prophets could I have warned thee? According to R. Isaac,[13] every day there was a prophet who warned Israel in the morning and a prophet who warned Israel at dusk, for it is written *The Lord forewarned Israel and Judah, by the hand of every prophet* [*who received the word by day*], *and of every seer* [*who saw visions at night*][14] (2 Kings 17:13). According to R. Nathan, every day there were two such Prophets in the morning and two

11. JV: *fail.*

12. JV: *What shall I take to witness for thee, what shall I liken to thee.* But *'ydk*, "take to witness for thee," may also mean "forewarn thee"; and *'dmk*, "liken to thee," may be extended to "what other circumstances favoring thee over other nations," etc.

13. "R. Isaac"—Pa; O: "R. [Judah the Prince]."

14. "*who saw visions at night*"—David Luria on Lam. Rabbah 2:13. Cf. Job 4:13.

The words "The *kĕṯiḇ* is 'all manner of Prophets,' " which follow in O, are deleted in accordance with O_1, S, and Pa.

such Prophets at dusk. For Scripture says, *I have sent unto you . . . the Prophets . . . betimes and often* (Jer. 7:25)—thus two in the morning; and says again *The Prophets, whom I send unto you . . . betimes and often* (Jer. 26:5)—thus two at dusk.

In another comment, the verse in Lamentations is taken to mean *With what other ornaments*[15] *might I have adorned thee?* (Lam. 2:13). With how many more ornaments could I have adorned thee, [O Israel]? For, as R. Johanan said, the day the Holy One went down to Sinai to give the Torah to Israel, there came down with Him sixty myriads of ministering angels and in the hand of every one of them was a crown to adorn each man in Israel.

R. Abba bar Kahana said in the name of R. Johanan: Twice sixty myriads of angels! One to set a crown upon each Israelite, and the other to gird him with a corselet of armor.

R. Huna Rabba of Sepphoris said: [Not with corselets of armor, but] with girdles of magistracy, as in the verse *He looseth the bond of kings, and bindeth their loins with a girdle* (Job 12:18).[16]

In another comment, the verse is read *What more booty*[17] *might I have given thee?* (Lam. 2:13). Have I not already given thee many booties—the booty of Egypt, the booty of the Red Sea, the booty of Sihon and Og, and the booty of the thirty-one kings of Canaan?

In another comment, the verse is read *Where else might I have met thee?*[18] (*ibid.*). In how many places did I meet with thee, [O Israel]!—in the Tent of Meeting in the wilderness, in Gilgal, in Shiloh, in Nob, in Gibeon, and twice in the eternal Habitation [in Jerusalem]. *What other circumstances favoring thee over other nations could I have brought about [for thy comforting]?* (*ibid.*). What other people have I treated like thee? What other people did I redeem with a mighty hand and bring ten plagues upon its enemies? For what other people did I divide the sea? For what other people did I sweep quail inland from the sea? What other people did I bring near to Mount Sinai and give My Torah to? What other people did I surround with clouds of glory? *O daughter Jerusalem* (*ibid.*)—O daughter, thy very name, which is made from *Jeru* (fear) and *salem* (peace) bids thee to fear Me and thus be at peace with Me.[19] [But since thou dost not fear Me], *how can I*

15. By metathesis *ʾʿydk*, "forewarn thee," is read as though written *ʾʿdyk*, "ornament thee."

16. Cf. PR 20:7.

17. *ʾʿydk*, previously rendered "forewarn" and "ornament," is now construed as though derived from *ʿd*, "booty."

18. *ʾʿydk*, previously rendered "forewarn," "ornament," and "booty" is now interpreted as though derived from *yd*, "to meet."

19. *Jeru* from *yrʾ*, "fear," and *salem* from *šlwm*, "peace."

e reconciled with thee[20] *and comfort thee, O virgin daughter whose name* *ion* [*indicates that you are to bear a sign, ṣywn*] (*ibid.*): O sons of Israel, ou who for My sake are to bear the sign of circumcision; the sign, upon ead and face, of hair unshaved;[21] the sign of fringes on the corners of your arments? For only when I am reconciled with thee—so R. Jacob bar Abuna nterpreted the verse *How can I be reconciled,* etc.—will I comfort thee. *But las, thy breach is great like the sea; only He can heal thee* (*ibid.*). Only He, aid R. Ḥilfai, who can heal the breach of the sea can heal thee.[22] R. Joshua ar R. Nehemiah said: He whom you extolled at the Red Sea with the words *Vho is like unto Thee?* (Exod. 15:11), He can heal thee. R. Abin read the onclusion of the verse from Lamentations as a question: Who can heal hee? *Such prophets* [*as*] *have seen visions for thee of vanity and delusion* Lam. 2:14)? And the Rabbis asked pointedly: Who can heal such prophets or thee?

4. [Yet there were two men among you, O Israel—Abraham and Isaiah —to each of whom I could say], *Thou hast loved righteousness, and hated vickedness; therefore God, thy God, hath anointed thee with the oil of gladness above thy fellows* (Ps. 45:8), [and given thee the power to bring comfort and healing to them]. It was R. Azariah, who citing R. Aḥa, nterpreted the Psalm, to begin with, as alluding to our father Abraham, and said, You find that before the Holy One brought a flood [of fire] upon the Sodomites, our father Abraham spoke up to the Holy One: Master of universes, Thou didst swear that Thou wouldst not bring again a flood to the world, as is said *I have sworn that the waters of Noah should no more go over the earth* (Isa. 54:9). Now, though Thou art not bringing on a flood of water, wilt Thou bring on a flood of fire? Dost Thou thus intend cunningly to evade Thine own oath? *That were a profanation for Thee to do after this manner* (Gen. 18:25); and Abraham went on to say, *The Judge of all the earth cannot exercise justice too strictly*[23] (*ibid.*). If Thou seekest strict justice, there will be no world, and if Thou seekest to have a world, strict justice cannot be exercised. Dost Thou think to take hold of the rope at both ends? Thou desirest Thy world, and Thou desirest true justice also. If Thou wilt not relent a little, the world will not endure. The Holy One replied to Abraham: *Thou hast loved righteousness, and hated wickedness* (Ps. 45:8) —thou hast loved making out My creatures to be righteous and hast hated making them out to be wicked. *Therefore God, thy God, hath anointed thee*

20. JV: *What shall I equal to thee?* But see Saul Lieberman's interpretation of the word *šwh* cited in PRKM, p. 267.

21. See Lev. 19:27.

22. The waters of the sea will be made sweet. See PR 33:12, and Exod. Rabbah 15:22.

23. JV: *shall not the Judge of all the earth do justly?*

with the oil of gladness[24] *above thy fellow creatures* (*ibid.*). What did God mean by *above thy fellow creatures*? In using these words, the Holy One meant: From the time I spoke to Noah to the time of My speaking to thee, I have spoken to no other creature of Mine. But with thee I make a new beginning of speaking: *After these things the word of the Lord came unto Abram* (Gen. 15:1).[25]

It was again R. Azariah, who now citing R. Judah bar R. Simon, interpreted the Psalm as alluding to Isaiah and said that Isaiah declared: As I walked about in my house of study, *I heard the voice of the Lord, saying: "Whom shall I send, and who will go for us?* etc. (Isa. 6:8). When I sent Amos, the children of Israel mockingly called him 'Tongue-heavy.' (Indeed, as R. Phinehas pointed out, his name, *Amos*, signifies tongue-heavy, *'amus*). Israel said derisively of My choice that the Holy One had set aside all the other children of men and caused His presence to dwell on none other than this Tongue-heavy, this man with a leaden tongue. And when I sent them Micah, they smote him[26] upon the cheek, as is said 'They smite the reprover of Israel with a rod upon the cheek' (Micah 4:14). Now *whom shall I send, and who will go for Me?*" (Isa. 6:8). Then Isaiah replied: "*Here am I; send me*" (*ibid.*). The Holy One warned him: "Isaiah, My children are obstinate, troublesome. Art thou willing to be smitten and put to shame by them?" Isaiah replied: "Even if such be my portion, *I am ready to give my back to the smiters, and my cheeks to them that pluck off the hair* (Isa. 50:6). But am I worthy of going to Thy children on a mission of Thine?" The Holy One then answered: Isaiah, *Thou hast loved righteousness* (Ps. 45:8), thou hast loved to make out My children to be righteous; *and hated wickedness* (*ibid.*), hated to make them out wicked. *Therefore God,* [*I*] *thy God, have Myself anointed thee with the oil of gladness above thy fellows* (*ibid.*). What is meant by *above thy fellows*? In using these words, the Holy One meant: As thou livest, all Prophets who prophesied before thee began to prophesy only through another prophet. As Scripture tells, *The spirit of Elijah rested on Elisha* (2 Kings 2:15); the spirit of Moses rested on the seventy elders, *The Lord . . . took of the spirit that was on him, and put it upon the seventy elders* (Num. 11:25). But thou alone wilt prophesy as from the mouth of the Divine Power, so that thou canst say, *The spirit of the Lord God is upon me; because the Lord hath anointed me* (Isa. 61:1). Nay more: all other

24. Words of prophecy are gladness. Cf. Jer. 15:16.

25. In a direct vision and not in a dream in the night or through the holy spirit, as earlier when *the Lord said unto Abram: Get thee out of thy country*, etc. (Gen. 12:1). See Naḥmanides on Gen. 12:7, and Maimonides, *Guide* (Eng. tr. Pines [Chicago, 1963], pp. 395 ff), 2:45.

26. Apparently the commentator construes "Micah" as *Mucah (Mukkeh)*, "one who is smitten." Cf. Piska 33:3.

Prophets who prophesied used single terms in their prophecies; but thou wilt prophesy in double terms [thus revealing that thou prophesiest with a double portion of the Divine Power]: *Awake, awake* (Isa. 51:9); *Awake, awake* (Isa. 51:17); *Rejoicing, I will rejoice* (Isa. 61:10); *I, even I* (Isa. 51:12); *Comfort ye, comfort ye My people* (Isa. 40:1).[27]

5. [Israel in its hope of being comforted pleaded with God]: *Oh, that Thou wert like a brother to me!* (Song 8:1). How like a brother? Like Cain to Abel? But Cain slew Abel. Like Ishmael to Isaac? But Ishmael hated Isaac. Like Esau to Jacob? But Esau hated Jacob. Like Joseph's brothers to Joseph? No, Joseph's brothers hated Joseph. Rather the other way around—like Joseph to his brothers. After all the evil things they did to him, what, according to Scripture, do you find Joseph saying? *"Now therefore, fear ye not, I will sustain you and your little ones." And he comforted them by speaking to their hearts* (Gen. 50:21). He said to them—so taught R. Simlai—You are the head, and I the body. Once the head is removed, what good the body? He went on to say: You, the Tribes of Israel, have been likened [in number] to the dust of the earth, the sand of the sea, and the stars in heaven. Would I go wage war against any of these? If I could prevail against these, I might then hope to prevail against you. But since I cannot prevail against these, I cannot prevail against you. He continued: Shall I set myself up as my father's adversary? What my father begot, am I to bury? Or as adversary of the Holy One? What He has blessed, am I to cut down with the sword? He went on: You, my brothers, are part of the order of the universe—twelve hours in a day, twelve hours in a night, twelve months in the year, twelve signs in the Zodiac, Twelve Tribes of Israel[28]—dare I annihilate one of the twelves that belong to the order of the universe?

Joseph said further: Before you came down to Egypt, the Egyptians treated me like a slave. But once you came down here to Egypt, you made known my honorable lineage.[29] If I kill you now, the Egyptians will say, "Joseph chanced upon some gang of young men and declared, 'These are my brothers.' Anyone can see for himself that Joseph lied,[30] since after a short time he found some pretext against them and killed them."

Joseph went on to reassure his brothers still more: "Besides, if I kill you now, the Egyptians will say: 'Joseph did not keep faith with his own broth-

27. Isaiah was thus given primogeniture, so to speak, as a prophet. See Benjamin Uffenheimer, "The Consecration of Isaiah," *Scripta Hierosolymitana* (Jerusalem, 1971), *22*, 236–38. But cf. PR 29/30A:5 (YJS, *18*, 576), n. 21, which suggests that at the time Isaiah was in a trance.

28. Cf. PR 4:1.

29. The word "He said further" in O is deleted in accordance with Pa.

30. Literally "that it was so."

ers. Is he likely, then, to keep faith with us?' " It was because of Joseph' concern for his brothers that Scripture declares: *He comforted them b speaking to their hearts*[31] (Gen. 50:21). Now does it not follow that i Joseph, who spoke persuasive, comforting words, to the hearts of his broth ers, succeeded in comforting them, surely the Holy One will succeed whe He comes to comfort Jerusalem, *When your God will say, Comfort ye comfort ye My people*? (Isa. 40:1).

6. [The words that Jeremiah uses of Israel and her suffering are muc the same as those used of Job and his suffering; hence what is intended b the parallels that follow is reassurance of Israel that as the outcome for Jo was comfort for his suffering, so the outcome for Israel will be comfort fo her suffering]: *All thy lovers have forgotten thee,* [*O Israel*], *they seek thee not; for I have wounded thee with the wound of an enemy* (Jer. 30:14) The words *the wound of an enemy* (*'wyb*), however, are to be read *the wounds of Job* (*'ywb*). Of Job it is written *The Chaldeans set themselves in three bands* (Job 1:17); and of Jerusalem it is written *The city is given into the hand of the Chaldeans* (Jer. 32:24). Of Job it is written *A fire of God is fallen from heaven* (Job 1:16); and of Jerusalem it is written *From on high He sent fire into my bones, and it prevaileth against them* (Lam. 1:13). Of Job it is written *And he took him a potsherd* (Job 2:8); and of Jerusalem it is written *The precious sons of Zion . . . how are they esteemed as earthen pitchers!* (Lam. 4:2). Of Job it is written *So they sat down with him upon the ground* (Job 2:13); and of Jerusalem it is written *They sit upon the ground, and keep silence* (Lam. 2:10). Of Job it is written *I have sewed sackcloth upon my skin* (Job 16:15); and of Jerusalem it is written *They have girded themselves with sackcloth* (Lam. 2:10). Of Job it is written *And have laid my horn in the dust* (Job 16:15); and of Jerusalem it is written *They have cast up dust upon their heads* (Lam. 2:10). Of Job it is written *Have pity upon me, have pity upon me, O ye my friends* (Job 19:21); and of Jerusalem it is written *Forasmuch as I will show you no pity* (Jer. 16:13). Of Job it is written *For the hand of God hath touched me* (Job 19:21); and of Jerusalem it is written *That she hath received of the Lord's hand double for all her sins* (Isa. 40:2). Now, taught R. Joshua bar Nehemiah, if Job who sinned was eventually given a double recompense,[32] so Jerusalem will eventually be given a double recompense of comfort: *Comfort ye, comfort ye My people* (Isa. 40:1).

7. [The disasters that befell Israel were of such a kind as to invite comfort from others who have likewise suffered disaster]. *Surely He stretcheth not*

31. That is, by appealing to their reason, the heart being in Rabbinic psychology the seat of intelligence. The argument that his own position in Egypt was linked to his brothers' well-being was persuasive.

32. See Job 42.

put His hand against a ruinous heap. On the contrary, when anyone has suffered disaster, He [*offers*] *him consolation*[33] (Job 30:24). The Holy One, said R. Abbahu, does not smite a people and leave her desolate. For when He brings disaster upon one people, He tries to console her [by citing comparable disasters] which came to another. And when He brings disaster upon the other, He tries to console her [by citing comparable disasters] which came to the one. Thus when God brought disaster to Assyria, He comforted Assyria by referring to a like disaster of Egypt's: *Art thou better than No-Amon?* (Nahum 3:8). And when He brought disaster to Egypt, He comforted her by referring to a like disaster of Assyria's: *Behold, the Assyrian was a cedar in Lebanon* (Ezek. 31:3). And so the reason that the Ten Tribes were banished first and the Tribes of Judah and Benjamin after them was to allow the Ten Tribes and the Tribes of Judah and Benjamin, so taught R. Jose, to comfort each other. Hence *Comfort each other, comfort each other, O My people* (Isa. 40:1).

8. *How then comfort ye me in vain? As for the words that you claim you bring back from God, all that I see remaining of them is ma'al*[34] (Job 21:34). [R. Abba bar Kahana and the Rabbis differ concerning the meaning of the last word in this verse]. According to R. Abba bar Kahana, Job meant by it that the words his friends claimed to have brought back from God showed faithlessness;[35] according to the Rabbis, however, Job meant by *ma'al* that the words his friends claimed to have brought back from God showed self-contradiction. [Now how is Job's charge of contradiction relevant to the verse *Comfort ye, comfort ye*]? It is relevant because the Holy One said to the Prophets: "Go, comfort Jerusalem"; [and as it turned out their words of comfort were contradictory]. Thus Hosea came to comfort her, saying: "The Holy One sent me to comfort thee." Jerusalem asked: What comfort do you bring me? Hosea replied: [The Holy One said through me], "Henceforth *I will be as the dew unto Israel*" (Hos. 14:6). Jerusalem retorted: Yesterday you reported God as saying *Ephraim is smitten, their root is dried up, they shall bear no fruit* (Hos. 9:16). And now you claim that He will be as *the dew unto Israel.* Which words am I to believe, yesterday's or today's?

Joel came to comfort Jerusalem, saying "The Holy One sent me to comfort thee." Jerusalem asked: What comfort do you bring me? Joel replied: [The Holy One said through me], *It shall come to pass in that day that the*

33. JV: *Surely none shall put forth his hand to a ruinous heap, neither because of these things shall help come in one's calamity.*

34. JV: *And as for your answers, there remaineth only faithlessness* (*ma'al*). Cf. PR 29/30B:2 (YJS, *18*, 583–84).

35. Lit. "required purgation [of dross]," or, "[of lies]." See MhG Gen., p. 880, where an anonymous teaching characterizes all prophecies predicting redemption as no more than a pack of lies.

mountains shall drop down sweet wine, and the hills shall flow with milk, etc. (Joel 4:18). Jerusalem answered: Yesterday you said to me, *Awake, ye drunkards, and weep, wail, all ye drinkers of wine, because of the sweet wine, for it is cut off from your mouth* (Joel 1:5); and now you say, *The mountains shall drop down sweet wine*. Which words shall I believe, yesterday's or today's?

Amos came to comfort Jerusalem, saying "The Holy One sent me to comfort thee." Jerusalem asked: What comfort do you bring me? Amos replied: [The Holy One said through me], *On that day will I raise up the Tabernacle of David that is fallen* (Amos 9:11). Jerusalem answered: Yesterday you said to me, *The virgin of Israel is fallen, she shall no more rise* (Amos 5:2). And now you say, *I will raise up the Tabernacle of David*. Which words am I to believe, yesterday's or today's?

Micah came to comfort Jerusalem, saying: "The Holy One sent me to comfort thee." Jerusalem asked: What comfort do you bring me? Micah replied: [Speaking through me, the Holy One declared of Himself], *Who is a God like unto Thee, that pardoneth the iniquity, and passeth by transgression?* (Micah 7:18). Jerusalem answered: Yesterday you said to me, *For the transgression of Jacob is all this, and for the sins of the house of Israel* (Micah 1:5). And now you say, *God pardoneth . . . iniquity*. Which words am I to believe, yesterday's or today's?

Nahum came to comfort Jerusalem, saying: "The Holy One sent me to comfort thee." Jerusalem asked: What comfort do you bring me? Nahum replied: [The Holy One said through me], *The wicked one shall no more pass through thee; he is utterly cut off* (Nahum 2:1). Jerusalem answered: Yesterday you said to me, *Out of thee came he forth, that deviseth evil against the Lord, that counseleth wickedness* (Nahum 1:11); but now you say to me, *The wicked one shall no more pass through thee*. Which words am I to believe, yesterday's or today's?

Habakkuk came to comfort Jerusalem, saying: "The Holy One sent me to comfort thee." Jerusalem asked: What comfort do you bring me? Habakkuk replied: [Speaking through me, the Holy One declared of Himself], *Thou art come forth for the deliverance of Thy people, for the deliverance of Thine anointed* (Hab. 3:13). Jerusalem replied to Habakkuk: Yesterday you said to me, *How long, O Lord, shall I cry, and Thou wilt not hear? I cry unto Thee of violence*, etc. (Hab. 1:2). And now you say to me, *Thou art come forth*. Which words am I to believe, yesterday's or today's?

Zephaniah came to comfort Jerusalem, saying: "The Holy One sent me to comfort thee." Jerusalem asked: What comfort do you bring me? Zephaniah replied: [The Holy One announced through me], *It shall come to pass at that time that I will free*[36] *Jerusalem for the sake of the lamps* (Zeph.

36. *Ḥpś*, "to search," is read as though written *ḥpš*, "to free." See PR 8:3.

1:12). Jerusalem said: Yesterday you spoke to me of *A day of darkness and gloominess, a day of clouds and thick darkness* (Zeph. 1:15). And now you speak of Jerusalem being freed. Which words am I to believe, yesterday's or today's?

Haggai came to comfort Jerusalem, saying: "The Holy One sent me to comfort thee." Jerusalem asked: What comfort do you bring me? Haggai replied: [The Holy One said through me], *Shall the seed ever again remain in the barn [unsown]? Shall the vine, the fig tree, the pomegranate, and the olive tree ever again bear no fruit? Indeed not! From this day I will bless thee* (Haggai 2:19). Jerusalem answered: Yesterday you said to me, *You sow much and bring in little* (Haggai 1:6). And now you say to me, *Shall the seed ever again remain in the barn [unsown]?* Which words am I to believe, yesterday's or today's?

Zechariah came to comfort Jerusalem, saying: "The Holy One sent me to comfort thee." Jerusalem asked: What comfort do you bring me? Zechariah replied: [The Holy One announced through me]: *I am very sore displeased with the nations that are at ease* (Zech. 1:15). Jerusalem said: Yesterday you declared: *The Lord hath been sore displeased with your fathers* (Zech. 1:2), and now you say, He is displeased with the nations. Which words am I to believe, yesterday's or today's?

Malachi came to comfort Jerusalem, saying: "The Holy One sent me to comfort thee." Jerusalem asked: What comfort do you bring me? Malachi replied: [The Holy One said through me], *All the nations shall call you happy; for ye shall be a delightsome land* (Mal. 3:12). Jerusalem answered: Yesterday you said, *I have no pleasure in you, saith the Lord of hosts* (Mal. 1:10). And now you say, *Ye shall be a delightsome land.* Which words am I to believe, yesterday's or today's?

Thereupon the Prophets came before the Holy One, saying to Him: Master of universes, Jerusalem refuses to be comforted by us. The Holy One replied: Then you and I together shall go to her and comfort her: *Comfort ye, comfort ye with Me*[37] (Isa. 40:1)—comfort Jerusalem, comfort her together with Me. Comfort her, ye who are in the regions above, comfort her, ye who are in the regions below. Ye who are alive comfort her, ye who are dead comfort her. Comfort her in this world, comfort her in the world-to-come. Comfort her for the Ten Tribes, comfort her for the Tribes of Judah and Benjamin. It is all these I mean by *ye* when I say, *Comfort ye, comfort ye with Me* (*ibid.*)—comfort Jerusalem, comfort her together with Me.

9. [To interpret *Comfort*, etc.], R. Abin posed two hypothetical questions. R. Abin asked this one first: If a king had a palace, and his enemies came into it and burned it down, who is to be comforted, the palace or the owner of the palace? Is it not the owner of the palace who should be com-

37. The word *'ammi*, "My people," is here vocalized *'immi*, "with Me."

forted? Likewise, the Holy One saying, The Temple is My palace, "And it is My palace that lieth waste" (Haggai 1:9), went on to ask, Who then requires comforting? Is it not I? Hence *Comfort, comfort, My people* (Isa. 40:1)—comfort Me, comfort Me, O My people.

R. Abin's other hypothetical question: If a king had a vineyard, and his enemies came into it and hacked at it and cut it down, who is to be offered comfort? The vineyard or the vineyard's owner? Is not the vineyard's owner to be comforted? Likewise the Holy One saying, Israel is My vineyard, *The vineyard of the Lord of hosts is the house of Israel* (Isa. 5:7), went on to ask, Who then requires comforting? Is it not I? Hence *Comfort, comfort, My people* (Isa. 40:1)—comfort Me, comfort Me, O My people.

R. Berechiah also posed two hypothetical questions, one in his own name and the other in the name of R. Levi. First R. Berechiah in his own name gave this analogy: If a king had a flock of sheep, and wolves came at it and tore it, who should be comforted? The flock of sheep or the flock's owner? Is not the flock's owner to be comforted? So, too, the Holy One saying, Israel are My flock, *Ye My sheep, the sheep of My pasture* (Ezek. 34:31), went on to ask, Who requires comforting? Is it not I? Hence, *Comfort, comfort My people* (Isa. 40:1)—comfort Me, comfort Me, O My people.

In the name of R. Levi, R. Berechiah told a parable to the same effect: A king had a vineyard which he proceeded to turn over to a tenant. When the vineyard produced good wine, the king used to say, "How good is the wine of my vineyard!" When it produced bad wine, the king used to say, "How bad is my tenant's wine!" Whereupon the tenant said: "My lord king, when the vineyard produces good wine you say, 'How good is the wine of my vineyard!' And when it produces bad wine you say, 'How bad is the wine [of my tenant]!' Yet good or bad, the wine is yours." Likewise, the Holy One just referred to Israel as "My people," saying to Moses: *Come now therefore, and I will send thee unto Pharaoh, that thou mayest bring forth My people, the children of Israel, out of Egypt* (Exod. 3:10), but after Israel did that unspeakable deed of theirs, what did He say? *Go, get thee down; for thy people . . . have dealt corruptly* (Exod. 32:7). Whereupon Moses replied: Master of universes, when the children of Israel sin, they are called mine; but when they are free from sin, they are called Thine. Yet sinful or sinless, they are Thine: *They are Thy people, and Thine inheritance* (Deut. 9:29). *Destroy not Thy people, and Thine inheritance* (Deut. 9:26). *Lord, why doth Thy wrath wax hot against Thy people?* (Exod. 32:11). Why wouldst Thou destroy Thy people? And Moses would not stop speaking endearingly of them—so said R. Simon—until God once again called them "My people": *And the Lord repented of the evil which He said He would do unto His people* (Exod. 32:14).

10. *Your God will keep saying*[38] (Isa. 40:1) [that He will comfort all succeeding generations]. R. Ḥanina bar Papa and R. Simon give different reasons for the phrasing of this verse. According to R. Ḥanina bar Papa, Israel said to Isaiah: Our teacher Isaiah, are we to suppose that you came to comfort only the generation in whose days the Temple was destroyed? He replied: I came to comfort all the generations. Hence Scripture does not say, "God said," but *Your God will keep saying* (*ibid.*). On the other hand, according to R. Simon, Israel said to Isaiah: Our teacher Isaiah, perhaps all the things you say you make up out of your own head. Isaiah replied: Scripture does not say "Your God [spoke to me alone]," but says *Your God will keep saying* [so that all the world will hear. Concurring with R. Simon], R. Ḥanina bar R. Abba pointed out that *Your God will keep saying* occurs eight times in Scripture[39] to prefigure the coming of eight Prophets, namely, Joel, Amos,[40] Zephaniah, Haggai, Zechariah, Malachi, Ezekiel, and Jeremiah, each of whom would prophesy [concerning what was to happen] after the destruction of the Temple.

11. [So that she may be comforted], *Speak ye to the heart of Jerusalem, and proclaim unto her*, etc. (Isa. 40:2). The children of Israel sinned with the head, they were smitten in the head, yet they will be comforted at the head. They sinned at the head: *Let us make a head, and let us return into Egypt* (Num. 14:4); and they were smitten in the head: *The whole head is sick* (Isa. 1:5); yet they will be comforted at the head: *Their king is passed before them, and the Lord at the head of them* (Micah 2:13). They sinned with the eye, they were smitten in the eye, yet they will be comforted by the eye. They sinned with the eye: *The daughters of Zion . . . walk . . . with wanton eyes* (Isa. 3:16); and they were smitten in the eye: *Mine eye, mine eye runneth down with water* (Lam. 1:16); yet they will be comforted by the eye: *For they shall see, eye to eye, the Lord returning to Zion* (Isa. 52:8). They sinned with the ear, they were smitten in the ear, yet they will be comforted by the ear. They sinned with the ear: *They stopped their ears, that they might not hear* (Zech. 7:11); they were smitten in the ear: *Their ears shall be deaf* (Micah 7:16); yet they will be comforted by the ear: *Thine ears shall hear a word, saying: "This is the way"* (Isa. 30:21).

They sinned by using the nose (*'af*) in obscene gestures, they were smitten with *'af*, yet they will be comforted with *'af*. They sinned by using the nose (*'af*) in obscene gestures: *And, lo, they put the branch to their nose*[41] (Ezek. 8:17); and they were smitten with *'af: I also* (*'af*) *will do this unto*

38. JV: *saith your God.*
39. The eight places are Isa. 1:11, 18; 33:10; 40:1, 25; 41:21 (twice); 66:9.
40. O_1: "Nahum."
41. Cf. Piska 3.11.

you (Lev. 26:16); yet they will be comforted with *'af: And yet ('af) for all that, when they are in the land of their enemies, I will not reject them* (Lev. 26:44). They sinned with the mouth, they were smitten by the mouth, yet they will be comforted by the mouth. They sinned with the mouth: *Every mouth speaketh wantonness* (Isa. 9:16). They were smitten with the mouth: *The Arameans . . . and the Philistines devour Israel with open mouth* (Isa. 9:11). Yet they will be comforted by the mouth: *Then was our mouth filled with laughter* (Ps. 126:2). They sinned with the tongue, they were smitten at the tongue, yet they will be comforted by the tongue. They sinned with the tongue: *They bend their tongue, their bow of falsehood* (Jer. 9:2). They were punished at the tongue: *The tongue of the sucking child cleaveth to the roof of his mouth for thirst* (Lam. 4:4). Yet they will be comforted by the tongue: *And our tongue with singing* (Ps. 126:2). They sinned with the heart, they were punished at the heart, yet they will be comforted by the heart. They sinned with the heart: *Yea, they made their hearts as an adamant stone* (Zech. 7:12). They were punished at the heart: *And the whole heart faint* (Isa. 1:5). Yet they will be comforted by the heart: *Speak ye to the heart of Jerusalem* (Isa. 40:2). They sinned with the hand, they were smitten by the hand, yet they will be comforted by the hand. They sinned with the hand: *Your hands are full of blood* (Isa. 1:15). They were smitten by the hand: *The hands of women full of compassion have sodden their own children* (Lam. 4:10). Yet they will be comforted by the hand: *The Lord will set His hand again the second time to recover the remnant of His people* (Isa. 11:11). They sinned with the foot, they were punished at the foot, yet they will be comforted by the foot. They sinned with the foot: *The daughters of Zion . . . walk . . . making a tinkling with their feet* (Isa. 3:16). They were smitten at the foot: *Your feet stumble upon the dark mountains* (Jer. 13:16). Yet they will be comforted by the foot: *How beautiful upon the mountains are the feet of the messenger of good tidings* (Isa. 52:7). They sinned with "this," they were punished by "this," yet they will be comforted by "this." They sinned with "this": *The people said . . . Up, make us a god . . . for as for this man Moses . . . we know not what is become of him* (Exod. 32:1). They were smitten with "this": *For this our heart is faint* (Lam. 5:17). Yet they will be comforted by "this": *It shall be said in that day: "Lo, this is our God"* (Isa. 25:9). They sinned with "He" (*hu'*), they were punished with "He," yet they will be comforted with "He." They sinned with "He (*hu'*)": *They have belied the Lord, and said, "It is not He"* (Jer. 5:12). They were punished with "He" (*hu'*): *Therefore He was turned to be their enemy, and Himself (hu') fought against them* (Isa. 63:10). Yet they will be comforted by "He" (*hu'*): *I, even I, am He (hu') that comforteth you* (Isa. 51:12). They sinned with fire, they were smitten by fire, yet they will be comforted by fire. They sinned with fire: *The children gather wood and the fathers kindle the fire*[42] (Jer. 7:18). They were smitten by fire: *From on high hath He sent fire into my bones* (Lam. 1:13). Yet they will be comforted by fire: *For I, saith the Lord, will be unto her a wall of fire round about* (Zech. 2:9). They sinned in double measure, they will be smitten in double measure, and will be comforted in double measure. They sinned in double measure: *Jerusalem sinned a sin* (Lam. 1:8). They will be smitten in double measure: *She hath received of the Lord's hand double for all her sins* (Isa. 40:2). And they will be comforted in double measure: *Comfort ye, comfort ye My people* (Isa. 40:1).

42. To make cakes for the queen of heaven, the moon goddess, possibly Astarte.

PISKA 17

SUMMARY

Why Zion should not despair

Because Israel's anguish has gone on for so long, it appears to them that there is no chance of their reconciling or of their being reconciled with God and that God's mercy has departed from them for ever. But God has not forgotten that He is merciful and gracious; nor has He forgotten that on six special occasions He chose to encamp in Israel's midst and lend them His strength. Hence Zion is not to say, "God has forsaken me" (Sec. 1). God's right hand which so often brought help to Israel has not changed—has not become powerless to help them. God is no more than wrathful with them: hence there is hope, and Zion is not to despair (Sec. 2). The people of Israel, being complainers and children of complainers, overlook the fact that God has already overthrown such enemies as Babylon, Media, and Greece; likewise He will overthrow Rome. Hence Zion should not say in complaint, "He has forsaken me" (Sec. 3).

The fact is that God's anger lasts only a single day. Indeed, had Israel resolved to return to God, on every one of the four days when their backslidings led Him to bring the four kingdoms successively upon them, He would have cooled His anger. In truth, on each of the four days God did to Israel what they had done to Him. Had He been in Israel's hearts, the different kinds of troubles and evils that befell them under the rule of the kingdoms would not have come upon Israel: hence if they take Him back into their hearts they need not despair (Sec. 4).

God's hand—His power—has not changed. He has merely bound—if one dare speak thus—His right hand behind His back as a sign to Israel that He is with them in their bondage. The redemption of Israel and the unbinding of God's right hand are certain to come as answers to the Psalmist's prayer for deliverance from wandering, poverty, and weakness. A Divine Voice will then echo on the mountain tops and proclaim that God's right hand has wrought salvation. Hence Zion is not to despair (Sec. 5).

In her complaints to God, Zion refers to the strength which Israel was the first to ascribe to God—the strength which should deliver her now instead of leaving her as forsaken as sheaves in the field. Zion further says, "The Lord forsook me and made me disgusting in the eyes of the nations." Yet it was the very disgust which the nations came to have for Israel that made them reject the daughters of Zion and thus kept the holy seed of Israel from mingling with the seed of the peoples of other lands (Sec. 6).

Finally, God assures Zion: Evil deeds I forget, but good deeds I do not forget—*I have graven thee upon the palms of My hands* (Isa. 49:16): a woman may forget her suckling child, but it is impossible for a man to forget the palms of his hands (Secs. 7–8).

PISKA 17

Yet Zion saith (Isa. 49:14).[1]

1. *I call to remembrance nĕḡinaṯi*[2] *in the night. Thereupon I commune with my heart, and have my spirit make diligent search* (Ps. 77:7). R. Aibu and R. Judah bar R. Simon differ as to the meaning of *nĕḡinaṯi.* R. Aibu took it to intimate that the congregation of Israel says plaintively to the Holy One: Master of universes, I call to remembrance the breaking of the power of the kingdoms, a breaking that at one time I was enabled by Thee to bring about. Thus R. Aibu takes *nĕḡinaṯi* to mean "the breaking of mine enemies' power," as in the verse "God the Most High . . . hath broken (*miggen*) thine enemies at thy hand" (Gen. 14:20). On the other hand, R. Judah bar R. Simon took *nĕḡinaṯi* to intimate that the congregation of Israel says plaintively to the Holy One: Master of universes, I call to remembrance the songs that at one time I sang to Thee on certain nights. Thus R. Judah takes *nĕḡinaṯi* to mean "my song" as in the verse "All the days of our life, [night and day], we sang songs (*nĕḡinoṯay*) to the stringed instruments in the house of the Lord" (Isa. 38:20). Therefore, in saying *I call to remembrance my song in the night* (Ps. 77:6), the Psalmist, speaking for the congregation of Israel, is alluding to a particular night, the night of Pharaoh's discomfiture, of which it is written "And it came to pass at midnight that the Lord smote all the first-born in the land of Egypt" (Exod. 12:29). The Psalmist is alluding also to another particular night, the night of Gideon's victory, of which it is written "And it came to pass the same night, that the Lord said unto him: 'Arise, get thee down upon the camp, for I have delivered it into thy hand' " (Judg. 7:9). The Psalmist is further alluding to another particular night, the night of Sennacherib's rout, of which it is written "And it came to pass that night, that the angel of the Lord went forth, and smote in the camp of the Assyrians a hundred fourscore and five thousand" (2 Kings 19:35). [And so the Psalmist, speaking for the congregation of Israel, is saying]: When I compare this night [of my anguish] with such nights in the past [when God was my help], *I commune with my heart, and have my spirit make diligent search* (Ps. 77:7)—I commune with my heart, have it search my deeds, and then hear it ask, *Will the Lord cast off for ever?* (Ps. 77:8). Thereupon I reply: Indeed, not! He has not cast Israel off, nor will He cast Israel off: "The Lord will not cast off for ever" (Lam. 3:31). [The Psalmist goes on to say, however: Though He has not cast off, yet it seems

1. In the seven-Sabbath cycle of consolation, Isa. 49:14–51:3 is the haftarah for *'Eḳeḇ*, the second Sabbath following the Ninth of Ab.

2. EV: *my song.*

that] *He will reconcile no more* (Ps. 77:8). In the past, Thou didst reconcile others for my sake. When Moses was angry, Thou didst reconcile him for my sake. [For Thou didst say to him, Go, return to the camp of Israel], "and he returned into the camp" (Exod. 33:11).[3] When Elijah was angry, Thou didst reconcile him for my sake, saying to him "Go to Damascus to [pursue] this wild way of thine—the speaking [of slander against Israel]"[4] (1 Kings 19:15). Yet at this moment there seems to be no chance of reconciling, or of being reconciled.

Has His mercy been let go ('afes) for ever?[5] *Is His promise come to an end for evermore?* (Ps. 77:9). (Here *'afes*, according to R. Reuben, is to be read [not in its usual sense of "cease," but] as the Greek word *apheis*, "let go"). With regard to the interpretation of *Is His promise come to an end for evermore?* R. Ḥanina bar Papa and R. Simon differ. R. Ḥanina bar Papa took the words to mean that the congregation of Israel is asking: Has the promise which Thou didst utter to Moses on Sinai, saying "From time to time I will be gracious, and from time to time I will show mercy"[6] (Exod. 33:19) come to an end for evermore? R. Simon, on the other hand, took the words to mean that the congregation of Israel is asking: Was Thy promise completely dissolved, brought to an end for evermore, as would appear from the words of Jeremiah who declared, "I have taken away My peace from this people, saith the Lord, even mercy and compassion" (Jer. 16:5)?

Hath God forgotten to be gracious? (Ps. 77:10) [the congregation of Israel asks, and replies in the conclusion of the verse]: *Though wroth in anger, His compassions endure for ever*[7] (*ibid.*). Thou canst not have forgotten that Thou art gracious—"a God merciful and gracious, a Lord slow to anger" (Exod. 34:6).

If the verse is read *Hath God forgotten the encampments?*[8] (Ps. 77:10), then it is saying, Thou canst not, O God, have forgotten Thine encampments

3. See MTeh 25:6.

4. JV: *Go, return on thy way to the wilderness of Damascus.* Since Elijah had not come to the area of Beer-sheba from Damascus, but from Carmel and Samaria, the commentator assumes these words to be God's silencing of Elijah who had just complained that "Israel have forsaken the covenant, thrown down [God's] altars, and slain [God's] Prophets" (1 Kings 9:14).

The word *mdbrh*, "wilderness," the commentator takes to be a form of *dbr*, "speak." See Song Rabbah 1:6.

5. If the verse were read *Has His mercy ceased for ever*, the phrase *for ever* would appear to be superfluous. Hence R. Reuben's comment.

6. See Rashi.

7. JV: *Hath He in anger shut up His compassions? Selah.* But *ḳfṣ*, "shut up," may by metathesis be read *ḳṣf*, "be wroth"; and, in Rabbinic exegesis, *selah* is taken to mean "for ever."

8. In this comment, *ḥannoṯ*, "be gracious," is associated with the stem *ḥanah* "encamp." On the meaning of God's encampment, see Piska 1.1–2.

—the Tent of Meeting, Gilgal, Shiloh, Nob, Gibeon,[9] and the two Temples which were meant to endure for ever, for the conclusion of the verse declares *Though wroth in anger, His compassions endure for ever* (*ibid.*): although He becomes angry, His compassions are near. Nevertheless, such is her anguish that Zion cries out, He has forsaken me, He has forgotten me: *Yet Zion saith, "The Lord hath forsaken me, the Lord hath forgotten me"* (Isa. 49:14).

2. The congregation of Israel goes on to say, *Because of the way we entreated* (*ḥalloṯi*),[10] *the right hand of the Most High has changed* (Ps. 77:11). R. Samuel bar Naḥman took this verse to mean that the congregation of Israel is saying: Because we did not entreat Him[11] in penitence, God's right hand was changed [and no longer protected us]. But R. Alexandri took the verse to mean that the congregation of Israel is saying: Because of me, the oath given us at Horeb was profaned (*ḥalloṯi*),[12] and God's right hand was changed.

[By way of proving that *ḥalloṯi* is not to be taken as intimating any weakness on God's part], R. Simon said: Have you ever in your life heard anyone say, "The orb of the sun has weakened and is unable to rise and do its work," or "The orb of the moon has weakened and is unable to rise and do its work?" Now if they who do His work show no signs of weakness, can one dare say that God shows signs of weakness?

R. Isaac illustrated the matter by a parable of a mighty man who lived in a certain province. The people of the province were confident that if hostile troops invaded it, he would go forth, face up to them, and at once they would run away. When hostile troops did come, he said to the people of the province: "I feel a weakness in my right hand." But the Holy One would never speak thus, for "The Lord's hand is not powerless, that it cannot save" (Isa. 59:1). You see, accordingly, that "It is nothing other than your own iniquities which have separated you from your God" (Isa. 59:2).

The right hand of the Most High has changed (Ps. 77:11). If the change in God's right hand has come about, said Resh Laḳish, because of [Israel's moral] weakness, there is hope, for he who suffers weakness is likely to

9. These are the places where, prior to the building of the Temple in Jerusalem, the Tabernacle was set up temporarily. See Josh. 4:19, Josh. 18:1, 1 Sam. 21:2–7, 1 Kings 3:4, 2 Chron. 1:3, and Piska 16.3. O reads "Nob, Shiloh, Gibeon"; but Pa has accurately "Shiloh, Nob, Gibeon."

10. JV: *This is my weakness* from *ḥalah*, "to be weak." However, in the comment which follows, *ḥalloṯi*, "my weakness," is derived from *ḥillah*, "to entreat [God]."

11. PRK has "entreat Thee," but a parallel version in Exod. Rabbah 45:2 reads "entreat the Holy One."

12. R. Alexandri derives *ḥalloṯi*, "my weakness," from *ḥll*, "to profane." Indeed O_1 and S read *ntḥllh*, "profaned," and not *ntḥlh*, "grew weak," the reading in O.

recover in the end. If, however, the change is in God's right hand itself, there is no hope. Such is Resh Laḳish's opinion, in keeping with what Resh Laḳish said on another occasion, when he began by citing the verse *If it is rejection, Thou didst reject us irretrievably; but Thou art only very wroth against us* (Lam. 5:22). That is, if God has rejected Israel, then there is no hope. If, however, He is no more than wrathful, then there is hope. For He who is angered is likely to be reconciled in the end. Nevertheless, such is her anguish that Zion cries out, He has forsaken me, He has forgotten me: *Yet Zion saith, "The Lord hath forsaken me, the Lord hath forgotten me"* (Isa. 49:14).

3. *Wherefore doth one living complain? A strong man* [*should complain only*] *about his sins* (Lam. 3:39). R. Abba bar Yudan took the verse to mean: If a man is alive, why should he complain? It is enough for a man that he is alive.[13] But R. Berechiah took the verse to mean that God says, If [the Torah], that utterance of Mine which makes living possible, is in your hand, and yet, [despite your disregard of Torah], you remain alive, why should you complain?

For his part, R. Levi took the verse to be saying: Why should a man complain against the One who lives for ever? If a man wants to show his strength by complaining, let him be *strong* [*in complaining*] *about his own sins* (*ibid.*).

Finally, R. Yudan took the verse to say: Let him stand up like a strong man, confess his sins, and not[14] complain. [To complain, however, has always been man's way]. Thus, according to R. [Judah], the Holy One said of mankind: They are complainers and children of complainers. Adam, for example: I busied Myself in his behalf and provided him with a help ("I will make him a help meet for him" [Gen. 2:18]), yet in My very presence, he complained, saying "The woman whom Thou gavest to be with me,[15] she gave me of the tree, and I did eat" (Gen. 3:12). Jacob did exactly the same thing to Me. I busied Myself with his son to have him govern Egypt ("And Joseph was the governor over the land" [Gen. 42:6]), yet Jacob complained in My very presence, saying "My way is hid from the Lord"[16] (Isa. 40:27). Jacob's children in the wilderness went on in exactly the same way about Me: I busied Myself choosing a light diet for them—the kind of diet that kings consume—so that not one of Jacob's children would overeat and

13. Particularly, as the verse concludes, since he is both strong and vigorous when he goes about committing sins.

14. Apparently, R. Yudan construes *mh* in Lam. 3:39 not as "wherefore," but as "not."

15. The words "with me," which the commentator deems unnecessary, are construed as both reproach and complaint.

16. In Isaiah this clause is introduced with the question "Why sayest thou, O Jacob?"

be seized by diarrhea, yet they complained to Me, saying "Our soul loatheth this light bread" (Num. 21:5). Zion, right now, is going on exactly in the same way about Me. In her behalf I busy Myself removing the kingdoms from the world. Have I not already removed Babylon, Media, and Greece, even as I shall remove [Rome], this present wicked kindgom? Nevertheless, Zion complains in My very presence, "He has forsaken me, He has forgotten me": *Yet Zion saith, "The Lord hath forsaken me, the Lord hath forgotten me"* (Isa. 49:14).

4. *Then My anger shall be kindled against them in that day, and I will forsake them, and I will hide My face from them, and they shall be devoured, and many evils and troubles shall come upon them*, etc. (Deut. 31:17). R. Aḥa said: The Holy One's burning anger lasts only one day. Hence, had Israel resolved to return to God, He would have cooled the anger that was kindled in Him on every one [of the four] day[s in Israel's past when their turning away from Him resulted in His bringing upon them the affliction of being ruled by "the kingdoms of the world"].

R. Tanḥuma [demonstrated that the passage from Deuteronomy quoted by R. Aḥa refers specifically to the four kingdoms]. Citing the Greek proverb *poiēsō soi hopōs poiēsas*,[17] he took God to be saying in the passage, "What they do, I do likewise." "What they do": *This people . . . forsake Me, and break My covenant* (Deut. 31:16); "I do likewise": *I . . . forsake them, and I . . . hide My face from them, and they are being devoured* (Deut. 31:17). The words *My anger shall be kindled against them* (*ibid.*) allude to Babylon's rule of them; the words *I will forsake them* (*ibid.*) allude to Media's rule of them; the words *I will hide My face from them* (*ibid.*) allude to Greece's rule of them; and the words *they are being devoured* (*ibid.*) allude to Edom's rule of them, in keeping with what is said in the verse "Behold [Edom] the fourth beast . . . devoured, and broke in pieces, and stamped the residue with its feet" (Dan. 7:7). And the words *Many evils and troubles shall come upon them* (Deut. 31:17) refer to all the different kinds of evils and troubles—a hundred less two—which are specified in the Torah [as coming upon them]. Deuteronomy goes on to quote Israel as *saying, On each day* [of the four which brought the rule of the kingdoms], *have not these evils come upon us because our God is not among us?* (*ibid.*)—that is, Had He been in our hearts, these evils would not have come upon us. Had He been in our hearts, we would not have had to go into exile. Nevertheless, such is her anguish [under the rule of the fourth kingdom], that Zion cries out against Him, He forsook me, He forgot me: *Yet Zion saith, "The Lord hath forsaken me, the Lord hath forgotten me"* (Isa. 49:14).

5. *If I forget thee, O Jerusalem, My right hand will be forgotten* (Ps.

17. R. Tanḥuma cites *I shall deal with thee as thou hast done* (Ezek. 16:59). See Lieberman, *GJP*, 59.

137:5). According to Bar Ḳappara, God said to Israel: "The time of My redemption[18] is in your hand, and the time of your redemption is in My hand." The time of My redemption is in your hand:[19] [Therefore, "Let not] thy heart grow haughty so that thou forgettest the Lord thy God" (Deut. 8:14); and the time of your redemption is in My hand: *If I forget thee, O Jerusalem, My right hand will forget* (Ps. 137:5). To R. Dosa this verse meant: If I forget thee, O Jerusalem, My right hand will forget how to perform miracles—[I will cease to be God].

R. Azariah and R. Abbahu said in the name of Resh Laḳish: You find that when Israel's sins brought it about that enemies invaded Jerusalem, the enemies seized Israel's warriors and bound their hands behind their backs. Thereupon the Holy One declared: Scripture says of Me, "I will be with him in trouble" (Ps. 91:15), and so since My children are deep in trouble, can I remain at ease? At once, [because Israel's hands had been bound by their enemies], "God bound His right hand behind His back"—if one dare speak thus—"on account of the enemy" (Lam. 2:3). Later on, however, God made known to Daniel the time when His right hand would again be visible, saying to Daniel: *Go on till the time of redemption* (Dan. 12:13). Daniel asked: "What then? Shall I be presenting myself for Divine scrutiny and judgment?" God replied: *Thou shalt rest* (*ibid.*). Daniel asked: "Rest for ever? [Not rise for the resurrection]?" God replied: *Thou shalt arise* (*ibid.*). Daniel said bluntly to God: "Master of universes, arise with whom? With the righteous or with the wicked?" God replied: "*With thy lot* (*ibid.*) —with righteous men like thyself." Daniel asked: "When?" God replied: "*At the end of yamin*" (*ibid.*). Again Daniel spoke up: "At the end of *yamin*, that is at the end of the world's days, or at the end of *yamin*, that is at the end of Thy right hand's being bound?" God replied: "At the end of My *yamin*—at the end of My right hand's being bound behind My back." By these words the Holy One was intimating to Daniel: "I have set a time for My right hand's being bound. As long as My children are bound in slavery, My right hand shall be bound with them. When I deliver My children, I shall deliver My right hand."[20]

David had God's redemption in mind when he said: *That they may be delivered for the sake of Thy beloved, or redeem* [*them*] *for Thy right hand's sake—answer me* (Ps. 60:7), and so David appealed directly to the Holy One: Master of universes, when Israel have merit, deliver them for the sake of Thy beloved, Abraham, Isaac, and Jacob. But when they have no merit, deliver them for Thy right hand's sake—*redeem* [*them*] *for Thy*

18. The redemption of My right hand which is thought to be chained or fettered (cf. Koran 5:69) while Israel is in exile.

19. Cf. PR 31:5.

20. See MTeh 137:7.

right hand's sake. [*Either way*], *answer me* (*ibid.*). [By the word *yeḥolṣun*, "that they may be delivered," David was implying Israel's deliverance from several kinds of affliction]. Thus David was challenging the Holy One: Master of universes, why is it that every one who loves Thee is made into a wanderer? Make them into those who find rest in one place, as we say in the prayer "Deliver us from the affliction of wandering" (*haḥăliṣenu*). (In keeping with this particular meaning of *haḥăliṣenu*, the Sages saw fit to bring the word into the Sabbath Grace after meals).[21] By this same entreaty David was further challenging the Holy One: Master of universes, why is it that every one that loves Thee is poor? Make them prosperous, if only by delivering them from poverty, as in the verse "He delivereth (*yĕḥalleṣ*) the poor from his poverty" (Job 36:15). By this entreaty, David was challenging the Holy One still further: Master of universes, why is it that every one that loves Thee is weak? Make them strong, in the sense of *yaḥăliṣ* in the verse "The Lord . . . will deliver (*yaḥăliṣ*) thy bones from weakness" (Isa 58:11).[22]

R. Eleazar taught in the name of R. Jose ben Zimra: [On the day of Israel's deliverance], a Divine Voice echoing on the mountain tops will proclaim, *O sing unto the Lord a new song . . . His right hand hath wrought salvation* (Ps. 98:1). R. Levi, citing R. Ḥama bar R. Ḥanina, taught: A Divine Voice echoing in the tents of the righteous will proclaim, *The voice of rejoicing and salvation is to remain in the tents of the righteous, because the right hand of the Lord is exalted* (Ps. 118:15). Even with such assurances from the Holy One, who goes on to declare, My right hand is to perform all these miracles for you, Zion still cries out, The Lord has forsaken me, has forgotten me: *Yet Zion saith, "The Lord hath forsaken me, the Lord hath forgotten me"* (Isa. 49:14).[23]

6. [In another reading, the word *'zbny*[24]—in the previous comments taken to mean "hath forsaken me"—is considered to be compounded of *'z*, "strength," and *bny*, "my children": hence] the verse, *Yet Zion saith, 'z bny* (Isa. 49:14), is read as though the congregation of Israel spoke reproachfully to the Holy One: Master of universes, Thou hast forgotten the acknowledgment of Thy strength (*'z*) which my children (*bny*) were impelled to utter before Thee at the Red Sea—"The Lord is my strength and song" (Exod. 15:2)—[Thy strength should deliver me now].

A further reproach: *The Lord hath forsaken me* (Isa. 49:14) as the owner of a field at harvest time must forsake the sheaves that he has forgot-

21. *APB*, 281, where the sense of "deliver us from wandering" would fit in the context of the Sabbath Grace.

22. Cf. Lev. Rabbah 34:15.

23. Cf. PR 31:6.

24. Inasmuch as "forsaken" and "forgotten" are almost synonymous, the first is regarded as "available" for special interpretation, namely *'z*, "strength," and *bny*, "my children."

ten, forsaking them in obedience to the command: "Thou shalt deem them forsaken for the poor and for the stranger" (Lev. 19:10).

In another comment the words *The Lord hath forsaken me* (Isa. 49:14) are read "The Lord made me be forsaken in disgust" in full view of the nations. According to R. Ḥanina, these were the words the daughters of Zion [cried out in their misery when they had to pay the consequences of their vanity and harlotry.[24a] In earlier years, before being compelled to cry out thus] *The daughters of Zion*, as Isaiah describes them, *are haughty, and walk with stretched forth necks, and painted eyes, walking and making themselves appear taller as they go, and their feet they beserpent* (Isa. 3:15). *The daughters of Zion are haughty*,—that is to say, they moved about with overweening arrogance; *and walk with stretched forth necks*: when one of them adorned herself, she would bend her neck in one direction and then in another to display her ornaments; *and painted*[25] *eyes* (*ibid.*): they painted their eyes with *siḳra*—a red dye—so said R. Nisa of Caesarea, or, according to Resh Laḳish, with collyrium; *walking and making themselves appear taller as they go* (*ibid.*): a woman who was tall would get two short women to accompany her, making certain that she walked between them in order to appear by contrast even taller than she was; on the other hand, a woman who was short would put on a shoe with thick soles and get two short women to accompany her, making certain that she walked between them in order to make herself look dashing. *And their feet they beserpent*[26] (*ibid.*): as R. Abba bar Kahana explained, each woman used to have the figure of a serpent imprinted upon her footwear. According to the Rabbis, each woman used to get the gullet of a hen, fill it with fragrant balsam, and set it between the heel of her foot and her shoe; then, when she got close to a group of young men, she would stop and press down upon the hen's gullet which would break, and the fragrance within it would go forth and overcome the young men as though it were a serpent's venom.

Because of these women's behavior, the Holy One said to Jeremiah: "Jeremiah, what are such women doing here? They must be banished from Jerusalem." And so Jeremiah went around among them, saying: My daugh-

24a. Zion's plaint in Isa. 49:14 is followed at once by the reassurance that God can no more forget Zion than a woman can forget the infant at her breast. But His having forsaken Zion God does not deny. Hence, as will become apparent, R. Ḥanina discerns divine benignity in the kind of "forsaking" God visited upon the daughters of Zion, and thus accounts for God's not reassuring Zion that neither she nor her daughters had in fact been forsaken.

25. EV relate *mĕśaḳroṯ* to *śḳr*, "look, glance"—hence *wanton glances of the eyes*.

26. EV: *making a tinkling as they go*. The commentator derives the verb *'ks* not from the Biblical *'ek̲es*, "anklet," but from the postbiblical *'ek̲es*, "viper, serpent."

ters, act in penitence so that Israel's foes do not come at you. And what did each one say in reply? *Let Him make speed, let Him hasten His work, that we may be seen*[27] (Isa. 5:19). A captain of a battalion will see me and take me as his wife, or even the prefect of a province will see me and take me as his wife. *Let the counsel of the Holy One of Israel draw nigh and come, that we may know it* (*ibid.*)—know whose counsel will prevail, ours or His.

When Israel's iniquities brought it about that [the Babylonians], Israel's foes, came into Jerusalem, the daughters of Zion, bedizened like harlots, went forth to greet them. When the captain of a battalion saw one of the daughters of Zion, he would grab her as his woman, pick her up, and seat her in his carriage. Or even when the prefect of a province saw one of them, he would grab her as his woman, pick her up, and seat her in his carriage.

Thereupon the Holy One said: The counsel of these women seems to prevail. Shall their counsel prevail, and Mine not prevail? What did the Holy One do then to the daughters of Zion? He smote them—so said R. Eleazar—with the shine of leprosy, as intimated in the verse *The Lord will smite with a scab* (*śpḥ*) *the crown of the head of the daughters of Zion* (Isa. 3:17). (The word *śpḥ* signifies a leprous scab, as in the verse "When a man shall have in the skin of his flesh a rising or a scab [*spḥt*]" [Lev. 13:2]).

R. Jose[28] bar R. Ḥanina said: God had the crowns of their heads swarm with family upon family[29] of lice.

R. Ḥiyya bar Abba said: The enemy made them handmaids[30] *mĕkuddanoṯ*, the word *mĕkuddanoṯ*, "forced to do hard labor," indicating that the daughters of Zion were reduced to the most menial kind of slavery.

R. Berechiah and R. Ḥilfo bar Zebud said in the name of R. Jose: The word *śpḥ* being written with a *šin* may be read *špḥ*, "family,"[31] thus implying that God was determined to preserve purity in the families of these daughters of Zion and keep the holy seed of Israel from mingling with the seed of the peoples of other lands.[32] When, despite all His efforts, the daughters of Zion did not return to God, the Holy One said: I know that the men of the nations of the earth do not abstain from intercourse with women who are having their menstrual flow or who have leprosy. So what did the Holy One do to the daughters of Zion? *He caused their privy parts to spill*[33] (Isa. 5:17). Why does the verse say *spill*, when one would expect it to say "flow?" Because the Holy One saw to it that the fountains of the women who

27. EV: *that we may see it*. A slight change in vowels changes the verb into the passive mood.
28. "Jose"—O_1, Pa; O: "Dosa."
29. He takes *spḥ* as a form of the word *mšpḥh*, "family [of lice]."
30. R. Ḥiyya associates *śpḥ* with *šp̄ḥh*, "handmaid."
31. They take *špḥ* to be a form of *mšpḥh*, "family."
32. Cf. Ezra 9:2.
33. The verb *'rh* may mean "lay bare" as in EV, or "spill."

were snatched up into the carriages of the Babylonian invaders spilled over and kept discharging so much blood that blood filled each Babylonian's carriage. And as each one looked with disgust at the blood, he transfixed upon the point of his sword the woman he had seated beside him, threw her under his carriage, and the carriage passing over her, cut her to pieces. The Babylonians then warned one another: "Depart from the daughters of Zion, for they are unclean." With reference to these words, the prophet admonished the daughters of Zion as to the disgust they might evoke [even among the heathen], citing the words, *"Depart ye," men cried to one another, "Unclean! depart, depart, touch not"* (Lam. 4:15).

The verse concludes *Because naṣu, they were banished*[34] (*ibid.*). Concerning the meaning of *naṣu*, R. Ḥanina bar Papa and R. Simon differ. R. Ḥanina bar Papa maintained that not until they condemned (*na'ăṣu*) the Holy One, [as did the daughters of Zion], were Israel banished. R. Simon maintained that not until they became fractious antagonists (*naṣu*)[35] of the Holy One, [as the daughters of Zion became], were Israel banished.

7. *Can a woman ('iššah) forget her sucking child ('ulah)?* (Isa. 49:15). Iḳa construed this verse [not as God's answer to Zion, but as a reiteration of Zion's cry of anguish, and took it to be saying] "Canst Thou forget the offerings made by fire (*'iššeh*), the whole burnt offerings (*'olah*)? Canst Thou have forgotten the offerings we used to bring to Thee?" According to R. Huna who cited R. Aḥa, the Holy One replied: Evil deeds I forget, but good deeds I do not forget. I forget evil deeds, such as are embodied in the words "These are thy gods, O Israel" (Exod. 32:4) which thou didst utter to a calf; but I do not forget good deeds, such as are embodied in thy saying to Me at Sinai "All that the Lord hath spoken we will do, and obey" (Exod. 24:7).[36]

8. R. Abbahu said: Of the two requests which Israel put to the Holy One, the Prophets told Israel: "You did not make your requests with the right words." Israel had said *Let Him come unto us as the rain, as the latter rain that watereth the earth* (Hos. 6:3). Of this request the Prophets said: You did not make your request with the right words. Rain—wayfarers find it troublesome, repairers of roofs find it troublesome, those who tread grapes in the winepress and those who beat grain on the threshing floor find it troublesome. The right words would have asked God to promise, *I will be as the dew unto Israel; he shall blossom as the lily* (Hos. 14:6): that is, like the dew wherein is the promise of life, wherein is no trouble for the world's inhabitants, so shall I be for you, [O Israel].[37] At another time Israel had

34. JV: *Yea, they fled away, and wandered.*
35. The meaning of *naṣu*, a *hapax legomenon*, is uncertain.
36. R. Huna construes Isa. 49:15 as *Yea, thy "these" I will forget, but [thy response to] "I," I shall not forget.*
37. "Like the dew . . . for you, [O Israel]"—O_1, Yalḳuṭ.

said: *Set me as a seal upon Thy heart* (Song 8:6). The Prophets said to Israel: You did not make your request with the right words. The heart—at times it is exposed, and at other times it is covered up. The right words would have asked that Israel be *A crown of beauty* [*exposed*] *in the hand of the Lord, and a royal diadem in the always open hand of thy God.*

According to R. Simon ben Ḳuzi, who cited R. Johanan, the Holy One said: Neither you nor your Prophets made your request with the right words. You should have requested Me to say, *I have graven thee upon the palms of My hands* (Isa. 49:16). [A woman may forget her sucking child, but] it is impossible for a man to forget the palms of his hands. Hence *these* [*women*] *may forget, yet will not I forget thee* (Isa. 49:15).

PISKA 18

SUMMARY

The comforting and rebuilding of Jerusalem

The outcry *O ye sons of men, how long will ye turn my glory into shame?* (Ps. 4:3) is first construed as David's reproach to Doeg and Ahithophel and then as God's reproach to the nations of the earth, for ultimately He was to vindicate David as well as the people of Israel (Sec. 1).

But before her vindication, Israel is to suffer because she has been poor in knowledge of Torah, poor in performance of good works, and poor in righteous men! Jerusalem will be razed to its foundations, and Israel will be tossed about as in a tempest (Sec. 2). Still, the very description of Jerusalem as *not comforted* (Isa. 54:11) holds the promise of the converse, that she will be comforted, for in singling out a shortcoming in a person or a people, Scripture does not intend to shame them (Sec. 3).

When comforting comes to Jerusalem, her walls will be beautifully strengthened and ornamented. The gleam of precious stones will illumine Jerusalem; the great gate of the Temple will be hollowed out of a pearl of purest ray. Indeed, precious stones will be as common as pebbles and will serve to mark the borders of Jerusalem. In keeping with such abundance, as well as in the abundance of men and women who love God's law, peace in the world will also be abundant (Secs. 4–6).

PISKA 18

O thou afflicted,
tossed with tempest (Isa. 54:1)[1]

1. *O ye sons of [distinguished] men ('iš), how long will ye turn my glory into shame?* etc. (Ps. 4:3). In the phrase *sons of [distinguished] men,* David was addressing Doeg and Ahithophel. And why did he call them *sons of [distinguished] men ('iš)*?[2] Because they were sons of Abraham, Isaac, and Jacob. Here *'iš* clearly applies to our father Abraham, with reference to whom it is said "Restore the wife of the man (*'iš*), for he is a prophet" (Gen. 20:7); *'iš*, here, applies also to our father Isaac, concerning whom Rebekah asked, "What man is this that walketh in the field to meet us?"[3] (Gen. 24:65); *'iš*, here, applies also to our father Jacob, of whom it is said "Jacob was a perfect[4] man" (Gen. 25:27). In asking, *How long will ye turn my glory into shame?* (Ps. 4:3) David meant: How long will you shame my glory by referring to me only as "the son of Jesse" [instead of calling me by my own name]: *Wherefore cometh not the son of Jesse?* (1 Sam. 20:27), *I have seen a son of Jesse* (1 Sam. 16:18), and *Will the son of Jesse give every one of you fields and vineyards?* (1 Sam. 22:7). Have I no name of my own? *How long will you take pleasure in vanity*? (Ps. 4:3)—how long will you take pleasure in dashing foolishly about with vain words, saying of me, "The Holy One has abandoned him, forgotten him; henceforth kingship will never return to him?" *You expect the loss to continue for ever?*[5] (*ibid.*). Do you really suppose that because my kingship was lost to me for a time that it will be for ever thus? *Know that the Lord hath set apart for Himself one that He favoreth* (Ps. 4:4): Long ago, God gladdened me with good tidings through Nathan the prophet who told me, "The Lord also hath put away thy sin; thou shalt not die" (2 Sam. 12:13).

A different comment: *O ye sons of the man* (Ps. 4:3). Here the nations of the earth are addressed; why are they called *sons of the man*? Because they are descendants of the children's children of Noah, "Noah [who] was a righteous and blameless man" (Gen. 6:9). The Holy One asked the nations

1. Isa. 54:1–10 is the haftarah for *Rĕ'eh*, the third Sabbath following the Ninth of Ab.

2. *'Iš* means a man of renown or distinction; *'enoš* means a small, obscure man.

3. "He was exceedingly glorious, garmented in and covered with a prayer shawl, his appearance like that of an angel of God" (MTeh 90:18).

4. JV: *quiet*. But *tam* can also mean "perfect."

5. Interpreting *kazab̲*, "falsehood," in the sense of *'ak̲zab̲*, "failing, drying up," and thus "loss of throne." As for the word *selah*, in Rabbinic exegesis it is usually translated "for ever" (cf. B.Er 54a). JV: *and seek after falsehood.*

of the earth: *How long will ye turn My glory*—the Temple—*into shame*? (Ps. 4:3). How long will you shame the glory of My House, spitting in it, befouling it, committing your transgressions within it? *Will you take pleasure in vanity?*—take pleasure in dashing madly about with foolish words, saying of Me, "The Holy One has abandoned the Temple, has forgotten it—henceforth the Presence will never return to it." *You expect the loss to continue for ever? (ibid.)*. Do you really suppose that because I removed My presence from the Temple for a time, it will be for ever thus? [It will not, for] *know that the Lord hath set apart for Himself one that He favoreth* (Ps. 4:4): that is, through the prophet Isaiah, long ago, God gladdened Israel with good tidings [of the Temple's restoration]: *O thou afflicted, tossed with tempest, and not comforted, behold, I will lay thy stones in stibium, and set thy foundations with sapphires* (Isa. 54:11).

2. In another comment, Isaiah's words are read *O thou poor, tossed with tempest* (*ibid.*)—*poor*, that is, in righteous men, poor in knowledge of Torah, poor in [the performance of] commandments and good works; *tossed*[6]—that is, tossed hither and thither—a people the nations of the earth toss about, as is said *Remember, O Lord, and hold against the children of Edom the day of Jerusalem['s destruction, the day] they said: Toss [Israel] hence, toss them hence, every last one of them*[7] (Ps. 137:7).

[R. Abba bar Kahana and R. Levi Berabbi differ concerning the meaning of *'aru, 'aru*, previously read "toss"]. R. Abba bar Kahana said it means "raze it, raze it," as in the verse *The broad walls of Babylon shall be razed* (*'ar'er*) (Jer. 51:58). R. Levi said it means "empty it, empty it," as in the verse *She hastened and emptied* (*tĕ'ar*) *her pitcher into the trough* (Gen. 24:20). According to R. Abba bar Kahana who said *'aru* means "raze it," the verse in the Psalm implies that the Edomites razed the city to its foundations [and stopped at that]. But according to R. Levi who said *'aru* means "empty it, empty it," the verse in the Psalm implies that the Edomites took away the very foundations of the city.[8]

3. Another comment: *O thou afflicted . . . and is not comforted* (Isa. 54:11). R. Levi taught: Whenever Scripture says that something is not, it is implying that the converse will be. Thus Scripture says, *Sarai was barren; she had not a child* (Gen. 11:30); afterwards she did have a child: *Sarah gave children suck* (Gen. 21:7). Likewise, *Peninnah had children, but Hannah had not children* (1 Sam. 1:2); afterwards Hannah did have children: *The Lord remembered Hannah, and she conceived, and bore three sons and two*

6. The word *s'rh* is read as though spelled *š'rh*, and linked with the stem *'r'r*, "to toss hither and yon." *Š'rh* is thus taken to mean "which is tossed hither and yon," the š being a mark of the *šaf'el*, the intensifying mode of the verb.

7. JV: *the day of Jerusalem, who said: Raze it, raze it, even to the foundation thereof.*

8. Cf. Piska 3.7.

daughters (1 Sam. 2:21). Finally, *She is Zion, there is not one that careth for her* (Jer. 30:17); but then one will come who does care: *And a redeemer will come to Zion* (Isa. 59:20).

4. *Behold, I will lay thy stones in stibium* (Isa. 54:11): black stibium [used as cement for the white stones in the walls would make them look whiter], explains R. Abba bar Kahana, [even as powdered stibium applied to eyelids makes the white of the eye look whiter and the eyes more beautiful], as is said "With stibium she painted her eyes, and then attired her head" (2 Kings 9:30). (Three things are said of stibium: it promotes growth of the eyelashes, stops tears, and cures that affliction of the eye which is called "the princess").[9]

And set thy foundations with sapphires (Isa. 54:11). R. Yudan and R. Phinehas differ about the meaning of the verse. R. Yudan took the verse to mean that each and every layer of stones to be set in Jerusalem's foundations would be as beautiful as a sapphire. But R. Phinehas [took the verse to mean that the foundations would be as hard as sapphire, and] went on: If you suppose that sapphire is soft, the story of a man who went down to Rome to sell a sapphire will show you how hard sapphire is. The prospective buyer made his purchase of the sapphire contingent upon his testing it. The seller consented. What did the buyer do? He took the sapphire, laid it on an anvil, and struck it with a hammer. The anvil split, the hammer was smashed, but the sapphire was in no way diminished.[10]

5. *And the turrets upon thy walls* (*šimšoṯayiḵ*) *I shall make of kaḏkoḏ* (Isa. 54:12). According to R. Abba bar Kahana, *kaḏkoḏ* means "this and that";[11] [thus Isaiah indicates that the stones of which the turrets are to be made will be alternately stibium and sapphire]. According to R. Levi, since [in Arabia the term for] bright red is *kaḏkaḏyenon*,[12] R. Joshua ben Levi taught that the stones will be bright red *kaḏkuḏaya* stones [which give off light in the dark].

Standing with [the prophet] Elijah on Mount Carmel, R. Joshua ben Levi asked him: "Will not my master show me these stones of *kaḏkuḏaya*?" Elijah said: "Yes," and contrived a miracle in order to show them to R. Joshua ben Levi. It so happened at that moment that a ship was sailing in the

9. "Princess" is the name not only of a certain disorder of the eye, but also of a demon afflicting the eye.

10. The sapphire, a crystalline mineral, is second in hardness only to the diamond. Nevertheless, if subjected to the test described above, it would shatter even as a diamond would. For this information grateful acknowledgment is made to Albert M. Schaler.

11. *Kaḏkoḏ*, which occurs only twice in the Bible, can be read *kaḏ kaḏ*, "this and that." See MTeh 87:1.

12. See *'Aruḵ*, *s.v. kaḏkoḏ*. R. Levi asserts that the Syriac word *kaḏkaḏyenon* was in use in Arabia.

Great Sea. The ship was filled with heathen, but on it there was also a Jewish lad. When a mighty tempest of the sea fell upon the ship, Elijah appeared to the lad and said to him: "Go on an errand for me to R. Joshua ben Levi—show him the *kaḏkuḏaya* stones [that you will now pick up from the sea bottom],[13] and I will save this vessel for your sake." The lad replied: "R. Joshua ben Levi, who is the greatest man of this generation, may not believe me." Elijah replied: "He will believe you, for he is a humble man. But when you show the stones to him, do not show them to him in the presence of any other person. Take him to a cave three miles distant from Lydda and there show them to him."

Thereupon, by a miracle, the lad got away safely from the ship. He then went to R. Joshua ben Levi, and finding him in the teacher's chair in the great academy of Lydda, said: "Sir, I have a private matter to confide to you." At once R. Joshua ben Levi rose and followed him. Come and see the humility of R. Joshua ben Levi, who, following the lad for three miles, did not inquire of him, "What is it that you want of me?" When they got to the cave, the lad said: "Sir, these are *kaḏkuḏaya* stones." As R. Joshua beheld them, their brightness shone forth so strongly that he was startled and let them fall to the ground where they disappeared.

Hence, in accordance with the view of R. Joshua ben Levi, [R. Levi concluded that] because of the brightness of the *kaḏkuḏaya* stones, of which the turrets upon Jerusalem's walls will be made, Isaiah calls these turrets *šimšoṯayiḵ*, "thy shining battlements"[14] (Isa. 54:12).

And thy gates of gems hollowed out[15] (*ibid.*). R. Jeremiah, citing R. Samuel bar Isaac, said: From a single pearl the Holy One will hollow out the east gate of the Temple together with its two wickets.

R. Johanan sat in his chair in the great synagogue of Sepphoris, expounding: The Holy One will hollow out the east gate of the Temple and its two wickets out of one pearl. A certain heretic, a seafaring man, who was present, said: "Why, you can't find a pearl even as large as a pigeon's egg, and this person, sitting in a teacher's chair no less, talks like this!"

Some time afterwards, as the heretic was sailing upon the Great Sea, his ship sank, and he went down to the bottom of the sea where he saw ministering angels hollowing, shaping, and carving designs in an object. He asked them: "What's that?" They replied: "It is the east gate of the Temple with its

13. See Ginzberg, *Legends*, 6, 333.

14. R. Joshua ben Levi associates *šimšoṯayiḵ*, a *hapax legomenon*, with *šemĕs*, "sun." [Gesenius-Brown regards *šimšoṯayiḵ* as an irregular plural of *šemeš*. L.N.]

15. The commentator interprets *ḳdḥ* in the sense of "to bore, hollow out," and not in the sense of "kindle" (hence "carbuncle, fiery red," as in JV). See Rashi on B.Sanh 100a.

two wickets being made out of one pearl." Forthwith by a miracle, he escaped safely thence.

A year later, the heretic returned and found R. Johanan sitting in his chair, expounding the same passage in Isaiah, and saying: The Holy One will hollow the east gate of the Temple with its two wickets out of one pearl. The man said: "Old man, old man, all that you have to tell us, tell; all the glowing things you can say, say. If mine own eyes had not seen what I saw, I would never have believed it." R. Johanan said: "Had your eyes not seen what you have seen, you would not have believed what I was saying in my instruction in Torah?" Thereupon R. Johanan lifted his eyes and looked at the man, and in that instant the man turned into a heap of bones.

A story of a pious man who, while walking on a beach in Haifa, wondered: Is it possible that the Holy One can hollow the east gate of the Temple with its two wickets out of a single pearl? Whereat a Divine Voice came forth and said: If you were not completely pious, the measure of justice would strike you down. The world—all of it—I made in six days, as is said *In six days the Lord made heaven and earth* (Exod. 31:17), and yet you are wondering whether the east gate of the Temple with its two wickets can be made out of a single pearl? Thereupon the pious man, entreating mercy for his life, said: Master of universes, it was only in my heart that I wondered—I did not utter the words with my lips.

At once a miracle was performed for him. The sea before him was divided, and he saw ministering angels hollowing, shaping, and carving designs in an object. He asked them: What is that? They replied: It is the east gate of the Temple with its two wickets being made out of one pearl.

6. *And thy entire border of precious stones* (Isa. 54:12). R. Benjamin ben Levi said: The borders of Jerusalem will be entirely marked out by precious stones and pearls of purest ray, and all Israel will come and take as many of them as they desire. For, in the world as we know it, borders of land are marked with stones and with cistus[16] whereas in the time-to-come borders will be marked with precious stones and pearls of purest ray. Hence *And thy entire border of precious stones.* As a matter of fact, said R. Levi, it would take an area of twelve by eighteen miles to accommodate all the precious stones and pearls of purest ray that will mark out Jerusalem's borders. [These will serve without fail to make peace among men in the world-to-come]. Now, in the world as we know it, when a man owes money to another, he is apt to say, "Let us go and try our case before a judge," who at times succeeds in making peace between them and at times does not succeed in making peace between them. In any event, both are not likely to come out satisfied. But in the time-to-come, when a man owes money to

16. A shrubby plant, with deep and straight roots, used for hedges to mark boundaries. See Ginzberg, *Legends*, *4*, 15–16.

another, he will say: "Let us go and try our case before the king Messiah in Jerusalem." Upon reaching the borders of Jerusalem, however, and finding within them an abundance of precious stones and pearls of purest ray, he will take two stones and give them to the other, saying: "Do I owe you more than the value of these?" And the other will say: "You did not owe me as much as these are worth—you are now absolved of obligation and are free of debt." Hence it is written *He maketh peace by means of thy borders* (Ps. 147:14).

All thy children shall be taught of the Lord; and abundant shall be the peace of thy children (Isa. 54:13). [In keeping with the abundance of precious stones and pearls of purest ray, the time of the Messiah is] four times referred to in Scripture as a time of abundant peace: *In his days shall the righteous flourish; and abundance of peace, till the moon be no more* (Ps. 72:7); *Abundant peace shall have they that love Thy law* (Ps. 119:165); *The humble shall inherit the land, and delight themselves in the abundance of peace* (Ps. 37:11); and the verse just quoted, *All thy children shall be taught of the Lord; and abundant shall be the peace of thy children* (Isa. 54:13).

PISKA 19

SUMMARY

Israel's obedience to three basic commands makes her worthy of being God's own people

Israel's enemies, exhibiting the figures of the cherubim which they had taken from the Temple, spread far and wide the slander that Israel, like other nations, had all along been worshiping idols—slander so malevolent that God promised Israel: *I, even I, will comfort you* (Sec. 1).

No fugitive from Israel could find comfort anywhere among the heathen nations. All of Israel's neighbors encompassed her with hostility, a hostility for which Israel blamed God because He had commanded His people not to intermarry with heathen nations. Hence God said *I will comfort you* (Sec. 2) like the most compassionate of fathers and soothe you like the most comforting of mothers (Sec. 3).

Until such comfort comes, Torah's promises of redemption give strength to Israel (Sec. 4). Moreover, to make up for Israel's long period of exile and suffering, when God redeems her, He will double her portion, such doubling being intimated by God's saying "I" twice—*I, even I, will comfort you.*

Israel's occasional giving up the hope of deliverance may be justified by the fact that when Jacob was to meet his brother Esau, he, too, was afraid and did not rely on God's promise of deliverance.

Israel is to know, however, that as long as heaven is not measurable by mortals, as long as the earth does not totter on its foundations, as long as the cycles of human life continue, God will not cast off Israel (Sec. 5), the people so dear to him that when Moses' staff with God's name graven upon it was shown to the Red Sea, the Sea fled in awe.

Torah, deeds of kindness, and the willingness to make offerings to God confer upon Israel the kind of distinction which led Him to say, *Thou art My people* (Sec. 6).

PISKA 19

I, even I, am He that comforteth you (Isa. 51:12).[1]

1. *An act of slander hath broken my heart—an overwhelming blow—I looked for some to show compassion, but there were none; and for comforters, but I found none* (Ps. 69:21). The verse alludes to the slander of Israel which Ammonites and Moabites spread far and wide. You find that when Israel's sins brought it about that heathen nations invaded Jerusalem, Ammonites and Moabites came with them. When the Ammonites and the Moabites came into the Holy of Holies, they took the figures of the cherubim, placed them on a common bier, and went around the streets of Jerusalem with them, exulting: Have not Israel been saying, "We do not worship idols"? But look—here is the proof that they do worship them. Of this slander, Scripture takes note in the verse *Moab and Seir say: Behold, the house of Judah is like unto all the nations*, etc. (Ezek. 25:8). And what did the children of Israel say in reply? All of them together cried out in lament: "Woe! Woe!" Ever since then the Holy One has been saying: "I have heard the slander of Moab and the revilings of the children of Ammon who, having crossed Israel's border, have taunted My people and glorified themselves. *Therefore, as I live," saith the Lord of hosts, the God of Israel: "Surely Moab shall be as Sodom, and the children of Ammon as Gomorrah"* (Zeph. 2:8–9). [Their slander, said Israel, was] *An overwhelming blow* (Ps. 69:2), an overwhelming blow, which utterly depleted my strength—*I looked* [*among men*] *for some to show compassion, but there were none, and for comforters* [*among them*], *but I found none* (*ibid.*). It was then that the Holy One said: *I, even I, am He that comforteth you* (Isa. 51:12).

2. *They have heard that I sigh; there is none to comfort me* (Lam. 1:21). R. Joshua of Siḵnin, citing R. Levi, took the verse to be expressive [of Israel's grief at the death] of Aaron the High Priest. You find that when Aaron the High Priest died, the Canaanites came and fought against Israel, as is said *When the Canaanite, the king of Arad, who dwelt in the South, heard tell that Israel's way of Atarim had set*[2] (Num. 21:1). What is meant by the words *way of Atarim*, etc.? That the life of Aaron, the great guide (*tayyar*) of the children of Israel who had led them through the ways of the wilderness,[3] had set like the sun. Hence, said Israel, *There is none to comfort me* (Lam. 1:21): not Moses, for he himself is a mourner, and not

1. In the seven-Sabbath cycle of consolation, Isa. 51:12–52:12 is the haftarah for *Šofĕṭim*, the fourth Sabbath following the Ninth of Ab.

2. JV: *that Israel came by the way of Atarim.*

3. Because of him, clouds of glory preceded Israel and made the way even for them.

Eleazar [Aaron's son], for he himself is a mourner. *All mine enemies have heard of my trouble, and were glad* (*ibid.*). They said: Now is the time to get at the children of Israel, the time to go and put an end to Canaan's enemies.

The Rabbis took the verse in Lamentations *They have heard that I sigh*, etc., to be expressive of [Israel's grief at] the rejection of them by the nations of the earth. You find that when Israel's iniquities brought it about that heathen nations invaded Jerusalem, they decreed that wherever Israel might flee, they be denied refuge. So when the children of Israel sought to flee to the south, heathen armies did not allow them to, [and hence the Lord condemned these heathen]: *Thus saith the Lord, For three transgressions of Gaza, yea, for four, I will not reverse it*[4] (Amos 1:6)—[My verdict against Gaza]. When the children of Israel sought to flee to the east, other heathen armies did not allow them to, [and these heathen the Lord also condemned]: *Thus saith the Lord, For three transgressions of Damascus, yea, for four, I will not reverse it* (Amos 1:3)—[My verdict against Damascus]. When the children of Israel sought to flee to the north, still other heathen armies did not allow them to, [and these heathen, too, the Lord condemned]: *Thus saith the Lord, For three transgressions of Tyre, yea, for four, I will not reverse it* (Amos 1:9)—[My verdict against Tyre]. When the children of Israel sought to flee to the west, still other heathen armies did not allow them to, [and these the Lord condemned as well, saying]: *The burden upon Arabia*[5] (Isa. 21:13)—[that is, the burden of guilt is upon Arabia]. Of the all-encompassing hostility of Israel's neighbors, the Holy One said to Israel: Your behavior towards them must have been outrageous [to provoke them to such hostility]. Israel retorted: Master of universes, hast Thou not done it?[6] [Art Thou not responsible for their hostility to us]? Israel's reply may be explained by a parable of a king wed to a noblewoman whom he admonished, saying: Do not talk with your neighbors. Neither lend anything to them, nor borrow anything from them. On one occasion she angered him, so he deposed her as queen and expelled her from his palace. Whereupon she went around looking for shelter among the houses of her neighbors, but not one of them took her in. Then the king said: Your behavior towards them must have been outrageous. She replied: My lord the king, is it not you who are responsible for their treatment of me? Did you not

4. The verse goes on to say: *Because they permitted an entire captivity to be carried away captive by delivering them up to Edom.* The phrase *entire captivity* suggests to the commentator that no one was permitted to escape.

As for Amos' prophesying concerning events that were to take place after the Temple's destruction, see Piska 16.10.

5. Even though Arabia lies east of the Land of Israel, it would appear that an Arabian army was stationed in the west.

6. Lam. 1:21 goes on to say *For Thou hast done it.*

specifically admonish me, saying, "Do not talk with your neighbors. Neither lend anything to them, nor borrow anything from them"? Had I [been neighborly and] borrowed from them or lent to them, which of them seeing me come into her house would not have gladly taken me in? Hence *Thou hast done it* (Lam. 1:21). So, too, Israel retorted to the Holy One: Master of universes, is it not Thou who art responsible for our neighbors' hostility towards us? Didst Thou not have it written for us in the Torah, *Neither shalt thou make marriages with them: thy daughter thou shalt not give unto his son, nor his daughter shall thou take unto thy son* (Deut. 7:3)? Had we allowed their sons to marry our daughters or our sons to marry their daughters, which of them upon seeing such daughters or sons standing at his door would not have gladly taken them in? Hence *Thou hast done it* (Lam. 1:21). [Then Israel went on to pray]: *Bring the day that Thou hast proclaimed when they will be like me* (*ibid.*)—that is, when the heathen nations will be like me when I am in distress, not like me when I am in ease. In the meantime, *There is none [among men] to comfort me* (*ibid.*). It was then that the Holy One said: *I, even I, am He that comforteth you.*

3. [Israel prayed further: *Be unto us*] *like as a father* [*who*] *hath compassion upon his children*, etc. (Ps. 103:13). Like any particular father? Like the most compassionate of the Fathers, R. Ḥiyya taught. And who was the most compassionate of the Fathers? That was—so said R. Azariah, citing R. Aḥa—our father Abraham. You find that before the Holy One brought a flood upon the Sodomites, Abraham said bluntly to the Holy One: Master of universes, Thou didst swear that Thou wouldst not bring again a flood to the world, as proved by the verse *I have sworn that the waters of Noah should no more go over the earth* (Isa. 54:9). Now, if Thou art not bringing a flood of water, art Thou perhaps about to bring a flood of fire? Dost Thou thus intend cunningly to evade Thine own oath? *That were a profanation for Thee to do after this manner*, etc. (Gen. 18:25). And, according to R. Levi, Abraham went on to say, *The Judge of all the earth cannot exercise justice too strictly*[7] (*ibid.*). If Thou seekest strict justice, there will be no world, and if Thou seekest to have a world, strict justice cannot be exercised. Dost Thou think to take hold of the rope at both ends? Thou desirest the world to endure, but Thou desirest true justice also. If Thou wilt not relent a little, the world will not endure.

R. Joshua bar Nehemiah applied the verse, *Like as a father hath compassion upon his children* (Ps. 103:13), to our father Jacob [when he was about to meet Esau]: *And he himself passed over before them and bowed*, etc. (Gen. 33:3). What is implied by the words *And he himself*? Jacob hastened to get ahead of his children so as to encounter any danger first, saying "I would rather have Esau strike me than strike my children." What

7. JV: *shall not the Judge of all the earth do justly?*

had he previously done in their behalf? He had armed them with weapons next to the skin and then clothed them in white garments. He thus prepared himself [and them] for three things: prayer, presents, or warfare. For prayer: *Deliver me, I pray Thee, from the hand of my brother* (Gen. 32:12). For presents: *The presents [for Esau] passed over before him* (Gen. 32:22). For warfare: *If Esau come to one camp, and smite it* (Gen. 32:9), then we proceed to wage war against Esau.

[As to God's compassion for Israel and His comforting of them], R. Samuel taught: It is the way of a father to have compassion: *Like as a father hath compassion upon his children* (Ps. 103:12); and it is the way of a mother to comfort: *As one whom his mother comforteth* (Isa. 66:13). The Holy One said: I will act like a father and I will act like a mother. I will act like a father: *Like as a father hath compassion upon his children.* I will act like a mother: *As one whom his mother comforteth.* And because He meant to be father and mother to Israel, the Holy One used "I" twice in the verse *I, even I, am He that comforteth you.*

4. R. Abba bar Kahana, citing R. Johanan, taught in a parable: A king who wed a noblewoman wrote out a pledge of a substantial settlement upon her: "Such-and-such elegant chambers, canopied over, I will provide for you. Such-and-such ornaments I will give you. Such-and-such treasures I will give you." Then he left her and went away to a far country by the sea where he remained many years. Eventually her companions began to mock her, saying: "How much longer will you wait around here? Get yourself a man while you are young and while your strength is with you." Thereupon she would go into her house, pick up her marriage settlement, read it, and be comforted. After many years, the king came back from the far country by the sea. He said to his wife: "My little one, I marvel that you could wait around for me all these years." She replied: "My lord the king, but for the substantial marriage settlement which you pledged to me in writing, my companions would long since have got me to give you up."

[As her companions mocked the king's wife], so, the world being what it is, the nations of the earth mock Israel and say to them: How long will you sacrifice yourselves for your God, giving up your lives for Him, letting yourselves be slain for His sake? How much pain He has brought upon you! How many plunderers He has brought upon you! How many afflictions He has brought upon you! Get yourselves over to us, and we shall make you captains, prefects, and commanders-in-chief! Israel's reply to the nations is to go into synagogues and into houses of study, take the Scroll, and read in it God's pledges to her: *I will have respect unto you, and make you fruitful, and multiply you; and will establish My covenant with you* (Lev. 26:9). And thus Israel comforts herself.

When the time of redemption arrives, the Holy One will say to Israel: "I marvel that you were able to wait for Me all these years," and Israel will reply to the Holy One: Master of universes, but for the Scroll which Thou didst write for us, the nations of the world would long since have got us to give Thee up. Of the Torah it is written *This*—[as in *This is the Torah* (Deut. 4:44)]—*I recall to my mind, therefore have I hope* (Lam. 3:21). And David said likewise: *Unless Thy Torah had been my delight, I should then have perished in mine affliction* (Ps. 119:92).[8]

5. Another comment: *I, even I, am He that comforteth you* (Isa. 51:12). R. Abun, citing Resh Laḳish, taught in a parable: A king who became angry at the noblewoman who was his wife deposed her as queen and put her out of his palace. After many years he wished to fetch her and restore her to her place. She said: "Let him double my marriage settlement for me, and then I will let him fetch me back." Even so the Holy One said to Israel: My children, at Sinai I used *'nky* only once in declaring to you *"I" am the Lord thy God* (Exod. 20:2). But in Jerusalem in the time-to-come I shall double My use of it to signify how greatly I mean to comfort you: *I, even I, am He that comforteth you* (Isa. 51:12).

[In another comment on this verse] R. Menaḥema, citing R. Abin, took God to be saying to Israel: Because of the comfort you gave Me at Sinai, when you said *All that the Lord hath spoken, we will do and obey* (Exod. 24:7), [I have doubled My assurance of comforting]. And since *Thou art the one* [*who exclaimed of Me "Who?"*],[9] *why art thou afraid?* (Isa. 51:12). Art thou not Israel, the very one who exclaimed of Me at the Red Sea "Who is like unto Thee, O Lord?" (Exod. 15:11). Why, then, *art thou afraid of man that shall die* (Isa. 51:12), or *of the son of man that shall be as grass?* (*ibid.*).

R. Berechiah, citing R. Ḥelbo, and R. Samuel bar Naḥman, citing R. Jonathan, said: In the days of Haman, Israel deserved extinction [for having given up the hope of deliverance]. They drew support, however, from the reaction of a certain elder [of Israel], for they said: If our father Jacob despaired[10] although the Holy One had promised him: *Behold, I am with thee, and will keep thee whithersoever thou goest* (Gen. 28:15), all the more so should we despair.

[It is because Israel despaired that] the prophet, chiding them, said: *And hast forgotten the Lord thy Maker, that stretched forth the heavens, and laid the foundations of the earth* (Isa. 51:13). You have forgotten what I said to you: *If heaven above be measured and the foundations of the earth searched out beneath, then will I cast off all the seed of Israel, for all that they have done, saith the Lord* (Jer. 31:37). Has heaven been measured? Is the earth

8. See PR 21:15.
9. JV: *Who art thou?*
10. *Then Jacob was greatly afraid* (Gen. 32:8). See Piska 23.2; Gen. Rabbah 76:1; and PR 33:5 (YJS, *18*, 638).

tottering on its foundations? From the fact that both heaven and earth are stretched out as of yore, you should draw the proper conclusion and not be afraid. Still, *thou fearest continually all the day because of the fury of the oppressor* (Isa. 51:13)—because, as R. Isaac explained, one oppression follows fast upon the other. *And yet where is the fury of the oppressor* (*ibid.*), of Haman and his helpers, *of him who made ready to destroy* (*ibid.*) "in the first month, which is the month of Nisan" (Esther 3:7)?

[*I . . . am He that comforteth you* (Isa. 51:12)]: *When he that is bent down* [*by illness*] *is speedily loosed, he shall not go down dying into the pit,* etc. (Isa. 51:14). The allusion in the words *He that . . . is speedily loosed,* R. Abbahu explained, [is to a loosening of bowels]. This is one of six bodily activities—namely, sneezing, sweating, sleep, seminal emission, dreaming, and regular bowel movement—each of which is a good sign of improving health in a sick person. Proof from Scripture that sneezing is a good sign? *His sneezings flash forth light* (Job 41:10). Proof that sweating is a good sign? *In the sweat of thy face shalt thou eat bread* (Gen. 3:19). Proof that seminal emission is a good sign? *Seeing seed, he will prolong his days* (Isa. 53:10). Proof that sleep is a good sign? *I should have slept, then I would have been at ease* (Job 3:13). Proof that dreaming is a good sign? *Thou didst cause me to dream, and make me to live* (Isa. 38:16). Proof that regular bowel movement is a good sign? *When that which is to be emptied*[11] *is quick to loose, he will not die and go down into the pit* (Isa. 51:14). That is, as R. Haggai pointed out, so long *as he does not lack his daily bread* (*ibid.*), these bodily activities are all good signs of improving health in a sick man.

6. *I am the Lord thy God, who stirred up the sea, that the waves thereof roared; the Lord Ṣĕḇa'oṯ is His name* (Isa. 51:15). What did the Red Sea see and flee from? On this point R. Judah and R. Nehemiah differ. According to R. Judah, the Sea saw Moses' staff and fled. But according to R. Nehemiah, His Name, the Ineffable Name of *The Lord Ṣĕḇa'oṯ*, was graven upon the staff, and seeing the Name, the Sea fled.

I have put My words in thy mouth, and have covered thee in the shadow of My hand, that I may plant the heavens and lay the foundations of the earth (Isa. 51:16). The implications of this verse we are taught in a passage of Mishnah which begins, "Simon the righteous was one of the last survivors of the Great Assembly," etc., implications which are specified in subsequent *halaḵoṯ*[12] (Aḇ 1:2). R. Huna, citing R. Aḥa, said: They who crossed the Red Sea had themselves already specified the implications of the verse. Their

11. See Rashi.

12. Wherein R. Simon is quoted as saying that the world endures because of Torah—*My words in thy mouth*; because of deeds of kindness—*covered thee in the shadow of My hand*; and offerings whereby it is possible to *plant the heavens and lay the foundations of the earth.*

words, *Thou in Thy kindness hast led the people that Thou hast redeemed* (Exod. 15:13), point to deeds of kindness. In their words *Thou hast guided them in Thy strength* (Exod. 15:14), *strength,* as in the verse "When the Lord gave strength to His people, He blessed them with peace" (Ps. 29:11), refers to Torah. Yet even after the giving of Torah, the world was tottering. When was the world put on a firm foundation? After Israel came *to Thy holy habitation* (Exod. 15:14), [these being the words by which those who crossed the Red Sea referred to the Temple where offerings were made].

In a Mishnah we are taught: Rabban Simeon ben Gamaliel said, "The world is established on three principles . . . all three of which are set forth in a single verse: *These are the things that ye shall do: speak ye every man the truth with his neighbor; exercise true justice; and make peace in your gates* (Zech. 8:16)" (Ab̲ 1:18). The three are, in fact, one. For when justice is exercised, truth is attained, and peace is achieved.

R. Joshua of Sik̲nin said in the name of R. Levi: The words *I have put My words in thy mouth* (Isa. 51:16) refer to words of Torah; the words *have covered thee in the shadow of My hand* (*ibid.*) refer to deeds of kindness. Thus you are taught that when a man engages himself in Torah and deeds of kindness, he merits refuge under the shadow of the wings of the Holy One. As Scripture says, "How precious is Thy lovingkindness which Thou didst command: because of it men take refuge in the shadow of Thy wings" (Ps. 36:8). In going on to say *that I may plant the heavens, and lay the foundations of the earth* (Isa. 51:16), Isaiah refers to Temple offerings [whereby the earth's foundations were laid]. Isaiah continues: *And say of thee who art distinguished*—[distinguished, that is, by obedience to the three commands specified in Zech. 8:16]—*"Thou art My people"*[13] (*ibid.*). R. Ḥanina bar Papa said: We went through all of Scripture, from first to last, and found no other verse where Israel is called "distinguished." No other indeed? No: only this one: *And say of thee who art distinguished, "Thou art My people"* (*ibid.*).

13. JV: *And say unto Zion: "Thou art My people."* But apparently R. Ḥanina construes *Zion* in its meaning of "distinguished." See *Ḳorban ha-'ed̲ah* on P.Ta 4:2.

PISKA 20

SUMMARY

Jerusalem's ultimate distinction and glory

Zion is the seventh in the number of notable mothers in Israel who were barren a long time before God blessed them with children. Like the others, Zion's time will come: no longer barren, no longer uprooted from the Land, she will find peace.

First among the mothers was Rachel: because so many matters of moment in Israel's past begin with her, the children of Israel are called by her name (Secs. 1–2).

In saying that something is not—such as not being blessed with children—Scripture does not intend to call attention to the lack, but rather to imply that the converse will be (Sec. 3). Hence Zion, though troubled now, will come to have peace, and her rejoicing will find expression in ten different ways (Sec. 4).

In the meantime, Zion's ruined precincts retain their holiness. Indeed, in its desolation, Zion brought to the fore more righteous men than when it was intact (Sec. 5).

That God does not intend to bring shame upon any creature or any thing involved in a transgression for which it was in no way responsible is shown by the fact that the kind of tree from which Adam ate remains unknown to this day (Sec. 6).

When Zion is restored, Jerusalem, in order to accommodate all who would crowd into her, will spread out to the south and to the north, to the east and to the west. Indeed she will not only spread outwards, but will rise upwards until she reaches the throne of glory where she will be protected by a wall of fire round about. Such is to be Jerusalem's distinction and surpassing glory (Sec. 7).

PISKA 20

Sing, O Barren (Isa. 54:1).[1]

1. *He maketh the barren woman to keep house, then to be a joyful mother of children* (Ps. 113:9). There were seven such barren women: Sarah, Rebekah, Rachel, Leah, Manoah's wife, Hannah, and Zion.[2] Hence the words *He maketh the barren woman to keep house* (*ibid.*) apply, to begin with, to our mother Sarah: "Sarai was barren" (Gen. 11:30); and the words *then to be a joyful mother of children* (Ps. 113:9) also apply to our mother Sarah: "Sarah gave children suck" (Gen. 21:7). Or the words *He maketh the barren woman to keep house* apply to Rebekah: "Isaac entreated the Lord for his wife, because she was barren" (Gen. 25:21); the words *then to be a joyful mother of children* also apply to Rebekah: "and the Lord let Himself be entreated of him, and Rebekah his wife conceived" (Gen. 25:21). Or the words *He maketh the barren woman to keep house* apply to Leah: "When the Lord saw that Leah was hated, He opened her womb" (Gen. 29:31), this statement implying that she had previously been barren; the words *then to be a joyful mother of children* also apply to Leah: "I have borne him six sons" (Gen. 30:20). Or the words *He maketh the barren woman to keep house* apply to Rachel: "Rachel was barren" (Gen. 29:31); so do the words *then to be a joyful mother of children:* "The sons of Rachel: Joseph and Benjamin" (Gen. 35:24). Or the words *He maketh the barren woman to keep house* apply to Manoah's wife: "The angel of the Lord appeared unto the woman, and said unto her: 'Behold now, thou art barren, and hast not borne' " (Judg. 13:3); the words *then to be a joyful mother of children* also apply to Manoah's wife: " 'but thou shalt conceive and bear a son' " (*ibid.*). Or the words *He maketh the barren woman to keep house* apply to Hannah: "Peninnah had children, but Hannah had no children" (1 Sam. 1:2); so do the words *then to be a joyful mother of children*: "Hannah conceived, and bore three sons and two daughters"(1 Sam. 2:21). Finally, the words *He maketh the barren woman to keep house* apply to Zion: "Sing, O barren, thou that didst not bear" (Isa. 54:1); so do the words *then to be a joyful mother of children*: "Thou, O Zion, shalt say in thy heart, Who hath begotten *me* these?" (Isa. 49:21).

2. R. Reuben read the word *Ranni* in *Ranni* ("sing") *O barren* (Isa.

1. In the seven-Sabbath cycle of consolation, Isa. 54:1–10 is the haftarah for *Ki ṯeṣe'*, the fifth Sabbath following the Ninth of Ab.

2. The theme of the seven barren women appears to be based on *the barren hath borne seven* (1 Sam. 2:5), which is construed "On seven occasions hath the barren borne."

54:1) as the Greek *eirēnē*, "Thou wilt come to have peace,[3] O uprooted one." [In construing *barren* as "uprooted" R. Reuben followed] R. Meir, who reading the word *'akarah*, "barren," as though spelled *'akurah*, "rooted up," took the verse to be saying "O people, whom the peoples of the earth uprooted!" Of this uprooting of Israel, Scripture says, *Remember, O Lord, and hold against the children of Edom the day of Jerusalem['s destruction, the day] they said: Raze it ('aru), raze it, even to the foundation thereof* (Ps. 137:7). According to R. Abba bar Kahana, the word *'aru* means "raze it, raze it," as in the verse *The broad walls of Babylon shall be razed ('ar'er)* (Jer. 51:58). (The rest of the comment on the etymology of *'aru* which is here abbreviated is in the Piska *O thou afflicted, tossed about* [18.2]).

R. Abba bar Kahana said: Most of the guests assembled at Boaz' wedding were descendants of Leah, [yet they blessed Ruth by saying *The Lord make (thee) . . . like Rachel and like Leah* (Ruth 4:11), naming Rachel first], for Rachel was held to be first among the wives, as is implied by the verse *And Rachel was 'krh*[4] (Gen. 29:31). R. Isaac's reading of this verse, [R. Abba goes on], led him to conclude that Rachel was the first among the wives, for he read *'krh* not as "barren" but as "root" (*ykrh*), metaphorically signifying that she was first. [R. Isaac thus came to a deduction from Scripture which] R. Simeon ben Yoḥai stated as follows: Because so many matters of moment in Israel's past go back to Rachel, therefore the children of Israel[5] are called by her name: *Rachel weeping for her children* (Jer. 31:14). They are called not only by her name, but also by her son's name: *It may be that the Lord, the God of hosts, will be gracious unto the remnant of Joseph* (Amos 5:15). And even by her son's son's name: *Ephraim is a darling son unto Me* (Jer. 31:19).

3. [*Sing, O barren*], *thou that didst not bear* (Isa. 54:1). [With Rachel, among others, in mind—the fact that she was barren and later bore a child]—R. Levi declared: Whenever Scripture says that something is not, it is implying that the converse will be. (The rest of R. Levi's comment, which is here abbreviated, is in the Piska *O Thou afflicted, tossed about* [18.3]).

4. *Break forth into singing, and cry aloud, thou that didst not travail* (Isa. 54:1). In Scripture, rejoicing is designated by ten different terms:[6] gladness, merriment, joy, exulting, jubilation; shouting, a ringing cry, a shrill cry, a

3. Why should one who is barren feel impelled to sing? Hence R. Reuben's comment in keeping with his practice elsewhere (Piska 14.1, and 17.1) to derive Hebrew words from the Greek.

Here the reading in Pa, *harinah*, which approximates *eirēnē*, "thou wilt come to have peace," is followed. See Brüll, *Jahrbücher*, *1*, 34, n. 8, referred to in B. Z. Bacher, *'Ăḡaḏaṯ 'amora'e 'ereṣ Yiśra'el* (Tel Aviv, 5690/1930), *3*, part 1, p. 79, n. 2.

4. Usually translated "barren."

5. "the children of Israel"—O_1; "her children"—O.

6. The number ten may be taken to symbolize the ten canopies which, according

resounding cry, and a trumpet blast. A trumpet blast, according to some, is excluded from this list and is replaced by "leaping," in the sense in which "leap" is used in the verse "Before him leapeth terror" (Job 41:14)—that is to say, rejoicing leaps up swiftly and suddenly like a flying fish from the water.

5. *For more are the children of the desolate than the children of the married wife, saith the Lord* (Isa. 54:1). R. Abba bar Kahana, citing the verse *When the Dwelling is become thy desolation*[7] (Song 4:3), said: Yea, even though the Temple is become a desolation, the ritually unclean incur guilt when they enter its ruined precincts, even as such incurred guilt when they entered its precincts at the time that it still stood. [Indeed it is more holy in its desolation—if one dare speak thus—than when it was standing]. According to R. Levi, God said that when the Temple was standing, it brought to the fore wicked men, such as Ahaz, Manasseh, and Amon. But when the Temple was in ruins, it brought to the fore righteous men, such as Daniel and his company, Mordecai and his company, Ezra and his company. In short, as R. Aḥa, citing R. Johanan, declared: God said that when the Temple was desolate, it brought to the fore for Me more righteous men than it did when it was intact.

6. *A stand of wheat that grows in the earth upon the top of the mountains, will like [a cedar of] Lebanon shake [down seed] from its fruit*[8] (Ps. 72:16). What was the plant Adam ate of? Wheat, according to R. Meir. The grape, according to R. Judah bar R. Il'a'i. According to R. Abba of Acco, it was the ethrog.[9] According to R. Jose, it was the fig. Each of these teachers cited proof for his answer. The proof of R. Meir who said that the plant was wheat: It is the way of the world that when a man has no understanding, people say of him, This man is "wise," God help him, because in all his days he never put bread made of wheat, [the source of wisdom], into his mouth.[10] With regard to R. Meir's opinion, R. Ze'era put the following question to R. Samuel bar R. Isaac: What Adam ate of is described in Scripture as a tree, so how can you say it was a grain—wheat? R. Samuel bar R. Isaac replied: [In the Garden of Eden], stalks of wheat were like trees,

---

to the Rabbis, the Holy One joined over Adam in the Garden of Eden. See Piska 4.4; and PR 14:10 (YJS, *18*, 280).

7. JV: *And thy mouth is comely*. But *midbarek*, "thy mouth," can also mean "thy wilderness, thy desolation"; and *n'wh*, "comely," is construed as though spelled *nwh*, "residence, Temple."

8. The verse is construed as speaking of the time-to-come when life will again be as it was in the Garden of Eden.

9. A kind of orange or citron used during the Feast of Sukkot.

10. Wheat was the first cereal to be domesticated. Hence it is considered both source and symbol of wisdom.

for they grew to the height of cedars of Lebanon and used to shake down their seed to the ground.

The proof of R. Judah bar R. Il'a'i who said that it was grapes: *Grapes of gall, they have clusters of bitterness* (Deut. 32:32)—those clusters that Adam ate brought bitterness into the world. The proof of R. Abba of Acco who said it was the ethrog: the words *Eve . . . ate of the tree* (Gen. 3:6) indicate a tree whose wood, like its fruit, may be eaten. And what tree is that? The ethrog.

The proof of R. Jose who said it was figs: *They sewed fig leaves together, and made themselves girdles* (Gen. 3:7). The import of this verse, R. Joshua of Si̱knin, citing R. Levi, illustrated by a parable of a king who had a son and also had many maidservants. The king instructed his son, saying to him: My son, beware of touching a single one of all these maidservants. But what did the son do? He proceeded to disgrace himself with one of the maidservants. When his father became aware of what his son had done, he deposed him and expelled him from the palace. The son then went about to all the houses of the other maidservants, and not one of them would take him in. You must therefore conclude that the one with whom he had disgraced himself was the one who opened her door and took him in. So it was with Adam. When he ate of the tree, he and his wife heard all the other trees repudiate him, saying: "Behold the thief! Behold the thief who sought to deceive his Creator, who sought to deceive his Master." Each one of the trees said, *Let not the foot of pride come unto me* (Ps. 36:12)—let not the foot that stepped forward in pride come unto me. *And let not the hand of the wicked shake me* (*ibid.*)—let him not lay his hand upon me to shake me or even take leaves from me. From the following verse you must therefore conclude that the tree which had given him fruit was the same one which had given him leaves: *They sewed fig leaves together, and made themselves girdles* (Gen. 3:7). And what was the name given to the fig tree? "Daughter of woe," so said R. Levi, for it brought woe and weeping to the world.

R. Berechiah, citing R. Simon who cited R. Joshua ben Levi, said: As to the identity of the tree from which Adam ate, the Holy One has not revealed, and will not reveal it. For a somewhat similar reason—[to spare mankind shame]—the Holy One said: It is written *If a woman approach any beast, and lie down thereto, thou shalt kill the woman and the beast* (Lev. 20:16). The human being commits a sin, to be sure, but what sin does the animal commit? None. However, because the animal is a stumbling block whereby a human falls into sin, therefore the Holy One said: Let it be stoned. Another reason for destroying the animal: That if it be allowed to live and be seen going through the marketplace, people will be tempted to say, "This is the animal on account of whom So-and-so was stoned to death."

And so the Holy One said: If, in regard to matters of this kind, I take such pains to spare Adam's descendants shame, all the more reason that I [do not make known the kind of tree whereby Adam sinned and thus] spare men the shame they would feel [whenever they saw the tree].

7. A story. R. Eleazar ben Azariah and R. Eleazar the Modiite sat engaged with the meaning of the verse *At that time they shall call Jerusalem the throne of the Lord* (Jer. 3:17). R. Eleazar ben Azariah asked R. Eleazar the Modiite: Can Jerusalem hold as many people [as will crowd into it when it becomes His throne]? R. Eleazar replied: The Holy One will say to Jerusalem: Extend thyself, enlarge thyself, receive thy hosts—*Enlarge the place of thy tent*, etc. (Isa. 54:2). R. Johanan said: Jerusalem is destined to grow to the gates of Damascus.[10a] And the proof? The verse *The burden of the word of the Lord. In the land of Hadrak and in Damascus shall be His resting place* (Zech. 9:1). As to the meaning of *Hadrak*, R. Judah and R. Nehemiah differ. According to R. Judah, the term *Hadrak* refers to the king Messiah, who will be rough (*ḥaḏ*) with the nations and gentle (*raḵ*) with Israel.[11] According to R. Nehemiah, Hadrak is actually the name of a place. For R. Jose, son of a woman from Damascus, said: I am from Damascus and I swear that a certain place there is called Hadrak. R. Judah then asked R. Nehemiah: If you take Hadrak to be merely the name of a place, how do you construe the verse's conclusion, namely, *and in Damascus shall be His resting place* (*ibid.*)? R. Nehemiah replied: As a fig tree is narrow at the base but spreads out at the top, so is Jerusalem destined to keep spreading out, and the banished will come and find rest therein to fulfill the pledge in the words *and in Damascus shall be His resting place* (*ibid.*). Here *resting place* refers to Jerusalem, as in the verse in which God said of Zion: *This is My resting place for ever; here will I dwell; for I have desired it* (Ps. 132:14). Then R. Judah asked: If Jerusalem is to extend to Damascus, how do you construe *The city shall be builded on her own mound* (Jer. 30:18)? R. Nehemiah replied: Jerusalem will not be moved from its original place: from each of its sides it will keep spreading out, however, and the banished will come and find rest therein, thus fulfilling the words *For thou shalt spread abroad on the right hand and on the left* (Isa. 54:3), phrases which refer to Jerusalem's length, [south and north]. Whence the proof that Jerusalem will also be enlarged in breadth, [east and west]? The verse *From the tower of Hananel*[12] *unto the king's "hollows"* (Zech. 14:10), the latter, according to R. Berechiah, referring to the Ocean;[13] but, according to the elder R. Zakkai, the phrase refers to the harbor of Jaffa. And the two do not really disagree as to the extent of Jerusalem's spreading to the west: for he who says, "unto the Ocean" construes the verse as referring to the "hollows" which the King who

10a. Cf. Gen. Rabbah 44:12.

11. R. Judah thus reads Zech. 9:1: "When Hadrak will be in the Land, Damascus shall be His resting place."

12. Probably located at the northeast corner of Jerusalem.

13. The Mediterranean.

is King of kings, blessed be He, hollowed out; while he who says "unto the harbor of Jaffa," construes the verse as referring to the one king Solomon hollowed out.[14] We thus have proof [of Jerusalem's being enlarged] in length and breadth. And whence the proof concerning its height? The verse *And there was an enlarging, and a winding about still upward on the sides thereof* (Ezek. 41:7).

R. Eliezer ben Jacob said: Jerusalem is destined to keep rising until it reaches the throne of glory where it will say to the Holy One, *The place* [*on earth*] *is too strait for me; give place where I may sit* (Isa. 49:20). Jose bar R. Jeremiah and R. Dostai, citing R. Levi, added: You still do not know what the full degree of Jerusalem's distinction is to be. However, from the verse *For I, saith the Lord, will be unto her a wall of fire round about, and I will be the glory in the midst of her* (Zech. 2:9), you may infer what is to be Jerusalem's distinction and surpassing glory.

14. His winepresses were in the city of Jaffa.

PISKA 21

SUMMARY

The radiance of Zion and God's bestowal of light

God and Israel together will give their light to Zion (Sec. 1). But the light which God and Israel are to give Zion will do no more than enhance the radiance of God's own glory with which Zion was endowed from the beginning of creation (Sec. 2). When the union of Israel and Zion takes place, the Holy One will say to Zion, "Rise, give light, for the light of your life has come" (Sec. 3). The glory of Zion's restoration will surpass the revelation on Sinai, the defeat of the heathen Sisera on Tabor, and the discomfiture of Jezebel's idols on Carmel. At the restoration Sinai, Tabor, and Carmel will hymn Moriah—Mount Zion—in song (Sec. 4).

From the beginning of creation, God envisioned the Temple's being built, destroyed, and rebuilt in Zion. When the Temple is rebuilt, God's light coming from it will provide light both day and night. Indeed, even in the past, the Temple's windows were made not so much to receive light from the world as to send light into the world.

Light first came into the world when God covered Himself with a white garment, and the world was made bright by the radiance of His majesty (Sec. 5).

God's bestowal of light, as well as His bestowal of darkness, serve His purpose in the world (Sec. 6).

PISKA 21

Arise, give light (Isa. 60:1).[1]

1. *Therefore glorify ye the Lord in the lights,* etc. (Isa. 24:15). On what occasions is He to be glorified? At the renewal of the radiance of the lamps. By this answer, said R. Abbahu, is meant the renewal of the two prime lights in heaven of which Scripture says, *God made the two great lights* (Gen. 1:16). [Thus the occasions on which He is to be glorified are the renewal of the cycle of the sun in the heavens and the renewal of the power of the moon over the earth]. How glorify Him on these two occasions? When the sun renews its cycle, the blessing ["Blessed is He who again and again does His work of creation"] is said; when the power of the moon over the earth is renewed, the same blessing is said.[2]

According to the Rabbis, the Holy One said to Israel: My children, since My light is your light, and your light is My light, let us—you and I—go and give light to Zion: *Arise, give light, for thy light is come* (Isa. 60:1).

2. R. Aḥa began his discourse with the verse *I am the Lord, that is My name* (Isa. 42:8), the name which I consented to be called by when I am with the ministering angels. *And My glory I do not give to a delayed one*[3] (*ibid.*) means, according to R. Menaḥema citing R. Abin, [that I did not give any kind of independent power] to the demons, [whose creation was delayed to the end of the sixth day of creation].[4] The Holy One goes on: *Neither do I endow anything tangible with the radiance of that glory which is Mine alone*[5] (*ibid.*). In all the creation which followed upon My creation of light there is only one tangible thing that I endow with the radiance of My glory, even though from time to time you ascribe such radiance to other tangible things.[6] Whom alone do I endow with the radiance of My glory?

1. In the seven-Sabbath cycle of consolation, Isa. 60:1–22 is the haftarah for *Ki tabo'*, the sixth Sabbath following the Ninth of Ab.

2. The renewal of the sun's cycle (*tĕḳufah*) occurs once every twenty-eight years. The moon in its power over the earth has reference to the spring equinox when the tides are greatest. See B.Ber 59b, and notes in Soncino tr., pp. 369–70.

3. EV: *another*; but in this comment the word *'ḥr* is apparently rendered in the sense of "delay."

4. See Ab 5:6, and Piska 7.1. For the preternatural power of demons, see MTeh 78:12.

5. JV: *Neither My praise to graven images.* But *tĕhillati*, "My praise," may mean "the radiance which is Mine"; and *pĕsilim*, "graven images," here seems to mean "things tangible."

6. "Only one tangible . . . the radiance of My glory" is a paraphrase of the Hebrew which reads "I do not endow another with the radiance of My glory, even though you ascribe such glory to tangible things."

Zion: *Arise, shine for the light which is thine alone is come* (Isa. 60:1).

3. *For with Thee is the fountain of life; in Thy light do we see light* (Ps. 36:10). R. Johanan and Resh Laḳish both made comments on this verse, R. Johanan making one and Resh Laḳish making two. In his one comment, R. Johanan said: The verse may be understood by a parable of a man who was walking along the road as the sun was setting. Someone came along and lighted a lamp for him, and it went out. Then another came and lighted a lamp for him, which also went out. Thereupon the man said: From now on I shall wait for the light of morning. So, too, Israel said to the Holy One: Master of universes, we made one lamp for Thee in the days of Moses, and it is now extinguished. We made ten in the days of Solomon,[7] and they also are now extinguished. From now on we shall wait for Thy light: *In Thy light do we [hope to] see light* (Isa. 60:1).

Resh Laḳish's two comments: To begin with, said Resh Laḳish, the verse may be illustrated by a parable of a king who had a son. When the king invited guests to his palace, he said to his son: My son, do you wish to dine with the guests? The son replied: No. The king then asked: And with whom do you wish to dine? The son replied: Only with you. Likewise the Holy One said to Israel: My children, do you wish to dine with the nations? They replied immediately: Master of universes, *Incline not my heart to any evil thing, to gather gleanings[8] of wickedness* (Ps. 141:4). God said: Is it because no more than gleanings are to be had that you do not wish to dine with the nations? Israel replied: Master of universes, *Let me not eat even of their delicacies* (ibid.)—even if the nations' portions are both delicious and generous, we do not desire them. What do we desire? Tasty and generous portions which come from Thee.

Resh Laḳish's other comment: The verse, Resh Laḳish said, may be illustrated by a parable of a king who had a daughter. There came a man who asked for her hand in marriage, but he was not worthy of her. There came another who asked for her hand in marriage, and he, too, was not worthy of her. But when there came yet another who proved worthy of her and asked for her hand in marriage, the king said [to his daughter what a father usually says when she becomes a bride]: Rise, give light, for the light of your life has come.[9] So, too, the Holy One will say to Israel: My children, since My light is your light, and your light is My light, let us go—you and I—and give our light to Zion: *Arise, give light, for thy light has come* (Isa. 60:1).

4. R. Phinehas said in the name of R. Reuben: There will come a time

---

7. See Exod. 27:20; and 1 Kings 7:49.

8. JV: *to be occupied in deeds.* But the commentator construes *ʿălilot,* "deeds," as though it read *ʿolělot,* "gleanings."

9. See B.Shab 116b.

when the Holy One will bring Sinai, Tabor, and Carmel together and build the Temple on top of them.[10] And the proof? The verse *It shall come to pass in the end of days that the mountain of the Lord's house shall be established on the top of the mountains* (Isa. 2:2). R. Huna responded: Is this all the significance you can find in the verse? The fact is that [at Zion's restoration the very mountains will burst into song: Moriah], the mountain of the Lord's House, will lead in the singing, and the lesser mountains will answer [with Psalms]. And the proof? The verse [*The mountain of the Lord's House*] . . . *shall be sung to* (*niśśa'*)[11] *by the hills* (Micah 4:1). That *niśśa'* denotes "be sung to" is shown by 1 Chron. 15:22 where *maśśa'*, the nominal form of *niśśa'*, is used in exactly this sense: [*Mount Moriah*] *which the Lord will establish shall be the leader of the Levites in song; because the mountain will enhance men's understanding of God, it shall be hymned in a lifting of song* (*maśśa'*).[12]

R. Hoshaia said in the name of R. Aphes: Jerusalem is destined to become a beacon for the nations of the earth, and they will walk in its light. And the proof? The verse *And nations shall walk at thy light,* etc. (Isa. 60:3).

R. Aḥa said: Israel is likened to an olive tree—*A leafy olive tree, fair with goodly fruit* (Jer. 11:16). And the Holy One is likened to a lamp—*The lamp of the Lord is the spirit of man* (Prov. 20:27). What use is made of oil? It is put into a lamp, and then the two together give light as though they were one. Hence the Holy One will say to Israel: My children, since My light is your light, and your light is My light, let us go together—you and I—and give light to Zion: *Arise, give light, for thy light has come* (Isa. 60:1).

5. R. Ḥiyya taught in a Baraita: [We are told in the first three verses of Genesis that] at the very beginning of the earth's creation the Holy One envisioned the Temple built, destroyed, and rebuilt: *In the beginning God*

10. R. Phinehas may mean the following: In the time-to-come, miracles to occur will surpass the revelation on Sinai, the defeat of the heathen Sisera on Tabor, and the discomfiture of Jezebel's idols on Carmel.

11. Since *the mountain of the Lord's house* is to be above mountains, it surely—the commentator reasons—will be exalted above hills which are lower than mountains. Hence, he renders *niśśa* not "exalted" but "sung to" in the way in which the leader may be said to be sung to by the members of a choir.

12. JV: *Kenaniah, chief of the Levites, was over the song; he was master in the song because he was skilful.* But the commentator takes *Kenaniah* as made up of *konen*, "to be established," and *yah*, "by the Lord"; takes *yasor*, "he was master," as *yaśor*, "shall be hymned"; construes *maśśa'*, "song," literally as "lifting in song"; and takes *meḇin*, "skilful," in the sense of "enhance men's understanding of God's word." Then, too, he regards the entire verse as being not an account of what has already taken place but rather a prediction of what will take place at the end of days.

created the heaven and the earth (Gen. 1:1)—the Temple built.[13] *And the earth was without form and desolate* (Gen. 1:2)—the Temple destroyed. *And God said: "Let there be light." And there was light* (Gen. 1:3)—the Temple completely rebuilt in the time-to-come.

R. Samuel bar Naḥman said: In the world which we know, men walk in the light of the sun by day and in the light of the moon by night. But in the time-to-come men will go and walk neither in the light of the sun by day, nor in the light of the moon by night. For at that time *The sun shall be no more thy light by day, neither for brightness shall the moon give light unto thee* (Isa. 60:19). In what light, then, will men walk? In the light of the Holy One. As the verse goes on to say, *The Lord shall be unto thee an everlasting light*, etc. (*ibid.*).

R. Ḥanina said: In the Temple there were windows, but light, [instead of coming into them], went out of them. And the proof of this assertion? The verse *And for the House he made windows, broad and narrow* (1 Kings 6:4). How could the windows be both broad and narrow? The openings for the windows were made narrow on the inside of the Temple, but were broadened out on the outside in order to send forth the greatest amount of light into the world. As R. Levi explained: In the way of the world, when a man builds himself a grand house, he has the openings for the windows made narrow on the outside but broad on the inside in order to have the greatest amount of light enter it. But the windows in the Temple were made otherwise: they were narrow on the inside and broad on the outside in order to send forth light into the world.

R. Berechiah, citing R. Baṣla, said: The verse *There were windows in* [*the House*] *and in the arches thereof round about* (Ezek. 40:25) does not go on to say *like those windows* (*kḥlwnwt*), but *khḥlwnwt*, a word compounded of *khwt* ("opaque") and *ḥlwnwt* ("windows"). That is to say, the windows were opaque, [insofar as they could not be seen through from the outside]: narrow on the inside and broad on the outside, they were so made as [not to admit light from the world, but] to send light out into the world.

R. Simeon ben Jehozadak sent a message to R. Samuel bar Naḥman, saying: I understand that you are a master of *'Ăgaḏah*; so tell me whence light went forth to the world? R. Samuel bar Naḥman replied: The Holy One covered Himself with a white robe, and the world—all of it—was made bright by the radiance of His majesty. But since R. Samuel bar Naḥman gave his reply in a whisper, R. Simeon ben Jehozadak pressed him further: Why whisper? Is not what you have just whispered said right out in the verse *Who coverest Thyself with light as with a garment* (Ps. 104:2)? Thereupon R. Samuel bar Naḥman answered: It was told to me in a whisper, so I answered

13. Heaven and earth are said to stand firm because of the service in the Temple. See Piska 19.6, and PR 5:3.

you in a whisper. Indeed, had not R. Isaac[14] expounded in public the theme that light came into the world from the robe with which the Holy One covered Himself, it would have been prohibited to say so in public, [even in a whisper].

Before R. Isaac expounded the theme, what used to be said of the light in the world? According to R. Berechiah, it was that the light went forth into the world out of the Temple site. And the proof? The verse *And, behold, the glory of the God of Israel came from the east; and His voice was like the sound of many waters; and the earth did shine with His glory* (Ezek. 43:2). Here *glory* refers to the Temple, which is addressed *Thou throne of glory, on high from the beginning, thou site of our Sanctuary* (Jer. 17:12).

6. [As the first verse of the chapter in hand speaks of His bestowal of light (*Arise, give light*), the next verse speaks of His bestowal of darkness]. *For, behold darkness shall cover the earth, and gross darkness the peoples* (Isa. 60:2). In their comments on this verse R. Abba bar Kahana and the Rabbis differ. R. Abba bar Kahana said: For three days both darkness and gross darkness served God's purpose in Egypt. (The rest of this discourse's beginning is as set down in *And it came to pass at midnight* [7.12]).

14. R. Isaac Nappaḥa (fl. 3rd century), pupil of R. Johanan, active in Tiberias and later in Caesarea, was a prolific and distinguished authority in 'Āgaḏah as well as in Halakah.

On the restrictions with regard to expounding mystical doctrines in public, see Ḥag 2:1.

PISKA 22

SUMMARY

The universal joy and glory which will come at the time of Israel's vindication

When Israel is quickened, God as well as all the earth's inhabitants will rejoice (Sec. 1). Israel will not only rejoice in Israel's deliverance but will also take delight in God and in His Torah. Thus Israel will both rejoice and give joy (Sec. 2). Israel's greatest cause of joy, however, will be that God their King will have come back (Sec. 3). Such joy will be vouchsafed to Israel because of the merit that came to them from Abraham and Isaac as well as the merit of reticence and modesty which is their own (Sec. 4). No wonder that in ten places in Scripture Israel is called "God's bride," even as on ten occasions in Israel's history God—Israel's Bridegroom—is said to clothe Himself in the garment appropriate to each occasion (Sec. 5). At the time of Israel's vindication, the Land of Israel will bring forth alive the dead within it earlier than the lands outside of Israel bring forth alive their dead. Moreover, he who utters Jerusalem's name contemptuously will be regarded as though he had uttered God's name blasphemously.

At the time of Israel's vindication, heaven and earth, heart and spirit, the name of the Messiah and the name of Jerusalem—all will be renewed.

Moreover, the name of Jerusalem will be revered like the name of its God (Sec. 5a).

PISKA 22

I will greatly rejoice in the Lord (Isa. 61:10).[1]

1. [Construing this verse *Rejoicing, I will cause joy to the Lord,*[2] note that] Scripture says elsewhere *Wilt Thou not quicken us again that Thy people may rejoice in Thee*? (Ps. 85:7). When Thou quickenest us, then, according to R. Aḥa, Thou[3] as well as Thy people and Thy city will rejoice.

[In further comment on the verse in Isaiah now construed *Rejoicing in the Lord, I will cause joy*, the following verse from Genesis is cited]: *Sarah said: God hath given me occasion for laughter; every one that heareth will laugh in joy with me*[4] (Gen. 21:6). R. Phinehas, R. Judah, and R. Ḥanan, quoting R. Samuel bar R. Isaac,[5] said: It is a question, however, whether a person's laughter—Reuben's say—is in itself enough to make someone like Simeon laugh with him. And yet Sarah said: *Every one that heareth will laugh in joy with me* (*ibid.*). The verse teaches, however, that when our mother Sarah gave birth to Isaac, at the same time all barren women were remembered by God, all the deaf were given hearing, all the blind were given sight, all the mute were given speech, all madmen restored to soundness of mind. And so all [who were otherwise afflicted] said: Would that Sarah had been remembered a second time, so that we, too, could have been remembered with her!

R. Berechiah, citing R. Levi, said: [Sarah's being remembered] added strength to the sun and the moon.[6] For you will note, in the account of the birth of Isaac, that the term "made" is used, *And the Lord made unto Sarah what He had spoken* (Gen. 21:1), and that in the account of the creation the same term is used, *And God made the two great lights* (Gen. 1:16). As "made" in this verse implies God's giving light to the world, so in the passage concerning Sarah, "made" implies adding even more light to the world. Note further that the Hebrew word for "made" also means "gave," so that Gen. 21:1 can be read *God gave unto Sarah what He had spoken.* The word is used in the same way in the story of Esther where it is said *The king . . .*

1. In the seven-Sabbath cycle of consolation, Isa. 61:10–63:9 is the haftarah for *Niṣṣabim*, the seventh Sabbath following the Ninth of Ab.

2. The infinitive absolute of "rejoice" is interpreted as another act of rejoicing besides the act of rejoicing indicated in the finite verb, which is given causative meaning.

3. "Thou"—O_1.

4. JV: *God hath made laughter for me; every one that heareth will laugh on account of me.*

5. "R. Phinehas, R. Judah, R. Ḥanan, quoting R. Samuel bar R. Isaac, said"—O_1; O: "R. Yudan, R. Simon, R. Ḥanin, R. Samuel bar Isaac."

6. See PR 42:4.

gave a release to the provinces (Esther 2:18). And as "gave" in the story of Esther means—so the account goes on to say—giving gifts to the world, so, too, the term "gave" in the story of Sarah means giving gifts to the world.

R. Berechiah, citing R. Levi, said: You find that when our mother Sarah gave birth, the nations of the world declared—and may we be forgiven for repeating what they said—: Sarah did not give birth to Isaac. It was Hagar, Sarah's handmaid—she gave birth to him, they said. [To prove that Sarah had indeed given birth to Isaac], what did the Holy one do? He withered up the nipples of the noblewomen of the world's nations, so that they came and kissed the dust at Sarah's feet, pleading with her: Do a good deed and give suck to our children. Thereupon our father Abraham said to Sarah: "Sarah, this is no time for modesty. Hallow the Holy One's name. Sit down in the marketplace and give suck to their children." Hence it is said *Sarah gave children suck* (Gen. 21:7). Note that the verse does not say "child," but *children*. Now from matters of this kind can we not draw the following inference? If a mortal, to whom joy came, rejoiced and caused every one else to rejoice, all the more reason to conclude that when the Holy One comes to bring joy to Jerusalem, Jerusalem will say, *Rejoicing in the Lord, I will cause joy* (Isa. 61:10).

2. *This is the day which the Lord hath made; we will rejoice and be glad bw* (Ps. 118:24). R. Abin said: We would not have known whether we are to rejoice in the day or in the Holy One,[7] had not Solomon proceeded to make it clear to us: *We will be glad and rejoice in Thee* (Song 1:4)—*in Thee*, in Thy Torah; *in Thee*, in Thy deliverance. R. Isaac said: *In Thee* (*bk*) means, "in the twenty-two letters which Thou hast written for us in the Torah," the letter *beṯ* having the numerical value of two, and the letter *kaf* the numerical value of twenty.

[The commentator now approaches the theme of rejoicing as follows]: In a Mishnah we learn: "If a man takes a wife and lives with her for ten years and she bears him no child, he is no longer permitted to nullify his obligation to be fruitful and multiply. After he divorces her, she may be married to another, and the second husband may also live with her [no more than] ten years [if she bears him no child. In either marriage], if she miscarry, the period of ten years is reckoned from the time of her miscarriage.

A man is under obligation to fulfill the commandment, 'Be fruitful and multiply,' but a woman is not under such obligation. R. Johanan ben Beroḳa taught, however: Of both man and woman Scripture says, *God blessed them; and God said unto them: 'Be fruitful and multiply'* (Gen. 1:28)" (Yeḇ 6:6).

7. The Hebrew *bw* may mean either *in it* as in EV, or *in Him*, the antecedent being *the Lord*.

In Sidon it happened that a man took a wife with whom he lived for ten years, and she bore no children. When they came to R. Simeon ben Yoḥai to be divorced, the man said to his wife: Take any precious object I have in my house—take it and go back to your father's house. Thereupon, R. Simeon ben Yoḥai said: Even as you were wed with food and drink [being served], so you are not to separate save with food and drink [being served]. What did the wife do? She prepared a great feast, gave her husband too much to drink [so that he fell asleep], then beckoned to her manservants and maidservants,[8] saying, "Take him to my father's house." At midnight he woke up from his sleep and asked: "Where am I?" She replied: "Did you not say, 'Whatever precious object I have in my house—take it and go back to your father's house'? I have no object more precious than you." When R. Simeon ben Yoḥai heard what the wife had done, he prayed in the couple's behalf, and they were remembered with children. For, even as the Holy One remembers barren women, righteous men [such as R. Simeon] also have the power to remember barren women. Now may not the matter be argued *a fortiori*? If one mortal saying to another mortal, I have no more precious object in the world than you, is able to rejoice and bring joy to everybody, all the more will Israel rejoice and give joy, Israel who for so many years and for ever so many ages have been looking forward to deliverance by the Holy One.[9] Hence *Rejoicing in the Lord I will give joy* (Isa. 61:10).

3. A parable of a noblewoman whose husband, sons, and sons-in-law[10] went to a far country by the sea. Presently she was told: "Your sons have come back!" She replied: "Let my daughters-in-law be glad." "And now look, your sons-in-law!" She replied: "Let my daughters rejoice." But when she was told, "Behold, your husband!" she replied, "Joy! Utter joy!" Likewise, when the Prophets will say to Jerusalem, *Thy sons come from far* (Isa. 60:4), Jerusalem will reply: *Let Mount Zion be glad* (Ps. 48:12). Told *Thy daughters are carried [to thee] on uplifted arms*[11] (Isa. 60:4), Jerusalem will reply: *Let the daughters of Judah rejoice* (Ps. 48:12). But when the Prophets will say to her: *Behold, thy King cometh unto thee* (Zech. 9:9), she will reply: "O joy! Utter joy!" *I will greatly rejoice in the Lord* (Isa. 61:10).

4. A parable of a fatherless child who grew up in a palace. When her time came to be wed, and she was asked, "Do you own anything?" she replied: "Yes, something from my father, something from my grandfather." Likewise the merit that Israel owns comes from Abraham, comes from our father Jacob. Thus the words *He hath clothed me with garments of salvation* (Isa.

8. "manservants and maidservants"—O_1; O: "her maidservant."

9. "If flesh-and-blood . . . deliverance by the Holy One"—O_1; O is not relevant to the parable preceding the conclusion.

10. "sons and sons-in-law"—O_1; O: "son and son-in-law."

11. JV: *thy daughters are borne on the side.*

61:10) have reference to the merit of our father Jacob, of whom it is said "Rebekah . . . clothed his hands with the skins of the kids of the goats"[12] (Gen. 27:16). The words *He hath covered me with the robe of righteousness* (Isa. 61:10) have reference to the merit of our father Abraham, of whom it is said "I have known him to the end that he may command his children . . . to do righteousness" (Gen. 16:19). *When the Bridegroom putteth on His royal diadem, then the bride bedecketh herself with her garments* (Isa. 61:10)—[that is, in her nuptials with God, Israel is bedecked with her own merit]. You find that when Israel stood at Mount Sinai, she bedecked herself like a bride who [in maidenly reticence] shows only one eye while keeping the other covered.[13]

5. In ten places in Scripture, Israel is called "bride"—six times by Solomon, three by Isaiah, and once by Jeremiah. Six times by Solomon: *Come with Me from Lebanon, My bride* (Song 4:8); *thou hast ravished My heart, My sister, My bride* (Song 4:9); *How fair is thy love, My sister, My bride*! (Song 4:10); *thy lips, O My bride, drop honey* (Song 4:11); *A garden shut up is My sister, My bride* (Song 4:12); *I am come into My garden, My Sister, My bride* (Song 5:1). Three times by Isaiah: *Thou shalt surely clothe thee with them as with an ornament, and gird thyself with them, like a bride* (Isa. 49:18); the verse already cited above, *When the Bridegroom putteth on His royal diadem, then the bride bedecketh herself with her garments* (Isa. 61:10); *As the Bridegroom rejoiceth over the bride* (Isa. 62:5). And once by Jeremiah: *The voice of joy and the voice of gladness, the voice of the Bridegroom and the voice of the bride* (Jer. 33:11).[14] Over against the ten places in Scripture in which Israel is spoken of as "bride," there are ten occasions on which the Holy One clothed Himself in the garment appropriate to each occasion. The first garment, one of glory and majesty—*Thou art clothed with glory and majesty* (Ps. 104:1)—the Holy One wore on the day of His creating the world. The second garment, one of overwhelming power—*The Lord reigneth, He is clothed with power* (Ps. 93:1)[15]—the Holy One wore to requite the generation of the flood. The third garment, one of strength—*The Lord is clothed, He hath girded Himself with strength* (Ps. 93:1)—the Holy One wore to give Torah to Israel. The fourth garment, white—*His raiment was as white snow*[16] (Dan. 7:9)—the Holy One wore

12. The skins of the goats Jacob put on made it possible for him to receive Isaac's blessing and the birthright. Thus these skins were to be Jacob's *garments of salvation.*

13. See Song 4:9.

14. Or, *Can a maid forget her ornaments, or a bride her attire?* (Jer. 2:32), in a context which refers specifically to Israel. See BM's note.

15. The Psalm goes on to speak of *the voices of many waters.*

16. The commentator takes white to symbolize God's forgiveness of Israel and also to symbolize the end of Israel's exile in Babylon. The exile coincided

on the occasion of the requital of the kingdom of Babylon. The fifth [and sixth] garments, garments of vengeance—*He put on garments of vengeance for clothing, and was clad with zeal as a cloak* (Isa. 59:17): thus it was two garments the Holy One wore to requite the kingdom of Media.[17] The seventh [and eighth] garments, garments of righteousness and vindication—*He put on righteousness as a coat of mail, and a helmet of deliverance upon His head*[18] (Isa. 59:17): thus it was these two the Holy One wore to requite the kingdom of Greece. The ninth garment, red—*Wherefore is Thine apparel red*? (Isa. 63:2)—the Holy One will wear to requite the kingdom of Edom.[19] The tenth garment, one of glory—*This one that is the most glorious of His apparel* (Isa. 63:1)—the Holy One will wear to requite Gog and Magog.[20] The congregation of Israel said to the Holy One: Of all the garments, none becomes Thee as well as this one: *This one that is the most glorious of His apparel.*

[5a]. [In connection with requital of Israel's enemies and with Israel's vindication, the following verse is cited]: *For as [a garden] the Land bringeth forth her growth* (Isa. 61:11). As a vegetable garden which is irrigated hastens to bring forth fruit earlier than a field which depends on the random fall of rain, even so will the Land of Israel bring forth alive the dead within it earlier than the lands outside of Israel bring forth alive their dead—some say, forty days earlier, and some say, forty years earlier. And the proof? The verse *He that [earlier] giveth breath to the people upon the Land* (Isa. 42:5).

Even so the Lord God will cause victory and glory to sprout for you as you contend with all the nations[21] (Isa. 61:11). Of this verse R. Phinehas and R. Hilkiah, citing R. Simon, said: Its implication is that of a man saying to his fellow: "The Holy One will cause victory to sprout quickly for you in your contention with your adversary [just as He causes a plant to sprout quickly in a well-irrigated field].[22]

---

with Babylon's downfall which was brought about by Daniel's prayers (Dan. 10:12). See Gen. Rabbah 99:2, and David Luria.

17. The rulers of Media brought to a halt the rebuilding of the Temple. See Ezra 4:11 ff.

18. Greek soldiers wore helmets (Gen. Rabbah 99:2). This fact may account for God's being described as helmeted in His encounter with Greece. Cf. MTeh 18:14.

19. The word "Edom" (= Rome) means "red," even as its deeds are red with blood. Hence God's garment in His encounter with Edom is to be red.

20. The defeat of Gog and Magog is to usher in God's kingdom in all its glory.

21. "As a vegetable garden which is irrigated . . . *all the nations*"—O_1.

22. The commentators find the use of agricultural imagery with reference to "victory" and "glory" (Isa. 61:11) puzzling. And so they cite the popular saying of a man meeting his neighbor who is heading for a court of law. The commentator's

And the nations shall see thy triumph (Isa. 62:2). R. Levi said: In this world, he who utters blasphemously the Holy One's ineffable name[23] is liable to the death penalty, for it is said *He that uttereth blasphemously the name of the Lord, he shall surely be put to death* (Lev. 24:16). Even so in the time-to-come he who utters Jerusalem's name contemptuously will be liable to the death penalty, for to Jerusalem it is said *Thou shall be called a new name, so that he who utters it contemptuously will be as one who so spoke of the Lord*[24] (Isa. 62:2).

R. Levi said: Six things the Holy One will renew in the time-to-come, namely, heaven and earth, heart and spirit, the name of the Messiah, and the name of Jerusalem. The proof for heaven and earth? *Behold, I create new heavens and a new earth* (Isa. 65:17). The proof for heart and spirit? *A new heart also will I give you, and a new spirit* (Ezek. 36:26). Proof for the name of the Messiah? *His name which will endure for ever, as long as the sun, shall be Yinnon*[25] (Ps. 72:17). Proof for the name of Jerusalem? *Thou shalt be called a new name* (Isa. 62:2).

R. Levi went on to say: Blessed is the city whose name is like the name of its king and the name of whose king is like the name of its God. "Whose name is like the name of its king": *The name of the city from that day shall be, "The Lord is there"* (Ezek. 48:35). "The name of whose king is like the name of its God": *In his day Judah shall be saved, and Israel shall dwell safely . . . And this is his name whereby he shall be called, The Lord is our righteousness* (Jer. 23:6).

---

conclusion: If in common parlance, one can speak of God's letting victory sprout, the prophet could well use agricultural terminology in speaking of "victory" and "glory" for Israel. Professor Jakob J. Petuchowski has supplied the interpretation of this difficult passage.

23. The tetragrammaton.

24. JV: *a new name which the mouth of the Lord shall mark out.* "The righteous, Messiah, and Jerusalem are to be named Lord" (B.BB 75b).

25. See B.Sanh 98b.

PISKA 23

SUMMARY

From judgment to mercy

True, the twenty-fifth day of Elul carries the distinction of being the first day of the creation of the world—the creation of the physical world, that is—but it is the sixth day of creation falling on the first day of Tishri, New Year's Day, the day Adam and Eve were created and judged, that carries the distinction of beginning the spiritual history of the world (Sec. 1).

New Year's Day has great significance for the children of Israel because it is the day when God judges Israel from His throne of mercy. If, in his dream, Jacob had dared climb and climb like the princes of the earth's nations, he and his children would have had no come-down. But because he lacked faith, despite God's encouragement of him, his children have been subjected to the four kingdoms. Israel's acts of charity, however, will bring God to act in their behalf. True, He may chastise them because of their disloyalty to His other commandments, but He will not destroy them (Sec. 2). Accordingly, year after year, directly after the harvest, when Israel's charitable deeds are numerous—year after year on New Year's Day, at the moment that the people of Israel take shofars and blow the *tĕḳiah*, the sustained note proclaiming redemption, the Holy One rises from the throne of judgment and takes His seat on the throne of mercy (Sec. 3). So significant is New Year's Day to God that He Himself sanctions the Sanhedrin's designation of a particular day as New Year's Day even when they err in such designation.

Only the people of Israel know how to propitiate their Creator when the shofar's tremolo sounds, a tremolo that bespeaks Israel's fear and anguish preceding judgment (Sec. 4).

The fact that the command for Israel to act charitably is followed directly by the injunction concerning judgment on New Year's Day, suggests that when passages in Scripture are scrutinized in context they lead *upward*, guiding men to a life of goodness (Sec. 5).

The month for blowing the shofar to propitiate God is called Tishri which means "Thou art ready to remit sins" (Sec. 6).

Since God's attempts to teach Israel the right way of life do not always avail, when Israel appear for judgment they should cite the merit of the Patriarchs (Sec. 7) through whom, particularly through Abraham, they will win expiation. Nevertheless, only when Israel resolve upon making their way of life acceptable to God, will God be filled with mercy for them (Sec. 8).

Since New Year's Day occurs in Tishri, the seventh month of the year, *šĕḇiʿi*, the Hebrew word for "seventh," is taken as pointing up several special characteristics of the month, as follows: (1) the month filled with commandments; (2) the month filled with plenty; (3) the month of God's oath that He will be filled with mercy for Israel (Sec. 9); (4) and the month that like anything which comes seventh in order is the most loved (Sec. 10).

When New Year's Day falls on a weekday, the shofar is to be blown, but it is not to be blown when New Year's Day falls on the Sabbath.

The children of Israel, who come before God for judgment on New Year's Day and go forth free of sin, are regarded by Him as if they were made anew on New Year's Day (Secs. 11–12).

PISKA 23

New Year's Day

1. *For ever, O Lord* [*of mercy*], *Thy word standeth fast in heaven*[1] (Ps. 119:89). In a Baraita, R. Eliezer taught: The creation of the world was begun on the twenty-fifth day of Elul. Rab's opinion [as expressed in his version of the Shofar Service] coincides with what R. Eliezer taught in the Baraita. In Rab's version of the Shofar Service it is said: "This day [of Tishri], when the intention of Thy works began to reveal itself [in the making of man], shall ever provide a reminder of [the judgment Thou didst pronounce] on the first New Year's Day, the day which, *as decreed by Israel ever calls for judgment by the God of Jacob*[2] (Ps. 81:5). Hence, on the first day of Tishri, New Year's Day, sentence is pronounced upon the countries of the world—those destined for war and those destined for peace, those for famine and those for plenty, those for death and those for life; on this day the lives of mortals are scrutinized to determine who is to have life and who is to have death." [This pronouncing of divine sentence on New Year's Day is] a reminder to mankind that on New Year's Day, the day Adam was created, [was the day he sinned and had divine sentence pronounced upon him]. In the first hour of the Day, he came into existence as a thought in God's mind;[3] in the second hour, God consulted the ministering angels [as to whether He should create him]; in the third hour, God gathered up the dust from which He was to make him; in the fourth, God kneaded the dust; in the fifth, God jointed the parts; in the sixth, God stood Adam up as a thing yet incomplete; in the seventh, God put the breath of life into him; in the eigth, God brought him into the Garden of Eden; in the ninth, God gave him a command; in the tenth, he transgressed the command given him; in the eleventh, he was brought to judgment; in the twelfth, he went forth from the Holy One's presence a free man. The Holy One said to him: Let the fact that thou goest forth free be a sign for thy children. Even as thou camest into My presence for judgment on this day and didst go forth free, so will thy children come into My presence for judgment on this day and go forth free. When?

1. The comments which follow are based on the ensuing verses: *Thy faithfulness is unto all generations: After Thou didst establish the earth so that it stood firm, that very day* [*Adam and Eve*] *were made to stand before Thee for judgments, since all things are Thy servants* (Ps. 119:90–91).

2. JV: *For it is a statute for Israel, an ordinance of the God of Jacob*. But *ḥoḳ*, "statute," also means "decree"; and *mišpaṭ*, "ordinance," also means "judgment."

3. The stages in God's making of man indicate that unlike the world which came into being by His decree, man is literally God's own handiwork.

[Year after year], *In the seventh month, in the first day of the month*[4] (Lev. 23:24).

2. Beginning his discourse with the verse *Therefore fear thou not, O Jacob, My servant . . . neither be dismayed* (Jer. 30:10), R. Naḥman applied it to the episode in Jacob's life when *He dreamed, and beheld a ladder . . . and angels of God* (Gen. 28:12). These angels, according to R. Samuel bar R. Naḥman, were the princes of the nations of the earth. Further, according to R. Samuel bar Naḥman, this verse proves that the Holy One showed to our father Jacob the prince of Babylon climbing up seventy rungs of the ladder, then climbing down; the prince of Media climbing up fifty-two rungs and no more; the prince of Greece, one hundred and eighty[5] rungs and no more; and the prince of Edom climbing and climbing, no one knows how many rungs. At the sight of Edom's climbing our father Jacob grew afraid and said: Is one to suppose that this prince will have no come-down? The Holy One replied: *Be not dismayed, O Israel* (Jer. 30:10): Even if—as though such a thing were possible!—thou were to see him seated next to Me, I would have him brought down thence. Indeed, Edom is told in Scripture, *Though thou make thy nest as high as the eagle, and though thou set it among the stars, I will bring thee down from thence, saith the Lord* (Ob. 1:4).

R. Berechiah, citing R. Ḥelbo who cited R. Simeon bar R. Jose in the name of R. Meir, said: The verse in Genesis teaches that the Holy One showed to our father Jacob the prince of Babylon climbing up and climbing down, the prince of Media climbing up and climbing down, the prince of Greece climbing up and climbing down, and the prince of Edom climbing up and climbing down. The Holy One then said: "Jacob, climb thou also." Thereupon Jacob grew afraid and said: Am I to suppose that as these princes are to have a come-down, I am to have a come-down too? The Holy One replied: "*Thou wilt not come down,*[6] *O Israel* (Jer. 30:10). If thou climbest up, thou wilt never have a come-down." But Jacob did not believe God and did not climb up. In regard to Jacob's lack of faith, R. Berechiah, citing R. Ḥelbo, who cited R. Simeon bar R. Yosina, said that R. Meir in expounding the verse *For all this they sinned still, and believed not in His wondrous works* (Ps. 78:32) attributed Israel's lack of faith [in other circumstances]to the example set by our father Jacob who lacked faith enough to climb up. [When Jacob would not climb up], the Holy One said to him: Hadst thou believed Me and climbed up the ladder's rungs, thou wouldst

4. Lev. 23:23–25 was originally the lesson for New Year's Day. See Meḡ 3:5. Tos Meḡ 4:6 gives Gen. 21:1 ff. as an alternative lesson.

5. The numbers 70, 52, and 180 are taken to represent the years of these kingdoms' dominance over Israel. See SOR, chap. 30, p. 71a, n. 52.

6. The Hebrew *teḥaṯ* may be translated "to come down," or "to be dismayed."

never have had to climb down. Since thou didst not believe and didst not climb up, the result for thy children in this world will be their subjection under the four kingdoms who will impose levies on entire communities of Israel, levies on crops and herds, and all sorts of exactions and poll-taxes. One might suppose that God was declaring that this subjection would last for ever. But not so, for He went on at once to say [words that were addressed to Israel as well as to Jacob]: *Thou wilt not suffer a come-down, O Israel; for lo, I will save thee from afar* (Jer. 30:10)—from Babylon; *and thy seed from the land beyond the sea*[7] *(ibid.)*—from Gaul, from Spain, and from the lands adjoining them; *and Jacob shall return* (*ibid.*) from Babylon; *and be quiet* [*in his heart*] (*ibid.*) with regard to Media; *and at ease* (*ibid.*) with regard to Greece; *and none shall make him afraid* (*ibid.*) because of Edom. [Furthermore, said the Holy One]: *On account of* [*their harvesting*] *"all the way" I will act against all the nations whither I have scattered thee*[8] (Jer. 30:11). It is of the nations who harvest their fields "all the way" [leaving nothing for the poor and the stranger] that God says, *On account of* [*their harvesting*] *"all the way," I will act* (*ibid.*). But to Israel who do not harvest crops "all the way," God says, *On account of* [*thy not harvesting*] *"all the way," I will not act thus against thee; I will correct thee in measure, and thus cleanse, but not destroy thee*[9] (*ibid.*). In the course of thy life as a people I will correct thee with chastisements in order to cleanse thee of thy disloyalty to Me, [but I will never destroy thee]. In what month [shall I, year after year, extend remission of thy disloyalty to My commandments]? *In the seventh month* (Lev. 23:24), [words which follow immediately upon My command that thou harvest not "all the way," but leave gleanings for the poor and the stranger].

3. Judah bar Naḥman, citing Resh Laḳish, began his discourse thus: The verse *God* [*'Elohim*] *is gone up amidst a tremolo* (*tĕru'ah*), etc. (Ps. 47:7) refers to the moment on New Year's Day when the Holy One, going up to sit on the throne of judgment, goes up with the intention of passing judgment without mercy: hence the words *God* [*'Elohim*] *is gone up amidst a tremolo* (*tĕru'ah*) [bespeak the fear and anguish that precede the rendering of His judgment]. The instant, however, that Israel take shofars and blow the *tĕḳi'ah*, [the sustained note, proclaiming redemption], the Holy One rises from the throne of judgment and takes His seat on the throne of mercy, as is said *Amidst this sound of the shofar the Lord will be* [YHWH *of mercy*][10] (*ibid.*). Filled with mercy for Israel and having mercy upon them,

7. Vocalizing *šiḇyam*, "their captivity," as *šeb-ba-yam*, "beyond the sea."

8. JV: *I will make full end of all the nations whither I have scattered thee.*

9. JV: *But I will not make a full end of thee; for I will correct thee in measure, and will not utterly destroy thee.*

10. *'Elohim* is taken to designate God as executor of judgment, while YHWH designates Him as dispenser of mercy and forgiveness.

again and again for their sake He turns the measure of judgment into the measure of mercy. When? [Year after year], *In the seventh month* (Lev. 23:24).

4. R. Josiah began his discourse with the verse *Blessed is the people who know the horn's tremolo* (Ps. 89:16). R. Abbahu, however, construed the verse *Blessed is the people who determine accurately the time for the horn's blast* [*on New Year's Day*], "the people" here being the five elders[11] who undertake to intercalate a year that requires intercalation.[12] What does the Holy One do when they begin their work? He leaves His councilors in heaven and comes down to this world, shrinking His presence to earthly dimensions. Thereupon the ministering angels say, "What a mighty One, what a mighty One [is He who can shrink His infinite being into finite dimensions]! What a God, what a God!" He of whom it is written *A God dreaded in the great council of the holy ones* (Ps. 89:8) leaves His councilors in heaven and goes down to earth where He shrinks His presence to earthly dimensions! Why this descent to earth? So that if "the people," the five members of the Sanhedrin, err in working out their intercalation of the year, the Holy One makes their faces shine with the light of His sanction of their procedure: *They "proceed," O Lord, in the light of Thy countenance* (Ps. 89:16).

R. Josiah, referred to just above, commenting on the verse *Blessed is the people who know the* [*horn's*] *tremolo* (*ibid.*), said: But as to the nations, do they not also know how to sound the horn's tremolo? Have they not many horns? Have they not many bugles? Have they not many trumpets? The verse speaks of only one people, however, saying *Blessed is* THE *people who know the* [*horn's*] *tremolo*. What the verse is really saying, then, is "Blessed is Israel, the people who know how to propitiate their Creator at the time of the horn's tremolo—[the tremolo that bespeaks the fear and anguish preceding judgment]." And when do they propitiate Him? [Year after year], *In the seventh month* (Lev. 23:24).

5. R. Berechiah, citing R. Jeremiah, began his discourse with the verse *The path of life goeth upward for the wise, that he may depart from the nether world beneath* (Prov. 15:24). *The path of life*—here *path of life* clearly means words of Torah, "She being a tree of life," etc. (Prov. 3:18). (Or, as in another comment on *The path of life, path of life* is taken to mean reproofs of chastisement, "Reproofs of chastisement being the way of life" [Prov. 6:23]). The eye of *the wise man* [who studies Torah] *goeth upward* [on the Scroll as he reads it] (Prov. 15:24) to see what has been said before, and he comes to ponder upon the order in which Torah's precepts are arranged. Thus when his eye goes directly *upward* of the verse in

11. "R. Simeon ben Gamaliel said: Five members of the Sanhedrin debate to determine whether to intercalate the year" (Sanh 1:2).

12. Thereby determining when New Year's Day is to fall.

hand, what does he read? The words *When you reap the harvest . . . you shall not reap "all the way" to the edges of your field* (Lev. 23:22)—that is, you shall not reap like the nations who harvest their fields "all the way," etc. (The rest of the discourse is as above [Piska 23.2]).

6. R. Berechiah began his discourse with the verse *Blow the shofar at the New Moon—when the crescent is not yet visible—on our feast day,* etc. (Ps. 81:4). But do not all other months [besides Tishri] begin with a New Moon?[13] Yes—hence the verse goes on to specify that the shofar is to be blown when the crescent is not yet visible. But is not the crescent invisible on other new moons as well? Yes—and for this very reason, the verse goes on to specify *on our feast day.* But the fact is that Nisan as well as Tishri not only has a New Moon on which the crescent is invisible but also has a feast day.[14] Nisan's feast, however, is by itself—[it takes place later on in the month]. So there is only one New Moon which begins not only when the crescent of the new moon is still invisible, but also has a feast that falls on the very day of the New Moon.[15] What month is that? Tishri. It is called Tishri because then Thou remittest (*tišre*) and forgivest our sins. When? [Year after year], *In the seventh month* (Lev. 23:24).

7. R. Levi, citing R. Ḥama bar Ḥanina, began his discourse with the verse *Thus saith the Lord thy redeemer, the Holy One of Israel: I am the Lord thy God, who teacheth thee* (*mĕlammeḏĕḵa*) *for thy profit, who wisheth to lead thee by the way that thou shouldst go* (Isa. 48:17). What elements of teaching are implied by the word *mĕlammeḏĕḵa*? That God endeavors to train you with a goad as one trains a heifer—[that is, by prodding you]. The goad is known by three names: *malmaḏ, marde'a, darḇan: malmaḏ,* because it trains (*mĕlammeḏ*) the heifer to plow [for her drink and fodder]; *marde'a* because it imparts an idea (*moreh de'ah*) to the heifer of what she is to do; *darḇan* because it impresses upon the heifer obedience (*maḏir binah*) to the goad.[16] The Holy One says sadly: A man provides a goad for his heifer, but he provides no such goad for his Impulse to evil.

Who wisheth to lead thee by the way that thou shouldst go (*ibid.*). R. Levi, continuing to cite R. Ḥama, illustrated these words by a parable of a prince who was on trial before his father in his capacity as judge. His father said: If you wish to win this case in which I am the judge, designate so-and-so, a sure winner, as your advocate and you will win the case.[17] Likewise

13. What then is the proof that the shofar is to be blown only on the New Moon of Tishri?

14. Why not assume, then, that the verse suggests blowing the shofar on Passover?

15. The moon's invisibility on New Year's Day is taken to suggest God's willingness on that day to consider Israel's sins as invisible. See Mah on Lev. Rabbah 29:6.

16. Cf. PR 3:2.

17. "Before me" is omitted as in S and Yalḳuṭ.

The Holy One said to Israel: My children, if you cite the merit of your Fathers, you will win your case that has come before Me. [Let Israel follow God's advice by designating Abraham, Isaac, and Jacob as their advocates]. Thus the phrase *in the one*[18] (Lev. 23:24) intimates that our father Abraham is to be designated, [for he was unique]—"Abraham was one" (Ezek. 33:24); the phrase *a memorial proclaimed with the blast of [a ram's] horn* (Lev. 23:24) intimates that our father Isaac is to be designated—"And he looked, and behold behind him a ram caught in the thicket by his horns" (Gen. 22:13); and the phrase *the holy one who is called*[19] (Lev. 23:24) intimates that our father Jacob is to be designated—"Hearken unto Me, O Jacob, My servant[20] and Israel My called" (Isa. 48:12). When are you to cite the merit of the Fathers so as to win your case that has come before Me? [Year after year], *In the seventh month* (Lev. 23:24).

8. R. Ḥiyya bar Marya, citing R. Levi, began his discourse with the verse *Surely Adam's sons, [what they say is] vanity, even men of high degree, [what they say is] a lie. In [God's] balances men and women go up—are brought together whilst they are mere breath* (Ps. 62:10). It is the way of the world for mortals to prognosticate "Such-and-such a man is going to marry such-and-such a woman", but since the prognosticators are *Adam's sons, [what they say is] vanity*. Or, "Such-and-such a woman is going to be married to such-and-such a man"—but even [if such prognosticators are] *men of high degree, [what they say is] a lie*. The truth is, R. Ḥiyya bar Marya went on, *In [God's] balances men and women go up* (*ibid.*)—that is, they are matched when they are no more than mere breath in their mothers' wombs. Thus men and women *are brought together whilst they are mere breath* (*ibid.*).

[Reading the verse *Surely the follies of the children of (Abraham), the man of high degree, yea, the lies of the children of (Abraham), the man of rank, "in the balance" they will go up, seem lighter than a breath* (*ibid.*)], R. Naḥman took it to mean: Notwithstanding all the follies that Israel commit and the lies that they utter in this world, Abraham is of sufficient merit to win expiation for all of Israel's deeds when they are scrutinized. And the

18. JV: *In the first day of the month, shall be a solemn rest unto you, a memorial proclaimed with the blast of horns.* But these words closely resemble Num. 29:1 where New Year's Day is likewise ordained. Since for the commentator the two texts are not simply a doublet, he considers the one in Leviticus "available" for special interpretation.

19. Reading not *miḳra'*, "calling together, convocation," but *mĕḳora'*, "one who is called."

20. "My servant" is not in MT, but it does occur in several MSS in Lev. Rabbah 29:5; in PR (Parma MS 1240) 40:5; and in MTeh 14:5 (Buber 58a). Accordingly, the evidence for "My servant" is more substantial than the "few MSS" to which Kittel, in his edition of Isaiah, refers.

proof? The verse "Because of Abraham, the greatest man among the mighty ones,[21] [the children of Israel in] the Land have surcease [from the painful effects of their] warfare [with the evil Impulse]" (Josh. 14:15). The words *"in the balance" they will go up* mean that [through Abraham] expiation will be won for you "in the Balance," that is, in the month whose zodiacal symbol is the Balance. What month is that? Tishri.

[The words previously rendered *Blow the shofar at the new moon* (Ps. 81:4) are now read] *Trumpet renewal*: renew your way of living; *become acceptable* [*to God*][22] (*ibid.*): make your way of life acceptable [to Me]. The Holy One meant further: If you make your way of life acceptable to Me, I will become like the shofar for your sake. What happens with a shofar? A man blows [harshly] into it from one end and his breath comes [gently] out of the other end. From the throne of judgment, I shall rise and take My seat on the throne[23] of Mercy, whence filled with mercy for you, I shall spare you and for your sake turn the harsh measure of justice into the gentle measure of mercy. When? [Year after year], *In the seventh* (*šĕḇi'i*) *month* (Lev. 23:24).

9. [Here follows a number of readings of *šĕḇi'i* (*ibid.*) other than in the sense of *seventh*]. *The month which is śĕḇi'i* is the month filled (*mĕśubba'*) with commandments: the commandment of the shofar is in it, the commandment of the Day of Atonement is in it, the commandment of the lulab cluster [is in it], and the commandment of the willow branch procession[24] is in it.

Or: *The month which is śĕḇi'i* is the month filled (*mĕśubba'*) with all kinds of plenty—it is the season for pressing wine, for threshing grain, for harvesting all kinds of fruits.

Or: *The month which is šĕḇi'i* R. Berechiah called "the month of God's oath (*šĕḇu'ah*)," in which God swore to Abraham, saying *By Myself have I sworn, saith the Lord*, etc. (Gen. 22:16). What need was there for such an oath? Because, according to R. Bebai bar Rabbah, citing R. Johanan, our father Abraham said bluntly to the Holy One: Master of universes, it is revealed and known unto Thee that when Thou saidst to me, *Take thy son, thine only one*, etc. (Gen. 22:2), there was in my heart an answer I could have given Thee. There was in my heart the temptation to say to Thee: Yesterday, Thou didst tell me, *In Isaac shall seed be called to thee* (Gen.

21. The other two mighty ones, being Isaac and Jacob. See Yalḳuṭ, Josh. 23.

22. EV: *Blow the shofar at the new moon*. But *ḥodeš*, "new moon," may also mean "renewal," and *šofar*, mean "acceptable."

23. The word *ks'*, "appointed time," or as rendered in Piska 23.6 "when the crescent is not yet visible," is here, in its spelling *ks'*, apparently taken to mean "seat" or "throne" and to suggest that God takes His seat on "the throne of mercy." Abraham Kanfer's suggestion.

24. See Suk 4:3.

21:12), and now Thou sayest to me *Take thy son, thine only one.* Accordingly, even though in my heart I felt an impulse to argue with Thee, still I restrained myself and did not argue with Thee. Hence, when Isaac's children put their hands to transgressions and evil deeds, remember for their sake their father's being bound on the altar and be Thou filled with mercy for them; have Thou mercy upon them and turn for their sake the measure of justice into the measure of mercy. [It was then God swore to Abraham]. When? [Year after year], *In the seventh month* (Lev. 23:24).

10. *And Abraham lifted up his eyes and looked, and beheld a ram caught in one thicket, and in another*[25] (Gen. 22:13). According to R. Yudan, the verse teaches that the Holy One showed our father Abraham the ram, released from one thicket, getting entangled in another thicket. Thereby the Holy One was intimating: Abraham, your children, like the ram, will be caught—caught first by transgressions and then entangled in troubles. But in the end their release will be announced with a ram's horn: *The Lord shall be seen over them, and His arrow shall go forth as the lightning, as the Lord God will blow the horn* (Zech. 9:14).

According to R. Ḥanina, the verse from Genesis teaches that the Holy One showed Abraham the ram, released from one thicket, getting entangled in another thicket, [and so on], by which the Holy One was implying: Abraham, thy children, like the ram, will be caught by the nations of the earth, entangled by the [four] kingdoms, and forcibly drawn from kingdom to kingdom—from Babylon to Media, from Media to Greece, from Greece to Edom. But in the end their redemption will be announced with a ram's horn: *The Lord shall be seen over them . . . as the Lord God will blow the horn*[26] (*ibid.*).

Anything that comes seventh in order is the one most loved. Thus in the order of the realms above, the seventh, the one closest to earth, is the one most loved: Heaven, heaven of heavens, expanse, vault, habitation, dwelling, and then sky—*Extol Him that chooseth to ride upon the sky* (Ps. 68:5) [because of all the realms it is closest to earth].[27] In the order of terrains also, the seventh is the one most loved: tilth, soil, sod, valley, desert, earth's foundation, and Land—*In mercy He judges the Land* [*containing all six of every other kind of terrain*][28] (Ps. 9:9). In the sequence of the generations also, the seventh is the one most loved: "Adam, Seth, Enosh, Kenan, Mahalalel, Jared, and Enoch" (1 Chron. 1:1-3)—*And Enoch walked with*

25. JV: *and looked, and behold behind him a ram caught in a thicket.* But the commentator takes *'ḥr*, "*behind* [*him*]," in the sense of "in another."

26. In this passage in Zechariah, the discomfiture of Javan (Greece) and the whirlwinds directed against Teman (Edom) are alluded to. Moreover, the phrase *The Lord shall be seen* (Zech. 9:14) echoes Gen. 22:14.

27. See B.Ḥag̃ 12b, and PRE, chap. 18.

28. See Sif Deut. 37 (ed. Finkelstein, p. 70).

God (Gen. 5:24). In the succession of the Patriarchs also, the seventh is the one most loved: Abraham, Isaac, Jacob, Levi, Kohath, Amram, and Moses —*And Moses went up unto God* (Exod. 19:3). Of [Jesse's] sons also, the seventh is the one most loved: Eliab, Abinadab, Shemael, Nethanel, Raddai, Ozem, and *David the seventh* (1 Chron. 2:15). In the royal line also, the seventh is the one most loved: Saul, Ish-bosheth, David, Solomon, Rehoboam, Abijah, Asa: *And Asa cried unto the Lord his God, and said: "Lord, there is none beside Thee to help, between the mighty and him that hath no strength; help us, O Lord our God, for we rely on Thee,"* etc. (2 Chron. 14:10).[29] In the succession of the years of remission of debts, the seventh, the year concluding the seventh of the seven-year cycles, is also the one most loved, [for it is followed by the Jubilee year]: *And ye shall hallow the fiftieth year* (Lev. 25:10). In the succession of years also, the seventh is the one most loved: *The seventh year shalt thou let [the Land] rest and lie fallow*, etc. (Exod. 23:11). In the succession of days also, the seventh is the one most loved: *And God blessed the seventh day, and hallowed it* (Gen. 2:3). Finally in the succession of months also, the seventh is the one most loved: *In the seventh month, in the first day of the month* (Lev. 23:24).

11. R. Abba bar R. Papi and R. Joshua of Siḵnin, citing R. Levi, said: Throughout the days of the year, Israel go about their usual business.[30] But on New Year's Day Israel take shofars, and as they blow the *tĕḳi'ah*, the Holy One, rising from the throne of justice, takes His seat on the throne of mercy whence filled with mercy for Israel, for their sake He turns the measure of justice into the measure of mercy. When? [Year after year], *In the seventh month in the first day of the month* (*ibid.*).

12. A story: R. Johanan and R. Simeon ben Laḳish were puzzled about the following passage in a Mishnah in which we learn "If New Year's festive day fell on Sabbath, the shofar was blown in the Temple, but not in the provinces" (RH 4:1). They said: If blowing the shofar is prescribed in the Torah, let the command to blow, override, in this respect, the keeping of the Sabbath in the provinces also; but if the blowing is not prescribed in the Torah it should not override, in this respect, the keeping of the Sabbath even in the Holy City. While they were sitting and puzzling over the matter, Kahana came along. They said: Look—the expert in the transmission of oral law is coming along; let us proceed to put the problem to him. And so they proceeded to ask him. He replied: One verse says of the first day in the seventh month, *It is a day of blowing the shofar unto you* (Num. 29:1), but

29. In response to Asa's prayer, God smote the Ethiopians, who, it is said, *were shattered before the Lord, and before His host* (2 Chron 14:12). These words intimate a kind of direct intervention by God, an intervention which no previous king of Judah had secured.

30. The comment appears to be based on the words *a ram caught in one thicket and in another* (Gen. 22:13).

another says of the day that it shall be for you a *Mentioning of the blowing of the shofar* (Lev. 23:24). How are the two verses to be reconciled? As follows: When New Year's Day falls during the week it shall be *a day of blowing the shofar unto you*; but when it falls on Sabbath, it shall be unto you merely a *Mentioning of the blowing of the shofar*—that is, the blowing of the shofar is to be mentioned, but the shofar is not to be blown.[31]

[Note that in what follows the authority who set forth the interpretation of the two verses in hand is not anonymous, but is identified as R. Simeon ben Yoḥai. The identification was made when] R. Ze'era urged his colleagues: "Go in and listen to the voice of R. Levi expound Torah, for it is unlikely that he would leave a lesson without instruction in halaḵah." When R. Ze'era's colleagues went into the house of study, R. Levi in their presence expounded the matter as follows: "One verse says of the first day in the seventh month *It is a day of blowing the shofar unto you* (Num. 29:1), but another says of that day *A mentioning of the blowing of the shofar* (Lev. 23:24). How are the two verses to be reconciled? As follows: When New Year's Day falls during the week, it shall be *a day of blowing the shofar unto you*; but when it falls on Sabbath there shall be merely *A mentioning of the blowing of the shofar*—the shofar is to be mentioned, but not blown. For, as R. Simeon ben Yoḥai taught: "In the Temple, where they knew precisely the time of the New Moon, the blowing of the shofar overrode the keeping of the Sabbath; but in the provinces, where they did not know precisely the time of the New Moon, the blowing of the shofar might not override the keeping of the Sabbath. And as R. Simeon ben Yoḥai further taught:[32] Indeed the verse *It is a day of blowing the shofar unto you . . . where ye make a burnt offering* (Num. 29:1, 2) clearly implies that [in the Temple], the place where offerings were brought, [the blowing of the shofar overrode the keeping of the Sabbath]."[33]

R. Taḥalifa of Caesarea noted: Elsewhere in the same passage Scripture says, *Ye shall present a burnt offering* (Num. 29:8, 13, 36), but here in reference to New Year's Day it says, *Ye shall make* (Num. 29:2). By these words the Holy One was implying: Since you come into My presence for judgment this day and go forth free, I regard you as though you had been made this very day—as though on this day I had brought you into being as a

31. The observance of the Sabbath thus supersedes specific requirements for the several festivals.

32. The Sanhedrin which sits in the Temple may have set the rising of Tishri's New Moon so late in the afternoon of the last day of Elul that there was not enough time to get word to the provinces.

33. R. Simeon's additional comment intends to answer the question: But what if the precise time of the New Moon is known in the provinces? In response, R. Simeon associates the blowing of the shofar with the bringing of offerings—acts which in the Temple overrode the keeping of the Sabbath. See P.RH 4:1, 59b.

newly made creature—*For as the heavens* [*which I have already made*] *stand before Me as though they were new, and the earth* [*which I have already made stands before Me*] *as though it were new, so shall your seed and your name stand before Me* [*as though they were newly made*] (Isa. 66:22).[34]

34. JV: *For as the new heavens and the new earth which I will make shall remain before Me, saith the Lord, so shall your seed and your name remain* (Isa. 66:22). Isaiah speaks of a time, however, when the children of Israel, having repented, are "clean vessels" (Isa. 66:20).

PISKA 24

SUMMARY

On repentance

As voiced by Hosea, God's plea to Israel to repent is both a shofar of warning and an appeal to seek God and live (Sec. 1). Even as one is always free to immerse himself in the sea, so the man who seeks repentance is free to repent at any time in any place. The Lord—Israel's pool of hope—is always nearby to cleanse repentant Israel (Sec. 2).

God gives those who are neither completely righteous nor completely wicked ten days between New Year's Day and the Day of Atonement to resolve to repent (Sec. 3).

How are you to cope with the Inclination to evil? Make it tremble with fear of evil's consequences; or make it tremble with frustration of its designs upon you. All the while, you are to seek every opportunity to pray to God, making sure, however, to refrain from the sin you might commit (Sec. 4).

God delights in "broken vessels"—in men whose hearts are broken in contrition (Sec. 5). By leading them to repentance, God mends such broken vessels, even as He enhances their strength (Sec. 6). Unlike Wisdom, Prophecy, and Torah, each of which prescribes punishment for a sinner, God asks no more of the sinner than that he mend his ways in order to be forgiven (Sec. 7). In human courts he who confesses to a crime suffers punishment; in God's court he who confesses to a sin goes forth a free man (Sec. 8). Reuben, first to repent, was to be the forebear of the prophet Hosea to whom God first spoke of Israel's returning to Him—of repentance (Sec. 9). A human magistrate reads the charge against an accused man, has him flogged to make him confess, sees to it that he does not retract his confession, and in the end has the accused executed. God, on the other hand, finds ways to summon to repentance the man who is guilty of transgression (Sec. 10).

Even if the repentance be half-hearted, God will accept it. Thus He accepted Cain's repentance although its genuineness was not at all certain; He accepted Ahab's repentance which was no more than a gesture; He accepted the repentance of the men of Anathoth, which, not being mentioned in Scripture, is only to be presumed; He accepted the repentance of the men of Nineveh whose repentance was largely calculated. God's acceptance of such dubious kinds of repentance is in keeping with His requiting of the wicked for only one wicked deed at a time, for He is always hopeful that the wicked will wholeheartedly repent. In keeping also with His practice of removing the weapons of His indignation to a distance, no wonder that He accepted even

Manasseh's repentance which came at the very last moment of his life. No wonder, too, that in order to accept Jeconiah's repentance God even set aside an oath which He had sworn. Should the people of Israel, then, have any doubt that He will accept their repentance? (Sec. 11). Even if they allowed God an opening in themselves as narrow as the eye of a needle, even if their repentance lasted no more time than it takes to wink an eye, even if their repentance were uttered in complete privacy, God would still accept Israel's repentance (Sec. 12). No matter how high the children of Israel heap up their iniquities, once they repent, God will disregard their iniquities (Sec. 13).

But if there is no repentance, God will ultimately bring the sinner to judgment, and his attempts to escape will prove futile (Sec. 14). God Himself acts as witness in behalf of those who repent and do good, even as He acts as witness against those who do not repent and persist in evil (Sec. 15).

Let Israel, as they contemplate repentance, ever remember that God bears them no grudge and that no matter what, He is their Father in heaven (Sec. 16).

In the meantime, Israel are to chip away bit by bit the Inclination to evil, the cause of the world's stumbling. But if they stumble, they should remember that any pain whatever that is visited upon them by way of punishment is meticulously noted down in heaven and mercifully included in the final reckoning of their punishment (Sec. 17).

Words of men who are eloquent, who chant Scripture well, and who expound it well help to stay God's judgment (Sec. 18). Equally effective are ordinary men's pleas and prayers to God, especially when combined with fasting and readiness to suffer persecution (Sec. 19).

PISKA 24

Return (Hos. 14:2).[1]

1. *When a shofar is blown in a city, and the people do not tremble, then if evil befall the city, the Lord hath not done it* (Amos 3:6). A parable of a city thrown into confusion by [news of] invaders approaching. There lived in the city a certain elder who kept warning all the people of the invasion of the city. Whoever heeded him [and fled] was saved; and whoever did not heed him [and stayed], the invaders came and slew. Thus it is written *So thou, son of man, I have set thee a watchman over the house of Israel* (Ezek. 33:7). *When I say unto the wicked: "O wicked man, thou shalt surely die," and thou dost not speak to warn the wicked from his way: that wicked man shall die in his iniquity, but his blood will I require at thy hand* (Ezek. 33:8). *Hence, if thou warn the wicked of his way to turn from it, and he turn not from his way, he shall die in his iniquity, but thou hast delivered thy soul* (Ezek. 33:9). So, too, *When a shofar is blown in a city*, on New Year's Day, *and the people*—Israel—*do not tremble, then if evil befall the city, the Lord hath not done it*, for the Holy One is not pleased by the death of the wicked. Thus it is written *Say unto them: As I live, saith the Lord God, I have no pleasure in the death of the wicked*, etc. (Ezek. 33:11). O people [of Israel], what do I require of you? *Turn ye, turn ye from your evil ways; for why will ye die, O house of Israel?* (*ibid.*). Some commentators take it that [God is pleading with Israel not so much to turn from evil and avoid death as] He is pleading with them to seek Him and live: *Seek ye Me, and live* (Amos 5:4). O people, what do I require of you? Only that ye seek Me and thus remain alive. Therefore, Hosea, admonishing Israel, said: *Return, O Israel, unto the Lord thy God* (Hos. 14:2).

2. *Awesome works—because Thou in righteousness afflictest us, O God of our salvation* (Ps. 65:6). R. Judah, citing R. Isaac, took the verse to mean: The awesome works Thou dost for us in this world are done to make up for the afflictions Thou bringest upon us in this world. But R. Haggai, likewise citing R. Isaac, took the verse to mean: The awesome works Thou wilt do for us in the world-to-come will make up for the afflictions Thou bringest upon us in this world.

Thou that art the confidence of all the ends of the earth (*ibid.*). Thou art the confidence of men of violence[2]—even such men trust in Thy name.

1. Hos. 14:2–10 is the haftarah for the Sabbath of Repentance.

2. The reference is to the saying "A thief on the rooftop calls upon the Merciful One not to let himself be caught." See B.Ber 63a margin. Professor Saul Lieberman has kindly provided the explanation.

Or: "Thou art the confidence of all whose hope of standing up to men of violence

Those who travel the highways have confidence when they invoke Thy name. Those who set forth on the seas have confidence when they invoke Thy name; so, too, do those who go forth with caravans.

Concerning the conclusion of the verse, *And of the sea, afar off* (*ibid.*), R. Ḥanina bar Papa asked R. Samuel bar Naḥman: What is meant by *And of the sea, afar off*? He replied: Repentance [for those far off from God] is likened to the sea.[3] As the sea is always open to all, so the gates of repentance are always open to all. Prayer [in a congregation], however, is likened to a ritual bath. As a ritual bath is open at some times and barred at other times, so the gates of prayer are open at some times and barred at other times. Just as a man at a ritual bath about to immerse himself, finding his father or his master there and ashamed to bare himself, goes away without bathing, [so a man sometimes feels ashamed to bare his heart in the presence of others and hence does not pray]. On the other hand, just as a man at the seashore need only go a short distance away to be alone when he immerses himself, [so the man who seeks repentance can repent at any time in any place].

R. Berechiah and R. Ḥelbo, citing R. 'Anan bar R. Jose, said: In truth, the gates of prayer are also always open, as R. Jose bar Ḥalafta implied by the question, Are there, indeed, set times for prayer? David's answer is explicit: When he says, *But as for me, let my prayer be unto Thee O Lord, in an acceptable time*, etc. (Ps. 69:14), David pleads directly with the Holy One: Master of universes, whenever I pray before Thee, let it be an acceptable time to Thee—*answer me with the truth of Thy salvation* (*ibid.*).

In the name of R. Eliezer, it is taught: "*The Lord is Israel's pool of hope* (*miḳweh*)[4] (Jer. 17:13) means that as the ritual pool of purification (*miḳweh*) is [nearby] to cleanse those who are impure, so the Holy One is [nearby] to cleanse Israel" (Yoma 8:9). Therefore Hosea, admonishing Israel, says to them, *Return, O Israel* (Hos. 14:2).

(so Pa) [has well nigh come to an end]—even such nearly hopeless men have confidence in Thy name."

For "ends of the earth" as referring to those whose hope having come to an end feel themselves beyond human assistance and therefore turn to God, see Ibn Ezra on Ps. 65:6. Professor Jakob J. Petuchowski has provided the interpretation given in this note as well as the reference to Ibn Ezra.

3. The two preceding verses, Ps. 65:4–5, speak of repentance and forgiveness of sins.

4. The word *miḳweh* means both "pool of hope" and "pool of cleansing." In a parallel passage (MTeh 4:9 [YJS, *13*, 2, 73]) the text continues as follows: "Which of the two can go to the other—the pool of cleansing to the unclean person, or the unclean person to the pool of cleansing? Obviously, the unclean person has to go to the pool of cleansing, let himself down, and immerse himself in it; so also must Israel go to the Holy One who will cleanse them."

3. *The Lord uttereth His voice before His army*, etc. (Joel 2:11). The words *The Lord uttereth His voice before His army* apply to [the blowing of the shofar on] New Year's Day; the words that follow, *for His camp is very great* (*ibid.*), apply to Israel; the words *for he is strong that executeth His word* mean that God increases the strength of the righteous who carry out His word; and the words *for the day of the Lord is great and very terrible* (*ibid.*) refer to the Day of Atonement, [which in the Land of Israel was called the Great Day].[5] As for the verse's concluding words, *And who can prevail against it—[against this Day]?* (*ibid.*), R. Ḳrispa, citing R. Johanan, stated: [No one, for between New Year's Day and *this day*], the names of those upon whom judgment is to be pronounced are set out in three registers—one with the names of the completely righteous, one with the names of the completely wicked, and one with the names of those who are neither completely righteous nor completely wicked. As Rabbi [Judah] stated it, *some to everlasting life* (Dan. 12:2): the completely righteous; *and some to reproaches and everlasting abhorrence* (*ibid.*): the completely wicked. *Blotted out of the book* (Ps. 69:29): the wicked; *remaining alive* (*ibid.*): the righteous; *and not written with the righteous* (*ibid.*): those neither completely righteous nor completely wicked, to whom the Holy One gives ten days between New Year's Day and the Day of Atonement: if they resolve to repent, they are inscribed with the righteous; but if they do not resolve to repent, they are inscribed with the wicked. Therefore Hosea, admonishing Israel, says to them: *Return, O Israel* (Hos. 14:2).

4. Concerning the verse *Tremble, and sin not. Commune with your own heart upon your bed*, etc. (Ps. 4:5), R. Jacob bar Abina and the Rabbis differ. According to R. Jacob bar Abina the verse means: Make your Inclination to evil tremble with fear [of sin's consequences], and it will be unable to make you sin. According to the Rabbis, the verse means: Make your Inclination to evil tremble with frustration [of its designs upon you], and you will not fall into the hand of sin.

In the name of R. Eliezer it is taught: *The Lord is Israel's pool of hope* (*miḳweh*) (Jer. 17:13). Hence the Holy One declared to Israel: I say unto you that you are to pray in the synagogue in your city; when you cannot pray in the synagogue, pray in your open field; when you cannot pray in your open field, pray in your house; when you cannot pray in your house, pray upon your bed; when you cannot pray upon your bed, commune with your heart—*Commune with your own heart upon your bed*, [but no matter where you are], *be still* (Ps. 4:5). This is to say, according to R. Yudan, that you must restrain yourself and refrain from the sin you might commit. Therefore Hosea, admonishing Israel, said to them: *Return, O Israel* (Hos. 14:2).

5. In their comments on the verse *The sacrifices of God are a broken*

5. Deut. Rabbah, ed. Lieberman, p. 52, n. 5.

spirit; a broken and contrite heart, etc. (Ps. 51:19), Zabdi bar Levi, R. Jose bar Peṭros, and the Rabbis differ.[6] One maintains that David said to the Holy One: Master of universes, if Thou acceptest me because of my repentance,[7] I know that Solomon my son will rise up, build the Temple, build the altar, and offer upon it all kinds of sacrifices.[8] If my *broken and contrite heart, O God, Thou wilt not despise* (*ibid.*), thereby, I know—*Through Thy favor* [*unto me*]—*Thou wilt do good unto Zion* (Ps. 51:20). *Thou wilt have occasion for delight in the sacrifices of righteousness . . . for then* [*children of Israel*] *will offer bullocks upon Thine altars* (Ps. 51:21). The other commentator, [saying that the verse in hand does not refer to David's repentance, but to any man who acts in repentance], goes on to ask: Whence the proof that the Holy One deems one who acts in repentance as though he had gone up to Jerusalem and there built the Temple, built the altar, and offered all kinds of sacrifices upon it? The proof is from the verse *A broken and contrite heart, O God, Thou wilt not despise* (Ps. 51:19), which is followed at once by the words *Then it will be, as though Thou hast already in Thy favor done good unto Zion, and already hast delight in the sacrifices of righteousness*, etc. (Ps. 51:20). The Rabbis[' view, however, is that the verse refers to prayers by him who stands before the ark as reader for the congregation, prayers for the rebuilding of the Temple and the restoration of the offerings, and in keeping with this view] ask: Whence the proof that the reader who stands before the ark is required to bow down as he prays for the rebuilding of the Temple and [the restoration of] the offerings? According to some, the Rabbis say that the proof comes from the blessing [in the *'Ămiḏah*], "O our God, favor us, come to dwell in Zion the city where Thy children will serve Thee with offerings, and in Jerusalem where we shall bow down to Thee."[9] But according to others, the Rabbis derived the rule that the reader is to bow down during this blessing from the very verse in hand: [*When praying for*] *the sacrifices of God, the spirit must be bowed and broken* (*ibid.*).[10]

R. Abba bar Yudan said: What God regards as unfit [for sacrifice] in an animal, He holds fit in a human being. In an animal, He regards as unfit one

6. Each will endeavor to explain the connection between *A broken and contrite heart Thou wilt not despise* (Ps. 51:19), and the words *Do good in Thy favor unto Zion* (Ps. 51:20) which follow directly.

7. For his abduction of Bath-sheba, the sin of which he confesses at the Psalm's beginning.

8. See 2 Sam. 7:13.

9. "where we shall bow down to Thee"—this clause is not in the blessing as found in the prayerbook now in use. It was, however, found in the Palestinian ritual published by Jacob Mann, *HUCA*, 2, 306.

10. "But according to others . . . *bowed and broken* (Ps. 51:20)"—Parallel in Lev. Rabbah 7:2.

that is *blind, or broken, or maimed, or having a wen* (Lev. 22:22); but in a human being He holds *a broken and contrite heart* (Ps. 51:19) to be fit for an offering to Him.

R. Alexandri said: If an ordinary person makes use of a broken vessel, it is taken as a reflection upon him. But the Holy One is unconcerned about His use of broken vessels—indeed His entire use is broken vessels: *The Lord is nigh unto them that are of a broken heart* (Ps. 34:19); *Who healeth the broken in heart* (Ps. 147:3); *A broken and contrite heart, O God, Thou wilt not despise* (Ps. 51:19). Hence, admonishing Israel, Hosea says to them: *Return, O Israel* (Hos. 14:2).

6. *Behold (hen) God enhances a man's strength; who is a teacher like unto Him?* (Job 36:22). According to R. Berechiah, *hen* is to be taken here as the Greek word for "one."[11] Thus the verse is to be read "Our God is the only one who enhances a man's strength," which is to say, He enhances the strength of the righteous who do His will. *Who is a teacher like unto Him*, a teacher who leads sinners to resolve upon repentance? Hence, admonishing Israel, Hosea says, *Return, O Israel* (Hos. 14:2).

7. *Good and upright is the Lord, because He doth instruct sinners in the way* (Ps. 25:8). When Wisdom is asked, "The sinner—what is to be his punishment?" Wisdom answers: *Evil which pursueth sinners* (Prov. 13:21). When Prophecy is asked, "The sinner—what is to be his punishment?" Prophecy replies: *The soul that sinneth, it shall die* (Ezek. 18:4). When Torah is asked, "The sinner—what is to be his punishment?" Torah replies: Let him bring a guilt offering in expiation and his sin shall be forgiven him.[12] When the Holy One is asked, "The sinner—what is to be his punishment?" the Holy One replies: In penitence let him mend his ways, and his sin shall be forgiven him. Hence it is written, [*At one and the same time*] *kind and strict in judgment is the Lord* (Ps. 25:8). R. Phinehas commented: How can He who is strict in judgment be called kind? And how can He who is kind be called strict in judgment? *Because He doth instruct sinners in the way* (*ibid.*)—that is, He teaches sinners the way to act in penitence. Therefore Hosea, admonishing Israel, said to them: *Return, O Israel* (Hos. 14:2).

8. *He that covereth his transgressions shall not prosper* etc. (Prov. 28:13). R. Simon and R. Joshua ben Levi, citing R. Simeon ben Ḥalafta, said: All other kinds of trees must have their roots covered in order to prosper, but the nut tree[13] does not prosper when its roots are covered.[14] Consider an analogy with a robber on trial before an examining magistrate:

11. Cf. Piska 9.6.
12. See Lev. 5:6.
13. A symbol of Israel. See PR 11:2.
14. The larvae of certain harmful beetles which deposit their eggs in the roots of nut trees are killed by exposure to air. Professor Y. Feliks of Bar-Ilan University has provided this information.

for as long as the robber protests his innocence, he is flogged, but after he confesses his guilt, he receives the written verdict [that commits him to prison]. The Holy One is a wholly different kind of magistrate: when a man refuses to confess his guilt, God gives him the written verdict [that commits him to prison]; but after he confesses, he goes forth a free man. Hence *He that covereth his transgressions shall not prosper*. On the other hand, as R. Judah said, *Whoso exposes his transgressions by confession, intending to forsake them, shall obtain mercy* (*ibid.*). Hence, admonishing Israel, Hosea says to them: *Return, O Israel* (Hos. 14:2).

9. *A man shall have his fill of good by the fruit of his mouth* (Prov. 12:14). It is written *And Reuben returned unto the pit* (Gen. 37:29). In their comments on this verse, R. Eliezer, R. Joshua, and the Rabbis differ. According to R. Eliezer, Reuben was so taken up with his sackcloth and his fasting in repentance over the incident [with Bilhah, Gen. 35:22] which had befallen him that he was not free [to look for Joseph]. But as soon as he was free of his sackcloth and his fasting, he came and peered down into the pit, *and, behold, Joseph was not in the pit*, etc. (*ibid.*). According to R. Joshua, however, Reuben was not free because responsibility for the affairs of the household was thrust upon him. But as soon as he became free of responsibility for the affairs of the household, he came and peered down into the pit, *and, behold, Joseph was not in the pit*, etc. (*ibid.*). According to the Rabbis, the Holy One said to Reuben: Thou didst seek to bring about the return of a well-loved son to his father. As thou livest, a son's son of thine will seek to bring about Israel's return to their Father in heaven. And who was the son's son? Hosea, of whom it is written *With Hosea the son of Beeri, the Lord first spoke* [*of return to Him*] (Hos. 1:1). We know that Hosea was a Reubenite because his father is so identified in Scripture: [*Baal's*] *son, Beerah, whom Tillegath-pilneser king of Assyria carried away captive; he was prince of the Reubenites* (1 Chron. 5:6). But why is he here called [not Beeri, as in Hosea, but] Beerah, "he of her well?" To indicate that he was a wellspring of Torah. But if Beerah was a wellspring of Torah, why did he die in exile? So that because of his merit, [at the time of resurrection], the Ten Tribes will return with him [to the Land], even as Moses died in the wilderness so that because of his merit, the generation of the wilderness will turn, [at the time of resurrection], unto [the Promised Land].[15]

[In agreement with the Rabbis as quoted just above], R. Berechiah declared: [Reuben was so taken up with turning back to God] that the Holy One said to him, "Thou wast first in an act of repentance.[16] As thou

15. See Num. Rabbah 19:13, and Deut. Rabbah 2:9.

16. *Reuben returned* (Gen. 37:29) may be translated, in disregard of the context, "Reuben repented."

livest, a son's son of thine will be the first to come and begin his discourse with the call to repentance: *Return, O Israel*" (Hos. 14:2).

10. *For My thoughts are not your thoughts, neither are your ways My ways, saith the Lord* (Isa. 55:8). A parable of a brigand on trial before an examining magistrate: at first the magistrate reads the charge against the accused and then, having had him flogged [to make him confess], has a hook put into his mouth [so that he cannot retract his confession]. The magistrate goes on to read the sentence of death, and then the brigand is led forth to be executed. Not such a magistrate is the Holy One. First, He read the charge against the Tribes: *Now they sin more and more, and have made them molten images of their silver* (Hos. 13:2). Then He had them flogged: *Ephraim is smitten, their root is dried up*, etc. (Hos. 9:16). Then having put a hook into their mouths—*The iniquity of Ephraim is bound up; his sin is laid up in store* (Hos. 13:12)—He read them the written pronouncement of their sentence: *Samaria shall bear her guilt, for she hath rebelled against her God* (Hos. 14:1). But then, [instead of having them executed], He found ways to summon them to repentance: *Return, O Israel* (Hos. 14:2).

11. What verse comes immediately before the lesson for the day from the Prophets? *Samaria shall bear her guilt* (Hos. 14:1). This is at once followed by the words *Return, O Israel* (Hos. 14:2). R. Eleazar, citing R. Samuel bar Naḥman, told a parable of a city which rebelled against its king. The king sent a general to lay it waste, but since the general was experienced and cool-headed, he said to the rebels: Take time to consider what you are doing lest the king lay waste your city as he laid waste such-and-such a city and its environs and such-and-such a province and its environs. So, too, Hosea said to Israel: My children, resolve upon penitence, so that the Holy One does not do to you what He did to Samaria and its environs. Thereupon Israel asked the Holy One directly: Master of universes, if we do resolve upon penitence, wilt Thou accept us [even though—human nature being what it is—our repentance may be imperfect]? He replied: I accepted Cain's repentance, and shall I not receive your repentance? Consider how Cain's repentance relieved the harshness of the decree that had been imposed on him. It was said to him, *When thou tillest the ground, it shall not henceforth yield unto thee her strength; a fugitive and a wanderer shalt thou be* (Gen. 4:12). But as soon as he vowed repentance, half the punishment specified in the decree was canceled for him. And whence the proof that he vowed repentance? Cain's saying *My sin is greater than can be forgiven* (Gen. 4:13). And what is the proof that half the punishment specified in the decree was canceled for him? The verse *And Cain went out from the presence of the Lord and dwelt in the land as a wanderer, on the east of Eden* (Gen. 4:16), Scripture here not speaking of him as both "a wanderer and a fugitive," but only *as a wanderer, on the east of Eden*. [But was Cain truly penitent? If he was], what is meant by the first part of the verse *Cain went out from the*

presence of the Lord?[17] According to R. Yudan, citing R. Aibu, the verse signifies that as Cain left the Lord's presence, he tossed off the words [*My sin is greater than can be forgiven*] as if by mouthing them he could blunt the Almighty's awareness of his sin. According to R. Berechiah, citing R. Eleazar bar R. Simeon, as Cain went out, thinking all the time to deceive his Creator, he put on a show [with the words *My sin is greater than can be forgiven*] just as a swine displays his cloven hoof [as if in proof of his purity].[18] But according to R. Huna, citing R. Ḥanina bar R. Isaac, Cain [did not speak deceitfully, but] went forth as one glad in heart, for here the phrase *went out* (*yoṣe'*) has the same connotation as in the verse "He goeth out (*yoṣe'*) to meet thee, he will be glad in his heart" (Exod. 4:14). As Cain went out, Adam met him and asked, "What was done in punishment of you?" Cain replied: "I vowed repentance and was granted clemency." Hearing this, in self-reproach Adam proceeded to strike himself in the face and said: "Such is the power of repentance, and I knew it not!" Then and there he exclaimed: *It is a good thing to confess to the Lord*, etc. (Ps. 92:2). According to R. Levi, the first verse of the Psalm just cited, a verse usually read *A Psalm, a song for the Sabbath day* (Ps. 92:1), is to be read *A Psalm, a song for the day of repentance*,[19] and the entire Psalm is to be taken as having been composed by Adam [after he was told by Cain that he had been granted clemency. Now we understand why God said to Israel: If I accepted Cain's], shall I not accept your repentance?

If I accepted Ahab's repentance, shall I not accept your repentance? A cruel decree had been imposed upon Ahab: *Thou shalt speak unto him, saying: Hast thou killed, and also taken possession? And thou shalt speak unto him, saying: Thus saith the Lord: In the place where dogs licked the blood of Naboth shall dogs lick thy blood, even thine* (1 Kings 21:19). *And it came to pass, when Ahab heard these words, that he rent his clothes, and put sackcloth upon his flesh, and fasted, and lay in sackcloth* (1 Kings 21:27). And in what manner did he fast? [In the manner of one who goes through the motions of fasting]: if he was accustomed to eat at the third hour, he ate at the sixth, and if he was accustomed to eat at the sixth hour, he ate at the ninth.[20] What is meant by the end of the verse *and he walked*

17. An impossible feat. Does not the Psalmist say, *Whither shall I go from Thy spirit* (Ps. 139:7)?

18. "just as a swine displays his cloven hoof [as if in proof of his purity]"—O_1, Pa. That is, a hypocrite is like a swine who, showing its cloven hoof (Lev. 11:7), pretends to be clean. O: "as though endeavoring to conciliate."

19. R. Levi associates *šbt*, "rest," with the root *šwb*, "return, repent."

20. The day being reckoned from six in the morning to six in the evening.

The "proof" from Scripture that Ahab fasted no more than three hours may be stated as follows: One would have expected the text to say that Ahab fasted, walked softly, and lay in sackcloth. The actual order suggests to the commentator that the

softly (*ibid.*)? According to R. Joshua ben Levi, [that he went through the motions of inflicting suffering upon himself] by taking his shoes off [and walking about gingerly]. Even so, what do we find Scripture saying? *The word of the Lord came to Elijah the Tishbite, saying: "Seest thou that Ahab humbleth himself before Me? Because he humbleth himself before Me I will not bring the evil in his days,"* etc. (1 Kings 21:28–29). Thus the Holy One, [who accepts even gestures of repentance], asked Elijah: "Hast thou seen Ahab avow penitence? *Seest thou that Ahab humbleth himself before Me?*" [Now we understand why God said to Israel: If I accepted Ahab's], shall I not accept your repentance?

I accepted the repentance of the men of Anathoth, and shall I not accept your repentance? God had imposed a cruel decree upon the men of Anathoth [because they had threatened Jeremiah with death]: *Thus saith the Lord concerning the men of Anathoth, that seek thy life, saying: "Thou shalt not prophesy in the name of the Lord that thou die not by our hand;" therefore thus saith the Lord:*[21] *Behold, I will punish them . . . there shall be no remnant unto them*, etc. (Jer. 11:21, 23). But when the men of Anathoth vowed to repent,[22] God accepted their repentance [and withdrew His decree], as is shown by the fact that they are specifically mentioned in the genealogical lists [of those who returned from Babylon]: *The men of Anathoth, a hundred and twenty-eight* (Ezra 2:23). [Now we understand why God said to Israel: If I accepted the repentance of the men of Anathoth], shall I not accept your repentance?

I accepted the repentance of the people of Nineveh, and shall I not accept your repentance? A cruel decree had been imposed upon the people of Nineveh: *Jonah began to enter into the city a day's journey, and he proclaimed, and said: "Yet forty days, and Nineveh shall be overthrown"* (Jonah 3:4). *And the tidings reached the king of Nineveh, and he arose from his throne, and laid his robe from him, and covered him with sackcloth, and caused it to be proclaimed through Nineveh by the decree of the king and his nobles, saying: "Let neither man nor beast . . . taste anything; let them not feed, nor drink water; but let them be covered with sackcloth, both man and beast, and let them cry mightily unto God"* (Jonah 3:7–8). According to Resh Laḳish, the people of Nineveh put on a great show of repentance. How did they do so? In the name of R. Simeon ben Ḥalafta, R.

---

verse be read "He fasted no more than [the additional time] he was wont to lie"—that is, he fasted no more than three hours, these being the additional hours of sleep into the day a king indulges in. See *Šĕyyare ḳorban ha'edah* on P.Sanh 10:2.

21. MT: *the Lord of hosts.*

22. The repentance of the men of Anathoth—not mentioned in Scripture—seems to be surmised from the fact that several decades later, in the days of Ezra, they did have a *remnant*. See Neh. 10:20.

Huna said: The people of Nineveh put their calves inside the cattle folds and the calves' dams outside the cattle folds so that the former could be heard from within lowing for their dams and the latter could be heard lowing from without for their calves. And as the calves were lowing from within and their dams from without, the people of Nineveh were moaning and crying out to God: If you do not heed our cries and show mercy to us, we shall not heed the cries of our cattle and show mercy to them.

According to R. Aḥa, the people of Arabia also make their cattle groan in order to gain God's attention and His mercy.[23] As Scripture tells us: *How the beasts groan! The herds of cattle are perplexed, because they have no pasture* (Joel 1:18).

What is meant by *mightily* in the proclamation of Nineveh's king: *Let them be covered with sackcloth, both man and beast, and let them cry mightily unto God* (Jonah 3:8)? What is meant, according to R. Simeon ben Ḥalafta, is that he who cries out most demandingly can prevail over the hardheartedness of a wicked man, and this being so, can all the more easily win over Him who is the Gentleness of the world. And what is meant by the conclusion of the verse in hand—*Yea, let them turn every one from his evil way—from the violence that is in their hands* (*ibid.*)? R. Johanan took these words to mean that of the objects the people of Nineveh had taken by violence they returned only those that were in plain sight, but those they had put away in a box, or in a chest, or in a closet they did not return.

And rend your hearts, so that you will not need to rend your garments (Joel 2:13), words which imply, said R. Joshua ben Levi, that if you rend your hearts in repentance you will have no occasion to rend your garments for the deaths of your sons and daughters. Why not? Because *He is gracious and compassionate, long in acts of patience* (*ibid.*). Both R. Aḥa and R. Tanḥum, citing R. Ḥiyya, who cited R. Johanan, pointed out that the text does not say "long in patience," but says *long in acts of patience* (*ibid.*) and means that He is long patient with the righteous and long patient with the wicked. He is long patient with the righteous, [delaying their immediate reward] and instead making them pay for the few wicked deeds they did in this world in order to give them their reward in full in the world-to-come. But He bestows ease in plenty upon the wicked in this world, thereby rewarding them in this world for their few good deeds in order to requite them in full in the world-to-come.

R. Samuel bar Naḥman, citing R. Johanan, said: The text, not saying "long in patience," but saying *long in acts of patience* (*ibid.*), is intimating that God exercises patience before deciding to requite the wicked, and even

23. "To this day, before praying for rain, Arabs in the Negeb first hurt their cattle and fowl to make them groan and cry out. Thereupon the Arabs proceed to pray: 'Send down rain for the cattle and fowl groaning from thirst.'" BM's note.

when He decides to requite them, in patience He requites them [for only one wicked deed at a time].[24] He who dares to assert, therefore, that the Merciful One is loose in the exercise of justice, said R. Ḥanina, gets loose bowels. The truth is that God long exercises patience, but finally makes requital.

R. Levi said: To me *long in acts of patience* (*ibid.*) implies that He moves a long way off the means by which He makes requital. Consider a parable of a king who had two fierce legions. The king said: If these stay with me in the city, then should the city's inhabitants provoke me, the two legions, on their own, will rise up and destroy them. Therefore, I shall send the legions a long way off, so that should the city's inhabitants provoke me, then before I send for the two legions, the inhabitants will have time to come and apologize to me, and I will accept the apologies. Hence Scripture: *They come from a country far away—from the end of heaven—the weapons of His indignation* (Isa. 13:5). Nay more, R. Isaac added: God keeps His weapons locked up; *The Lord hath unlocked His armory, and hath brought forth the weapons of His indignation* (Jer. 50:25), [and while He delays using His weapons]—unlocking and locking His armory—[so as to give men time to repent], His mercies come nigh. As R. Meir taught, the words *Behold, the Lord cometh forth out of His place*[25] (Isa. 26:21) mean that in Israel's behalf He comes forth out of the place where He exercises justice to the place where He exercises mercy.[26] [And now we understand why God said to Israel: If I did not choose to use My weapons against Nineveh, but accepted her repentance instead], shall I not accept your repentance?

I accepted Manasseh's repentance: shall I not accept yours? A cruel decree of punishment had been imposed upon Manasseh. Scripture says: *The Lord spoke to Manasseh, and to his people; but they gave no heed. Wherefore the Lord brought upon them the captains of the host of the king of Assyria, who took Manasseh with hooks*, etc. (2 Chron. 33:10, 11). What is meant by *with hooks*? With manacles, so said R. Abba bar Kahana. The verse goes on to say, *and imprisoned him in copper work*[27] (*ibid.*). What is meant by *in copper work*? According to R. Levi bar Ḥaita, there was contrived for the punishment of Manasseh a copper caldron in the shape of a jackass,[28] with

24. In the hope that in the meantime the sinner will repent. So *Ḳorban ha-'edah* on P.Beṣ 3:8.

25. Since the whole earth is full of His glory, how can God be said to leave *His place?* Therefore R. Meir suggests that *His place* means "the place where He should be in His exercise of strict justice." See *Ḳorban ha-'edah* on P.Ta 2:1. See also Piska 23.8, and 11.

26. See Piska 23.3.

27. JV: *and bound him with fetters.*

28. See W. Bacher, "Le Taureau de Phalaris dans l'Agada" in *Revue des Études Juives, 44* (1902), 291–95.

many holes made in the caldron. After Manasseh was put into the caldron, a slow fire was started under it. When Manasseh saw, then, that his trouble was real trouble, there was not an idol anywhere in the world, not a one, that he failed to call upon by name: O idol so-and-so, come and deliver me![29] When he realized that his appeal was availing him nothing at all, he said: I remember that my father had me read a particular verse, *In thy distress, when all these things are come upon thee, in the end of days, return to the Lord thy God, and hearken unto His voice; for the Lord thy God is a merciful God; He will not fail thee, neither destroy thee* (Deut. 4:30, 31). All right, then, I will call upon my father's God: if He answers me, well and good, but if not, then all deities are alike worthless. At this point the ministering angels began shutting heaven's windows so that Manasseh's prayer could not come up before the Holy One. They put the question to the Holy One: A man who set up an idol in the Temple—can the repentance of such a man be accepted? The Holy One replied: If I do not receive him in his repentance, I shall be barring the door to all who would repent. What did the Holy One proceed to do for Manasseh? He contrived an opening (*ḥtyrh*) for his sake under His very own throne of glory [where the angels could not interfere with] His hearing Manasseh's supplication. Hence it is written *And he prayed unto Him; and He was entreated* (*wy'tr*) *of him*, etc. (2 Chron. 33:13), where the *kĕṯiḇ*, *wyḥtr*,[30] implies that God Himself made the opening so that *He could hear his supplication*, etc. (*ibid.*). [This reading of the *kĕṯiḇ* is justified by the fact that] in Araba, as R. Eleazar bar R. Simeon pointed out, the Aramaic *'tyrt'*,[31] "a hole dug in the earth," is pronounced *ḥtyrt'*.[32] The verse in hand goes on to say, *And brought him back to Jersualem into his kingdom* (*ibid.*). How did He bring Manasseh back? R. Samuel bar Naḥman, citing R. Aḥa, said that God brought him back on a wind, for the word *hšyḇ*, "brought back," has the specific connotation of *mšyḇ*, "brought back by being blown back," as in the statement, "Thou bringest the wind to blow."[33] [Thus having been brought back on a wind], *Manasseh knew that the Lord He was God* (*ibid.*), and Manasseh exclaimed: Where there is judgment, there is a Judge.[34]

[Now we understand why God said to Israel: If I accepted Manasseh's repentance], shall I not accept your repentance?

I accepted the repentance of Jeconiah: shall I not accept your repentance? A cruel decree had been imposed upon Jeconiah: Scripture says, *This man Coniah is a despised, shattered image* (*'ṣb*) (Jer. 22:28), for Jeconiah,

29. "deliver me"—O_1; O: "deliver him."
30. This is no such *kĕṯiḇ* in MT.
31. The nominal form of the verb *wy'tr*, "He was entreated."
32. The nominal form of *wyḥtr*, "He let Himself be dug into." Cf. Piska 27.3.
33. See Hertz, APB, p. 133.
34. Cf. PR 51:5.

according to R. Abba bar Kahana, was like a man's skull (*'ṣm*)[35] which once shattered is utterly useless, or, according to R. Ḥelbo, like a wrapper of reed matting that dates are packed in, which, once emptied, is utterly useless.[36] And Scripture goes on to say of Jeconiah: *He is a vessel that none reaches for with delight* (*ibid.*), a vessel, said R. Ḥama bar R. Ḥanina, such as a urinal; or a vessel, said R. Samuel bar Naḥman, such as is used for drawing off blood. [These comments on Jeconiah derive from] R. Meir's statement: The Holy One swore that He would raise up no king out of Jeconiah king of Judah. Thus Scripture: *As I live, saith the Lord, though Coniah the son of Jehoiakim . . . were the signet on a hand, yet by My right, I would pluck thee hence* (Jer. 22:24), words by which God was saying, explained R. Ḥanina bar R. Isaac, "Beginning with thee, Jeconiah, I pluck out the kingship of the house of David." It is to be noted, however,[37] that the Hebrew for "pluck thee" is not as one would expect *'tḳk*, but the fuller and less usual *'tḳnk*, which may also be rendered "mend thee"—that is, mend thee by thy repentance. Thus in the very place, [the kingship], whence Jeconiah was plucked, amends would be made to him: [his line would be renewed].

R. Ze'era said: I heard the voice of R. Samuel bar Isaac expounding from the teacher's chair a specific point concerning Jeconiah, but I just cannot remember what it was. R. Aḥa Ariḵa asked: Did it perhaps have some connection with this particular verse—*Thus saith the Lord: Write ye this man childless, a man* [*who*] *will not prosper in his days* (Jer. 22:30)? "Yes, that's it!" said R. Ze'era. Thereupon R. Aḥa Ariḵa went on to give R. Samuel bar Isaac's interpretation of the verse: In his days Jeconiah, so long as he is childless, will not prosper, but when he has a son, then he will prosper by his son's prosperity.

R. Aḥa bar Abun bar Benjamin, citing R. Abba bar R. Papi, said: Great is the power of repentance, which led God to set aside an oath even as it led Him to set aside a decree. Whence the proof that a man's repentance led Him to set aside the oath He made in the verse *As I live, saith the Lord, though Coniah the son of Jehoiakim were the signet on a hand, yet by My right, I would pluck thee hence* (Jer. 22:24)?[38] The proof is in the verse where Scripture says [of one of Jeconiah's descendants] *In that day, saith the Lord of hosts, will I take thee, O Zerubbabel . . . the son of Shealtiel . . . and will make thee as a signet* (Haggai 2:23). And the proof that a man's repentance led God to set aside a decree He issued in the verse *Thus saith the Lord: Write ye this man childless*, etc. (Jer. 22:30)? The proof is in the

35. There is here a play on *'ṣb*, "image," and *'ṣm*, "bone," the labials "b" and "m" being interchangeable.

36. Jer. 22:30 goes on to say of Jeconiah, *Write ye this man childless.*

37. A paraphrastic rendition of "Another comment."

38. An oath which meant the end of David's dynasty and, presumably, of the hope for restoration of the Jewish people's sovereignty in its own land.

verse where Scripture says, *The sons of Jeconiah—the same is Asir—Shealtiel his son*, etc. (1 Chron. 3:17). R. Tanḥum bar Jeremiah said: Jeconiah was called *Asir*, "one imprisoned," because he had been in prison (*'ăsurim*);[39] and his son called "Shealtiel" because he was like a sapling, newly set out (*huštĕlah*), through whom David's line would be continued.

R. Tanḥuma said: Jeconiah was called *Asir*, "imprisoned," because God imprisoned Himself by His oath in regard to him; and Jeconiah's son was called Shealtiel, "God consulted," because God consulted the heavenly court, and they released Him from His oath.

12. R. Judah II the Patriarch, citing R. Judah bar R. Simon, said: Ordinarily, if a man shoot an arrow, how far will it go? Over as much ground as is required to plant one or two *kor*[40] of seed in. The power of repentance, however, is so great that it shoots all the way up to the throne of glory!

R. Jose said: By the verse *Open to Me* (Song 5:2) the Holy One meant: Make for Me an opening in you, an opening as narrow as the eye of a needle, and I shall make the opening so wide that camps full of soldiers and siege engines could enter it.[41]

R. Tanḥuma citing R. Ḥanina, and R. Aibu citing Resh Laḳish, said: Vow repentance for as little time as it takes to wink an eye,[42] *and you will be aware that I am the Lord* [*of mercy*] (Ps. 46:11). For, as R. Levi said: Were Israel to vow repentance for but one day, they would be redeemed forthwith. And the proof? *We would be the people of His pasture, and the flock of His hand, if only for but one day you would hearken to His voice* (Ps. 95:7).

R. Judah bar R. Simon took the verse *Return, O Israel, unto the Lord thy God* (Hos. 14:2) to signify that even if the iniquity of Israel went so far as to deny the Root of the universe, [He would accept their repentance and let them return to Him].[43]

R. Eleazar said: The way things go in the world, if a man proceeds to abuse his fellow in public and then after a time wants to make up with him,

39. See 2 Kings 25:27.

40. 75,000 and 150,000 square cubits, respectively.

41. Cf. Piska 5.6, and PR 15:6.

42. The Hebrew *harpu, let be* (Ps. 46:11), which directly precedes *and you will be aware that I am God* (thus MT), is apparently construed in a dual sense: (1) *harpu*, "Let go [of your sins and repent]"; (2) *harpu*, taken as made up of *heref 'ayin*, "wink of an eye."

43. The implication of the verse is thus: "Return, O Israel, even if your rebellion extended 'unto [the person] of the Lord thy God.' "

An alternative rendition: "R. Judah bar R. Simon read the verse *Return, O Israel, towards ('ad) the Lord thy God* (Hos. 14:2) and took it to signify that if the iniquity of Israel went so far as refusal to admit the existence of the Root of the

his fellow is apt to say, "You abuse me in public, but now want to make up with me in private. Go fetch the people in whose presence you abused me, and then I will make up with you." The Holy One does things differently. Even if a man proceeds to blaspheme and revile Him in the market place, the Holy One says, "Repent and make up with Me even if in complete privacy, and I will accept thee."

13. R. Issachar of Kefar Mindu interpreted the verse *For He knoweth false men; indeed He seeth iniquity, but He considereth it not*[44] (Job 11:11) as follows: It is man's way in the world to heap up iniquities, but once he vows repentance, then, though God *seeth* [*his*] *iniquity, He considereth it not*, if one dare say such a thing.

It is taught in the name of R. Meir: *Return, O Israel* (Hos. 14:2)—return, that is, while He is still [the Lord] standing in the measure of mercy; if thou dost not return, He will become *thy God* (*ibid.*), [the God of stern judgment]—return, therefore, before mercy's defense turns into justice's accusation.

14. Samuel Paṭigrisah[45] cited in the name of R. Meir the verse *Rejoice, O young man, in thy youth . . . and walk in the ways of thy heart* (Eccles. 11:9)[46] . . . In regard to this verse, R. Samuel bar Isaac said: The Sages were about to suppress the Book of Ecclesiastes, having found ideas in it which smacked of heresy. They asked: Should Solomon have given utterance to advice such as *Rejoice, O young man, in thy youth*, etc. (*ibid.*), despite the fact that Moses had said, *Go not about after your own heart and your own eyes* (Num. 15:39)? Solomon dared further to say, *Walk in the ways of thy heart, and in the sight of thine eyes* (Eccles. 11:9), as though all restraint be removed and there be neither justice nor Judge. Since Solomon went on, however, to say *But know thou, that for all these things God will*

---

universe, [yet God will accept their repentance if they do no more than admit His existence as the Root of the universe]."

Because the verse uses the preposition *'aḏ* for "unto" instead of *'el*, R. Judah takes *'aḏ* as here signifying "towards," the point being that if Israel were to do no more than incline in repentance towards Him, He would still accept their repentance in the hope that eventually they would return in entire repentance unto Him. Thus the implication of the verse as read by R. Judah would be: "Return, O Israel, even if it be no more than acknowledging that the Lord thy God exists."

44. JV: *And when He seeth iniquity, will He not then consider it?*

45. Possibly a corruption of *Podagriṭa*, "a man suffering from podagra"; or a corruption of *Pragmaṭoṭes*, "a merchant." So A. A. Hal-Lewi in Deut. Rabbah (Tel Aviv, 5723/1963), 2:24, p. 60.

46. The continuation of R. Meir's comment, missing here, is found in Deut. Rabbah 2:24. So Buber in PRKB, 164, n. 143.

bring thee into judgment (*ibid.*), the Sages decided that Solomon had, after all, spoken well.

[In regard to God's judgment], R. Ḥiyya the elder and R. Simeon ben Ḥalafta differ in their comments. R. Ḥiyya the elder cited a parable of a robber who, as he was fleeing from the examining magistrate, was told, "Cut out your running, so that you won't be exhausted and will be able to stand upon your feet when you are dragged back here for sentencing": *Know thou, that for all these things God will bring thee to judgment* (Eccles. 11:9). R. Simeon ben Ḥalafta cited a parable of [a robber] who sought to get away by swimming across a body of water and who was told, "Cut out your trying to swim away, so that you won't be half-drowned when you are dragged back here for sentencing": *Know thou, that for all these things God will bring thee to judgment* (*ibid.*).

R. Josiah cited a parable of a man who used to bring in merchandise without paying the duty on it. When he was finally caught, he was told, "Pay the duty," and he replied, "Here it is—take it." He was then told, "Do you suppose that we demand it for just this one time? We demand you pay for all the times you brought in merchandise without paying the duty": *Know thou, that for all these things God will bring thee to judgment* (*ibid.*).

R. Levi cited a parable of a bird put in a cage. Another bird came and, observing the caged one, said: "How happy you must be that the feed you require is provided for you!" The bird in the cage responded: "All you see is the feed: you don't see the bars of the cage": *Know thou, that for all these things God will bring thee to judgment* (*ibid.*).

R. Tanḥuma told a parable of a cheat who came into a tavern where he said to the tavernkeeper: "Serve me good wine, fine bread, and fat meat." After the cheat had eaten and drunk, the tavernkeeper said to him, "Pay your bill." The cheat replied: "Here's my belly, go ahead and cut it open." The tavernkeeper said: "And do you expect to put me off like this?" Being a clever man, what did he do? He grabbed the cheat, wrapped him up in a mat of reeds, propped him up at the door at the tavern, and said to every passer-by: "How about making a contribution in behalf of this dead man? I want to get enough to bury him." A mean-spirited man passed by and asked: "How long are you going to keep this game up?" The tavernkeeper replied: "Until I get enough to cover what he owes me." After what was owed him was collected, the tavernkeeper told the cheat: "Get up and go to the grave of your father and say to him, 'Your son will come to a bad end'." *Know thou, that for all these things God will bring thee to judgment* (*ibid.*).

15. According to R. Eliezer ben R. Jose the Galilean, Israel said to the Holy One: Master of universes, if we resolve upon repentance, who will bear witness that we have done so? God replied: "Since I act as witness against those of you who are guilty of evil, shall I not also act as witness in behalf of those of you who do good? I act as witness against those of you guilty of

evil: *I will come near you to judgment; and I will be a swift witness against the sorcerers and against the adulterers* (Mal. 3:5). And shall I not be a witness in behalf of those of you who do good?[47] [I acted as witness against Ahab the son of Kolaiah, and I acted as witness against Zedekiah the son of Maaseiah].

Ahab the son of Kolaiah and Zedekiah the son of Maaseiah were false prophets who committed adultery with their neighbors' wives, as it is written [*The pair*] *wrought vile deeds in Israel, and have committed adultery with their neighbors' wives* (Jer. 29:23). How did they go about it? One of them would go to a married woman and say, "In a vision it was made known to me that my colleague would come to you and that you would give birth to a prophet in Israel." And thus the one acted as go-between for the other, and the other for the one. When it came time for the women to give birth, they went to Nebuchadnezzar's wife, and told her "Thus-and-thus happened." She replied: "I can do nothing at all without the king's being told." When Nebuchadnezzar arrived, she said: "Thus-and-thus happened." He replied: "How could it happen? The God of this people hates adultery. I know what to do. I will put to the ordeal this pair of so-called prophets, even as I put to the ordeal Hananiah, Mishael, and Azariah. If the pair come out alive, then what they told the women is true; but if they do not, they are false prophets." What did he do? For the ordeal of the pair he had had fabricated a kind of huge frying-pan with a great many holes in the bottom, and then, having placed the pair in the pan, started a slow fire under them. And when they saw that their trouble was real trouble, they said that the High Priest Joshua the son of Jehozadak was in on their cheats and so should be placed together with them in the pan, saying to themselves at the same time, "Through his merit we might be saved." What did the Holy One do to them? They were roasted by the fire, but the High Priest came out alive, so that it used to be said of him, "Is not this man a brand plucked out of the fire?" (Zech. 3:2). Hence Scripture: [*Of the pair*] *shall be taken up a curse by all the captivity of Judah that are in Babylon, saying: "The Lord make thee like Zedekiah and like Ahab whom the king of Babylon roasted in the fire"* (Jer. 29:22). The text does not say, "whom the king of Babylon burned," but says, *whom the king of Babylon roasted*[48] *in the fire* (*ibid.*)—roasted them, as we say, like parched ears of grain.

16. R. Levi and R. Isaac differ in their comments [on God's reasons for accepting Israel's repentance]. According to R. Levi, the Holy One told Jeremiah: Go, say to Israel, "Vow repentance." When Jeremiah went and

47. R. Eliezer's comment is based on reading Hos. 14:2 as *Return, O Israel and the Lord thy God will be a witness*. By a slight change in vowels, *'aḏ*, "unto," can be read *'eḏ*, "witness." See PR 44:10 (YJS, *18*, 780–81).

48. The commentator calls attention to the similarity between *ḳll*, "to curse," and *ḳlh*, "to parch, to roast."

exhorted them, they replied: "Our master Jeremiah, how shall we vow repentance? With what countenance may we come into the presence of Him who is everywhere? Have we not provoked Him? Have we not made Him jealous? Those mountains and hills where we sacrificed to idols—*They sacrifice upon the tops of the mountains, and offer upon the hills* (Hos. 4:13)—are they not still standing? Therefore *Let us lie down in our shame, and let our confusion cover us*" (Jer. 3:25). When Jeremiah came into the Holy One's presence and reported Israel's reply, God said: Go, tell them [that because of their misconduct they deserve to have Me cast them off]. Did I not have set down in My Torah the words *The soul that turneth unto the ghosts, and unto the familiar spirits, to go astray after them, I will set My face against that man, and will cast him off from among his people* (Lev. 20:6)? But have I acted thus toward you? Have I not, instead, promised, *I will not frown upon you; for I am merciful, saith the Lord. I will not bear grudge for ever* (Jer. 3:12)?

According to R. Isaac, the Holy One told Jeremiah: Go, say to Israel, "Vow repentance." When Jeremiah went and exhorted them, they replied: "Our master Jeremiah, how shall we vow repentance? With what countenance may we come into the presence of the Holy One? Have we not provoked Him? Have we not made Him jealous? Those mountains and hills where we sacrificed to idols—*They sacrifice upon the tops of the mountains, and offer upon the hills* (Hos. 4:13)—are they not still standing? Therefore *Let us lie down in our shame, and let our confusion cover us*" (Jer. 3:25). When Jeremiah came into the Holy One's presence and reported Israel's reply, God said: Go tell them this: If you do come in repentance, will you not be coming to your Father in heaven? *I am a father to Israel, and Ephraim is My first-born* (Jer. 31:9).

17. *For thou hast stumbled over that which leads thee to evil* (Hos. 14:2). [In comment on man's Inclination to evil], R. Simon compared it with a stone sticking up[49] at a certain crossroads, a stone which men were always stumbling over. The king of the region said: Keep chipping away at the stone until the time comes for me to have it removed entirely from its place. So, too, the Holy One said to Israel: My children, the Inclination to evil is the outstanding cause of the world's stumbling. Keep chipping away at it until the time comes for Me to have it removed entirely from the heart of man. Hence Scripture: *I will take away the stony heart out of your flesh, and I will give you a heart of flesh* (Ezek. 36:26).

R. Isaac said: When a man stumbles into a transgression and because of the transgression incurs the penalty of death from heaven, it generally happens that [instead of his dying] one of his oxen may die, or one of his hens may perish, or one of his flasks may shatter, or one of his fingers may get

49. The Inclination to evil is likened elsewhere to a mountain. See B.Suk 52a.

broken.[50] Thus what belongs to him or what is part of him is considered by heaven to stand for all of him, [so that he does not have to suffer the death penalty].

Another comment: *Adding one thing to another, to settle*[51] *the account* (Eccles. 7:27). Any pain whatever that is visited by way of punishment upon a transgressor is meticulously noted down by heaven and is reckoned with all the other pains he has suffered, so that by pain being added to pain, little by little the account of his guilt is settled. To what extent is this procedure followed in settling a man's account [with heaven]? To the extent of including in the reckoning even the least of a man's punishments.

18. *Take with you words* (Hos. 14:3). R. Judah and R. Nehemiah differ in their comments on this verse. According to R. Judah, God meant: Did you not previously at Sinai succeed in beguiling Me with words?—*They beguiled Him with their mouth, and lied unto Him with their tongue* (Ps. 78:36). According to R. Nehemiah, the plea *Take with you words* (*ibid.*) means, Take along men whose words[52] are eloquent, men who chant Scripture well, who expound it well—men such as Levi ben Sisi and his companions. Consider what Levi ben Sisi did when marauding soldiers were approaching the city he lived in. When the soldiers were about to enter, he took a Scroll of the Law, went up to a roof top, and called upon God: Master of universes, if I ever set aside a single word in this book, have these marauders come in; but if I never did, have them go hence. Thereupon when the marauders were looked for, they were not to be found. Levi's disciple in similar circumstances also called upon God: thereupon, though his hand withered, the marauders went hence. A pupil of a disciple of Levi's in similar circumstances likewise called upon God, and his hand did not wither, but neither did the marauders depart. To such a person one might apply the saying, "There is no point in jabbing a fool: like a corpse he does not feel the knife."

19. *And return unto the Lord; say unto Him: "Forgive all iniquity,"* etc. (Hos. 14:3). R. Judah and R. Nehemiah differ in their comments on this verse. [Interpreting the words *Forgive all iniquity* to mean, "The iniquity of all Thou puttest up with"], R. Judah understood Hosea as suggesting that Israel plead, "Thou puttest up with all, and wilt Thou not put up with our iniquities?" But R. Nehemiah, [interpreting the words as "Art Thou resolved to take payment[53] for all iniquity?"], understood Israel to be pleading "Take not payment for all our iniquity. Take payment for one half and

50. "may get broken"—O_1; O: "may get hurt" (?).

51. JV: *to find.* But *mṣ'*, "find," is read as though it were *mṣh*, "settle," (literally "to wring out").

52. Evidently R. Nehemiah read here not *dĕḇarim* but *dabbarim.*

53. *Tiśśa'* means "forgive," as well as, among other meanings, "take payment."

leave the other half without taking payment for it. *Take [in a way that is] good [for Israel]" (ibid.).*

R. Nathan and R. Aḥa, citing R. Simon, said: *Ṭwb*, "good," is a cipher[54] for *nfš*, "life." Hence *Take good* means "Take life"—[that is, instead of the live offerings we used to bring, take our very fat and flesh, such as we give up in Thy name when we are fasting or when we are suffering persecution].

So will we pay for bullocks with the offering of our lips (ibid.). R. Abbahu said: How are we to compensate Thee for the bullocks we used to offer to Thee? Our lips will pay by means of the prayer we offer to Thee.

R. Isaac said: Prayer is the means of expiation: in return for prayer Thou grantest expiation for our [sinful] lives. How much to be marveled at is the good Thou dost us in permitting prayer as the means of saving our lives! In return, what word that best befits Thee shall we *take* as the utterance of our mouths? *Good (ibid.)*—"In praising the Lord, [say to Him that] He is good"[55] (Ps. 92:2); "O praise the Lord, [by saying] 'Behold the good' "[56] (Ps. 118:1).

54. By the *Atbash* method of interchanging the first letter of the Hebrew alphabet, *'alef*, with the last letter, *taw*; the second, *beṯ*, with the next to the last, *šin*; and so on.

55. JV: *It is good to confess unto the Lord.* But the Hebrew for "confess" also means "praise."

56. JV: *O praise the Lord, for He is good.*

PISKA 25

SUMMARY

God's acts of patience

God enhances the strength of the righteous to enable them to do His will; and, in turn, His own strength is enhanced by righteous men. On the other hand, when men do not do His will, they weaken Him.

Moses acknowledged the truth of all God told him, except for one thing—God's patience in punishing a man who sins. In the end, however, Moses admitted the need for God's patience with the man who sins and His forbearance in punishing the sinner only a little at a time (Sec. 1). In His exercise of patience God lifts out from the pan of iniquities one of the writs attesting a man's guilt, so that the good deeds in the other pan of the scales tip the balance. He even brings Himself to forget man's iniquities (Sec. 2). Insofar as Israel is concerned, God can do so, because in Israel the children of wicked fathers are rarely themselves wicked (Sec. 3). Hence Moses could boldly plead with God that He forgive Israel's sins. Even though Moses presented his petition in the name of his ancestry, God was so pleased by his bold petition that He granted it in Moses' own name (Sec. 4).

PISKA 25

Sĕliḥot[1]

1. *Yet the righteous holdeth on his way, and he that hath clean hands enhances strength* (Job 17:9). *The righteous* is the Holy One, of whom it is said "The Lord is righteous, He loveth righteousness" (Ps. 11:7); *and he that hath clean hands* is also the Holy One, to whom it is said "Thou that art of eyes too clean[2] to behold evil" (Hab. 1:13); *he . . . enhances strength* is again the Holy One who enhances the strength of the righteous to enable them to do His will.

Another comment: *The righteous holdeth on his way* applies to Moses, of whom it is said "He persisted in executing the righteousness of the Lord, and His ordinances with Israel" (Deut. 33:21); *and he that hath clean hands* also applies to Moses who was able to say to the people, "I have not taken one ass from them" (Num. 16:15); *he . . . enhances strength* also applies to Moses who enhanced the strength of the Almighty, as when he said "And now, I pray Thee, let the strength of the Lord be enhanced" (Num. 14:17). Thereby—as R. Jacob bar Aḥa citing R. Jose bar R. Ḥanina, and the Rabbis citing R. Johanan taught—Moses meant: May the strength of Thy mercy be enhanced, so that the measure of mercy prevail over the measure of justice: "And now, I pray Thee, let the strength of the Lord be enhanced [to this end]" (*ibid.*).

R. Yudan told a parable of a strong man who was exercising with a block of stone that came from a stonecutter. A passer-by saw him and said: Your strength is marvelous. May your strength be enhanced by your exercise, as the strength of the Mighty One's mercy is enhanced by His exercise of it: "And now, I pray Thee, let the strength of the Lord be enhanced" (*ibid.*).

R. Azariah, citing R. Judah bar R. Simon, said: Whenever righteous men do the Holy One's will, they enhance the strength of the Almighty. [This is to say that Moses' doing of God's will gave God the strength to hold back from destroying Israel]. Hence Moses' plea, "And now, I pray Thee, let the

1. "God's acts of forgiveness." The term has come to designate prayers which entreat God's forgiveness.

Abraham Goldberg suggests that the Piska *Sĕliḥot* was linked with the Fast of Gedaliah on the third of Tishri, or perhaps with those days between New Year's Day and the Day of Atonement when the Torah was read. See *Ḳirjath Sefer, 43* (5768/1967), 77.

2. This is the only instance in Scripture where the word "clean" with reference to God is used to qualify a part of the body: The commentator infers the cleanness of God's hands from the cleanness of His eyes.

strength of the Lord be enhanced" (*ibid.*), [was answered]. On the other hand, when men do not do His will, then, if one dare say such a thing, "The Rock that begot thee, thou dost weaken"[3] (Deut. 32:18).

R. Judah bar R. Simon, citing R. Levi ben Peraṭa, said: Whenever Israel do the Holy One's will, they enhance the power of the Almighty, as shown by the verse "When we are with God, we increase [His] valor"[4] (Ps. 60:14); but when Israel do not do His will, they "are gone without Strength before the persecutor" (Lam. 1:6). R. Aḥa said: Just as when Israel went into exile, they had to yield to the pressure of a powerful persecutor, so, when they are redeemed, they will be redeemed by the pull of a powerful redeemer. Note that the Hebrew word for "persecutor" is given here in the text not in its briefer form *rdf* but in its full form *rwdf* in order to signify the fullness of the persecutor's power; so, too, in order to signify the fullness of the redeemer's power[5] the Hebrew word for "redeemer" is given here in the text not in its briefer form *g'l*, but in its full form *gw'l*, as in the verse *A redeemer* (*gw'l*) *will come to Zion* (Isa. 59:20).

R. Isaac said: Except for one thing, Moses acknowledged the truth of all God told him. Moses, speaking boldly to the Holy One, complained: Master of universes, when a man sins, Thou art too patient in punishing him—collect from him at once what is due Thee. The Holy One replied: As thou livest, [for Israel's sake] thou wilt have need of such patience from Me. And where in Scripture is Moses shown to have need of God's patience? The place where Scripture tells the incident of the spies who returned with an evil report about the Land—*The Lord be long in acts of patience* (Num. 14:18). We have no verses in Scripture to prove that, except for one thing, Moses admitted the truth of all God had told him. However, as we know from two verses, Moses admitted that God had to have patience. [One of the verses is cited just above: *The Lord be long in acts of patience*]. The other is [the verse *O God, Lord of vengeances*[6] (Ps. 94:1) which is]

3. The word *tšy*, "thou wast unmindful," may be taken as a form of *tšš*, "to weaken."

The Masorah points up the enhancing of God's strength by putting a majuscule *yoḏ* at the beginning of *yigḏal*, "let the strength of the Lord be 'majusculated' "; and points up the depletion of God's strength by putting a miniscule *yoḏ* at the end of *tšy*, "[The Rock] . . . thou dost weaken—thou dost 'minisculate.' "

4. JV: *Through God we shall do valiantly.*

5. "The full redemption will never again be followed by servitude." Mah as quoted by A. Cohen in Lam. Rabbah, Soncino tr., 108.

It should be noted that *rwdf*, "persecutor," in Lam. 1:6, and *gw'l*, "redeemer," in Isa. 59:20 are the only instances in Scripture where, according to the Masorah, these two words are spelled *plene*—that is, with the letter *waw* (the *w* in each word) serving as a vowel.

6. To R. Tanḥum, the apostrophe *O God, Lord of vengeances* is puzzling. How

mentioned by R. Tanḥum bar Ḥanila'i in reporting the following incident: "While passing by a synagogue whose congregation consisted of people who had come from Babylon [to Palestine], I heard the voice of a youngster recite *Thy testimonies are very sure . . . O Lord, for prolonging of days* (Ps. 93:5) and go on to recite the verse which directly follows it *O Lord, God of vengeances* (Ps. 94:1). [It came to me, then, what Moses meant by this verse: not vengeance impatiently taken all at once, but vengeances taken as painlessly as possible—that is, as the plural indicates, vengeance taken only a little at a time]."

That this is the significance of the verse is shown, according to R. Aḥa and R. Tanḥum bar R. Ḥiyya, who cited R. Johanan, [by the fact that the plural *vengeances* is paralleled] by the plural *patiences* in Numbers 14:18 where the verse does not say "long in patience," but *long in patiences.* (The rest of the comment is to be found in Piska *Return* [24:11]).

2. [In going on to describe God's attributes, Moses says], *The Lord . . . is plenteous in mercy, lifting*[7] *up iniquity* (Num. 14:18). R. Eleazar and R. Jose bar R. Ḥanina differ in their comments on this verse. R. Eleazar said: When both pans of the scale of justice balance exactly, a man's iniquitous deeds on one side and his good deeds on the other, the Holy One lifts out from the pan of iniquities one of the writs attesting the man's guilt, so that the good deeds [in the other pan] tip the balance. Hence we understand that what is meant by the words *lifting up 'awon* ("iniquity") (Num. 14:18) is "lifting out iniquity, and thus tipping the balance (*'ayin*)."[8]

R. Huna said in the name of R. Abbahu: If one dare even mention such a thing, forgetfulness is not one of God's attributes. But for Israel's sake He makes Himself be one who forgets. And the proof? The verse *Who is a God like unto Thee, that forgets*[9] *iniquity and passeth by transgression* (Micah 7:18). David said likewise: *Thou forgettest*[10] *the iniquity of Thy people, and thus Thou ever pardonest all their sin* (Ps. 85:3).

3. [Continuing, Moses speaks of God as] *Clearing, but not clearing*[11] (Num. 14:18). That is, God clears those who repent of the transgressions they are charged with, but does not clear those who do not repent. God clears [transgressors who repent] in this world, but does not clear [transgressors who wait to repent] in the world-to-come. [Moses goes on fur-

---

can Lord (YHWH), the name of God which denotes mercy, be addressed as *Lord of vengeances?* Hence the comment that follows.

7. *Nośe'* means "lifting up" as well as "forgiving."

8. By an untranslatable play on words, R. Eleazar uses "iniquity" as well as "balance," the two meanings implicit in *'awon.*

9. Reading *nośe'*, "forgives," as though written *nošeh*, "forgets."

10. Reading *naśa'ṯa*, "forgivest," as though written *našiṯa*, "forgettest."

11. JV: *and that will by no means clear.* But in this comment, the phrase is rendered literally. See Rashi on Exod. 34:6–7.

thermore to describe God as] *Visiting the iniquity of the fathers upon the children—upon the third, and upon the fourth generation* (*ibid.*). Consider the implications of this verse by analogy with a four-level storehouse, one level above the other: on one there is wine; on another, oil; on still another, honey; and on still another, water. If a fire begins on any one of the levels, what is above it will extinguish the fire. But if all four levels should have oil on them, all four will burn down. Likewise, if children persist, generation after generation, in the wicked ways of their forefathers, punishment therefor will be visited upon them. But if there be an alternating of the generations, with one generation righteous and the next wicked, and so on, then *The fathers shall not be put to death for the children, neither shall the children be put to death for the fathers*, etc. (Deut. 24:16). Hearing this, Moses rejoiced, saying, "In Israel there is no destroyer of grape vines who is also the son of a destroyer of grape vines."

4. [Moses prayed to God]: *Pardon, I pray Thee, the iniquity of this people, according unto the greatness of Thy lovingkindness* (Num. 14:19). R. Jose bar R. Ḥanina and R. Samuel bar Naḥman differ in their comments on this verse. According to one, the Holy One replied to Moses, "*From Egypt even till now* (*ibid.*)—have they not sinned against Me?" But according to the other, it was Moses who, acknowledging Israel's guilt in the words *from Egypt until now*, went on to plead with the Holy One: Master of universes, hast Thou not pardoned and forgiven them in the past? Even so, pardon and forgive them in the future.

R. Alexandri told a parable of two men who presented written petitions to the king. One presented it in his own name; it was granted [not in his name], however, but in the name of his ancestor. The other presented his petition in his ancestor's name, but it was granted to him in his own name.

Thus Hezekiah presented a petition in his own name: *Remember now, O Lord, I beseech Thee, how I have walked before Thee in truth,* etc. (2 Kings 20:3); but it was granted in the name of his ancestor: *I will defend this city for Mine own sake, and for My servant David's sake* (2 Kings 20:6). Moses presented a petition in the name of his ancestry, but it was granted in his own name. He presented it in the name of his ancestry: *Remember Abraham, Isaac, and Israel, Thy servants,* etc. (Exod. 32:13), but it was granted in his own name: *I have pardoned according to thy word* (Num. 14:20).

PISKA 26

SUMMARY

On God's judgment

The death of Aaron's two sons points up the fate which befalls all kinds of people—the good, the bad, and the indifferent (Sec. 1). Indeed, everywhere grief is mingled with joy. Thus a young man, as illustrated by a story, may die on the day he is to be wed. Even God's joy in the beneficence which He bestowed upon the generation of the flood and upon the people of Sodom and Gomorrah came to be mingled with grief when justice demanded that the generation of the flood and the inhabitants of Sodom and Gomorrah be destroyed. So, too, God's joy was mingled with grief when Aaron's two sons who came to present their offerings had to die (Sec. 2). Nevertheless, human beings distracted by grief are not to let grief entwine itself permanently in their lives. At the same time, the wicked are not to suppose that they can find joy unmingled with grief in God's world. Adam for all his splendor, Abraham for all his love of God, Elisheba for all the triumphs which were hers—each came to taste grief. How then can the wicked expect to escape it? (Sec. 3).

As High Priest, Aaron could command God to mount up His presence upon the Ark or to remove it from the Ark. As High Priest, he could tell in advance the kind of year the people of Israel were to have. And when Aaron's two sons died, God Himself remained as mourner (Sec. 4). How, then, is one to explain the death of Nadab and Abihu, a death which, Job said, made his heart leap out of its place in terror? (Sec. 5). The truth is that Aaron's two sons were taken by way of punishing Aaron for his transgression. But they were also taken because they were guilty of a kind of presumptuousness which expressed itself in their daring to render a legal decision in the presence of Moses their master (Sec. 6/7). Some commentators suggest that Nadab and Abihu incurred the penalty of death because in bringing their offering they were guilty of certain infractions stemming in part from presumptuousness. But whatever their guilt, they were not guilty of dissolute practices in secret (Sec. 8). Other commentators suggest that Aaron's sons were guilty of four offenses: tasting wine before entering the Sanctuary; entering the Sanctuary without washing their hands and feet; entering it while lacking the prescribed number of garments; being childless at the time they entered it. They were childless because in utter disregard of the High Priest's obligation to marry, they refused to take wives; in their presumptuousness, they deemed no maiden in Israel worthy of themselves.

So great was the presumptuousness of Nadab and Abihu that they all but trod on Moses' and Aaron's heels, saying: "In no time at all we shall assume authority over Israel." Even in God's presence on Sinai the two brothers were not humble, for they feasted their eyes upon the Presence in the manner of a man who is eating and drinking without restraint. Moses, on the other hand, in his humility did not feast his eyes on the Presence and so was given the privilege of inspiring awe in others.

Nadab's and Abihu's presumptuousness notwithstanding, their death—the death of children of a righteous man—was twice as grievous for God as it was for their father.

Actually, according to one commentator, Nadab and Abihu received their sentence of death at Sinai, but God, not wishing to confound the day of Torah's joy, preferred to have them punished on the day of His own joy, the day He was to enter the Tent of Meeting (Sec. 9).

The question whether the son of a High Priest may or may not officiate as High Priest during the life of his father is discussed; and the circumstances under which such officiating may take place is illustrated by the story of Ḳimḥith whose seven sons all served in the office of High Priest (Sec. 10).

The death of the righteous atones for Israel's sins. Hence Scripture mentions the death of Nadab and Abihu in connection with the Day of Atonement, even though their death occurred on the first of Nisan (Sec. 11).

PISKA 26

DISCOURSE ON THE PASSAGE *After the death of Aaron's two sons* (Lev. 16:1).[1]

1. [In meditating upon the death of Aaron's two sons], R. Simeon bar R. Abin began his discourse with the verse *All things come alike to all: like things befall the righteous and the wicked* (Eccles. 9:2). The words *like things befall the righteous* apply to Noah, of whom it is said "Noah was in his generations a man righteous" (Gen. 6:9). Concerning what befell him, R. Phinehas [in the name of] R. Johanan, citing R. Eleazar ben R. Jose the Galilean, said: When Noah went forth from the ark, a lion sprang upon him and mutilated him, so that he was not ritually fit to bring offerings, and in his stead his son Shem had to bring offerings. The words *like things befall . . . the wicked* (Eccles. 9:2) apply to Pharaoh-necoh. When he sought to sit on Solomon's throne, he did not know its workings, so that a part of its mechanism, made in the semblance of a lion, sprang up and mutilated him.[2] Thus the one died a cripple, and the other died a cripple: *like things befall the righteous and the wicked* (*ibid.*).

Like things befall . . . the good, the clean, and the unclean (*ibid.*). The words *the good* apply to Moses, of whom it is said "And when his mother saw the infant [Moses], behold he was goodly" (Exod. 2:2), that is, she saw that he had been born circumcised.[3] The words *the clean* apply to Aaron whose business was the cleansing of Israel.[4] The words *the unclean* apply to the spies. The latter, whose mouth spoke foully of the Land, were not permitted to enter it. On the other hand, the two completely righteous men, [Moses and Aaron], were not permitted to enter it either. Hence *like things befall . . . the righteous, the wicked, the good, the clean, and the unclean* (Eccles. 9:2).

The words *Like things befall . . . him that sacrificeth* (*ibid.*) apply to Josiah, of whom it is written "Josiah gave to the children of the people, of the flock, lambs and kids, all of them for the Passover offerings" (2 Chron.

1. Lev. 16:1–34 is the lesson for the Day of Atonement.

2. After slaying Josiah (2 Kings 23:29), Pharaoh-necoh is said to have taken Solomon's throne from which, when he sought to mount it, a secret mechanism sprang upon him and mutilated him. Thus the epithet *necoh* in Pharaoh's name is associated with *nkh*, "spring upon." Likewise the word *'k*, "only," which is used in describing Noah as the flood's survivor (Gen. 7:23), is associated with *nkh*, "spring upon," implying that Noah had been mutilated.

3. The commentator seems to be construing *'tw*, "him," as though it read *'wtw*, "his mark [of circumcision]." The foreskin is regarded as a mark of imperfection in man.

4. Through the ash of the Red Heifer and through bringing offerings.

35:7). And the words *befall . . . him that sacrificeth not* (Eccles. 9:4) apply to Ahab who abolished the practice of bringing offerings to the altar [of God]. But does not Scripture say, "Ahab sacrificed for him" (2 Chron. 18:2)? Yes, Ahab sacrificed for Jehoshaphat's[5] sake, but not with the sincerity of intention that offerings require. Yet Josiah died shot through with arrows, and Ahab died shot through with arrows. The one died shot through with arrows: "The archers shot at king Josiah" (2 Chron. 35:23); and the other died shot through with arrows: "A certain man drew his bow at a venture, and smote the king of Israel between the lower armor and the breastplate," etc. (2 Chron. 18:33). Hence *like things befall . . . him that sacrificeth, and him that sacrificeth not* (Eccles. 9:4).

The words *like things befall the good and the sinner* (*ibid.*) apply to David, of whom it is said that he was "goodly to look upon" (1 Sam. 16:12). And the words *the sinner* apply to the wicked Nebuchadnezzar, who was told "Break off thy sins by almsgiving"[6] (Dan. 4:24). The one built the Temple[7] and reigned forty years, and the other destroyed the Temple and reigned forty-five years. Hence *like things befall . . . the good, and the sinner* (*ibid.*).

Like things befall him that sweareth an oath and him that feareth an oath (Eccles. 9:4). The words *him that sweareth an oath* apply to Zedekiah, of whom it is written "And he also rebelled against king Nebuchadnezzar, who had made him swear by God," etc. (2 Chron. 36:17). By what holy object did Nebuchadnezzar make Zedekiah swear? By the altar,[8] so said R. Jose bar R. Ḥanina. The words *him that feareth an oath* apply to Samson, of whom it is written "Samson said unto the [people of Judah]: 'Swear unto me that ye will not fall upon me yourselves' "[9] (Judg. 15:12). The one died through having his eyes put out, and the other died through having his eyes put out. The one died through having his eyes put out: "They . . . put out the eyes of Zedekiah"[10] (2 Kings 25:7); and the other died through having his eyes put out: "The Philistines laid hold of him, and put out his eyes" (Judg. 16:21). Hence *like things befall . . . him that sweareth an oath and him that feareth an oath* (Eccles. 9:4).

Another comment: *Like things befall the righteous* (*ibid.*) such as

5. Jehoshaphat came to visit Ahab in Samaria.
6. See Piska 2.5.
7. He made all preparations for its building. See PR 6:7 (YJS, *18*, 129).
8. The king of Babylon brought Zedekiah "under an oath" (Ezek. 17:13). Apparently the commentator construes the word *'lh*, "oath," as though it were spelled *'lh*, corresponding to the Syriac *'elata*, "altar."
9. The fact that Samson was ready to rely upon their oath proves that he himself would not violate one.
10. A man who is prone to swearing in God's name dares do so in His very eyes, so to speak, in punishment whereof the man's eyes are put out.

Aaron, of whom it is written "He walked with Me in peace and uprightness" (Mal. 2:6). *And befall . . . the wicked* (Eccles. 9:4) such as Korah's congregation, concerning whom Moses said to the people of Israel: "Depart, I pray you, from the tents of these wicked men" (Num. 16:26). The latter came in quarrelsomeness to bring offerings and were burnt; the sons of the former came not in quarrelsomeness to bring offerings but likewise were burnt, as it is written *After the death of the two sons of Aaron* (Lev. 16:1).

2. *I said of laughter: "It is mingled"* (Eccles. 2:2), words which R. Abba bar Kahana understood to mean: How mingled[11] with grief is the laughter in which the heathen nations of the world indulge in their theatres and circuses! *And of joy: "What would it there?"* (*ibid.*)—that is, [since an unmixed joy attends study of Torah], what point would there be in the attendance of the disciples of the wise at theatres and circuses?

In another comment the words [previously rendered *I said of laughter: "It is mingled"*] are now rendered *I said of that which is punishable:*[12] *It is radiant.*[13] According to R. Aḥa, Solomon said: I was drawn by their radiance to three things which the measure of justice deems punishable [and warns against]. Scripture warns, *Neither shall* [*a king*] *multiply wives* (Deut. 17:17), yet it is said of me "He had seven hundred wives, princesses, and three hundred concubines" (1 Kings 11:3); Scripture warns, [*A king*] *shall not multiply horses to himself* (Deut. 17:16), yet it is said of me, "Solomon had forty thousand stalls of horses for his chariots, and twelve thousand horsemen" (1 Kings 5:6); Scripture warns, *Neither shall he greatly multiply to himself silver and gold* (Deut. 17:17), yet it is said of me, "The king made silver to be in Jerusalem as abundant as stones," etc. (1 Kings 10:27). But was not so much silver likely to be stolen? It could not be stolen—so said R. Jose bar R. Ḥanina—because the ingots were as large as unhewn stones of ten cubits by eight cubits. So abundant was gold in Solomon's days, taught R. Simeon ben Yoḥai in a Baraita, that even the scales were made of gold, "Silver being nothing accounted of in the days of Solomon" (2 Chron. 9:20).

[Because things that are punishable, thou didst deem radiant], *Therefore of mirth* (Eccles. 2:2)—[that is, of Solomon's joy in his kingship], the Holy One [deeming that Solomon had forfeited the kingship], said to him: *"What doth it here?* (*ibid.*), the crown on thy head?[14] Get off My throne."

11. R. Abba equates the word *mhwll*, in JV, "mad," with *mhwl*, "mingled."

12. The commentator construes *śĕḥoḳ*, "laughter," as a form of the Syriac *šeḥaḳa*, "punishment," or "punishable."

13. R. Aḥa takes *mĕholal*, "mingled," in its other meaning of "radiant."

14. *The crown wherewith his mother hath crowned him . . . in the day of the mirth of his heart* (Song 3:11).

In that instant an angel in Solomon's guise came down and seated himself upon the throne,[15] while Solomon found himself going around to all the houses of assembly and all the houses of study in Jerusalem, saying: *I Koheleth was [and still am] king over Jerusalem* (Eccles. 1:12). But he was told in reply: King Solomon is sitting on his throne. You are crazy to say, "I am king Solomon." Then what did the people do to him? They tapped him with a length of reed [as is done to quiet a crazy man] and gave him a dish of boiled grits to eat. In that instant he said: *Vanity of vanities, saith Koheleth*, etc. (Eccles. 1:2).

In another comment, R. Phinehas, taking the words as previously read *I said of laughter: "It is mingled [with grief]"* (Eccles. 2:2), went on to say: If laughter must be mingled with grief, is there any place for pure joy in the world? Consider a story of one of Kebul's[16] notables. He was to have his son wed on the fourth day of the week[17] and prepared a feast for the representatives of the family. During the feast he said to his son: Go and fetch a jar of wine from the upper chamber. When the son got there, a serpent bit him, and he died. The father waited for him to come down, but when he did not come down, the father said: I will go up and see what's happened to my son. When he came up, he found that a serpent had bitten his son and that he was dead, lying prone among the wine jars. What did the father do? [Not wishing to bring grief into his guests' mirth], he waited until the guests had finished eating and drinking. After the guests had finished eating and drinking, he said to them: "Know now that you are not here to say in my son's honor the bridegroom's Grace after Meals, but rather to say the mourner's Grace after Meals. You are not here to escort my son to his bridal chamber: you are here to escort him to his grave." Presently, when R. Zakkai of Kebul arrived, [he gave voice to the grief of all present, and] lamenting the son's death, quoted the verse *I said of laughter: "It is mingled [with grief]"* (*ibid.*).

Another comment: *I said of laughter: "It is mingled [with grief]."* How mingled with grief was the derisive laughter that the measure of justice burst into when the generation of the flood came to brazen defiance of Him, despite all He had provided for them! *Their bull gendered, and failed not; their cow calved, and cast not her calf. They sent forth their little ones already grown up like a flock of sheep, and their children were able to dance [at birth]. They sang to the timbrel and harp, and rejoiced at the sound of the pipe. They spent their days in prosperity, and peacefully they went down to the grave* (Job 21:10–13).[18] Nevertheless, [despite the fact that He had

15. In the guise of Solomon, Ashmedai placed himself on the throne. See MTeh 78:12.

16. A city in western Galilee near Acco.

17. The day virgins are wed. See Ket̲ 1:1.

18. See Gen. Rabbah 36:1.

always provided for them], they began to question His providence, saying *What is the Almighty, that we should serve Him? And what profit should we have, if we pray unto Him?* (Job 21:14). Thereupon, the measure of justice required the Holy One to say to them: *Of mirth,* [such as My providence hath brought you], *what doth it here?* (Eccles. 2:2). By your lives, [the measure of justice requires that] I blot you out[19] from the face of the earth, as is written *And He blotted out all of them who rose up* [*against Him*][20] (Gen. 7:23).

Another comment: *I said of laughter: "It is mingled* [*with grief*]*"* (Eccles. 2:2). How mingled with grief was the derisive laughter the measure of justice burst into at the inhabitants of Sodom and Gomorrah! Of their land it is written: [*Sodom's and Gomorrah's*] *ground out of which came bread was of a sudden turned upside down, and appeared as though it were on fire.*[21] [Before the overthrow], *though men had been aware that* [*Sodom's and Gomorrah's*] *stones were a source of sapphires and that it had dust of gold,* [*yet the path thereto they did not know, for the path was impenetrable*]:[22] *indeed not even a bird of prey knew it, no falcon's eye had seen it, proud beasts did not tread it, nor did a lion pass thereon* (Job. 28:5–8). [But not content with the plenty and the security of their land's riches],[22a] the inhabitants of Sodom and Gomorrah had gone so far as to say: "Let us so arrange matters that even the fact that wayfarers' feet were once permitted among us will be forgotten," as is written *The passage through the brook was blocked against strangers so that their very feet were forgotten as, languishing* [*for lack of food and drink*] *among men* [*of Sodom and Gomorrah*], *they were forced to wander hence*[23] (Job 28:4). Thereupon the Holy One declared: *Of mirth,* [such as My providence hath brought you], *what doth it here?* (Eccles. 2:2). By your lives, [the measure of justice requires that]

19. A play on the words *smḥh*, "mirth" and *š'mḥh*, "I will blot out," may be intended here (so David Luria in his Novellae on Eccles. Rabbah), the meaning being that excessive mirth leads to a blotting out of mankind from the face of the earth.

20. JV: *And He blotted out every living substance.* But the word *yĕḳum*, "living substance" may also be read "they who rose up." Such indeed may well be *yĕḳum*'s overtone in Deut. 11:6, the word's only other occurrence in Scripture, where Dathan and Abiram rose up against Moses.

21. JV: *As for the earth, out of it cometh bread, and underneath it is turned up as it were by fire.*

22. For an account of the foliage shielding Sodom and Gomorrah, see S2.3.

22a. Cf. Ezek. 16:49.

23. So, apparently, the commentator construes the verse. JV: *He breaketh open a shaft away from where men sojourn; they are forgotten of the foot that passeth by; they hang afar from men, they swing to and fro.*

I force you out of My world: *Then the Lord caused to rain upon Sodom and upon Gomorrah brimstone and fire . . . and He turned those cities upside down* (Gen. 19:24, 25), [dumping out their inhabitants].

Another comment: *I said of laughter: "It is mingled* [*with grief*]" (Eccles. 2:2). How mingled with grief was the ironical laughter that burst from the measure of justice at Elisheba, daughter of Amminadab! In one day Elisheba, daughter of Amminadab, knew four great joys. She saw her husband made High Priest, her brother-in-law made king, her brother made prince, and her two sons[24] made adjutants of the High Priest. But when [Nadab and Abihu, her other two sons], came in to present their offerings in the Tabernacle, and [the measure of justice required that they be] taken out, [their souls] having been burnt [out of them],[25] her rejoicing was turned to mourning. As Scripture says, *After the death of Aaron's two sons* (Lev. 16:1).

3. R. Levi began his discourse with the verse *I say unto those whose joy has become mingled* [*with grief*], *do not let your grief overcome you entirely*[26] (Ps. 75:5). I plead with such of you who are so distracted by grief that your hearts are filled with every kind of gloomy thought, do not allow grief to entwine itself permanently in your lives. Else, said R. Levi, you will become grief-mongers,[27] spreading your gloom everywhere you go in the world. On the other hand, R. Levi went on, God says *to the wicked: "Lift not up the horn"* (*ibid.*), by which the Holy One was telling the wicked: Righteous men did not get to rejoice in My world, yet you expect to rejoice in My world. Adam did not get to rejoice in My world, yet you expect to rejoice in My world. R. Levi, citing R. Simeon ben Menasya, continued: [Consider how the splendor of Adam might have led him to rejoice], for the very round of his heel outshone the globe of the sun. And do not wonder at this! Human nature is such that when a man has two salvers made for him, one for himself and one for his steward, whose salver does he have made the more beautiful? Not his own? So Adam was created for the service of the Holy One, and the globe of the sun was created for the service of lesser creatures. Does it not follow, then, that the very round of Adam's heel

24. Aaron, Moses, Nahshon, and Eleazar and Ithamar, respectively.

25. Into their nostrils there entered something like two threads of fire which burned their souls but left their bodies intact. See B.Sanh 52a, and Rashi on Lev. 10:5.

26. JV: *I say unto the arrogant: "Do not deal arrogantly.*" But R. Levi construes *holĕlim*, "arrogant," as "those whose joy has been mingled with grief"; and reading the word as *ḥolĕlim* takes it also in the sense of "those whose grief overcomes them entirely."

27. R. Levi now reads *holĕlim*, as though written *'olelim*, a verbal form of *'alĕlai*, "alas, alack."

outshone the globe of the sun? How much more brightly, then, must have shone the countenance of his face! Furthermore, said R. Levi in the name of R. Ḥama bar R. Ḥanina, the Holy One joined together thirteen canopies over Adam in the Garden of Eden, (and so on as set forth in the Piska of the Red Heifer [4.4]), yet despite all the splendor that was bestowed upon Adam, [God told him] "Dust thou art, and unto dust shalt thou return" (Gen. 3:19).

Abraham did not get to rejoice in My world, yet you, [the wicked], expect to rejoice in My world! Consider Abraham: when he was one hundred years old, a son was born to him, and eventually the Holy One said to him: *Take now thy son*, etc. (Gen. 22:2). Thereupon Abraham proceeded on a three days' journey: *On the third day Abraham lifted up his eyes, and saw the place afar off* (Gen. 22:4). What did he see? He saw a cloud clinging to the mountain. And he asked his son, "Do you see what I see?" Isaac replied: "Yes." Abraham asked: "What do you see?" Isaac replied: "I see a cloud clinging to a mountain." Abraham then turned to his young servants: "Do you see what we see?" They replied: "No." He said to them: "Since you do not see anything, and the ass does not see anything, *Abide ye here with the ass* (Gen. 22:5), ye people[28] who see no more than the ass." What did Abraham do then? He took his son Isaac, went up to the top of the mountain, built an altar, set up a pile of wood, arranged the kindling, bound his son upon the altar, and took the knife in his hand to slay him. Indeed, had not the Holy One said to Abraham *Lay not thy hand upon the lad* (Gen. 22:12), Isaac would have been slain.

When Isaac got back to his mother, she asked him: My son, what did your father do to you? He replied: My father took and led me up mountains and down the hills below them until he brought me finally to the top of one mountain where he built an altar, set up a pile of wood, arranged the kindling, bound me upon the altar, and took the knife into his hand to slay me. Had not the Holy One said to him *Lay not thy hand upon the lad* (*ibid.*), I would have been slain. His mother then said: Alas for you, son of a mother so hapless that if the Holy One had not said *Lay not thy hand upon the lad* (*ibid.*), you would have been slain. Scarcely had she finished speaking when her soul left her. Then, says Scripture, *Abraham came to mourn for Sarah, and to weep for her* (Gen. 23:2). Whence did he come? From Mount Moriah. [Know from this account that even as righteous a man as Abraham could not expect to know lasting joy in this world].

Indeed, if one dare say such a thing, the Holy One Himself does not get to rejoice in His world, and yet you, [the wicked], expect to rejoice in His

28. By a slight change in vowels, the word *'im*, "with," may be read *'am*, "people."

world. Note that Scripture does not say, "The Lord rejoiced in His works," but says *The Lord will rejoice in His works* (Ps. 104:31), signifying that only in the [untroubled] time-to-come will the Holy One get to rejoice in the works of the righteous.

Israel likewise does not get to rejoice in My world, yet you, [the wicked], expect to rejoice in My world. Note that Scripture does not say, "Israel rejoiced in his Maker," but says, *Israel will rejoice in his Maker* (Ps. 149:2), signifying that only in the time-to-come will Israel rejoice in the Holy One's works.

Elisheba, daughter of Amminadab, did not get to rejoice, yet you, [the wicked], expect to rejoice in My world. In one day, Elisheba, daughter of Amminadab, knew four joys: her husband as High Priest, her brother-in-law as king, her brother as prince, and two of her sons as adjutants of the High Priest. But when her other two sons came [into the Tabernacle] and were taken out [their souls] burnt [out of them],[25] her joy was turned to mourning: *After the death of Aaron's two sons* (Lev. 16:1).

4. R. Yudan of Gallia[29] began his discourse by pointing to [two allusions in Scripture to the Presence. The first is in] the verse in which God asks Job, *Doth the eagle mount up at thy command*, etc? (Job 39:27), [the eagle here symbolizing the Presence.[30] The second is in the same verse]. Here the Holy One is considered to be saying to Aaron: At thy command I made My presence mount up and rest upon the Ark; or, at thy command, I removed My presence from upon the Ark.[31]

[The next verse, going on to say] *She dwelleth and abideth on the rock* (Job 39:28), refers to the abiding of the Presence in the First Temple; as for her abiding in the Second [and in the Third Temple, the verse, continuing with the words] *upon the crag of the rock, and the stronghold*[32] (*ibid.*), is referring to her two other abidings. [As for what is signified by *the crag of the rock*], we learn in a Mishnah: "Though the Ark was taken away, the bare crag of the rock was still on the site of the Temple, the crag, which ever since the days of the early Prophets,[33] had been called *šĕṯiyah*, 'Foundation.'

29. See Piska 9, note 58.

30. The commentator may construe *nšr*, "eagle," as a nominal form of the verb *šrh*, "abide." Hence, "the Lord's abiding presence." So *Yĕfeh to'ar* on Lev. Rabbah 20:4.

31. R. Yudan derives his comment from Job 39:27b which he construes *Or removeth from His nest*, that is, from His Ark of the Covenant.

32. The commentator construes *The crag of the rock* as a reference to the time of the Second Temple when the Ark was no longer there; and he takes *the stronghold* to refer to the Third Temple which is to be built. See PR 47:3; and Lev. Rabbah M, 454, n. 2.

33. The days of David and Solomon.

And why was it called *šĕṯiyah*? Because—so said R. Jose bar Ḥalafta—the earth was founded (*hušaṯ*)[34] upon it" (Yoma 5:2).

[In the days when the Temple still stood], how did the prayer of the High Priest on the Day of Atonement go? "May it be Thy will, O Lord our God and God of our Fathers, that the coming year be supplied with rain, alternating with sunshine; be blessed with dew; be a year when the cost of living is low; be a year of plenty; a year of favor; a year of blessing; a year of good business; be a year when Thy people, the household of Israel, will not require help from one another; a year when Thy people, the household of Israel, will not lord it over one another." The Rabbis of Caesarea said: [The High Priest prayed in particular] concerning our brethren in Caesarea that they would not lord it over one another. The Rabbis of the South said: [The High Priest prayed in particular] concerning our brethren who live in the Sharon region[35] that their dwellings might not become their tombs [because heavy rains could cause their houses to collapse].

[Of the High Priest's prayer, Scripture goes on to say], *From within [the Temple] he spieth out food* (Job 39:29): that is, from within the Temple he can make out the prospect for food for all the days of the coming year. *His eyes behold afar off* (*ibid.*), since on New Year's Day he foresees what is to be at the year's end. How? [By watching the direction of the smoke rising from the altar]. When he saw the smoke of the kindling on the altar rise toward the south, he knew that the south would be blessed with plenty; rise toward the west, he knew that the west would be blessed with plenty; rise toward the north, he knew that the north would be blessed with plenty; toward the east, that the east would be blessed with plenty. And when the smoke rose straight up to the sky, he knew that all the world would be blessed with plenty. But all this God-given honor to the High Priest notwithstanding, *His young rolled convulsively upon the ground*[36] (Job 39:30): Aaron saw his young ones rolling *upon the ground*, and he stayed silent. Nevertheless, [lest we conclude from this grievous event that God had turned away from Aaron], the verse goes on to say, *Where the slain are, there is He* (*ibid.*)—there is God's presence as Mourner. For note—as R. Yudan citing R. Joshua ben Levi, and R. Berechiah citing R. Ḥiyya bar Abba, pointed out—that in the verse *Draw near, carry your brethren from before the Holiness* (Lev. 10:4), Scripture does not say "from before the Ark" but *from before the Holiness*, as though a man were saying to his companion, "Take away the dead from before the Mourner. How long can

34. Or: "called *šĕṯiyah*, 'spindlestone.' And why was it called *šĕṯiyah?* Because . . . the earth was spun (*hušaṯ*) from it." Cf. MTeh 91:7; and Ginzberg, *Legends*, 5, 15. Or, to venture a bolder reading, "Because the earth was set spinning upon it."

35. The northern part of the coastal plain.

36. The word *dam*, "blood," the commentator appears to construe as a contraction of *'ădamah*, "ground."

this Mourner endure His distress?" [That the Presence continued to abide in the Tabernacle even after the grievous event] is implied in the verse *After the death of Aaron's two sons they continued in nearness to the presence of the Lord*[37] (Lev. 16:1).

5. R. Ahawa bar R. Ze'era began his discourse as follows: [Even though on the Day of Atonement Aaron entered the Sanctuary with a treasury of merits to support him, he had nevertheless to suffer the death of his two sons]: *At this,*[38] *my heart trembleth* [said Job], *indeed, all but leapeth out* (*yittar*) *of its place* (Job 37:1). (How are we justified in translating the rare word *yittar* as *leapeth out*? By the fact that in its only other appearance in Scripture, it is used to describe certain insects as "leaping [*natter*] on the ground" [Lev. 11:21]. That "leap" is the sense of the word in this particular verse is confirmed by the Aramaic Targum where it is translated by its synonym "jump"). Thus Job in his indignation cried out: Aaron's sons were not even accorded the treatment given Aaron's rod. Aaron's rod was dry when it was brought into the Tent of the Testimony, but was full of sap when it was brought forth: indeed, it put forth buds—"put forth buds, and bloomed blossoms" (Num. 17:23). Even Titus, wicked as he was, could venture into the Holy of Holies, slash both veils, and go forth in peace. But Aaron's sons, who came into the Tabernacle to present an offering, were taken out, [their souls] burnt [out of them]: *After the death of Aaron's two sons* (Lev. 16:1).

6/7. R. Berechiah began his discourse with the verse *To punish the righteous beyond measure is not good* (Prov. 17:26), by which the Holy One meant: If the two sons I took [had been innocent and I had taken them] only for the sake of imposing punishment upon Aaron,[39] it would not have been good. *To punish* [in this way] *the righteous*, [such as Aaron, would be going] *beyond measure* (*ibid.*). But [to take Nadab and Abihu], as indicated in the passage *After the death of Aaron's two sons* (Lev. 16:1)—that is, *to strike princes because right requires it*[40] (Prov. 17:26), that is another matter. [As to the particular offense that Nadab and Abihu were guilty of], it is taught in the name of R. Eliezer: Nadab and Abihu came to deserve the death penalty for no reason other than that they

37. JV: *When they drew near before the Lord.*

38. The word *this* in the verse *With this shall Aaron come into the holy place* (Lev. 16:3) R. Aḥawa takes to refer to the many meritorious deeds that entered with him on the Day of Atonement—the merit of the Patriarchs, of the Matriarchs, of Manasseh and Ephraim, of the Tribes, of circumcision, of the Torah, and of Israel. See PR 47:4 (YJS, *18*, 806–07). Lev. 16, it should be added, was uttered to Moses on the New Moon of Nisan, the day Nadab and Abihu died. See B.Giṭ 60a.

39. For having made the golden calf.

40. See Julius H. Greenstone, *Proverbs*, Philadelphia, 1950, p. 190. JV: *To punish also the righteous is not good, nor to strike the noble for their uprightness.*

presumptuously rendered a legal decision in the presence of Moses our master.[41] Consider a story of the pupil who rendered a legal decision in the presence of R. Eliezer. Thereupon R. Eliezer said to Imma Shalom his wife:[42] "This young man will not live out the week." And he did not live out the week. R. Eliezer's disciples asked him: Rabbi, are you a prophet? He replied: "I am neither a prophet, nor the son of a prophet" (Amos 7:14), but the tradition was transmitted to me that any pupil who renders a legal decision in the presence of his master brings the death penalty upon himself. The fact is, R. Eliezer continued, that a pupil is enjoined against rendering a legal decision unless he is more than twelve miles[43] away from his master. The master's presence is considered to extend a distance of twelve miles because twelve miles was the extent of the camp of Israel [under Moses' jurisdiction], as we gather from the verse *And they pitched by the Jordan, from Beth-jeshimoth even unto Abel-shittim*,[44] etc. (Num. 33:49). On a certain occasion, R. Tanḥum bar R. Jeremiah was in Hefer where people were asking him questions on matters of law and he was giving them answers. One of them asked: "Pardon, O master, but did you not teach us, O master, that a pupil is enjoined against rendering a legal decision unless he is more than twelve miles away from his master, twelve miles having been the extent of the camp of Israel in the wilderness? Is not [your master] R. Mani at this moment living in Sepphoris [only three miles away]?" R. Tanḥum replied: "May evil come upon me if I knew that he was living there!" From that moment on he rendered no further legal decisions.

8. In four instances Scripture, in mentioning the death of Aaron's sons, also mentions the sin[45] they were guilty of, so as to have you know that the sin specified was the only sin that could be charged against them. As R. Eleazar the Modiite said: Go forth and see how heavily the death of Aaron's

41. "What legal decision did they render? That the verse *The sons of Aaron the priest shall put fire upon the altar* (Lev. 1:7) means: although fire for the altar will come down from heaven, yet it is obligatory [for the sons of Aaron] to bring fire made in an ordinary way" (B.Yoma 53a). The decision of Nadab and Abihu was correct, but they incurred the death penalty for presuming to render such a decision in the presence of Moses their master instead of requesting him to render it for them.

Samuel Edels (on B.Er 63a) suggests that the comment just made is inferred from the verse *Nadab and Abihu offered strange fire*, [fire made in the ordinary way], *before the Lord, which he*, [Moses], *had not commanded them* (Lev. 10:1). See BM's note.

42. R. Eliezer (1st century C.E.) was the son of Hyrcanus, and his wife was a sister of Rabban Gamaliel.

43. A mile is 2,000 cubits.

44. A distance of twelve miles. See Lev. Rabbah 20:7.

45. Lev. 10:1–2, 16:1; Num. 3:4, 26:61.

two sons weighed upon the Holy One, for whenever Scripture mentions their death, it also specifically mentions their sin. And for what reason? In order not to give the earth's inhabitants an occasion for loose talk and not to give people a chance to say: Aaron's sons were guilty of dissolute practices in secret, and it was because of these that they were brought to death.

Bar Ḳappara said in the name of R. Jeremiah bar Eleazar that Aaron's sons died because of four things they had done: because of venturing near to God's presence, because of a superfluous offering they brought, because of the strange fire they brought, and because they took no counsel with each other. Because of venturing near to God's presence: they dared to come into His presence within the Tabernacle's Holy of Holies. Because of a superfluous offering they brought: they brought an offering which they were not commanded to bring. Because of the strange fire they brought: they brought fire from an oven into the Tabernacle [instead of taking fire from the altar]. Because they took no counsel with each other, for, as R. Ḥiyya taught: The *word maḥtaṯo* in the passage *Nadab and Abihu . . . took each of them his censer* (*maḥtaṯo*) (Lev. 10:1) is to be read *mĕḥitaṯo*, "his own breach, his own downfall," implying that each had gone his own way without taking counsel of the other.

9. R. Mani of Sha'ab said in the name of R. Joshua of Siḵnin, citing R. Levi: Aaron's sons were taken because of four offenses, the penalty for each one being death. Death was decreed for Aaron's sons because they entered the Sanctuary having tasted wine beforehand, although Scripture says, "Drink no wine nor strong drink . . . that ye die not" (Lev. 10:9). [Death was decreed for them] because they entered the Sanctuary without washing their hands and feet, though Scripture says, "Aaron and his sons shall wash their hands and their feet thereat" (Exod. 30:19), and goes on to say, "When they go into the Tent of Meeting, they shall wash with water, that they die not" (Exod. 30:20). Death was decreed for Aaron's sons because they lacked the prescribed number of garments, of which Scripture says, "[These garments] shall be upon Aaron, and upon his sons, when they go in unto the Tent of Meeting . . . that they bear not iniquity and die" (Exod. 28:43). What garment did they lack? They lacked the robe,[46] of which Scripture says, "It shall be upon Aaron to minister; and the sound [of the bells] thereon shall be heard when he goeth in unto the holy place . . . that he die not" (Exod. 28:35). Death was decreed for them because they had no children,[47] it being said of them "Nadab and Abihu died before the Lord, when they offered strange fire before the Lord . . . and they had no children"

46. Possibly inferred from the fact that Nadab and Abihu were carried out from the Sanctuary in their tunics. David Luria on Lev. Rabbah 34:14.

47. Deliberate avoidance of procreation is so punishable. See B.Yeḇ 63b, and Gen. Rabbah 34:14.

(Num. 3:4). The fact is—so said Abba Ḥanin—[Nadab and Abihu had no children], because they had no wives [to bear them children], even though Scripture commands that the High Priest " 'shall make atonement for himself and for his house' (Lev. 16:6), his wife being signified by the words 'his house' "[48] (Yoma 1:1).

According to R. Levi, Nadab and Abihu [did not marry because they] were arrogant. Many young women sat grieving, waiting in vain to be asked in marriage by Nadab and Abihu. But what did the two say? They said: Our father's brother is king, our mother's brother is prince, our father is High Priest, we are adjutants of the High Priest. What woman is worthy of us? In this connection R. Menaḥema said in the name of R. Joshua bar Nehemiah: Why does Scripture say, *Fire devoured their young men* (Ps. 78:63)? Because *Their virgins had no marriage song* (*ibid.*).

The arrogance of Nadab and Abihu may be further inferred from the following: *Unto Moses He said: "Come up unto the Lord, thou, Aaron, Nadab, Abihu, and seventy of the elders of Israel"* (Exod. 24:1). This verse intimates that Moses and Aaron walked first, with Nadab and Abihu treading on their heels,[49] saying: "In no time these two old men will die, and in their place we shall assume authority over the community [of Israel]." According to R. Yudan, who cited R. Aibu, these words actually came from their mouths; but according to R. Phinehas, they meditated them privately in their hearts. According to R. Berechiah, the Holy One told them: "Boast not thyself of tomorrow, for thou knowest not what a day may bring forth" (Prov. 27:1). Many a young ass has died and had its skin turned into saddlecloths for its dam's back.

And further proof of the arrogance of Aaron's sons, said R. Phinehas, is to be had from the following verse: *And upon the nobles of the children of Israel He laid not His hand*, etc. (Exod. 24:11) from which it may be inferred that they deserved to have a hand laid upon them. For, as R. Hoshaia said, when Scripture tells us that at Sinai *They beheld God, and did eat and drink* (*ibid.*), are we to understand that food and drink went up with them at Sinai?[50] No, what the verse is telling us is that they feasted their eyes upon the Presence in the manner of a man who is eating and drinking without restraint.

According to R. Johanan, however, they were actually nourished by be-

48. [In conversation among men it was considered improper to refer to another person's wife, the word "house" or "family" being used instead. L.N.]

49. Thus God Himself, in allowing Nadab and Abihu to precede the elders, gave in to their arrogance.

50. An inadmissible supposition, since it is said of Moses that during his forty days and forty nights on Sinai he ate no bread and drank no water. See Exod. 34:28.

holding Him, as is proved by the verse *In the light of the King's countenance is life*[51] (Prov. 16:15).

But according to R. Tanḥuma, Exodus 24:11 teaches that Aaron's sons stood and stared in a gross way, feasting their eyes boldly on the Presence. In contrast to such behavior—so said R. Joshua of Sikn̲in, citing R. Levi—Moses did not feast his eyes on the Presence and so unwittingly derived benefit from the Presence. Proof that he did not feast his eyes on the Presence? The verse *And Moses hid his face* (Exod. 3:6). And proof that he derived benefit from the Presence? The verse *Moses knew not that the skin of his face sent forth beams* (Exod. 34:29).

Another comment: Because *Moses hid his face, for he was afraid* (Exod. 3:6), [he himself was allowed the privilege of inspiring awe, for], as Scripture says, *They were afraid to come nigh him* (Exod. 34:30). Because *he was afraid to look upon God* (Exod. 3:6), [he was allowed the privilege], *the similitude of the Lord to behold* (Num. 12:8). Nadab and Abihu, however, having feasted their eyes upon the Presence, derived no benefit from the Presence. Besides inferring their arrogance from the verses already cited, we may also infer it from the following verse: *Nadab and Abihu died before the Lord, when they offered strange fire in the wilderness of Sinai* (Num. 3:4), [signifying that the fire of their consuming curiosity in the wilderness of Sinai was the cause of their death].

R. Johanan asked: But does the verse in hand mean to say that Nadab and Abihu actually died right before the Lord[52] [in the Holy of Holies]? No. What the verse tells us is that when the children of a righteous man have to die during their father's lifetime, it is as grievous to the Lord as though they had died right before Him.

According to R. Simon, R. Naḥman of Jaffa put the following question to R. Phinehas bar Ḥama: Why are the words *before the Lord* said twice—once here in Leviticus 10:2 and once in Numbers 3:4—whereas the words *in the presence of Aaron their father*[53] (*ibid.*) are said only once? To teach that their death was twice as grievous for the Holy One as it was for their father.

The verse goes on to say that Nadab and Abihu died *in the wilderness of Sinai* (Num. 3:4). But did they die in the wilderness of Sinai?[54] Not in fact. But the verse means us to understand that having received the sentence of

51. Cf. Piska 6.1.

52. Did they not in fact, in keeping with the opinion of R. Eliezer, die outside the Holy of Holies, in a place where even Levites were permitted to enter? For R. Eliezer's opinion, see Sif Lev., *Šĕmini, Millu'im, 1*, 35, ed. Weiss 45d.

53. The words in the verse are transposed by the commentator and construed *Nadab and Abihu died . . . in the presence of Aaron their father* (Num. 3:4).

54. Did they not actually die in the Tent of Meeting?

death at Mount Sinai,[55] [they were as good as dead]. In this connection, consider a parable of a king who was about to give his daughter in marriage. There was discovered, however, among the representatives of the groom's family a wrongdoing requiring drastic punishment. The king said: If I slay them now, I shall confound my daughter's day of joy. My day of joy is to come later. I would rather have them punished during my day of joy and not during my daughter's day of joy. Likewise the Holy One said: If I slay Nadab and Abihu now, I will confound the day of Torah's joy. My day of joy is to come later. I would rather have them punished during My day of joy than during Torah's day of joy. The day of Torah's joy—that is, *The day of His espousals* (Song 3:11)—refers to God's marrying of the Torah to Israel on Sinai; and the day of God's joy—that is *the day of His heart's joy* (*ibid.*)—refers to [God's entrance into] the Tent of Meeting.

10. *And they had no children* (Num. 3:4). R. Jacob bar Abuy said in the name of R. Aḥa: If Nadab and Abihu had children, the children would have taken precedence over Eleazar and Ithamar, [the younger brothers of Nadab and Abihu],[56] for he who precedes in the line of inheritance also precedes in the inheritance of rank, provided, of course, that he conducts himself honorably after the manner of his forebears.

Eleazar and Ithamar ministered[57] *in the priest's office in the presence of Aaron their father* (*ibid.*), words which R. Isaac took to mean that they ministered during Aaron's lifetime, but which R. Ḥiyya bar Abba took to mean that they ministered after Aaron's death. In support of R. Isaac's opinion that their ministry occurred during Aaron's lifetime, [the following analogy is offered]: The phrase *in the presence of* is used here in Numbers 3:4 and also in Genesis: *Haran died in the presence of his father Terah* (Gen. 11:28). As in Genesis, the phrase signifies the death of a child in the father's lifetime, so here in Numbers 3:4 it signifies the ministry of a son in the father's lifetime. On the other hand, in support of R. Ḥiyya bar Abba's opinion that Eleazar and Ithamar did not minister until after their father's death, [the following analogy is offered]: The phrase *in the presence of* is used here in Numbers 3:4 and also in Genesis: *Abraham rose up from the presence of his dead* (Gen. 23:3). As in Genesis where the phrase refers to a time after Sarah's death, so here in Numbers 3:4 it refers to a time after Aaron's death.

In keeping with the opinion of R. Isaac that Eleazar's and Ithamar's

55. The words *in the wilderness of Sinai* are thus read "that which had been decreed at Sinai": *midbar*, "wilderness," is here construed as a nominal form of the verb *dbr*, "to speak, to decree."

56. Since, in inheritance, children take precedence over brothers.

57. Since the word *ministered* is taken to mean, "ministered as High Priests," it is possible to differ as to whether Eleazar and Ithamar ministered as such during Aaron's lifetime (e.g. when he was incapacitated), or only after his death.

ministry occurred during Aaron's lifetime, we are to understand that whenever a ritual uncleanness befell Aaron, Eleazar ministered as High Priest and that whenever a ritual uncleanness befell Eleazar, Ithamar ministered. It happened, for example, that Simeon the son of Ḳimḥith went out one day to talk with the king of the Arabs, and a jet of saliva chanced to spurt from the king's mouth onto Simeon's garments, making him ritually unclean. Thereupon his brother Judah took over and ministered as High Priest in his stead. On that day, their mother beheld her two sons as High Priests. According to the Sages, Ḳimḥith had seven sons and all of them served in the office of High Priest. When the Sages came to visit her, they asked her: What good deeds are there to your credit [that you should be so honored in your sons]? She replied: The ceiling beams of my house have never beheld the hair of my head.[58]

It used to be said: Flour (*ḳimḥaya*) is flour, but Ḳimḥith is the very flower of flours.[59] To Ḳimḥith was applied the verse *The true glory of a king's daughter is within*[60] (Ps. 54:15).

In keeping with R. Ḥiyya's opinion that Eleazar's and Ithamar's ministries occurred after Aaron's death, we are to understand that his son Eleazar served after Aaron died and that Ithamar served after Eleazar died.

11. R. Abba bar Zebina said: Why is the account of Miriam's death (Num. 20:1) put next to the passage on the ash of the Red Heifer (Num. 19)? To teach that as the ash of the Red Heifer atones for Israel's sins,[61] so the death of Miriam atoned for Israel's sins. R. Yudan said: Why is the account of Aaron's death (Deut. 10:6) put next to a passage which speaks of the breaking of the Tablets (Deut. 10:2)? To teach that Aaron's death was as grievous in the sight of the Holy One as was the breaking of the Tablets.

R. Ḥiyya bar Abba said: Since Aaron's sons, [Nadab and Abihu], died on the first of Nisan,[62] why does Scripture mention their death in connection with the Day of Atonement?[63] To teach that as the Day of Atonement atones for Israel's sins, so the death of the righteous atones for Israel's sins. And the proof that the Day of Atonement atones for sin? The verse *By means of this day shall atonement be made for you* (Lev. 16:30). And the proof that

58. Uncovering the hair was an act of immodesty.

59. An attempt to reproduce the pun of *ḳimḥaya* and *Ḳimḥith.* Literally: "All flours (*ḳimḥaya*) are coarse flours, but the flour of Ḳimḥith is fine flour." That is, "Smiths are Smiths, but this one is a Smythe."

60. The verse concludes [*In reward therof*] *her raiment is of chequer work inwrought with gold,* words which are taken to be an allusion to the garments worn by the High Priest. See Rashi on B.Yoma 47a.

61. See B.MḲ 28a and Tosafot; Piska 4.7; and PR 14:14.

62. At the time of the dedication of the Tabernacle.

63. See Lev. 16:1 ff.

the death of the righteous atones for sin? The verse *And they buried the bones of Saul and Jonathan his son in the country of Benjamin in Zela, in the sepulchre of Kish his father; and they performed all that the king commanded. And after that God was entreated for the Land* (2 Sam. 21:14).[64]

64. PRKB's continuation on pages 174b–178a is not found in any PRK MS. However, the *'Aruḳ*, *s.v. sḳbṭr*, cites the word as being in Piska *'Aḥăre moṯ*. Hence, under the assumption that at one time chap. 21 of Lev. Rabbah was part of Pĕsiḳta dĕ-Raḇ Kahăna, Buber in his edition of PRK included Lev. Rabbah, *'Aḥăre moṯ* (chap. 21), in which the word *sḳbṭr* occurs.

PISKA 27

SUMMARY

Lessons of the Feast of Sukkot

Instruction in Torah is more precious than silver. Thus, while collectors of charity who put pressure upon people for contributions they cannot afford will, according to Scripture, be punished, collectors of money in behalf of instructors in Bible and Mishnah are free to collect as much as they are able. As to compensation for teaching even one word in the Torah, no human being can ever be paid enough.

R. Johanan disposed of all his possessions so that he might devote himself entirely to Torah. He is one of three men whose devotion to Torah is eulogized.

Obedience is to be given to Torah's precepts, and the apparent cost of obedience is not to be reckoned, for obedience to a command, such as the one concerning the high-priced lulab, may well bring a reward beyond human calculation (Sec. 1).

Ps. 16:11, the introductory verse of a *pĕṯiḥah*, is construed *In Thy presence are seven joys*. The seven joys are identified first as the seven companies of righteous men who will be received by the Presence; and then as the seven requirements for the Feast of Sukkot, requirements which include the four plants in the lulab cluster (Sec. 2). In the time-to-come, when Israel is created anew, Israel will still take the lulab cluster and therewith praise the Holy One (Sec. 3).

The phrase *All the trees of the wood* (1 Chron. 16:33), in the introductory verse of the next *pĕṯiḥah*, is taken to refer to trees which bear fruit as well as those that do not; hence the lulab cluster is likewise to be made up of plants which bear fruit and plants which do not (Sec. 4).

The several parts of the verse *I will wash my hands in innocency; so will I compass Thine altar, O Lord, that I may make the voice of thanksgiving to be heard, and tell of all Thy wondrous works* (Ps. 26:6–7) are construed as meaning that the lulab cluster must be obtained honestly, not dishonestly; that men with lulabs circle the altar once on each day of Sukkot; that festal thank offerings are to be made on Sukkot; and that the Hallel Psalms are to be chanted so that all can hear them (Secs. 5–6).

In referring to the time of the year when the Feast of Sukkot is to be celebrated, Scripture changes from counting by days in the month to counting by days in the festival. The reason for the shift is explained by a parable. On the Feast of Sukkot, Israel go and fetch myrtles and willows and palm branches and build sukkahs and sing praises to God because He has made atonement for them on the Day of Atonement. So, on the first day of the Feast, God says: Let bygones be bygones. From this moment on commences a new reckoning. Today, the first day of Sukkot, is to be the first day in the new reckoning of iniquities (Sec. 7).

Other observations on the lulab cluster follow: it must be taken on the first day even if the first day falls on a Sabbath; the ethrog used in the cluster is identified as growing on a tree whose wood and fruit have the same aroma; the fronds of the palm in the cluster must be tied together; two willow withes and three myrtle twigs are required in the cluster (Sec. 8).

The lulab cluster is variously understood to represent God's glory, the Patriarchs, the Matriarchs, and the Sanhedrin; the four plants in the cluster are also understood to represent four different kinds of Jews (Sec. 9).

So great is the merit of the cluster ordained to be taken *on the first day* (Lev. 23:40) that in reward for its observance God, revealing Himself as First, will inflict punishment on Esau, first among Israel's enemies; will build the Temple spoken of as "first"; and bring the Messiah, he whom Scripture describes as "first unto Zion" (Sec. 10).

PISKA 27

And ye shall take for your own sake on the first day the fruit of goodly trees (Lev. 23:40), etc.[1]

1. R. Abba bar Kahana began his discourse by quoting *Take My instruction, and not silver; knowledge rather than choice gold* (Prov. 8:10), which R. Abba bar Kahana interpreted as God's plea, "Take My instruction of Torah, and not silver." Then R. Abba went on to quote *Wherefore do ye weigh out silver? Because there is no bread*[2] (Isa. 55:2). Why are you forced to weigh out silver as tribute to the children of Esau? Is it not *because there is no bread*—because you have not taken your fill of the bread of Torah? *And the forced labor which you must give* (*ibid.*). Why must you give forced labor [to sustain yourselves] while the nations of the earth are filled with food? *Because you have not had enough* (*ibid.*)[3]—because you have not eaten enough of the bread of Torah, nor drunk enough of the wine of Torah, of which it is written "Come, eat of My bread, and drink of the wine which I have mingled" (Prov. 9:5).

R. Berechiah and R. Ḥiyya, his father, taught in the name of R. Jose bar R. Nehorai: It is written *I will punish all that oppress* [*the people of Jacob*] (Jer. 30:20), a statement that applies even to collectors of charity [when they put pressure upon people for contributions people cannot afford]. But the statement does not apply to those who collect money in behalf of teachers of Mishnah and teachers of Bible, payment which the teachers of Mishnah and the teachers of Bible merit because they do not labor at some other employment in their own behalf. As to compensation for teaching even one word in the Torah, for such teaching no human being can give adequate compensation.[4] Indeed in a Baraita it is taught: In heaven, on New Year's Day, the amount of money allotted for a man's needs is specified, except that no limit is set upon the amount which he expends for celebration of festivals, Sabbaths, New Moons, festivals' half-festive days,[5] and the amount which children take as payment to their schoolmaster's house. When a man expends less for such purposes, his total allotment is made less; and when he gives more, his total allotment is made more.

In connection with the study of Torah, a story is told of R. Johanan who was taking a walk up from Tiberias to Sepphoris, leaning on the shoulder of

1. Lev. 23:40 and ff; the lesson for the first day of the Feast of Sukkot.
2. JV: *Wherefore do ye spend money for that which is not bread.*
3. JV: *And your gain for that which satisfieth not?*
4. Apparently R. Berechiah construes Prov. 8:10: *Take My instruction, and reckon not its cost in silver.*
5. The days intervening between the first and last days of Passover or Sukkot.

R. Ḥiyya bar Abba. When they came to a certain farm, R. Johanan said: This farm was mine, and I sold it because I wanted to devote myself entirely to the study of Torah. When they came to a vineyard, R. Johanan said: This vineyard was mine, and I sold it because I wanted to devote myself entirely to the study of Torah. When they came to an olive orchard, R. Johanan said: This olive orchard was mine, and I sold it because I wanted to devote myself entirely to the study of Torah. Thereupon R. Ḥiyya bar Abba began to weep. When R. Johanan asked, "Why are you weeping?" his companion replied: I weep because my master did not put anything aside for his old age. R. Johanan said: Ḥiyya, my son, is what I did really as foolish as you seem to think? I gave up something which took no more than six days to provide and acquired something which took forty days and forty nights to provide. For God gave to the creation of the entire world no more than six days, as is written *In six days the Lord made heaven and earth* (Exod. 31:17); but to give the Torah He took forty days and forty nights, as is written *And* [*Moses*] *was there with the Lord forty days and forty nights* (Exod. 34:28).

When R. Johanan was laid to rest, his generation applied to him the verse *When a man giveth all the substance of his house for love* (Song 8:7): for such love as R. Johanan had for the Torah, *he will be given* [*in the world-to-come*] *rich spoil*[6] (*ibid.*). When Abba Hoshaia of Teria was laid to rest, people saw his bier flying through the air [as a sign of God's love for him]; his generation spoke of him in contrast to *the man who gives all the substance of his house for* [*a woman's*] *love* (*ibid.*), thinking to get in exchange such love as the Ground of Being had for Abba bar Hoshaia of Teria—but *such a man would be utterly contemned* (*ibid.*). When R. Eleazar bar Simeon was laid to rest, his generation applied to him the verse *Who is this that cometh up out of the wilderness like pillars of smoke, perfumed with myrrh and frankincense, with all powders of the merchant?* (Song 3:6). What did they mean by *with all powders of the merchant*? That R. Eleazar had rare powers—that he was a teacher of Scripture and Mishnah, a precentor,[7] a composer of hymns and songs; and that, in addition, he used to discourse on Scripture to public assemblies.

In another comment, the verse is read *Take My instruction, and reckon not its apparent cost* (Prov. 8:10). R. Abba bar Kahana said: The great reward for taking the lulab cluster you may infer from the reward for the act of "taking" in Egypt, as referred to in the verse *Ye shall take a bunch of hyssop*, etc. (Exod. 12:22). What was the value of the hyssop? Four farthings, five farthings at most. Yet it was this bunch of hyssop, [by which Israel survived the plague of the first-born], that eventually enabled Israel to

6. So Targum *ad loc.* JV: *he would be utterly contemned.* But the stem *bz* can mean both "contemn" and "spoil, booty."

7. See Lev. Rabbah M, p. 690, n. 5.

take possession of the spoil of Egypt, of the spoil at the Red Sea, of the spoil of Sihon and Og, and of the spoil of the thirty-one kings of Canaan. Now for the taking of the lulab cluster, which costs a man ever so much more money [than hyssop] and with which ever so many more precepts are associated, how much greater and greater is the reward! Hence Moses charged Israel, saying *Take for your own sake on the first day the fruit of goodly trees* (Lev. 23:40).

2. *Make me know the path of life; in Thy presence is fullness of joy* (Ps. 16:11). David begged the Holy One: Master of the universe, make me know which gate is open toward life in the world-to-come. R. Yudan and R. Azariah differ as to the reply God gave David. According to R. Yudan, the Holy One said to David: "David, desirest thou life there? Look as from a watchtower to a life lived in fear of the Lord, since *The fear of the Lord prolongeth days*" (Prov. 10:27). According to R. Azariah, the Holy One replied: "David, desirest thou life there? Look as from a watchtower for affliction [which brings understanding], since *Reproofs of affliction are the way of life*" (Prov. 6:23).

In another comment the verse is read *May there be the fullness of joy* (*śmḥwt*)[8] *which is in Thy presence* (Ps. 16:11): fill us with the five kinds of joy—[each letter in *śmḥwt* stands for one of them]—which are in Thy presence, namely, Scripture, Mishnah, Talmud, Toseft[a], and 'Ăḡaḏah.

Another comment: *In Thy presence is fullness* (*śoḇa'*) *of joy* (Ps. 16:11). Do not read *śoḇa'*, "fullness," but *šeḇa'*, "seven"—seven joys in Thy presence. The verse thus refers to the seven companies of righteous men who will be received by the Presence, so that their faces will shine [like the seven radiances of the world]—like the sun, like the moon, like the firmament, like the lightnings, like the stars, like light-reflecting lilies [i.e. Prophets], and like the lampstand in the Temple. Their faces shine like the sun? Yes, as Scripture says, *Clear as the sun* (Song 6:10). Their faces shine like the moon? Yes, as Scripture says, *Fair as the moon* (*ibid.*). Shine like the firmament? Yes, as Scripture says, *They that are wise shall shine as the brightness of the firmament* (Dan. 12:3). Shine like the lightnings? Yes, as Scripture says, *The appearance of them is like torches, they run to and fro like the lightnings* (Nahum 2:5). Shine like the stars? Yes, as Scripture says, *They that turn the many to righteousness shall be as the stars for ever and ever* (Dan. 12:3). Shine like light-reflecting lilies—[Prophets]? Yes, as Scripture says, *For the leader; upon light-reflecting lilies.*[9] *A Psalm of David* (Ps. 69:1). Shine like the lampstand in the Temple? Yes, as Scripture says, *I have seen, and behold a lampstand all of gold,*[10] etc. (Zech. 4:2).

8. Apparently the unnecessary plural, *śmḥwt*, "joys," suggests to the commentator the exposition which follows.

9. JV: *Shoshannim*. See MTeh 45:5.

10. Since the statement *Not by might, nor by power, but by My spirit* (verse 6)

At Thy right hand stand those who give pleasure (*nĕʿimoṯ*) (Ps. 16:11). David asked the Holy One: Master of universes, is it possible to tell which company of the righteous is the more loved and gives God the more pleasure? Two Amoraim differ as to the answer. [Of the company standing at the right hand of God], one Amora maintains: It is the company of the righteous backed by the strength of Torah and good deeds.[11] The other Amora maintains: It is the company of conscientious teachers of Bible and teachers of Mishnah who have scrupulously given instruction to children and hence will abide at the right hand of God. Either way, *At Thy right hand stand those who give pleasure.*[12]

Another comment: *In Thy presence are seven joys* (Ps. 16:11), these being the seven requirements for the Feast of Sukkot: the four plants represented in the lulab cluster, the sukkah, the festal peace offering, and a joyous peace offering. Since the festal peace offering is enjoined, why a joyous peace offering also? Or if a joyous peace offering, why a festal offering also?[13] R. Abin replied by way of an analogy: Consider two contestants who appear before a judge. We do not know which is victorious until one of them carries off the palm. Then we know that he was adjudged the victor. So, too, when Israel and the counterparts in heaven of the princes of the earth's nations appear before the Holy One on New Year's Day, preferring charges against each other, at first we have no way of knowing which will be the victor. When Israel, however, come forth from the presence of the Holy One with their palms and their ethrogs in their hands, we know that Israel is adjudged the victor. Therefore Moses charges Israel: *Take ye on the first day the fruit of goodly trees* (Lev. 23:40).

3. *He hath regarded the prayer of the destitute man* (Ps. 102:18). R. Reuben said: We cannot easily fathom David's moods. There are times when he calls himself *king*, and there are times when he calls himself *the afflicted*. The explanation must be that when he foresaw and beheld that righteous men, men such as Asa, Jehoshaphat, Hezekiah, Josiah, would issue from him, he called himself *king*, saying *Give the king Thy judgments, O God, and Thy righteousness unto the king's son* (Ps. 72:1). But when he foresaw and

---

occurs in the context, the commentator assumes that the righteous are alluded to in the symbol of the lampstand. Cf. PR 8:4.

11. "with regard to which it is said *At His right hand is the fiery law* (Deut. 33:2)." So MTeh 16:12 goes on to say.

12. Since teachers of Bible and of Mishnah intoned the words of the texts which they used (Sof 3:10), the second Amora takes *nĕʿimoṯ* to mean "those whose words of instruction are intoned."

13. Since eating the meat of either offering is considered fulfillment of the obligation to bring offerings during the festival, why bring two offerings? Because, as R. Abin will explain somewhat obliquely, the additional offering symbolizes Israel's celebration of victory in the judgment.

beheld that wicked men, men such as Ahaz, Manasseh, and Amon, would issue from him, he thought of himself as destitute and called himself *the afflicted,* as when he said *A prayer of the afflicted, when he fainteth* (Ps. 102:1).

This verse R. Alexandri read *When a man delayeth his prayer* (*Tĕfillah*),[14] *he will be poor*, and applied it to a workingman. Thus, a workingman, [who fears his employer's displeasure], keeps watching throughout the day for his employer to go away for a while, [so that he can take time off from his work to say his daily *Tĕfillahs*, but if his employer does not leave], then the workingman must often delay saying them to the very end of the times set for them.[15] [Accordingly, R. Alexandri] takes the word *'tf,* usually read *fainteth* (*A prayer of the afflicted, when he fainteth* [Ps. 102:1]), to mean *delayeth*, as in the verse *On account of the delayings* (*'ṭfym*), those [*of the flocks which might have been Jacob's*] *were Laban's*[16] (Gen. 30:42), for, as R. Isaac bar Ḥaḳila used to say of this verse, how can the word *delayings* be construed except as a reference to Jacob's delays in saying his daily prayers?

[*He will regard the prayer of a destitute man, and not despise their prayer* (Ps. 102:18)]. Resh Laḳish said: The conclusion of this verse is not consistent with its beginning, and its beginning is not consistent with its conclusion. Since the verse begins by saying *He will regard the prayer of a destitute man*, it should have concluded with "and not despise *his* prayer." On the other hand, since the verse concludes with *and not despise their prayer*, it should have begun with "He will regard the prayer of destitute *men*." The inconsistency is explained by the fact that when David said *He will regard the prayer of a destitute man* he was referring to Manasseh king of Judah [who was destitute in his lack of good deeds]; and when David said *and not despise their prayer* he was referring to Manasseh's own prayer and to his forebears' prayers in his behalf. Hence it is written that "destitute" *Manasseh . . . prayed unto Him, and He was entreated* (*'tr*) *of him, and heard their prayers*[17] (2 Chron. 33:13). That is, God let Himself be dug into—as the

14. There are set times for the morning and afternoon *Tĕfillah*. See PR 49:1, and Glossary.

R. Alexandri takes *'ani*, "afflicted," in its other meaning of "poor," and *ya'ăṭof*, "faint," in its other meaning of "delay."

15. The point is that a man at work in a tree or upon a stone wall must stop his work and descend to the ground to say the *Tĕfillah* (Ber 2:4). If he is fearful of his employer's displeasure, he is apt to put off his descent and, as a result, find himself even poorer because he missed saying the *Tĕfillah* at the proper time.

16. JV: *So the feebler were Laban's*. See MTeh 102:1.

17. The prayer of David, for example, which he prayed when he saw that Manasseh would issue from him. *And heard their prayers*—Pa; MT: *And heard his supplications.*

kĕtib ḥtr indicates—so that His mercy poured out.[18] *'tr,* so R. Eleazar bar R. Simeon pointed out, is the same as *ḥtr*, for in the Araba[19] dialect of Aramaic *'trth*, " a hole dug in the earth," is pronounced *ḥtrth*. *And He brought him back to Jerusalem* (*ibid.*). How did He bring him back? R. Samuel bar R. Jonah, citing R. Aḥa, said that God brought him back on a wind, for the word *hšyb*, "brought back," here suggests *mšyb*, "cause to blow," as in the statement "Thou causest the wind to blow."[20] Having been [thus miraculously brought back], *Manasseh knew that the Lord He was God* (*ibid.*), and Manasseh thereupon exclaimed: Where there is judgment, there is a Judge.

R. Isaac began his discourse by saying [that Ps. 102:18 is to be read *May He regard the prayer of the destitute, and not despise their prayer*, and] that it alludes to the generations of our time [whom persecution has made destitute[21] so that] they have neither king nor prophet, neither Urim nor Thummim: all they have left is prayer. Said David to the Holy One: Master of universes, this prayer, which is all that the destitute have—do not despise it.

This shall be written for a vergent generation; a people that shall be created shall praise the Lord (Ps. 102:19). In David's saying to the Holy One, *This shall be written for a vergent generation*, he had in mind [Manasseh's being restored to Jerusalem as proof] that God receives the penitent man [even when he is on the verge of death]. And in saying *a people that shall be created shall praise the Lord*, he meant that God gives a new life to each man that repents.[22]

Another comment: The word *This* in *This shall be written for a vergent generation* (*ibid.*) alludes to Hezekiah's generation which was on the verge of death.[23] And the words which follow, *a people that shall be created shall praise the Lord* (*ibid.*), mean that the Holy One gave them a new life.

Another comment: The word *This* in *This shall be written for a vergent generation* alludes to Mordecai's and Esther's generation which was on the verge of death. And the words *a people that shall be created shall praise the Lord* mean that the Holy One gave them a new life.

Another comment: The word *This* in *This shall be written for the vergent generation* alludes to the present generations which are on the verge of death.

18. Cf. Piska 24.11, and PR 11:3.

19. Araba is in the northern part of the area west of the Jordan. See Ezekiel Kutscher in *Tarbiṣ*, *23* (5712/1952), 45, n. 107.

20. These words are said in the daily *Tĕfillah* during the winter season. See Hertz, *APB*, p. 133. On the story of Manasseh's repentance, cf. Piska 24.11.

21. R. Isaac reads the words *for the generation to come* which follow, as "the vergent generation." So David Luria on Lev. Rabbah 30:3. See the next paragraph.

22. See Lev. Rabbah M, p. 698, n. 5.

23. See 2 Kings 18:17 ff.

And the words *a people that shall be created shall praise the Lord* mean that the Holy One will give us a new life.[24] And what will He expect of us? That we will take the lulab cluster and the ethrog and praise the Holy One. Hence Moses charges Israel, saying to them *Take ye on the first day*, etc. (Lev. 23:40).

4. *Let the field exult, and all that is therein; then shall all the trees of the wood sing for joy* (Ps. 96:12). The word *field* in *Let the field exult* stands for the world, having the same sense here as in the verse where it is said of Cain and Abel that "they were in the field"[25] (Gen. 4:8). The phrase *all that is therein* refers to the world's inhabitants, as in the verse "The earth is the Lord's and the fullness thereof" (Ps. 24:1). With regard to *Then shall all the trees of the wood sing* (Ps. 96:12), and also with regard to the parallel verse *Then shall all the trees of the wood sing* (1 Chron. 16:33), R. Aḥa said that the phrase *trees of the wood* usually refers to trees which do not bear fruit, but since the phrase is qualified by the word *all*, the reference is to trees which bear fruit as well as to those that do not. [The lulab cluster is likewise made up of plants which bear fruit and plants which do not]. Before whom is the one who holds such a cluster to sing with joy? *Before the Lord* (Ps. 96:13). for, as the Psalm goes on to say, *He is come* (*ibid.*) on New Year's Day, [and says again *He is come* (*ibid.*)] on the Day of Atonement. To do what? *To judge with righteousness the Land* [*containing all the features of the six other kinds of land*],[26] *and with equity the* [*earth's*] *peoples* (*ibid.*).

5. *I will wash my hands*[27] *in innocency; so will I compass Thine altar, O Lord* (Ps. 26:6). The words *I will wash my hands in innocency* (*ibid.*) imply that the lulab cluster must be got through honest purchase, not through stealing. And the words *so will I compass Thine altar, O Lord* (*ibid.*), which follow, are to be read in the light of what is taught in a Mishnah: "On each [of the seven days of the Feast of Sukkot] men circled about the altar once, reciting 'We beseech Thee, O Lord, save now! We beseech Thee, O Lord, make us now to prosper!' (Ps. 118:25)." (Suk 4:5) [After the verse beginning *I will wash my hands*, etc.], the Psalm reads *That I may make the*

24. An alternative interpretation would start what follows as a new paragraph: "[To return to the theme of the trial in heaven between the princely counterparts of the earth's nations and Israel. After the trial's triumphant conclusion for Israel], what will He expect of us," etc. Cf. MTeh 102:3.

25. And, according to one tradition, argued about dividing the world between the two of them. See Gen. Rabbah 22:7.

26. "The Land containing all the features of the six other kinds of land" is the Land of Israel. See Piska 23.10, and Sif Deut. 37. JV: *He will judge the world with righteousness, and the peoples in His faithfulness.*

27. The commentator takes the word *kappoṯ* to mean "handshaped branches (or fronds) of palm trees."

voice of thanksgiving to be heard (Ps. 26:7), *thanksgiving* referring here to the festal thank offerings. The end of the verse, *and tell of all Thy wondrous works* (*ibid.*), refers—so said R. Abun—to the recitation of the *Hallel* Psalms which tell of God's wondrous works in times gone by, in the present time, in the time of the Messiah, in the time of Gog and Magog,[28] and in the time-to-come. Thus the Psalm *When Israel went out of Egypt* (Ps. 114:1) tells of God's wondrous works in times gone by; the Psalm *Not unto us, O Lord, not unto us, but unto Thy name give glory* (Ps. 115:1) tells of God's wondrous works in the present time; the Psalm *I love the Lord, because He hath heard my voice and my supplications* (Ps. 116:1) tells of God's wondrous works in the time of the Messiah; the words *Order the festal procession with boughs [to celebrate what befell those who penetrated Jerusalem] as far as the horns of the altar*[29] (Ps. 118:27) refer to God's wondrous works in the time of Gog and Magog; finally in the same Psalm, the verse *Thou art my God, and I will praise Thee* (Ps. 118:28) refers to God's wondrous works in the time-to-come.

6. *And ye shall take that which is yours*[30] (Lev. 23:40). The statement —so taught R. Ḥiyya—implies that the obligation of taking the lulab cluster rests on each and everyone of you. The words *that which is yours* further imply that the cluster must be truly yours—not got by stealing.

R. Levi taught: A man who uses a lulab cluster got by stealing—to whom may he be likened? To a highwayman who sat at a crossroads, robbing all those who came and went. Once, even as a legionary was passing on his way to collect the tax of a certain province, the highwayman, springing out upon him, got the better of him and robbed him, taking all the legionary had with him. After a time the highwayman was captured and thrown into prison. When the king's legionary heard the news, he went to the highwayman and said to him: "Up and give me all that a certain person robbed me of and took away, and I shall plead for you." The highwayman answered: "Of all that a certain person seized upon and took away from you there is naught left except this rug which belongs to you." The legionary said to him: "Give it to me, and I shall plead for you before the king." And as the highwayman gave it to him, the legionary said: "Tomorrow you will be taken out for judgment before the king, and when he calls out to you, saying, 'Is there any man that will plead for you?' you say, 'Such and such a legionary.' Thereupon he will send a messenger summoning me, and I will plead in your behalf."

28. The combined armies of the heathen nations under the leadership of Gog and Magog, barbarian tribes of the North (Ezek. 38–39), who will contend with the Messiah.

29. According to Zech. 14:2, Gog and Magog will succeed in reaching the center of Jerusalem where the altar was located. So interpreted in *Ḳorban ha-'eḏah* on P.Meḡ 2:1.

30. JV: *And ye shall take you.*

The next day when the highwayman was taken out for judgment, the king called out to him: "Have you a man to plead for you?" The highwayman replied: "Such and such a legionary." The king then sent for the legionary, summoned him and asked: "Know you anything good of this man?" The legionary answered: "I do indeed! On the day you sent me to levy the tax of a certain province, this man, springing out upon me got the better of me and robbed me, taking away all that I had with me. This very rug is witness to what he did." Whereat everyone exclaimed: "Woe to the man whose advocate turns accuser!" Even so, when a man in order to gain God's favor brings a lulab cluster but got it by robbery, the cluster itself cries out before the Holy One: "I was got by robbery! I was got by violence!" And the ministering angels exclaim: "Woe to this one whose advocate turns accuser!"[31]

7. *Ye shall take you on the first day* (Lev. 23:40). Scripture has fixed the day of the Festival as *the fifteenth day of the seventh month* (Lev. 23:39), and yet Scripture speaks here of *the first day* as though the month's first day were meant. [Why should Scripture have shifted over from counting by days in the month to counting by days in the festival]? R. Mani of Shaab and R. Joshua of Sik̲nin, citing R. Levi, replied as follows: The matter may be explained by the parable of a city which owed the king a balance on its tax. The king went forth to collect it, but when the notables of the city came out about ten miles[32] from the city and sang his praise, the king remitted a third of the sum the citizens owed. When the councilors of the city came out about five miles from it and also sang his praise, the king remitted another third of what the citizens owed. When the king entered the city, all the city's inhabitants came forth to sing his praise. Thereupon the king said: "Let bygones be bygones; from this moment on we shall commence a new reckoning."

Likewise on New Year's Day, when Israel come and resolve upon repentance, the Holy One remits one third of the punishment for Israel's iniquities. During the Ten Days of Repentance, when men notable for their piety fast, the Holy One remits most of the punishment for Israel's iniquities. Finally, when the Day of Atonement comes and all Israel fast, the Holy One forgives all punishment for their iniquities. For the words *with Thee is forgiveness* (Ps. 130:4) imply—so taught R. Aḥa—that from the beginning forgiveness is kept with Thee in trust. Why? *That Thou mayest be feared* (*ibid.*) which is to say that the uncertainty of forgiveness may instill the fear of Thee in all Thy creatures.

Between the Day of Atonement and Sukkot all in Israel are engaged in obeying God's commandments, this one engaged with building his sukkah and that one with getting his lulab cluster. Finally, on the Festival's first day, taking in their hands their lulab clusters and their ethrogs, they sing the Holy

31. Cf. MTeh 26:5.

32. A Roman mile is about one and a half kilometers.

One's praise. And the Holy One says to them: "I have already forgiven you that which has taken place. From now on reckon your iniquities anew." Therefore Scripture says, *on the first day*. What is implied by *on the first day*? That the Festival's first day is to be regarded as though it were the first day in a man's activities and consequently first in the reckoning of his iniquities.

8. *On the first day* (Lev. 23:40)—in the daytime, not the nighttime. The lulab cluster must be taken on the first day even if the first day falls on a Sabbath. *On the first day* further implies that the Sabbath is set aside only for the Festival's first day, [and not for any other during the Festival].[33]

The words *Fruit* [*which is like its parent*] *tree, the hadar,* (*ibid.*) point to the requirement that the wood of the tree selected for the lulab cluster and the fruit of the tree have the same aroma.[34] Thus we know that the *hadar* is the ethrog. Moreover, as Ben Azzai said, the word *hadar* suggests a fruit [such as the ethrog] which from year to year remains [*had-dar*, "dwells"] on the tree that bears it. For further proof that the *hadar* and the ethrog are the same, note that Aquila in his translation represents *haddar* by *hidor*—that is, a fruit which lives in proximity to water[35] [as the ethrog does: hence the ethrog].

Branches (*kappoṯ*) *of palm trees*: the word *kappoṯ*, said R. Ṭarfon, signifies that the palm tree's branches must be *kafuṯ*, "tied together": hence when the fronds are spread out, it is required that they be tied together.

And boughs of a tree screened by its network of foliage[36] (*ibid.*)—that is, a tree whose boughs resemble the plaiting of a net, namely, the myrtle, [must be represented in the lulab cluster]. *And willows of the brook* (*ibid.*) —words that would seem to indicate "willows which grow only by a brook [must be represented]." What is the proof that willows growing in a valley or in the hills may be used as well? Because Scripture says *And willows*[37]—[*all kinds, as well as those*] *of the brook*. Abba Saul said: The plural *willows* implies that two bunches of willow withes were required—one bunch for the lulab cluster and another bunch for the Temple.[38]

33. In fact, in the Land of Israel the Sabbath was set aside for any one of the other days of the Festival as well. In Babylonia, however, after the Festival's first day, the lulab cluster and ethrog were not made use of on the Sabbath. See B.Suk 43a; and Lieberman, *YKF*, 278.

34. Or, literally "have the same taste." (Cf. Suk 4:7). Young branches of the ethrog tree used to be eaten. So Mošeh Mirkin in his edition (Tel Aviv, 5717/1956) of Gen. Rabbah 15:7.

35. *Hydōr* is the Greek for water.

36. JV: *And boughs of thick trees.* But *'bt*, written defectively without the *waw*, may mean "thick" or "network of foliage."

37. The plural *willows* is taken as signifying that the use of all kinds of willows is permitted.

38. Wherewith to circle the altar. See Suk 4:5.

R. Ishmael taught: The phrases *fruit of the tree hadar and branch*[39] *of palm trees* (*ibid.*) signify that one piece of fruit and a single branch of the palm are to be used; the phrase *boughs of a tree screened by its network of foliage* (*ibid.*) signifies that three twigs of myrtle are to be used; and *willows of the brook* (*ibid.*) signifies that two willow withes are to be used. It is permitted that two of the myrtle twigs may be used even if their tops have been lopped off, provided that the third one has not had its top lopped off. According to R. Ṭarfon, however, all three may be used even if their tops have been lopped off.

9. R. 'Aḳiḇa said:[40] In the phrase *The fruit of the tree hadar* (Lev. 23:40), the word *hadar* is a symbol of the Majestic One, of whom it is said "Thou art clothed with glory and majesty (*hadar*)" (Ps. 104:1). *A branch of palm trees* (Lev. 23:40) likewise is a symbol of the Holy One, of whom it is written "The Righteous One shall flourish like the palm tree" (Ps. 92:13). *And a tree whose boughs are leafy* (Lev. 23:40) is likewise a symbol of the Holy One who is present among the righteous, as it is said "And He stood among the myrtle trees that were in the bottom" (Zech. 1:8). *And willows* (*'arḇe*) *of the brook* (Lev. 23:40) are likewise a symbol of the Holy One, of whom it is written "Extol Him that rideth upon the skies (*'ărabot*)" (Ps. 68:5).[41]

Another comment: *Take ye . . . the fruit of the tree hadar* (Lev. 23:40). *Hadar* stands for our father Abraham to whom the Holy One gave a majestic bearing in his old age, for it is written "When Abraham was well on in years, he was majestic in age" (Gen. 24:1). *A branch* (*kappoṯ*) *of palm trees* (Lev. 23:40) stands for our father Isaac who was tied (*kafuṯ*) and bound upon the altar. *And a tree whose boughs are leafy* (*ibid.*) stands for our father Jacob: even as the myrtle tree is rich in leaves, so Jacob was rich in sons. *And willows of the brook* (*ibid.*) stand for Joseph: as the willow in the lulab cluster wilts and dries up before the other three plants in the cluster do, so Joseph died before his brothers did.[42]

39. JV: *Branches.* But since *kappoṯ*, "branches," is written defectively, without the *waw*, R. Ishmael read *kappaṯ*, "one branch."

40. In R. 'Aḳiḇa's comment which follows, the ethrog represents God's majesty; the palm, His rewarding the righteous; the myrtle, His presence among the righteous as an indication of favor (B.Sanh 93a); and the willow, His governance of the world.

41. Since *'ăraḇoṯ*, "willows," is a homonym for *'ăraḇoṯ*, "skies," it is assumed that in His mercy He that rides in majesty upon the skies will send down rain from the sky after the feast of Sukkot, during which Jews had taken up withes of willow and of three other plants in a cluster.

In the order of the seven realms above, *'ăraḇoṯ* is the one closest to earth. See Piska 23.10.

42. See Gen. 50:24–26. According to this comment, the Jew, in combining the

Another comment: *Take ye . . . the fruit of the tree hadar* (Lev. 23:40). *Hadar* stands for our mother Sarah to whom the Holy One gave a majestic bearing in her old age, as is written "When Abraham and Sarah were old, they were majestic in age" (Gen. 18:11). *A branch of palm trees* (Lev. 23:40) stands for our mother Rebekah: like the palm tree which bears both fruit and thorns, so Rebekah bore a righteous man and a wicked man. *And a tree whose boughs are leafy* (*ibid.*) stands for our mother Leah: as the myrtle tree is rich in leaves, so Leah was rich in children. *And willows of the brook* (*ibid.*) stand for our mother Rachel: as the willow in the lulab cluster wilts before the other three plants in the cluster do, so Rachel died before her sister did.

Another comment: *Take ye . . . the fruit of the tree hadar* (Lev. 23:40). *Hadar* stands for Israel's Great Sanhedrin whom the Holy One honored for their hoary-headed majesty, as is written "Thou shalt rise up before the hoary head, and honor (*haḏarta*) the face of the man who got wisdom"[43] (Lev. 19:32). And *branches* (*kappoṯ*) *of palm trees* (Lev. 23:40) stand for disciples of the wise who make sacrifice of their physical comfort (*kofin*) to learn Torah from one another. *And boughs of a leafy tree* (*ibid.*) refer to the three boughs of myrtle in the lulab cluster, the three standing for the three rows of the Sages' disciples who sat before the Sanhedrin. *And willows of the brook* (*ibid.*) refer to the two willow withes, the two standing for the two scribes of the judges who were stationed in attendance upon the Sanhedrin, one on the right and one on the left.[44]

In another comment the verse is read *Take for your own sake . . .* [*a cluster including*] *the fruit of goodly trees*, etc. (Lev. 23:40), *the fruit of goodly trees* [the ethrog] standing for [a kind of men in] Israel: even as the ethrog has aroma and has edible fruit, so Israel have men in their midst who have knowledge of Torah and also have the merit of good deeds. *And branches of palm trees* (*ibid.*) also stand for [a kind of men in] Israel: as the palm tree has edible fruit but no aroma, so Israel have men in their midst who have knowledge of Torah but do not have the merit of good deeds. *And branches of a tree screened by its network of foliage* (*ibid.*) also stand for [a kind of men in] Israel: as the myrtle tree has aroma but does not have edible fruit, so Israel have men in their midst who have the merit of good deeds but do not have Torah. *And willows of the brook* (*ibid.*) also stand for [a kind of men in] Israel: even as the willow has neither edible fruit nor aroma, so Israel have men in their midst in whom there is neither knowledge

---

four plants, is invoking the merit of the Patriarchs so that God will send down rain.

43. JV: *the old man.* But the commentator apparently takes *zḳn*, "old man," as portmanteau for *zh šḳnh* [*ḥkmh*], "one who got wisdom."

44. See Sanh 4:3–4.

of Torah nor the merit of good deeds. The Holy One says: In order to make it impossible for Israel to be destroyed, let all of the different kinds of men be bound together as plants of different kinds are bound into a cluster, so that the righteous among them [by their knowledge of Torah and the merit of their good deeds] will atone for the others. Hence Moses charged Israel: *Take for your own sake on the first day* [*a cluster*], etc. (Lev. 23:40).

10. R. Berechiah taught in the name of R. Abba bar Kahana: Through the merit of your obeying the precept *Take ye on the first day*, etc., I, [says God], shall reveal Myself to you as "the First," and in your behalf inflict punishment upon "the first," and build you "the first," and bring you "the first." I shall reveal Myself to you as "the First," for it is written of Me *I the Lord am the first, I the last—I am He*[45] (Isa. 41:4); and will inflict punishment in your behalf upon "the first"—upon the wicked Esau, of whom it is written *The first came forth ruddy* (Gen. 25:25); and build you "the first"—the Temple, of which it is written *Throne of glory on high from the first, counterpart of the place of our Sanctuary*[46] (Jer. 17:12); and bring you "the first"—the Messiah, of whom it is written *The first unto Zion will I give* [*who will say*]*: "Behold, behold them* [*returning to Zion*]*," and to Jerusalem a messenger of good tidings* (Isa. 41:27).

45. MT: *I, the Lord, who am the first, and with the last am the same.*

46. JV: *Thou throne of glory on high from the beginning, thou place of our Sanctuary*. But see Ḳimḥi, and MTeh 30:1.

PISKA 28

SUMMARY

The Eighth-Day Festival as exemplifying God's gracious dealing with Israel

Jews are grateful for what God gives them, in contrast to the heathen who, when He gives them ease, are likely to blaspheme and revile Him just the same. Moreover, the heathen observe holidays riotously, while Jews observe them peacefully. It is because of their exemplary conduct that after the seven days of Sukkot Jews are given an additional day, the Eighth-Day Festival, to celebrate (Sec. 1).

Discourse on the Eighth-Day Festival exemplifying God's gracious dealing with Israel is introduced by the *pĕṯiḥah* verse *The wicked borroweth, and payeth not, but the righteous dealeth graciously, and giveth* (Ps. 37:21). The different kinds of wicked are described: he who raises a hand against his fellow, he who borrows and does not repay, he who makes strife, he who is brazen-faced, the heathen nations who eat and drink and rejoice but say no blessing over the food. On the other hand, the righteous, such as Israel, after eating and drinking give thanks to God in the Grace after Meals, even as the Righteous One of the universe *dealeth graciously, and giveth.*

To illustrate God's gracious dealing, His distribution of festivals throughout the year is considered. He had intended to give to Israel a festival for every month during the summer, but on account of the business of the golden calf He deprived the months of Tammuz, Ab, and Elul of the festivals He had intended for them. To make up, however, for Israel's being deprived of the festivals He had intended them to celebrate during the three previous months, He assigned all three festivals for celebration during Tishri, the following month. Then God said: Since Tishri makes up for the other months and has not been given a festival of its own, let it have its own day—the Eighth-Day Festival (Sec. 2).

In exposition of the reason for the Eighth-Day Festival, Eccles. 7:14 is cited as a *pĕṯiḥah*'s introductory verse. The middle part of the verse, *in the day of adversity consider*, is construed as suggesting the many things—prayer, turning in repentance to God, charity, a change of name, a change in conduct, a change of residence, and fasting—which can avert a harsh decree of God's. The final part of the verse, *God hath set the one against the other*, is construed as explaining the reason for the creation of righteous men and wicked men, for the equal dimensions of the Garden of Eden and of Gehenna and for their being placed next to each other. Finally, the first part of the verse, *In the day of prosperity be joyful*, is construed as exhorting us to be joyful in a fellow man's prosperity, even as in the day of his adversity we should seek to save him from adversity; to participate with others joyfully in studying Torah and obeying its precepts; and to be joyful on the Eighth-Day Festival through the observance of which Israel are saved from drought and come to enjoy prosperity (Sec. 3).

In further exposition of the reasons for the Eighth-Day Festival's being so named, Israel's prayer to God, *Give a portion* [*of prosperity*] *because of seven and also because of eight* (Eccles. 11:2), is cited as the introductory verse of a *pĕṯiḥah*: seven refers to the Sabbath, and eight to the eight days of circumcision; seven refers to the seventh generation from Abraham which Moses circumcised, and eight refers to the eighth generation from Abraham which Joshua circumcised; seven refers to the seven days of Passover, and eight to the eight festal days that are made up of the seven days of the Feast of Sukkot and the Eighth Day that comes right after; seven refers to the seven days of menstruation during which Israel refrain from sexual intercourse, and eight to the eighth day after the birth of a child, the day on which the child is circumcised; and finally, seven refers to the seven days of the Feast of Sukkot, and eight to the Eighth-Day Festival (Sec. 4).

Another reason for the Eighth-Day Festival: Because God regards Himself as glorified by the sacrifices brought by a humble man and hence takes delight in the offerings brought by Israel, He charged Israel to celebrate the Eighth-Day Festival for His glory and delight (Sec. 5).

The Eighth-Day Festival is a festival in its own right. Special lots are cast to determine what priests are to perform the various ceremonies in its celebration. It has its own sacrifice, its own Psalm, and its own benediction. Pertaining to it are certain regulations concerning the kiddush on the eve of the festival and the manner in which one may eat in the sukkah on the eve of the festival.

One might have expected the Eighth-Day Festival to follow Sukkot after an interval of fifty days, as Pentecost follows Passover. But because Sukkot falls during the rainy season when the burden of a journey to Jerusalem would be heavy, the Eighth-Day Festival follows directly after Sukkot (Secs. 6–7).

The word *'Aṣereṯ*, the Hebrew name for the festival, suggests that God and Israel are drawn together, and accordingly the season of Sukkot and the Eighth-Day Festival, in particular, are considered to be the right time to ask God for rain (Sec. 8).

While the Feast of Sukkot brings Israel to make offerings in behalf of the nations of the earth, the Eighth-Day Festival is a day of rejoicing solely for Israel and God, a day when Israel rejoice both in God and in His Torah (Sec. 9).

Some day the Temple will be rebuilt, and again the keeping of such ordinances as the offerings in the Temple and the tithes will be observed in fulfillment of the promise *Ye that cleave to the Lord your God will be alive every one of you* [*as you are*] *this day* (Deut. 4:4) (Sec. 10).

PISKA 28

On the Eighth-Day Festival

a. A query concerning law: Is a Jew permitted to eat in his sukkah on the Eighth Day? Our Sages taught as follows: "Yes, but in order to give the Eighth-Day Festival its due honor, on the afternoon of the seventh day of Sukkot he must start fetching down[1] the furnishings of the sukkah"[2] (Suk 4:8). R. Joshua ben Levi, however, maintained that on the Eighth Day a man should see to it that he stay away from his sukkah, since the Torah clearly says *Ye shall dwell in booths seven days* (Lev. 23:42), not eight days. Still, if eating in the sukkah is pleasing to him, what is he to do? He is to go into his house, so said R. Hoshaia, and there say the kiddush [for the Eighth Day]; then he may go into his sukkah and there have his meal. Another opinion: [If a man wishes to eat in his sukkah on the Eighth Day], he is required to invalidate the sukkah before the end of the seventh day. How does he invalidate it? He invalidates it by removing one palm branch from it.

Why does the Torah put a man to the trouble of going back into his house on the Eighth Day [instead of allowing him to remain in the sukkah]? Because the Eighth Day is a festival in its own right. As the Rabbis emphatically say: The Eighth Day is a festival in its own right. Special lots are cast to determine what priests are to perform the various ceremonies in its celebration.[3] It has its proper sacrifice, and its proper blessing. This "proper blessing" R. Eleazar understood to indicate that on the Eighth Day the blessing to be said is "Thou . . . hast enabled us to reach this season."[4] You can see for yourself that the Eighth Day is a festival in its own right. For, according to R. Abun the Levite, as R. Aḥa pointed out: With regard to all the other days in the Feast of Sukkot, Scripture says, *And on the day* (Num. 29:17, 29:20), indicating by *and* the consecutiveness of the days; but with regard to the Eighth-Day Festival Scripture says simply *On the . . . day* (Num. 29:35), thereby indicating to you that it is a festival in its own right. And the proof? The verse in the lesson: *On the Eighth Day ye shall have a solemn assembly* (Num. 29:35).

b. In the verse *Thou increasest the heathen, O Lord, yea, Thou increasest*

1. Since sukkahs were often built on the flat roofs of houses (Suk 2:3), the term "fetch down" is appropriate.

2. Into the house where he would ordinarily have his meals in the evening at the end of the seventh day and thereafter, on the Eighth-Day Festival.

3. Yoma 2:2, and Suk 5:6.

4. See Hertz, *APB*, p. 810.

the heathen, but art Thou honored?[5] (Isa. 26:15), what is implied by *Thou increasest the heathen,* etc.? That the prophet said to God: Master of universes, when Thou givest ease to a heathen, does he praise Thee for it? When Thou givest him a son, he does not circumcise him, but lets his foreskin remain and lets his locks grow.[6] Thou givest him a house, and he set up an idol therein. Hence *Thou increasest the heathen, O Lord.* Does he acknowledge Thee? Art Thou honored by him? When Thou increasest a man in Israel, however, Thou art honored. Thou givest him a son, and after eight days he circumcises him. Thou givest him a house, and he fixes a mezuzah upon it. Thou givest him a roof, and he builds a parapet around it.[7] Hence the verse [previously taken as referring to the heathen], may be read also as referring to Israel *Thou increasest* THE *nation*[8] . . . *Thou art honored* (*ibid.*).

c. Another comment: The verse *Thou increasest* THE *nation,*[8] etc. (Isa. 26:15), the Rabbis took to mean: As Thou increasest festivals for us, we increase offerings to Thee.[9]

R. Levi said: God desired to give to the children of Israel a festival for each and every month during the summer and so gave them Passover in Nisan, the minor Passover[10] in Iyar, and Pentecost, the festival that in Sivan, follows upon Passover. But as He was about to give them a notable feast in Tammuz, they made themselves the golden calf,[11] and therefore He took away the festivals He had intended for the months of Tammuz, Ab, and Elul. He made up, however, for Israel's being deprived of the festivals He had intended them to celebrate during the three previous months, by assigning them to the following month, Tishri, and having the three festivals—New Year's Day, the Day of Atonement, and Sukkot—celebrated within Tishri's span. Then said the Holy One: Since Tishri has been used to make up for the other months and has not been given a festival that is its own, let it be given its own day. Hence: *On the Eighth Day, ye shall have* [*an additional*] *solemn assembly* (Num. 29:35).

d. With regard to the meaning of the two numbers in the verse *Give a portion* [*of prosperity*] *because of seven, and also because of eight* (Eccles.

5. JV: *Thou hast gotten Thee honor with the nations, O Lord, yea, exceeding great honor with the nations; Thou art honored.*

6. At puberty locks of hair were offered to the gods.

7. Deut. 22:8.

8. In this context the word *goy* has a dual meaning: it may mean either "Gentiles who are heathen" or "The nation [of Israel]."

9. As against heathen who spend such days in riotous living. See Piska 28.1, end.

10. See Num. 9:10 ff.

11. On the seventeenth of Tammuz, after which Israel remained in disgrace until the tenth of Tishri, the day God pardoned Israel's sin. See PR 26:6; B.Ta 28b, and Rashi.

11:12), R. Eliezer and R. Joshua differ. R. Eliezer said: The words *Give a portion* [*of prosperity*] *because of seven* allude to the seven days of the week which culminate with the Sabbath; and the words *and also because of eight* allude to the eight days of circumcision.

R. Joshua said: The words *Give a portion* [*of prosperity*] *because of seven* allude to the seven days of Passover; and the words *and also because of eight* allude to the eight days in the festal season of Sukkot.

Another comment: What is meant by the words rendered *Give a portion* [*of honor*] *to seven*? That you are to give—so said R. Levi—a portion of honor to Sukkot's seven days. *And also to* [*the day which brings the number up to*] *eight?* That the Holy One also charged you with regard to the Eighth Day's holiness, since He said, *On the Eighth Day,* etc. (Num. 29:35).

Another comment: What is meant by the words rendered *Give a portion* [*of restraint*] *to seven for the sake of eight,* etc.? If you give—so taught R. Judah bar R. Simon, citing R. Meir—a measure of restraint to the seven days of menstruation [during which Israel refrain from sexual intercourse], you will earn the reward of My giving you a son whom you will circumcise when he is eight days old.

e. In another comment, the words are rendered: *On the eighth day there is to be a solemn confining* (Num. 29:35). With regard to the confining enjoined at Passover, Scripture says in Deuteronomy, *Solemn confining by the Lord thy God* (Deut. 16:18), while here in Numbers, with regard to the Eighth-Day Festival, Scripture says *solemn confining by you* (Num. 29:35). R. Ḥanina bar Ada explained: For your sake on Passover, says God, I confine the winds and rains in order that you may occupy yourselves with harvesting your fields. But during the present season, during Sukkot, when for My sake, you [make pilgrimages to Jerusalem and there] confine yourselves [in sukkahs, in your absence from your fields], I open for the sake of your crops treasuries wherein are winds as well as treasuries wherein are rains. Hence *On the eighth day there is to be a solemn confining by you.*

Another comment: In Deuteronomy *the solemn confining* [is God's], while here in Numbers *the solemn confining* is Israel's. R. Levi, citing R. Ḥama bar Ḥanina, said: What parable explains the inconsistency? The one of two merchants who went into a city together. One of them spoke up and said to his fellow: If both of us open for business [and offer our wares] in the city at the same time, we shall cause a stoppage of work in the city.[12] So you offer your wares during one week, and I shall offer mine during the following week.

R. Ḥanina bar Ada, citing the verse *How beautiful are thy steps in sandals* (Song 7:2), pointed out that the [last word should be understood not as *sandals* (*nĕʿalim*) but as "closings" (*nĕʿilim*); moreover, that the] text has

12. Since all the laboring people will run to market on one and the same day.

the word not in the singular but in the plural, signifying two "closings": the "closing" of Passover and the "closing" of Sukkot. For the Holy One says to Israel: For My sake you "enclose" yourselves during Passover, and so during Sukkot [while you are in your sukkahs in Jerusalem], I, too, "enclose" Myself throughout the Festival: [I hold back the winds and the rains in Jerusalem, but in your absence from your fields], for the sake of your crops, I cause winds to blow, clouds to rise, rains to come down, dews to bespangle the ground, plants to spring up, fruits to grow plump. Then during Passover you again enclose yourselves for My sake [as pilgrims in Jerusalem, away from your work], but [after Passover] you are able to go forth to the harvest, finding your fields full of all manner of plenty [because of the winds, the rains, and the dews I brought to your fields during Sukkot]. Therefore Scripture deems it necessary to say *On the Eighth Day the solemn assembly is for you* (Num. 29:35).

f. Another comment: Why were Israel "enclosed" for solemn assembly for an additional day? Rab said: By what parable may the question be answered? By that of a king to whom came an occasion for rejoicing, during which his tenants arrived and accorded him honor, and the people in his household arrived and accorded him honor. To all these the royal consort kept hinting, saying: "Now, while the king is rejoicing, get at him for satisfaction of your wishes." When they did not see what she was hinting at, the royal consort pressed the king for an additional day of feasting during which the people might get satisfaction of their wishes from the king. Even so, the Torah keeps hinting to Israel: "Ask for satisfaction of your wishes." How does the Torah do so? [As follows]: The verse prescribing the drink offerings for the second day, uses the word *nskyhm* (*their drink offerings*)[13] (Num. 29:19); the verse prescribing drink offerings for the sixth day, uses the word *wnskyh* (*the drink offerings thereof*)[14] (Num. 29:31); and the verse prescribing them for the seventh day, uses the word *kmšpṭm* (*after the ordinance thereof*)[15] (Num. 29:33). [The variations in spelling indicated by the letter *mem* at the end of the first word, by the letter *yoḏ* within the second word, and by the letter *mem* at the end of the third word show what the Torah is hinting, for the three letters together spell] *mym* ("water")—[in short, the Torah was hinting to the children of Israel that the right time to ask God for a pouring out of rain upon the fields was during the Feast of Sukkot]. But since they did not see what the Torah was hinting at, the Torah itself pressed in their behalf for an additional day, the Eighth-Day Festival.[16]

13. The usual formula is *the drink offering thereof*, as in Num. 29:21, 25, 28.

14. The usual formula is *the drink offering* (singular) *thereof*, as in Num. 29:16, 23, 26, etc.

15. The usual formula is *after the ordinance*, as in Num. 29:18, etc.

16. When the recital of the prayer "Thou causest the wind to blow and the rain to fall" (*APB*, p. 44) is resumed.

When you consider the matter, you would say that as the concluding festival of Pentecost follows Passover after an interval of fifty days, so the festival at Sukkot's conclusion should follow Sukkot after an interval of fifty days. Why, then, does the festival come right after Sukkot? In answer, R. Joshua ben Levi asked, What parable is apt here? and replied: The one of a king who had many sons, some conducting their affairs in a place far away and some conducting their affairs in a place nearby. Whenever they wished to, those conducting their affairs in the place nearby would come visit him, and then, when they wished to go away, he was not distressed. Why not? Because, the journey being short, whenever they wished to come and return they could come and go in one day. But when those who were conducting their affairs in a distant place came to him and then wished to go—them, he would press to remain with him for one more day. Likewise, on Passover the days of summer begin soon enough, so that after a fifty days' interval Israel may conveniently come up to Jerusalem for Passover's concluding festival, Pentecost. But the season after Sukkot, which we are dealing with, is the rainy season when the roads are troublesome. Therefore the Holy One said: While the children of Israel are here, let them also observe the concluding festival. Hence *On the Eighth Day, for your own sake, ye shall have a festival* (Num. 29:35).

g. *On the Eighth Day . . . ye shall present a burnt offering, an offering made by fire: one bullock, one ram* (Num. 29:36). R. Phinehas ben Ḥama said: The seventy bullocks which Israel offered during Sukkot[17] were in behalf of the earth's seventy [heathen] nations[18] that they might live in prosperity. These offerings, R. Berechiah used to reckon in the following way: Thirteen bullocks on the first day and seven on the seventh day, thus twenty; twelve on the second day and eight on the sixth day, again twenty; eleven on the third day and nine on the fifth day, once again twenty; adding the ten on the fourth day, you have a total of seventy. The Holy One said: My children, throughout the days of Sukkot we are completely taken up with our guests. On this Eighth Day, let Me and you feast together. Hence, *one bullock, and one ram* (*ibid.*).

R. Ḥunya bar Yudan said: As long as Israel continue to go up to Jerusalem and bring Sukkot's offerings, the Holy One showing them a cheerful countenance—if one dare speak thus—says to them: My children, you will again observe this day in the midst of prosperity [that has been restored to you],[19] and you will again come to Me. And the proof? The verse *These ye shall* [*again*] *offer unto the Lord in your appointed seasons* (Num. 29:39).

17. See Num. 29.
18. Reckoned by name in Gen. 10.
19. When the Temple will be rebuilt. See Piska 28.10.

[Additional Piska] from Another Source

1. *On the Eighth Day, ye shall have a solemn assembly,* etc. (Num. 29:35).[20] "Thou hast increased a heathen, O Lord, Thou hast increased a heathen; art Thou glorified?" (Isa. 26:15). When Thou didst increase ease for the wicked Pharaoh, did he in gratitude glorify Thee as Lord? Rather, did he not blasphemously and revilingly say, *Who is the Lord, that I should hearken unto His voice?* (Exod. 5:2). When Thou didst increase ease for the wicked Sennacherib, did he in gratitude glorify Thee as Lord? Rather, did he not blasphemously and revilingly say, *Who are they among all the gods of the countries, that have delivered their country out of my hand, that the Lord should deliver Jerusalem out of my hand?* (2 Kings 18:35). Thou didst increase ease for Nebuchadnezzar. Did he in gratitude glorify Thee as Lord? Rather, did he not blasphemously and revilingly say, *Ye shall be cast . . . into the midst of a burning fiery furnace; and who is the God that shall deliver you out of my hands?* (Dan. 3:15). On the other hand, "Thou hast increased the nation,[21] Thou art honored" (Isa. 26:15). When Thou didst increase ease for David, he blessed Thee thus: *David blessed the Lord before all the congregation* (1 Chron. 29:10). When Thou didst increase ease for his son Solomon, he blessed Thee thus: *Blessed be the Lord that hath given rest unto His people Israel* (1 Kings 8:56). When Thou didst increase ease for Daniel, he blessed Thee thus: *Blessed be the name of God* (Dan. 2:20).

And because "Thou art honored" by Israel, Isaiah went on to pray: *Remove far all the ends of the earth*[22] (Isa. 26:15). R. Levi took these words to signify that since Thou dost scrutinize those who are near Thee and dost scrutinize those who are far from Thee, bring even nearer those who are near Thee and remove farther off those who are far from Thee. Bring nigh those who are near Thee, in keeping with the verse "The Lord is nigh unto all them that call upon Him" (Ps. 145:18); remove farther those who are far from Thee, in keeping with the verse "The Lord is far from the wicked" (Prov. 15:29).

Another comment: "Thou hast increased the nation [of Israel] and consequently Thou art honored" (Isa. 26:15). Consider how it is with the

20. Num. 29:35 ff. is the lesson for *Šĕmini 'Aṣeret*, the Eighth-Day Festival, which follows upon the conclusion of the Feast of Sukkot.

21. The Hebrew *goy* may mean "nation" as in this comment, or "heathen" as in the previous comment.

22. "The ends of the earth" will be construed, "those who are far removed from God." JV: *unto the farthest ends of the earth.*

heathen nations of the world: when Thou givest a male child to one of their people, he disguises the circumcision [if the child is born so marked][23] and lets his son's locks grow.[24] As the child begins to grow up, he takes him to his heathen temple and thus provokes Thee. With Israel, on the other hand, when Thou givest a male child to one of them, he counts up eight days and then circumcises him; and if the child is a first-born redeems him after thirty days.[25] Then, when the child grows up, he takes him to synagogues and to schools where each and every day Thou art honored in the child's blessing of Thee: "Bless ye the Lord who is to be blessed."[26]

Another comment: "Thou hast increased the nation" (*ibid.*). It is the way of the nations of the earth when Thou increasest holidays for them, that they eat, drink, and carouse and attend their theaters and circuses and provoke Thee with their utterances and their deeds. But it is the way of Israel when Thou increasest holidays for them, that they eat, drink, and rejoice and attend synagogues and schools and increase the number of their prayers, increase the number of their additional offerings, increase the number of their regular offerings.[27] Therefore Scripture deems it necessary to say, *On the Eighth Day, ye shall have an [additional] solemn assembly* (Num. 29:35).

2. *The wicked borroweth and payeth not,* etc. (Ps. 37:21). R. Isaac said: There are three sorts of men who are called wicked, namely, he who raises a hand against his fellow, he who borrows and does not repay, and he who makes strife. Whence the proof that the man who even raises a hand against his fellow is to be called wicked? The verse which says, *And he said to the wicked, "Wherefore wouldst thou smite thy fellow?"* (Exod. 2:13). The verse's implication—as R. Ze'era pointed out—is not that he smote his fellow: even if he did no more than raise his hand against his fellow, but did not actually smite him, he is called wicked. Note the language of Scripture: *And he said to the wicked, "Wherefore wouldst thou smite thy fellow?"* The verse does not say, "Wherefore didst thou smite?" but says, *"Wherefore wouldst thou smite,"* implying that the man had it in mind to smite his fellow, but as yet had not smitten him. R. Samuel bar Tanḥum reported: I stated this inference in the presence of R. Tanḥuma, and he remarked: He who is brazen-faced is also called wicked, for it is written *A wicked man hardeneth his face* (Prov. 21:29). And whence the proof that he who borrows and does not repay is to be called wicked? The verse which says, *The wicked borroweth, and payeth not* (Ps. 37:11). And whence the proof that

23. That is, he has his son's foreskin restored by surgery.
24. To be cut off at puberty and offered to the gods.
25. These words are said before the blessings preceding the Shĕma'. See Hertz, *APB*, p. 1034.
26. *Ibid.*, p. 108.
27. Cf. Maimonides' Code, III, IV, vi, 20 (YJS, *3*, 304).

he who makes strife is to be called wicked? The verse concerning Korah's band which says, *Depart, I pray you, from the tents of these wicked men* (Num. 16:26). Incidentally, the verse *Depart, I pray you, from the tents of these wicked men* was the one that R. Judah used to recite when he was about to administer an oath to a man [willing to take it].[28]

Another comment: *The wicked borroweth and payeth not* (Ps. 37:21). By *wicked* are meant those nations of the earth who eat and drink but say no blessing over the food. By the words *But the righteous when dealt with graciously gives*[29] (*ibid.*) are meant Israel who eat and give thanks to God in the Grace after Meals.

Resh Laḳish said: You find that after the Holy One gives to a righteous man what he had sought of Him, He then returns and of His own will graciously gives him even more. Hence it is written *But the righteous dealeth graciously, and giveth* (*ibid.*), meaning that the Righteous One of the world deals graciously by giving more.

R. Levi said: What God intended was this—to give to Israel a festival for every month during the summer: Passover in Nisan, the minor Passover[30] in Iyar, Pentecost in Sivan. But on account of the transgressions and evil deeds that they came to own,[31] God took away the three festivals He had intended for the months of Tammuz, Ab, and Elul. He made up, however, for Israel's being deprived of the festivals He had intended them to celebrate during the three previous months by assigning three festivals to the following month, Tishri, and having them celebrated within Tishri's span: New Year's Day to make up for the missing festival in Tammuz; the Great Fast to make up for the missing festival in Ab; the seven days of the Feast of Sukkot to make up for the missing festival in Elul. Then said the Holy One: Since Tishri makes up for the other months and has not been given a festival that is its own, let it be given its own day. Therefore Scripture deems it necessary to say, *On the Eighth Day, ye shall have* [*an additional*] *solemn assembly* (Num. 29:35).

3. *In a day that offers an opportunity for goodness, then engage in goodness*[32] (Eccles. 7:14). R. Abba bar Kahana said: When a day for doing a

28. There was general disapproval of a man who was willing to take an oath in the middle of a dispute in order to settle it, disapproval which found expression in the saying "Right or wrong do not enter into an oath." See PR 22.6 (YJS, *18*, 467), Lev. Rabbah 6:3, and B.BM 49a.

29. JV: *The righteous dealeth graciously*. But in this comment, the verb *ḥwnn*, "dealeth graciously," is apparently taken in a passive sense, "When dealt with graciously, gives [grace to God]."

A man who eats and drinks without a blessing is said to be an embezzler. See MTeh 16:1.

30. See Num. 9:10 ff.

31. By making the golden calf.

32. JV: *In the day of prosperity be joyful, and in the day of adversity, consider.*

good deed comes your way, do it at once, for it is written *In a day that offers an opportunity for goodness, then engage in goodness*. The verse goes on *And in a day that has led you to do evil, consider*: that is, if you find yourself facing a day on which you have done evil, consider how best to repent, so as to be delivered from the evil of the Day [of Judgment].

R. Yudan said in the name of R. Eleazar: Three things—prayer, charity, and turning in repentance to God—avert a harsh decree, as is indicated in a single verse wherein all three are specifically referred to: *If My people, upon whom My name is called, shall humble themselves, and pray, and seek My face, and turn from their evil ways, then will I hear from heaven, and will forgive their sin, and will heal their Land* (2 Chron. 7:14). Here the word *pray* refers to prayer; the next words in the verse, *and seek My face*, refer to acts of charity, as when Scripture says, "As for me, I shall behold Thy face through charity" (Ps. 17:15); the following words in the verse, *and turn from their evil ways*, refer to turning in repentance to God. And with regard to Israel's practice of the three, how does the verse conclude? *Then will I hear from heaven, and will forgive their sin, and heal their Land* (*ibid.*).

R. Huna said in the name of R. Jose: A change of name or a change of conduct can also avert a harsh decree. A change of name, as is shown by the instance of our father Abraham: *Neither shall thy name any more be called Abram, but thy name shall be Abraham* (Gen. 17:5). Abraham as Abram could not beget children, but when he was renamed Abraham, he could beget them. A like instance: *As for Sarai thy wife, thou shalt not call her name Sarai, but Sarah shall her name be* (Gen. 17:15). Sarah as Sarai could not bear children, but when she was renamed Sarah she could bear them. That a change in conduct can avert a harsh decree may be seen from what happened to the people of Nineveh: *And God saw their works that they turned from their evil way; and God repented of the evil, which He said He would do unto them* (Jonah 3:10).

And some say that a change of residence also can avert a harsh decree, as may be seen from what happened to our father Abraham. For after *The Lord said unto Abram: "Get thee out of thy country"* (Gen. 12:1), there follow directly, the words *And I will make thee into a great nation* (Gen. 12:2).

R. Mana said: A fast also, as is said *The Lord answer thee in the day of self-mortification* (Ps. 20:2). Apropos of fasting, Rabbah bar [Meḥasya and] R. Ḥama bar Gurya said in the name of Rab: Fasting does away with a bad dream, even as fire does away with tow, provided, however, R. Ḥisda said, the fast is observed the same day; even if that day be the Sabbath, R. Joseph added.

God hath set the one over against the other (Eccles. 7:14). That is, the

---

But *ṭoḇah*, "prosperity, joy," can also mean "goodness"; and *ra'ah*, "adversity," can also mean "evil."

Holy One made righteous men as well as wicked ones, as Scripture tells: *And after that came forth his brother, and his hand had hold on Esau's heel* (Gen. 25:26). R. Phinehas and R. Hilkiah stated in the name of R. Simon that not even the thinness of a caul separated Esau and Jacob, and yet the one came out a righteous man and the other a wicked man. Why does the Holy One create both righteous men and wicked men? In order that the ones should atone for the others,[33] as is indicated by the verse *God hath set the one over against the other.*

Another comment: *In the day of prosperity be joyful* (Eccles. 7:14). R. Tanḥum bar R. Ḥiyya said: In the day of your fellow man's prosperity rejoice with him. *And in the day of adversity consider* (*ibid.*)—if adversity confronts your fellow, consider how to do him a kindness and save him.

[Keep in mind and do] what the mother of R. Tanḥum bar R. Ḥiyya used to do. She would set out on a day to buy one pound of meat in her son's behalf, but she would end up by buying two pounds,[34] one for him and one for the poor. Or on another day she would set out to buy one bunch of vegetables for him, but she would end up buying two, one for him and one for the poor. But why does the Holy One create both poor people and rich people? In order for them to draw riches from each other,[35] as is indicated by the verse *God hath made the one for the other*, etc. (*ibid.*).

In another comment, the verse is read *In the day meant for rejoicing, be joyful* (*ibid.*). R. Aḥa said: On the day when [men rejoice in partaking of] the goodness of Torah, [studying it and practicing its precepts], you also partake of its goodness, and rejoice, for the same reason, *so that in the day of adversity thou wilt be one who beholds.* This is to say that when the Day of Judgment arrives, the day of which it is written *The sinners in Zion are afraid*, etc. (Isa. 33:14), you will be among those who behold the punishment of the sinners rather than among those who are beheld receiving punishment; you will be among the spectators rather than among the gladiators;[36] you will be among those of whom it is written *They shall go forth, and look upon the carcasses of the men that have rebelled against Me* (Isa. 66:24), and not among those of whom it is written *Their worm shall not die, neither shall their fire be quenched; and they shall be an abhorring unto all flesh* (*ibid.*).

Why did the Holy One create both Gehenna and the Garden of Eden [so

33. See PR 51:2, end.

34. "by buying two pounds—C; O: "by buying him two pounds."

35. The poor are enriched by the charity they receive, and the rich are enriched by the merit of the charity they give.

36. See Lieberman, *GJP*, 38, n. 51a. [The particular sort of gladiator meant here is one who is engaged in combat with savage beasts (Greek *kynēgos*). The whole phrase seems to be an otherwise unrecorded Greek proverb. L.N.]

close to each other and give equal space to each]? In order that one may borrow room from the other, [for when the righteous are more numerous then the Garden of Eden borrows room from Gehenna, and when the wicked are more numerous, Gehenna borrows room from the Garden of Eden].[37] But how much space is there between Gehenna and the Garden of Eden? R. Johanan said: No more than the thickness of a wall. R. Ḥanina said: No more than the breadth of a hand. But the Rabbis said: The two are right next to each other.

Finally, R. Levi, [taking the phrase *In the day of prosperity* (Eccles. 7:14) to refer to the Eighth-Day Festival, through the observance of which Israel are saved from drought], said that the Holy One declared to Israel: My children, those offerings which I caused to be prescribed in the Torah, be heedful of them: you have no better intercessor than the offerings for the bringing down of rain. Hence the Holy One deemed it necessary to command Moses to say to Israel: *On the Eighth Day, for your own sake, ye shall have a solemn assembly*[38] (Num. 29:34).

4. *Give a portion* [*of prosperity*] *because of seven, and also because of eight* (Eccles. 11:2). As to what the two numbers mean, R. Eliezer, R. Nehemiah, and R. Joshua differ. R. Eliezer said: The words *Give a portion* [*of prosperity*] *because of seven* contain an allusion to the Sabbath, of which it is written "And it came to pass because of the seventh"[39] (1 Kings 18:44).[40] The words *and also because of eight* contain an allusion to the

37. Gehenna and the Garden of Eden are each made to contain half the world's population, as though one half of the world were righteous and the other half wicked. Accordingly, when the righteous are more numerous, the Garden of Eden "borrows" space from Gehenna, and *vice versa* when the wicked are more numerous.

According to another tradition, Gehenna and the Garden of Eden are each made to hold the world's entire population. See B.Ḥag̃ 15a. Professor Saul Lieberman explained this passage.

38. Or, R. Levi may regard the saying *God also hath set the one over against the other* (Eccles. 7:14) as meaning that over against the withholding of rain (*'ṣyrh*) God set an additional day of "holding of oneself" (*'ṣrt*) in the presence of God. For both interpretations of R. Levi's comment, see David Luria in his Novellae on Eccles. Rabbah 7:14.

39. JV: *at the seventh time*. The previous verse mentions, however, that at Elijah's bidding the lad was to go up seven times and look toward the sea for a sign of rain; and so the next verse might have read "at the last time" and not *at the seventh time*. Therefore R. Eliezer takes Scripture's use of *the seventh* as an allusion to the Sabbath, the merit of which Elijah invoked in his appeal for rain.

40. The Hebrew text cites here *And it came to pass on the seventh day* (Exod. 16:27), which appears to be a scribal error; and so 1 Kings 18:44 is substituted here, the verse cited in PR 54:2, and Eccles. Rabbah 11:12.

eight days of circumcision, of which it is written "Elijah . . . put his face between his knees"[41] (1 Kings 18:42). These two verses from Kings intimate that Elijah said to the Holy One: Master of the universe, even if Israel have fulfilled no commandments other than those concerning the Sabbath and circumcision, the merit of these two is such as to have Thee send down the rain because of them.

R. Nehemiah said: The words *Give a portion* [*of prosperity*] *to seven* allude to the generation which Moses circumcised—the seventh generation [from Abraham]. The words *and also because of eight* refer to the generation which Joshua circumcised—the eighth generation [from Abraham].[42] The Holy One said to Joshua: Thy master, Moses, circumcised Israel in the seventh generation from Abraham, do thou circumcise them in the eighth, as is said *At that time the Lord said unto Joshua: "Make thee knives of flint, and circumcise again the children of Israel the second time"* (Josh. 5:2). The words *the second time* intimate that God was saying, "Circumcise them once again; thou wilt not have to circumcise them a third time, [for hereafter they will perform the rite of circumcision for themselves]."[43]

R. Joshua said: The words *Give a portion* [*of prosperity*] *because of seven* allude to the seven days of Passover. The words *and also because of eight* allude to the eight festal days that are made up of the seven days of the Feast of Sukkot and the Eighth-Day Festival that comes right after them. By the words *and also* is meant that we entreat Thee [not only because of the aforementioned three festivals but] also because of Pentecost, New Year's Day, and the Day of Atonement to *Give a portion* [*of prosperity*].[44]

R. Simon interpreted the verse as alluding to two of the princes—one, a descendant of Ephraim, and the other, a descendant of Manasseh—who were given the honor of bringing offerings at the dedication of the Tabernacle's altar in the wilderness]. The words *Give a portion* [*of prosperity*] *because of seven* refer to the first prince of whom Scripture says, *On the seventh day . . . the prince of the children of Ephraim* (Num. 7:48); and the words *and also because of eight* refer to the second prince of whom Scripture

41. The phrase "between his knees" is construed as meaning that in his appeal for rain Elijah invoked the merit of circumcision.

42. Abraham, Isaac, Jacob, Levi, Kohath, Amram, Moses, and Joshua. These two circumcisions were regarded as crucial in Israel's history. But for them, Israel would not have been freed from Egypt, nor been able to enter the Land of Israel. During the years in the desert, the cooling north wind did not blow; and so circumcisions could not be performed. See Ginzberg, *Legends*, *4*, 7, and notes thereto; and Gen. Rabbah 46:9.

43. See Mek̲, *3*, 204–05.

44. *And* alone would have sufficed; the addition of *also* implies to R. Joshua that the preceding three holidays are referred to as well.

says, *On the eighth day . . . the prince of the children of Manasseh*[45] (Num. 7:54).

R. Azariah said in the name of R. Judah bar R. Simon: The words *Give a portion because of seven* allude to the period of the priests' preparation for serving in the Tabernacle—*He shall consecrate you seven days,* etc. (Lev. 8:33), says Scripture. And the words *and also because of eight* allude to the eighth day when the priests began to serve in the Tabernacle—*And it came to pass on the eighth day that Moses called Aaron*, etc. (Lev. 9:1), says Scripture.

R. Judah bar R. Simon, citing R. Meir, took the words *Give a portion because of seven* as alluding to the seven days of menstruation during which Israel refrain from sexual intercourse, and he took the words *and also because of eight* as alluding to the eighth day after the birth of a child, the day on which the child is circumcised. Accordingly, in construing the verse, he took it that the Holy One was saying: "If thou refrain from sexual intercourse during the seven days of menstruation, then I shall give thee a male child whom thou wilt circumcise on the eighth day," for in the very next verse after the one concerning menstruation, Scripture says, *And in the eighth day the flesh of his foreskin shall be circumcised* (Lev. 12:3).

R. Levi said: The words *Give a portion because of seven* refer to the seven days of the Feast of Sukkot; and the words *and also because of eight* are understood by reference to *On the Eighth Day, ye shall have a solemn assembly* (Num. 29:35).

5. *Since the Lord taketh pleasure in His people*, etc. (Ps. 149:4). R. Joshua of Sik̲nin said in the name of R. Levi: The Holy One takes pleasure in the offerings of Israel. The words *He adorneth the humble with His heeding*[46] (*ibid.*) mean that the Holy One regards Himself as glorified by the sacrifice brought by a humble man. That *heeding* (*yšwʿh*) here refers to God's heeding of sacrifices is shown by the verse *And the Lord gave heed* (*yšʿ*) *unto Abel and his offering* (Gen. 4:4). *Since the Lord taketh pleasure in His people* (Ps. 149:4), that is, since the Holy One takes pleasure in the offerings of Israel, therefore Moses charged Israel *On the Eighth Day ye shall have* [*an additional*] *solemn assembly* (Num. 29:35).

6. R. Johanan said: [Though the Eighth Day comes right after the seven days of the Feast of Sukkot], it is a festival in its own right. Special lots are

45. The other princes represented each an entire Tribe, whereas the princes of Ephraim and Manasseh represented each one half of what should have been the Tribe of Joseph. Nevertheless, they were accorded the same privilege of bringing a particular offering at the dedication of the Tabernacle's altar in anticipation, as it were, of the historical role of Ephraim and Manasseh as separate and full-sized Tribes.

46. JV: *with salvation.*

cast to determine what priests are to perform the various ceremonies in its celebration.[47] It has its proper sacrifice, and its proper benediction. As to being a festival in its own right, R. Bun said: With regard to all the other days in the Feast of Sukkot Scripture says, *And on the day* (Num. 29:17, 20, 23, 26, 29, 32), indicating by *and* the consecutiveness of the days, but with regard to the Eighth Day, Scripture says simply: *On the . . . day* (Num. 29:35). Hence we know that thc Eighth Day is a festival in its own right.[48] As to the lots for various ceremonies performed by the priests, we are taught the following in a Mishnah: "On the Eighth Day they cast lots as they do at the other feasts" (Suk 5:9). As to its proper sacrifice, Scripture says, *one bullock, one ram*,[49] etc. (Num. 29:36). As to its proper benediction, R. 'Illa said: It is required that on the Eighth Day the blessing "Thou . . . hast enabled us to reach this season"[50] be said.

7. In a Mishnah we read: "It is required that the [practices associated with the] sukkah continue for a full seven days. Thus after a man has finished eating [the last meal of the Feast],[51] he should not pull down the sukkah at once. However, in order to give the Eighth-Day Festival its due of honor, on the afternoon of the seventh day of Sukkot he must start fetching down[52] the furnishings of the sukkah"[53] (Suk. 4:8). R. Abba bar Kahana [and] R. Ḥiyya bar Ashi said in the name of Rab: [If a man wishes to eat in his sukkah on the Eighth Day], he is required to invalidate the sukkah in one way or another[54] sometime during the seventh day. R. Joshua ben Levi said: Of such a man it is only required that on the eve of the Eighth Day he say its proper kiddush[55] in his house [and not in the sukkah].[56]

And R. Jacob bar Aḥa said in the name of Samuel: If a man says kiddush in one abode and then decides to eat his meal in another abode, he must say the kiddush a second time [in the other abode].

47. See Yoma 2:2, and Suk 5:6.

48. On the Eighth-Day Festival, dwelling in a sukkah is not required. See Tos Suk 4:17; B.Suk 48a, and Rashi.

49. In contrast to the seven bullocks, two rams, and fourteen lambs offered up on the seventh day of the Feast of Sukkot. See Num. 29:32.

50. See Hertz, *APB*, p. 810.

51. On the morning of the seventh day of Sukkot.

52. Since sukkahs were often built on top of the flat roofs of houses (Suk. 2:3), the term "fetch down" is used.

53. Into the house, where he would ordinarily have his meals in the evening and thereafter on the Eighth-Day Festival.

54. By diminishing the sukkah's size (see *Ḳorban ha-'edah* on P.Suk 4:5); or by removing a palm branch from it (see PRKB, 194b). In this way the man makes it clear that he is not observing the Feast of Sukkot for eight days.

55. See Hertz, *APB*, p. 808.

56. And so there is no need to invalidate the sukkah inasmuch as the kiddush in the house has already marked the Eighth Day's distinctiveness.

R. Aḥa and R. Ḥanina said in the name of R. Hoshaia: In the event that a man's sukkah is pleasing to him, on the eve of the Eighth-Day Festival he may say its proper kiddush in his house, and then go up to his sukkah and eat his meal without having to say the kiddush again.

R. Abun pointed out that Samuel's teaching may be construed as being in agreement with R. Ḥiyya's,[57] and that R. Hoshaia's teaching may be construed as being in agreement with R. Joshua ben Levi's.[58]

R. Mana said: In truth, there is no difference of opinion between Samuel and R. Joshua ben Levi. What Samuel said applies to a man who intends to eat in one house, [but then goes and eats in another]. And what R. Joshua ben Levi said applies to a man who does not intend to eat in the house in which he is saying the kiddush.[59]

R. Joshua ben Levi said: By rights the Festival at Sukkot's conclusion should have followed Sukkot after an interval of fifty days.[60] A parable will explain how the matter may be understood. The parable tells of a king who had married daughters in a place nearby and other married daughters in a place far away. The married ones who lived nearby could come [visit him] and go back on the same day; but the married ones who lived far away could not come [visit him] and go back on the same day. And so the king said to the latter: Let us, you and I, rejoice in each other one more day [without a separation intervening]. Likewise, [in regard to the length of the interval between Sukkot and the Eighth-Day Festival]: Inasmuch as Passover comes at the time when Israel is passing from the rainy season into the dry season, the burden of the journey to Jerusalem is not heavy—indeed, Israel can come

57. R. Ḥiyya required that during the seventh day of Sukkot the sukkah be invalidated. Hence, a man who goes into the sukkah to eat must say the kiddush a second time. Since the sukkah is partly dismantled, it is apparent that he does not intend to use it for more than seven days.

58. R. Joshua ben Levi does not require invalidating the sukkah on the seventh day of Sukkot. Hence, saying the kiddush in the sukkah on the eve of the Eighth-Day Festival would make it appear that he intends to continue using the sukkah after the seventh day.

59. See Lieberman's note in PRKM, p. 475.

60. The name *'Aṣereṯ*, "bound [to the festival which precedes it]" or "concluding festival," is applied to Pentecost as well as to the Eighth-Day Festival, the celebration of both of which was fixed not through reckoning time by the moon but by reference to Passover and Sukkot which precede them. Hence, prior to the month of Sivan in which Pentecost falls, the court in Jerusalem sent out no messengers to report witnessing the arrival of the new moon, since "the time for Pentecost was set" (P. RH 1:4, 57b) on the fiftieth day after the second day of Passover.

Inasmuch as the Eighth Day is deemed to be the concluding festival of Sukkot, even as Pentecost is regarded as the concluding festival of Passover, R. Joshua ben Levi undertakes to explain why, unlike Pentecost which comes fifty days after Passover, the Eighth-Day Festival comes directly after Sukkot.

and return on the same day—and therefore [Pentecost], the festival at the conclusion of Passover, comes after an interval of fifty days. Sukkot, on the other hand, comes at the time of Israel's passing from the dry season into the rainy season when the burden of the journey to Jerusalem is heavy—it would be impossible to come and return on the same day—and therefore the Festival at Sukkot's conclusion is not set to take place after an interval of fifty days. Hence the Holy One said to Israel: "Let us, you and I, rejoice in each other for one more day." Accordingly, Scripture deems it necessary to say *On the Eighth Day, ye shall have* [*an additional*] *solemn assembly* (Num. 29:35).

8. [As to the meaning of *'Aṣereṯ*, the name given to the Eighth-Day Festival], R. Yudan said in the name of R. Isaac: As long as Jews draw together for the celebration of festivals in synagogues and houses of learning, the Holy One shows by His presence that He is drawn to them. And the proof? The words spoken by Manoah to the angel: *I pray thee, let us draw* (*'aṣar*) *thee to us, that we make ready a kid for thee* (Judg. 13:15).

But R. Haggai, in the name of R. Isaac, did not agree with R. Yudan, saying: If Jews do no more than collect in synagogues and in houses of learning, the Holy One shows by His presence that He is pleased to collect with them. And the proof? *I collected constantly*[61] [*with my fellows*], *O Lord, and He inclined unto me, and heard my cry* (Ps. 40:2). R. Alexandri said: In this connection, consider the parable of a king to whom came an occasion for rejoicing. During the subsequent seven days of feasting, his royal consort kept hinting to the people of the palace, saying: "Now is the time, while the king is rejoicing, to get at him for satisfaction of your wishes." When they did not see what she was hinting at, the royal consort herself got on their account an additional day of feasting from the king. Even so the Torah keeps steering Israel to their opportunity by hinting to them: "Ask for rain." You can see for yourself that the Torah is doing so by noting the variation in spelling of certain words in the following verses that specify the drink offerings for the Feast of Sukkot: The verse prescribing the drink offerings for the second day, uses the word *nskyhm* (*their drink offerings*)[62] (Num. 29:19); the verse prescribing the drink offerings for the sixth day uses the word *wnskyh* (*the drink offerings thereof*)[63] (Num. 29:31); and the verse prescribing them for the seventh day, uses the word *kmšpṭm* (*after the ordinance thereof*)[64] (Num. 29:33). The variations in spelling indicated by the letter *mem* at the end of the first word, by the letter *yoḏ* within the second word, and by the letter *mem* at the end of the third word show what

61. JV: *I waited patiently*. But *ḳwh* may mean either "wait" or "gather, collect."

62. The usual formula is *the drink offering thereof*, as in Num. 29:21, 25, 28.

63. The usual formula is *the drink offering* (singular) *thereof*, as in Num. 29:16, 23, 26, etc.

64. The usual formula is *after the ordinance*, as in Num. 29:18, 20.

the Torah is hinting at, for the three letters together spell *mym* ("water")—in short, the Torah was hinting to Israel that during the Feast of Sukkot was the right time to ask of God a pouring out of rain upon their fields. But since they did not see what the Torah was hinting at, the Torah itself got an additional day, the Eighth-Day Festival, for them. Hence Torah charges Israel *Let the Eighth Day be for you* [*an additional*] *solemn assembly* (Num. 29:35).

9. R. Alexandri told the parable of a king to whom an occasion for rejoicing came. Throughout the seven days of feasting, the king's son was busy with the guests. But after the seven days of feasting had run their course, the king said to his son: My son, I know that throughout the seven days of feasting you were burdened with the guests, but now let you and me rejoice for one day, and I shall not burden you further except to require from you one cock and one pound of meat. So, too, throughout the seven days of feasting Israel are occupied with offerings for the heathen nations. As R. Phinehas said: All those seventy bullocks which Israel offer during Sukkot in behalf of the earth's seventy nations [are offered] so that the world may not be depopulated of them [in punishment for their sins].

But since *In return for my love, they are my adversaries* (Ps. 109:4), why did Israel persist in bringing offerings in behalf of the seventy nations? Because *I am all for prayer* (*ibid.*)—because we of Israel trust in the efficacy of prayer.[65]

After Sukkot's seven days had run their course, the Holy One said to Israel: My children, I know that throughout Sukkot's seven days you were engaged with offerings for the earth's nations. Now let you and Me rejoice together, and I shall not burden you much except for requiring you to offer Me one bullock and one ram.

When Israel heard God speak thus, they began to praise the Holy One, saying *This is the day which the Lord hath made; we will rejoice and be glad* (*bw*) (Ps. 118:24). R. Abin said: From the word *bw* we could not tell whether we were to rejoice in the day or in the Holy One.[66] But when Solomon came, he made it clear: *We will be glad and rejoice in Thee* (*bk*) (Song 1:4). *In Thee*—in Thee who hast given us thy Torah. *In Thee*—in Thee who deliverest us. R. Isaac said, however: What Solomon had in mind by *bk* was the twenty-two letters which Thou, O God, didst use in writing the Torah for us, the letter *beṯ* equaling two and the letter *kaf* equaling twenty.

10. *These ye shall offer unto the Lord in your appointed seasons* (Num.

65. Which went with the offerings whose purpose was not only to preserve the world but also to cause the nations to change their evil mode of life. So Professor Jakob J. Petuchowski. "The High Priest of the Jews makes prayers . . . on behalf of the whole human race." Philo, *The Special Laws, 1*, 97 (Loeb Classical Library [London and Cambridge, 1937], *7*, 155).

66. The Hebrew *bw* may be rendered "in it" or "in Him."

29:39). R. Ḥanina taught in the name of R. Tanḥum bar R. Yudan: Scripture does not say here of the offerings "These ye have offered," but says *These ye shall offer*. The Torah is thus telling Israel by way of a hint that there will be a second time [for such offerings, the time when the Temple is rebuilt].

R. Berechiah taught in the name of R. Abba bar Kahana: It is written *Thou shalt therefore keep this ordinance in its season from year to year* (Exod. 13:10). The Torah is thus telling Israel by way of a hint that there will be a second time [for the keeping of the ordinance of Passover, the time when the Temple is rebuilt].

R. Judah bar R. Simon said: Scripture entreats God: *Look forth from Thy holy habitation, from heaven* (Deut. 26:15). What does the next verse say? *This day the Lord thy God commandeth thee to do these statutes and ordinances* (Deut. 26:16). Now what does the one verse have to do with the next? This: As long as Israel do the will of God and continue, [even after the destruction of the Temple], to pay their tithes as is proper, so that each one of them is able to say, *I have [in payment] removed the hallowed things—[the tithes]—out of my house* (Deut. 26:13), then, as the Torah tells Israel by way of a hint, there will be a second time when, [because God is looking forth from His holy habitation upon you], *Ye that cleave to the Lord your God will be alive, everyone of you, [as you are] this day* (Deut. 4:4).

SUPPLEMENT 1

And this is the blessing

1. *wherewith Moses blessed* (Deut. 33:1).[1] Let our teacher instruct us: If he who stands before the ark as reader for the congregation[2] makes a mistake [in his reading of the *Tĕfillah*[3]], what is to be done? Our Masters taught as follows: When he who stands before the ark as reader for the congregation makes a mistake, a new reader takes his place. [At what point in the reading of the *Tĕfillah* is the new reader to resume]? R. Jose said: If, [in the reading of the *Tĕfillah*], the first reader makes a mistake in any one of the first three blessings, the new reader must go back and resume the reading with the first of the three blessings.[4] Or if the first reader makes a mistake in any one of the intermediate blessings,[5] the new reader must go back and resume the reading with the first of the intermediate blessings, "Thou favorest man with knowledge."[6] Or if the first reader makes a mistake in any one of the last three blessings, the new reader must go back and resume the reading with the first one of the last blessings, "Accept, O Lord our God, thy people Israel."[7]

Another comment asserts, however: When a reader makes a mistake, a new reader takes his place. At what point in the reading of the *Tĕfillah* does the new one resume? At the beginning of the blessing in which the first reader made the mistake. From whom did our Masters learn that the foregoing procedure is the proper one? From the Fathers of the world, each of whom took particular care to begin his blessing at the point where the Father before him had stopped. For example? Abraham blessed Isaac: *Unto Isaac all that*

1. The reading of Deut. 33:1 ff., which in the Land of Israel, marked the completion of the triennial cycle was an occasion for a Šimḥaṯ Torah, observed triennially. See Ezra Fleischer, *Šimḥaṯ Torah šel 'Ereṣ Yiśra'el, Sinai* 59 (5726/1966), 211 ff. Professor Joseph Heinemann provided the information as well as the reference.

2. Literally "one who passes before the ark."

3. See Glossary.

4. The one ending with the words "Shield of Abraham." See APB, p. 44. Inasmuch as the first three blessings are concerned with the praise of God, the three are considered as though they are one, and the new reader resumes with the first blessing.

5. Blessings 4–15 (or 16, if the blessing against slanderers is included), all of which being personal petitions, are considered as though they are one.

6. APB, p. 46.

7. APB, p. 50, the first of the last three, each of which is an expression of gratitude. See B.Meḡ 18a.

Abraham had he gave (Gen. 25:5). As to what Abraham gave, R. Judah and R. Nehemiah differ. One said: It was the birthright that Abraham gave, as may be inferred from the words "Esau . . . turned over his birthright unto Jacob"[8] (Gen. 25:35). The other said: It was the bestowal of blessing that he gave, as may be inferred from "So God thee give"[9] (Gen. 27:28). When Isaac arose to bless Jacob, he asked himself: "Where am I to begin?" "Where my father stopped." "Where did my father stop?" "With the word 'give.' And so I will begin with it: 'So God thee give' (*ibid.*)." And with what word did Isaac stop in his blessing? With the word "call," as is said "And Isaac did call Jacob, and blessed him" (Gen. 28:1). And so when Jacob arose to bless the Tribes, he did not begin with any word other than "call": "Jacob did call unto his sons" (Gen. 49:1). And with what word did he stop? With the word "this," as is said "Their father spoke unto them, and blessed them, saying, It is with this"[10] (Gen. 49:28). Therefore, when Moses stood up to bless Israel, he said, Jacob concluded with the word "this," and so I shall begin with "this," as is said *This is the blessing* (Deut. 33:1).

2. Another comment. Let our teacher instruct us: He who ascends the dais to read from the Torah—is he permitted to read before he says the appropriate blessing, or is he not? Our Masters taught as follows: First he says the blessing and then he reads from the Torah, as did Moses, who had the privilege of receiving the Torah from the Holy One's hand. First, Moses said the blessing over the Torah, and then he read. What blessing, asked R. Eleazar, did Moses say before reading the Torah? "Blessed art Thou, O Lord, who hast chosen this Torah, hast hallowed it, and taken delight in those who carry out its teaching"—taken delight, that is, not so much in those who study Torah industriously or meditate in it, but in those who carry out its teaching, heeding Torah's precepts for the precepts' sake. Thus to a Jew who says: "I learned no Torah, learned no wisdom—am I then worthless?" the Holy One replies: All Torah, all wisdom, is but a small matter: he who fears Me and carries out Torah's precepts—in the heart of such a man is the entire Torah and entire wisdom, as is said *Wisdom's beginning is the fear of the Lord* (Ps. 111:10), and also *The fear of the Lord is His treasure* (Isa. 33:6).

3. [In another comment, the verse is read] *Because of this blessing wherewith Moses blessed the children of Israel, he became the man of*

8. For if an older son was able to transfer his title to a blessing to his younger brother, how much more so is a father, Abraham, able to bestow it on Isaac, a younger son.

9. Since the word "give" in Gen. 27:28 implies bestowal of blessing, it is assumed that in Gen. 25:5 it likewise implies such bestowal.

10. Here the word *this* is probably taken to refer to Torah (see PR 47:4 [YJS, *18*, 808]) which, in his blessing, Jacob promised was to be given to his sons.

God[11] (Deut. 33:1), "Inasmuch as the Lord waits (*yĕḥakkeh*) for him who bestows grace upon you"[12] (Isa. 30:18). Note, said R. Berechiah, that for the verb "wait" the text does not use the unambiguous *yĕṣappeh*, but the ambiguous *yĕḥakkeh* [which means "wait," but also means "to fish with a hook (*ḥakkah*)]": God is like a fisherman who sits waiting to raise up his catch.[13] Indeed, said R. Aḥa, we find that whenever a man speaks up out of concern for Israel, the Holy One raises him up in the world, for the verse goes on to say "He raises him up who has compassion on you" (*ibid.*). From whose experience, R. Yudan asked,[14] do we know this? From that of Ahimaaz the son of Zadok: *Then said Ahimaaz the son of Zadok: "Let me now run, and bear the king tidings,"* etc. (2 Sam. 18:19). *And the king said: "Is it well with the young man Absalom?"* (2 Sam. 18:29). *And Ahimaaz answered: "I saw a great tumult, but I knew not what it was"* (*ibid.*). *And the king said: "Turn aside, and stand [in a higher rank] here." And he turned aside, and so stood* (2 Sam. 18:30). What is meant, asked R. Abba bar Kahana, by the text's saying *he turned aside, and so stood?* That if Ahimaaz had been a captain, thereupon he was made a prefect, and if he had been a prefect, thereupon he was made commander-in-chief. *And, behold, the Cushite came; and the Cushite said: "Tidings for my lord the king,"* etc. (2 Sam. 18:31). *And the king said unto the Cushite: "Is it well with the young man Absalom?" And the Cushite answered: "The enemies of my lord the king . . . be as that young man is"* (2 Sam. 18:32). *And the king was greatly agitated, and went up to the chamber over the gate*, etc. (2 Sam. 19:1). What is intimated by the words *And the king was greatly agitated?* That he signaled to his spearmen, so said R. Isaac bar Ḥanina, and they pierced the Cushite.

Reasoning from these circumstances *a fortiori*, we come to the following conclusion: If Ahimaaz, the son of Zadok, who, [in order to spare the king], reported neither good nor evil of the king's son was rewarded with such distinction, all the more so is he rewarded who, out of compassion, speaks up in behalf of the Holy One's sons. The truth of this you can see for yourself. In all of Moses' lifetime he was not called "man of God" until he

11. JV: *And this is the blessing, wherewith Moses the man of God blessed the children of Israel.*

12. JV: *And therefore will the Lord wait that He may be gracious unto you.* But *laḥănanḵem*, "that He may be gracious unto you," may be read "to him that is gracious to you," or "bestows grace upon you." Professor Saul Lieberman's suggestion.

13. Whether Israel want it or not, God will be gracious to them.

14. JV: *And therefore will He be exalted that He may have compassion upon you.*

The words "for it is written 'God raises up the man who has compassion upon you' " which follow are deleted as in O_1, C, and Yalḳuṭ.

spoke up compassionately in behalf of Israel. Thus: *Because of this blessing, wherewith Moses blessed the children of Israel, he became the man of God*[15] (Deut. 33:1).

4. *He that withholdeth corn, people shall curse him,* etc. (Prov. 11:26). The words *He that withholdeth corn* apply to the wicked Pharaoh who withheld corn during a time of want;[16] the words *people shall curse him* mean that such as he will become a curse word among the peoples of the world. And the words that follow, *but blessing shall be upon the head of him that selleth it* (*ibid.*), apply to Joseph who sold corn freely during a time of want.

Another comment: The words *He that withholdeth corn* refer to one who withholds the corn which is Torah; the words *people shall curse him* mean that such a one becomes a curse word among people. On the other hand, the words *but blessing shall be upon the head of him that bestoweth it unstintingly*[17] refer to him who unstintingly teaches Torah.

Another comment: The words *He that withholdeth corn* apply to the wicked Balaam who held back from blessing Israel; the words *people shall curse him* mean that he became a curse word among people. On the other hand, the words *but blessing shall be upon the head of him that bestoweth it unstintingly* apply to Moses who unstintingly bestowed blessing upon Israel.

[In connection with the blessing of Israel], R. Isaac declared: Scripture says, *And when Balaam saw that it pleased the Lord to bless Israel,* etc. (Num. 24:1). What was it that Balaam saw? He saw that Moses was to bestow four blessings upon Israel, and that he, Balaam, was expected to bestow seven blessings upon Israel.[18] So he said: If I bestow seven blessings, and Moses bestows four, there will be eleven. Thereupon the Holy One declared: "The eye of this wicked one looks askance at so much blessing for Israel. And so I shall settle for the three blessings he grudgingly brings himself to bestow upon them. Let Moses, however, whose eye lights up when he blesses Israel, come and bestow four blessings upon them." These are the three blessings which Balaam bestowed upon them: *How goodly are thy tents, O Jacob* (Num. 24:5); *Who hath counted the dust of Jacob?* (Num. 23:10); *None hath beheld iniquity in Jacob* (Num. 23:21). And these are

15. In the next verse, Moses goes on to say, *The Lord came to Sinai; after having [first] risen at Seir unto the people thereof* (Deut. 33:2), unto the people of Seir who rejected the Torah unlike the children of Israel—Moses concluded—who did accept it. See PR 21:2/3 (YJS, *18*, 417).

16. The words *the people cried to Pharaoh for bread* (Gen. 41:55) are construed as implying that not until the people came crying did Pharaoh sell them corn. So Mah on Gen. Rabbah 91:5.

17. *Mašbir*, "selleth," is read as though spelled *masbir*, "bestoweth unstintingly."

18. To correspond to the seven altars he built. So Yalḳuṭ, *Bĕraḵah*, 951. See Num. 23:1, 14, 29.

the four blessings which Moses bestowed: *The Lord, the God of your fathers, make you a thousand so many more as ye are, and bless you* (Deut. 1:11); *And Moses and Aaron went into the Tent of Meeting, and came out, and blessed the people* (Lev. 9:23);[19] *And Moses saw all the work, and behold, they had done it; as the Lord had commanded, even so had they done it. And Moses blessed them* (Exod. 39:43). In this last instance, just what was the blessing he bestowed upon them? He began by saying "May it be [God's] will that the Presence rest upon the work of your hands," and he continued in the words of the Psalm [he composed]: "May the graciousness of the Lord our God be upon us; establish Thou also upon us the work of our hands" (Ps. 90:17). And [the fourth blessing that Moses bestowed upon Israel was this one], the one in hand, *And this is the blessing* (Deut. 33:1).

5. In another comment on *And this is the blessing* (Deut. 33:1), the *And* not only points up the blessings but points also to the words of solace that went with them. Inasmuch as at the beginning of Deuteronomy, Moses rebukes Israel—*These are the [sharp] words which Moses spoke unto all Israel* (Deut. 1:1)—therefore at the conclusion of the Book, Moses turns around and blesses them—*And this is the blessing.*

In another comment on *And this is the blessing* (Deut. 33:1) it is noted that the verse could have begun *This*, etc., but in actually beginning with *And this*, etc., it not only points up the blessings, but also points to the words of solace that went with them. For, though Moses speaks sharply to them at the beginning of the lesson for the Sabbath—*the wasting of hunger, and the devouring of the fiery bolt* (Deut. 32:24)—at the conclusion of the lesson he says, *Blessed art thou, O Israel* (Deut. 33:29).

6. In another comment on *And this is the blessing* (*bĕraḵah*) (Deut. 33:1), do not read *bĕraḵah*, ("blessing"), but *bĕreḵah* ("pool"). Even as a pool of water serves to purify persons whose impurity has kept them from the God of Israel, so Moses served to bring near [to God] those who were far [from Him]: early in his life, he brought Bithiah near to Him, [Bithiah, who was the daughter of a Pharaoh],[20] and at the end of his life, he brought Reuben near to Him, [Reuben who had sinned with Bilhah]. For Reuben's sake, he said: *Let Reuben live, and not die*[21] (Deut. 33:6).

7. In further comment on *And "this" is the blessing* (Deut. 33:1), R. Aibu and the Rabbis differ. According to R. Aibu, the utterance of prayer

19. Immediately after the blessing, the glory of the Lord appeared to the people, and fire came forth from before the Lord. See Lev. 9:23–24.

20. Bithiah, Pharaoh's daughter, saved Moses, became a convert, and married Caleb. See 1 Chron. 4:18; and Lev. Rabbah 1:3, M, 11.

21. Reuben will live in this world and not die in the world-to-come, for the incident with Bilhah (Gen. 35:22) will no longer be remembered against him. So Rashi.

precedes bestowal of blessing. What is the proof from Scripture? The verse *Before the soul is wrung out of his body, the prayer of a wholly pious man precedes "this"*[22] (Ps. 32:6)—[that is, precedes his bestowal of blessing]: thus after Moses' prayer came his blessing.

According to the Rabbis, however, the bestowal of blessing precedes the utterance of prayer. And the proof? The verse *Blessed be the Lord for evermore. Amen, and Amen* (Ps. 89:53), which is followed immediately by the words *A prayer of Moses the man of God* (Ps. 90:1).

8. R. Banai taught in the name of R. Huna that Moses wrote thirteen Scrolls of the Law: twelve for the Twelve Tribes and one for the Tribe of Levi. Thus, if any one of the Tribes were considering the excision of even a single word from the Torah, the Tribe of Levi would bring forth its Scroll of the Law and thereby maintain the correctness of the text.[23]

Moses blessed eleven of the Tribes. Why did he not bless the Tribe of Simeon? Because in Moses' heart there was a grievance against Simeon for the deed he was guilty of at Shittim. As Scripture tells us: *When Israel abode in Shittim* (Num. 25:1), *One of the children of Israel,* [*a Simeonite*] . . . *brought unto his brethren a Midianitish woman* (Num. 25:6). On this account, Moses did not bless Simeon. Nevertheless, Moses attached Simeon to the Tribe of Judah, saying, *This one is to be a part of Judah,* [*the one of whom it was said at his birth*] *in a voice which praised the Lord, "The Lord heard* (*šama'*)"[24] (Deut. 33:7). That the verse refers to Simeon is shown by the words *The Lord heard*, for they were the words Simeon's mother used when he was born, saying "The Lord heard (*šama'*) that I am hated" (Gen. 29:33). [In explanation of Simeon's being made a part of Judah], R. Joshua of Sikhnin, citing R. Levi, told a parable of an ox whose actions became savage, and so it was suggested, "Shape the figure of a lion near the ox's trough, so that looking at the figure of the lion, the ox will be afraid and quiet down." If we think of Simeon as the ox[25] and Judah as the lion, we can understand why Moses attached Simeon to Judah. And because Moses did not bless Simeon, no king[26] was appointed out of his Tribe. But does not

22. JV: *For this let every one that is godly pray unto Thee in a time when Thou mayest be found.*

However, R. Aibu renders *'al zo'ṯ*, "for this," as "precedes 'this' " and transposes the phrase to the end of the verse; he renders *kol ḥasiḏ*, "every one that is godly," as "the wholly pious man"; and *mĕṣo'*, "be found," he associates with *mṣh*, "wring"—hence "soul wrung out of the body." See Gen. Rabbah 92:1.

23. See Lieberman, *HJP*, 85–86.

24. JV: *And this for Judah, and he said: Hear, Lord, the voice of Judah.* However, the commentator reads *šĕma'*, "hear," as though vocalized *šama'*, "heard"—hence "the Lord heard." The second occurrence of *Judah* in Deut. 33:7, the commentator construes in its etymological sense of "praise the Lord." See Gen. 29:35.

25. Simeon's star is in the zodiacal sign of the Ox. See MTeh 90:3.

26. "king"—O_1; O and 3 other MSS: "judge," or "ruler."

Scripture say, *Zimri*[27] *reigned seven days in Tirzah* (1 Kings 16:15)? "Maybe so," said R. Yudan, "but a seven-day reign would amount to nothing anyway."

Moses composed eleven Psalms appropriate to the eleven Tribes he blessed. They are as follows: The Psalm *Thou turnest man to contrition, and sayest: "Return, ye children of men"* (Ps. 90:3) is appropriate to the Tribe of Reuben who were contrite before God.[28] The Psalm *O thou that dwellest in the covert of the Most High, and abidest in the shadow of the Almighty* (Ps. 91:1) is appropriate to the Tribe of Levi which abode in the Temple's court [and thus in the shadow of the Almighty]. The Psalm *For the Sabbath day. It is a good thing to give thanks unto the Lord and to sing praises unto Thy name* (Ps. 92:1) is appropriate to the Tribe of Judah, of whom his mother said: " 'This time will I praise the Lord.' Therefore she called his name Judah ('Praise')" (Gen. 29:35). The Psalm *O come, let us sing unto the Lord* (Ps. 95:1)[29] is appropriate to the Tribe of Issachar who devoted themselves to Torah, [singing its words as they studied them].[30] The Psalm *Holiness becometh thy house* (Ps. 93:5) is appropriate to Benjamin in whose territory the Temple was built.[31] The Psalm *Thou God, to whom vengeance belongeth* (Ps. 94:1) is appropriate to the Tribe of Gad who are destined to destroy the foundations of heathen nations.[32]

R. Joshua ben Levi said: Thus far have I heard from my teachers of the Psalms appropriate to several of the Tribes. From here on, reckon the others out for yourself.

9. *A man, God*[33] (Deut. 33:1). When Moses went up on high, he was very much a man; but when he came down below, he was like unto God: *And when Aaron and all the children of Israel saw Moses . . . they were afraid to come nigh him* (Exod. 34:30).

Another comment on *A man, God* (Deut. 33:1). When he fled from Pharaoh's presence, Moses was very much a man; but when the Egyptians sank in the sea, he was like unto God.

In another comment, the phrase *The man of God* (Ps. 90:1) is read *The*

27. Zimri the king is not identified as of the Tribe of Simeon. There may have been however, a tradition that he was, a tradition based perhaps on the fact that Zimri, who brought unto his brethren a Midianite woman, was head of a Simeonite clan (Num. 25:14).

28. See Piska 24.9.

29. See BM's note, and MTeh 90:3.

30. See B.Yoma 26a, Gen. Rabbah 72:5, PR 46:3, and Piska 1.8.

31. See MTeh 78:19.

32. See Rashi on Gen. 49:19.

The reference may be to Elijah (so, my friend Meir Ayyali in an unpublished essay). Cf. MTeh 90:3 (YJS, *13*, 2, 87), and *Yalkuṭ*, *Zo'ṯ hab-bĕrakah*, 900.

33. JV: *the man of God.*

spouse of God, [for *'iš* can mean "spouse" as well as "man"]. R. Jonathan [took the phrase not only as signifying Moses' espousing of the Shekinah—she who is the Divine Presence—but also as intimating that Moses had the authority over the Shekinah that a spouse has over his wife. In confirmation of his reading R. Jonathan] cited from Numbers a verse which asserts the authority of a spouse over his wife, *Her spouse may cause her to rise up, or her spouse may make void her vow*[34] (Num. 30:14). He makes connection of this verse with the phrase *the spouse of God* by pointing to the parallel between the words "rise up" in *Her spouse may cause her to rise up* and Moses' command "Rise up" in the verse "And it came to pass, when the Ark set forward that Moses said, 'Rise up, O Lord'" (Num. 10:35). What is more, according to R. Jonathan, the words *her spouse may void her vow* allude to Moses' voiding of God's vow to destroy Israel for their worship of the golden calf.[35] Having thus turned aside God's wrath,[36] Moses exercised still further his authority as *the spouse of God* by demanding "'Turn, O Lord, thousands of Israel into myriads!' (Num. 10:36)—I mean not to budge from this place until Thou hast promised me to make Israel's thousands into myriads."[37]

10. The words *The blessing wherewith Moses . . . blessed the children of Israel* (Deut. 33:1) indicate that at the time of his death Moses blessed all of Israel with one blessing. A short time before, as the words *Ye are standing this day, all of you, before the Lord your God: your heads, your Tribes, your elders, and your officers, even all the men of Israel, your little ones and your wives* (Deut. 29:9) indicate, he had singled out for blessing each one of the children of Israel, blessing them Tribe by Tribe. Then, at the conclusion of blessing them Tribe by Tribe (Deut. 33:1-27), he had included all Israel in a single blessing: *Blessed art thou, O Israel, who is like unto thee?* (Deut. 33:29). The fact is, R. Abin said, that all of his life Moses had wished to bless Israel, but the angel of death, [knowing that Moses' blessing of Israel would limit death's dominion], did not allow Moses to bestow the blessing. What did Moses finally do? He seized and bound the angel of death, and, having cast him down at his feet, blessed Israel in the very presence of the angel. So, says Scripture, *This is the blessing, wherewith Moses the man of God blessed the children of Israel in the presence*[38] *of his death* (Deut.

34. JV: *Her husband may let it stand, or her husband may make it void.*

35. See Exod. Rabbah 43:4.

36. "Having thus turned God's wrath" is a paraphrase of JV's *and when it rested* (Num. 10:36).

37. "Of righteous men it is written *Thou shalt decree a thing, and He shall establish it unto thee* (Job 22:28)." See B.Shab 59b.

38. JV: *before his death.* The commentator seems to wonder why Scripture finds it necessary to say that Moses blessed Israel before his death, as though he could have done so after his death.

33:1) [and thus saved the people of Israel from death's dominion]. In whose presence was the blessing bestowed? In the presence of the one cast down at Moses' feet. And what blessing did he bestow upon them? *Save Thy people, and bless Thine inheritance; minister unto them, and carry them* [*on in life*] *for ever* (Ps. 28:9).

11. In another comment on *And this is the blessing* (Deut. 33:1), R. Berechiah began his discourse with the verse *Many illustrious sons of mankind have bestowed strength by their blessing*[39] (Prov. 31:29): Moses' predecessors bestowed many blessings, each of them in his own generation, but among all the blessings, no blessing was as excellent as Moses' blessing, the words *thou excellest them all* (*ibid.*) referring to the fact that Moses' blessing excelled all others. When Noah came into the world and blessed his sons, strife followed his blessing, for although he blessed one, he also cursed one. He cursed one son: *And he said, Cursed be Canaan* (Gen. 9:25); and blessed one son: *May Shem be blessed by the Lord God*[40] (Gen. 9:26). When Isaac came and blessed Jacob, a quarrel followed the blessing, for Esau's anger was kindled at Jacob because of the blessing his father bestowed upon Jacob—*And Esau hated Jacob*[41] (Gen. 27:41). When our father Jacob came and blessed the Tribes, a quarrel followed, since he rebuked Reuben for his affair [with Bilhah], saying to him *Unstable as water, have not thou the excellency; because thou wentest up to thy father's bed* (Gen. 49:4).

And from whom did Moses' predecessors learn that each of them was to bestow blessing when there was need for it? They learned to do so from no other than the Holy One. For when Adam came into the world, the Holy One blessed him—*Male and female created He them, and blessed them* (Gen. 5:2)—and the world was maintained by this blessing until the generation of the flood came and brought upon themselves the annulment of the blessing. It was then that the Holy One appeared: *The Lord said, "I will blot out man"* (Gen. 6:7). When Noah [and his company] came forth from the ark, the Holy One, seeing that His previous blessing had been annulled and hence no longer maintained them, appeared at once above Noah and blessed him: *And God blessed Noah and his sons* (Gen. 9:1). The world was maintained by this blessing until Abraham came into the world; for his sake the Holy One added another blessing: *I will make of thee a great nation, and I will bless thee* (Gen. 12:2). Then the Holy One said: Henceforth it is not becoming for Me to be called upon to bestow blessing upon My creatures. And so I shall turn over the bestowal of blessings to thee, [Abraham]—

39. JV: *Many daughters have done valiantly*. But see Piska 12, note 2.

40. JV: *Blessed be the Lord, the God of Shem.*

41. The verse goes on to say *because of the blessing wherewith his father blessed him.*

whomsoever thou bestowest blessing upon, I shall place My seal on the blessing thou bestowest. But since the bestowal of blessing had been turned over to Abraham, why did he not bless Isaac? Because he foresaw concerning Isaac that Esau would issue from him. So he reasoned: If I bestow the blessing upon Isaac, Esau will be blessed through him. Accordingly Abraham said: I have years whose number has already been reckoned out [and before long I shall be gone], whereupon the power to bestow blessings will return to the place it first came from, to its Master [who can tell better than I whom to bless or not bless]. In determining to let the Holy One settle the matter of bestowing blessing or not, with whom may Abraham be compared? With [the tenant in] the parable of a householder who had a vineyard which he had put in the tenant's care. In the vineyard a tree yielding the elixir of life overhung another tree yielding deadly poison. The tenant said: If I cultivate this vineyard, the tree yielding deadly poison will flourish alongside the tree yielding the elixir of life. But if I do not cultivate this vineyard, the tree yielding the elixir of life will die. Finally, he said: I am no more than a tenant. So I shall simply keep an eye on this vineyard—the householder will have to decide in regard to his vineyard whether he will cultivate it or not.

Likewise Abraham said: If I give Isaac my blessing, Esau will be blessed forthwith. But if I do not give Isaac my blessing, it will not be fair to Jacob who, after all, deserves the blessing. However, I have years whose number has already been reckoned out [and before long I shall be gone], whereupon the power to bestow blessing will return to its Master [who knows better than I upon whom to bestow it].

At length, when our father Jacob—peace upon him!—came into the world, he received five blessings: two from his father Isaac, the one that had been given to Abraham, one from an angel, and one from the Holy One. [With regard to the first of the two that came to Jacob from his father], we are told *And Isaac trembled very exceedingly*, etc. (Gen. 27:33). Why, R. Eleazar ben Pědaṯ asked, did our father Isaac tremble very exceedingly at the instant he was about to bestow the blessing? Because he had a vision of the Day of Judgment. When he was about to bless Esau, he did not know how depraved Esau had become. Since Esau used to come and inquire of his father whether water and salt do or do not require tithing, Isaac reasoned: If Esau is willing to tithe water and salt, he must be all the more willing to give all the other kinds of tithes. But when Esau's evil deeds were made known to Isaac, he suddenly had a vision of the Day of Judgment that was awaiting Esau,[42] and so he trembled exceedingly, as is said *And Isaac trembled very exceedingly*, [and thereupon declared of Jacob], *Yea, and he shall be*

42. See Gen. Rabbah 67:2.

blessed[43] (*ibid.*). Thus Jacob was given the first of his father's two blessings. The second of his father's blessings is noted as follows: *Isaac called Jacob, and blessed him* (Gen. 28:1). Next came the blessing that originally had been given to Abraham: *And give thee the blessing of Abraham* (Gen. 28:4). Then came the angel's blessing: *And Jacob asked him, and said: "Tell me, I pray thee, thy name? . . . And* [*the angel*] *blessed him there* (Gen. 32:30). Finally came the Holy One's blessing: *And God appeared unto Jacob again . . . and blessed him* (Gen. 35:9). When Jacob came to bless the Tribes, he blessed them with the five blessings which he possessed, and added a sixth blessing, as is said *All these* [*had already been given to*] *the Twelve Tribes of Israel, and also this one which their father was to speak unto them, as he blessed them* (Gen. 49:28). What is implied by *and also this one*? That he gave the Tribes a sixth blessing. When Moses came, he gave Israel a seventh blessing, as is said *And this is the blessing* (Deut. 33:1), meaning that he was adding a blessing to all the preceding blessings.

[There is another tradition, however, concerning Moses and the number of blessings he bestowed upon Israel, a tradition that has to do with Balaam's grudging bestowal of blessing upon Israel]. When the wicked Balaam came to bless Israel, he should have bestowed upon them seven blessings to correspond to the seven altars.[44] Grudgingly he bestowed only three blessings upon Israel, but Balak reproached him even for bestowing these, saying *Thou hast already blessed them these three times* (Num. 24:10). As for the Holy One, He said to Balaam: "O wicked one, thine eye looks askance at bestowal of blessing upon Israel. And therefore I shall not put it in thy power to finish out thy blessings of Israel." Then came our teacher Moses, his eye full of blessings, and he blessed Israel. It was Moses whom Solomon had in mind when he said, *He that hath a bountiful eye, shall be blessed* (Prov. 22:9), for the latter words are to be read not *shall be blessed*, but "will bless"[45]—that is, our teacher Moses will bless. Indeed, so full of blessings was Moses' eye that he bestowed upon Israel the four further blessings which Balaam had begrudged them. The four blessings were these: *And Moses saw all the work . . . And Moses blessed them* (Exod. 39:43); *And Moses and Aaron went into the Tent of Meeting, and came out, and blessed the people* (Lev. 9:23); *The Lord, the God of your fathers, make you a thousand times so many more as ye are* (Deut. 1:11); and the one he finished with, *And this is the blessing* (Deut. 33:1). Hence Scripture: *Many illustrious sons of*

43. Isaac's blessing in Gen. 27:28 is not reckoned, since it had been bestowed in error.

44. See S1.4.

45. A slight change in the vowels of *ybrk*, "shall be blessed," makes the second reading possible.

mankind have bestowed strength by their blessing, but thou excellest them all (Prov. 31:29).

12. *Wherewith Moses . . . blessed* (Deut. 33:1). It was fitting for Moses to bless Israel, because [his love for them was so strong that] at every instant he was ready to give up his life for their sake.[46]

13. *The spouse of God* (Deut. 33:1). Resh Laḳish said: Were it not written in Scripture, it would be impossible to say such a thing as this: that just as a man gives an order to his wife to have something done, so Moses gave orders to the Holy One to have things done.[47] It was Israel's merit that conferred such power upon Moses—*Because of the children of Israel* (*ibid.*).

14. *Before his death* (Deut. 33:1). Can anyone possibly imagine such a thing as Moses' blessing Israel *after* his death? What, then, is intimated by the words *before his death*? That in the very presence of the angel of death, Moses blessed Israel. For when the Holy One said to him—to Moses—*And die in the mount* (Deut. 32:50), the angel of death supposed that authority over Moses' life had been given him then and there, and so the angel of death came and stationed himself directly above him. Thereupon Moses declared to him: Long ago the Holy One promised me that [when I die] He would not give thee the power to take me.[48] Thereupon, in the very presence of the angel of death, as is said *before his death* (*ibid.*), Moses blessed Israel.

15. *The Lord came unto Sinai, after having* [*first*] *risen at Seir, then having shined forth at Mount Paran*[49] (Deut. 33:2). The verse indicates that the Holy One went around among all the peoples of the world to have them accept the Torah, but they would not accept it. With regard to this matter Scripture says, *All the kings of the earth praised Thee when they heard the words of Thy mouth* (Ps. 138:4), a statement which, until Micah the Morashtite came and explained what really happened, might have led to the conclusion that upon hearing God's words the peoples had been willing to accept the Torah. Micah quoted God as saying, however, *I will execute*

46. The words *before his death* (Deut. 33:1) may have suggested to the commentator the idea that Moses was ever ready to lay down his life for Israel whom he loved.

47. The Hebrew text reads "so the Holy One gave orders to Moses to have things done," which appears to be a euphemism employed to avoid what is outwardly a blasphemous statement, that a mortal man could give an order to God. See S1.9.

48. Moses is said to have died *by the mouth of the Lord* (Deut. 34:5), a statement taken to mean that the angel of death exercised no power over Moses. See B.BB 17a.

49. Seir is a reference to Edom, and Paran to Ishmael. See Rashi; and PR (YJS, *18*, 417, n. 11). JV: *The Lord came from Sinai, and rose from Seir unto them, He shined forth from Mount Paran.*

vengeance in anger and fury upon the peoples, because they hearkened not (Micah 5:14). Thus you learn that the peoples heard God's words, but did not accept them. It was in regard to God's offer of the Torah to the peoples that David raised His voice in praise, saying *Thou art the God that dost wonders; Thou hast offered to make known Thy strength among the peoples* (Ps. 77:14), *Thy strength* here clearly referring to Torah, as in the verse "The Lord gave strength unto His people" (Ps. 29:11).[50] Hence David was exclaiming to the Holy One: O what wonders didst thou wish to do in Thy world when Thou didst offer to make known Thy Torah to the peoples of the world!

R. Abbahu said: It was revealed and known to Him who had only to speak to have the world come into being that the peoples of the world would not accept the Torah [when He offered it to them]. Why, then, did He offer it? Because if He did not, then they would have cause to reproach Him. And this is the way the Holy One always does things. He does not impose punishment before making sure that His creatures have no cause to reproach Him. Only after He has made sure does He banish them from the world: the Holy One does not proceed with arbitrary power against His creatures.

Another explanation: Why did He make sure with regard to His offering of the Torah that the peoples of the earth would have no cause to reproach Him? Because of the merit of the Fathers.[51]

16. The words *He* 'A<u>T</u>A' *among the myriads holy* (Deut. 33:2) indicate that the Holy One stood out[52] in the midst of His host. Come and see that the nature of the Holy One is not like the nature of flesh-and-blood. The nature of flesh-and-blood is such that within the [range, say, of a mortal king's] entourage, there are apt to be men who are more comely or have greater strength than he, men who are shorter or taller than he. Not so the Holy One—He stands out, unique among all His myriads. *Who is like unto Thee, O Lord, among the mighty?* (Exod. 15:11).

17. The saying *At His right hand was a fiery law unto them* (Deut. 33:1) indicates that the Torah was given by God's right hand.

Since the Torah is called *fiery law*, said R. Johanan, he who is about to engage in the study of Torah should consider himself as standing within fire.[53] Hence Scripture says, *At His right hand a fiery law unto them.*

18. *Yea, He showeth love to the peoples* (Deut. 33:3) [by giving them

50. See MTeh 28:6.

51. Abraham and Isaac being the forebears of Ishmael and Esau.

52. The word *'aṯa'*, "come," is construed as the Aramaic *'aṯa'*, "sign," hence, "stood out." See Piska 12.22.

53. Even as fire is given from heaven, so is Torah; even as fire is a source of life, so is Torah; even as those who make use of fire in their work (e.g. a blacksmith) bear the signs of fire upon their persons, so are disciples of the wise recognized by their walk, their speech, and their dress. See Sif Deut. 343, ed. Finkelstein, 399–400.

suzerainty over Israel].[54] Hence Moses dared to reproach the Holy One: Master of the universe, [by showing such love], Thou settest two yokes upon Thy children—that of Torah and that of enslavement to the kingdoms. The Holy One replied to Moses: *All His holy ones will be in thy hand* (*ibid.*)—every one who engages in Torah will be safe in thy hand. In the words that follow—*They who wear themselves out to get to thy feet*[55] (*ibid.*)—God was saying: As for those whose feet are worn with travel because they have sought [thee or the masters who succeed thee in order] to study Torah, from such as they I will remove the yoke of the kingdoms.

The words [*They who wear themselves out*, etc.] are also rendered *Though they are smitten*,[56] *still at thy feet*—that is, even though they are smitten like slaves, [they will remain at thy feet], *weighing thy words* (*ibid.*), and they will not stir from thy tabernacles of Torah.

19. *Moses commanded us a law, an inheritance of the congregation of Jacob* (Deut. 33:4). But who are of *the congregation of Jacob?* Only such as occupy themselves with Torah's words deserve to share in the inheritance of Jacob, as is said *If thou delight thyself in the Lord, then I will make thee to ride upon the high places of the earth, and I will feed thee of the inheritance of Jacob thy father*[57] (Isa. 58:14).

20. The word *there* in the verse *The small and the great are there alike*, etc. (Job 3:19), said R. Johanan, refers to the day of death, for even if a man be wise, or strong, or rich, he still cannot save himself on the day of death, as is said *There is no man that hath power over the wind . . . neither hath he power over the day of death* (Eccles. 8:8). As for the word *small* (Job 3:19), it is taken to refer to king David—peace upon him!—who is called "small" in the verse "And David was the small one" (1 Sam. 17:14), and the word *great* (Job 3:19) is taken to refer to Moses, of whom it is said "Moreover the man Moses was very great," etc. (Exod. 11:3). *The servant* in the words that follow, *and the servant is free from his master* (Job 3:19), is taken to refer to Israel, for when a man dies he is free of God's commandments [that governed him in this world].

The death of Moses is mentioned ten times in Scripture: (1) *Behold, thy days approach that thou must die* (Deut. 31:14); (2) *and die in the mount* (Deut. 32:50); (3) *I must die* (Deut. 4:22); (4) *I know that after my death* (Deut. 31:29); (5) *how much more after my death* (Deut. 31:27); (6) *before his death* (Deut. 33:1); (7) *So Moses . . . died there* (Deut. 34:5); (8) *and Moses was a hundred and twenty years old when he died* (Deut. 34:7); (9) *Moses My servant is dead* (Josh. 1:2); (10) *Now it*

54. See Rashi. JV: *Yea, He loveth the peoples.*
55. JV: *and they sit down at thy feet.*
56. *Tukku* may mean "wear themselves out" or "are smitten."
57. The inheritance is not, so to speak, automatically transmitted.

came to pass after the death of Moses (Josh. 1:1). [But the harsh decree of death for Moses was not finally sealed until the High Court revealed itself to him and decreed: "It is My decree that you should not pass over"].[58] It was then that the Holy One said to Moses: Moses, thou didst exalt Me above all the beings of the world and didst make Me the only object of love in My world. I, for My part, shall exalt thee above all the inhabitants of the world, and I shall make thy name so known in My world that all will know there can be none like thee in this world. And in the world-to-come I shall raise thee above all the righteous—all of them: I shall have thee own fifty-five more rivers of balsam oil than they,[59] as is said *Fifty-five rivers*[60] (*lhnḥyl*) *to him that loves Me* (*'hby*) *with such an abundance* [*of love*] (Prov. 8:21).

[Abraham, Isaac, and Jacob each loved God in his own way. So did Moses. But such was the abundance of Moses' love of God that it included not only his own way of loving God but the ways of Abraham, Isaac, and Jacob as well. The proof is as follows]: The letter *'alef* in the word *'hby*, "him that loves Me," stands for Abraham; the letter *he'* stands for Isaac; the letter *beṯ* for Jacob; and the letter *yoḏ* for Moses himself. And how do we know that the letter *'alef* refers to Abraham? Because it is said "The seed of Abraham who loves Me (*'hby*)" (Isa. 41:8). And how do we know that the letter *he'* in *'hby* stands for Isaac? Because it is said "And, behold (*hnh*) Isaac" (Gen. 26:8).[61] [To understand how great was the merit of Abraham], consider that the Holy One created the world because of Abraham, as is said *The coming into being of heaven and earth was on account of hbr'm*[62] (Gen. 2:4), the letters of *hbr'm* being the very letters that make up the name Abraham (*'brhm*). [To understand how great was] the merit of Isaac who offered himself bound on the altar, consider that because of Isaac the Holy One will quicken the dead, as is said *From heaven did the Lord look down to hear the groaning of the one bound,* [*and will look down*] *to free the children of men from death* (Ps. 102:21). And how do we know that the letter *beṯ* in *'hby* refers to Jacob? The verse *O house* (*beṯ*) *of Jacob, come*

58. "But the harsh decree of death . . . My decree that you should not pass over"—parallel in Deut. Rabbah 11:10.

59. Thirteen such rivers are said to be bestowed upon the righteous (see Tanḥuma, *Bĕre'šiṯ*, 1; and B.Ta 25a); the number corresponds to God's thirteen attributes (Exod. 34:6–7).

60. The numerical value of the letters *he'* (5) and *nun* (50) in *lhnḥyl*, "give," add up to fifty-five; and the letters *nḥl* are taken to mean "river." JV: *That I may cause those that love me to inherit substance.*

61. The equivalent of *hnh* in Aramaic being *ha*, that is, a way of spelling the letter *he'*. Or [the author suggests that the additional *he'* of the fuller form *hnh* (instead of the shorter form *hn*) is what implies the connection with Isaac. L.N.]

62. JV: *These are the generations of the heaven and the earth when they were created* (*hbr'm*).

ye, and let us walk in the light of the Lord (Isa. 2:5). Even as *beṯ* signifies both letter and "house" (*beṯ*), so the name *Jacob* signifies both the man and the house of Israel (*beṯ Yiśra'el*), as intimated by *How goodly are thy tents, O Jacob* (Num. 24:5). And how do we know that the letter *yoḏ* in *'hby* refers to Moses himself? The verse *But Moses' hands* (*wyḏy*) *were weighty* [*with God*][63] (Exod. 17:12). Even as the *yoḏ* signifies both the letter and "hand" (*yaḏ*), *Moses* signifies both the man and the Torah, as is said *Remember ye the Torah of Moses My servant* (Mal. 3:22). Or: Read not only *yoḏ* but also *yaḏ*, "hand," for not only did the hand of Moses receive the Torah, but the numerical value of *yoḏ* is ten which indicates the Ten Commandments, the *fiery law*, of which Scripture says, *his right hand a fiery law unto them* (Deut. 33:2).

Moses replied sadly to the Holy One: Among sixty myriads of the children of those who hallowed Thy name, I praised Thee, saying *Behold* (*hn*)! *unto the Lord thy God belongeth the heaven, and the heaven of heavens*, etc. (Deut. 10:14). And with the same word [*Behold* (*hn*)! *thy days approach that thou must die* (Deut. 31:14)], Thou didst decree death for me. God replied: Even as thou didst praise Me [in this world], so in the time-to-come fifty-five myriads of the completely righteous will be praising thee from their midst.

[And how do we know that there will be fifty-five myriads]? Because the sum of the numerical values of the letters in the word *hn*, "Behold!" is fifty-five.

63. So that the children of Israel discomfited Amalek.

SUPPLEMENT 2

Another Piska [for Sukkot][1]

1. R. Ḥinena bar Papa—some say R. Simla'i—commented as follows: In the time-to-come, the Holy One will bring out a Scroll of Torah, hold it to His bosom, and say, "Whosoever has occupied himself with a Scroll such as this, let him come and get his reward." At these words all the peoples of the world will come together in a motley crowd, as is said *All the peoples come together in motley: Let them assemble in kingdoms, however. Who among them can declare* [*that they have occupied themselves with*] *"This"? Let them at least lay claim to* [*fulfillment of commands*] *before "This" was given.*[2] *Then let them bring evidence* [*that those previous commands had been fulfilled*], *and thus be justified* [*in seeking reward*],[3] etc. (Isa. 43:9). By these words the Holy One meant: Come not before Me in motley, but let each and every people come by itself with its own archivists: By "people" (*l'wm*), we are to understand "kingdom," for in the words *Let them assemble in l'wmym, l'wmym* is read as in the verse "one kingdom (*l'wm*) shall be stronger than the other kingdom" (Gen. 25:23). Does God say "Come not before Me in motley" because the eye of heaven can be confused by the diversity of mankind? No: His command intends that mankind separate into their respective kingdoms, so that being unmingled they will be able to understand what is said to them, etc. This comment goes on as at the beginning of the tractate 'Ăḇoḏah zarah (2a-b) and continues to the passage where it is asked "What did He seek in Seir? What did He seek in Paran"?[4] By these questions concerning God's seeking, Scripture informs us that the Holy One had gone around and offered the Torah to all the peoples of the world, but they did not accept it: finally, it was Israel who came and accepted the Torah. Therefore the Holy One will be moved to compassion for Israel [on the Day of Judgment], as is said *There shall be a sukkah for shade from the searing heat of the Day* [*of Judgment*][5] (Isa. 4:6). For, so

1. The discourse is probably intended for the second day of Sukkot.

2. The demonstrative pronoun "This" alludes to Torah (see PR 47:4 [YJS, *18*, 808]). The commands *before "This" was given* are the commands given in Noah's time, which applied to all mankind, and not to Israel alone. See Piska 12.1.

3. JV: *All the nations are gathered together, and the peoples are assembled; who among them can declare this, and announce to us former things? Let them bring their witnesses that they may be justified.*

4. See Deut. 33:2. Seir is Edom, representing Rome's predecessors; and Paran represents Ishmael's descendants (see Gen. 21:21).

5. JV: *There shall be a booth for a shadow in the daytime from the heat.*

taught R. Levi, the Holy One says of him who fulfilled the command of the sukkah in this world, "Since he fulfilled the command to dwell in a sukkah—[i.e. in awareness of God's presence]—in this world, I shall shelter him from the fire of the Day of Judgment." Note, according to R. Yannai and Resh Laḳish, [that Gehenna is here identified not as a place, but as a time—specifically a day], as in the verse *Behold, the day cometh, it burneth as a furnace* (Mal. 3:19).

In not putting the sun in the heaven that we mortals see, the Holy One showed great consideration for the world we live in. The Holy One set the luminaries in heaven's firmament, as is said *And God set them* (Gen. 1:17): note, however, taught R. Yannai and R. Ḥanina, that Scripture does not say He set them "in heaven," but *in the firmament of the heaven. What* is *the firmament of the heaven?* It is the firmament which is above the heaven [we mortals see]. As R. Abbahu pointed out: There is an explicit verse to the effect that the Holy One put the sun in the firmament, the verse *Thou art the Lord, even Thou alone; Thou hast made heaven* (Neh. 9:6). Here the verse does not go on to say "with all their host," but proceeds to say *the heaven of heavens*, and then goes on *with all their host.* Accordingly, where are you led to conclude is the Holy One's host set? [Not in heaven, but] in *the heaven of heavens*, a phrase which makes you understand that the Holy One put the sun in the upper firmament. Why in the upper? Had it been put in this firmament, the one we mortals see, the sun, following its course, would in its summer solstice have burned up the creatures below. God, therefore, set it in the upper firmament.

You are to know that it is a journey of five hundred years between firmament and firmament and that the sun makes this journey covered as with a tent: *In the heavens hath He set a tent for the sun* (Ps. 19:5). Thus the sun goes forth on its journey of one thousand and five hundred years,[6] its intensity dimmed both by its being enveloped and by the length of its journey so that it can do no injury to creatures below. But in the time-to-come the Holy One will roll open the upper firmament, as is said *The heaven shall be unrolled as a scroll* (Isa. 34:4), and will remove the tent from over the sun, which, following its course, will requite the wicked [by consuming them in its summer solstice], as is said *Behold, the day cometh, it burneth as a furnace; and all the proud, and all that work wickedness, shall be stubble; and the day that cometh shall set them ablaze . . . that it shall leave them neither root nor branch* (Mal. 3:19). In that day the Holy One will make a sukkah for the righteous and hide them therein, as is said *He hideth me in His sukkah in the day of trouble*, etc. (Ps. 27:5), and as is also said *There*

6. From the upper firmament to the first is a journey of 500 years; across the first firmament, another 500 years; from the first firmament to the earth, another 500 years. See P.Ber 9:1, 13a.

shall be a sukkah for shade from the searing heat of the day (Isa. 4:6)—that is, from the searing heat of the Day of Judgment. According to the Sages, however, the fire in the time-to-come will be [not from the sun but] from Gehenna, of which it is said *The Lord, whose fire is in Zion, and His furnace in Jerusalem* (Isa. 31:9).

2. It[7] is written *Behold, the day of the Lord cometh, when thy spoil shall be divided in the midst of thee* (Zech. 14:1). This verse is to be read in the light of what the Psalmist says, *O God the Lord, the strength of my salvation, who hast sheltered my head as in a sukkah in the day of battle* (Ps. 140:8). R. Phinehas the Priest ben Ḥama commented: Where were Israel when Pharaoh's hosts shot their arrows? The Holy One enclosed Israel with clouds of glory, sheltering them therewith as in a sukkah so that the arrows could not injure them, as is said "Thy cloud standeth over them" (Num. 14:14). Hence it is said *Who hast sheltered my head as in a sukkah in the day of battle* (Ps. 140:8).

Another comment on *Who hast sheltered my head as in a sukkah in the day of battle* (Ps. 140:8). The Holy One meant: "My head as well as Israel's is thus sheltered." For in the time-to-come, when all the nations of the earth gather against the Land of Israel and make war upon its people—*I will gather all nations against Jerusalem to battle* (Zech. 14:2)—what will the Holy One do? He will go forth and fight against the nations, as is said *Then shall the Lord go forth, and fight against those nations* (Zech. 14:3). In what way will He fight? In the way He fought in the day of Pharaoh, as is said *As when he fought in the day of battle* (*ibid.*). And what will He do? He will shelter as in a sukkah the heads of Israel, as is said *Who hast sheltered my head as in a sukkah in the day of battle* (*nešeḳ*) (Ps. 140:8). What is the literal meaning of *nešeḳ*? "Contact,"[8] so said R. Samuel bar Naḥmani: it refers to the day when the two worlds, this world and the world-to-come, will be brought into contact (*yaššiḳu*) with each other. And what is the day referred to? [The Day of Judgment, as is said] *Behold, the day of the Lord cometh* (Zech. 14:1).

Another comment on *Behold, the day of the Lord cometh.* Why will the nations come to Jerusalem on that day? R. Samuel bar Naḥmani said: Because Gehenna is set in Jerusalem where the Holy One will sit in judgment upon them, declare them guilty, and send them down into Gehenna. And whence the proof that Gehenna is set in Jerusalem? From the words *Saith the Lord, whose fire is in Zion, and His furnace in Jerusalem* (Isa. 31:9). How will the Holy One get the nations to come to Jerusalem? He will beguile them and bring them up to Jerusalem, and there He will judge them. R. Samuel

7. This verse, which in the Hebrew text concludes Sec. 1, obviously forms the beginning of Sec. 2.

8. The word *ḳĕrab̲*, "battle" (Zech. 14:3), may also mean "contact."

bar Naḥmani said: In the place that the robber despoiled, there will he be crucified. Out of Jerusalem the nations brought forth their spoil and led Israel into captivity: hence they will be crucified in Jerusalem, as is said *Behold, the day of the Lord cometh, [O Jerusalem], when thy spoil (šĕlaleḵ) shall be divided up in the midst of thee* (Zech. 14:1). R. Phinehas the Priest ben Ḥama commented: What is meant by *šĕlaleḵ*? "The spoil which was taken from thee." Why is this uncommon word for "spoil" used here? Because its components are such as to intimate "that which was formerly thine" (*šellaḵ*) as well as "that which was never thine" (*šello' laḵ*). For when the nations of the world came up to Jerusalem and laid it waste, they proceeded first to empty it of all of Israel's wealth, as is said *He hath set me down as an empty vessel* (Jer. 51:34). Then the nations [invaded the Temple and] overturned all of its precious vessels, broke them up, and took the pieces away—they left nothing at all in the Temple, but looted it of every single thing, as is said *That which was of gold, in gold, and that which was of silver, in silver, the captain of the guard looted* (2 Kings 25:15). *And the brazen sea and the oxen*[9] *. . . did the Chaldeans break in pieces, and carried the brass of them to Babylon* (2 Kings 25:13). Thereupon the Holy One said to Israel: As ye live, you will lose nothing. It now lies with Me to bring gold to you: *For brass I will bring gold, and for iron will I bring silver* (Isa. 60:17). Israel asked: Master of the universe, but suppose the nations come up again, wage war against us, and take away all that we have, of what avail the gold to us? The Holy One replied: As ye live, there will be no more war, as is said *And they shall beat their swords into plowshares, and their spears into pruning hooks; nation shall not lift up sword against nation, nor learn war any more* (Isa. 2:4); also *I shall see to it that the orders of the day concerning thee are peace*[10] (Isa. 60:17). Further it is said *He maketh wars to cease unto the ends of the earth; He breaketh the bow, and cutteth the spear in sunder; He burneth the chariots in the fire* (Ps. 46:10). How else is *He maketh wars to cease* to be understood except that God is saying "I shall have you live in unceasing tranquillity?" But Israel will say to the Holy One:[11] Granted that Thou wilt make cease the wars of nations of the earth against us and that Thou wilt doubtless bring us gold to replace our brass. But what of the blood that was spilt? What wilt Thou do? God replied: As for an assurance of wealth, I have already given you My word. But the blood weighs sorely upon Me. Indeed, I can leave unpunished everything else that needs punishment, but the spilling of Israel's blood I shall not leave unpunished, as is said *I will leave unpunished, but their blood I will not leave*

9. The words *and the oxen* are not in MT.

10. See Rashi and Ḳimḥi. JV: *I will also make thy officers peace.*

11. The words "But the Holy One said" are emended to read "But Israel will say to the Holy One." See BM's note.

unpunished;[12] *for the Lord sitteth in Zion* (Joel 4:21). The fact that the words *The Lord sitteth in Zion* are not only the last in the verse but also the last in the Book signifies that the last act on the Day of Judgment will be God's sitting in Zion. Until then, God's judgment upon mankind will be held in abeyance—"Not until then," God says, "shall I sit in Zion and judge the nations and pronounce the judgment they deserve," as is said *There will I sit to judge all the nations round about* (Joel 4:12). Israel asked Him: Master of the universe, when will this judgment take place? He replied: In this matter you have no choice but to wait for Me, as is said *Therefore wait ye for Me, saith the Lord, until the day that I rise up to the prey; for My determination is to gather the nations*, etc. (Zeph. 3:8). They asked Him: And how will judgment be carried out? Will the nations be put in the hands of the angels for punishment, or will they be punished in Gehenna? The Holy One replied: It will all be left to you. You will have the authority to impose on them any form of death you wish, as is said *The avenger of blood shall himself put the murderer to death* (Num. 35:15). Nay more!—[you will be acting in My behalf]. Any one in this world who has waged war against you will be deemed to have waged it against Me. Indeed the Holy One said much the same thing to Moses: *Avenge the children of Israel of the Midianites* (Num. 31:2), but then, so that Israel would be acting in His behalf, the Holy One had Moses order Israel *to execute the Lord's vengeance on Midian* (Num. 31:3). On the other hand, [because certain Israelites did not come to fight beside Deborah against Israel's enemies], she contemned them [because, as she said, they had not fought in the Lord's behalf]: *Because they came not to the help of the Lord, to the help of the Lord against the mighty* (Judg. 5:23). [You must expect, the Holy One warns Israel, that as in the past], so in the future, all the peoples of the earth will stand together to cut you off from being a nation. Thus the Psalmist: *They have said: "Come, and let us cut them off from being a nation; that the name of Israel may be no more in remembrance*" (Ps. 83:5). They will stand together not only against you, but against Me also, as is said *The kings of the earth stand up, and the rulers take counsel together, against the Lord, and against His anointed* (Ps. 2:2). And what have I decided to do to them? I shall turn them over into your hand, and you will take vengeance upon them in My behalf, as is said "I will lay My vengeance upon Edom by the hand of My people Israel" (Ezek. 25:14). *This shall come to pass on that day when there shall not be light, yet precious things will be perspicuous*[13] (Zech. 14:6).

3. Another comment: *There shall be a* [*sheltering*] *sukkah for shade in*

12. JV: *I will hold their blood as innocent that I have not held as innocent.*

13. JV: *And it shall come to pass in that day that there shall not be light, but heavy clouds and thick.* See, however, Piska 4.7 and PR 14:13 (YJS, *18*, 289, n. 87).

the daytime from the heat (Isa. 4:6). Whosoever obeys the command to dwell in the sukkah—[that is, in the awareness of My presence]—in this world, is so sheltered from malevolent things that they will not be able to hurt him. Thus the Psalmist: *With His pinions He will shelter thee as in a sukkah* (Ps. 91:4).

Another comment: *There shall be a sukkah for shade in the daytime from the heat* (Isa. 4:6). Whosoever obeys the command to dwell in the sukkah in this world, the Holy One will give him a portion in the time-to-come, in such a sukkah as Sodom was, ["the Garden of the Lord (Gen. 13:10)," as Scripture tells us, before it turned to iniquity]. This sukkah of Sodom, the Holy One will divide into many, many portions for the righteous to dwell in. Thus the Psalmist: *God spoke to His holy one, "When I exult, when I divide into portions, when I mete out the valley of 'sukkah upon sukkah'* "[14] (Ps. 60:8). Who is the *holy one* in the words *The Lord spoke to His holy one?* It is—so said R. Joshua bar Nehemiah—our father Abraham, peace upon him! By *When I exult*, God was referring to His exultation when His kingdom will shine forth in the world. At that time, [says the Holy One], *I divide into portions*: "I will divide Sodom, 'the Garden of the Lord,' into many, many portions for thy children." And the proof that it is the division of Sodom that God intends? The words *When I mete out the valley of "sukkah upon sukkah."* In these words God was saying: I shall divide into portions the extraordinary sukkah of Sodom, a sukkah covered with the foliage of seven trees, the foliage of one shading the one below it, and so on: the foliage of the vine, fig, pomegranate, peach, almond, nut, and the palm shading all the inhabitants below.

[In regard to Sodom's sevenfold shade], R. Isaac said in the name of R. Johanan ben Šahina:[15] There is a kind of falcon [so keen-sighted] that even when it soars twenty-five miles up in the sky, it can see what is on the ground, as R. Meir, R. Jose, and the Sages agreed. According to one, however, it can see down below on the ground a vessel only three handbreadths wide. According to another, even a vessel a handbreadth and a half wide. And according to still another, even a vessel three fingerbreadths wide.[16] [Concerning His reward for the righteous], the Holy One declared: Whosoever obeys the command to dwell in a sukkah in this world, to such a man I will give a portion in the sukkah of Sodom whose foliage is so luxuriant that

14. JV: *God spoke in His holiness, that I would exult; that I would divide Shechem, and mete out the valley of Succoth.* But *Shechem* may be construed as "portion," and the plural *Succoth* may be rendered "sukkah upon sukkah."

15. "Šahina"—parallel in Lev. Rabbah M, 102; S: "Šiṭnah," "hatred," an implausible name. *Šahina* (Persian-Arabic *shăhīn*) is a gerfalcon, a large species of hunting falcon.

16. See Lev. Rabbah 5:2, M, 102–03.

no bird, [however keen-sighted], can peer through it. As Scripture says, *That path no bird of prey knoweth; neither hath the falcon's eye seen it* (Job 28:7).

4. In another comment the verse is read *There shall be a sukkah for shade from the searing heat of the Day* [*of Judgment*] (Isa. 4:6). R. Levi said: In this world, whosoever obeys the command to dwell in a sukkah—[that is, in awareness of the presence of God]—him, in the world-to-come, the Holy One will have dwell, [safe from His fiery wrath], in a sukkah made of the Leviathan's skin, as is said in the verse in which God asked Job: [Dost thou not realize that even the tiniest gap in] *the walls of the sukkah* [*of the righteous*] *will be filled in with skin from the Leviathan?*[17] (Job 40:31).

You find that when affliction came upon Job, he stood up and raised a cry against the measure of justice, saying *Oh that I knew where I might find Him* (Job 23:3), *I would know the words which He would answer me* (Job 23:5). The Holy One replied: [In the world-to-come thou wilt find Me attentive upon the righteous]. For with skin from the Leviathan, I shall make for the righteous in the world-to-come a sukkah [impervious to My fiery wrath]. Even if the smallest strip be lacking to fill a gap in the walls of the sukkah, I shall have the gap filled in only with skin from the Leviathan, as is said [Dost thou not realize that even the tiniest gap in] *the walls of the sukkah* [*of the righteous*] *will be filled in with skin from the Leviathan?*[18] (Job 40:31). Lest you suppose that the skin of the Leviathan is not something extraordinary, consider what R. Phinehas the Priest ben Ḥama and R. Jeremiah citing R. Samuel bar R. Isaac said of it: The reflection of the Leviathan's fins makes the disk of the sun dim by comparison, so that it is said of each of the fins "It telleth the sun that it shines weakly" (Job 9:7). For *The* [*Leviathan's*] *underparts, the reflections thereof,* [*surpass*] *the sun: where it lieth upon the mire, there is a shining of yellow gold*[19] (Job 41:22). It is said, moreover, that the words *Where it lieth upon the mire, there is a shining of yellow gold* (*ḥaruṣ*) mean [not only that the Leviathan's underparts shine, but] that the very place it lies upon is *ḥaruṣ*—that is, golden. Hence *Where it lieth upon the mire, there is a shining of yellow gold.* Still further it is said: Ordinarily, there is no place more filthy than the one where a fish lies. But the place where the Leviathan lies is purer even than yellow gold. Hence *Where it lieth upon the mire, there is a shining of yellow gold* (Job 41:22). *The rows of his shields*—that is, of his scales—*are*

17. See B.BB 75a.

18. JV: *Canst thou fill his skin with barbed irons?* But *tĕmalle'*, "canst thou fill," is apparently read as a third person feminine with "skin" as the subject, even though "skin" is generally masculine; and *śukkoṯ*, "barbed irons," is read *sukkoṯ*, "booths."

19. JV: *Sharpest potsherds are under him, he spreadeth a threshing sledge upon the mire.* But *ḥaddude*, "sharpest," can mean "reflections"; *ḥeres*, "potsherds," can mean "sun"; and *ḥaruṣ*, "threshing sledge," can mean "gold." See Rashi.

a pride (Job 41:7), for *They hold to one another fast like a seal closed tight* (*ibid.*). On the meaning of these words, R. Abba bar Kahana and our Masters of the South differ. According to one opinion, the Leviathan's scales are closed tight in the manner of a two-scroll document, one rolled up inside the other, the inner scroll being closed tight by a row of seals; according to the other opinion, the Leviathan's scales are held tight as a single-scroll document is held tight by a cord with a sealed knot.

Or the words *They hold to one another fast like a seal closed tight* signify, according to R. Berechiah the Priest, that the Holy One said: [As though the Leviathan's scales were a double-scroll document], I closed the inner layer of scales, sealed it tightly, and then rolled it up together with the outer layer of scales.[20] [Out of this compacted skin of the Leviathan, says the Holy One, I take such strips of skin as are required to make the sukkahs of the righteous in the world-to-come impervious to My fiery wrath on the Day of Judgment].

A different comment [on the extraordinary qualities of the Leviathan]: *The rows of his shields are his pride* (Job 41:7). The Leviathan has the pride which is proper only to Him who is on high, and so the Holy One says to the ministering angels: Go down and wage war against him. At once they go down to wage war against him. But when the Leviathan raises up his visage, and the ministering angels see it, affrighted by the fearful countenance, they flee, as is said *When he raiseth himself up, the mighty are afraid* (Job 41:17). *The mighty* are none other than the ministering angels, of whom it is said[21] *Who among the sons of might can be likened unto the Lord* (Ps. 89:7).

By reason of the breaches, they find themselves shot into them (*yiṯhaṭṭa'u*) (Job 41:17). What is meant by the words *By reason of the breaches they find themselves shot into them?*[22] They mean that when the Leviathan wishes to eat, he strikes the water with his tail and makes such a breach in the sea that the fish are drawn towards the breach and are shot into it, whereupon he eats them. The word *yiṯhaṭṭa'u* means "be shot into," as in the verse *Every one could sling stones at a hair-breadth and not fail to shoot each one accurately* (*yaḥăṭi'*) (Judg. 20:16).

When the Holy One again commands the angels, "Take swords and go down against Leviathan," they at once take swords and attack him, but

20. Professors Saul Lieberman and Yigael Yadin explained the analogy of the Leviathan's scales with the double-scroll and single-scroll documents used in Graeco-Roman times.

21. The words *Who in the skies can be compared unto the Lord* are omitted.

22. JV: *By reason of despair, they are beside themselves.* But *šĕḇarim*, "despair," may mean "breaches"; and *yiṯhaṭṭa'u*, "they are beside themselves," may be construed "they find themselves shot into."

swords are of no concern to him,[23] as is said *If one lay at him with the sword, it will not hold; nor the spear, the dart, nor the pointed shaft* (Job 41:18). As the spear recoils from armor, so it bounds back from the Leviathan's skin. Even iron is esteemed mere straw by him, as is said *He esteemeth iron as straw, and brass as rotten wood* (Job 41:19). Then the angels take up arrows and send them straight at him. But can such concern him, of whom it is said *The arrow cannot make him flee* (Job 41:20)? So then they take up slingstones which they throw at him, and he deems them stubble, as is said *Slingstones are turned with him into stubble. Clubs are accounted as stubble* (Job 41:20-21). [Of his great powers] Scripture goes on to say, *He maketh the deep to boil like a pot; he maketh the sea like a pot of perfume* (*merḳaḥah*) (Job 41:23): he makes the entire sea into rich perfume, the word *merḳaḥah* being understood as in the verse "a perfume compounded (*mirḳaḥaṯ*) after the art of the perfumer" (Exod. 30:25).[24]

He maketh a path to shine after him; he thinks to grow hoary in the deep (Job 41:24). Because his dwelling in the sea is over the deep, he believes that there he will continue to live safely, as is said *He thinks to grow hoary in the deep.* What will the Holy One do about it? He will bring Behemoth to Leviathan, and they will engage in close combat with each other, as is said *One is so close to the other, that no air* (*ruaḥ*) *can come between them* (Job 41:8). Read not *ruaḥ*, "air," but *rewaḥ*, "space": [there is no space between them]. Or, the words *no air can come between them* refer to the ministering angels who are called "airy winds," as in the verse "Who makest winds Thine angels" (Ps. 104:4): [hence not even ethereal angels can come between them]. Behemoth and Leviathan will be joined to each other, as is said *They are joined one to another* (Job 41:9). And once joined they will not be sundered, as is said *They stick together, that they cannot be sundered* (*ibid.*). What will the Holy One then do? He will signal to Leviathan, who thereupon will strike Behemoth with his fins and thus slaughter him; at the same time He will signal to Behemoth who will strike Leviathan with his tail and slay him.[25] Then what will the Holy One do at once? He will take skin from the Leviathan and use it in making sukkahs for the righteous, as is said

23. "but swords are of no concern to him"—Yalḳuṭ. S reads, "But is it of concern to you?" a reading which makes for difficulty.

24. Can this possibly be a reference to ambergris, which is a waxy secretion of the sperm whale much valued in perfumery?

25. Leviathan, being a fish, requires no ritual slaughtering; hence the blow from Behemoth's tail, which kills the Leviathan without cutting its windpipe and gullet, is sufficient to make the latter's flesh fit for human consumption. But Behemoth, an animal, requires full ritual slaughtering (*šěḥiṭah*); hence Leviathan must strike it with his sharp fins, thus cutting its windpipe and gullet to make its flesh fit for human consumption (see Piska 4.3). For a description of Behemoth, see Piska 6.1.

[*The gaps in the walls of*] *every sukkah* [*of the righteous*] *will be filled in with skin from the Leviathan* (Job 40:31).

Thereafter, [*banging*] *a cymbal* [*to attract customers, the righteous will hawk*] *the Leviathan's head as a fish delicacy*[26] (*ibid.*). On this verse, R. Naḥman, R. Huna the Priest, and R. Judah the Levite bar R. Shallum made different comments. One said: [Like fishmongers] the righteous will bang a cymbal and cry, "Let everyone who has obeyed the command of going up to Jerusalem in pilgrimage come and partake of the Leviathan's head, whose delicious taste is like the taste of the head of a fish from the Sea of Tiberias." A colleague said: Like fishmongers the righteous will bang a cymbal and cry: "Let everyone who has obeyed the command of going up to Jerusalem in pilgrimage come and partake of the Leviathan's head, whose delicious taste is like the taste of the head of a fish from the Great Sea."[27] At once, all those who are summoned—associates, so called—come together and make a banquet of Leviathan, as is said *The associates*—associates by virtue of their all having obeyed the command to go up to Jerusalem in pilgrimage—*make a banquet of him* (Job 40:30)

Another comment: *The associates*—members of many, many different associations—*make a banquet of him*, some of the associations being concerned with study of Scripture, some with study of Mishnah, some with Talmud, some with Haggadah, some with deeds of charity, some with the proper performance of precepts; each and every association comes and takes its portion of Leviathan. Lest you suppose there is strife among the associations [over the various portions], the verse goes on to say, *They shall part him as among merchants* (*ibid.*). When merchants who jointly own a precious stone sell it and then proceed to divide the money realized from it, they do not engage in quarreling: each one comes and takes his portion in accordance with the money he invested. So in the time-to-come there will be no quarreling among those banqueting on the Leviathan. Each and every one of the righteous will come and take his reward according to his deeds. Hence *They shall part*

26. JV: *or his head with fish-spears*. But *ṣilṣal*, "spear," also means "cymbal."
27. The Mediterranean.

The Leviathan, like the manna provided for Israel in the wilderness, was one of God's special creations, and, like manna, was intended by Him to serve a purpose beyond the bodily nourishment of Israel. The miraculous nature of manna was such that it was absorbed into all two hundred and forty-eight parts of the body: hence unhindered by the ordinary processes of digestion and excretion the people of Israel were ready to receive the revelation at Sinai (MTeh 78:3). In the days of the Messiah, the Leviathan's head was to serve the same purpose as manna and thus prepare the people of Israel for instruction in Torah, instruction which God Himself was to impart (Piska 12.21). See Baḥya ben Asher's comment on Gen. 1:21, (ed. Šewel [Jerusalem, 5726 (1966)], 38–40); and *Kiṯbe Rabbenu Bachye*, ed. Šewel (Jerusalem, 5730/1969), 501–04.

him as among kĕna'ănim (*ibid.*), *kĕna'ănim* meaning "merchants," as in the verse "whose traffickers are princes, whose merchant (*kĕna'ănim*) are the honorable of the earth" (Isa. 23:8).

5. Another comment: *There shall be a sukkah for shade from the searing heat of the Day* [*of Judgment*] (Isa. 4:6). These words are to be considered in the light of the verse *Deliverance belongeth unto the Lord. Blessing Thee is incumbent on Thy People*[28] (Ps. 3:9). Israel said bluntly to the Holy One: Master of the universe, Thine is the obligation to provide miracles and deliverance for us, as is said *Deliverance belongeth unto the Lord.* And, for our part, what are we to utter in blessing Thee? Songs and Psalms. What the Psalm says, namely, that performing miracles and bringing deliverance is the Lord's obligation—*unto the Lord* (Ps. 3:9)—is likewise implied in the verse *There shall be a sukkah for shade from the searing heat of the Day* [*of Judgment*] (Isa. 4:6). And when Thou performest all these miracles for us, we shall not be ingrates—for our part, we shall utter Songs and Psalms, as indeed, in the very next verse from Isaiah, Scripture goes on to say, *Let me sing to my Well-beloved, a song to my Well-beloved concerning His vineyard* (Isa. 5:1).

6. It is written *Thou shalt keep the Feast of Sukkot seven days* (Deut. 16:13). Why do Israel make the sukkah? Because of the miracles the Holy One performed for them when they went forth out of Egypt, for clouds of glory surrounded them and sheltered them, as is said *I had the children of Israel dwell in sukkahs* (Lev. 23:43), a verse which the Aramaic Targum translates "I had the children of Israel dwell in cloud-sukkahs." Accordingly, when Scripture asserts, *Ye shall dwell in sukkahs seven days* (Lev. 23:42), the reason, says God, is *that your generations may know that I had the children of Israel dwell in* [*miraculous*] *sukkahs* (Lev. 23:43). For the Holy One said to Israel: "My children, be sure to make sukkahs and dwell therein seven days in order that you be reminded of the miracles that I performed for you in the wilderness." Hence, even though you build a sukkah, you are not being particularly generous to God—you are only requiting Him, who is quoted as saying *I had the children of Israel dwell in* [*miraculous*] *sukkahs*, etc. (*ibid.*). So, too, says God, in obeying My command to take the lulab̠ cluster and shake it before Me, even though you do so, you are not being particularly generous to Me—you are only requiting Me. For when I brought you forth out of Egypt, I made the mountains shake before you, as is said *The mountains skipped like rams* (Ps. 114:4). And in the time-to-come I shall again perform miracles like this for you, as it is said *The mountains and the hills shall break forth before you into singing* (Isa. 55:12).

7. In comment on the verse *After that thou hast gathered in from thy*

28. "Marius"—parallel in Yalḳuṭ where it appears as "Marus"; S: "Maryom."

threshing floor, and from thy winepress (Deut. 16:13), R. Eleazar bar Marius[29] said: Why do we build the sukkah right after the Day of Atonement? [Because the sukkah may serve God's purpose in the judgment He decrees on the Day of Atonement]. As you well know, on New Year's Day the Holy One sits in judgment upon all the world's inhabitants, and on the Day of Atonement He seals the judgment. Now it may be that the judgment decreed for Israel is banishment. Therefore, when Israel build the sukkah and then banish themselves from their homes to dwell in the sukkah, the Holy One considers this banishment as equivalent to their dwelling in exile in remote Babylonia, as is said *Be in pain, and labor to bring forth, O daughter of Zion, like a woman in travail; now as thou goest forth out of the city, and dwellest in the field, it shall be as though thou comest unto Babylon; there shalt thou be rescued; there shall the Lord redeem thee from the hand of thine enemies* (Micah 4:10).

8. *And thou shalt rejoice in thy Feast* (Deut. 16:14). You find three verses that command you to rejoice in the Feast of Sukkot: *And thou shalt rejoice in thy Feast* (*ibid.*); *And thou shalt be altogether joyful* (Deut. 16:15); *And ye shall rejoice before the Lord your God seven days* (Lev. 23:40). For Passover, however, you will not find even one command to rejoice. Why not? Because in the season of Passover, judgment is passed with regard to field crops;[30] and since no man knows whether the year will bring forth crops or not, therefore Scripture gives no command to rejoice during Passover.

Another answer to the question, Why does Scripture give no command to rejoice during Passover? Because the Egyptians died during Passover. Therefore, though we read the entire *Hallel*[31] on each of the seven days of Sukkot, [an entirely joyful feast], on Passover we read the entire *Hallel* only on the first day and on the night preceding it, because of what is said in the verse which Samuel loved to quote *Rejoice not when thine enemy falleth* (Prov. 24:17).[32]

In regard to Pentecost we are given only one command to rejoice, the one which reads *Thou shalt keep the Feast of Weeks unto the Lord thy God . . . and shalt rejoice, thou and thy household*[33] (Deut. 16:10-11). And why is there only one command to rejoice during Pentecost? Because the field crops have already been brought in. Then why not two commands to rejoice? Because, though the field crops have been brought in, judgment is still to be passed in regard to the fruits of the tree, and therefore for Pentecost Scripture does not give us a second command to rejoice. As for New Year's Day,

29. JV: *Thy blessing be upon Thy people.*
30. RH 1:1.
31. Psalms 113–18, as used for liturgical recitation.
32. See Ab̲ 4:19.
33. MT: *thou and thy son.*

Scripture does not give us even one command to rejoice. Why not? Because it is the day when men's lives are judged, and a man is more anxious about his life than about his possessions. On Sukkot, however, [all is joyful]: men's lives have received pardon on the Day of Atonement—*For on this day shall atonement be made for you* (Lev. 16:30)—field crops have been brought in, fruits of the tree have been gathered, and hence for Sukkot we are given three commands to rejoice: *And thou shalt rejoice in thy feast* (Deut. 16:14); *Ye shall rejoice before the Lord your God* (Lev. 23:40); *And thou shalt be altogether joyful* (Deut. 16:15).

In another comment, the verse just cited is read *Howbeit thou shalt be joyful* (Deut. 16:15). What is implied by *Howbeit . . . be joyful?* That in this world, a man may indeed rejoice: howbeit, his joy is not complete. Why not? In this world, when a man has children born to him, he is troubled about them, troubled whether the children are likely to survive or not. But in the world-to-come, the Holy One will destroy death, as is said *He will swallow up death for ever* (Isa. 25:8). Then men's rejoicing will be complete, as is said *Then will our mouth be filled with laughter, and our tongue with singing* (Ps. 126:2).

Another comment on *Howbeit thou shalt be joyful* (Deut. 16:15). In this world a man who wants to rejoice when a festival comes, gets meat and cooks it in his house by way of celebrating the festival. But no sooner does he begin to eat, having first dealt out a portion to each of his sons, than he is apt to hear, "My brother's portion is bigger than mine," and so, even in the midst of his joy, he is vexed. But in the time-to-come, when pots are cooking away and a man sees them, his soul rejoices at the sight [because he knows he will eat his meal in peace]. Hence Scripture: *Lord, Thou wilt set on peace for us* (Isa. 26:12), "set on" being a term used also when pots are put to cooking on the fire. It was R. Phinehas the Priest ben Ḥama who pointed out that Scripture uses the term "set on" in connection with cooking. Thus: *Set on the pot, set it on, and also pour water into it* (Ezek. 24:3). Only in the time-to-come will a man experience complete joy [in his feasting]. Hence *Lord, Thou wilt set on peace for us* (Isa. 26:12).

SUPPLEMENT 3

[Midrashic Miscellany: *The Inclination to Good and the Inclination to Evil*]

1. Why dost Thou show favor to Israel, as indicated by the verse *That which is a statute for Israel is an ordinance for the God of Jacob* (Ps. 81:4)? God replied: I show them favor out of consideration for the merit of their Fathers.

2. *Better is a poor and wise child than an old and foolish king* (Eccles. 4:13). R. Nathan said: The words *A poor and wise child* stand for the Inclination to good.[1] And why is the Inclination to good called *child*? Because the Inclination to good, [in contrast to the Inclination to evil, does not come into being until the children of men reach the age of thirteen, and only then] begins to guide them in the right path. Why is it called *poor*? Because too few people pay attention to it. Why is it called *wise*? Because it wisely guides a man from the age of thirteen on. The words *an old and foolish king* stand for the Inclination to evil. Why is it called *old*? Because it is part of a man from the time he is expelled from his mother's womb to the time he is hoary-headed, as is said "For the disposition of man's heart is evil from his youth" (Gen. 8:21)—that is, from the time he is expelled from his mother's womb.[2] And why is the Inclination to evil called *foolish*? Because it directs men into the path of folly. Like the very king of those who lie in ambush, it waits to ensnare men. As Scripture says, *Out of the bushes*[3] *he comes forth to rule* (Eccles. 4:14). The verse concludes, however, with reassurance: *Behold! In his very kingdom, the poor is brought forth* (*ibid.*)—that is, the Inclination to good is brought forth in the very kingdom of the Inclination to evil.

The Inclination to evil, as the Sages tell us, is thirteen years older than the Inclination to good. Since a man's Inclination to evil is born as he leaves his mother's womb, it keeps growing even as he grows. Accordingly, if he proceeds to violate the Sabbath [before he has reached the age of thirteen], there is nothing to stay his hand. And if he proceeds to commit an act of unchastity [before the age of thirteen], there is nothing to stay his hand.

1. Margin reads: "from the age of thirteen on. And why is it called *poor?* Because not all people pay attention to it. And why is it called *wise?* Because it wisely guides men in the right path."

2. Play on *nĕʻuraw*, "his youth," and *ninĕʻar*, "expelled." The following attempts to reproduce the play on words in the original: "For the disposition of your heart is evil from your *youth*" (Gen. 8:21)—that is, from the time *you th*rust yourself from your mother's womb."

3. The word *surim*, "prison," is read as though spelled *sirim*, "bushes."

Only when a man reaches the age of thirteen is the Inclination to good born within him. Then, if he would profane the Sabbath, it says to him, "Wretch! Scripture declares, *Everyone that profaneth it, shall surely be put to death*" (Exod. 31:14). If he would take a life, it says to him, "Scripture declares *Whoso sheddeth man's blood, by man shall his blood be shed*" (Gen. 9:6).

When a man, his imagination heated, proceeds to commit an act of unchastity, all the parts of his body obey him. But when he sets out to fulfill a religious obligation, all the parts of his body protest from deep within him because the Inclination to evil in his innermost being is king over the two hundred and forty-eight parts that make up a man; the Inclination to good, however, may be likened to a king who is shut up in a prison, as is said *For out of prison he comes forth to rule* (Eccles. 4:14), that is, the Inclination to good [finally comes out in a man and rules his conduct].

Another comment: The words *For out of prison he came forth to rule* apply to Joseph, of whom it is said "Then Pharaoh sent and called Joseph" (Gen. 41:14). Of the righteous Joseph—concerning the time when Potiphera's wife said to him, "Lie with me," and he refused: "He refused, and said unto his master's wife . . . 'How can I do this great wickedness?' " (Gen. 39:8, 9)—the following is told: When she threatened, "I shall shut you up in prison," he replied, *The Lord looseth prisoners* (Ps. 146:7). When she threatened, "I shall put out your eyes," he replied, *The Lord openeth the eyes of the blind* (Ps. 146:8). When she threatened, "I shall make a humpback out of you," he replied, *The Lord raiseth up them that are bowed down* (*ibid.*). When she threatened, "I will make you into a stranger—banish you,"[4] he replied, *The Lord preserveth the strangers* (Ps. 146:9).

And do not be astonished at Joseph. Witness R. Zadok who showed even greater restraint when he was taken as a captive to Rome where a prominent noblewoman purchased him [in the slave market] and sent a beautiful maidservant to tempt him to lie with her. When he saw the maidservant, he fixed his eyes upon the wall and sat silent and motionless all night. In the morning the maidservant went and complained to her mistress, saying, "I would rather die than be given to this man [and be rebuffed by him]." When the noblewoman asked R. Zadok: "Why did you not do with this woman what men generally seek to do?" he replied: "I am of a family from which High Priests are chosen, and I thought: Shall such as I lie with such as she and multiply bastards in Israel?"

At once the noblewoman gave orders that R. Zadok be freed with great honor.

And do not be astonished at R. Zadok. Witness R. 'Aḳiḇa who showed even greater restraint than he. When R. 'Aḳiḇa went to Rome, it was slan-

4. See *The Fathers According to R. Nathan*, tr. Judah Goldin, YJS, *10*, p. 193, n. 7. Or: "I will give you the status of an Aramean slave, a starving nomad."

derously said of him before a certain general [that he enjoyed the company of loose women]. Thereupon the general sent two very beautiful women to him. These were bathed, anointed, and adorned like brides for their grooms. All night, they kept thrusting themselves at R. 'Aḳiḇa, one saying, "Turn to me," and the other saying, "Turn to me." Sitting between them, he spat in disgust at both.

In the morning the women went off and complained to the general, saying to him, "We would rather die than be given to this man [and be rebuffed by him]." Whereupon the general asked R. 'Aḳiḇa: "Why did you not do with these women what men generally seek to do? Are they not beautiful? Are they not human beings like yourself? Did not He who created you create them?"[5] R. 'Aḳiḇa replied: "What could I do? The odor of their bodies, as foul as the stench of carrion or of swine overcame me."

Of men such as Joseph, R. Zadok, R. 'Aḳiḇa, and their like, Scripture says, *Bless the Lord, ye messengers of His, ye mighty in strength, that fulfill His word* (Ps. 103:20).

Another comment: The Inclination to evil dwells at the very entrance of the heart [and is like a fly, an enemy[6] to fly from]. As Scripture says, *Flies of death cause the ointment of the perfumer to stink and putrefy* (Eccles. 10:11). Thus, when an infant still in his cradle puts his hand on glowing coals, what is the cause of his doing so? Is it not the Inclination to evil, [an enemy to the person it dwells in]? So, too, when one goes up to a rooftop and falls off, what brought the fall about? Is it not the Inclination to evil which flings him headlong? On the other hand, take a look at a kid or a lamb: as soon as such younglings see an open hole [they might fall into], they draw back. For there is no Inclination to evil in an animal.

R. Simeon ben Eleazar said: With what may the Inclination to evil be compared? With iron put into fire. So long as the iron is in the fire, one may make of it any implement one pleases. It is the same with the Inclination to evil: the only means of coping with it are [the fiery] words of Torah, as is said *Is not My word like as fire? saith the Lord* (Jer. 23:29).

It is also written *If thine enemy be ready to eat thee up, get him to eat the bread* [*of Torah*] (Prov. 25:21). Thus, as the school of R. Ishmael taught: My son, if this ugly enemy comes at you, get him to come into the house of study. [If you wonder at the strength of the Inclination to evil, remember that from the very beginning of time the Inclination to evil has had allies]. As R. Judah the Prince said: With whom may the Inclination to evil be compared? With a brigand. When he was captured, he was asked, "Who

5. These questions reflect the tone of contemporary polemics against so-called Jewish separatism. See *The Fathers According to R. Nathan*, tr. Judah Goldin, YJS, *10*, 193, n. 12.

6. See B.Ber 61a. Professor Jakob J. Petuchowski suggests that the commentator is playing on the Aramaic words *diḇaḇa'*, "fly," and *dĕḇaḇa'*, "enmity."

were your mates?" and he replied, "So-and-so, and So-and-so," saying to himself, "Since I am to be executed, let them also be executed with me." Therefore he who heeds the Inclination to evil will fall into Gehenna, [as did Satan, the father of the Inclination to evil, and his allies].[7]

[And why do the wicked keep falling into Gehenna?] Because, as it is said, *The eyes of the wicked fail* (Job 11:20). The wicked—repentance is open to them, yet they do not turn towards repentance. A parable of a band of renegades who rebelled against their king: when the king seized them and shut them up in prison, what did they do? They made an opening [in the prison wall] and got away, except for one who did not flee. In the morning, when the king found him, the king said: "Fool, the opening was before you, and yet you did not free yourself. Your companions who have freed themselves, how can I possibly punish them?" Likewise—[in the conclusion of the verse cited above]—the Holy One says to the wicked who fail to see that they can free themselves: *they lose the chance to flee* (*ibid.*).

As for the righteous who do not heed the Inclination to evil, the fire of Gehenna can no more have dominion over them than can fire have dominion over the salamander which is begotten from fire. And just as fire can have no effect upon one who is anointed with the salamander's blood, all the more certain is it that fire can have no effect upon the disciples of the wise whose entire being is on fire with Torah, which is itself fire, as is said *Is not My word like as fire? saith the Lord* (Jer. 23:29).

7. In his rebellion against God, Satan is said to have had companion angels associated with him. See Ginzberg, *Legends*, 5, 85.

SUPPLEMENT 4

Tithe, and then thou shalt again tithe[1] (Deut. 14:22)

1. *Tithe, and then thou shalt again tithe all the increase of thy field* (Deut. 14:22). "All kinds of provender, except water or salt, may be purchased with second-tithe money"[2] (Er 3:1). [Why not water or salt]? Because it was with these two staples that two earlier generations provoked God—the generation of the flood by saying that rain did not come from Him,[3] and the Sodomites by refusing to give salt to strangers.[4] Hence it was with water and salt that God punished these two generations. Accordingly, since the second tithe must be brought in a spirit of joy, the Holy One said: [In expending the second tithe] do not include [in your purchases water or salt], a sign of My cursing of the generations, with [the fruit of the earth, which is] a sign of My blessing of the generations.

2. Moses said reproachfully to the Holy One: Dost Thou not know that though Thou didst command us to set aside a tithe, a tenth part, we find it difficult to do so because [of the exactions] of the nations of the earth? Deal with us considerately, as is said *Give ear, O Shepherd of Israel, deal Thou with the flock like Joseph*[5] (Ps. 80:2). Why did Moses bring in here an allusion to Joseph? Because he was implying the following in Israel's behalf: "Master of universes, how many evils did the Tribe fathers inflict upon Joseph! Yet in requital he did not mete out any cruelty to them, but said instead *I will sustain you, and your little ones* (Gen. 50:21). So do Thou conduct Thyself, O Lord, with us as Joseph did with his brothers." God replied: When Joseph ruled in Egypt he took [a substantial levy], one part out of five, as is said *Ye shall give a fifth unto Pharaoh* (Gen. 47:24), even though Pharaoh did not control dew and rain as I do. I, however, protect the seeds, cause winds to blow, clouds to rise, rains to come down, dews to descend, plants to spring up—yet all I ask of you is only one part in ten. Hence *Thou shalt surely tithe*[6] (Deut. 14:22).

1. EV: *Thou shalt surely tithe.* But such a translation glosses over a repetition of the verb.

2. The second tithe, which the owners give in the first, second, fourth, and fifth year of the six-year cycle of tithing, they had to use up in Jerusalem either by eating the produce they brought from their fields, or by selling it and spending the proceeds in Jerusalem. See Deut. 14:22 ff.

3. See B.Sanh 108a; Sif Deut. 43 (ed. Finkelstein, p. 92); Gen. Rabbah 5:1, 28:2; and Piska 26.2.

4. See Rashi on Gen. 19:26.

5. JV: *Thou that leadest Joseph like a flock.*

6. Only the first tithe is given to God. The second tithe, the owners themselves

3. [In another comment the verse is read] *Tithe, and then thou shalt again tithe* (Deut. 14:22). Abraham was the first man to set aside a tithe from a heap of crops, which [up to his time] had been used entirely for secular purposes. In fact, he set aside the tithe from the middle, [the best part], of the heap. Therefore, the Holy One plucked him away from the domain of idols as well as from things used entirely for secular purposes and raised him up into the firmament, as is said *He is the One that raised up the man of the east and summoned Ṣeḏeḳ, [Jupiter], to light his way*[7] (Isa. 41:2). Isaac also set aside a tithe, as is said *Isaac sowed in that land, and counted in the same year a hundredfold increase* (Gen. 26:12). The reason he thus measured his crop was in order to set aside a tithe from it. Therefore, he was blessed, as the verse goes on to say, *and the Lord blessed him* (*ibid.*). Jacob also set aside a tithe, for he said: *Of all that Thou shalt give me I will surely give the tenth unto Thee* (Gen. 28:22).[8] Therefore, [like our Fathers], we, too, are to give the first tithe to the Tribe of Levi and give the portion of the crop due to Aaron in order to procure God's pardon for our iniquities and to utter songs [in celebration of our pardon]. We infer the setting aside of a second tithe from the passage in Deuteronomy wherein it is said *Thou shalt eat before the Lord thy God* (Deut. 14:23)—[that is, you shall eat in Jerusalem another tithe, a second one, which the previous verse (Deut. 14:22) enjoins you to set aside].

---

must consume in Jerusalem; or, in the third and sixth years of the six-year cycle of tithing, give it to the poor. See Deut. 14.22 ff.; and PR 25:1 (YJS, *18*, 513).

7. That is, God brought Abraham out of the secular, terrestrial sphere, indeed elevated him above the planets, so that Jupiter was no more than a lamp for his feet. See Rashi on Gen. 15:5. JV: *Who hath raised up one from the east, at whose steps victory attendeth?* But *ṣeḏeḳ*, "victory," may also mean "Jupiter."

8. See PR 25:3 (YJS, *18*, 519).

SUPPLEMENT 5

How beautiful upon the mountains (Isa. 52:7)

1. *How beautiful upon the mountains are the feet of the messenger of good tidings, that announceth peace* (Isa. 52:7). These words are to be considered in the light of what Solomon, king of Israel, was inspired by the holy spirit to say, *Thy tablets because they offer all kinds of instruction are as beautiful as precious ornaments*[1] (Song 1:9), a verse which Solomon uttered with regard to the congregation of Israel. For, as he envisioned Israel's eventual redemption, he voiced praise and glory to the Holy One. Solomon said: Even as the Commandments on the tablets were beautiful when brought down by our teacher Moses, so will the messengers of good tidings be beautiful when they come to Zion. The day when the exiles are gathered in will be as great as the day when the Torah was given to Israel on Mount Sinai. And what is to be the order of the procession when the exiles are gathered? The Presence will walk at the head of them, as is said *Their King is passed on before them* (Micah 2:13), the Patriarchs of the world behind them, the Prophets at both sides of them, and the Ark and the Torah with them. All Israel will be clothed in majesty, mantled in great glory, so that their splendor will illumine the world from one end to the other. At that time the hands of the peoples of the world will grow powerless, so that no man of might will be able to raise his hand to lift a weapon, as is said *Not one people will lift up a sword* (Isa. 2:4). There will be no weapon that will remain unbroken, as is said *They shall beat their swords into plowshares* (*ibid.*), and there will not be an idol or image that will remain unshattered, as is said *The idols shall utterly pass away* (Isa. 2:18). The peoples of the world will come, pick up their shattered idols, and cast them away, as is said *In that day a man shall cast away his idols of silver, and his idols of gold* (Isa. 2:20). Why all this? In order to remove from God's presence every kind of idolatry in the world, as is said *The Lord alone shall be exalted in that day* (Isa. 2:11), and the Holy One will then reign from world's end to world's end. Hence Solomon foretells with praise the beauty of the congregation of Israel when redemption comes: as Scripture says, *Thy tablets because they offer all kinds of instruction are as beautiful as precious ornaments; and thy disciples who strain* (*ḥozĕrim*) *to hear words of Torah are like strings of jewels* (*ḥăruzim*)[2] *around thy neck* (Song 1:9).

1. JV: *Thy cheeks are comely with circles.* But the commentator connects *leḥi*, "cheek," with *luaḥ*, "tablet"; and *torim*, "circlets, ornaments," with *torah*, "instruction," or "kinds of instruction."

2. The word *ḥăruzim*, "strings of pearls," is, by metathesis, also construed as

2. *How beautiful upon the mountains are the feet of the messenger of good tidings* (Isa. 52:7). R. Joshua said: Why of all the work of creation are the mountains to be distinguished in that the messengers of good tidings are to appear upon them first? Because the Fathers of the world are mountains, metaphorically speaking, as they are addressed in the verse *Hear, O ye mountains, the Lord's controversy, and ye enduring rocks, the foundations of the earth*, etc. (Micah 6:2).[3] And why do the messengers of good tidings appear first to the Fathers of the world? Because, when Israel were banished, [from their graves] the Fathers of the world assembled with the Mothers of the world and appeared before the Holy One where they put together a great lament. At once, from the heavens above, the Holy One responding to them, asked: *Wherefore are My beloved in My House?*[4] (Jer. 11:15)—why have My beloved put together a great lament, as if for the dead, in My House? They answered Him bluntly: Master of the universe, wherein have our children sinned that Thou hast done such a thing as to banish them? He replied: *They have wrought lewdness*[5] (Jer. 11:15) by seeking to disguise circumcision which was the stamp of holiness on their flesh.[6] And so they have been condemned to banishment. Thereupon the Fathers asked Him: Master of the universe, is it possible that Thou wilt forget them in their banishment among the peoples of the world? He replied: By My great name, I swear that I shall not forget them among the peoples of the world, but instead will restore them to their place, as is said *And there is hope for thy future, saith the Lord; for thy children shall return to their own border* (Jer. 31:16). Thus did the Holy One comfort the Fathers, and they went and lay down again in their graves. For this reason—[that is, because the Fathers spoke up in Israel's behalf]—when he who brings good tidings of the redemption comes, he will first come to the graves in the Cave of Machpelah. And who will be the ones bringing the good tidings? They will be, said R. Joshua, the descendants of Jonadab the son of Rechab, who will be the first with good tidings to Israel, for it is said *There shall not be cut off unto Jonadab the son of Rechab a man to stand before Me for ever* (Jer. 35:19). Indeed, Jonadab's descendants

---

ḥozĕrim, "strain," and taken to describe disciples straining their necks to hear from their masters all kinds of instruction in Torah as though they had never heard them before. The translation of Song 1:9 follows the parallel in Song Rabbah.

3. See Piska 3.c; PR 3:3, and 12:5.

4. JV: *What hath My beloved to do in My House.* But a slight change in vowels makes it possible to construe *My beloved* (singular) as a plural.

5. MT: *She hath wrought lewdness.*

6. See Jer. 11:15. That is, they had their sons' foreskins restored by surgery. Cf. Piska 28.1.

The words may also be rendered "as is shown by the fact that they had given up circumcision, the stamp of holiness on their flesh." See PR 14:15 (YJS, *18*, 294, n. 105), and 15:13 (YJS, *18*, 325, n. 79).

will go up [to Jerusalem] where they will be the first to bring offerings, since of them it is said *a man to stand before Me for ever,* words which include an allusion, one may infer, to the days of the Messiah.[7]

R. Dosa said: The mountains themselves will be the first to bring good tidings to Israel, since at the time Israel were banished, they mourned for Israel, as is said *I beheld the mountains, and, lo, they trembled* (Jer. 4:24). A parable of a king of flesh-and-blood: he had two sons, one of whom died; whereupon the people of the principality donned black. The king said to the people: Since you donned black at the one's dying, I shall have you don white at the other's rejoicing.[8] Likewise the Holy One said to the mountains: Since you took up a weeping at My children's banishment, as is said *With the mountains will I take up a weeping and wailing* (Jer. 9:9), out of you, O mountains, I shall bring tidings of My children's rejoicing, as is said *How beautiful upon the mountains are the feet of the messenger of good tidings* (Isa. 52:7).

3. *The voice of thy watchmen! They lift up the voice, together do they sing* (Isa. 52:8). These words are to be considered in the light of the verse *Be strong, and let your heart take courage, all ye that wait for the Lord* (Ps. 31:25). Of whom did David utter this verse? He uttered it of Israel who had been waiting and yearning for the time God would return to His Temple and thus cause His Torah to rejoice.[9] Indeed, the Holy One also yearns and waits for the time when He will be returning to His Temple and cause Israel to rejoice. When will that time be? When He has requited wicked Edom. Then Israel will say: Master of the universe, Edom caused us much grief. It destroyed our Sanctuary, slew our Sages, put us into bondage, and consumed the fruit of our labor; and now, hungry and thirsty [for Thy requital of her], I sit and wait for the day when Thou wilt come and in my behalf punish her, as is said *My soul thirsteth for the God [of requital], for the living God* (Ps. 42:3).

R. Ḥiyya bar Abba said in the name of R. Johanan: It is written *Hope deferred maketh the heart sick; but desire fulfilled is a tree of life* (Prov. 13:12). When a man waits for a particular thing to happen, and what he awaits is not brought about for him, his heart is sick. But when what he awaits is brought about for him, it seems to him as though new life had been given him. And so the congregation of Israel says: Master of universes, every hope in the world has a set time for its fulfillment, but the hope for the Messiah has no such set time. The Holy One answers: Come, and I will reassure thee, as is said *The Lord will comfort Zion, He will comfort all her*

7. See Ginzberg, *Legends*, *3*, 380; *6*, 154.
8. See variants in BM's apparatus for corrected text.
9. Many commandments in the Torah that have to do with Temple procedures obviously cannot be fulfilled if the Temple is not functioning.

waste places (Isa. 51:3). And what will He say to her? *Arise, shine, for thy light is come, and the glory of the Lord is risen upon thee* (Isa. 60:1). The congregation of Israel replies: Rise Thou up at the head of us, and we shall follow Thee. Thereupon the Holy One will rise, as is said *Now will I arise, saith the Lord; now will I be exalted; now will I lift Myself up* (Isa. 30:10). And again *Now will I arise, saith the Lord; I will set him in safety at whom they puff* (Ps. 12:6). And wherewith will the Holy One comfort Israel? By Zion's ingathering of her sons in joy, as is said *Lift up thine eyes round about, and behold: all these gather themselves together, and come to thee,* etc. (Isa. 49:18). Of such hope of redemption, David said: *Be strong, and let your heart take courage* (Ps. 31:25).

The voice of them that wait in thy behalf! They lift up the voice, together do they sing; [*for they shall see, eye to eye, how the Lord returneth to Zion*] (Isa. 52:8). R. Meir said: By *them that wait in thy behalf*[10] are meant ministering angels who have been waiting for the rebuilding of Jerusalem, weeping and mourning for Jerusalem ever since she was destroyed, as is said *The celestial beings cry, "*[*The Temple's destruction*] *is an outrage";*[11] *the angels of peace weep bitterly* (Isa. 33:7). A parable of a king of flesh-and-blood who left his palace and went away to [makeshift residence in] an inn. The members of his household were grief-stricken, and the servants wore themselves out during the journey—in short, everyone felt bereaved because the king had left his palace. Likewise the Holy One left His palace, saying, *I have forsaken My House, I have cast off My heritage, I have given the dearly beloved of My soul into the hand of her enemies* (Jer. 12:7). What servants of His may be said to have been grief-stricken? The celestial beasts who carry the throne of glory. And what members of His household may be said to have been worn out? The ministering angels who felt bereaved when the King, the King of kings, the Holy One, went forth out of the Temple. Of His return at the time set for redemption Scripture says, *Rejoice for joy with Jerusalem, all ye that mourn for her* (Isa. 66:10).

Or: In comment on *The voice of them that wait in thy behalf! They lift up the voice;* [*for they shall see, eye to eye, how the Lord returneth to Zion*] (Isa. 52:8), R. 'Aḳiḇa said: By *them that wait in thy behalf* is meant the Prophets who await Israel's redemption. Even though the Prophets had spoken words of rebuke to Israel, they turned about and brought them good tidings and comforting.[12] A parable of a king's daughter: Her father appointed a guardian for her, and when she did the king's bidding, self-governance was allowed her. But when she rebelled, self-governance was not

10. According to R. Meir, only angels are capable of such a feat, while R. 'Aḳiḇa will say that only Prophets are capable of it.
11. JV: *Behold, the valiant ones cry without.* But see PR 40:6 (YJS, *18*, 718).
12. Cf. Piska 16.8.

allowed her. Likewise, when Israel did the bidding of Him who is everywhere, the Prophets spoke words of praise and promises of self-governance to them—in short, heartened them. But when Israel rebelled, the Prophets spoke words of rebuke to them.

4. *How beautiful upon the mountains are the feet of the messenger of good tidings* (Isa. 52:7). These words mean to teach you that the Holy One will bring down Jerusalem, built anew, from heaven and will set it [as upon four pillars] upon the tops of the four mountains, Sinai, Tabor, Hermon, and Carmel[13] [that in the time-to-come will mark the boundaries of the new Jerusalem].[14] Thus, standing upon the four mountains, Jerusalem will bring to Israel the good tidings of the time set for redemption. And why will Jerusalem be established upon the mountains? Because, said God, from the kind of place where Israel received the Torah as well as transgressed it, I shall bring them good tidings. Hence *How beautiful upon the mountains are the feet of the messenger of good tidings*. Those bringing good tidings will be the descendants of Jonadab the son of Rechab,[15] who upon entering the Temple will bring offerings, procure expiation, and bring tidings of redemption to Israel, for it is said of Jonadab's descendants, "There shall not be cut off unto Jonadab the son of Rechab a man to stand before Me for ever" (Jer. 35:19). Also "beautiful upon the mountains" is he *that announceth peace* (Isa. 52:7), namely, Moses, supreme among Prophets: Even when the Holy One turned Sihon over to Moses to do with as he liked, he announced his wish to make peace with Sihon, saying "I sent messengers out of the wilderness of Kedemoth unto Sihon king of Hebron with words of peace" (Deut. 2:26). Also "beautiful upon the mountains" is *the harbinger of good tidings* (Isa. 52:7), namely, Isaiah, who said of himself, "The spirit of the Lord God is upon me, because the Lord hath anointed me to bring good tidings unto the humble" (Isa. 61:1). Also "beautiful upon the mountains" is he *that announceth redemption* (Isa. 52:7), namely, the redeemer of whom it is said "The redeemer shall come unto Zion" (Isa. 59:20). Also "beautiful upon the mountains" is David, king of Israel, *who saith unto Zion: "Thy God reigneth"* (Isa. 52:7). Hence it is said *How beautiful upon the mountains* (Isa. 52:7).

13. See Piska 21.4. Mount Hermon settled down between the two shores of the Red Sea, enabling Israel to cross the sea. See Ginzberg, *Legends*, *3*, 83.

14. See Piska 20.7.

15. Descendants of Jethro, a proselyte. See S5.2; and Ginzberg, *Legends*, *6*, 134, 409.

SUPPLEMENT 6

I will greatly rejoice (Isa. 61:10)

1. *I will greatly rejoice in the Lord, my soul shall rejoice in my God; for He hath clothed me with the garments of salvation, He hath covered me with the robe of victory* (Isa. 61:10). What comes directly before the verse that begins the lesson? *Their seed shall be known among the nations, and their offspring among the peoples; all that see them shall acknowledge them, that they are the seed which the Lord hath blessed* (Isa. 61:9). And directly after this verse come the words *I will greatly rejoice in the Lord.*

You will find that Isaiah said to Israel no word of rebuke whose hurt he did not subsequently heal [by saying the very opposite]. He began with *Ah sinful nation* (Isa. 1:4), but ended with *Open ye the gates, that the righteous nation that keepeth faithfulness may enter in* (Isa. 26:2). He began with *A seed of evil-doers, children that deal corruptly* (Isa. 1:4), but ended with *children that will not deal falsely* (Isa. 63:8). Nay, more: Isaiah soothed the pain of the grief that [Jeremiah and] others had voiced. Jeremiah said *How is she become as a widow!* (Lam. 1:1), but Isaiah said *As the bridegroom rejoiceth over the bride* (Isa. 62:5). Jeremiah said *How is she become tributary!* (Lam. 1:2), but Isaiah said *Behold, thou shalt call a nation that thou knowest not, and a nation that knew not thee shall run after thee* (Isa. 55:5). Jeremiah said *She weepeth sore in the night* (Lam. 1:2), but Isaiah said *Thou shalt weep no more; He will surely be gracious unto thee at the voice of thy cry, when He shall hear, He will answer thee* (Isa. 30:19). Jeremiah said *Her tears are on her cheeks* (Lam. 1:2), but Isaiah said *The Lord God will wipe away tears from off all faces* (Isa. 25:8). Jeremiah said *The ways of Zion do mourn, because none come to the solemn assembly* (Lam. 1:4), but Isaiah said *And I will make all My mountains a way* (Isa. 49:11), and *Cast up, cast up the highway, gather out the stones* (Isa. 62:10), and also *Cast ye up, cast ye up, clear the way* (Isa. 57:14). Jeremiah said *All her gates are desolate* (Lam. 1:4), but Isaiah said *Go through, go through the gates, clear ye the way of the people* (Isa. 62:10). Jeremiah said *She hath none to comfort her among all her lovers* (Lam. 1:2), but Isaiah said *I, even I, am He that comforteth her* (Isa. 51:12). Jeremiah said *I will cause to cease from them the voice of mirth* (Jer. 25:10), but Isaiah said *I will greatly rejoice in the Lord* (Isa. 61:10).

2. What is intimated by *Rejoicing, I will cause to rejoice in the Lord,* [another reading of the verse from Isaiah 61:10 cited just above]? That the congregation of Israel said to the Holy One: Since Thou didst cause us to

rejoice, let everyone rejoice with us, so that we be not like others who rejoiced while everyone else did not rejoice with them. The Holy One responded: Indeed, thou wilt be like Sarah thy mother who rejoiced and whom everyone else rejoiced with, as when she said: *God hath given me occasion for joy; everyone that heareth will laugh in joy with me*[1] (Gen. 21:6).

R. Samuel bar Naḥman said: Whoever mourned over Jerusalem upon its destruction will rejoice over it upon its rebuilding. The Holy One mourned over it, as is said *For it is a day of trouble, and of trampling, and of perplexity for the Lord, the God of hosts, in the Valley of Vision* (Isa. 22:5). And the Holy One will rejoice over it, as is said *As the bridegroom rejoiceth over the bride, so shall thy God rejoice over thee* (Isa. 62:5). The ministering angels mourned, as is said *Behold, the celestials cry, "[The Temple's destruction is] an outrage"; the angels of peace weep bitterly* (Isa. 33:7). And the ministering angels will rejoice in its rebuilding, as is said *I will set upon thy walls, O Jerusalem, [angelic] watchmen [who will be ever wakeful] day and night* (Isa. 62:6). The sun and the moon mourned, as is said *The sun darkened in his going forth, and the moon did not cause her light to shine* (Isa. 13:10). And the sun and the moon will rejoice in its rebuilding [by shining more radiantly], as is said *Moreover the light of the moon shall be as the light of the sun, and the light of the sun shall be sevenfold* (Isa. 30:26). Heaven and earth mourned, as is said *I clothe the heaven with blackness, and I make sackcloth their covering* (Isa. 50:3); *I beheld the earth, and lo, it was waste and void* (Jer. 4:23). And heaven and earth will rejoice with Israel, as is said *Sing, O ye heavens, for the Lord has done it; shout, ye lowest parts of the earth* (Isa. 44:23). Trees mourned, as is said *The fig tree did not blossom, there was no fruit in the vines; the labor of the olive failed* (Hab. 3:17). And the trees will rejoice with Israel, as is said *The tree will bear its fruit; the fig tree and the vine will yield their strength* (Joel 2:22); and also *Ye, O mountains of Israel, ye shall shoot forth your branches, and yield your fruit to My people Israel, for they are at hand to come* (Ezek. 36:8). The hills and the mountains mourned, as is said *I beheld the mountains, and lo, they trembled, and all the hills moved to and fro* (Jer. 4:24). And the hills and the mountains will rejoice with Israel, as is said *The mountains and the hills shall break forth before you into singing, and all the trees of the field shall clap their hands* (Isa. 55:12). The righteous mourned, as is said *To appoint unto them that mourn in Zion*, etc. (Isa. 61:3). And the righteous will rejoice, as is said *Rejoice ye with Jerusalem, and be glad with her, all ye that love her*, etc. (Isa. 66:10).

All the foregoing is implied in Israel's saying *Rejoicing, I will cause to rejoice in the Lord* (Isa. 61:10).

1. See Piska 22.1.

3. [Heaven and earth] wanted [to be linked with Jerusalem in the accounts of its rejoicing, but they did not find themselves so linked][1a] until Joel the son of Pethuel came and said [with regard to heaven]: *Be glad then, ye children of Zion, and rejoice in the Lord your God; for He giveth you the former rain in just measure* [*from heaven*] (Joel 2:23). Then Isaiah came and said with regard to earth, heaven's counterpart: *I will greatly rejoice in the Lord . . . for as the earth bringeth forth her growth,* etc. (Isa. 61:10). Then came Solomon who summed up in one verse what Joel and Isaiah had said [about heaven and earth rejoicing with Jerusalem]: *I am my Beloved's, and my Beloved is mine, that feedeth among the lilies*[2] (Song 6:3).

4. *Rejoicing, I will rejoice* (*śoś 'aśiś*) *in the Lord* (Isa. 61:10). What led Isaiah to say *in the Lord*, rather than "in God?" Because in the usual kinds of rejoicing, distress follows upon gladness whose celebration generally depends upon stuffing down a large quantity of meat and gulping down a large amount of red wine. Therefore, it is no accident that *śimḥah*, "gladness," is written with a *šin*, suggesting *šimhah*, "desolation."[3] But the kind of rejoicing Isaiah speaks of, a rejoicing coming through the Lord, is a gladness upon which no distress follows. Hence in the verse quoted above Isaiah's use of "Lord" instead of "God" is in keeping with Scripture's usage. For whenever Scripture says "Lord," the measure of mercy is meant, as is indicated by the words *The Lord, Lord, God merciful and gracious* (Exod. 34:6). On the other hand, whenever Scripture uses the term "God" (*'Elohim*), the measure of justice is meant, as indicated by the words *Thou shalt not revile God* (*'Elohim*)—[that is, God the judge] (Exod. 22:27).

5. *Rejoicing, I will rejoice in the Lord* (Isa. 61:10). A parable of a king of flesh-and-blood who had gone together with his sons and sons-in-law to a city by the sea. After a while when people came and said to the queen, "Good news! Your sons are back," she replied: Go out and make my daughters-in-law glad. When people came and said to her: "Good news! Your sons-in-law are back," she replied: Go out and make my daughters glad. But when people came and said to her: "Good news! the king is back," she replied: Surely, this is my very own gladness!

For His part, [the King], the Holy One, said to the congregation of

1a. See Saul Lieberman's note in PRKM, 476; and *Yalkuṭ on Isaiah*, ed. Spira (Berlin, 1894), p. 251.

2. In Jerusalem, where there are lilies growing in a field nourished by rain from heaven.

3. See Saul Lieberman's note, PRKM, 476. [As a matter of fact, *śoś 'aśiś* is also spelled with *Śin* throughout. The author, for the sake of his argument, assumes that the latter terms are spelled with the equivalent letter *samek̲*, which cannot possibly be read as a *Šin*. L.N.]

Israel: [Good news]! *Lift up thine eyes round about, and see: [Thy children] are all gathered together, and come to thee*, etc. (Isa. 60:4).

The words *For He hath clothed me with the garments of salvation* (Isa. 61:10) refer to the seven garments which, according to Scripture, the Holy One will have put on successively from the time the world was created until the time He requites wicked Edom. When He created the world, He put on glory and majesty, as is said *Thou are clothed with glory and majesty* (Ps. 104:1). When He appeared over the Red Sea, He put on haughtiness, as is said *The Lord reigneth; He is clothed in haughtiness* (Ps. 93:1). When He gave the Torah, He put on strength, as is said *The Lord puts on strength for the sake of His people* (Ps. 29:11). When He forgives the iniquities of Israel, He will put on a white garment, as is said *His raiment was as white snow* (Dan. 7:9). When He requites the peoples of the world, He will put on garments of vengeance, as is said *And He put on garments of vengeance for clothing* (Isa. 59:17). When the Messiah appears, God will put on the sixth garment: He will be clothed in righteousness, as is said *He put on righteousness as a coat of mail, and a helmet of salvation upon His head* (*ibid.*). When He requites Edom, He will put on the seventh garment: He will put on red apparel, as is said *Wherefore is Thine apparel red?* (Isa. 63:2). The splendor of the garment He puts on the Messiah will stream forth from world's end to world's end, as implied by the words *As a bridegroom putteth on a priestly diadem* (Isa. 61:10). Israel will live in his radiance and say: Blessed is the hour in which the Messiah was created! Blessed is the womb whence he came! Blessed is the generation whose eyes behold him! Blessed is the eye which has been given the privilege of seeing him whose lips open with blessing and peace, whose diction is pure delight, whose garments are glory and majesty, who is confident and serene in his speech, the utterance of whose tongue is pardon and forgiveness, whose prayer is a sweet savor, whose supplication during his study of Torah is purity and holiness.

Blessed are Israel. How much is laid up for them! As is said *Oh how abundant is Thy goodness which Thou hast laid up for them that fear Thee* (Ps. 31:20).

And as a bride adorneth herself with jewels (Isa. 61:10). Even as a bride is distinguished among her companions by her jewels, even so the congregation of Israel puts to shame enemies only by the light it clothes itself in, as is said *For, behold, though darkness will cover the earth*, etc., *nations shall walk at thy light, and kings at the brightness of thy rising* (Isa. 60:2,3).

Another comment: A bride is adorned with grace in the eyes of all who see her. But since a bride—once the days given over to her bridal bower are done—must go back to household tasks, is the congregation of Israel likewise to go back to its servitude? No, says Scripture, *The ransomed of the Lord shall return . . . and everlasting joy shall be upon their heads* (Isa. 35:10, 11).

SUPPLEMENT 7

Seek ye (Isa. 55:6)

1. *Seek ye the Lord while He may be found* (Isa. 55:6), [said Isaiah]. And David said: *Seek ye the Lord and His strength* (Ps. 105:4). What did he have in mind in going on to say in the same verse *Seek His face evermore* (*ibid.*)? To teach you that the Holy One, may His name be blessed, is at times seen and at times not seen, at times listens to prayer and at times does not listen to it, [at times answers prayer and at times does not answer it], at times lets Himself be sought out and at times does not let Himself be sought out, at times may be found and at times may not be found, at times is near and at times is not near. Thus He showed Himself to Moses, as is said *And the Lord spoke unto Moses face to face* (Exod. 33:11), but then He turned away and hid from him, so that Moses had to say, *Show me, I pray Thee, Thy glory* (Exod. 33:18). He likewise showed Himself to Israel at Sinai, as is said *They saw the God of Israel* (Exod. 24:10), and *The appearance of the glory of the Lord was like devouring fire* (Exod. 24:17), but then He turned away and hid from them, as is said *Take ye therefore good heed unto yourselves—for ye saw no manner of form* (Deut. 4:15), and *Ye heard the voice of words, but ye saw no form* (Deut. 4:12). While Israel were in Egypt, it is written *And God heard their groaning* (Exod. 2:24), but then when they sinned, *The Lord hearkened not to your voice, nor gave ear unto you* (Deut. 4:45). God answered Samuel in Mizpah, as is said *And Samuel cried unto the Lord . . . and the Lord answered him* (1 Sam. 7:9), but then He turned away and did not answer him, as when *The Lord said unto Samuel: "How long wilt thou mourn for Saul, seeing I have rejected him from being king over Israel?"* (1 Sam. 16:1). He answered David, as is said *I sought the Lord, and He answered me* (Ps. 34:5), but then He turned away and did not answer him, as when *David fasted, and as often as he went in, he lay all night upon the earth* (2 Sam. 12:16), and finally was told *The child also that is born unto thee shall surely die* (2 Sam. 12:14). At a time When Israel vow repentance, the Lord can always be found by them, as is said *Ye will seek the Lord thy God; and thou shalt find Him,* etc. (Deut. 4:29), but at a time when they vow no repentance, it is written *With their flocks and with their herds they shall go to seek the Lord, but they shall not find Him; He hath withdrawn Himself from them* (Hos. 5:6). At times He is near, as is said *The Lord is nigh unto all them that call upon Him* (Ps. 145:18), but at times He is not near, as is said *The Lord is far from the wicked* (Prov. 15:29).

Scripture says, *The Lord will regard thy person* (Num. 6:26), but then says, *The Lord . . . regardeth not persons* (Deut. 10:17). If a man vows repentance, God has regard for his person. One supposes that God's regard for persons applies to every kind of person, but to indicate otherwise, the verse concludes with the words *thy person* (Num. 6:26)—that is, the verse applies to a person of Israel and not to a person from another people. When Israel vow no repentance however, He has no regard for their persons. Thus it is said *O Jerusalem, wash thy heart from wickedness, that thou mayest be saved. How long shall thy baleful thoughts lodge with thee?* (Jer. 4:14). When, accordingly, will you be saved? When you vow repentance. But if you do not, what does Scripture say? *Though thou wash thee with niter, and take thee much soap, yet thine iniquity is marked before Me* (Jer. 2:22). Thus with Israel's repentance in mind, Isaiah said: *Seek ye the Lord while He may be found* (Isa. 55:6).

2. By what parable may the preceding comment be explained? By that of a king who said to his servants: Go forth and proclaim in my entire kingdom that I am about to sit and adjudicate civil cases. Before I sit in judgment on capital cases, however, let anyone who has a complaint against his fellow appear before me, and I will judge him in scales weighted in his favor. Likewise the Holy One, may His name be blessed and His title exalted, says to Israel: "My children, know ye that I pass judgment at four successive times in the year." [The four times are as follows]: At the time of Passover, He adjudicates cases concerning the produce of the field; at the time of Pentecost, cases concerning the fruit of the tree; at the time of the New Year, cases concerning all the inhabitants of the world who pass before Him in single file; at the time of Sukkot, cases concerning the supply of water.[1] "During three of these times," God continues, "I judge civil matters, [and at these times, without weighting the scales in anyone's favor, as a king of flesh-and-blood does], I make some people rich and some people poor, give more to some and less to others. But New Year's Day is the time for judging capital cases—for deciding death or life." As is said in Rab's Version of the Shofar Service: On the first day of Tishri, sentence is pronounced upon the countries of the world—those destined for war and those destined for peace. On this day the lives of mortals are scrutinized to determine who is to have life and who is to have death.[2] "Now," God declares, "if you vow repentance before Me, I will receive you and, [like a king of flesh-and-blood], will judge you in scales weighted in your favor. The gates of heaven are open, and I yearn to hear your prayers, hopefully looking down, as I do, through the windows of heaven and peering out through its lattices up until the moment when I have no choice but to seal the decree on the Day of Atonement."

Hence, with the judgment on New Year's Day in mind, Isaiah said: *Seek ye the Lord while He may be found* (Isa. 55:6).

1. A paraphrase of RH 1:2.
2. See Piska 23.1.

3. R. Samuel bar Naḥman said in the name of R. Jonathan: By what parable may the verse just above be explained? By that of a king who lived in a certain principality. When the people of the principality provoked him, the king was angered [and would not abide in their midst]. He removed himself some ten miles from the city before he stopped. A man who saw him went to the people in the city and said: Know that the king is angry at you and may well send legions against the city to destroy it. Go out and appease him before he removes himself still further away from you. Thereupon a wise man who was standing by said to the people: Fools, while he was in your midst, you did not seek him. Now, before he moves further away, seek him out. He may receive you. Hence it is said *Seek ye the Lord while He may be found* (Isa. 55:6)—that is, seek Him during the Ten Days of Repentance while He is abiding in Israel's midst. [At other times], as Ezekiel said in His name, *There may be a wall between Me and you*[3] (Ezek. 43:8). Therefore, *Call upon Him while He is near; let the wicked forsake his way, and the man of iniquity his thoughts; and let him return unto the Lord, and He will have compassion upon him, and to our God, for He will abundantly pardon* (Isa. 55:6–7).

ABBREVIATIONS

Aḇ	’Aḇoṯ
Ar	‘Ărakin
AZ	‘Ăḇoḏah Zarah
BB	Baḇa Baṯra
Beḵ	Bĕḵoroṯ
Ber	Bĕraḵoṯ
Beṣ	Beṣah
Bik	Bikkurim
BḲ	Baḇa Ḳamma
BM	Baḇa Mĕṣi‘a
Eḏ	‘Eḏuyyoṯ
Er	‘Eruḇin
Giṭ	Giṭṭin
Ḥag	Ḥăḡiḡah
Ḥal	Ḥallah
Ḥul	Ḥullin
Kel	Kelim
Ker	Kĕritoṯ
Keṯ	Keṯubboṯ
Ḳid	Ḳiddušin
Kil	Kil’ayim
Mak	Makkoṯ
Meḡ	Mĕḡillah
Men	Mĕnaḥoṯ
Mid	Middoṯ
MḲ	Mo‘eḏ Ḳaṭan
MSh	Ma‘ăśer Šeni
Naz	Nazir
Neḏ	Nĕḏarim
Neḡ	Nĕḡa‘im
Nid	Niddah
Oh	’Ŏhaloṯ
Or	‘Orlah
Par	Parah
Pes	Pĕsaḥim
RH	Roš haš-Šanah
Sanh	Sanheḏrin
Sem	Śĕmaḥoṯ
Shab	Šabbaṯ
Sheb	Šĕḇi‘iṯ
Sheḇu	Šĕḇu‘oṯ
Sheḳ	Šĕḳalim
Sof	Sofĕrim
Soṭ	Soṭah
Suk	Sukkah
Ta	Ta‘ăniṯ
Tam	Tamiḏ
Tef	Tĕfillin
Tem	Tĕmurah
Ter	Tĕrumoṯ
Ṭoh	Ṭoharoṯ
Uḳṣ	Uḳṣin
Yaḏ	Yaḏayim
Yeḇ	Yĕḇamoṯ
Zeḇ	Zĕḇaḥim

B. prefixed to the name of a tractate indicates a reference to the Babylonian Talmud; P. indicates a reference to the Palestinian (Jerusalemite) Talmud; and Tos a reference to the Tosefta (ed. Zuckermandel, Pasewalk, 1880; 2d ed., Jerusalem, 1937). Otherwise the reference is to tractates of the Mishnah.

Unless another edition is specified, the Midrash Rabbah used—on the Pentateuch as well as on the Five Scrolls—is the Wilno, 1878, edition.

OTHER SOURCES AND COMMENTARIES

‘Ănaf Yosef	Chanoch Zundel ben Yosef [d. 1867], Commentary on Midrash Rabbah (Wilno, 1897)

APB	*The Authorized Daily Prayer Book of the United Hebrew Congregations of the British Empire*, with a translation by Simeon Singer [1848–1906], 13th ed., London, 1925
'Aruk̲	Nathan ben Jehiel of Rome [11th century], *Aruch Completum*, ed. Alexander Kohut [1842–94], facsimile reprint, 8 vols., Vienna, 1926
AV	The Authorized version of the English Bible, first published in 1611
B (appended to a title-abbreviation)	ed. Solomon Buber
B.	Babylonian Talmud
b.	*ben* (Hebrew) or *bar* (Aramaic), "son of"
Bertinoro	Obadiah ben Abraham of Bertinoro [d. ca. 1500], Commentary on the Mishnah
BM	Bernard Mandelbaum
C	Carmoly Add. 1479, late fifteenth or early sixteenth century manuscript of PRK
Cas	Casanata Sacerdote 3324, seventeenth century manuscript which includes all but the last nine Piskas of PRK, Piskas from Pĕsiḳta Rabbat̲i, as well as sections from other midrashim
chap.	chapter
David Luria	David Luria [1798–1855], Comments on Midrash Rabbah, in the Wilno, 1878, edition
'En Ya'ăḳob̲	Jacob ben Solomon ibn Ḥab̲ib̲ [ca. 1460–1516], Compilation of the haggadic passages in the Babylonian Talmud and in the orders *Zĕra'im* and *Mo'ed̲* of the Palestinian Talmud, 4 vols., New York, 1955
'Eṣ Yosef	Chanoch Zundel ben Yosef [d. 1867], Commentaries on Tanḥuma (ed. Warsaw, after World War I) and on Midrash Rabbah on the Pentateuch (Wilno, 1897)
EV	English versions of Scripture (as distinguished from special interpretations made by a Rabbinic commentator)
G	Genizah fragments cited in PRKM

Gen. Rabbah TA	Genesis Rabbah, ed. Julius Theodor [1849–1923] and Chanoch Albeck [1890–1972], Berlin, 1912–31
Gesenius-Brown	Wilhelm Gesenius, *A Hebrew and English Lexicon of the Old Testament*, translated by Edward Robinson, edited by Francis Brown, S. R. Driver, and Charles A. Briggs, Oxford, 1907
Ginzberg, *CPT*	Louis Ginzberg [1873–1953], *Commentary on the Palestinian Talmud* (in Hebrew), 4 vols., New York, 1941–61
Ginzberg, *Legends*	Louis Ginzberg, *Legends of the Jews*, 7 vols., Philadelphia, 1908–38
Hertz, *APB*	*The Authorized Daily Prayer Book*, revised ed., by Joseph Herman Hertz [1872–1946], New York, 5714/1954
Ibn Ezra	Abraham ibn Ezra [1092–1167], Commentary on the Bible
Jastrow	Marcus Jastrow [1829–1903], *A Dictionary of the Targumim, the Talmud Babli and Yerushalmi, and the Midrashic Literature*, 2 vols., London and New York, 1903
JE	*The Jewish Encyclopedia*
JQR	*The Jewish Quarterly Review*
JV (Jewish Version)	*The Holy Scriptures according to the Masoretic Text*, Philadelphia, The Jewish Publication Society of America, 5677/1917
Kĕli yĕḳar	Ephraim ben Aaron of Lenicziza [d. 1619], Annotations on the Pentateuch (printed in Rabbinic Bibles)
Ḳimḥi	David Ḳimḥi [ca. 1160–1235], Commentary on the Bible
Ḳorban ha-ʿeḏah	David Fränkel [ca. 1704–64], Commentary on the orders Moʿeḏ, Našim, and Nĕziḳin of the Palestinian Talmud (ed. Wilno, 1922)
Krauss, *Lehnwörter*	Samuel Krauss [1866–1948], *Griechische und lateinische Lehnwörter*, 2 vols., Berlin, 1898–99
KY	Baruch ben Jonah Etelson, *Kanfe Yonah*, Commentary on Song Rabbah, Warsaw, 1876
Leḳaḥ Ṭoḇ	Tobiah ben Eliezer [11th century], Midrash Leḳaḥ Ṭoḇ, ed. Buber, Wilno, 1880

Lev. Rabbah M	Leviticus Rabbah, ed. Mordecai Margulies [1910–68], 5 vols., Jerusalem, 1953–60
Levy, *Wörterbuch*	Jacob Levy [1819–92], *Neuhebräisches und chaldäisches Wörterbuch über die Talmudim und Midraschim*, 4 vols., Leipzig, 1876–89
Lieberman, *GJP*	Saul Lieberman [1898–], *Greek in Jewish Palestine*, New York ,1942
Lieberman, *HJP*	Saul Lieberman, *Hellenism in Jewish Palestine*, New York, 1950
Lieberman, *TKF*	Saul Lieberman, *Tosefta ki-fĕšuṭah*, 12 vols. (in progress), New York, 1955–73
Lieberman, YKF	Saul Lieberman, *Hay-Yĕrušalmi ki-fĕšuṭo*, Jerusalem, 1934
L. N.	Leon Nemoy [1901–]
Mah	Zĕ'eḇ Wolf Einhorn [d. 1862], Commentary on Midrash Rabbah, Wilno, 1878
Mattĕnoṯ kĕhunnah	Issachar Ber ben Naphtali hak-Kohen [16th century], Comments on the Midrash Rabbah (in the Wilno, 1878, ed. of that Midrash)
MC	Ephraim Zalman Margolioth [1762–1828], Commentary on the Pĕsiḳta Rabbaṯi (in the Lemberg ed. of that Midrash; reprinted in the Warsaw ed.)
Meḳ	Mĕḳilta dĕ-Rabbi Ishmael, ed. Jacob Zallel Lauterbach [1873–1942], 3 vols., Philadelphia, 1933
MhG. Exod.	Midraš hag-Gaḏol on Exodus, ed. Mordecai Margulies, Jerusalem, 1956
MhG. Gen.	Midraš hag-Gaḏol on Genesis, ed. Mordecai Margulies, Jerusalem, 1947
MhG Num.	Midraš hag-Gaḏol on Numbers, ed. Solomon Fisch [1898–], 2 vols., London, 1957–63
Minḥaṯ šay	Jedidiah Norzi [ca. 1560–1626], Masoretic commentary on the Bible (printed as a supplement in Rabbinic Bibles)
Mishnah (ed. Albeck)	*The Mishnah*, ed. Chanoch Albeck, 6 vols., Jerusalem, 1952–58; and introductory volume, Jerusalem, 1959
Montefiore, *RA*	Claude Goldsmid Montefiore [1859–1939] and Herbert Loewe [1882–1940], *Rabbinic Anthology*, London, 1938

MSS — The manuscripts which Bernard Mandelbaum used in his edition of PRK

MT — Masoretic text of Scripture

MTeh — Midrash Tĕhillim, ed. Solomon Buber, [Wilno, 1891]; translated by William G. Braude [1907–], New Haven, 1959 (YJS, *13*)

Naḥmanides — Moses ben Naḥman [1194–ca. 1270], Commentary on the Pentateuch (printed in Rabbinic Bibles)

O — Oxford Neubauer 151 (1), thirteenth century manuscript upon which PRKM is based

O_1 — Oxford Neubauer 2334–11, sixteenth century manuscript of PRK whose table of contents begins with the Piska for New Year's Day

O_2 — Oxford Neubauer 152, fifteenth century manuscript of PRK which is an abridgment of C

Onkelos — *see* Targum

P. — Palestinian Talmud

Pa — Parma De Rossi 261, thirteenth or fourteenth century manuscript which contains eleven chapters of PRK

Pĕne Mošeh — Moses Margalit [18th century], Commentary on the orders *Našim, Zĕra'im*, and *Mo'eḏ* of the Palestinian Talmud, ed. Wilno, after World War I

PH — *The Pentateuch and Haftarahs*, ed. Joseph Herman Hertz, London, 1956

PR — Pĕsiḳta Rabbaṯi, ed. Meir Friedmann [1831–1908], Vienna, 1880; translated by William G. Braude, New Haven, 1968 (YJS, *18*)

PRE — Pirḳe dĕ-Rabbi Eliezer, Warsaw, 1852; translated by Gerald Friedlander [1871–1923], London, 1916

PRF — Pĕsiḳta Rabbaṯi, ed. Friedmann, Vienna, 1880

PRK — Pĕsiḳta dĕ-Raḇ Kahăna

PRKB — Pĕsiḳta dĕ-Raḇ Kahăna, ed. Solomon Buber [1827–1906], Lyck, 1868

PRKM — Pĕsiḳta dĕ-Raḇ Kahăna, ed. Bernard Mandelbaum [1922–], 2 vols., New York, 1962

Rashi — R. Solomon ben Isaac of Troyes [1040–1105], author of commentaries on the Hebrew Bible and on the Babylonian Talmud

RV — Revised version of the English Old Testament (first published in 1885)

S — Safed (sixteenth century) manuscript of PRK which Buber used as the basis for his edition

S (followed by a numeral) — Supplement

Samuel ben Meir — Samuel ben Meir [ca. 1085–ca. 1174], Commentary on the Bible

Samuel Edels — Samuel Eliezer ben Judah Edels [1555–1631], Novellae on the Babylonian Talmud (in the Wilno, 1880, ed.)

Sif — Sifre, Sifra

Šiyyure ḳorban — David Fränkel [ca. 1704–64], Notes on the Palestinian Talmud (ed. Wilno, 1922)

Soncino tr. — The English translations of the Babylonian Talmud (1935–52), the Midrash Rabbah (1939), and the Zohar (1931–34), issued by the Soncino Press in London

SOR — Seder ʻOlam Rabbah, ed. Ber Ratner [1852–1916], Wilno, 1894

Strashun's Novellae — Samuel Strashun [1794–1872], Novellae on Midrash Rabbah (in the Wilno, 1878, ed. of that Midrash)

Table of Scriptural Lessons — The Table of Scriptural Lessons in *The Holy Scriptures*, Philadelphia, 5677/1917

Tanḥuma — ed. Warsaw, after World War I

Tanḥuma B — ed. Solomon Buber, Wilno, 1885

Targum — Ancient translations or paraphrases of the Bible into Aramaic. The most important of these is the translation of the Pentateuch that is ascribed to Onkelos, the Proselyte, a Mishnaic teacher of the first century.
The Targum Jonathan is a freer paraphrase of the Bible, ascribed to Jonathan ben Uzziel, a pupil of Hillel.

Torah šĕlemah — Menahem Kasher [1895–], Compilation of Rabbinic comments on the Pentateuch and commentary thereon, Jerusalem, 1927–69

Torat̲ Ḥayyim — Ḥayyim ben Joseph [18th century], Commentary on

	parts of 'En Ya'ăḳoḇ (in the New York, 1955, ed.)
Tosafoṯ	Critical and explanatory glosses on the Talmud by the successors of Rashi
tr	transmitter
Yalḳuṭ	The compilation or catena on Scripture known as Yalḳuṭ Šimě'oni
Yěfeh to'ar	Samuel ben Isaac Jaffe [16th century], Comments on Midrash Rabbah (in the Wilno, 1878, ed. of that Midrash)
YJS	Yale Judaica Series
Yoreh de'ah	Joseph Caro [1488–1575], *Šulḥan 'aruḵ*, Part II, ed. Wilno, 1894
Zayyiṯ ra'ănan	Abraham Abele Gumbiner [ca. 1635–83], Comments on the Yalḳuṭ (in the Warsaw, 1876, ed. of that compilation)
Zunz, *had-Děrašoṯ*	Yom Ṭoḇ Lippmann Zunz [1794–1886], *had-Děrašoṯ bě-Yiśra'el*, translated by Chanoch Albeck, Jerusalem, 5707/1947
[ ]	Interpolation made for the sake of clarity or based on a parallel reading in another source
< >	Insertion made by Mandelbaum in his ed. of Pěsiḳta dě-Raḇ Kahăna

GLOSSARY

Ab
see Months

Adar
see Months

Afternoon Prayer (*Minḥah*)
recited from half an hour after midday until sunset, corresponding to the time set for the daily burnt offering of the afternoon

'Ăḡaḏah (pl. *'Ăḡaḏoṯ*)
that part of Talmudic (and of later Rabbinic) literature which does not deal with legal matters

Altar
unless otherwise specified, refers to the Outer Altar, also known as the Altar of Burnt Offering (Exod. 25:6), situated in the courtyard of the Tabernacle or the Temple Court; upon it were burned all sacrifices except the incense and were offered all sprinklings of blood except those of certain sin offerings

Amalek
a people totally evil—hence *the* symbol of evil

'Ămiḏah (literally "standing")
see Tĕfillah

Amoraim
literally "expounders," "expositors"; Talmudic authorities who flourished about 200–500 C.E., and whose discussions are embodied in the Gemara

Analogy
the use of a similar expression occurring elsewhere in Scripture in order to apply to one subject a rule, characteristic, or concept already known to apply to another

Atbash (*'tbš*)
a method of interchanging the first letter of the Hebrew alphabet, *'alef*, with the last letter, *taw*; the second, *beṯ*, with the next to the last, *šin*; and so on

Baraita
an extraneous Mishnah, containing a Tannaitic tradition not incorporated in the Mishnah as collected by Rabbi Judah the Prince (ca. 200 C.E.), but cited in the Gemara, the Midrash, or the Tosefta

Berabbi
an honorific title given to a Sage or scholar

Bible
the Hebrew Bible consists of three main groups: (1) the Law, i.e. the five books of the Pentateuch; (2) the Prophets, subdivided into Prior Prophets (Joshua through Kings) and Latter Prophets (Isaiah through Malachi); and (3) the Writings (Psalms through Chronicles); *see also* Oral Law

Blessing, seasonal
benediction ending with the words "who has kept us alive, and preserved us, and enabled us to reach this season"; *see* Maimonides' Code, III, x, i, 3 (YJS, *14*, 454–55) for the full text

Burnt offering
offered because of sinful desire or evil thoughts that come into one's mind; cf. Lev. Rabbah 7:3

Clean and unclean animals
cf. Lev. 11

Daily burnt offerings
two he-lambs were offered daily in the Temple, one in the morning and one in the afternoon at dusk; cf. Num. 28:1–8

Day and night
in the Jewish system of time reckoning, the day begins with the preceding night; the night is counted from dusk to dawn, and the day from dawn to dusk or sunrise to sunset; a daylight hour means a twelfth part of the day as thus defined

Denar
a silver coin, which is worth a quarter of a *sela'*, approximately twenty-five cents, or one twenty-fourth of the gold denar

Diverse kinds
of seeds or plants, may not be sown together; of garment stuffs, may not be worn together; of cattle, may not be bred to each other; cf. Lev. 19:19; Deut. 22:9–11

Edom
a Rabbinic designation of Rome

Eighteen Benedictions (*Šĕmoneh 'eśreh*)
see Tĕfillah

Elul
see Months

Ephah
standard Biblical dry measure equal to ten *'omer* (Exod. 16:36) or three *sĕ'ah*, approximately the contents of seventy eggs—1 bushel

'Erub̲
literally "intermingling, blending"; specifically, a symbolic act of "blending" several domains or limits together for the purpose of making it lawful on the Sabbath to walk or transport things from one place to another

Esau
a Rabbinic designation of Rome

Ethrog
a species of citron (*Citrus medica L.*) used with the festive cluster on the Feast of Sukkot; *see also* Lulab

Festal peace offering (*ḥăḡiḡah*)
brought on each of the pilgrimage festivals; cf. Deut. 16:16; Exod. 23:14–17; Ḥaḡ 1:1–2; Pes 6:3–4; and YJS, *4*, 43–44, 49

First fruits
a portion of the first ripe fruits brought by the owner of the field to the Temple in thanksgiving and then consumed by the priests; *see* Num. 18:17, 18

Firstling
the first-born male of cattle and sheep brought by the owner to the Temple as a hallowed offering and consumed by the priests; see Num. 18:17, 18

Four Kingdoms
Babylonia, Media and Persia, Greece, and Rome, which kept Israel in subjection; cf. Dan. 7

Gemara
that part of the Talmud which contains the comments of the Amoraim upon the Mishnah

Habdalah
the Benediction of "Separation" recited at the close of the Sabbath or holy day

Haftarah
the selection from the Prophets read in the synagogue service after the lesson from the Pentateuch

Halaḵah (pl. *Halaḵoṯ*)
that part of Talmudic (and of later Rabbinic) literature which deals with legal matters; also a Section of a chapter in the Mishnah

Hallel
Psalms 113–18, as used for liturgical recitation

Hanukkah
minor Jewish festival of eight days, beginning on the 25th day of Kislev, commemorating the rededication of the Temple by the Maccabees in 165 B.C.E.

Heave offering
a portion of the produce (about two percent on the average) which was given to the priests who alone were permitted to eat it; cf. Num. 18:8; Lev. 22:10; Deut. 18:4

Heave offering of the tithe
out of the tithe which he received, the Levite was obliged to give a tenth part to the priest; in other words, one hundredth of the original produce harvested by the Israelite; cf. Num. 18:25–32

Heshvan
see Months

Holy spirit
the quickening of man's natural faculties by divine inspiration—a level of

inspiration below that of prophecy, whereby a prophet receives divine communications in a supranatural manner, see Maimonides, *Guide*, 2:45

Homer
11 bushels

Hours, Daylight
see Day and night

Immersion pool
must contain 40 *sĕ'ah* (approximately 60 gallons or 270 liters) of water, which may not be drawn, but must be taken directly from a river or spring, or must consist of rain water led straight into the bath (YJS, *8*, 509–10)

Iyar
see Months

Jubilee year
the year concluding a series of seven Sabbatical cycles comprising 49 years; cf. Lev. 25:8–16

Ḳab̲
4 pints

Ḳĕri
the Masoretic instruction for reading as opposed to the *kĕṯib̲*, the traditional spelling of Biblical words

Kĕṯib̲
the traditional spelling of Biblical words as opposed to the *Ḳĕri*, the Masoretic instruction for reading

Kiddush
the ceremony of drinking wine after a blessing in the synagogue or home, by which the advent of the Sabbath or festivals is sanctified

Kislev
see Months

Kor
11 bushels

Law, the
see Bible

Levite
(a) a descendant of the Tribe of Levi (see Num. 3:5 ff.); (b) as contrasted to "priest" and "[lay] Israelite"

Loḡ
a liquid measure said to be equal to the displacement of six eggs (cf. B.Er 83a)—1 pint

Lulab
the palm branch carried with the festive cluster during the Festival of Sukkot—cf. Lev. 23:40; or, more generally, the cluster of palm branch, myrtle, and willow used with the ethrog on that festival

Mezuzah

literally "doorpost" (Deut. 6:9); a piece of parchment bearing the verses Deut. 6:4–9, 11:13–21, enclosed in a cylinder and fastened to the righthand doorpost

Midrash

exposition or exegesis of Scripture

Mishnah (literally "teaching")

the collection of legal decisions of the Sages of the first two centures C.E. (the Tannaim), edited and arranged into six orders by Rabbi Judah the Prince (ca. 200 C.E.); the Mishnah provides the text to which the Gemara is the commentary, the two together constituting the Talmud

Months

the Hebrew names of the months are as follows: Nisan, Iyar, Sivan, Tammuz, Ab, Elul, Tishri, Heshvan (Marheshvan), Kislev, Tebet, Shebat, Adar; in an intercalated year a thirteenth month, called 2nd Adar, is added

Musaf (Additional offering)

special offering for the Sabbaths, New Moons, and festivals, brought in addition to the regular daily offerings; cf. Num. 28:9–31; after the destruction of the Temple, replaced by the Additional Prayer

Nazirite

one who vows to dedicate himself to the service of God; his vow implies (a) abstention from all products of the grapevine; (b) letting his hair grow; (c) avoidance of contact with a dead body (see Num. 6:2–8)

Nisan

see Months

Noachide Commandments

seven universal precepts held to be incumbent not only upon Israelites but also upon all the "sons of Noah," i.e. upon the whole human race; cf. Maimonides' Code, XIV, v, ix, 1 (YJS, *3*, 230–31) *a*nd MTeh (YJS, *13*, 2, 417–18)

'Omer

the sheaf of barley, also called the sheaf of waving, brought as an offering on the 16th day of Nisan; cf. Lev. 23:9–14

Oral Law

unlike the written Torah which Moses received at Sinai, the Oral Law or Oral Torah, its authoritative exposition, was never meant to be, but eventually was, committed to writing

Parasang

a distance of 8,000 cubits or 4 miles

Peace offering

sacrifice betokening nearness and communion between God and man

Pĕṯiḥah
a brief, dramatic sermon or homily, which on a Sabbath or feast day preceded the reading of the lesson for the day in the Torah Scroll

Piska
literally "a passage in Scripture designated as an annual lesson," or "a lesson in Scripture that is brief." In the translation of Pĕsiḳta dĕ-Raḇ Kahăna the term is used as a synonym for chapter

Priestly watch
the priests and Levites were divided into 24 guards or watches, each one of which was on duty for one week every half year; cf. 1 Chron. 24:4; Ta 4:2

Prophets
see Bible

Purim
the Feast of Lots, observed on the fourteenth day of Adar in commemoration of the salvation of the Jews in Persia; its full story is recorded in the Book of Esther

Rabbi
literally "my master"; a term of respect used in direct address by a disciple to his teacher and generally by the public to a scholar known for his learning. It was only much later that the term assumed its present meaning of the spiritual leader of a Jewish community

Ram's horn
see Shofar

Representatives of the Family
relatives designated to represent a groom or bride in negotiating betrothal or other matters pertaining to the well-being of either

Ritual bath
see Immersion pool

Sabbath limit
one may not walk on the Sabbath beyond the distance of 2,000 cubits from the city or place where one resides

Sages
see Scribes

Sanhedrin
council, high court; the Great Sanhedrin, the Supreme Court consisting of 71 members; a Small Sanhedrin, a high court consisting of 23 members

Sĕ'ah
peck and a half or 12 quarts

Scribes
or Sages; the post-Biblical scholars dating back to Ezra the Scribe (ca. 440 B.C.); the term, however, is loosely used to apply to the Rabbis of the subsequent period who preserved and transmitted the Oral Law

Scripture
see Bible

Sheaf of barley
see ‘Omer

Shebat
see Months

Shekinah
“the Presence [of God]”; used as a circumlocution when Scripture speaks of God’s dwelling in a place or removing from one

Shĕma‘
the name and the first word (“Hear, [O Israel]!”) of a group of passages from Scripture (Deut. 6:4–9, 11:13–21; Num. 15:37–41) which must be recited daily in the morning and in the evening

Shofar
ram’s horn sounded on New Year’s Day and on other occasions; cf. Num. 29:1; Lev. 25:9; the notes produced by it were the following: sustained note (*tĕḳi‘ah*), tremolo (*tĕru‘ah*), and broken note (*šĕḇarim*)

Sivan
see Months

Sukkah
the booth used in observance of the Festival of Sukkot

Talmud
the two collections of Rabbinic law and lore comprising Mishnah and Gemara; one, the Palestinian, also known as Jerusalemite Talmud, redacted by the disciples of R. Johanan, ca. 300 C.E.; the other, the Babylonian, redacted by R. Ashi and Rabina, ca. 450 C.E.

Tammuz
see Months

Tannaim
authorities who are cited in the Mishnah and the Baraita and who flourished up to about the year 200 C.E.

Tebet
see Months

Tĕfillah
the name of one of the principal prayers in the daily services, consisting on weekdays of 19 (originally 18) benedictions. Hence called also “Eighteen Benedictions” (*Šĕmoneh ‘eśreh*), and also, since it is usually recited while standing, *‘Ămiḏah* (“Standing [Prayer]”)

Tefillin (phylacteries)
small leather cases, one worn on the arm and the other on the head during the recital of week-day prayers. Each case contains parchment strips upon which are written four passages from Scripture: Exod. 13:1–10, 11–16; Deut. 6:4–9, 11:13–21

Tĕḳi'ah
  see Shofar
Tĕru'ah
  see Shofar
Tishri
  see Months
Tithe (*ma'ăśer*)
  a tenth part of a man's harvest given either as a due or in charity: the first tithe was given to the Levite in each of the first six years of the Sabbatical cycle; the second tithe was separated in the first, second, fourth, and fifth years of the cycle and was consumed by the owner in Jerusalem; the poor man's tithe was given to the poor in the third and sixth year of the cycle
Torah
  see Bible
Tosefta
  a collection of those legal decisions of the Tannaim which were not included in the Mishnah; redacted by R. Ḥiyya, disciple of Rabbi Judah the Prince
Urim and Thummim
  the twelve precious stones set in the "breastplate of judgment" upon which were engraved the names of the Twelve Tribes of Israel (Exod. 28:15–30); the letters served as an oracle
Writings
  see Bible

PASSAGES CITED

SCRIPTURE

Genesis

1:1	12.24, 21.5
1:2	21.5
1:3	21.5
1:5	7.5
1:14	5.1
1:15	5.1
1:16	21.1, 22.1
1:17	5.1, S2.1
1:20	4.3
1:26	4.3
1:28	22.2
2:3	23.10
2:4	S1.20
2:10	6.1
2:15	12.7, 15.1
2:16	12.1, 12.7, 15.1
2:17	12.1, 14.5
2:18	17.3
2:19	4.3
2:20	4.3, 4.4
3:6	20.6
3:7	20.6
3:8	1.1, 5.3
3:9	15.1
3:11	15.1
3:12	4.4, 17.3
3:17	14.2
3:19	4.4, 14.2, 19.5, 26.3
3:23	4.4, 15.1
3:24	12.7, 15.1
4:4	9.4, 28.5
4:8	27.4
4:12	24.11
4:13	24.11
4:16	24.11
4:25	5.2
5:2	S1.11
5:24	23.10
6:7	S1.11
6:8	9.4, 12.1
6:9	18.1, 26.1
6:16	12.12
7:1	12.7
7:2	4.2
7:11	9.1
7:23	26.2
8:1	9.1
8:4	9.1
8:16	12.7
8:21	1.1, 6.3, S3.2
9:1	S1.11
9:4	12.1
9:6	12.1, S3.2
9:13	11.15
9:14	11.15
9:25	S1.11
9:26	S1.11
10:7	12.23
11:28	26.10
11:30	18.3, 20.1
12:1	13.1, 28.3
12:2	28.3, S1.11
12:17	7.4
14:14	8.2
14:15	7.5
14:20	17.1
14:22	10.6
15:1	16.4
15:9	5.2
15:12	5.2
15:13	5.7
15:15	3.1
15:17	5.2
15:18	5.2
16:19	22.4
17:5	28.3
17:8	8.4
17:9	8.4, 12.1, 12.7
17:12	4.3
17:15	28.3
18:1	5.8
18:7	9.9
18:11	27.9
18:18	11.15
18:25	16.4, 19.3
18:27	3.2
19:24, 25	26.2
20:7	18.1

21:1 9.4, 22.1
21:4 12.1
21:6 22.1, S6.2
21:7 18.3, 20.1, 22.1
21:12 14.2, 23.9
21:23 11.9
21:28 11.9
22:2 23.9, 26.3
22:4 26.3
22:5 26.3
22:12 26.3
22:13 9.9, 23.7, 23.10
22:16 23.9
23:3 26.10
23:9 10.1
23:15 10.1
23:16 10.1
24:1 27.9
24:17 6.2
24:20 3.7, 18.2
24:65 18.1
25:5 S1.1
25:21 20.1
25:22 3.1
25:23 S2.1
25:23–26 3.1
25:25 5.18, 27.10
25:26 28.3
25:27 10.10, 18.1
25:29 3.1, 11.5
25:30 6.2
25:35 S1.1
26:1 13.1
26:4 2.8
26:8 S1.20
26:12 10.6, S4.3
26:28 9.4
27:1 3.1, 5.18
27:9 9.9
27:15 5.18
27:16 22.4
27:22 15.5
27:28 S1.1
27:33 S1.11
27:36 3.11
27:41 9.11, S1.11
28:1 S1.1, S1.11
28:4 S1.11
28:7 5.9, 13.1
28:12 23.2
28:14 2.8
28:15 19.5
28:22 10.6, S4.3
29:31 20.1, 20.2
29:33 S1.8
29:35 S1.8
30:20 20.1
30:42 27.3
31:4 4.3
31:36 14.1
31:37 14.1
32:9 19.3
32:12 19.3
32:22 19.3
32:28–29 7.3
32:30 S1.11
32:33 12.1
33:3 19.3
35:8 3.1
35:9 3.1, S1.11
35:10 7.3
35:18 13.14
35:22 24.9
35:24 20.1
37:2 3.13
37:29 24.9
38:8 12.1
39:2 9.4
39:8, 9 S3.2
39:11 14.2
41:14 S3.2
42:6 17.3
42:18 3.13
45:12 11.6
46:4 14.2
46:26, 27 11.13
47:12 4.3
47:24 S3.2
48:5 10.6
49:1 S1.1
49:4 S1.11
49:28 S1.1, S1.11
50:11 11.9
50:21 16.5, S4.2

Exodus

1:7 11.11
1:10 14.4
1:14 3.e, 3.2, 5.9
1:16, 22 9.11
1:22 11.2, 11.5
2:2 12.13, 26.1
2:13 28.2
2:24 S7.1

3:6 26.9
3:8 14.4
3:10 14.5, 16.9
3:12 12.18
3:16 5.3
4:14 24.11
4:22 1.4
4:28 12.6
5:2 11.1, 14.5, 28.1
5:20 5.8
6:6 5.11
6:13 14.5
6:25 13.12
7:1 12.23
8:12 7.11
8:16 11.1
9:3 7.11
9:24 1.3
9:27 11.1, 14.5
9:29 1.4
10:22 5.9, 7.12
11:2 11.6
11:3 S1.20
11:4 5.6, 5.9, 7.3, 7.5
11:5 7.6/9
11:7 11.12
12:1 5.9
12:1–2 5.2
12:2 5.1, 5.3, 5.4, 5.5, 5.6, 5.7, 5.10, 5.11, 5.13, 5.14, 5.18
12:3 5.17, 5.18
12:6 5.18
12:8 5.17
12:9 5.19
12:11 5.19
12:12 1.2, 5.8, 5.9, 7.3
12:16 5.13
12:21 5.17
12:22 27.1
12:29 7.3, 7.5, 7.6/9, 17.1
12:30 7.5, 7.6/9
12:33 7.5
12:36 11.3
12:37 2.8
12:42 7.6/9
12:43 12.16
13:10 28.10
13:17 11.1, 11.3, 11.4, 11.6, 11.7, 11.8, 11.9, 11.10
13:18 11:11
13:19 11.12, 11.25
13:20 12.14
13:21 11.8
13:22 11.8
14:7 12.5
14:15 8.2
14:21 5.9
14:29 9.4, 12.11
14:30 12.6
14:31 1.2, 5.8
15.2 5.9, 17.6
15:3 4.10, 5.17
15:4 11.2
15:8 1.4
15:9 11.1, 12.2
15:11 16.3, 19.5, S1.16
15:13 19.6
15:14 19.6
15:15–16 3.10
15:17 5.4
15:18 2.7, 5.6
15:25 12.8
16:4 11.8, 12.11
16:16 8.1
16:26 14.5
16:27 14.5
16:31 12.25
17.2 3.a
17:4 3.15
17:7 3.a, 3.9
17:8 3.a
17:9 3.b, 3.c
17:10 3.c, 3.d
17:12 S1.20
17:13 3.b, 3.c, 3.d
17:14 3.2, 3.15, 3.16
17:16 3.16
18:4 4.7
18:11 11.5
18:21 12.16
18:27 12.9, 12.16
19:1 12.1, 12.2, 12.3, 12.4, 12.7, 12.9, 12.11, 12.12, 12.13, 12.15, 12.16, 12.17, 12.18, 12.19, 12.20, 12.21
19:2 12.14, 12.15
19:3 1.4, 12.11, 23.10
19:4 11.8
19:7 12.19
19:8 5.16, 12.19
19:11 5.8, 12.13
19:14 1.4

19:17 5.16
19:20 1.4, 5.8, 12.11, 12.15
20:2 5,8, 13.8, 19.5, 12.22, 12.24
20:3 12.4, 13.8
20:4 2.1
20:7 13.8
20:8 13.8
20:12 13.8
20:13 13.8
20:14 13.8
20:15 5.16
20:18 12.19
21:1 12.8, 12.11
21:14 11.5
22:13 10.1
22:19 2.1, 14.5
22:27 12.1, 12.23, S6.4
23:11 23.10
23:19 10.9
23:20 10.9
24:1 26.9
24:7 2.7, 4,4, 5.6, 5.16, 9.6, 12.19, 14.4, 17.7, 19.5
24:10 S7.1
24:11 26.9
24:17 5.3, S7.1
25:8 2.1, 2.10, 3.14, 6.4
25:22 1.2, 6.4
25:40 1.3
26:6 1.6
26:11 1.6
26:15 1.2, 1.3
26:29 1.2
26:31 1.2
27:10 1.2
27:20 2.7
27:41 9.11
28:2 11.9
28:35 26.9
28:43 26.9
29:38–42 6.3
29:39 5.17
30:2 2.1, 2.7
30:12 2.2, 2.3, 2.5, 2.7, 2.8, 2.9, 2.10, 6.4
30:13 2.4, 2.10, 6.4
30:19 26.9
30:20 26.9
30:25 S2.4
30:31 2.7
31:13 2.7, 5.1
31:14 S3.2
31:17 2.4, 18.5, 27.1
32:1 2.4, 16.11
32:4 2.1, 9.6, 9.8, 17.7
32:7 16.9
32:8 4.4, 9.3, 14.4, 14.5
32:11 16.9
32:13 25.4
32:14 14.5, 16.9
32:24 2.4
32:28 2.8
33:5 2.7
33:11 17.1, S7.1
33:18 S7.1
33:19 17.1
34:5 3.c, 4.5
34:6 17.1, S6.4
34:6–7 6.1
34:26 10.9
34:27 10.9
34:28 6.1, 27.1
34:29 5.4, 26.9
34:30 5.3, 26.9, S1.9
39:43 S1.4, S1.11

Leviticus

2:14 8.1
3:5 6.3
6:2 6.3
6:12 2.4
8:33 28.4
9:1 28.4
9:4 4.5
9:23 S1.4, S1.11
10:1 26.8
10:2 26.9
10:4 26.4
10:9 26.9
11:4 4.2
11:5 4.2
11:6 4.2
11:7 4.2
11:21 26.5
11:29 5.15
12:3 9.1, 9.10, 28.4
13:2 17.6
13:46 7.10
13:52 7.10
13:56 7.10
14:40 7.10
14:45 7.10
15:25 12.15
16:1 26.1, 26.2, 26.3, 26.4,

26.5, 26.6/7
16:6 26.9
16:26 4.6
16:29 4.6
16:30 2.7, 9.9, 26.11, S2.8
17:13 15.7
18:5 4.6
18:16 4.6
19:9 5.5
19:10 17.6
19:19 4.6
19:32 27.9
19:34 12.17
20:2 2.7
20:6 24.16
20:10 2.1
20:16 9.3, 20.6
20:18 12.15
20:26 5.5
21:1 4.4
22:22 24.5
22:27 9.1, 9.2, 9.3, 9.4, 9.5, 9.6, 9.7, 9.9, 9.10
22:28 9.11
22:29 9.12
23:4 5.13
23:10 8.1, 8.2
23:11 8.3
23:15 8.1
23:22 23.5
23:24 23.1, 23.2, 23.3, 23.4, 23.6, 23.7, 23.8, 23.9, 23.10, 23.12
23:39 27.7
23:40 27.1, 27.2, 27.3, 27.6, 27.7, 27.8, 27.9
23:42 28.a, S2.6
23:43 S2.6
24:2 2.7, 15.1
24:11 11.6
24:16 12.1, 22.5a
25:10 23.10
26:1 12.4
26:9 19.4
26:13 12.17
26:16 16.11
26:44 16.11

Numbers

1:18 4.3
2:2 2.8
3:4 26.9, 26.10
3:13 7.5
5:15 8.4
6:24 1.5, 5.8, 13.13
6:25 13.13
6:26 1.5, 13.13, S7.1
7:1 1.1, 1.2, 1.3, 1.4, 1.5, 1.6
7:2 1.7
7:3 1.7, 1.8
7:4 1.8
7:5 1.8
7:48 28.4
7:54 28.4
7:89 1.2
8:4 5.15
8:17 7.5
8:19 2.7
9:20 4.5
10:35 S1.9
10:36 S1.9
11:8 12.25
11:22 4.3
11:25 4.5, 16.4
11:31 12.11
12:3 2.3
12:5 4.5
12:7 4.3, 5.4, 7.3
12:8 26.9
14:4 12.14, 16.11
14:14 S2.2
14:17 25.1
14:18 25.1, 25.2, 25.3
14:19 25.4
14:20 25.4
15:39 8.1, 24.14
16:15 25.1
16:26 26.1, 28.2
17:23 26.5
18:20 13.12
18:26 10.6
19:1 4.7, 12.10
19:1–2 4.2
19:2 4.1, 4.4, 4.5, 4.6, 4.7, 4.9, 4:10
19:3 4.9, 4.10
19:5 4.9, 4.10
19:6 4.10
19:9 4.10
19:17 4.4
20:1 26.11
20:10 14.5
20:12 14.5
20:16 7.3

21:1 19.2
21:5 17.3
21:17 11.8, 12.11
21:34 8.2
23:9 3.c
23:10 S1.4
23:21 S1.4
23:23 9.2
24:1 S1.4
24:5 S1.4, S1.20
24:10 S1.11
24:20 3.5
25:1 S1.8
25:6 S1.8
25:11 13.12
25:22 2.10
26:7, 14 11.6
26:19–56 2.8
26:52 5.9
28:2 2.10, 6.1, 6.2, 6.3, 6.4
28:3 2.10, 6.4
28:4 2.10, 6.4
28:6 6.1, 6.4
28:7 6.1
29:1 23.12
29:1–2 23.12
29:2 23.12
29:8, 13, 36 23.12
29:17, 29:20 28.a
29:17, 20, 23, 26, 29, 32 28.6
29:35 28.a, 28.c, 28.d, 28.e, 28.f, 28.1, 28.2, 28.4, 28.5, 28.6
29:36 28.6
29:19 28.f, 28.8
29:31 28.f, 28.8
29:33 28.f, 28.8
29:34 28.3
29:35 28.7, 28.8
29:36 28.g
29:39 28.g, 28.10
30:14 S1.9
31:2 S2.2
31:3 S2.2
33:3 5.1
33:49 26.6/7
33:55 13.5
34:18 5.9
35:15 S2.2

Deuteronomy

1:1 13.7, S1.5
1:11 S1.4, S1.11
1:12 15.6
2:26 S5.4
4:4 1.8, 28.10
4:6 4.4
4:7 5.13
4:12 S7.1
4:15 S7.1
4:22 S1.20
4:29 S7.1
4:30, 31 24.11
4:31 15.7
4:34 5.11
4:44 19.4
4:45 S7.1
5:4 1.2
5:5 12.13
5:27 5.8
6:7 9.5
7:3 4.3, 19.2
7:4 4.3
7:23 4.3
8:4 11.21
8:14 17.5
9:2 26.1
9:19 5.3
9:26 16.9
9:29 16.9
10:2 26.11
10:6 26.11
10:14 S1.20
10:17 S7.1
10:21 11.13
10:22 2.8, 11.13
13:7 5.9
14:2 9.4
14:4 6.1, 9.5
14:5 6.1, 9.5
14:21 10.9, 10.10
14:22 10.1, 10.3, 10.4, 10.5, 10.6, 10.7, 10.8, 10.9, 10.10, S4.1, S4.2, S4.3
14:22, 23 10.2
14:23 10.10, S4.3
14:25 10.7
14:29 10.10
15:10 10.4

15:11 10.4
15:14 5.5, 10.4
16:10–11 S2.8
16:13 S2.6, S2.7
16:14 10.10, S2.8
16:15 S2.8
16:18 28.e
16:19 1.7
17:15 3.14
17:16 1.7, 26.2
17:17 1.7, 26.2
18:18 13.6
20:17 13.5
22:6 9.11
22:9 5.5
22:10 5.5
22:11 4.6
22:25 3.1
23:8 3.e, 3.3
23:11 3.10
23:20 4.4
24:16 25.3
24:19 5.5
25:4 5.5
25:5 4.6
25:11–12 3.6
25:13–14 3.4
25:16 3.4
25:17 3.a, 3.e, 3.1, 3.3, 3.4, 3.6, 3.7, 3.8, 3.9, 3.10
25:18 3.10, 3.11, 3.12, 3.13
25:19 3.2, 3.5, 3.14, 3.15
26:11 10.2
26:13 10.7
26:15 28.10
26:16 12.5
28:12 10.10
28:24 10.10
28:50 13.13
29:9 S1.10
29:22 13.10
31:14 S1.20
31:16 17.4
31:17 17:4
31:27 S1.20
31:29 S1.20
32:10 3.a
32:13 12.11
32:18 25.1
32:24 13.7, S1.5
32:30 5.2
32:32 20.6
32:50 S1.14, S1.20
33:1 S1.1, S1.3, S1.4, S1.5, S1.6, S1.7, S1.9, S1.10, S1.11, S1.12, S1.13, S1.14, S1.17, S1.20
33:1–27 S1.10, S1.11
33:2 5.8, 12.22, S1.15, S1.16, S1.20
33:4 S1.19
33:3 S1.18
33:6 2.7, S1.6
33:7 S1.8
33:8 5.4
33:21 25.1
33:29 8.4, S1.5, S1.10
34:5 S1.20
34:7 S1.20
34:10 13.6

Joshua

1:1 S1.20
1:2 S1.20
1:8 15.5
1:10 5.9
2:6 13.4
2:12 13.4
2:13 13.4
2:16 13.4
3:11 15.10
4:19 5.17
5:2 28.4
6:25 13.5
7:10 8.2
9:17 13.12
14:15 23.8

Judges

1:22 10.8
5:4 5.6, 12.15
5:20 8.2
5:23 S2.2
5:31 8.1
7:9 17.1
7:13 8.4
11:37 5.7
13:3 20.1
13:15 28.8
15:12 26.1
18:27 10.8
20:16 S2.4
26:16 12.12

1 Samuel

1:2 18.3, 20.1
2:6 1.4
2:21 18.3, 20.1
3:14 5.11
6:1 11.9
7:9 S7.1
9:12 4.5
10:25 4.5
11:8 2.8
14:47 5.3
15:4 2.8
15:32 3.6
15:33 3.6
16:1 S7.1
16:12 26.1
16:18 18.1
17:14 S1.20
17:24 11.1
17:32 16.2
20:1 14.1
20:27 18.1
22:7 18.1
23:12 4.2
24:12 4.2
26:14 4.2
28:5 5.3

2 Samuel

1:13 3.16
1:16 3.16
2:14 4.2
3:12 4.2
12:13 2.1, 18.1
12:14 S7.1
12:16 S7.1
17:2 5.3
18:19 S1.3
18:29 S1.3
18:30 S1.3
18:31 S1.3
18:32 S1.3
19:1 S1.3
20:19 11.13
21:14 26.11
24:9 2.8

1 Kings

3:9 16.2
4:20 2.9
5:2 6.1
5:3 6.1
5:6 26.2
5:9 4.3
5:10 4.3
5:11 4.3
5:12 4.3
5:13 4.3
6:4 21.5
6:37 12.19
6:38 12.19
8:2 12.19
8:27 6.4
8:56 28.1
10:19 1.7
10:27 26.2
11:3 26.2
13:1–2 2.6
13:4 2.6
13:6 2.6
14:4 3.1
16:15 S1.8
17:1 1.4
17:23 1.4
18:13 4.2
18:22 4.2
18:42 28.4
18:44 28.4
19:15 17.1
21:19 24.11
21:27 24.11
21:28–29 24.11

2 Kings

1:15 1.4
2:8 1.4
2:11 1.4
2:15 16.4
3:4 2.5, 6.2
3:15 7.4
3:27 2.5
4:1 2.5
4:7 11.15
5:26 16.2
6:17 9.4
9:30 18.4
17:13 16.3
18:25 2.5
18:35 28.1
19:26 10.9
19:35 17.1
20:3 25.4
20:6 25.4

25:7 4.10, 5.12, 26.1
25:9 4.10
25:13 S2.2
25:15 S2.2

Isaiah

1:3 9.8
1:4 S6.1
1:5 16.11
1:10 14.3
1:15 16.11
1:18 6.4, 9.5
1:19–20 14.3
1:21 5.17, 6.4, 15.6, 15.7
1:22 15.8
1:23 15.9
1:24 15.10, 15.11
1:26 15.11
1:27 15.11
2:2 21.4
2:4 S2.2, S5.1
2:5 S1.20
2:9 2.3
2:11 S5.1
2:18 S5.1
2:20 S5.1
3:10 9.1
3:11 9.1
3:15 17.6
3:16 16.11
3:17 17.6
4:3 5.9
4:6 S2.1, S2.3, S2.4, S2.5
5:1 S2.5
5:7 16.9
5:17 17.6
5:19 17.6
5:24 15.5
6:2 1.3, 9.3, 16.1
6:8 16.4
8:2 13.12
8:6 6.2
8:7 6.2
9:11 16.11
9:16 16.11
10:30 13.1
11:11 16.11
11:12 4.10
13:5 24.11
13:10 S6.2
14:2 12.17
14:5 5.9
17:12 2.1
19:18 7.5
21:13 19.2
22:5 S6.2
22:8 15.7
22:12 15.3
23:5 7.11
23:8 S2.4
23:13 7.10, 14.3
24:5 10.5
24:15 21.1
24:16 16.1
25:8 S2.8, S6.1
25:9 16.11
26:2 S6.1
26:11 24.11
26:12 S2.8
26:15 28.b, 28.c, 28.1
27:7 11.4
27:8 11.4
28:20 10.8
28:22 13.2
29:1 13.15
29:15 9.1
30:10 S5.3
30:18 S1.3
30:19 S6.1
30:20 3.16
30:21 16.11
30:22 13.2
30:26 S6.2
30:32 8.4
31:9 S2.2
33:6 S1.2
33:7 S5.3, S6.2
34:4 S2.1
34:6 4.9, 5.18
34:6–7 7.11
34:9 7.11
34:11 7.11
35:5 5.16, 12.19
35:6 5.16, 12.19
38:16 19.5
38:20 17.1
39:1 2.5
40:1 16.1, 16.4, 16.5, 16.6, 16.7 16.8, 16.9, 16.10, 16.11
40:1, 2 16.2
40:2 16.6, 16.11
40:16 2.10, 6.4
40:17 9.6, 16.1
40:27 17.3

41:2 S4.3
41:4 5.18, 27.10
41:8 S1.20
41:24 9.6
41:27 27.10
42:5 22.5a
42:8 4.3, 7.2, 21.2
42:13 9.11
42:16 4.7
43:9 S2.1
43:12 12.6
44:23 S6.2
44:26 7.3
45:17 12.25
48:12 23.7
48:17 23.7
49:3 2.7
49:11 S6.1
49:12 12:22
49:14 17.1, 17.2, 17.3, 17.4, 17.5 17.6
49:15 17.7, 17.8
49:16 17.8
49:18 22.5, S5.3
49:20 20.7
49:21 20.1
49:23 9.4
50:3 15.3, S6.2
50:6 16.4
51:2 5.2
51:3 S5.3
51:4 1.3
51:9 16.4
51:12 16.4, 16.11, 19.1, 19.5, S6.1
51:13 19.5
51:14 19.5
51:15 19.6
51:16 19.6
51:17 16.4
52:7 5.9, 16.11, S5.1, S5.2 S5.4
52:8 16.11, S5.3
52:12 5.19
53:10 19.5
54:1 20.1, 20.2, 20.3, 20.4, 20.5
54:2 12:22, 20.7
54:3 20.7
54:9 16.4, 19.3
54:11 18.1, 18.3, 18.4
54:12 18.5, 18.6
54:13 12.21, 18.6
55:2 27.1
55:3 14.2
55:5 S6.1
55:6 S7.1, S7.2, S7.3
55:6–7 S7.3
55:8 24.10
55:12 S2.6, S6.2
56:7 10.10
57:14 S6.1
58:11 17.5
58:13 10.2
58:14 10.2, S1.19
59:1 17.2
59:2 17.2
59:15 5.9
59:17 22.5, S6.5
59:20 18.3, 25.1, S5.4
60:1 21.1, 21.2, 21.3, 21.4 S5.3
60:1–2 5.14
60:2 7.12, 21.6
60:2, 3 S6:5
60:3 21.4
60:4 22.3, S6.5
60:17 S2.2
60:19 21.5
61:1 16.4, S5.4
61:3 S6.2
61:9 S6.1
61:10 16.4, 22.1, 22.2, 22.3, 22.4, 22.5, S6.1, S6.2, S6.3, S6.4, S6.5
61:11 22.5a
62:2 22.5a
62:5 22.5, S6.1, S6.2
62:6 S6.2
62:10 S6.1
63:1 22.5
63:2 22.5, S6.5
63:8 S6.1
63:10 16.11
65:10 6.1
65:17 22.5a
66:6 7.11
66:10 S5.3, S6.2
66:13 19.3
66:22 23.12
66:24 13.14, 28.3

Jeremiah

1:1 4.10, 13,1, 13.2, 13.3, 13.5, 13.6, 13.7, 13.8, 13.9, 13.12, 13.13, 13.14
1:1–3 13.15
2:4 14.3, 14.4
2:5 14.3, 14.5, 4.6, 14.7
2:7 15.1
2:8 14.1
2:22 S7.1
2:27 13.4, 13.8, 16.1
3:1 12.1
3:12 24.16
3:17 3.15, 20.7
3:22 13.11
3:25 24.16
4:7 13.1, 13.15
4:14 S7.1
4:22 9.8
4:23 S6.2
4:24 S5.2, S6.2
4:31 3.1
5:2 13.4, 13.8
5:12 16.11
5:24 8.1
7:9 13.8
7:18 16.11
7:25 16.3
7:26 14.2
8:8 15.6
9:2 13.8, 16.11
9:4 13.4
9:9 13.10, S5.2
9:11 15.5
9:12 15.5
9:16 15.4
10:10 4.2
10:15 14.7
10:16 14.7
10:19 15.4
11:15 S5.2
11:16 21.4
11:21, 23 24.11
12:7 S5.3
13:11 2.7
13:16 13.9, 16.11
15:1 15.1
15:2 13.13, 14.2
15:17 15.2
16:5 13.13, 17.1
16:11 15.5
16:13 13.13, 16.6
17:8 6.1
17:12 21.5, 27.10
17:13, 24.2 24.4
20:7 13.14
22:24 24.11
22:28 24.11
22:30 24.11
23:6 22.5a
23:24 10.7
23:29 S3.2
25:10 S6.1
26:5 16.3
26:20 13.12
29:22 13.13, 24.15
29:23 24.15
30:10 23.2
30:11 23.2
30:14 16.6
30:17 18.3
30:18 20.7
30:20 27.1
31:9 24.16
31:10 13.9
31:11 13.9
31:13 13.15
31:14 20.2
31:16 S5.2
31:19 20.2
31:33 10.6, 12.21
31:37 19.5
32:7 13.14
32:24 16.6
33:11 9.12, 22.5
33:13 2.8
35:19 S5.2, S5.4
37:12 13.4
39:12 13.9
40:1 13.9
40:3 2.5
40:4 13.9
40:5 13.9
43:11 13.7, 13.8
46:20 4.9
48:11 12.22
49:20 3.13
50:25 24.11
50:33 11.5
50:34 11.5
51:34 S2.2

51:58 3.7, 18.2, 20.2
51:64 13.14
52:13 4.10

Ezekiel

1:3 13.2, 13.12
1:7 9.3
1:26 4.4
3:13 16.1
4:9 8.4
8:17 3.11, 16.11
9:3 13.11
10:3 13.11
10:4 13.11
10:5 16.1
10:18 13.11
10:19 13.11
11:23 13.11
16:6 7.4
16:9 11.8
16:10 11.8, 12.11
16:14 4.4
16:19 10.8, 12.25
16:31 13.4
18:4 24.7
20:25 14.4
22:7 13.4, 13.8
22:8 13.8
22:14 16.2
24:3 S2.8
24:7 15.7
24:8 15.7
25:8 19.1
25:14 S2.2
27:27 4.9, 5.19
28:12 4.4
28:13 4.4
29:16 9.3
30:18 7.5
31:3 16.7
31:15 9.1
33:7 24.1
33:8 24.1
33:9 24.1
33:11 24.1
33:24 23.7
34:31 16.9
34:14 9.1
34:31 2.3
36:8 S6.2
36:25 4.10
36:26 22.5a, 24.17
37:4 14.4
38:22 7.11
39:17–19 7.11
40:25 21.5
41:7 20.7
43:2 21.5
43:8 S7.3
43:11 6.3
43:14 3.6
48:35 22.5a

Hosea

1:1 13.7, 24.9
1:9 13.7
1:22 15.8
1:23 15.9
1:24 15.10
2:1 2.8
2:10 9.8
2:11 10.10
2:16 5.8
3:2 5.10, 12.4
3:3 12.4
4:2 15.7
4:13 5.7, 13.4, 24.16
4:16 4.10
5:6 S7.1
5:11 12.1
5:15 13.11
6:3 17.8
6:7 15.1
7:3 9.7
7:13 15.4
8:3 15.5
8:10 6.3
9:15 15.1
9:16 16.8, 24.10
10:14 9.11
11:1 1.2
12:3 9.5
12:10 5.8
12:12 1.8
13:2 24.10
13:12 24.10
13:13 3.d
14:1 24.10, 24.11
14:2 24.1, 24.2, 24.3, 24.4, 24.5, 24.6, 24.7, 24.8, 24.9, 24.10, 24.11, 24.12, 24.13, 24.17
14:3 24.18, 24.19

14:6 16.8, 17.8
14:10 2.2

Joel

1:5 16.8
1:18 24.11
2:11 24.3
2:13 24.11
2:22 S6.2
2:23 S6.3
3:3 7.11
4:12 S2.2
4:15 15.3
4:18 16.8
4:19 3.e
4:21 S2.2

Amos

1:3 19.2
1:6 19.2
1:9 19.2
1:11 3.1
3:6 24.1
3:8 13.15
4:7 5.9
5:1 15.4
5:2 16.8
5:4 24.1
5:15 20.2
7:7 13.11
7:14 26.6/7
9:1 13.11
9:11 16.8
9:13 7.10

Obadiah

1:2 3.13, 5.18
1:4 23.2
1:5 3.1
1:18 3.b, 15.5

Jonah

3:4 24.11
3:7–8 24.11
3:8 24.11
3:10 28.3

Micah

1:5 16.8
2:2 13.8
2:13 16.11, S5.1
4:1 21.4
4:10 S2.7
4:14 16.4
5:14 S1.15
6:2 9.5, S5.2
6:3 9.5
6:9 13.11
6:11 3.4
7:6 5.9, 11.1
7:15 5.8
7:16 16.11
7:18 16.8, 25.2
7:19 6.4
7:20 10.6
12:4 9.5

Nahum

1:3 15.3
1:11 16.8
2:1 16.8
2:5 27.2
3:8 16.7

Habakkuk

1:2 16.8
1:13 4.10, 25.1
3:13 16.8
3:17 S6.2

Zephaniah

1:5 13.4, 13.8
1:12 16.8
1:15 16.8
2:8–9 19.1
3:8 S2.2

Haggai

1:6 16.8
1:9 16.9
2:9 5.9
2:19 16.8
2:23 24.11

Zechariah

1:2 16.8
1:5 13.3, 13.4
1:8 27.9
1:15 16.8
2:3 5.9
2:9 16.11, 20.7
3:2 24.15
4:2 27.2
7:11 16.11

7:12 16.11
8:16 19.6
9:1 20.7
9:9 22.3
9:14 23.10
10:11 10.8
13:2 4.7
14:1 S2.2
14:2 S2.2
14:3 9.11, S2.2
14:6 4.7, S2.2
14:9 5.9
14:10 20.7
14:12 7.11

Malachi

1:4 3.5
1:10 16.8
1:11 6.3
2:6 5.4, 26.1
3:5 24.15
3:12 16.8
3:17 6.4
3:19 S2.1
3:20 16.1
3:22 4.5, S1.20

Psalms

2:2 9.11, S2.2
3:3 2.1
3:4 2.1
3:9 S2.5
4:3 18.1
4:4 18.1
4:5 24.4
8:5 4.3, 5.13
9:7 3.5, 3.16
9:8 3.16
9:9 23.10
11:6 12.9
11:7 25.1
12:6 S5.3
12:7 3.6, 4.2
12:8 4.2
16:9 16.2
16:11 27.2
17:14 11.14
17:15 11.14, 28.3
18:18 12.2
18:19 12.2
18:20 12.2
19:5 S2.1
19:8 12.19
19:11 12.5, 12.13
20:2 12.24, 28.3
22:4 5.8
24:1 27.4
25:1 11.14
25:8 24.7
26:6 27.5
26:7 27.5
27:1 5.3
27:5 S2.1
28:9 S1.10
29:4 12.25
29:11 19.6, S1.15, S6.5
30:2–4 8.4
30:5–6 8.4
30:7–8 8.4
30:9–10 8.4
30:11–12 8.4
30:13 8.4
31:20 12.20, S6.5
31:25 S5.3
32:6 S1.7
32:9 3.3
34:5 S7.1
34:19 24.5
35:10 11.1
36:7 9.1
36:8 16.1, 19.6
36:9 9.1
36:10 21.3
36:12 20.6
37:3 10.2
37:11 18.6, 28.2
37:21 28.2
37:29 1.1
40:2 10.4, 28.8
40:5 5.2
40:9 10.6
42:3 S5.3
43:3 5.4
45:8 16.4
45:11 1.3
46:10 S2.2
46:11 24.12
47:6 1.4
47:7 23.3
48:12 22.3
49:8–9 2.10, 6.4
50:7 12.23
50:10 6.1
50:12 6.1

51:19	24.5	78:29	3.12
51:20	24.5	78:32	23.2
51:21	24.5	78:36	24.18
54:2	4.2	78:44	7.11
54:15	26.10	78:48	7.10
56:13	9.12	78:51	7.10
57:5	4.2	78:61	11.9
57:6	4.2	78:63	26.9
57:9	7.4	79:12	3.6
58:4	3.1	80:2	S4.2
60:7	17.5	81:4	23.8, S3.1, 23.6
60:8	S2.3	81:5	5.13, 23.1
60:14	25.1	81:6	4.3
62:10	23.8	82:1	5.8
63:4	3.1	82:6	4.4, 12.25
65:6	24.2	83:5	S2.2
66:3	11.2	85:3	25.2
66:12	5.2	85:7	22.1
66:15	6.3	85:9–10	1.5
68:5	23.10, 27.9	89:1	4.3
68:7	2.4	89:7	S2.4
68:10	8.1	89:8	23.4
68:13	5.3	89:16	23.4
68:15	10.4	89:38	5.12
68:18	12.22	89:52	5.9
69:1	27.2	89:53	5.9, S1.7
69:2	19.1	90:1	S1.7, S1.9
69:14	24.2	90:3	S1.8
69:21	19.1	90:17	S1.4
69:29	24.3	91:1	S1.8
72:1	27.3	91:4	S2.3
72:5	3.16, 9.1	91:10	1.5
72:7	18.6	91:15	5.6, 17.5
72:16	20.6	92:1	24.11, S1.8
72:17	22.5a	92:2	24.11, 24.19
73:16	7.1	92:13	27.9
73:25	4.9	93:1	22.5, S6.5
73:26	5.6	93:5	25.1, S1.8
75:3	4.7	94:1	25.1, S1.8
75:5	26.3	95:1	S1.8
75:8	2.4	95:7	24.12
76:9	12.6	96:12	27.4
77:6	17.1	96:13	27.4
77:7	17.1	98:1	17.5
77:8	17.1	99:6	4.5
77:9	17.1	99:7	4.5
77:10	17.1	101:6	10.2
77:11	17.2	102:1	27.3
77:14	S1.15	102:18	27.3
77:16	5.11	102:19	27.3
78:9	11.10	102:21	S1.20
78:18	3.12	103:12	19.3

103:13 19.3
103:20 S3.2
104:1 22.5, 27.9, S6.5
104:2 21.5
104:2–3 1.3
104:4 6.1, S2.4
104:19 5.1
104.31 26.3
104:32 10.7
105:4 S7.1
105:33 7.10
106:23 9.4
109:4 28.9
109:14 3.1
109:15 3.1
111:2 6.1
111:10 S1.2
113:9 20.1
114:1 27.5
114:4 S2.6
115:1 27.5
115:16 12.11
116:1 27.5
118:1 24.19
118:15 17.5
118:24 22.2, 28.9
118:25 27.5
118:27 27.5
118:28 27.5
119:4 6.3
119:15 12.12
119:54 5.9
119:62 7.4
119:89 23.1
119:92 19.4
119:104 12.12
119:140 12.5
119:165 18.6
121:4 11.8
122:4 11.6
126:2 16.11, S2.8
127:1 15.5
130:4 27.7
132:14 20.7
135:4 9.4
136:10 7.6/9
137:5 17.5
137:7 3.e, 3.7, 18,2, 20.2
138:4 S1.15
139:9 16.1
139:12 7.5
140:8 S2.2
141:4 21.3
144:15 2.10, 6.4
145:18 28.1, S7.1
146:5 2.10
146:7 11.5, S3.2
146:8 S3.2
146:9 S3.2
147:2 13.15
147:3 24.5
147:14 18.6
149:2 26.3
149:4 28.5
149:5 12.5

Proverbs

1:22 13.2
1:23 13.2
1:33 14.2
3:9 10.3
3:17 12.14
3:18 23.5
3:19 4.4
4:2 10.2, 15.5
6:20 10.6
6:23 23.5, 27.2
8:10 27.1
8:15 5.3
8:20 12.8
8:21 S1.20
9:5 12.13, 27.1
10:20 2.6
10:27 27.2
11:1 3.4
11:2 3.4
11:26 S1.4
12:10 9.11
12:14 24.9
13:12 5.3, S5.3
13:21 24.7
13:25 6.2
13:35 6.2
14:10 12.9, 12.16, 16.2
14:34 2.5
15:19 2.2
15:24 23.5
15:29 28.1, S7.1
16:7 11.1
16:15 6.1, 12.22, 26.9
17:2 13.4
17:10 11.3
17:26 26.6/7
18:16 5.3

18:23 14.3
19:17 9.2
19:25 3.a, 3.d
20:27 21.4
21:9 13.11
21:22 4.4
21:29 28.2
22:9 S1.11
22:20 12.5, 12.12
23:23 15.5
24:17 S2.8
25:12 4.3
25:21 11.1, S3.2
25:22 11.1
25:28 4.3
27:1 26.9
28:8 10.1
28:13 24.8
28:22 10.1
30:4 1.4
30:5 12.13
31:18 7.6/9
31:21 10.4
31:27 5.4
31:29 12.1, S1.11
31:30 12.1
31:31 12.1

Job

1:14 7.10
1:15 7.10
1:16 7.10, 16.6
1:17 7.10, 16.6
2:8 7.10, 16.6
2:13 16.6
3:13 19.5
3:19 S1.20
4:17 16.1
5:5 8.2
6:11–12 5.3
9:7 S2.4
11:9 12.20
11:11 24.13
11:20 S3.2
12:7 6.1
12:8 6.1
12:9 6.1
12:10 1.4
12:18 16.3
13:12 3.2
13:28 3.2
14:4 4.1
14:20 4.4
16:15 16.6
17:9 25.1
18:13 3.6
19:21 16.6
21:10–13 26.2
21:14 26.2
21:34 16.8
23:3 S2.4
23:5 S2.4
23:40 S2.8
25:2 1.3
26:8 1.4
28:5–8 26.2
28:4 26.2
28:7 S2.3
28:10 4.7
30:4 5.8
30:24 16.7
31:34 7.10
31:38 10.7
31:39 10.7
31:40 10.7
34:10 14.1
36:15 17.5
36:22 24.6
37:1 26.5
37:23 2.10, 6.4
39:27 26.4
39:28 26.4
39:29 26.4
39:30 26.4
40:15, 20 6.1
40:15, 23 6.1
40:30 S2.4
40:31 S2.4
41:3 9.2
41:7 S2.4
41:8 S2.4
41:9 S2.4
41:10 19.5
41:14 20.4
41:17 S2.4
41:18 S2.4
41:19 S2.4
41:20 S2.4
41:20–21 S2.4
41:22 S2.4
41:23 S2.4
41:24 S2.4

Song of Songs

1:2 12.5
1:4 9.1, 22.2, 28.9
1:6 14.4
1:9 S5.1
2:3 12.10
2:5 12.3
2:8 5.7
2:9 5.8
2:10 5.8, 5.9
2:11 5.9
2:12 5.9
2:13 5.9
3:6 27.1
3:7–8 5.3
3:9 1.2
3:10 1.2
3:11 1.3, 26.9
4:3 20.5
4:7 4.10
4:8 22.5
4:9 22.5
4:10 22.5
4:11 11.21, 22.5
4:12 11.6, 22.5
4:13 11.6
4:15 11.21
4:16 1.1
5:1 1.1, 1.3, 22.5
5:2 5.6, 24.12
5:10 12.22
5:15 12.24
6:3 S6.3
6:9 4.10
6:10 27.2
7:2 28.e
8:1 16.5
8:6 17.8
8:7 27.1

Ruth

1:3 7.10
1:5 7.10
2:11 16.1
2:12 16.1
2:13 16.1
2:14 6.2, 16.1
3:10 7.4
4:11 20.2

Lamentations

1:1 13.8, 15.1, 15.2, 15.3, 15.4, 15.6, S6.1
1:2 S6.1
1:4 S6.1
1:6 25.1
1:8 16.11
1:13 16.6, 16.11
1:16 16.11
1:21 19.2
2:1 13.8, 15.6
2:3 17.5
2:10 16.6
2:13 16.3
2:14 16.3
2:17 15.3
2:18 16.2
3:6 13.13
3:21 19.4
3:28 15.3
3:31 17.1
3:39 17.3
4:1 13.8, 15.6
4:2 16.6
4:4 16.11
4:7 4.10
4:10 16.11
4:15 17.6
5:6 3.e
5:17 16.11
5:21 13.14
5:22 13.14, 17.2

Ecclesiastes

1:2 26.2
1:3 8.1
1:5 8.1
1:9 5.8
1:12 26.2
1:16 16.2
2:2 26.1, 26.2
2:8 5.3
3:1 12.7
3:15 9.4
4:13 S3.2
4:14 S3.2
5:15 8.1
6:4 9.1
7:14 28.3
7:27 24.17

7:29 4.3
8:1 4.4
8:8 S1.20
9:2 26.1
9:4 26.1
10:8 11.17
10:11 4.2, S3.2
10:18 12.15
11:2 28.4
11:9 8.1, 24.14
11:12 28.d

Esther

2:16 5.11
2:18 22.1
3:7 3.d, 19.5
3:13 9.11
4:3 8.2
6:1 5.17

Daniel

2:20 28.1
2:38 4.9, 5.18
2:46 9.4
3:15 14.4, 28.1
3:22 4.10
3:27 10.8
4:24 26.1
7:7 17.4
7:9 15.3, 22.5, S6.5
7:11 4.9
8:12 15.5
8:16 4.4
9:7 10.8
9:11 15.1
9:27 13.10
10:6 1.3
12:2 24.3
12:3 27.2
12:11 5.8
12:12 5.8
12:13 17.5
16:14 S2.8
16:15 S2.8

Ezra

1:2 5.9
2:23 24.11
2:64 2.8
5:12 4.10
10:3 4.3

Nehemiah

5:18 6.1
9:6 6.1, S2.1
9:7 9.4
13:28 14.6

1 Chronicles

1:1–3 23.10
2:15 23.10
2:55 3.d
3:17 24.11
5:6 24.9
12:33 1.8
15:22 21.4
16:33 27.4
23:13 4.5
23:14 4.5
24:5 12.5
26:10 7.6/9
27:25 10.6
29:10 28.1
29:23 5.12

2 Chronicles

7:5 1.8
7:14 28.3
9:20 26.2
14:10 23.10
18:2 26.1
18:33 26.1
32:20 8.2
33:10, 11 24.11
33:13 24.11, 27.3
35:7 26.1
35:23 26.1
36:17 26.1

MISHNAH AND TOSEFTA

Běrak̲ot̲

6:6 6.1

Šabbat̲

23:2 3.d
24.3 6.2

'Eruḇin

| 3:1 | S4.1 |

Šĕḵalim

| 4:2 | 4.7 |

Yoma

1:1	26.9
5:2	26.4
8:9	24.2

Sukkah

| 4:5 | 27.5 |
| 4:8 | 28.a, 28.7 |

Roš haš-Šanah

| 3:2 | 9.3 |
| 4:1 | 23.12 |

Yĕḇamoṯ

| 6:6 | 22.2 |

Baḇa Ḳamma

| 7:7 | 4.4 |

'Aḇoṯ

1:2	19.6
1:18	19.6
6:2	15.5

Mĕnaḥoṯ

| 10:4 | 8.1 |

Ḥullin

| 4:3 | 4.1 |

Nĕḡa'im

| 8:2 | 4.1 |

Parah

| 1:1 | 4.7 |
| 4:4 | 4.1, 4.6 |

Niddah

| 2:1 | 12.15 |

Tos Tĕmurah

| 1:13 | 1.8 |

AUTHORITIES CITED OR REFERRED TO*

The Rabbis and scholars whose commentary and activity makes up the bulk of the Pĕsiḳta dĕ-Raḇ Kahăna are known as Tannaim and Amoraim; they flourished between the first and the fifth centuries of the Common Era (C.E.).

The period of the Tannaim, from the death of Hillel and Shammai to that of Judah the Patriarch, corresponds approximately to the first two centuries of the Common Era. The Tannaim quoted or referred to in Pĕsiḳta dĕ-Raḇ Kahăna are identified in the index by the letters T and the numbers 1 to 5, corresponding to the five generations by which the Tannaim are designated:

First Generation (T1)—ca.10–ca.80 C.E.
Second Generation (T2)—ca.80–ca.120 C.E.
Third Generation (T3)—ca.120–ca.140 C.E.
Fourth Generation (T4)—ca.140–ca.165 C.E.
Fifth Generation (T5)—ca.165–200 C.E.

The period of the Amoraim runs approximately from the third century C.E. through the fourth; and the Amoraim are also listed in the index by generations as follows:

First Generation (1)—approximately the first half of the third century C.E.

Second Generation (2)—approximately the second half of the third century C.E. (e.g. Johanan b. Nappaḥa, d. 279; Simeon b. Laḳish, d. 275).

Third Generation (3)—approximately the first half of the fourth century C.E.

Fourth Generation (4)—approximately the third quarter of the fourth century C.E.

Fifth Generation (5)—approximately the fourth quarter of the fourth century C.E.

The letter P after an Amora's name indicates that he lived in Palestine; the numeral following the letter designates the generation. The letter B after an Amora's name indicates that he lived in Babylonia; the numeral following the letter designates the generation. When the generation is uncertain, the letter P or B is followed by a question mark.

* In preparing this index, the following works were made use of:

Aharon Hyman, *Tolĕdoṯ Tanna'im wĕ-'Amora'im*, 3 vols., London, 5670/1910

George Foot Moore, *Judaism in the First Centuries of the Christian Era*, 3 vols., Cambridge, Mass., 1927–40

Hermann L. Strack, *Introduction to the Talmud and Midrash*, Philadelphia, 1931

The Mishnah, translated by Herbert Danby, London, 1933

Mordecai Margulies, *Enṣiḳlopedyah lĕ-Ḥaḵme hat-Talmuḏ we-hag-Gĕ'onim*, 2 vols., Tel Aviv, 1958

Chanoch Albeck, *Maḇo' lam-Mišnah*, Tel Aviv, 5720/1959

Chanoch Albeck, *Maḇo' lat-Talmudim*, Tel Aviv, [5729]/1969

The letter "b" occurring in a Rabbi's name stands for "ben" or "bar," meaning "son of." The letter S stands for "Supplement"; references to individual Supplements are indicated by the numerals 1 through 7. "Tr.," following the number of the Piska and Section or Supplement and Section, indicates that the Rabbi therein cited is the transmitter of a comment or teaching in the name of an older master or a colleague.

Abaye (P3), 5.9
Abba, of Acco (P3), 20.6
Abba b. Aḥa (PB2), 7.6/9
Abba Ḥanin (T3 and 4), 26.9
Abba Hoshaia of Teria (P4), 27.1
Abba b. Kahana (P3), 1.1, 1.2, 1.8, 2.6, 3.4, 3.6, 3.7, 3.16, 5.3, 5.9, 6.2, 6.3, 7.10, 10.6, 10.10, 13.1, 13.4, 15.2, 15.15, 16.3(tr.), 16.8, 17.6, 18.2, 18.4, 18.5, 19.4(tr.), 20.2, 21.6, 24.11, 26.2, 27.1, 27.10, 28.3, 28.7(tr.), 28.10, S1.3, S2.4
Abba b. Papi (P4), 23.11(tr.), 24.11
Abba [Rabbah] b. Huna (B3), 10.9
Abba Saul (T3 and 4), 4.7
Abba b. Yudan (P5), 5.2(tr.), 12.11, 17.3, 24.5
Abba b. Zĕbina (P4), 26.11
Abbahu (P3), 1.8, 4.4, 5.5, 5.17, 8.4, 9.3, 11.1, 15.1(tr.), 16.7, 17.5(tr.), 17.8, 19.5, 21.1, 23.4, 24.19, 25.2, S1.15, S2.1
Abdimi, of Haifa (P3), 12.22
Abin [Abun, Bun] (BP 3 and 4), 1.3, 1.7, 2.7, 4.2, 4.3(tr.), 4.7(tr.), 5.9, 5.11, 5.18, 6.13, 7.2, 7.6/9(tr.), 8.1, 8.3, 12.5, 13.14, 14.14(tr.), 16.1, 16.3, 16.9, 19.5, 19.5(tr.), 21.2, 22.2, 27.2, 27.5, 28.6, 28.7, 28.9, S1.10
Abin b. Judah (P?), 2.5
Abun, *see* Abin
Abun, the Levite [Berabbi] (P3?), 12.13, 28.a
Addi (P2), 11.6
Aḥa (P3 and 4), 1.3, 1.7, 3.1(tr.), 4.3, 4.7, 4.7(tr.), 5.2, 5.13, 5.15(tr.), 5.16, 6.3(tr.), 7.2, 7.6/9(tr.), 8.1(tr.), 9.4(tr.), 9.5, 9.5(tr.), 12.5, 12.10(tr.), 12.24, 13.2, 13.3, 13.9, 14.3, 14.4(tr.), 15.7, 16.4, 17.4, 17.7, 19.3, 19.6, 20.5(tr.), 21.2, 21.4, 22.1, 24.11, 24.19(tr.), 25.1, 25.1(tr.), 26.2, 26.10, 27.3, 27.4, 27.7, 28.a(tr.), 28.3, 28.7(tr.), S1.3
Aḥa b. Abun b. Benjamin (P5), 24.11(tr.)
Aḥa Arika (BP3), 24.11
Aḥa (Abba?) b. Kahana (P?), 7.11
Aḥa b. 'Ulla (BP3 and 4), 10.6
Aḥawa b. Zĕ'era [Zĕ'ira] (P4), 12.10, 26.5

Aibu (P2), 1.1, 1.6, 3.1, 3.2, 4.8, 5.3, 12.18, 17.1, 24.11, 24.12(tr.), 26.9, S1.7
'Aḳiḇa (T3), 4.7, 9.1, 10.10, 14.3, 28.9, S3.2, S5.3
Alexandri (P2), 3.15, 17.2, 24.5, 25.4, 27.3, 28.8, 28.9
Ammi (P3), 10.1, 15.5
'Anan b. Jose (P3?), 24.2
Aphes (P1), 21.4
Asi (P3), 5.5, 15.5
Azariah (P5), 1.1(tr.), 1.2(tr.), 3.14(tr.), 4.7 (tr.), 5.9, 10.9(tr.), 12.10, 14.1(tr.), 16.4(tr.), 17.5(tr.), 19.3(tr.), 25.1(tr.), 27.2, 28.4
Azariah, of Kefar Hiṭṭaya (P2), 6.3
Banai [Benaiah] (P5), 3.4(tr.), 8.1, S1.8(tr.)
Bar [Ben] Ḥuṭa (P4), 12.5, 12.12
Bar Ḳappara (P1), 1.8, 4.3, 6.2, 8.2, 10.3, 11.6, 15.3, 15.7, 15.9, 17.5, 26.8(tr.)
Basla (P5), 21.5
Bebai (P3), 2.8, 2.9(tr.), 5.9, 12.7
Bebai b. Rabbah (P3), 23.9(tr.)
Ben Azzai (T3), 6.4, 12.12, 27.8
Ben Ḥuṭa, *see* Bar Ḥuṭa
Benaiah, *see* Banai
Benjamin b. Japheth (P3), 7.5(tr.)
Benjamin b. Levi (P4), 8.1, 13.4, 18.6
Berechiah (P4), 1.3, 2.4, 2.6(tr.), 2.7, 2.10(tr.), 3.1, 3.4, 3.7, 3.12, 3.16(tr.), 4.2(tr.), 4.5(tr.), 4.9, 5.1, 5.1(tr.), 5.2(tr.), 5.5(tr.), 5.8(tr.), 5.11(tr.), 5.11, 5.12, 5.17(tr.), 5.18(tr.), 6.1(tr.), 7.3(tr.), 7.11, 8.1, 9.5, 9.9(tr.), 9.11(tr.), 11.1, 12.22, 12.24, 13.7(tr.), 13.13, 15.9, 16.9, 16.9(tr.), 17.3, 17.6(tr.), 19.5(tr.), 20.6(tr.), 20.7, 21.5(tr.), 21.5, 22.1(tr.), 23.2(tr.), 23.5(tr.), 23.6, 23.9, 24.2(tr.), 24.6, 24.9, 24.11(tr.), 26.4(tr.), 26.6/7, 26.9, 27.1(tr.), 27.10(tr.), 28.f, 28.10(tr.), S1.3, S1.11, S2.4
Berechiah, the Priest, *see* Berechiah
Bun *see* Abin
Dosa (P3), S5.2
Dosṭai (P4), 20.7(tr.)
Dosṭai, of Kokaba (T4), 6.2
Eleazar (P2), 28.3
Eleazar b. Araḵ (T2), 2.5, *see* Eliezer b. Araḵ
Eleazar b. Azariah (T2), 12.22, 20.7
Eleazar b. Jose [the Galilean] (T4), 1.3, 5.7, 7.6/9, 24.15, 26.1
Eleazar b. Jose [Joseph] (P5), 4.5, 5.16
Eleazar b. Marius (P4?), S2.7

Eleazar b. Menahem (P3), 7.4, 9.1
Eleazar, the Modiite (T3), 12.22, 20.7, 26.8
Eleazar [b. Pedaṯ] (P3), 1.5, 2.9(tr.), 4.2, 4.7, 7.11, 8.1, 10.8, 11.5, 11.9, 12.5, 12.11, 12.22, 13.7(tr.), 13.9, 13.14, 15.9, 17.5(tr.), 17.6, 24.11(tr.), 24.12, 25.2, 28.a, 28.f, S1.2, S1.11
Eleazar b. Simeon (T5), 11.16, 11.18, 11.19, 11.20, 11.21, 11.22, 11.23, 11.24, 24.11, 27.1, 27.3
Eliezer [b. Araḳ] (T2), 2.5, 3.16, 4.7, 23.1, 24.2, 24.4, 24.9, 26.6/7, 28.c
Eliezer [b. Hyrcanus] (T2), 4.7
Eliezer b. Jacob (T4), 2.9, 5.7, 20.7
Eliezer b. Jose, the Galilean *see* Eleazar b. Jose [the Galilean]
Eliezer, the Modiite *see* Eleazar, the Modiite
Eliezer [b. Pedaṯ] *see* Eleazar [b. Pedaṯ]
Eliezer [b. Zadok?] (T4), 28.4
Gamaliel (T2), 1.2, 2.5, 11.22, 12.15
Haggai (P4), 4.3, 5.8(tr.), 6.1(tr.), 10.2(tr.), 19.5, 24.2(tr.), 28.8(tr.)
Ḥama (B5), 5.8(tr.), 7.10
Ḥama b. Gurya (B2), 28.3(tr.)
Ḥama b. Ḥanina (P2), 1.8, 3.16, 4.4, 5.2(tr.), 5.5, 5.8, 5.11, 7.11, 8.4, 11.8, 11.13, 12.11, 17.5, 23.7, 24.11, 26.3, 28.e
Ḥami b. 'Oḳba (P3), 8.3(tr.)
Ḥanan, *see* Ḥanin
Ḥanan b. Pazzi (P4), 4.2
Ḥanin (P3), 1.3, 5.3, 6.3, 22.1
Ḥanina b. Abba [Adda?] (P4), 16.10, 28.e
Ḥanina b. Abbahu (P3), 13.10
Ḥanina b. Adda, *see* Ḥanina b. Abba
Ḥanina [b. Ḥama] (P1), 1.1, 4.7, 5.1, 5.8, 10.1, 13.10, 17.6, 21.5, 23.10, 24.11, 24.12, 28.3, 28.7(tr.), 28.10(tr.), S2.1
Ḥanina b. Isaac (P3), 24.11
Ḥanina b. Papa [Ḥinena b. Papa] (P3), 5.2, 6.3, 12.25, 16.10, 17.1, 17.6, 19.6, 24.2, S2.1
Ḥanina b. Šilka (P3 or 4), 3.6(tr.), 3.11(tr.)
Ḥelbo (BP3), 5.17(tr.), 9.9, 19.5, 23.2(tr.), 24.2(tr.), 24.11
Ḥilfai, *see* Ḥilfo
Ḥilfo (P3?), 8.1, 16.3
Ḥilfo b. Zebud (P4?), 17.6(tr.)
Hilkiah (P4), 5.13(tr.), 7.5(tr.), 22.5a(tr.), 28.3(tr.)
Hillel, disciples of (T1), 6.4
Ḥinena b. Papa *see* Ḥanina b. Papa
Ḥisda (P4), 28.3
Ḥiyya, *see* Ḥiyya b. Abba

Ḥiyya b. Abba (P3), 1.3, 4.9, 5.3, 5.6, 5.9, 5.13, 5.15(tr.), 5.17(tr.), 6.1, 11.6, 11.14, 12.24, 14.4(tr.), 15.5, 17.6, 24.11(tr.), 26.4, 26.10, 26.11, 27.1, 27.6, S5.3(tr.)
Ḥiyya b. Adda (P2), 10.3
Ḥiyya b. Adda, of Jaffa (P4), 5.17
Ḥiyya b. Ashi (B2), 28.7(tr.)
Ḥiyya [the elder] (P1), 2.9(tr.), 8.1, 10.7, 12.4, 12.17, 15.7, 19.3, 21.5, 24.14, 26.8, 28.7
Ḥiyya, father of Berechiah (P3), 27.1
Ḥiyya b. Marya (P5), 23.8(tr.)
Hizkiah (P1), 10.4, 11.15(tr.)
Hoshaia (P1), 1.8, 5.8, 5.13, 10.7, 11.6, 12.17, 14.6, 15.7, 21.4(tr.), 26.9, 28.a, 28.7
Huna [Huna, the Priest, Ḥunya] (BP4), 1.3, 1.8(tr.), 2.5, 2.6(tr.), 2.10(tr.), 3.1, 3.4, 3.6, 3.10, 5.7(tr.), 6.1(tr.), 6.2, 6.3, 6.4(tr.), 7.6/9(tr.), 7.10(tr.), 8.1(tr.), 9.4(tr.), 9.8(tr.), 10.6, 11.6(tr.), 12.8, 12.10(tr.), 13.10(tr.), 15.5(tr.), 17.7(tr.), 19.6(tr.), 21.4, 24.11(tr.), 25.2(tr.), 28.3(tr.), S1.8, S2.4
Huna, the Priest *see* Huna
Huna Rabba, of Sepphoris (P3), 16.3
Huna b. Yeḳo (PB4), 6.1
Ḥunya, *see* Huna
Ḥunya b. Yudan (B4), 28.f
Idi (P2), 2.6, 5.2(tr.), 9.8(tr.)
Iḳa (P4), 17.7
'Illa (P2), 28.6
Illa (P2), 28.6
Isaac (P3), 1.1, 1.3, 3.6, 3.7, 3.12, 3.16, 4.3, 4.7, 5.4, 5.8, 5.9, 5.13, 5.18, 6.1, 6.2, 9.1, 9.10, 10.1, 10.2, 10.5, 10.9, 12.3, 14.5, 14.7, 16.3, 17.2, 19.5, 20.2, 21.5, 22.2, 24.2, 24.11, 24.16, 24.17, 25.1, 26.10, 27.3, 28.2, 28.8, 28.9, S1.4, S2.3
Isaac (T4), 11.15
Isaac b. Ḥaḳila (P2), 27.3
Isaac b. Ḥanina (B3), S1.3
Isaac b. Marion (P3), 5.8, 10.9(tr.)
Isaac b. Zĕ'era (P3), 6.2
Ishmael (T3), 4.3, 5.3, 9.1, 11.3, 27.8, S3.2
Issachar, of Kefar Mindi (P?), 24.13
Jacob b. Abaye [Jacob b. Abuy] (P4), 8.4(tr.), 26.10(tr.)
Jacob b. Abina [Abuna] (P3), 16.3, 24.4
Jacob b. Abuna, *see* Jacob b. Abina
Jacob b. Abuy, *see* Jacob b. Abaye
Jacob b. Aḥa (P3), 25.1(tr.), 28.7(tr.)

Jacob, of Kefar Ḥanin (P3), 1.3, 4.2(tr.), 15.3
Jacob, of Kefar Nibburin [Nubrai] (P4), 4.3
Jacob, of Nubrai *see* Jacob, of Kefar Nibburin
Jacob b. Yuda (P3), 2.2(tr.)
Jacob b. Zaḇdi (P4), 9.3(tr.)
Jeremiah (P4), 15.5(tr.), 18.5(tr.), 23.5, S2.4(tr.)
Jeremiah b. Eleazar (P4), 9.2, 26.8
Johanan (P2), 1.3, 1.5, 1.7, 2.10, 3.6, 3.11, 4.2, 4.3(tr.), 4.4, 5.1, 5.2, 5.9, 5.10(tr.), 5.13, 5.15, 5.17, 6.1, 6.4, 7.5, 8.4, 9.12, 11.1, 11.2, 11.13, 12.2, 12.3, 12.4, 12.23, 13.9, 13.14, 14.4, 15.4, 15.9, 16.3, 17.8, 18.5, 19.4, 20.5, 20.7, 21.3, 23.9, 23.12, 24.3, 24.11, 25.1, 26.1(tr.), 26.9, 27.1, 28.3, 28.6, S1.17, S1.20, S5.3
Johanan b. Beroḳa (T3), 22.2
Johanan, the High Priest (1st century B.C.E.), 11.1
Johanan b. Pazzi (P?), 5.11
Johanan b. Sahina (P2), S2.3
Johanan b. Zakkai (T1), 2.5, 2.10, 4.7, 4.10, 7.5
Jonah (P4), 2.4
Jonah, of Bozrah (P5), 2.4
Jonathan (P3), 9.1(tr.), 12.9, 13.11, 19.5, S1.9, S7.3
Jonathan, of Beth Gubrin (P2), 2.2, 2.3, 2.9, 3.1, 9.1, 12.9, 13.11, 19.5
Jonathan b. Haggai (P4), 10.9(tr.), 14.1(tr.)
Jose, *see* Jose b. Ḥalafta
Jose (P3), 6.1, 6.3, 11.10, 13.10, 16.7, 17.6, 24.12, 28.3
Jose b. Bun (P5), 6.1
Jose [hak-Kohen?] (T2), 11.7, 11.11
Jose b. Ḥalafta (T4), 2.4, 3.15, 8.4, 11.7, 13.10, 20.6, 24.2, 26.4, S2.3
Jose b. Ḥanina (P2), 2.7, 3.1, 4.7, 5.8, 5.13, 7.11, 8.3, 10.9, 12.24, 15.1, 17.6, 25.1, 25.2, 25.4, 26.1, 26.2
Jose b. Il'a'i (P2?), 5.14
Jose b. Jeremiah (P4–5), 12.1, 20.7(tr.)
Jose b. Ḳaṣri (P1), 1.8
Jose b. Menasya (B2), 6.1(tr.)
Jose, of Mimlaḥ (P2), 4.2
Jose b. Nehorai (P1), 9.4, 27.1
Jose b. Peṭros (P1), 24.5
Jose, son of a woman of Damascus (T2–3), 20.7
Jose b. Zimra (P1), 2.9, 12.10, 17.5
Joseph (B3), 9.4, 28.3, S3.2
Joseph b. Judah (T5), 4.5
Joshua b. Abin (P4), 7.10(tr.)
Joshua [b. Hananiah] (T2), 2.5, 3.16, 24.9, 28.d, S5.2
Joshua b. Ḳorḥa (T4), 4.5, 11.19, 28.4

Joshua b. Levi (P1), 1.4(tr.), 1.5(tr.), 2.6, 3.6, 3.15(tr.), 4.2, 5.11, 5.13, 6.1, 8.1, 8.3, 8.4, 9.1, 11.1, 11.5, 11.6, 11.15, 12.11, 12.23, 14.4, 15.5, 18.5, 20.6, 24.8(tr.), 24.11, 26.4, 28.a, 28.f, 28.7, S1.8
Joshua b. Nehemiah (P4), 2.8, 2.10(tr.), 5.11(tr.), 7.5, 10.8, 16.3, 16.6, 19.3, 26.9, S2.3
Joshua, of Sik̲nin (P4), 1.2(tr.), 1.3(tr.), 3.6(tr.), 3.11(tr.), 4.2(tr.), 4.4(tr.), 4.6(tr.), 5.6(tr.), 9.10(tr.), 10.2(tr.), 11.9(tr.), 13.4(tr.), 19.2(tr.), 19.6(tr.), 20.6(tr.), 23.11(tr.), 26.9(tr.), 27.7(tr.), 28.5(tr.), S1.8(tr.)
Josiah (P3), 23.1, 23.4, 24.14
Josiah (T2), 9.1
Judah (B2), 28.2
Judah (P3), 3.3(tr.), 4.2(tr.), 6.1, 6.10, 10.8, 24.2, 24.8
Judah Berabbi [b. Ḥiyya] (P1), 5.8, 9.1, 10.4
Judah b. Giyoraya (T4), 11.14
Judah b. Gurya (P3), 3.6
Judah [b. Il'a'i] (T4), 1.2, 1.3, 2.10, 3.1, 3.10, 3.12, 3.14, 4.4, 5.7, 6.3, 8.3, 9.4, 10.8, 11.4, 11.15, 12.5, 12.6, 12.24, 15.6, 15.11, 19.6, 20.6, 20.7, 24.18, 24.19, S1.1
Judah, the Levite, b. Shallum (P5), 12.23, S2.4
Judah b. Manasseh (P3), 4.2
Judah b. Naḥman (P2–3), 5.3(tr.), 5.4(tr.), 23.3(tr.)
Judah b. Pazzi *see* Judah b. Simon [b. Pazzi]
Judah II, the Patriarch (P3), 15.5, 24.12(tr.)
[Judah] b. Pedaiah (P1), 4.4
Judah, the Prince (T5), 4.4, 9.1, 11.24, 13.10, 17.3, 24.3, S3.2
Judah b. Simon [b. Pazzi] (P4), 1.1, 1.2, 1.3, 2.6(tr.), 2.7, 2.10(tr.), 3.14(tr.), 6.1, 6.4, 6.4(tr.), 7.6/9, 8.4, 9.1, 9.4, 9.5, 9.8, 10.1, 10.8, 10.10, 11.6(tr.), 12.1, 12.19, 12.22, 12.23(tr.), 13.6, 13.12, 14.5, 15.5, 16.4, 17.1, 22.1, 24.12, 25.1, 28.d(tr.), 28.4, 28.4(tr.), 28.10
Judah b. Zeb̲ida (P3), 6.1
Justa (P3), 5.1(tr.)
Ḳrispa (P3), 5.13(tr.), 24.3(tr.)
Levi (P3), 1.2, 1.3, 1.6, 1.8, 2.10(tr.), 2.10, 3.a, 3.e, 3.1, 3.4, 3.5, 3.6(tr.), 3.6, 3.7, 3.8(tr.), 3.9, 3.11(tr.), 3.12, 3.16(tr.), 4.2, 4.3, 4.4(tr.), 4.4, 4.6, 5.2, 5.5, 5.8, 5.9, 5.10(tr.), 5.11(tr.), 5.14(tr.), 7.3, 7.4, 7.10, 7.11(tr.), 8.1, 8.4, 9.6, 9.7, 9.10, 9.11, 9.12(tr.), 10.1, 10.2, 10.3, 11.8(tr.), 11.9, 11.13(tr.), 12.3, 12.11, 12.11(tr.), 12.22, 12.25, 13.4, 14.2, 14.3, 14.4, 15.9, 16.9, 17.3, 17.5(tr.), 18.2, 18.3, 18.5, 18.6, 19.2, 19.3, 19.6, 20.3, 20.5, 20.6, 20.7, 21.5, 22.1, 22.5a, 23.7(tr.), 23.8, 23.11, 23.12, 24.11, 24.12, 24.14, 24.16, 26.3, 26.3(tr.), 26.9, 27.6, 27.7, 28.c, 28.e(tr.), 28.1, 28.2, 28.3, 28.4, 28.5, S1.8, S2.1, S2.4
Levi Berabbi, *see* Levi

Levi b. Ḥaita (P4), 24.11
Levi b. Peraṭa (P2), 25.1
Levi b. Sisi (P1), 24.18
Levi b. Zechariah (P5), 7.11(tr.)
Levi, son-in-law of Zechariah (P5), 7.11(tr.)
Luliani, of the South [Daroma] (P?), 10.10(tr.)
Lulianos b. Tiberius (P4), 4.7(tr.)
Mana [Mani] (P2), 2.5, 4.4, 7.2, 28.3, 28.7
Mani (P5), 26.6/7
Mani, of Shaab (P3–4), 4.4(tr.), 26.9(tr.), 27.7(tr.)
Mari b. Jacob (P3?), 4.5
Marinus b. Hoshaia (P1–2), 11.6
Meir (T4), 1.8, 2.9, 6.1, 6.2, 6.4, 7.11, 8.1, 10.6, 11.1, 11.4, 13.7, 20.2, 20.6, 23.2, 24.11, 24.13, 24.14, 28.d, 28.4, S2.3, S5.3
Menahem, of Gallia (T5), 9.12
Menaḥema (P5), 2.8(tr.), 2.9(tr.), 5.8(tr.), 7.2(tr.), 19.5(tr.), 21.2(tr.), 26.9(tr.)
Naḥman (P5), 5.14, 5.15, 5.16, 23.2, 23.8, S2.4
Naḥman, of Jaffa (P?), 26.9
Nahum b. Simai (P1), 5.17
Nathan (P4), 11.6, 24.19(tr.)
Nathan (T4), 3.8, 7.6/9, 11.7, 11.15, 16.3, S3.2
Nehemiah (P4), 3.1, 7.2(tr.), 13.1(tr.)
Nehemiah (T4), 1.3, 1.8, 2.10, 3.10, 3.12, 5.7, 6.3, 9.4, 8.3, 11.4, 12.5, 12.24, 15.6, 15.11, 19.6, 20.7, 24.18, 24.19, 28.4, S1.1
Nehorai (P2), 5.9
Nehorai (T4), 11.11
Neḥunya b. haḳ-Ḳanah (T2), 2.5
Nisa, of Caesarea (P4), 17.6
Nunya, of Caesarea (P4?), 7.1
Phinehas (P4), 2.10, 3.1(tr.), 3.13(tr.), 5.13(tr.), 7.4(tr.), 8.1, 8.4, 9.12(tr.), 11.6(tr.), 13.2(tr.), 14.6(tr.), 15.7(tr.), 16.4, 18.4, 21.4(tr.), 22.1(tr.), 25.5a (tr.), 24.7, 26.1(tr.), 26.2, 26.9, 28.3(tr.), 28.9
Phinehas b. Abin [Abun] (P4?), 5.3(tr.)
Phinehas b. Ḥama (P4), 12.23, 26.9, 28.f, S2.2, S2.4(tr.), S2.8
Phinehas, the Priest, b. Ḥama, *see* Phinehas b. Ḥama
Rab (B1), 2.10, 6.4, 10.9, 13.4, 23.1, 28.3, 28.7, S7.2
Rabbah [b. Meḥasya] (B2–3), 28.3(tr.)
Rabbi [?], 5.2, 9.1
Rabbi [Judah?] *see* Judah, the Prince
Rabbis, 2.1, 2.4, 2.5, 3.1, 3.6, 3.10, 3.12, 4.2, 4.3, 4.4, 5.7, 5.9, 5.13, 6.1, 6.3, 7.5, 7.11, 8.1, 8.4, 11.1, 11.5, 11.9, 11.10, 12.5, 12.23, 15.4, 15.10, 16.3, 16.8, 17.6, 21.1, 21.6, 24.4, 24.5, 24.9, 25.1(tr.), 28.c, 28.3, S1.7

Rabbis, of Caesarea, 26.4
Rabbis, of the South, 26.4
Resh Laḳish (P2), 1.5, 1.6, 2.10, 4.2, 4.4, 5.3, 5.4, 6.1, 8.2(tr.), 8.4, 10.10, 11.9, 12.22, 12.23, 15.4, 17.2, 17.5, 17.6, 19.5, 21.3, 23.3, 23.12, 24.11, 24.12, 27.3, 28.2, S1.13, S2.1
Reuben (P3), 14.5, 17.1, 20.2, 21.4, 27.1
Sages, 8.1, 11.9, 11.20, 24.14, 26.10, S2.3, S3.2, S5.3
Samuel (P4), 5.15, 15.5, 19.3, 28.7
Samuel b. Abdimi (P5), 3.6
Samuel b. Ammi (P3), 2.1
Samuel, of Cappadocia (P3), 4.3
Samuel b. Ḥalafta (P2?), 12.11
Samuel b. Ḥiyya b. Judah (P2), 5.8(tr.)
Samuel b. Isaac (BP3), 4.9, 5.18, 6.1, 8.1, 13.2, 14.1, 15.5, 18.5, 20.6, 22.1, 24.11, 24.14, S2.4
Samuel b. Jonah (P5), 27.3(tr.)
Samuel b. Naḥman [Naḥmani] (P2–3), 1.5, 1.8, 2.7, 2.9(tr.), 3.1(tr.), 3.12, 4.2, 4.3, 4.4, 5.11, 5.18, 8.4, 9.5, 9.8, 10.8, 11.1, 12.5, 12.9(tr.), 13.5, 13.12, 13.14, 14.3, 15.10, 17.2, 19.5(tr.), 21.5, 23.2, 24.2, 24.11 24.11(tr.), 25.4, S2.2, S6.2, S7.3(tr.)
Samuel Paṭigrisah (T5?), 24.14(tr.)
Samuel b. Tanḥum (P5), 28.2
Samuel b. Yeba (P4?), 5.15(tr.)
Shammai, disciples of (T1), 6.4
Shela, of Kefar Tamarta (P2), 5.1(tr.), 5.10
Simai (P1), 11.8
Simeon b. Abba (BP3), 5.2(tr.)
Simeon b. Abin (?), 26.1
Simeon b. Eleazar (T5), S3.2
Simeon b. Gamaliel (T4), 4.3, 19.6
Simeon b. Ḥalafta (P1), 3.8, 10.7, 24.8, 24.11, 24.14
Simeon b. Ḥilfa (P1), 9.4
Simeon b. Jehozadak (P1), 21.5
Simeon b. Jose, *see* Simeon b. Jose B. Leḳonya
Simeon b. Jose b. Leḳonya (T5), 11.20, 11.21, 23.2(tr.)
Simeon, the Just (3rd Century B.C.E.), 4.7
Simeon b. Laḳish, *see* Resh Laḳish
Simeon b. Menasya (T5), 4.4, 26.3
Simeon b. Nezira (P1), 13.2
Simeon b. Yoḥai (T4), 1.3, 1.4, 1.5, 2.7, 4.3, 5.10, 5.15, 6.1, 7.5, 11.7, 11.15, 11.16, 11.17, 11.23, 12.6, 15.5, 20.2, 22.2, 23.12, 26.2
Simeon b. Yosina [Yosne] (P2), 1.1, 23.2
Simlai (BP2), 5.15(tr.), 16.5, S2.1

Simon (P3), 4.5, 5.1, 5.2, 5.13, 5.17, 6.1, 7.5, 8.3(tr.), 8.4, 14.1, 15.7, 16.10, 17.1, 17.6, 20.6(tr.), 22.5a, 24.8(tr.), 24.17, 24.19, 26.9, 28.3, 28.4
Simon b. Ḳuzi (P3?), 17.8(tr.)
Taḥalifa, of Caesarea (P2), 1.6, 23.12
Tanḥum (P4), 24.11(tr.)
Tanḥum b. Abun (?) 3.1(tr.)
Tanḥum b. Ḥanila'i (P2), 3.2, 4.2, 11.13, 12.22, 13.8, 15.10, 25.1
Tanḥum b. Ḥiyya (P3), 25.1(tr.), 28.3
Tanḥum, of Jaffa (P5), 7.1(tr.)
Tanḥum b. Jeremiah (P5), 24.11, 26.6/7
Tanḥum, son-in-law of Eleazar b. Abina (P4), 1.1(tr.)
Tanḥum b. Yudan (P?), 4.5, 28.10
Tanḥuma (P5), 1.8, 4.2, 5.8(tr.), 5.9, 5.10, 6.1, 7.5, 9.2, 13.7(tr.), 17.4, 24.12(tr.), 24.14, 26.9, 28.2
Ṭarfon (T2), 27.8
Yannai (P3), 5.5, 5.9, 6.1, 8.1, S2.1
Yudan (P4), 1.2, 1.6, 1.8(tr.), 2.6, 2.7(tr.), 2.7, 3.1(tr.), 4.4, 4.5(tr.), 5.2(tr.), 5.3(tr.), 5.5(tr.), 5.7, 5.11, 5.17(tr.), 6.2, 7.6/9, 7.10, 8.1, 10.8, 11.9, 11.12, 13.2, 15.5, 15.7, 17.3, 18.4, 23.10, 24.4, 24.11(tr.), 25.1, 26.4(tr.), 26.9(tr.), 26.11, 27.2, 28.3(tr.), 28.8(tr.), S1.3
Yudan, of Gallia (P3), 26.4
Yudan b. Simeon [Simon] (P2), 4.4, 5.11
Zabdi b. Levi (P1), 24.5
Zadok (T4), S3.2
Zakkai (P1), 3.1
Zakkai, the elder (P4), 20.7
Zakkai, of Kebul (P1), 26.2
Zakkai, of Shaab (P1), 4.4(tr.)
[Zĕʿera] (Zĕʿira) (P4), 1.5, 2.5, 5.1(tr.), 13.10, 20.6, 23.12, 24.11, 28.2
Zeʿir (P4), 2.5
Zĕʿira, *see* [Zĕʿera]

SUBJECTS AND NAMES

Aaron: radiance of, at Red Sea, 11.13; conversed with God in pillar of cloud, 4.5; beauty of priestly garments of, 11.9; at bidding of, God's presence would mount or leave Ark, 26.4; passage on Red Heifer dedicated to, 4.5; death of, encouraged king of Arad to attack Israel, 19.2

Ab, significance of zodiacal sign of, in relation to Jerusalem's destruction and rebuilding, 13.15 n. 44

Abba Hoshaia, of Teria, eulogy for, 27.1

Abbahu, R., returned from Caesarea with his face aglow, 4.4

Abel, city of, wise woman of, identified as Serah, 11.13

Abihu. *See* Nadab and Abihu

Abimelech, oath sworn to, by Abraham, 11.9

Abner: lion in understanding of Torah, 4.2; slain because he did not let Saul be reconciled with David, 4.2; because he arrogantly put own name before David's, 4.2; because he did not protest slaying of priests of Nob, 4.2; because he made sport of young men's blood, 4.2

Abraham: accompanied only by Eliezer when he pursued four kings, 8.2; pursued four kings on night of fifteenth of Nisan, 7.5; conquered Nimrod by prayer, 8.2; first man after Noah, addressed by God in direct vision, 16.4; shown by God: Torah, Temple offerings, Gehenna and the yoke of kingdoms, 5.2; chose yoke of kingdoms for his children, 5.2; choice directed by God, 5.2; commanded to observe practice of circumcision, 12.1; told to sit in God's presence, 5.8; how recent was oath he swore to Abimelech, 11.9; refrained from protesting to God His command to bind Isaac, 23.9; consequence of his giving seven ewe lambs to Philistines, 11.9; why Philistines slew seven descendants of, 11.9; saw cloud clinging to mountain, 26.3; servants of, saw only ass, 26.3; God transferred bestowal of blessing to, S1.1, S1.11; why he did not bless Isaac, S1.11; money of, coveted by Ephron, 10.1; life of, shortened to avoid his learning of Esau's evil deeds, 3.1; first to set aside tithe, S4.3; giving of tithes by, 10.6; earned Canaan through merit of *'omer*, 8.4; called Ethan, 4.3; raised up into firmament, S4.3; merit of, caused Presence to return from seventh to sixth heaven, 1.1; Israel blessed through merit of, 5.8; bullock as offering invokes merit of, 9.9; most compassionate of Patriarchs, 19.3; defended God's creatures, 16.4; foresaw Israel's troubles and redemption, 23.10; made God swear to have mercy for Israel, 23.9; God created world because of, S1.20; world never without thirty men like him, 11.15; willingness of, to sacrifice Isaac, Mesha sought to outdo, 2.5. *See also* Patriarchs

Abyss, wicked used as cover for, 9.1

Acronyms, 12.24; 28.8

Adam: found no iniquity in God, 14.5; stood erect while listening to God, 5.3; on first day of Tishri, received command, disobeyed, was judged, was freed, 23.1; given six commandments, 12.1; round of heel of, outshone sun, 4.4, 12.1, 26.3; gave God the name "Lord," 4.3; called God "Lord," to which he consented, 7.2; God joined thirteen (eleven, ten) canopies over him in Garden of Eden, 4.4, 26.3; how he named animals, 4.3; crouched to hide, 5.3; height of, diminished to one hundred cubits, 5.3; tree he ate of, not identified, 20.6; after sinning, found God's voice harsh, 5.3; would not have died but for his sin, 9.4; God lamented transgression and expulsion of, 15.1; sin of, caused Presence to remove to first heaven, 1.1; greatest sin of, was ingratitude, 4.4; learned power of repentance from Cain, 24.11; composed Psalm for repentance, 24.11; formerly felt no desire in wife's absence, 5.2
Affection, bestowed on world when Tabernacle was set up, 1.5
Affliction, meaning of, 27.2
Afflictions: of Israel, shared by God, 5.6; of this world, will be compensated for by wonders in world-to-come, 24.2
Africa, principality in, visited by Alexander, 9.1
Afterlife, countenances of righteous will be restored in, 8.1
'Ăḡaḏah: God's face joyous at revelation of, 12.25; why preferred, 12.3; as metaphysics, 21.5
Agag: flesh of, cut in olive-sized pieces and fed to ostriches, 3.6; male parts cut off, 3.6; torn apart, 3.6; Samuel's treatment of, symbolic requital for Amalek, 3.6
Agricultural advice, given in Torah, 10.7
Ahab: men in time of, not guilty of slander, 4.2; sacrificed to God for Jehoshaphat's sake, 26.1; made only gestures of repentance, 24.11
Ahab, son of Kolaiah: false prophet, 24.15; committed adultery with neighbor's wife, 24.15; roasted in frying pan, 24.15
Ahijah, made blind so that he should not see disciple Jeroboam's wickedness, 3.1
Ahimaaz, concern for David led to promotion of, S1.3
Ahithophel: delighted in lapping up slander, 4.2; reproached by David, 18.1
'Aḳiḇa, R.: matters not revealed to Moses, revealed to, 4.7; restrained desire when tempted by two beautiful women, S3.2
'Alef, letter: giving of Torah inaugurated with, 12.24; raised cry because world was created with *beṯ*, 12.24. *See also* Letters
Alexander of Macedon: victorious when he saw visage of Simeon the Just, 4.9; visited king who dispensed justice equitably, 9.1; visited principality ruled by women who gave him sound counsel, 9.1
Allegory, examples of: 4.9, 5.6, 5.7, 5.9, 5.10, 5.18
Altar: drains of, must be stopped for pouring of drink offering, 6.1; cost High Priest sixty centenaries of gold, 4.7
Altar smoke, High Priest could foretell year's crops from direction of, 26.4

Amalek: took Israelites' genealogical rolls from Egypt, 3.10; polluted Israel by pederasty, 3.10; first to use male member as instrument of derision, 3.11; attacked when Israel ruminated as to God's presence among them, 3.a; smote those who hung back from obeying God's commands, 3.12; attack by, encouraged attacks by others, 3.10; merits which Moses invoked against, at Rephidim, 3.c; allies of, not smitten in battle with Joshua, 3.d; brought on by dishonesty in weights and measures, 3.4; God's face is hidden while his seed endures, 3.16; will fall only at hand of Rachel's descendants, 3.13; likened to dog licking up blood, to fly greedy for open wound, to locust, 3.8; totally evil, 3.3; God swore no proselytes would be received from, 3.16; cut all the way down to foundations of Sanctuary, 3.6; cut off male parts from live Israelites, 3.6; tore up Scrolls of Torah, 3.6; symbolic crushing of, in days of Samuel, 3.6. *See also* Edom, Esau, Rome

Amasa, lion in understanding of Torah, 4.2

Ammi, R., sent to check teaching of Torah in villages of Land of Israel, 15.5

Ammonites: said cherubim had been objects of worship in Temple, 19.1; regulations concerning marriage with, 16.1

Amos: accused by Israel of contradicting own words, 16.8; called "Tongue-heavy," 16.4

Amram: court of, 5.7; merit of, caused Presence to return from second to first heaven, 1.1

Amraphel, Nimrod identified with, 8.2 n. 21

Anathoth, repentance of men of, 24.11

Angel, seated himself on Solomon's throne, 26.2

Angel of conception, charged by God to shape the embryos of Israelites with their fathers' features, 11.6

Angel of death, Moses blessed Israel in presence of, S1.10, S1.14

Angels: require no food, 6.1; but for Israel's acceptance of Torah, would have had to destroy Israel, 12.22; seen by Jacob, were princes of nations, 23.2; have been weeping since Jerusalem's destruction, S5.3; protested God's acceptance of Manasseh's prayer, 24.11; tablet with God's name on heart of every one of them, 12.22; frightened by Leviathan, S2.4; draw sustenance from splendor of Presence, 6.1; hollow east gate for Temple, 18:5

Angels, at Sinai: innumerable, 12.22; as many as males in Levites' camp, 12.22; 60 (120) myriads of, came down to crown each Israelite, 16.3; 60 (120) myriads of, came down to gird each Israelite with armor, 16.3

Angels, names of, Anger and Hot Displeasure, 5.3; Michael, Gabriel, 1.3, 12.22; Raphael, 12.22

Anger, of God, lasts only one day, 17.4

Animal(s): flesh cut from living, prohibited, 12.1; reasons for killing of, if woman copulated with them, 9.3; why they must be at least eight days old for offering, 9.1, 9.10; named by Adam, 4.3; when slaughtered must have gullet and windpipe cut, 4.3. *See also* Beasts

Apostates, will share heathens' fate, 4.9, 5.19
Apple tree, why Israel was compared to, 12.10
Araba, dialect of, 24.11, 27.3
Arabia: people of, made cattle groan to gain God's attention and mercy, 24.11
Arad, king of, encouraged by death of Aaron to attack Israel, 19.2
Ark of the Covenant, reason for seven months' captivity among Philistines of, 11.9
Arks, significance of the two, accompanying Israel in wilderness, 11.12
Asa, in royal line, seventh and most loved, 23.10
'Aṣereṯ, meaning of, 28.8
Associations (*Ḥăḇuroṯ*), for religious purposes, S2.4
Assyrians, put Manasseh into jackass-shaped cauldron over slow fire, 24.11
Atonement, Day of. *See* Day of Atonement
Azariah. *See* Hananiah, Mishael, and Azariah

Babylon: palm trees planted in, forty years before exile, to provide fruit whose sweetness accustomed Israel's tongue to study of Torah, 13.10; at Daniel's bidding, God answered Israel in, 5.9; chronology of exile in, 5.9
Balaam, philosopher among nations, 15.5; was expected to bestow seven blessings upon Israel, S1.4
Barak, conquered Sisera with prayer, 8.2
Barbaria, 5.7
Barburim, definitions of, 6.1
Bar Ḳappara, R., Mishnah of, 15.7
Barley: added by Ezekiel to bread dough, 8.4; dog would not eat bread made with excess of, 8.4; sheaf of, *see 'Omer*
Beasts, which may be eaten, three subject to human control, seven not subject, 6.1, 9.5. *See also* Animals
Beerah: Hosea's father, 24.9; well-spring of Torah, 24.9; why he died in exile, 24.9
Behemoth: drinks limitless waters of Yubal from Eden, 6.1; manner of, in feeding and drinking, 6.1; in close combat with Leviathan, S2.4; will slay Leviathan with his tail, S2.4
Belshazzar, one of three descendants of Merodach-baladan, each of whom became world conqueror to reward Merodach's homage to God, 2.5
Bestiality, why animal involved in, is put to death, 20.6
Beṯ, letter, world created with, 12.24. *See also* Letters
Betrothal and marriage, 5.3. *See also* Marriage
Bezer, Bozrah mistaken for, 4.9
Bible, teachers of, will abide at God's right hand, 27.2. *See also* Scripture, Torah
Birds: went into exile, 13.10; all returned, 13.10

Birth, chance for survival at, one in ninety-nine, 9.6

Bithiah: daughter of Pharaoh, was first-born, 7.6/9; brought near to God by Moses, S1.6; survived through merit of Moses' prayer, 7.6/9

Blessing(s): Balaam was expected to bestow upon Israel seven, S1.4; bestowal of, from Abraham to Moses, S1.1; of Moses, contain words of solace for prior words of sharpness, S1.5; must precede reading from Torah, S1.2; priests spread fingers in bestowing, 5.8

Boaz: hinted at Solomon's descent from Ruth, 16.1; restrained his sexual desire, 7.4; most guests at wedding of, descendants of Leah, 20.2

Bondage: of Israel due to lack of Torah, 27.1; imposed on Israel when they sin, 2.5

Bozrah, mistaken for Bezer, city of refuge for prince of Edom, 4.9

Bride: of God, Israel so termed in ten places in Scripture, 22.5; term for Israel, S6.5; permission of, must be given to groom, before he enters bridal bower, 1.1

Brigand, wife of, acting as enemy, 11.1

Bullock: as offering, invokes merit of Abraham, 9.9; why God asks offering of, despite Israel's sin with, 9.6; why Scripture designates sacrificial calf as, 9.3

Burnt offerings: continuation of, after wanderings in wilderness, questioned by Israel, 6.3; daily intercession of, for Israel, 6.3. *See also* Lambs, Offerings, Sacrifices

Caesarea, center of learning, 4.4

Cain: repentance of, questioned, 24.11; cancelled decree that made him fugitive, 24.11; taught Adam power of repentance, 24.11

Calcol, name for Joseph, 4.3

Caleb, conquered thirty-one kings of Canaan with prayer, 8.2

Calendar: God follows decrees of Israel's courts concerning, 5.13; reckoning of, turned over to Israel after exodus, 5.2, 5.11, 5.13. *See also* Festivals, New Moons

Calf, golden: before sin of, Israel did not fear seven seas of fire, 5.3; after making of, Moses could not gaze on angels' faces, 5.3; when made by Israel, nations of earth gloated, 2.1; God avoids reminding Israel of their iniquity concerning, 9.3; Israel not guilty of making, 9.8; Red Heifer symbolic atonement for, 4.8

Calumny. *See* Slander

Camel, how fed on Sabbath, 6.2

Canaan: thirty-one kings of, conquered by prayer of Joshua and Caleb, 8.2; inhabitants of, not utterly destroyed, 13.5; land of, earned by Israel through merit of *'omer*, 8.2

Canaanites: spared immediate invasion by Israel, 11.9; recentness of their show of respect for Jacob, 11.9
Candlestick for Tabernacle, making of, baffled Moses, 5.15
Carmel, Mount: with Mts. Sinai, Tabor, and Hermon, will support Jerusalem, S5.4; with Mts. Moriah, Sinai, and Tabor brought together, will support Temple in time-to-come, 21.4
Carp. *See Šibbuṭa*
Cattle, God's concern for, His reason for preserving man, 9.1
Cavilling, at God's commandments, prompted by Impulse to evil, 4.6
Census: of Israel, taken on ten occasions, 2.8; of Tribes, based by Moses on number value of first letters of names of Tribes, 2.8; unnecessary, followed by population decrease, 2.9
Chaos, dark, will be summoned against Rome, 7.12
Charity: acts of, by Israel, bring God to act in their behalf, 23.2; can avert evil decree, 28.3; collectors for, may not pressure contributors beyond their means, 27.1; God's, in allowing Danites' success, 10.8; in allowing house of Joseph to worship idol, 10.8; in sending manna, 10.8
Chastity: of R. 'Aḳiḇa, S3.2; of R. Zadok, S3.2; of Israel, sole reason why God let them leave Egypt, 11.6
Cherubim, said by Ammonites and Moabites to have been objects of worship in Temple, 19.1
Chicken, skin of feet of, is fishlike, 4.3
Children: in David's days knew subtle distinctions of law, 4.2; Oenomaus of Gadarah, philosopher, advises that Israel is vulnerable when Torah is not studied by, 15.5
Chilion. *See* Mahlon and Chilion
Chronology: of Egyptian oppression, 5.7, 5.9; of exodus, 5.9; of Babylonian exile, 5.9
Circumcision: inaugurated with Isaac, 12.1; not performed by Hebrews in Egypt, 5.11; performed by Moses upon Israel before exodus, 5.6, 5.9; one of two commandments obeyed by Israel before leaving Egypt, 7.4; performed by Joshua upon Israel when they arrived in Land, 5.9; observance of, discontinued in Jeremiah's time, 4.10, 5.9; disguised by people of Israel before exile, S5.2; why performed on eighth day after birth, 9.10; performed on Sabbath or Day of Atonement for Jew, not Gentile, 4.3; one of three signs borne by Israel, 1.3. *See also* Epispasm
Circumlocution, in Scripture, to avoid unseemly speech, 4.2
Circuses, avoided by Jews, 15.2
Clothes, worn by Israel while in wilderness, 11.21
Cloud of Glory, Danites expelled for idolatry from shelter of, 3.12; hovered over Samuel's courtyard, 4.5
Cloud-sukkahs, in wilderness, S2.6

Coin of fire, shown to Moses, meaning of, 2.10

Colors, four, used in Tabernacle, 1.3

Commandments: six hundred and thirteen, two hundred forty-eight positive, three hundred sixty-five negative, 12.1; reward for obedience to, 27.1; three, startled Moses, 2.10. *See also* Negative commandments, Positive commandments

Commands: given to Noah, disregarded by nations, S2.1; of God, to be exclusive, blamed by Israel as cause of nations' hostility, 19.2

Compensation, none adequate for teaching of Torah, 27.1

Confession, leads to God's mercy, 24.8

Conjunction of moon, 5.1, 5.15

Contrition, God delights in men whose hearts are broken by, 24.5

Courts of Israel, God follows decrees of, concerning calendar, 5.13

Courts of nations, do not require two eyewitnesses nor warn accused of consequences of crime, 3.6

Covenant of God with Israel, fundamental observances of, are circumcision and Sabbath, 5.6

Cow, horns of, why not proper for shofar, 9.3

Craftsmen, four. *See* Four craftsmen

Crag of rock on Mount Moriah, earth founded upon, 26.4

Creation, doctrine of, probed in days of Jeremiah, 4.10

Creeping things named in Pentateuch, hunting of on Sabbath, forbidden because they have skins, 4.3

Crops of coming year, foreseen by High Priest from direction of altar smoke, 26.4

Cup, from which woman suspected of infidelity drank and died, not to be used by another woman likewise suspected, 9.3

Curriculum of study. *See* Study

Curtains in Tabernacle, original dimensions of, not altered by wrinkles or creases, 1.6

Cuthean, debated with R. Meir about tithing, 10.6; who mocked R. Simeon b. Yoḥai, fate of, 11.16

Cutheans, survival of, in Land which was brimstone and salt after exile, 13.10

Dan, Tribe of, expelled from shelter of cloud of glory because of idolatry, 3.12

Daniel: at bidding of, God answered Israel in Babylon, 5.9; vision of, concerning time of redemption, 17.5

Danites, served idol which brought them luck, 10.8

Darda, name for generation of wilderness, 4.3

Darkness, plague of, in Egypt, wicked among Israel died during, 5.9

Daughters of Zion, wanton behavior of, 17.6

David: children in days of, knew subtle distinctions of the law, 4.2; in succession of Jesse's sons, seventh and most loved, 23.10; contrasted with Saul, 5.3; concern for, led to promotion of Ahimaaz, S1.3; reproached Doeg and Ahithophel, 18.1; began rule two years after anointment, 5.3; foresaw character of descendants, 27.3; harp of, hung against window, so that north wind blew through strings, 7.4; put harp and psaltery at his head to play on them at midnight, 7.4; harp over bed of, served to awaken him at midnight to study Torah, 7.4; exercised care in tithing, 10.6; delighted to do God's will, 10.6; was incited to sleep late by Inclination to evil, 7.4; expressed to God his distress at death of martyrs, 11.14; reference of, to Gehenna, 10.4; came into God's presence not through hallowing His Name, but by His charity, 11.14; assured by God of life eternal, 11.14; men in generation of, guilty of slander, 4.2

David, son of. *See* Messiah

Day of Atonement: circumcision may be performed on, for Jew, not Gentile, 4.3; prayer of High Priest on, 26.4; sukkah deemed equivalent to banishment which may have been decreed on, S2.7. *See also* New Year's Day, Repentance, Ten Days of Penitence

Day of Judgment: for Esau, foreseen by Isaac while blessing him, S1.11; God will shelter Israel on, as in sukkah, S2.2; fulfilling command of sukkah provides shelter from, S2.7

Dead: will be quickened by God because of Isaac, S1.20; will be brought forth by Land of Israel earlier, in time-to-come, 22.5a

Death: deserved by man who does not tithe for poor, 10.9; of righteous, atones for Israel's sins, 26.11; of righteous man's son, grieves God, 26.9; will be destroyed in world-to-come, S2.8

Deborah, conquered Sisera with prayer, 8.2

Dbr, stern word, 13.7

Decisions, by pupil, forbidden within twelve miles of master, 26.6/7

Decree: evil, means of averting, 28.3; God's, set aside by power of repentance, 24.11

Defective spelling, exposition of, 25.1 n. 5

Demons: came to an end when Tabernacle was set up, 1.5; ruled over by Solomon before he sinned, 5.3; have no independent power, 7.2, 21.2

Dew(s): brought down by generous tithing, 1.4; withheld because of miserly tithing, 1.4; noxious, 8.3; boon of, 17.8; term for Written Torah, 5.6

Disciples, duties of, provided for their masters, 11.8

Dispersion, generation of. *See* Generation of dispersion

Diverse kinds, Impulse to evil tries to discredit proscriptions concerning, 4.6

Divine Root. *See* Presence

Divine Voice. *See* Voice, Divine

Document, two-scroll, single-scroll, S2.4

Doeg: Amalekite proselyte, 3.16; delighted in lapping up slander, 4.2; reproached by David, 18.1

Dog, would not eat bread made with excess of barley, 8.4; loyalty of, 11.1
Dog-faced generation, Messiah will come in, 5.9
Dogs, make-believe, served as guardians of Joseph's coffin, 11.12
Donkeys, raised and lowered from roof by Eleazar bar R. Simeon b. Yoḥai, 11.18
Dough, Israel punished through having to set aside two offerings of, 14.4
Dove, term for Israel in their relationship with God, 5.6
Dream of Jacob, presented span of four kingdoms' rule, 23.2
Drink offering: altar drains must be stopped for pouring of, 6.1; God speaks of drinking, filling Himself, satiety, intoxication, with reference to, 6.1

Eagle, symbolized Presence, 26.4
Earth: founded upon crag on Mount Moriah, 26.4; became stable when Tabernacle was set up, 1.4, 1.5; root of Presence originally fixed in, 1.1; as long as it does not totter, Israel will endure, 19.5
East: kings of, amount of food consumed by, 6.2; men of, do not kiss on mouth, or tear food with teeth, 4.3; take counsel only in open field, 4.3
Ecclesiastes, Book of: ideas in, smacked of heresy, 8.1; Sages were about to suppress, 8.1, 24.14
Eden. *See* Garden of Eden
Edom (Rome): God's patience with, 3.e; pre-eminent among all peoples, 7.11; prince of, will mistakenly flee not to Bezer, but to Bozrah, 4.9; will be thrust from heaven, 4.9; requital of, will signal God's return to Temple, S5.3; sanguinary prophecies against, 7.11. *See also* Amalek, Esau, Rome
Edomites, took away foundation of Jerusalem, 18.2
Egypt: Hebrews in, were uncircumcised and unshorn, 5.11; worshiped idols, 5.7; Hebrew language forgotten in, 12.24; during plague of darkness in, wicked among Israel died, 5.9; first-born of, slew sixty myriads of their fathers, 7.6/9; God first destroyed property of, then slew first-born, 7.11; first-born of, during tenth plague, smitten at midnight and died on following day, 7.5; prince of, smitten in daytime, 7.5; details of tenth plague among first-born of, 7.6/9; before leaving, Israel obeyed commandment of circumcision, 7.4; circumcision performed in, 5.6; Moses circumcised Israel in, before exodus, 5.9; Israel united in, 14.4; bitter servitude in, lasted eighty-six years, 5.9; Israel resided in, as free aliens, for one hundred ninety years; as slaves, for two hundred ten years, 5.7; woe of, at letting Israel slip out of their land, 11.7; God's patience with, 3.e; Israelites' genealogical rolls in, taken by Amalek, 3.10; redemption of Israel from, despite what measure of justice required, 5.11; hasty deliverance from, contrasted with that in world-to-come, 5.19. *See also* Pharaoh
Egyptians: tested Joseph in seventy languages, 4.3; horrified at sight of lambs tied to Israelites' bedsteads, 5.17; smitten by stick or sword with which they

smote Israel, 11.4; schemes of, against Israel, turned against them, 11.5; received measure for measure for what they intended for Israel, 11.2; woe of, at letting Israel slip out of their land, 11.7; death of, cause of no command to rejoice on Passover, S2.8; sins of, in Abraham's day, caused Presence to remove to fifth heaven, 1.1; sins of, in Moses' day, caused Presence to remove to seventh heaven, 1.1. *See also* Pharaoh

Eight, number, meanings of, 28.d, 28.4

Eighth-Day Festival: characteristics of, 28.a, 28.6; observance of, saves from drought, 28.3; offerings of, solely for God and Israel, 28.9; regulations for kiddush on eve of, 28.a, 28.7; regulations concerning eating in sukkah on, 28.a; why it follows Sukkot directly, 28.7, 28.8; Tishri's own festival, 28.c

Eleazar b. Arak̲, R., exegesis of, preferred by R. Johanan b. Zakkai to R. Eliezer's and R. Joshua's, 2.5

Eleazar b. R. Simeon, R.: expended his strength in learning, 11.22; eulogy for powers of, 27.1

Eleazar b. R. Simeon, R., wife of: laughed and wept at his deathbed, 11.23; went to recover body of, 11.23; widowed, refused remarriage to R. Judah, 11.24

Elements, even when hostile, can dwell and work together, 1.3

Eliezer: only companion of Abraham in pursuit of four kings, 8.2; satisfied by one drink from Rebekah's pitcher, 6.2; numerical value of letters in name of, 8.2

Eliezer, R., descended from Moses, 4.7; pupil of, rendered decision, 26.6/7

Elijah: compelled by God to be reconciled with Israel, 17.1; taught number of chariots that came down with God on Sinai, 12.22; showed R. Joshua b. Levi stones of bright red *kad̲kud̲aya*, 18.5; taught Eleazar bar R. Simeon b. Yoḥai the Sifra, 11.22; power of, 1.4; never died, because he never sinned, 9.4

Elisheba: knew four joys in one day, 26.3; measure of justice grieved and laughed ironically at, 26.2

Elul, month, physical creation of world was begun on twenty-fifth of, 23.1

Emptiness, will be summoned against Rome, 7.12

Enemy: construed as meaning "dog," 11.1; as meaning "snake," 11.1; as referring to man's wife, 11.1

Enoch, seventh in sequence of generations, and most loved, 23.10

Enosh, generation of. *See* Generation of Enosh

Ephraim, descendants of, slain in battle with Egyptians, 11.10

Ephrn, exceptional spelling of Ephron, 10.1

Ephron, covetousness of, 10.1

Epispasm, S5.2

Esau: at birth, ripped Rebekah's womb, so that she did not bear twelve Fathers of Tribes, 3.1; was separated from Jacob not even by thinness of caul, 28.3; did not learn righteousness from Isaac and Rebekah, 3.13; was lecher and murderer, 3.1; thief, 3.1; opened mouth wide as camel to eat pottage, 6.2; hawked up phlegm and exhibited member to deride circumcised Jacob, 3.11; criticised Cain's folly, 9.11; "gracious" giving of, to poor, 10.1; would ask Isaac if water and salt require tithing, S1.11; at blessing of, Isaac foresaw his Day of Judgment, S1.11; Rebekah had no public funeral because of, 3.1; wars against those who do not tithe, 10.10; Israel's payment of tribute to, caused by lack of Torah, 27.1; prefigured in Exod. 12:2, 5.18. *See also* Amalek, Edom, Rome

Esoteric doctrines. *See* Mystical doctrines

Esther: conquered Haman by prayer, 8.2; in generation of, Amalek will be crushed, 3.16; prefigured in Exod. 12:3, 5.18

'Eṯ, measure of time, 7.5

Ethan, name for Abraham, 4.3

Ethrog, wood and fruit of, have same aroma, 27.8

Eulogies, 27.1

Evil-merodach, one of three world-conquerors made descendants of Merodach-baladan, to reward the latter's homage to God, 2.5

Exile: God had Himself bound in chains at, 13.9; Israel in, haunted by songs of deliverance from of old, 17.1; will occur through pressure of powerful persecutor, 25.1

Exiles: Jeremiah cast in his lot with, 13.9; day of gathering of, will be great as day Torah was given, S5.1

Exodus: circumcision performed by Moses on Israel before, 5.6, 5.9; God gave Israel task of calendar reckoning after, 5.2, 5.11

Expiation for Israel, won through Abraham's merit, 23.8

Ezekiel: added barley to bread dough, 8.4; offering of *'omer* helped Israel in days of, 8.4; one of four reputed to have come from blemished stock, 13.12

Falcon, keen-sightedness of, S2.3

Fasting, can avert evil decree, 28.3; means of giving one's fat and flesh in place of offerings, 24.19

Fate, similar, befalls good, bad, and indifferent, 26.1

Fathers. *See* Patriarchs

Fear of God, 27.2

Feast of Conclusion. *See* Eighth-Day Festival

Fees, for schoolmasters, not allotted on New Year's Day, 27.1

Festivals: amount expended for, not allotted on New Year's Day, 27.1; punishment of Israel by having to observe two days of, 14.4; were intended to be one for each summer month, 28.c, 28.2

Figs, topped baskets of first fruits, 5.9

Fingers, spread by priests in blessing, 5.8

Fire, mingled with hail in Egypt, 1.3

Firmament: sun set in, above heaven, to diminish its intensity, S2.1; distance from next, five hundred years, S2.1
First-born: Egyptian, pleaded with their fathers to let Hebrews go, 7.6/9; slew sixty myriads of their fathers, 7.6/9; smitten at midnight and died on following day, 7.5; details of tenth plague among, 7.6/9; God destroyed property first, then slew first-born, 7.11; ransom required for Tribe Fathers' sale of Joseph, Rachel's first-born, 2.10; of Israel, hallowed only on day first-born of Egypt died, 7.5
First fruits, baskets of, topped by figs, 5.9
Firstling, substitution for, violates negative command, 4.4
Fish: seven hundred species of clean, went into exile, 13.10; and all returned, 13:10; from Sea of Tiberias, from Great Sea, S2.4; do not require ritual slaughter, 4.3
Five hundred years, distance between firmaments, S2.1
Five, number, significance of, in regard to Egyptians, 11.11
Flood, generation of. *See* Generation of flood
Flood of fire in Sodom, 16.4
Forces, opposite, do not injure each other when both surrender to God, 1.3
Forty-five righteous men, ever present part of Israel, 5.10
Forty-nine arguments in interpreting Torah, 4.2
Foundation of earth, crag of rock on Mount Moriah, 26.4
Four craftsmen, Elijah, king Messiah, Melchizedek, and priest, anointed in time of war to exhort Israel, 5.9
Four kingdoms: Israel's adversaries, 12.25; span of rule of, seen in Jacob's dream, 23.2
Four kings, pursued by Abraham on night of fifteenth of Nisan, 7.5
Fowl, windpipe or gullet of, must be cut in slaughtering, 4.3
Friendship, bestowed on world when Tabernacle was set up, 1.5
Fringes, on corners of garments, one of three signs borne by Israel, 1.3

Gabriel, identified with fear, 1.3
Galilee, will be laid waste in generation of Messiah, 5.9
Gamaliel, R., asked by heathen why God revealed Himself in thorn bush, 1.2
Gamaliel II, Rabban, reassured by maidservant concerning ritual purity of vessels, 12.13
Garden of Eden: God joined thirteen (ten, eleven) canopies over Adam in, 23.6; in this world also each and every righteous man has his own, 9.1; location of, with respect to Gehenna, 28.3; source of river Yubal, 6.1
Garments: seven, of God, S6.5; in which God will clothe Himself on ten occasions, 22.5
Gaulan, will be desolate in generation of Messiah, 5.9
Gehenna: one of four things God showed Abraham, 5.2; description and loca-

tion of, 28.3; darkness in, 9.1; punishment of wicked in, 10.4; surrender of souls of wicked in, 10.4; fire of, has no dominion over righteous, S3.2; is place in Jerusalem, S2.1; not place, but day, burning as furnace, S2.1

Gematria, examples of: 3.1, 6.2, 8.2, 11.5, 13.11, S1.20. *See also* entries in Index of "Plays on Words and Letters"

Gems, will be common as dust in time-to-come, 18.6

Generation of dispersion, sins of, caused Presence to remove to fourth heaven, 1.1

Generation of Enosh, sins of, caused Presence to remove to second heaven, 1.1

Generation of flood: sins of, caused Presence to remove to third heaven, 1.1; asserted that rain did not come from God, S4.1; questioned God's providence, 26.2; measure of justice grieved and laughed derisively at defiance of God by, 26.2

Generation of Messiah, will be dog-faced generation, 5.9

Generation of wilderness, called Darda, 4.3

Genesis, Book of, Temple envisioned in as built, destroyed, and rebuilt at beginning of, 21.5

Gentile, descent of, traced through Gentile mother in mixed marriage, 9.3. *See also* Heathen, Nations

Gerah, ten, equal half-shekel, 2.10

Gideon, offering of *'omer* stood by Israel in days of, 8.4

Gifts, requested by God, small return for that which God gives man, 9.2

Gilgal, God answered Israel at Joshua's bidding in, 5.9

Giscala, burial place of R. Eleazar bar Simeon, 11.23

Goat, as offering, invokes merit of Jacob, 9.9

God: arrangement of sub-entries

1) Scriptural-chronological sequence
2) relationship to Israel at exile and after
3) God and Torah
4) God as Judge
5) God's powers and manifestations
6) God's timeless or universal attributes

1) present on earth at beginning of time, 1.1; joined thirteen canopies over Adam in Garden of Eden, 26.3; consented to be called "Lord" by Adam, 7.2; gave no independent power to demons, 7.2; lamented transgression and expulsion of Adam, 15.1; created world because of Abraham, S1.20; showed Torah, Temple offerings, Gehenna, and the yoke of kingdoms to Abraham, 5.2; directed Abraham's choice of yoke of kingdoms for his children, 5.2; told Abraham to sit in His presence, 5.8; turned over bestowal of blessing to Abraham, S1.11; counted as seventieh of those who came with the house of Jacob to Egypt, 11.13; promised that no dog would snarl when Israel left Egypt, 11.12; after exodus, turned over reckoning of calendar to Israel, 5.2; led and protected Israel in wilderness, 11.11; Israel let

themselves be drawn after Him without hesitation, 9.1; charged angel of conception to give embryos of Israelites features of their fathers, 11.6, charity of, in sending manna, 10.8; Moses gave orders to, S1.13; patience of, criticised by Moses at first, 25.1; reconciled Moses with Israel, 17.1;

at Sinai: spoke to each and every person in keeping with his capacity, 12.25; gave Torah as eagerly as mother gives breast to child, 12.2; sought to give Torah to all nations of earth, 5.2, S1.15, S2.1; "bought" Israel by precepts which gave sustenance to resist straying, 5.10; told Moses when to take down Ten Commandments, 10.9;

at Aaron's bidding, made His presence mount or leave Ark, 26.4; asks offering of bullock, despite Israel's sin, 9.6; offerings are not food for, 6.1; enjoys fragrance of obedience and good deeds in offerings, 6.1; studied passage of Red Heifer, 4.7; return of, to earth, signified by Tabernacle, 1.2; symbolized in lulab, 27.9; mourned death of Nadab and Abihu, 26.4; at Gilgal, answered Israel at Joshua's bidding, 5.9;

questioned Job, 10.7; assured David that martyrs' portion is in life eternal, 11.14;

asks for no more than tithe in return for all He gives, 10.8; gives crop according to measure of tithes, 10.10; punishes for not tithing, 10.9; symbolically takes offerings of lambs in Temple, 5.17; glory of, always remains on Temple site, 5.8; compelled Elijah to be reconciled with Israel, 17.1; confirms word of His prophets, 7.3; follows decrees of Israel's courts concerning calendar, 5.13; sanctions New Year's Day designated by Sanhedrin, 23.4;

2) at exile, had Himself bound in chains, 13.9; mourned for Judah and Benjamin, 15.4; lamented over Israel like king of flesh and blood, 15.3; lamented transgressions and expulsion of Israel, 15.1; shares Israel's afflictions, 5.6; will not leave unpunished spilling of Israel's blood, S2.2; war against Israel deemed war against Him, S2.2; will cease to be should He forget Israel, 17.5; Israel's patron, 12.23; Israel's pool of hope always nearby Israel, 24.2; is heart of Israel, 5.6; loves Israel so much that He mentions them five times in single verse, 2.7; called Israel "Mother" in endearment, 1.3; does not come to Israel with burdensome demands, 6.1; demands of, commensurate not with His majesty, but with Israel's capacity, 2.10, 6.3; imposed poverty upon Israel to induce repentance, 14.3; commands of, to be exclusive, blamed by Israel for nations' hostility, 19.2; nations of earth glad when He came to argue with Israel, 9.5; forgets Israel's evil deeds, 17.7; makes Himself be one who forgets, for Israel's sake, 25.2; avoids reminding Israel of their iniquity, 9.3; brought to act in behalf of Israel by their acts of charity, 23.2; devices of, of mercy toward Israel, 5.7; may contract limits of periods before redemption, 5.7; will cleanse Israel from all sins in time-to-come, 4.10;

3) not lenient about neglect of study of Torah, 15.5; inner force of Torah

brings students back to, 15.5; will teach Israel Torah in world-to-come, 12.21; glory of, stands, while Israel sit, in houses of prayer and study, 5.8; is pleased to be with Jews who merely collect in synagogues, 28.8;

4) reckons sins closely, 24.14; tips balanced scales of justice in sinner's favor by lifting out iniquities, 25.2; righteousness of judgment of, acknowledged, 10.8; dispensation of judgment of, to righteous and to wicked, 9.1; seeks the pursued, 9.4; does not act arbitrarily against His creatures, S1.15; anger of, lasts only one day, 17.4; "Good," epithet for, 24.19; compassion of, like that of father or mother, 19.3; thirteen attributes of mercy of, 6.1; meaning of patience of, 24.11; delays taking human life in exercising justice, 7.10; punishment inflicted by, calculated to minimize pain and severity, 24.17; more severe than punishment by hand of Pharaoh or Sennacherib, 15.2; meaning of vengeances of, 25.1; right hand of, changed by lack of penitence, 17.2; eager to summon to repentance, 24.10; grieves at death of righteous man's son, 26.9; consoles mourners, 3.1;

5) manifold powers and manifestations of, 1.4; providence of, 8.1; rewards those who bring joy to His household, 10.10; enhances strength of righteous to do His will, 24.6, 25.1; when pleased by man's ways, makes man's enemies his allies, 11.1; called Lion, 13.14; awesomeness of doings of, 11.2; opposite forces surrender to, so that neither injures other, 1.3; has power to make His creations surrender to His creatures, 1.3; delivers weak Impulse to good from strong Impulse to evil, 11.1; strength of, enhanced by righteous men, 25.1; transmutes and purifies "this," term of contempt, 2.4; hidden at times, S7.1; is not present, when there are no witnesses, 12.6; seven garments of, S6.5; will clothe Himself with garments on ten occasions, 22.5; Name of, *see* Name of God; Throne of, *see* Throne of God; places respect due righteous man above respect due Him, 2.5; requests gifts which are small return for that which He gives man, 9.2;

6) honoring of, with one's substance, 10.3; with one's exceptional qualities, 10.3; reason for anthropomorphic description of, by Prophets, 4.4; arguments for inducing belief in promises of, 9.4; does not yet rejoice in world, but will in time-to-come, 26.3; *See also* Parables and analogies, Presence

Gog and Magog, criticised folly of Israel's earthly foes, 9.11

Golden calf. *See* Calf, golden

Grammata, six, equal half-shekel, 2.10

Grasshoppers, clean, eight hundred species of, went into exile, 3.10; and all returned, 3.10

Grave, cannot abide wicked, 9.1

Graven image. *See* Image, graven

Greek words, identified with, or putative source of, Hebrew words: 3.1, 9.6, 14.5, 17.1, 27.8

Grief, not to be entwined into one's life, 26.3

Groom, not to enter bridal bower until given leave by bride, 1.1

Habakkuk, accused by Israel of contradicting his own words, 16.8
Ḥăḇuroṯ, *see* Associations
Hadrian, tortured those who hallowed the Name, 11.14
Haggai: accused by Israel of contradicting his own words, 16.8; prophecy entrusted to, in Jeremiah's time, 13.14
Hail, mingled with fire in Egypt, 1.3
Hair, unshaved on head and face, one of three signs borne by Israel, 1.3
Half-shekel: equals ten gerah, 2.10; equals six grammata, 2.10; equals one *ṭeḇa'*, 2.10; is ransom for sin with golden calf, 2.10
Hallel: S2.5; read in entirety only on first day of Passover, S2.8; significance of, 27.5
Hallowing the Name, suffering entailed by, 11.14
Haman: father of, was barber and bath attendant at Karnaim, 8.4; led horse for Mordecai, 8.4; conquered by prayer of Esther, 8.2; by prayer of Mordecai, 8.2; criticised Pharaoh's folly, 9.11; prefigured in Exod. 12.3, 5.18; boldness of Israel, in eating lambs in Egypt, stood by them in days of, 5.17; *'omer* stood by Israel in days of, 8.4
Hananiah, Mishael, and Azariah: cast into fiery furnace by Jews forced to do so, 4.10; verse recited by, on leaving furnace, 10.8
Hand, right, of God, changed by lack of penitence, 17.2
Hannah, one of seven barren women, 20.1
Harbingers of good tidings in time-to-come, identity of, S5.4
Harlot, pretense of, to good name, 10.1
Harp, David's: played at midnight, 7.4; hung over his bed to waken him to midnight study of Torah, 7.4; hung against window, so that north wind blew through strings, 7.4. *See also* Psaltery
Harvest, uncertain, therefore no command given to rejoice on Passover, S2.8; blending of atmosphere and dew required for, 8.1
Hasmoneans, descendants of, prefigured in Exod. 12.3, 5.18
Head, uncovered, Roman token of respect, 9.5
Health, six signs of improvement of, in sick person, 19.5
Hearkeners, four kinds of, 14.2
Heart, characteristics and importance of, 16.2
Heathen (singular): asked R. Gamaliel why God revealed Himself in thorn bush, 1.2
Heathen (plural): given ease, blaspheme, 28.1; not grateful to God, 28.b; observe holidays riotously, 28.1; do not believe in world-to-come, 6.2. *See also* Gentile, Nations
Heaven, as long as immeasurable, Israel will endure, 19.5
Hebrew language, forgotten by Israel in Egypt, 12.24

Hebrews in Egypt: uncircumcised and unshorn, 5.11; worship idols, 5.7
Heifer, Red. *See* Red Heifer
Heresy, suggestion of, in Book of Ecclesiastes, led Sages to consider suppressing it, 24.14
Hermon, Mount, with Mts. Carmel, Sinai, and Tabor, will support Jerusalem, S5.4
Ḥesed, varities of meaning of, 2.4
Hezekiah: conquered Sennacherib with prayer, 8.2; instituted practice of immersion after menstrual period, 6.2; meager daily fare of, 6.2; petition of, presented in own name, granted in name of ancestor, David, 25.4; offering of *'omer* by, helped Israel in days of, 8.4
High Priest(s): could foretell year's crops from direction of altar smoke, 26.4; prayer of, on Day of Atonement, 26.4; each, built runway for Red Heifer at own cost, 4.7
Hills, stand for courts of righteous, 5.7
History, view of, 5.2
Ḥiyya, R., Mishnah of, 15.7
Holy Ark, three required to go before it, 3.d
Honor: given to God with one's substance, 10.3; given to God with one's exceptional qualities, 10.3
Horse: six characteristics of, 3.3; unaware of help intended for him, 3.3
Hosea: accused by Israel of contradicting his own words, 16.8; descendant of Reuben, 24.9
Hoshaia, R., Mishnah of, 15.7
Houses of prayer (study), while Israel sit in, God's glory stands, 5.8
Human life, in exercising justice God delays taking of, 7.10

Idol(s): worship of, by house of Joseph, allowed as instance of God's charity, 10.8; brought luck to Danites, 10.8; called "rival," 10.8; offered manna by Israel, 10.8
Idolatry, designated "excrement," 13.2
Image, graven, Israel passed over Red Sea with, 10.8
Imma Shalom, wife of R. Eliezer, was told prediction of pupil's doom, 26.6/7
Impulse to evil. *See* Inclination to evil
Impulse to good. *See* Inclination to good
Inclination to evil: led Johanan the High Priest to become Sadducean, 11.1; has allies, S3.2; part of man from birth, S3.2; dwells at entrance of heart, S3.2; king over two hundred forty-eight parts that make up man, S3.2; compared to stone sticking up at a crossroads which men stumble over, 24.17; strongest despoiler, 11.1; enduring enmity of, 11.1; enmity of, countered by Torah, 11:1; overcome by study of Torah, S3.2; tries to discredit four precepts, each of which has notable exception, 4.6; should be made to tremble

with fear of its consequences and with frustration of its designs, 24.4; will be removed from heart of man in time-to-come, 24.17; incited David to sleep late, 7.4

Inclination to good: begins to guide individual at age of thirteen, S3.2; weak, 11.1; delivered by God from stronger Impulse to evil, 11.1

Ingratitude, Adam's greatest sin, 4.4

Inheritance, line of, 26.10

Iniquities, lifted by God from pan of scales of justice, to tip balance in sinner's favor, 25.2

Intercourse: sexual, 5.2; Jews refrain from, during menstruation, 28.4

Isaac: when Sarah gave birth to, barren women bore, handicapped were healed, sun's light was intensified, 22.1; binding of, on New Year's Day, 23.9; on hearing of the binding of, Sarah died, 26.3; circumcision began with, 12.1; why not blessed by Abraham, S1.11; set aside tithe, 10.6, S4.3; eyes of, grew dim so that he should not see Esau's wickedness, 3.1; on blessing Esau, foresaw Day of Judgment for him, S1.11; merit of, caused Presence to return to fifth heaven, 1.1; because of, God will quicken dead, S1.20. *See also* Patriarchs

Isaiah: conquered Sennacherib with prayer, 8.2; nephew of King Amaziah, 14.3; accused of making things up out of his own head, 16.10; reprimanded sharply, 14.3; reversed every word of rebuke he had uttered, S6.1; humility of, 16.4; soothed the pain of grief voiced by other Prophets, S6.1; prophesied from mouth of Divine Power, with double portion of Divine Power, 16.4; came to comfort all generations, 16.10

Israel: blessed through merit of Abraham, 5.8; expiation for, won through Abraham's merit, 23.8; in lack of faith, likened to Jacob who did not climb ladder, 23.2; occasional loss of hope of deliverance justified by Jacob's similar despair, 19.5; length of servitude of, in Egypt, 5.7; in Egypt, had forgotten the Hebrew language, 12.24; worshiped idols, 5.7; were united, 14.4; chastity of, sole reason God let them go forth from Egypt, 11.6; departed from Egypt in fifth generation after Jacob, 11.11; obeyed commandment of circumcision before leaving Egypt, 7.4; boldness of, in taking lambs in Egypt, stood by them at crossing of Jordan and in days of Haman, 5.17; Egypt's woe at having let them slip out of country, 11.7; proportion of, who went up out of Egypt, 11.11; redemption of, from Egypt, for four reasons, 11.6; reckoning of calendar (time) turned over after exodus, to, 5.2, 5.11, 5.13; to reckon year by moon, 5.1; reason for lunar calendar, 5.14; concerning calendar, God follows decrees of courts of, 5.13;

answered by God at Red Sea at Moses' bidding, 5.8; passed over Red Sea with graven image, 10.8; let themselves without hesitation be drawn after God, 9.1; offered manna to idols, 10.8; hands of, grew slothful in committing transgressions at Rephidim, 12.15; lost faith in God at Rephidim, 3.12;

at Sinai: at giving of Torah, Sinai was enlarged to accommodate, 12.22; something of God's splendor bestowed upon, after they accepted Torah, 4.4; became God's people only after accepting Torah, 12.23; became sound in body at acceptance of Torah, 12.19; but for their acceptance of Torah, angels would have had to destroy, 12.22; before sin of golden calf, did not fear seven seas of fire, 5.3; after sin of golden calf, could not gaze at face of God's intermediary, 5.3; not guilty of making calf, 9.8; God asks bullock as offering from, despite their sin, 9.6; led about and protected by God in wilderness, 11.11; led through wilderness by God's own providence, 11.8; clothes worn by, while in wilderness, 11.21; attack on, by king of Arad, encouraged by death of Aaron, 19.2; Balaam was expected to bestow seven blessings upon, S1.4; why Moses delayed blessing of, until end of life, S1.10; questioned continuation of burnt offering after wanderings in wilderness, 6.3; reply of, to nations' taunt concerning the two arks in wilderness, 11.12; enjoined by Moses to tithe, 10.1, 10.3, 10.5, 10.6, 10.7, 10.8; delight of, gained by merit of Sabbath and merit of tithes, 10.2; commanded to do three things upon entering Land, 3.14; Canaanites spared immediate invasion by, 11.9; answered by God at Gilgal at Joshua's bidding, 5.9; denied refuge after Jerusalem's destruction, 19.2; Patriarchs and Matriarchs lamented at banishment of, S5.2; in exile, haunted by songs of deliverance from of old, 17.1; God lamented transgressions and expulsion of, 15.1;

afflictions of, shared by God, 5.6; spilling of blood of, will not go unpunished by God, S2.2; war against, deemed war against God, S2.2; God forgets evil deeds of, 17.7; for sake of, God makes Himself be one who forgets, 25.2; God is patron of, 12.23; regarded by God as though created on New Year's Day, 23.12; not reminded by God concerning their iniquity, 9.3; so loved by God that He mentions them five times in single verse, 2.7; called "bride," S6.5; called God's bride in ten places in Scripture, 22.5; called "mother" in endearment by God, 1.3; should God forget, He will cease to be God, 17.5;

sin of, brings harsh reprimand from nations, 2.5; brings bondage, 2.5; sins of, atoned for by death of righteous, 26.11; atoned for by Miriam's death, 26.11; poverty imposed by God upon, to induce repentance, 14.3; blame God's commands for nations' hostility, 19.2; even tasty portions of nations spurned by, 21.3; nations of earth glad when God came to argue with, 9.5; taunted by the nations as being children of Egyptians, 11.6;

unique activities of, compared with other peoples, 5.5; set apart from heathen peoples to give latter hope of elevation, 5.5; purity of lineage of, 17.6; chastity of, sufficient to bring about Israel's redemption, 11.6; reticence and modesty of, 22.4; fertility of, 11.11; acts of charity of, bring God to act in their behalf, 23.2; has alternating generations of good and wicked men, hence no unbroken succession of wicked, 25.3;

God makes demands upon, commensurate with their capacity, 6.3; alive or dead, are made to hearken, 14.4; given strength by promises of redemption in Torah, 19.4; given sustenance by God's precepts, to help them resist straying, 5.10; unafraid of Gehenna because of obedience to precepts, 10.4; as full of obedience to commandments as pomegranate is full of seeds, 11.6; sit in houses of prayer and of study, while God's glory stands, 5.8; is vulnerable, according to philosopher Oenomaus of Gadarah, when children do not study Torah, 15.5;

bodily parts of, which sinned and were smitten, will yet give comfort, 16.11; words of, used in sin, will yet give comfort, 16.11; to bear three signs, 1.3; three traits of, which lead God to make them His very own, 19.6; four kinds of people in, 27.9; forty-five righteous men ever-present part of, 5.10; God's six meeting places with, 17.1; why compared to apple tree, 12.10; symbolized in lulab, 27.9; compared with moon, 5.12; likened to pomegranate, when leaving Egypt, 11.6; likened to sand, 2.9; called Mahol, "people given pardon," 4.3; concern for, causes man to be elevated in world, S1.3; paean of, at Messiah's coming, S6.5; will rejoice in requital of Edom, S5.3; will rejoice in Maker only in time-to-come, 26.3; will re-experience redemption only in time-to-come, 5.16; will endure as long as heaven is immeasurable and earth does not totter, 19.5; righteous share pain of, 8.4; will be taught Torah by God in world-to-come, 12.21. *See also* Israelites

Israel, Land of: seventh and most loved, in order of lands, 23.10; boundaries of, as holy as Land itself, 5.3; fertility of, 13.10; punishes those deceitful in tithing, 10.5; overflown by no bird, during fifty-two years after Temple's destruction, 13.10; at resurrection, will receive Ten Tribes and Israelites who died in wilderness, 24.9; will bring forth her dead earlier in time-to-come, 22.5a

Israelites: lambs tied to bedsteads of, horrified Egyptians, 5.17; genealogical rolls of, in Egypt, taken by Amalek, 3.10; identification of, as true sons of Tribe Fathers, 11.6; protectors of in Egypt, beaten, and later made princes in wilderness, 1.7. *See also* Israel, Jews

Issachar, Tribe of: advised making wagons to carry Tabernacle parts, 1.8; knew what should be done at right time, 1.8; knew intercalary days and months, 1.8; provided two hundred heads of courts of justice, 1.8

Jacob: not separated from Esau by even thinness of caul, 28.3; received five blessings, S1.11; in dream saw span of four kingdoms' rule, 23.2; saw angels who were princes of nations, 23.2; prepared himself with prayer, presents, warfare, 19.3; took not even pin from Laban, 14.1; Canaanites' show of respect for, 11.9; went ahead of his children so as to face danger from Esau first, 19.3; despaired before meeting Esau, 19.5; giving of tithes by, 10.6; bestowed six blessings upon Tribes, S1.11; goat as offering invokes merit of, 9.9; merit of, caused Presence to return to fourth heaven, 1.1. *See also* Patriarchs

Jeconiah: why called "Asir," 24.11; deemed utterly useless, yet his line was renewed, 24.11

Jedo, accorded Jeroboam respect due royalty, 2.5

Jeremiah: reason for birth of, in land of Benjamin, 13.14; one of four reputed to have come from blemished stock, 13.12; descendant of Rahab, 13.4; anguish of, about himself as priest who bestows no blessings, 13.13; went to Anathoth to receive his priestly portion, 13.4; went to Anathoth to portion out direful prophecies, 13.4; cast in his lot with exiles, 13.9; was scolded by Nebuzaradan for doing so, 13.9; reprimanded gently, 14.3; picked up and kissed severed fingers and toes of Israel, 13.9; whether ended prophecy with words of reproof, 13.14; last of Prophets, 13.14; compared with Moses, 13.6; God's adjutant, 4.10;

in days of: Israel violated all Ten Commandments, 13.8; circumcision not observed, 4.10; doctrine of creation probed, 4.10;

meanings of name: "desolation," 13.12; "the Lord rises," 13.12; "the Presence journeyed up and away in ten stages," 13.11; "void, destitute," 13.8. *See also* Jeremiah, in Index of "Plays on Words and Letters"

Jeroboam: accorded respect due royalty by Jedo, 2.5; brazen or delicate in saying to Jedo "thy God," 2.5

Jerusalem: meaning of name of, 16.3; name of, will be revered like name of its God, 22.5a; abuse of widows and orphans common in, 15.9; venality of judges in, 15.9; before destruction, debasers of coin and wine numerous in, 15.8; one who lodged full day in, did not remain sinful, 5.17, 6.3, 15.7; destroyed only after Jeremiah's departure, 13.14; Edomites took away foundations of, 18.2; wealth in, at its restoration, 18.6; suffering and restoration of, compared with Job's, 16.6; Vespasian destroyed 480 synagogues in, 15.7; those who mourned destruction of, will rejoice over its rebuilding, S6.2; nations will battle against, in time-to-come, S2.2; whosoever will utter contemptuously name of, will incur death penalty, 22.5a; Gehenna is place in, S2.1; will be extended in time-to-come, 20.7; will reach throne of glory, 20.7; is God's throne, 3.15; heavenly, will be set on Mts. Sinai, Tabor, Hermon, and Carmel, S5.4

Jethro: left before giving of Torah, 12.9, 12.16; descendants of, first to bring offerings to rebuilt Temple, S5.2; will bring offerings, S5.4; sat as judges in Chamber of Hewn Stones and were reckoned part of Israel, 3.d

Jew(s): forced to cast Hananiah, Mishael, and Azariah into furnace, 4.10; avoided theatres and circuses, 15.2; so regarded, when descended from Jewish woman in mixed marriage, 4.3; God is pleased to be even with those who only collect in synagogues, 28.8; three distinguishing precepts of, 16.3; given ease, honor God, 28.1; grateful to God, 28.b; observe holidays with prayers and offerings, 28.1. *See also* Israel, Israelites

Job: play on name of, 16.6; wanted to fight Chaldeans but realized strokes were from God, 7:10; oxen and asses of, died, 7.10; accused friends of uttering contradictory words, 16.8; questioning of, by God, 10.7; speaks to God about tithing, 10.7; angered at fate of Aaron's sons, 26.5; suffering and restoration of Jerusalem compared with, 16.6; meaning of by *the words of Job are ended*, 10.7; given anticipation of world-to-come, 7.10

Jochebed, counted as seventieth of house of Jacob in Egypt, 11.13

Joel, accused by Israel of contradicting his own words, 16.8

Johanan, High Priest, became Sadducean through Impulse to evil, 11.1

Johanan, R.: asked R. Abbahu why his face was aglow, 4.4; sold all he had in order to study Torah, 27.1; eulogy for, 27.1

Johanan b. Zakkai, R.: discussed Red Heifer with heathen, 4.7; greatness of God acclaimed in his study house, 4.10; preferred the exegesis of R. Eleazar b. 'Arak̠ to those put forth by R. Eliezer and R. Joshua, 2.5

Jonadab, Rechab's son, descendants of, first to bring offerings in rebuilt Temple, S5.2, S5.4

Joram, received children from Obadiah's wife as pledges for money she and her husband borrowed to maintain Prophets in hiding, 2.5 n. 19

Jordan, river: at crossing of, Israel was sustained by their boldness in taking lambs in Egypt, 5.17; twelve months' flow of, not enough to moisten Behemoth's mouth, 6.1

Jose, R., sent to check teaching of Torah in villages of Land of Israel, 15.5

Jose b. Ḥalafta, R., discussed with Roman lady: Ezekiel's sufferings, 8.4; God's matchmaking, 2.4; God's making of ladders for different persons to ascend and descend, 2.4

Joseph: gentleness of, S4.2; hand of, pure because of chastity, 14.2; and Potiphar's wife, S3.2; did not learn wickedness from Pharaoh and Potiphar, 3.13; tested in seventy languages by Egyptians, 4.3; called Calcol, 4.3; comforted his brothers, 16.5; why he swore oath again and again, 11.25; he and two sons counted among house of Jacob who entered Egypt, 11.13; bones of, taken up from Egypt by Moses, 11.12; coffin of, called up by Moses from bottom of Nile, 11.12; burial place of, made known to Moses, 11.12

Joshua: chosen to fight Amalek because of descent from Joseph, 3.b; smote only Amalek in battle and not their allies, 3.d; God answered Israel at Gilgal at bidding of, 5.9; conquered thirty-one kings of Canaan with prayer, 8.2

Joshua b. Ḳorḥa, R., reproached Eleazar bar R. Simeon b. Yoḥai for being executioner, 11.19

Joshua b. Levi, R.: not regarded as equal by R. Simeon b. Yoḥai, 11.15; humility of, 18.5; saw marble pillars in Rome protected with wrappings, 9.1; shown stones of *kad̠kud̠aya* by Elijah, 18.5

Joshua, son of Jehozadak: claimed by false prophets to be a fellow lecher,

24.15; survived ordeal of frying pan while two false prophets roasted, 24.15
Joy, five kinds of, bestowed by Presence, 27.2
Judah, R., inferior in holiness to R. Eleazar bar R. Simeon, 11.24
Judah b. R. Il'a'i, R.: effect of four cups of Passover wine on, 4.4; seen by heathen with face aglow, 4.4
Judea, could not supply food for Nehemiah, 6.1
Judgment, Day of. *See* Day of Judgment
Judgment of God, dispensation of, to righteous and to wicked, 9.1
Justice: balanced scales of, made to tip in sinner's favor, when God lifts out iniquities, 25.2; in God's exercise of, He delays taking human life, 7.10; strict, cannot be exercised by God in world, 16.4, 19.3
Justice, measure of: grieved and laughed derisively when generation of flood defied God, 26.2; grieved and laughted derisively at Sodom and Gomorrah's selfishness, 26.2; at Elisheba, 26.2; redemption from Egypt occurred despite requirements of, 5.11

Kaḏkuḏaya, Elijah showed R. Joshua b. Levi bright red stones of, 18.5
Ḳarṭigna, principality ruled by women, visited by Alexander, 9.1
Ḳaṣia, end of the world, 9.1 n. 8
Kebul, notable of, hid grief from wedding guests, 26.2
Ḳĕri. See Kĕṯiḇ and *ḳĕri*
Kĕṯiḇ and *ḳĕri*, examples of, 2.5, 4.7, 5.8, 9.1, 11.14, 24.11, 27.3
Kiddush, regulations for: on eve of Eighth-Day Festival, 28.7; on Eighth-Day Festival, 28.a
Ḳimḥith: modesty of, 26.10; seven sons of, all High Priests, 26.10
Kindness, one of three traits of Israel which lead God to make people His very own, 19.6
King, reminded by herald of six commandments as he ascended each of six steps of throne, 1.7
King of the universe. *See* God.
Kings, sleep till nine o'clock in the morning, 7.4
Knowledge of Torah, less important than practice thereof, S1.2
Kohath, merit of, caused Presence to return to second heaven, 1.1

Laban, Jacob took not even a pin from, 14.1
Lambs: tied to Israelites' bedsteads, horrified Egyptians, 5.17; daily offered on northeast and southwest altar corners respectively, 6.3; permit Israel's two daily meals as acknowledgment of God's sovereignty, 6.3; use of, for morning and evening sacrifice, to be determined in advance, 6.3; symbolize "taking" of God, 5.17; will serve as Israel's advocates on Day of Judgment, 6.3; *See also* Burnt offerings, Offerings, Sacrifices

Land, The. *See* Israel, Land of
Land of Israel. *See* Israel Land of
Leah, one of seven barren women, 20.1
Leper, ritual cleansing of, discussed by Solomon, 4.3
Leprosy, God strikes with it first man's house and garments, then his body, 7.10
Letters: giving of Torah inaugurated with *'alef*, 12.24; raised cry because world was created with *beṯ*, 12.24; world created with *beṯ*, 12.24
Letters, numerical value of. *See* Gemaṭria, examples of
Levi, merit of, caused Presence to return to third heaven, 1.1
Levi, R., was unlikely to leave lesson without instruction in halaḵah, 23.12
Levi b. Sisi, power of prayer of, 24.18
Leviathan: angels frightened by, S2.4; angels' swords recoil from armor of, S2.4; in close combat with Behemoth, S2.4; will slay Behemoth with fin, S2.4; fins of, dim sun's disk by comparison, S2.4; head of, will be eaten by righteous, S2.4; lair of, pure, S2.4; skin of, will make material for sukkah promised to those who dwell in earthly sukkah, S2.4; underparts of, shine, S2.4
Levirate marriage, Impulse to evil tries to impugn, 4.6
Levite, deserves tithe from finest part of crop, 10.10
Leviticus, Book of, why children start their studies with, 6.3
Libations, passage on, expounded by R. Simeon b. Yoḥai, 11.15
Life, eternal, David assured by God of martyrs' portion in, 11.14
Light, how created by God, 21.5
Lineage: purity of Israel's, 17.6; son of Jewish mother and Gentile father is Jew, 4.3; son of Gentile mother and Jewish father is Gentile, 4.3
Lion, name for God, 13.14
Lion of God, name for Temple, 13.14
Lord: Adam's name for God, to which He consented, 7.2; overcame wickedness of Pharaoh, 11.1; bestowed on world when Tabernacle was set up, 1.5
Lovingkindness, act of, when performed by nations, masks sin, 2.5
Lulab(s): must be honestly purchased, 27.5; requirements of, for plants in cluster, 27.8; held by men circling altar each day of Sukkot, 27.5; taking of, on Sabbath, 27.8; obedience to command of, may bring incalculable reward, 27.1; will bring redemption, 27.10; sign of, triumphant conclusion of Israel's trial on New Year's Day, 27.2; meaning of four plants in, 27.9; God, Patriarchs, Matriarchs, Great Sanhedrin, Israel symbolized in, 27.9

Machpelah, cave of, S5.2
Mahlon and Chilion, animals of, died before they did, 7.10
Mahol, name for Israel, 4.3

Malachi: accused by Israel of contradicting his own words, 16.8; prophecy entrusted to, in Jeremiah's time, 13.14
Males, signified by "a fountain sealed" (Song 4:12), 11.6
Malevolence, sukkah shelters from, S2.3
Man: gifts and obedience of, to God, are small return for that which he receives from God, 9.2; unmarried, who supports schools, will some day be rewarded by having own child, 9.2
Mana, R., effect of four cups of Passover wine on, 4.4
Manasseh, king: put into copper caldron shaped like jackass, over slow fire, 24.11; returned from captivity on wind, 27.3; exclaimed "Where there is judgment, there is a Judge," 24.11; repentance of, at last moment of life, 24.11; power of prayer of, 27.3; angels protested God's acceptance of prayer of, 24.11
Mankind, called "complainers and children of complainers," 17.3
Manna: taste of, varied to suit each person, 12.25; offered to idols by Israel, 10.8; sending of, instance of God's charity, 10.8; will appear in days of Messiah, 5.8
Manoah, wife of, one of seven barren women, 20.1
Marriage(s): determined by God when embryos are but breath in mothers' wombs, 23.8; childless, to be dissolved after ten years, 22.2; of female convert, captive, or emancipated slave, must be delayed three months, 12.17; levirate, Impulse to evil tries to impugn, 4.6. *See also* Betrothal and marriage
Married women, signified by "a spring shut up" (Song 4:12), 11.6
Massah-and-Meribah, "trying-and-strife," actually name of Rephidim, 3.a
Master(s): presence of, extends twelve miles, within which no pupil may render decisions, 26.6/7; pupil's decisions in presence of, bring on death penalty, 26.6/7; provided for by their disciples, 11.8
Matchmaking by God, discussed by R. Jose b. Ḥalafta with Roman lady, 2.4
Matriarchs: lamented at banishment of Israel, S5.2; symbolized in lulab, 27.9
Measure for measure, 17.4
Media: why permitted by God to worship idols, 4.9; prefigured in Exod 12:3, 5.18
Meeting places, of God and Israel, 16.3
Meir, R., debated with Cuthean about tithing, 10.6
Menstruation, Jews refrain from sexual intercourse during, 28.d, 28.4
Mercy: bestowed on world when Tabernacle was set up, 1.5; God's thirteen attributes of, 6.1; God's devices of, toward Israel, 5.7
Merit of Abraham, wins expiation for Israel, 23.8
Merit of Fathers. *See* Merit of Patriarchs
Merit of Patriarchs, 3.c, 17.5, 22.4, 23.7, S3.1
Merodach-baladan: took three steps in homage, upon learning that God had made sun go back ten degrees, 2.5; three world-conquerors descended from, in reward for his homage to God, 2.5

Meron, people of, saw R. Simeon b. Yoḥai in their dreams, 11.23

Mesha: sought to outdo Abraham's willingness to sacrifice Isaac, 2.5; unrestrained desire of, for sheep, 6.2

Messiah: will come after seven year period of affliction, 5.9; will come in dog-faced generation, 5.9; will come at Elijah's bidding, 5.9; after first appearance, will disappear for forty-five days, 5.8; manna will appear in days of, 5.8; rough (*ḥaḏ*) with nations, gentle (*raḵ*) with Israel, 20.7; Israel's paean at coming of, S6.5; time of, 18.6; hope for, has no set time, S5.3

Micah, prophet: accused by Israel of contradicting his own words, 16.8; smitten on cheek, 16.4

Michael, angel, identified with merciful dominion, 1.3

Midnight, no creature can apprehend instant of, 7.1

Miriam: means "bitterness," 5.9; death of, atoned for Israel's sins, 26.11

Mishael. *See* Hananiah, Mishael, and Azariah

Mishnah: God's face equanimous at revelation of, 12.25; reason for neglect of, 12.3; teachers of, will abide at God's right hand, 27.2

Moabites: regulations concerning marriage with, 16.1; said cherubim had been objects of worship in Temple, 19.1

Modesty and reticence of Israel, 22.4

Moon: created to dissuade nations of earth from sun worship, 5.1; created as means of proclaiming New Moons and New Year's Days, 5.1; conjunction of, 5.15; does not set instant of month's departure, 5.1; renewal of power of, over earth, 21.1; mystery of changes of, baffled Moses, 5.15; Israel to reckon year by, 5.1; why Israel reckons year by, 5.14; Israel compared with, 5.12

Mordecai: saying Shĕma' when Haman approached with horse, 8.4; conquered Haman with prayer, 8.2; prefigured in Exod. 12:3, 5.18; studying precept of *'omer* when Haman approached with horse, 8.4

Moriah, Mount: earth founded upon crag of earth on, 26.4; and Mts. Sinai, Tabor, and Carmel to be brought together, Temple to be built on, in time-to-come, 21.4; will be sung to by other mountains in time-to-come, 21.4

Morons, term applied to Israel by Moses, which cost him entry into Land, 14.5

Moses: born circumcised, 26.1; appeared, then disappeared, as first Messiah, 5.8; power of, 1.4; rod of, had God's seventy names emblazoned upon it, 3.c; staff of, 19.6; petition of, presented in name of ancestry, granted in own name, 25.4; prayer of, saved Bithiah, 7.6/9; brought Bithiah near to God, S1.6; circumcised Israel before exodus, 5.9; matters not revealed to, revealed to R. 'Aḳiḇa, 4.7; made Joseph's coffin float up from bottom of Nile, 11.12; imaginary dogs were present when he made Joseph's coffin float up from bottom of Nile, 11.12; excellence of, in taking Joseph's bones out of Egypt, 11.12; radiance of, at Red Sea, 11.13;

went up to heaven to receive Torah, 4.4; conversed with God in pillar of cloud, 4.5; refrained from staring at Presence, 26.9; knew reasons for precept of Red Heifer, 4.7; instructions of, concerning Red Heifer, will continue through lineal descendant, 4.7; ash of Red Heifer used by, will endure to rebuilding of Temple, 4.7; enjoined Israel to tithe scrupulously, 10.1, 10.3, 10.5, 10.6, 10.7, 10.8; set down precepts in Torah in groups of sixty (seventy), 5.10; wrote thirteen Scrolls of Law, S1.8; told by God when to take down Ten Commandments, 10.9; interpreted Written Torah to Israel, 4.4; fate of, depended on Israel's behavior, 5.9; argued with God after sin of golden calf, 16.9; gave orders to God, S1.13; critical at first of God's patience, 25.1; found no iniquity in God, 14.5; as God's intermediary, 5.3; ready to give up life for Israel, S1.12; called "man of God" after speaking compassionately for Israel, S1.3; was reconciled with Israel by God, 17.1;

served as High Priest in wilderness whenever God chose, 4.5; but did not wear priestly garments, 4.5; baffled by three things, 5.15; startled by commandments to make Sanctuary, ransom for soul, and daily offerings, 2.10, 6.3; shown meaning of coin of fire, 2.10; shown fiery colors by God (on the Mount) as pattern for Tabernacle, 1.3; set up and took down Tabernacle each day during seven (eight) days of investiture, 1.5; anointed Tabernacle vessels for world as we know it and for world-to-come, 1.6; distraught, because God had not previously communicated to him command that princes bring oxen to convey Tabernacle, 1.8; counted Israel by numerical values of first letters of Tribes' names, 2.8; sought to make peace with Sihon, S5.4; composed eleven Psalms for eleven Tribes, S1.8;

blessed Israel in presence of angel of death, S1.10, S1.14; why he waited until end of life to bless Israel, S1.10; bestowed upon Israel four blessings which Balaam had begrudged them, S1.11; blessing of, exceeded all blessings bestowed previously, S1.11; did not bless Tribe of Simeon because of deed at Shittim, S1.8; interceded for Reuben, 2.7; brought Reuben near to God, S1.6; denied entry into Land because he called Israel "morons," 14.5; why he died in wilderness, 24.9; death of, mentioned ten times in Scripture, S1.20; in succession of Patriarchs, seventh and most loved, 23.10; Eliezer descended from, 4.7; Jeremiah compared with, 13.6; authority of, over Shekinah, like that of spouse over wife, S1.9; seat of, resembles royal throne, 1.7; merit of, caused Presence to return to earth, 1.1; in world-to-come, will own fifty-five more rivers of balsam oil than the righteous, S1.20; in time-to-come, fifty-five myriads of righteous will praise, S1.20

Moses and Aaron, conquered Pharaoh, Sihon and Og with prayer, 8.2

Moth, nibbled behind ear of corpse of R. Eleazar bar R. Simeon, 11.23

Mother, God's term of endearment for Israel, 1.3

Mount of Olives, Presence lingered for three and a half years on, before soaring up, 13.11

Mountains: messengers of good tidings at redemption, S5.2; term for courts of righteous, 5.7; term for temples of idolatry, 5.7

Mourning, practices of, 15.3

Mystical doctrines (teaching), imparted at Sinai, 12.22; must be conveyed in whisper, 21.5

Nadab and Abihu: remained single through arrogance, 26.9; impatient to succeed Moses and Aaron, 26.9; presumptuously rendered decision in presence of their master Moses, 26.6/7; stared grossly at Presence, 26.9; died on first day of Nisan, 26.11; died for four offenses, 26.8, 26.9; souls of, burnt out, but bodies untouched, 26.3 n. 22, 26.5; innocent of secret dissolute practices, 26.8; mourned by God, 26.4

Nahum, accused by Israel of contradicting his own words, 16.8

Naḳai, mocked R. Simeon b. Yoḥai, fate of, 11.16

Name, change of, can avert evil decree, 28.3

Name of God, made up of seventy-two letters, 5.11; "Lion," 13.14; *Naṭrona*, "Supreme Guardian," 5.18

Nations: disregarded commands given to Noah, S2.1; princes of, appeared to Jacob as angels, 23.2; Moses sought to give Torah to, S1.15; reason for solar calendar of, 5.14; Israel spurned even tasty portions of, 21.3; hostility of, ascribed by Israel to God's commands to be exclusive, 19.2; exactions of, made giving tithe difficult, S4.2; give harsh reprimand when Israel sins, 2.5; courts of, do not require two eyewitnesses nor warn accused of consequences of crime, 3.6; acts of lovingkindness of, mask for sin, 2.5; seventy bullocks offered on behalf of, during Sukkot, 28.9; will battle against Jerusalem in time-to-come, S2.2; moon created to dissuade them from sun worship, 5.1; asked by God to accept Torah, 5.2; glad when God came to argue with Israel, 9.5; gloated when Israel made golden calf, 2.1; Israel set apart from, to give nations hope of elevation, 5.5; to reckon year by sun, 5.1. *See also* Gentile, Heathen

Naṭrona, "Supreme Guardian" (name of God), 5.18

Nebuchadnezzar: was dwarf, 13.8; one of three world-conquerors descended from Merodach-baladan, to reward latter's homage to God, 2.5; wife of, thwarted false prophets' schemes of lechery, 24.15; urged by Divine Voice to destroy Jerusalem, 5.9; prefigured in Exod. 12:2, 5.18

Nebuzaradan: scolded Jeremiah for casting his lot with exiles, 13.9; sought reason for seething of blood on Temple rock, 15.7

Negative commandments, correspond to three hundred and sixty-five days in solar year, 12.1. *See also* Commandments

Nehemiah, Judea could not supply food for, 6.1

New Moon: procedure for determining arrival of, 5.15; amount expended for, not allotted on New Year's Day, 27.1; festive meal on, 27.1

New Year's Day: God judges cases of mankind during, S7.2; no command to rejoice on, because men's lives judged during, S2.8; God regarded Israel as though created on, 23.12; God sanctions date of, designated by Sanhedrin, 23.4. *See also* Day of Atonement, Repentance, Ten Days of Penitence

Niggardliness: of Jew to Jew, 10.1; consequence of, 10.1

Nimrod: identified with Amraphel, 8.2 n. 21; conquered by Abraham's prayer, 8.2

Nineveh, people of: made cattle groan to gain God's attention, 24.11; made show of repentance, 24.11

Nisan: night of fourteenth of, 5.17; on night of fifteenth of, Abraham pursued four kings, 7.5

'nḵy ("I"), reason for double use of, in promise of redemption, 19.5

Noah: mutilated by lion as he was leaving ark, 26.1; forbidden to eat flesh cut from living animal, 12.1; commands given to, disregarded by nations, S2.1

Noḳeḏ, meaning of, 2.5

Numerical value of letters. *See* Gemaṭria

Oath: of Abraham, sworn to Abimelech concerning three generations, 11.9; of God, set aside by power of repentance, 24.11

Obadiah, wife of, pledged children for money borrowed to maintain prophets in hiding, 2.5

Obedience to commandments, reward for, 27.1

Oblations, study of pertinent ordinances equivalent to bringing, 6.3

Oenomaus of Gadarah, philosopher, advised that Israel is vulnerable when children do not study Torah, 15.7

Offerings: Moses startled by commandment of, 6.3; are one of three acts of Israel which lead God to make Israel His very own, 19.6; only beasts subject to human control required for, 6.1, 9.5; consist of animals easily overcome by pursuers, 9.4; reason for offering on Sukkot the kind known as "festal peace" and also the kind known as "joyous peace," 27.2; are not food for God, 6.1; God enjoys fragrance of obedience and good deeds in, 6.1; God's acceptance of, signifies return to His favor, 1.1; replaced by fasting, which offers up one's own fat and flesh, 24.19; replaced by prayer, as means of expiation, 24.19; study of pertinent ordinances equivalent to bringing, 6.3; all will cease, except thank-offering, in time-to-come, 9.12. *See also* Burnt offerings, Lambs, Sacrifices

Og, conquered by prayer of Moses and Aaron, 8.2

Olives, Mount of. *See* Mount of Olives

'Omer: Abraham earned Canaan through merit of, 8.4; Israel earned Canaan through merit of, 8.2; stood by Israel in days of Ezekiel, Gideon, and Hezekiah, 8.4; stood by Israel in days of Haman, 8.4; makes peace between husband and wife, 8.4; manner of waving of, 8.3; procedure in, and measuring of, sheaf of barley, 8.1

Orphans, abuse of, common in Jerusalem, 15.9

Oxen: for pulling Tabernacle, sold by princes to congregation, 1.8; longevity and youth of, 1.8

Paean of Israel at Messiah's coming, S6.5

Palm trees, planted in Babylon forty years before exile to provide fruit whose sweetness accustomed Israel's tongue to study of Torah, 13.10

Parables and analogies: banker's son against whom due bill was issued, 14.7; bird in cage, 24.14; bride adorns herself with jewels, S6.5; brigand betrays fellows, S3.2; brigand sentenced and executed after flogging and confession, 24.10; carpenter turned tools over to son, 5.13; cheat was chastened by tavern keeper, 24.14; city confused by imminent invasion, 24.1; city rebelled against its king, 24.11; cover for wine vessels, 9.1; ear is like fumigating vessel, 14.2; elders concerned for particular headdress, 2.7; fatherless child about to wed, 22.4; fig tree narrow at base, spreading at top, 20.7; four-level storehouse on fire, 25.3; gazelle leaps and skips, 5.8; God as cook, 8.1; God as watchman, 8.1; heir let property slip through fingers, 11.7; heir sold field for trifle, 11.7; heir sold tree trunk for trifle, 11.7; highwayman's victim became his advocate, then his accuser, 27.6; Holy One appeared as statue with faces on every side, 12.25; iron put in fire, S3.2;

king, angered at people, left city, S7.3; king asked son to dine with guests, 21.3; king asked steward to make garment of precious stones, 1.3; king became angry at noblewoman (wife), 19.5; king betrothed noblewoman, 12.11; king called daughter "mother" in endearment, 1.3; king concerned for particular purple cloak, 2.7; king concerned for particular undergarment, 2.7; king counted years of era from daughter's wedding month, 12.11; king deposited possessions with steward, 14.5; king fenced in vineyard with biting dog within, 3.9; king forebore to mar joy of daughter's marriage day, 26.9; king had son and many maidservants, 20.6; king had son of marriageable age, 12.19; king had twelve sons, 15.4; king had two cooks, 6.3; king had two fierce legions, 24.11; king invited son to feast with him when guests departed, 28.9; king invited two foes to feast, 3.e; king journeyed along highway, 6.3; king judged civil cases, S7.2; king kissed palace walls when departing, 13.11;

king left palace for inn, S5.3; king made pavilion for daughter who had come of age, 1.2; king married many women but did not record nuptials, 5.11; king numbered flock, 2.8; king of whose two sons one died, S5.2; king questioned tutor constantly about son, 2.7; king reclined on dining couch, 6.3; king remitted city's taxes in return for its praise, 27.7; king sent proclamation to province, 9.5; king strides forth into field, 12.22; king struck two sons (R. Johanan), 15.4; king struck two sons (R. Simeon b. Lakish), 15.4; king turned son over to tutor, 14.5; king turned timepiece (arm ring, finger ring, keys to treasuries) over to son, 5.13; king visited by married daughters from near and far, 28.7; king visited by sons from near and far, 28.f; king wanted to marry woman of goodly stock (R. Eleazar), 12.11; king wanted to marry woman of goodly stock (R. Levi), 12.11; king wed noblewoman and bade her be exclusive, 19.2; king wed noblewoman and pledged substantial settlement, 19.4; king went away with sons and sons-in-law, S6.5; king withdrew decree forbidding foreign marriages, 12.11;

king's consort urged people to hint for additional feast-day, 28.8; king's consort urged subjects to petition him, 28.f; king's daughter had guardian, S5.3; king's daughter had unworthy suitors, 21.3; king's daughters were gossiped about as wanton, 11.6; king's flock despoiled, 16.9; king's palace burned down, 16.9; king's restored wife wanted offerings from his hand, 1.1; king's servant brought him rotten fish, 11.3; king's son was captured, 5.11, 12.11; king's vineyard hacked down, 16.9; king's vineyard produced good wine and bad, 16.9;

man carried foolish son to market, 3.a; man evaded paying duty, 24.14; man had ten gold coins, 15.11; man in province was mighty, 18.2; man walked on road during sunset, 21.3; merchants sell gem jointly, divide profits fairly, S2.4; noblewoman brought two myrtles to king, 14.4; noblewoman's husband, sons, and sons-in-law went to far country, 22.3;

ox acted savagely, S1.8; palace falls into ruin, 14.3; passerby urges jewels be set in king's crown, 2.7; physician turned medicine cabinet over to son, 5.13; pool of scalding water, 3.10; prince walked in marketplace, 12.11; renegades rebelled against king, S3.2; robber ran from magistrate, 21.14; robber received verdict of prison after confession, 24.8; robber swam away to escape sentence, 24.14; rock at crossroads caused men to stumble, 24.17; Roman lady could not match God's matchmaking, 2.4; Roman lady had two family representatives in household, 14.3; sick man attended by physician, 14.5; strong man exercised with block of stone, 25.1; tenant cultivated vineyard, S1.11; Tent of Meeting like cave at edge of sea, 1.2; two contestants appear before judge, 27.2; two men presented written petitions to king, 25.4; two merchants were open for business alternately, 28.e; woman brought charges against son, 9.5; woman observed by three representatives of family, 15.6. *See also* Way of the World

Paradoxes: man with single spot of leprosy unclean, but with spot spread over entire body clean, 4.1; midwife touching dead embryo in womb unclean, but mother clean until embryo leaves her body, 4.1; caring for Red Heifer makes one's garments unclean, but Red Heifer itself makes the unclean clean, 4.1

Passover: no command to rejoice on, because of Egyptians' death, S2.8; no command to rejoice on, because harvest uncertain, S2.8; entire *Hallel* read only on first day of, S2.8; God judges harvest cases during, 7.2; lambs of, 5.17

Patience of God: criticised by Moses at first, 25.1; meaning of, 24.11

Patriarchs: distribution of tithes by, 10.6; lamented at banishment of Israel,

S5.2; faithfulness of, 10.2; gentleness of, 14.1; merit of, 3.c, 17.5; symbolized in lulab, 27.9; were wanderers, 13.1
Pavilion of Solomon, signifies Tabernacle, 1.2
Peace, bestowed on world when Tabernacle was set up, 1.5
Penitence. *See* Repentance
Penitence, Ten Days of. *See* Ten Days of Penitence
Pentecost: God judges cases of fruits of trees on, S7.2; only one command to rejoice on, because judgment on fruits of trees is still pending, S2.8
Persecutor mighty, will bring about exile, 25.1
Pests, are at peace with righteous, 11.1
Pharaoh: asked by Egyptian first-born to let Hebrews go, 7.6/9; smitten to make him let Israel go, 11.4; criticised Esau's folly, 9.11; wickedness of, overcome by God, 11.1; afflicted by God as he would have afflicted Israel, 11.3; conquered by prayer of Moses and Aaron, 8.2; received measure for measure for what he intended for Israel, 11.4; found no iniquity in God, 14.5; punishment by, not as severe as punishment by God, 15.2. *See also* Egypt, Egyptians
Pharaoh-necoh (Pharaoh-the-lame), mutilated by lion in mechanism of Solomon's throne, 26.1; outwitted by Solomon, 4.3
Philistines: why Ark was in seven months' captivity among, 11.9; responsibility of, for destroying seven shrines, 11.9
Phinehas, one of four reputed to have come from blemished stock, 13.12
Pillar of cloud, was means by which God conversed with Moses, Aaron, Samuel, 4.5
Pillars of marble, protected with wrappings in Rome, 9.1
Plene, exposition of, 25.1 n. 5
Pomegranate, Israel likened to, when they left Egypt, 11.6
Pool of hope, of Israel, in that God is always nearby, 24.2
Poor and rich, created to sustain each other, 28.3
Population decline, follows unnecessary census, 2.9
Positive commandments, correspond to two hundred and forty-eight parts of human body, 12.1. *See also* Commandments
Potiphar's wife, and Joseph, S3.2
Poverty: follows delay in recitation of *Tĕfillah*, 27.3; imposed by God upon Israel to induce repentance, 14.3
Practice of Torah, more important than knowledge thereof, S1.2
Prayer: can avert evil decree, 28.3; precedes (follows) blessing, S1.7; is means of expiation, instead of offerings, 24.19; gates of, open at times, closed at times, open always, 24.2; granted, as reward for tithing, 10.10; of High Priest, on Day of Atonement, 26.4; places where one may pray, 24.4; power of, 8.2; of righteous, power of, 24.18; sole possession of persecuted generations, 27.3
Precentor, power of intercessory prayer of, 24.18

Precepts: are God's means of "buying" Israel, by giving them sustenance wherewith they may resist straying, 5.10; obedience to, only small return for that which God gives man, 9.2; set down by Moses in groups of sixty (seventy), 5.10

Presence (reverent metonymy for God): symbolized by eagle, 26.4; bestows five kinds of joy, 27.2; root of, originally fixed in earth, 1.1; lingered for three and a half years on Mount of Olives before soaring up, 13.11; journeyed up and away in ten stages, 13.11; removed from earth to seventh heaven because of sins of seven successive generations, 1.1; returned from seventh heaven to earth because of merit of righteous in seven successive generations, 1.1; filled all of Tabernacle, 1.2. *See also* God

Priests: defiled by contact with dead, purified by ash of Red Heifer, 4.4; spread fingers when blessing, 5.8; were Sages, 12.5

Princes: of nations, appeared to Jacob as angels, 23.2; of Egypt, smitten in daytime, 7.5; in wilderness, fame of, 5.9; when in Egypt had endured beating to protect Israelites, 1.7; offered six wagons of intricate workmanship, 1.8

Procreation, obligation, of man, woman, or of both, to fulfill commandment of, 22.2

Profit, in study of Torah, 8.1

Prohibition, of seething kid in its mother's milk, 10.9

Prophets: reason for their use of anthropomorphism, 4.4; accused by Israel of contradicting their own words, 16.8; all begin with words of reproof but conclude with words of comfort, 13.14; God confirms word of, 7.3; maintained in hiding by money for which Obadiah's wife pledged children, 2.4; likened to women, 12.1; words of, endure, 13.3

Prophets, false, claimed Joshua son of Jehozadak was a fellow lecher, 24.15

Proselytes: none from Amalek would be received by God, 3.16; from Egypt, made calf, 9.8; Torah given under zodiacal sign of Twins, to hint readiness to accept, 12.20

Prosperity, is reward for tithing, 10.10

Proverbs and sayings: Many a young ass has died, and had its skin turned into saddlecloths for its dam's back, 26.9; Flour (*ḳimḥaya*) is flour, but Ḳimḥith is the very flower of flours, 26.10 n. 54; It is pointless to jab a fool—like a corpse he does not feel the knife, 24.18; Though you pound a fool in an artisan's mortar, you cannot make anything worthwhile out of him, 2.5; One who sets apart the good from the bad is more likely to seek more of the good than one who sets apart the bad from the good, 5.5; In Israel no destroyer of grape vines is also the son of a destroyer of grape vines, 25.3; A harlot who sells herself for apples tries to better her name by giving them to the sick, 10.1; Where there is judgment, there is a Judge, 24.11, 27.3; Make an opening for Me in you, as narrow as the eye of a needle, and I shall make it so wide that camps full of soldiers and siege engines could

enter it, 5.6; Poverty is as becoming to the daughter of Jacob as a red ribbon on the neck of a white horse, 14.3; A robber will be crucified in the place he despoiled, S2.2; Dost Thou think to take hold of the rope at both ends?, 16.4, 19.3; Seeing is the custom of his household, 5.3; One twin feels the headache of his brother, 5.6; "What they do, I do likewise" (Greek; God speaking to man), 17.4; He who rears a wicked son or a wicked disciple will have his eyes grow dim, 3.1; If you have acquired wisdom, what do you lack? If you lack wisdom, what have you acquired?, 4.3; A man who lacks wisdom is like a city without a wall, 4.3
Providence: of God, 8.1; led Israel through wilderness, 11.8; mysterious ways of God's, 17.6; questioned by generation of flood, 26.2
Psalms, eleven composed by Moses, for eleven Tribes, S1.8
Psaltery, put at David's head, for midnight playing, 7.4. *See also* Harp
Punishment: of Israel, through having to observe two days of festivals, 14.4; through having to set aside two offerings of dough, 14.4; by God, calculated to minimize pain and severity, 24.17; of wicked in world-to-come, is endless, 9.1; in Gehenna, twelve months, 10.4
Pursued, sought by God, 9.4
Pupils, may render no decisions within twelve miles of master, 26.6/7

Rab, Version of Shofar Service of, 23.1, S7.2
Rachel: first among wives, 20.2; one of seven barren women, 20.1
Rahab, Jeremiah descendant of, 13.4
Rain(s): brought down by generous bestowal of tithes, 1.4; withheld by miserly bestowal, 1.4; did not come from God, according to generation of flood, S4.1; could cause dwellings in Sharon to collapse, 26.4; Sukkot right time to ask for, 28.f, 28.8; troublesomeness of, 17.8
Ram, as offering, invokes merit of Isaac, 9.9
Ransom of soul, Moses startled by commandment of, 6.3
Reader for congregation: directions for, when preceding reader errs in *Tĕfillah*, S1.1; practices of, 24.5
Reading from Torah, must be preceded by blessing, S1.2
Rebekah: had no public funeral because of Esau, 3.1; one of seven barren women, 20.1
Red Heifer: rite of, decreed by God, 4.1, 4.7; reasons for precept of, known to Moses, 4.7; God studied passage on, 4.7; Moses' instructions concerning, will continue through lineal descendants, 4.7; come seven times seven, 4.2; ash of, used by Moses, will endure to rebuilding of Temple, 4.7; use of ash of, is mysterious act of God which brings clean out of unclean, 4.1; ash of, purifies priests defiled by contact with dead, 4.4; why female, unlike other communal offerings, 4.8; High Priests built runway for, each at his own cost, 4.7; discussed by R. Johanan b. Zakkai with heathen, 4.7; Impulse to

evil tries to impugn rite of, 4.6; is symbolic atonement for golden calf, 4.8; allegorical treatment of passage on, 4.9
Red Sea: God answered Israel at Moses' bidding at, 5.9; Israel accompanied by graven image over, 10.8; waters of, shone through radiance of Moses and Aaron, 11.13; formed wall for Israel, 11.3
Redeemer, mighty, will bring about redemption, 25.1
Redemption: from Egypt, occurred despite what measure of justice required, 5.11; occurred for four reasons, 11.6; Daniel's vision of time of, 17.5; mountains are messengers of good tidings at, S5.2; promises of, in Torah, give strength to Israel, 19.4; will occur through pull of powerful redeemer, 25.1; God may contract limits of periods before, 5.7; will be re-experienced by Israel only in time-to-come, 5.16; in world-to-come, neither in haste nor in flight, 5.19. *See also* Time-to-come, World-to-come
Reḡa', measure of time, 7.5
Registers, three, with names of righteous, wicked, and those in between, set out between New Year's Day and Day of Atonement, 24.3
Rejoicing, designated by ten different terms, 20.4
Repentance: can avert evil decree, 28.3; effect of, on God, S7.2; effective even if fleeting as wink of eye, 24.12; lack of, changed God's right hand, 17.2; leads God to set aside oath and decree, 24.11; God widens opening small as needle's eye, into one wide enough for siege engines, 5.6, 24.12; God's call to, for prevention of death and preservation of life, 24.1; equals pilgrimage to Jerusalem, building of Temple and altars, and offering of sacrifices, 24.5; in privacy, may make up for blasphemy in marketplaces, 24.12; possible for Israel in spite of provocations, 24.16; poverty imposed by God upon Israel to insure, 14.3; man who resolves upon, will have God Himself as his witness, 24.15; likened to sea in which one may always bathe, 24.2; soars up to throne of glory, 24.11. *See also* Day of Atonement, New Year's Day, Ten Days of Penitence
Rephidim: not place-name, but designation of Israel's moral lapse, 3.a; actual name Massah-and-Meribah (Trying-and-Strife), 3.a; Israel at peace with one another at, 12.14; Israel's hands grew slothful in committing transgressions at, 12.15
Reptiles forbidden for food, identification of, baffled Moses, 5.15
Residence, change of, can avert evil decree, 28.3
Respect, shown by Jews for their elderly, children, and Sages, 11.9
Resurrection: Israelites who died in wilderness will go to Land of Israel at time of, 24.9; Ten Tribes will go to Land of Israel, 24.9
Reuben: responsible for affairs of Jacob's household, 24.9; brought near to God by Moses, S1.6; Moses interceded for, 2.7; repentance of, 24.9; reward of, for seeking Joseph's return to his father, 24.9; Hosea was descendant of, 24.9
Reward, of righteous in world-to-come, endless, 9.1

Rezin, appetite of, 6.2
Rich and poor, created to sustain each other, 28.3
Righteous: were created to atone for wicked, 28.3; countenance of, will be restored in afterlife, 8.1; share Israel's pain, 8.4; will feast on (head of) Leviathan, S2.4; have power to cause barren women to be remembered, 22.2; enhance God's strength, 25.1; strength of, enhanced by God, 24.6, 25.1; death of, atones for Israel's sins, 26.11; reward of, in world-to-come, endless, 9.1; fire of Gehenna has no dominion over, S3.2; God's dispensation of His judgment to, 9.1; in time-to-come God will make sukkah for, S2.1; each and every, has his own Garden of Eden, 9.1; world never without thirty, 11.15; forty-five, are ever present part of Israel, 5.10; seven companies of, will be received by Presence, 27.2; God grieves at death of son of, 26.9
Ritual baths of purification, instituted by Hezekiah, require 40 *sĕ'ah* of water, 6.2
Ritual slaughtering, discussed by Solomon, 4.3
Rod of Moses, God's seventy names emblazoned upon, 3.c
Roman lady, had discussions with R. Jose b. Ḥalafta: on Ezekiel's sufferings, 8.4; on God's making of ladders, 2.4; on God's matchmaking, 2.4
Rome: pre-eminent among all peoples of Edom, 7.11; rapacious levies of, 2.2; never accepted yoke of God, 4.9; R. Joshua b. Levi saw marble pillars protected in, 9.1; dark chaos and emptiness will be summoned against, 7.12; will be punished with same means as used against Egypt, 7.11. *See also* Amalek, Edom, Esau
Root, Divine. *See* Presence
Rosh ha-Shanah. *See* New Year's Day
Ruth: Boaz hinted at Solomon's descent from, 16.1; conduct of, 16.1; required little food, 6.2; counted among Matriarchs, 16.1

Sabbath: circumcision may be performed on, for Jew, not Gentile, 4.3; expenditures for, not allotted on New Year's Day, 27.1; merit of, 10.2
Sacrifices, God does not consider magnitude of offering of, 6.1. *See also* Burnt offerings, Lambs, Offerings
Sadducean, High Priest Johanan became, through Impulse to evil, 11.1
Sages, nearly suppressed Book of Ecclesiastes for its seeming heresy, 8.1, 24.14
Salt: not given to strangers by Sodomites, S4.1; Esau asked Isaac if tithing required for, S1.11; second-tithe money may not purchase, S4.1
Samuel: conversed with God in pillar of cloud, 4.5; equal to Moses and Aaron, in that God spoke to him in pillar of cloud, 4.5; Book of Torah inscribed to, 4.5; in generation of, Amalek will be symbolically crushed, 3.16; treatment of Agag by, was symbolic requital for Amalek, 3.6
Sanctuary, Moses startled by commandment to make, 6.3. *See also* Tabernacle

Sanhedrin: God sanctions New Year's Day designated by, 23.4; symbolized in lulab, 27.9
Sapphire, hardness of, 18.4
Sarah: when delivered of Isaac, barren women gave birth, handicapped were healed, sun's light was intensified, 22.1; one of seven barren women, 20.1; chastity of, is example to all Israelite women, 11.6; suckled children of nations, 22.1; died upon hearing of the binding of Isaac, 26.3
Sarmatia, 5.7
Satan, father of Inclination to evil, and allies, fell into Gehenna, S3.2
Saul: began rule immediately after anointment, 5.3; spent own money freely to save Israel's, 5.3; why Philistines slew him and his three sons, 11.9; humble, 5.3; deemed servant's honor equal to his own, 5.3; observed Levitical rules of purity, 5.3; scholar in Torah, 5.3
Scales of justice, when balanced, will tip in sinner's favor, as God lifts out iniquities, 25.2
Scapegoat, Impulse to evil tries to discredit precept concerning, 4.6
Scoffing, requital for, 13.2
Scripture: God's face severe at revelation of, 12.25; Israel called God's bride in ten places in, 22.5; thirteen qualities of mercy attributed to God in, 6.1; passages in, to be studied in context, 23.5; does not call attention to lack but implies its converse, 20.3; in singling out shortcoming does not intend to shame, 18.3; speaks in roundabout way to avoid unseemly speech, 4.2. *See also* Bible, Torah
Scrolls of Law, thirteen written by Moses, S1.8
Sĕ'ah, of water, forty required for ritual bath of purification instituted by Hezekiah, 6.2
Seat of Moses, resembled royal throne, 1.7
Sĕḇi'i (seventh month), meanings of, 23.9
Second tithe money, may not purchase water or salt, S4:1
Sĕmini 'Ăṣereṯ. *See* Eighth-Day Festival
Sennacherib: conquered by prayer of Hezekiah, 8.2; conquered by prayer of Isaiah, 8.2; punishment by God more severe than punishment by hand of, 15.2
Separation of Jews from heathen, confers holiness, 5.5
Serah, daughter of Asher: was maidservant in Egypt, 7.6/9; identified herself as seventieth of house of Jacob in Egypt, 11.13; made Joseph's burial place known to Moses, 11.12; presence of, at Red Sea, 11.13; identified as wise woman of Abel, 11.3
Seraphim: covered soles of feet, 9.3; paralleled by standing shittim cedars in Tabernacle, 1.3
Serpent, claims to be less virulent than slander, 4.2
Servitude, bitter, in Egypt, lasted eighty-six years, 5.9
Settlements, guarded by teachers of Scripture and Mishnah, 15.5

Seven, number, meanings of, 28.d; 28.4
Seven companies of righteous, 27.2
Seven garments of God, S6.5
Seven trees, foliage of, covered Sodom's sukkah, S2.3
Seventh day, most loved, 23.10
Seventh month, most loved, 23.10
Seventh year, most loved, 23.10
Sevenths most loved: sky, Land of Israel, Enoch, Moses, David, Asa, seventh year, seventh day, seventh month, 23.10
Seventy, number of house of Jacob who entered Egypt, 11.13
Seventy bullocks, offered in behalf of nations during Sukkot, 28.9
Seventy-two, letters in Name of God, 5.11
Sexual intercourse, Jews refrain from, during menstruation, 28.d, 28.4
Sharon, dwellings in, could collapse during rain, 26.4
Shealtiel, meaning of, 24.11
Shekel, meanings of, 10.1
Shelomith, guilty of wantonness, 11.6
Shĕma', informality in reading of, 9.5
Shittim, because of deed at, Tribe of Simeon not blessed by Moses, S1.8
Shittim cedars, standing in Tabernacle, parallel seraphim standing above, 1.3
Shofar: blown in Temple when New Year's Day fell on Sabbath, but not in provinces, 23.12; calls for renewal, and for life acceptable to God, 23.8; makes measure of justice move back, brings measure of mercy near, 23.8; horn of cow not proper for, 9.3; Rab's Version of Service of, 23.1, S7.2
Shrines, reason for destruction of seven, 11.9
Shuthelah, sons of, slain in battle with Egyptians, 11.10
Šibbuṭa (carp), did not return from exile, 13.10
Sick person, six signs of returning health in, 19.5
Sifra: recited by Eleazar bar R. Simeon b. Yoḥai after thirteen years' instruction from Elijah, 11.22; study of, consumes strength, 11.22
Sihon, conquered by prayer of Moses and Aaron, 8.2
Simeon, Tribe of: not blessed by Moses because of deed at Shittim, S1.8; no king from, S1.8
Simeon b. Jose, R.: answered questions of son-in-law Eleazar b. Simeon, about Israel's clothing in wilderness, 11.21; fed son-in-law Eleazar b. Simeon whole ox, trough of bread, cask of wine, 11.20. *See also* Stories
Simeon b. Yoḥai, R.: bathed and was healed in springs of Tiberias, 11.16; likened to rainbow, 11.15; praise of, 11.15; sold produce at low prices, 11.16. *See also* Stories
Simeon the Just: built separate runways for each Red Heifer, 4.7; visage of, seen by Alexander of Macedon before victories, 4.9
Sin(s): cleansed or put out of sight, controversy about, 6.3; closely reckoned by God, 24.14; of eating untithed produce, 10.9; of Israel, atoned for by

death of Miriam, 26.11; of Israel, atoned for by death of righteous, 26.11; no one who lodged full day in Jerusalem, remained possessed of, 6.3; masked by lovingkindness performed by nations, 2.5; subject man to fear and awe, 5.3

Sinai, Mount: was enlarged to accommodate Israel at giving of Torah, 12.22; mystical teaching imparted at, 12.22; revelation at, was day of God's betrothal of Israel, 1.7; together with Mts. Tabor, Hermon, and Carmel, will support Jerusalem, S5.4; together with Mts. Tabor, Carmel, and Moriah, will support Temple in time-to-come, 21.4. *See also* God, Israel

Sinner: avenues to forgiveness for, 24.7; kinds of punishment for, 24.7; balanced scales of justice tipped in favor of, when God lifts iniquities out of pans, 25.2

Sisera, conquered by prayer of Barak, 8.2

Sister, term for Israel in their relationship with God, 5.6

Sivan, month, Torah given on sixth of, 12.4

Six commandments, given to Adam, 12.1

Six wagons, offered by princes, significance of number of, 1.7

Sky, in order of realms, seventh and most loved, 23.10

Slander: men of David's generation guilty of, 4.2; men of Ahab's generation not guilty of, 4.2; slays three: person speaking, person spoken to, person spoken of, 4.2; worse than serpent's sting, 4.2

Slingstones, became as stubble against Leviathan, S2.4

Smoke of altar, direction of rising of, told High Priest of year's crops, 26.4

Snake, tame, loyalty of, to master, 11.1

Snakes, two fiery, walked before people of Meron, 11.23

Sodom and Gemorrah: flood of fire in, 16.4; measure of justice grieved and laughed derisively at selfishness of, 26.2

Sodomites: gave no salt to strangers, S4.1; sins of, caused Presence to remove to sixth heaven, 1.1

Solomon: descent of, from Ruth, hinted at by Boaz, 16.1; in days of, silver ingots were eight by ten cubits, 26.2; scales were made of gold, 26.2; mode of dining of, 6.1; outwitted Pharaoh-the-lame, 4.3; throne of, had lion in its mechanism which mutilated Pharaoh-necoh, 26.1; angel seated himself on throne of, 26.2; drawn to three things which measure of justice deems punishable, and sinned through them, 26.2; before sinning, ruled over demons, 5.3; deemed crazy, 26.2; forfeited kingship, 26.2; explained the meaning of ritual cleansing of lepers, 4.3; discussed ritual slaughter, 4.3;

wisdom of: wiser than Adam, 4.3; wiser than Abraham, Moses, Joseph, and generation of wilderness, 4.3; equaled all of Israel's, 4.3; held back his turbulent desires, 4.3; every verse of, had two or more implicit parables, 4.3; every verse of, illustrated by three thousand parables, 4.3; every parable of, had one thousand and five applications, 4.3; could not fathom passage of Red Heifer, 4.3

Son of David. *See* Messiah
Son of righteous man, God grieves at death of, 26.9
Songs of deliverance, from of old, haunted Israel, 17.1
Soul, knows that it will be punished with brimstone, 12.9
Spices, sprinkled on coals brought in after banquet, 6.1
Springs of Tiberias, R. Simeon b. Yoḥai bathed and was healed in, 11.16
Stew, cooked up by Egyptians, 11.5
Stibium, black: used as cement for walls of Jerusalem, 18.4; cosmetic, 18.4; qualities of, 18.4
Stones: of hollowed-out pearl will make up Temple gate, 18.5; of bright red *kad̠kud̠aya* shown to R. Joshua b. Levi by Elijah, 18.5
Stories: brigand's wife who falsely accused husband, was later executed on false charge, 11.1; dogs and snakes who are friends and foes of men, 11.1; heathen prepared banquet, lacking only soft-shelled nuts, 6.2; inspector of measures, 10.2; notable of Kebul spared guests at son's wedding the news of his death, 26.2; man sold cloak, 10.7; man sold maidservant, 10.7; man whose cloak was stolen, 15.9; man went to Rome to sell sapphire, 18.4; man scrupulous in paying tithes, had niggardly son, 10.1; man who always paid tithes, 10.3; man who never paid tithes, 10.3; pious man walked on beach in Haifa, 18.5; Roman lady discussed with R. Jose b. Ḥalafta: Ezekiel's sufferings, 8.4; God's making of ladders for different persons to ascend and descend, 2.4; and God's matchmaking, 2.4; woman whose kettle was stolen, 15.9; woman who presented silver lamp to judge, 15.9;
R. 'Aḳib̠a resisted wiles of two women, S3.2; pupil of R. Eliezer rendered decision, 26.6/7; maidservant of Rabban Gamaliel examined herself religiously, 12.15; steward of Rabban Gamaliel lost all strength through study of Sifra, 11:22; Hananiah, Mishael, Azariah, and nations of world, 10.8; R. Johanan sold all he had in order to study Torah, 27.1; R. Johanan and R. Simeon consulted R. Kahana on blowing shofar on Sabbath, 23.12; Levi b. Sisi turned away marauders by swearing upon Scroll of Law, 24.18; Mordecai saw Haman approach leading horse, 8.4; Moses made Joseph's coffin float up from bottom of Nile, 11.12; Simeon son of Ḳimḥith made unclean by royal Arabian spittle, 26.10;
R. Simeon b. Yoḥai: made Naḳai, the mocking schoolmaster, into heap of bones, 11.16; made serpent bite man who was greedy for aftergrowths, 11.17; could fill valley with golden denar, 11.15; told Elijah that worth of R. Joshua b. Levi was put in question by rainbow, 11.15; promised to bring generations of man close to God, from his time to time of Messiah, 11.15; thought himself sole righteous man in his generation, 11:15;
R. Simeon b. Yoḥai and son R. Eleazar: sight of captive bird gave them courage to emerge from hiding, 11.16; in gratitude, sold goods at low prices, 11.16; purified streets of Tiberias, 11.16; turned mocking Cuthean into corpse, 11.16;

Eleazar bar R. Simeon b. Yoḥai: consumed whole ox, trough of bread, cask of wine at house of father-in-law, 11.20; his prodigious appetite matched by prodigious strength, 11.18; discussed with father-in-law long-wearing ever-fresh garments of Israel in wilderness, 11.21; called "vinegar, son of wine" by R. Joshua b. Ḳorḥa for serving as executioner, 11.19; persuaded by Elijah to leave manual labor for pursuit of learning, 11.22; after thirteen years' instruction by Elijah, could recite Sifra, 11.22; once ignored blasphemy, hence was punished in grave, 11.23; corpse of, was removed from Giscala to beside father's grave, 11.23; superiority of, in holiness to R. Judah, demonstrated by control over afflictions, 11.24; widow of, spurned R. Judah for his inferior holiness, 11.24;

R. Tanḥum bar Jeremiah rendered no decisions in Hefer while his master R. Mani was only three miles away, 26.6/7; mother of R. Tanḥum b. Ḥiyya bought as much for poor as for son, 28.3; R. Zadok resisted temptation by maidservant, S3.2

Stubble, become as slingstones against Leviathan, S2.4

Students, brought back to God by inner force of Torah, 15.5

Study: children's, starts with Leviticus, 6.3; of laws of sacrifice, is surrogate for act, 6.3; of Torah, God not lenient about neglect of, 15.5; profit in, 8.1; not for its own sake, leads to study for its own sake, 15.5

Sukkah: regulations for, on seventh day of feast, 28.7; regulations concerning eating in, on Eighth-Day Festival, 28.a; invalidation of, 28.a; dwelling in, deemed equivalent to banishment which may have been decreed on Day of Atonement, S2.7; fulfilling command of, will shelter from Day of Judgment, S2.1; shelters from malevolent things, S2.3; serves as reminder of miracles in wilderness, S2.6; dwelling in, ensures portion in sukkah made from skin of Leviathan, S2.4; ensures portion in sukkah luxurious as Sodom's, S2.3; Sodom's, covered with foliage of seven trees, S2.3; will be made by God for righteous in time-to-come, S2.1. *See also* Cloud-sukkahs

Sukkot: three commands to rejoice on, because men have been pardoned, field crops harvested, fruits gathered, S2.8; seven requirements for, 27.2; seventy bullocks offered during, in behalf of nations, 28.g, 28.9; on each day of, men holding lulabs circled altar, 27.5; marks new reckoning of sins, 27.7; God judges cases concerning water at time of, S7.2; is right time to ask for rain, 28.f, 28.8; pilgrimage during, and observance of, ensures rebuilding of Temple, 28.g, 28.9

Sun: only orb created to give light, 5.1; dim compared to Leviathan's fins, S2.4; round of Adam's heel outshine globe of, 4.4, 12.1; renewal of cycle of, 21.1; why nations of earth reckon year by, 5.1, 5.14; set in firmament above heaven, to reduce its intensity, S2.1; in time-to-come, God will remove tent from, S2.1

Synagogue(s): of people who had come from Babylon to Palestine, 25.1; while

Israel sit in, God's glory stands, 5.8; God is pleased to be with Jews who do no more than collect in, 28.8

Tabernacle: wagons for conveying of, 1.7, 1.8; maintained by single head tax, 2.2; vessels of, anointed for world as we know it and for world-to-come, 1.6; dimensions of curtains of, will remain unchanged, 1.6; four colors used for, 1.3; colors of, like pattern God showed to Moses, 1.3; standing shittim cedars in, parallel seraphim standing above, 1.3; filled by Presence, 1.2; visible sign of God's return to earth, 1.2; God's means of private communication with Israel, 1.2; Israel's nuptial chamber, 1.3;
set up and taken down by Moses each day of seven (eight) days of investiture, 1.5; when set up, demons came to end, 1.5; earth became stable, 1.4, 1.5; love, affection, friendship, and peace bestowed on world, 1.5; wrangling ceased, 1.5. *See also* Candlestick for Tabernacle, Sanctuary, Tent of Meeting

Tabor, Mount: together with Mts. Sinai, Carmel, and Hermon, will support Jerusalem, S5.4; together with Mts. Sinai, Carmel, and Moriah, will be foundation of Temple in time-to-come, 21.4

Talmud: God's face friendly at revelation of, 12.25; reason for neglect of, 12.3

Tanḥum b. Ḥiyya, R., charity of mother of, 28.3

Tanḥum b. Jeremiah, R., when in Hefer, rendered no decisions while his master R. Mani was in Sepphoris, three miles away, 26.6/7

Teachers of Scripture and Mishnah: when unpaid, villages in Land of Israel uprooted, 15.4; guard settlements, 15.5; will abide at God's right hand, 27.2

Ṭeḇa', equals half-shekel, 2.10

Tĕfillah: directions for next reader, if congregation reader errs in, S1.1; delay in recitation of, brings poverty, 27.3

Tĕḳi'ah: at tone of, God takes seat of mercy, 23.3; turns measure of justice into measure of mercy, 23.11; sustained note proclaiming redemption, 23.3

Temple: building, destruction, and rebuilding of, envisioned at beginning of Genesis, 21.5; day of building of, signifies God's nuptials with Israel, 1.3; Ammonites and Moabites said cherubim had been objects of worship in, 19.1; windows of, opaque, 21.5; light went forth from, 21.5; offerings of lambs in, serve as symbolic taking of God, 5.17; called "Lion of God," 13.14; standing, brought wicked men to fore, 20.5; in ruins, brought righteous men to fore, 20.5; requital of Edom will signal God's return to, S5.3; will be built on Mts. Moriah, Sinai, Tabor, and Carmel brought together, 21.4; east gate of rebuilt, will be hollowed out by angels, 18.5; gate of, will be made of hollowed out pearl, 18.5

Temple, Second, western wall of, will never be destroyed, 5.8

Temple offerings, one of four things God showed Abraham, 5.2

Ten Commandments: laws ahead of, and laws after, 12.8; Moses told by God when to take down, 10.9; all violated by Israel in Jeremiah's day, 13.8
Ten Days of Penitence, for those neither completely wicked nor completely righteous, 24.3. *See also* Day of Atonement, New Year's Day, Repentance
Ten Plagues: details of, 7.6/9; execution of, emulated military tactics, 7.11
Tent of Meeting: like crown, topped with blue, purple and scarlet, 1.3; God's entrance into, on day of His nuptials with Israel, 1.3. *See also* Sanctuary, Tabernacle
Tĕru'ah, expresses fear and anguish that precede judgment, 23.3
Thank offering, sole offering in time-to-come, 9.12
Theatres and circuses, avoided by Jews, 15.2; laughter and grief mingled therein, 26.2
Thirteen, age of, Inclination to good begins to guide individual at, S3.2
Thirty righteous men, world never without, 11.15
"This," term of contempt, transmuted and purified by God, 2.4
Three: required to go before Holy Ark, 3.d; prevalence of number, 12.13
Throne: of king, what herald said as king ascended each of six steps of, 1.7; resembled seat of Moses, 1.7; of Solomon, angel sat on, 26.2; had lion in its mechanism which mutilated Pharaoh-necoh, 26.1
Throne of God: incomplete while Amalek's seed endures, 3.16; term for Jerusalem, 3.15
Tiberias, fish from, S2.4
Time: reckoning of, turned over by God to Israel, 5.2, 5.13; measures of: *'eṯ*, *regă'*, *zĕman*, 7.5; physical, spiritual, 23.1; right, for different events, 12.7
Time-to-come: description of, S5.1; identity of harbingers of good tidings in, S5.4; Inclination to evil will be removed from hearts of men in, 24.17; God will make sukkah for righteous in, S2.1; all offerings except thank offering, will cease in, 9.12; Temple will be built in, on Mts. Moriah, Sinai, Tabor, and Carmel brought together, 21.4; Mount Moriah will be sung to by other mountains in, 21.4; Land of Israel will bring forth her dead earlier in, 22.5a; Jerusalem will be extended in, 20.7; nations will battle against Jerusalem in, S2.2; whoever utters Jerusalem's name contemptuously in, will incur death penalty, 22.5a; spilling of Israel's blood will not go unpunished in, S2.2; God Himself will cleanse Israel from all sins in, 4.10; Israel will rejoice in Maker only in, 26.3; Israel will re-experience redemption only in, 5.16; God will renew six things in, 22.5a; will see God remove tent from over sun, S2.1; will see God rejoice in world, though He does not yet do so, 26.3. *See also* Redemption, World-to-come
Tishri, month: means "Thou art ready to remit sins," 23.6; filled with commandments, with all kinds of plenty, 23.9; on first day of, spiritual history of world began, 23.1; Adam received command, disobeyed, was judged, and was set free, 23.1; God's oath to Abraham in, 23.9; judgment pronounced on first day of, 23.1

Tithes: distribution of, by Patriarchs, 10.6; given by Abraham, Isaac, Jacob, S4.3; given by Isaac, 10.6; given by Jacob, 10.6; difficult to give because of nations' exactions, S4.2; merit of, 10.2; ungenerous, withhold dew and rain from world, 1.4; generous, bestow dew and rain on world, 1.4

Tithing: connection of, with prohibition of seething kid in its mother's milk, 10.9; of present year's produce, 10.10; help to the needy, 10.4; performed by merchants and seafarers for men who labor in Torah, 10.10; Job's words to God about, 10.7; debate about, between Cuthean and R. Meir, 10.6; faithfulness in, 10.2; consequence of faithfulness in, 10.1; prayer for rain granted as consequence of, 10.10; prosperity reward for, 10.10; consequence of niggardliness in, 10.1; punishment of those deceitful in, 10.5; evasion of: sinful, 10.9; punished by wicked Esau, 10.10; punished by God, 10.9; brings death of Israel's sons, 10.10

Titus, slashed Temple veils, yet went forth in peace, 26.5

Torah: one of four things God showed Abraham, 5.2; offered to all peoples by God, 5.2, S2.1; given by God as eagerly as mother gives breast to child, 12.2; giving of, inaugurated with *'alef*, 12.24; given to Israel after they became one brotherhood, 12.14; giving of, in relation to prohibition of seething kid in its mother's milk, 10.9; given on sixth of Sivan, 12.4; given under zodiacal sign of Twins to hint readiness to accept proselytes, 12.19; given by written word and by word of mouth, 12.5; reason for delay in giving of, 12.3; Sinai was enlarged to accommodate Israel at giving of, 12.22; but for Israel's acceptance of, angels would have had to destroy Israel, 12.22; Israel became sound in body at acceptance of, 12.19; precepts of, set down by Moses in groups of sixty (seventy), 5.10; Written and Oral, 15.5; Written, called "dew," 5.6; agricultural advice in, 10.7; forty-nine arguments in interpreting, 4.2; likened to wine, honey, and peppers, 12.13; engagement in one of three particularities of Israel which lead God to make the people His very own, 19.6; lack of, causes Israel's bondage, 27.1; promises of redemption in, give strength to Israel, 19.4; day of gathering of exiles will be as great as day Israel received, S5.1;

Practice, study, and teaching of: not to be like antiquated decree, 12.12; should be like freshly issued decree which all rush to read, 12.5; man must make himself ownerless like wilderness to engage in, 12.20; blessing must precede reading from, S1.2; bread and water of, counter Impulse to evil, 11.1; counsel always found in, 12.12; defined as "good," 10.2; Inclination to evil overcome by, S3.2; inner force of, brings its students back to God, 15.5; profit at laboring at, 8.1; God not lenient about neglect of, 15.5; practice of, more important than knowledge of, S1.2; not for its own sake, leads to study for its own sake, 15.5; when studying, man should consider self as within fire, S1.17; unmixed joy, 26.2; teaching of, cannot receive adequate compensation, 27.1; men who labor in, to be paid from tithes, 10.10; Oenomaus of Gadarah, philosopher, advised that Israel is vulnerable

when children do not engage in, 15.5; R. Jose and R. Ammi sent to villages in Land of Israel to check, 15.5; words of, are not to seem antiquated, 12.21; retaliate against him who does not give them labor required for understanding, 12.5; words of, stand up for him who valorously gives them labor required for understanding, 12.5. *See also* Bible, Scripture
Torture, by Hadrian of those who hallowed Name, 11.14
Tosefta, ancient, heard by R. Abbahu in Caesarea, 4.4
Tree: from which Adam ate, 20.6; sickly, must have roots covered with earth to live, 24.8
Tribe Fathers, bones of, to be carried by each Tribe from Egypt, 11.25
Tribes: Jacob bestowed six blessings upon, S1.11; counted by Moses according to numerical values of first letters of names, 2.8; Moses composed eleven Psalms for eleven, S1.8; one of the twelves that belong to order of the universe, 16.5
Trying-and-strife (Massah-and-Meribah), actually name of Rephidim, 3.a

Uncovered head, Roman token of respect, 9.5
Undefiled, term for Israel in their relationship with God, 5.6
Unmarried man, who supports schools, will some day be rewarded by having children of his own, 9.2
Unseemly speech, avoided in Scripture by way of circumlocution, 4.2
Uriah: one of four reputed to have come from blemished stock, 13.12; slain in Jerusalem, 15.7

Vengeance of God, meaning of, 25.1
Vespasian, destroyed 480 synagogues in Jerusalem, 15.7
Villages in Land of Israel, R. Jose and R. Ammi sent to check teaching of Torah in, 15.5
Virgins, designated by "a garden barred" (Song 4:12), 11.5
Voice, Divine: 9.2, 11.23, 15.5, 17.5, 18.5

Wagons, six, offered by princes, significance of number of, 1.7; intricate workmanship of, 1.8
War against Israel, deemed war against God, S2.2
Water: Esau asked Isaac if tithing required for, S1.11; second-tithe money may not purchase, S4.1
Waving, of *'omer*, described, 8.3
"Way of the earth," (Exod. 13:17), eight examples of, signifying "in the usual manner," 11.8
Way of the world: when man buys meat, he goes to much trouble to prepare

it, 8.1; man may eat spoiled food for a time, but will later draw away with loathing, 13.2; man heaps up iniquities in world, 24.13; man's heart keeps bitter memory of wrong done to him, 3.e; promises of king of flesh-and-blood are only as good as his life is long, 4.2; man who suffers public abuse wants public apology, 24.12; man has more beautiful salver made for himself than for his steward, 26.3; when man washes cloak, he goes to much trouble to dry it, 8.1; in grand house, window openings are narrow on outside, broad on inside, 21.5

Weapons, five kinds of, provided for Israel leaving Egypt, 11.11

Weights and measures, dishonesty in, brings on Amalek, 3.4

Western wall of Temple, will never be destroyed, 5.8

White, symbol of God's forgiveness, 22.5

Wicked: kinds of, 28.2; deeds of, produce no fruit, 9.1; grave cannot abide, 9.1; used as cover for abyss, 9.1; God's dispensation of His judgment to, 9.1; punishment of, in Gehenna, twelve months, 10.4; in world-to-come, endless, 9.1

Widows, abuse of, common in Jerusalem, 15.9

Wife, man's desire for, implanted by God, 5.2

Wilderness: clothes worn by Israel while wandering in, 11.21; cloud-sukkahs in, S2.6; God's own providence led Israel through, 11.8; sukkah reminder of miracles in, S2.6

Wine: effect on R. Judah b. Il'a'i of four Passover cups of, 4.4; effect on R. Mana, 4.4

Wings of earth, morning star, sun, cherubim, creatures of chariot, 16.1

Woman suspected of infidelity, not to use cup of another woman likewise suspected, who drank and died, 9. 3

Women rulers of principality, gave Alexander of Macedon good counsel, 9.1

World: physical creation of, begun on twenty-fifth of Elul, 23.1; spiritual history of, began on first day of Tishri, 23.1; never without thirty righteous men, 11.15; God does not yet rejoice in, but will in time-to-come, 26.3

World-to-come: deliverance in, contrasted with hasty deliverance from Egypt, 5.19; God will teach Israel Torah in, 12.21; endless punishment of wicked in, 9.1; endless reward of righteous in, 9.1; wonders in, will compensate for afflictions in world as it is now, 24.2; death will be destroyed in, S2.8; life in, how obtained, 27.2. *See also* Redemption, Time-to-come

Wrangling, ceased after Tabernacle was set up, 1.5

Yoke of kingdoms: one of four things God showed Abraham, 5.2; chosen by Abraham for his children, under God's direction, 5.2

Yubal, river of limitless waters flowing from Eden, which Behemoth drinks, 6.1

Zadok, R., restraint of, when tempted by maidservant, S3.2
Zechariah: accused by Israel of contradicting his own words, 16.8; prophecy entrusted in Jeremiah's time to, 13.14
Zechariah [the son of Jehoiada]: seven transgressions were committed in Jerusalem at slaying of, 15.7; blood of, kept seething on Temple rock, 15.7
Zedekiah, blinding of, seemed to symbolize death of Israel, 4.10
Zedekiah, son of Maaseiah, false prophet: committed adultery with neighbor's wife, 24.15; roasted in frying pan, 24.15
Zĕman, measure of time, 7.5
Zephaniah, accused by Israel of contradicting his own words, 16.8
Zion: "sign" for three distinguishing precepts for Jews, 16.3; one of seven barren women, 20.1; endowed with radiance of God's glory, 21.2; in behalf of, God removes kingdoms from the world, 17.3; messengers, coming to, with good tidings, will be as beautiful as Commandments on tablets, S5.1; God and Israel will together give light to, 21.3
Zion, daughters of: hoped to be taken by Babylonian generals, 17.6; wanton behavior of, 17.6; seemed loathsome to Babylonian generals, 17.6
Ziz, a bird that darkens the sun with its wings, 6. 1
Zodiacal signs, 12.20, 13.15

PLAYS ON WORDS AND LETTERS

‘aḏ=“in eternity” (*‘aḏ*=“the Eternal”) 1.1 n9
‘aḏ=“unto” (*‘eḏ*=“witness”) 24.15 n46
’Aḏon=“lord” (*’Adn, ’Adm*=“man”) 4.3 n44
’af=“nose” (*’af*=“also”) 16.11
’afes=“cease” (Greek *apheis*=“let go”) 17.1
’aḥoṯ=“sister” (*’aḥuy*=“akin” or “stitched together”) 5.6 n32
‘ăḵarah=“barren” (*‘ăḵurah*=“uprooted”) 20.2
‘alil=“crucible” (*‘olal*=“young child”) 4.2 n12
‘ălilоṯ=“deeds” (*‘olělоṯ*=“gleanings”) 21.3 n8
Allon (Greek *allon*=“another occasion”) 3.1
’ămahoṯ=“maidservants” (*’immahoṯ*=“Matriarchs”) 16.1 n10
Amalek (*‘am*=“people”+*yeleḵ*=“locust”) 3.8
(*‘am*=“people”+*laḵ*=“lick”)
’ammi=“My people” (*‘immi*=“with Me”) 16.8 n37
Amos (*‘amus*=“tongue-heavy”) 16.4
‘anah=“spoke” (*‘anah*=“answered”) 5.9
‘ani=“afflicted” (*‘ani*=“poor”) 27.3 n14
‘arḇe=“willows” (*‘ărаḇоṯ*=“skies”) 27.9 n39
‘aru=“raze” (*‘aru*=“empty”) 3.7 n48
‘aru=“toss” (*‘ar‘er*=“razed”) 18.2
(*tě‘ar*=“emptied”) 20.2
‘Ăṣereṯ (*‘aṣar*=“draw near”) 28.8
Asir (*’asurim*=“in prison”) 24.11
’ăšišoṯ=“dainties” (*’iššoṯ*=“fires”; *mě’uššašoṯ*=“closely reasoned and precisely expressed”) 12.3
‘aśśer=“tithe” (*’aššer*=“prosper”) 10.10 n36
’aṭ (*l’ṭ, lě-’aṭ*=“go softly”) 6.2 n36
’aṯa’=“come” (Aramaic *’aṯa’*=“sign”) 12.22 n67
(*’oṯ*=“stood out”) S1.16 n52
‘awon=“iniquity” (*‘awon*=“affliction”) 3.1
(*‘ayin*=“balance”) 25.2 n8
’ayyekkah=“where art thou?” (*’ayka, ’ykh, ’eykah*=“how?”) 15.1 n3
ba=“in” (*ba’*=“is come”) 12.11 n38
12.18
bakkošaroṯ (*běḵi*=“weeping”+*široṯ*=“song”) 2.4
banoṯ=“daughters” (*bnh*=“build”) 12.1 n2
bdrk=“away” (*bd’rky*=“records or archives”) 3.10 n54
Beeri (*bě’erah*=“he of her well”) 24.9
běraḵah=“blessing” (*běreḵah*=“pool”) S1.6
bḵ=“in Thee” (*beṯ* 2+*kaf* 20=22 letters in Hebrew alphabet) 22.2
28.9

bmlḥmwt tnwfh="battles of wielding"
(*bmlḥmwt tnwfh*="bread of waving") 8.4 n32
dam="blood" (*ădamah*="ground") 26.4 n36
darḇan="goad" (*maḏir binah*="impresses obedience") 23.7
Darda'=(*dor*="generation"+*de'ah*="knowledge") 4.3
dĕḇarim="things" (*dabbarim*="men
whose words are eloquent") 24.18 n51
diḇaḇa="fly" (*dĕḇaḇa*="enemy") S3.2 n6
diḇre="words" (*deḇer*="pestilence")
(*dĕḇari*="My word")
(*dĕḇaray*="My words") 13.8
(*dabray*="as to leading") 13.9
dmḵ="thy blood" (*dmyḵ*="thy bloods") 3.16 n68
'dr="lack" (*'dr*="flock" or "band") 5.9 n82
drwlmsyy'="wrought destruction"
(Greek *dorilēpsia*="capture by spear"
or *dorialōsia*="capture by storm") 7.11 n44
dwdy="my beloved" (Greek *deui*="come hither"+
Theos="God") 5.8
'eḇen="gemstone" (*'eḇen*="weight") 3.4 n37
'el="out of" (*'al*="without") 8.2 n20
Eleazar (*'el 'ozer*="unto God who helps") 4.9
(*'el 'ozer*="God's adjutant") 4.10
Eliezer (*'alef* 1+*lameḏ* 30+*yoḏ* 10+*'ayin* 70+
zayin 7+*reš* 200=318 men) 8.2 n23
'ĕmune="faithful" (*minyan*="count"+
ne'ĕman="faithful") 11.13 n46
'ešma'="I understood" (*'ašmia'*="I make myself
understood in") 4.3
'eśśa'="lift up" (*'eššа'* or *'eššaḥ*="bent low") 11.14 n49
'fsy="ends of" (*'fsy*="those who have come to naught
in . . . " or "those who have been
gathered into [the earth]") 1.4 n37
ḡaḇ="eminence" (*gbh*="collect, impose, or visit punishment for sin") 3.2 n32
Gallim (*gallim*="waves"; *golim*="wanderers") 13.1 n2, 3
gĕmul="good deed" (*gamul*="child weaned from milk") 9.2 n20
g'l (*gw'l*="fullness of the Redeemer's power") 25.1 n5
gnni="my garden" (*ginuni*="my bride's bower") 1.1
goy="nation" (*goy*="heathen") 28.c n8
28.1 n21
haḏar="ethrog" (*had-dar*="dwells";
Greek *hydōr*="water") 27.8
haḏar="the tree 'haḏar' " (*haḏarta*="thou shalt honor") 27.9
Hadrak (*ḥad*="rough"+*raḵ*="soft") 20.7 n11
haḵi="is not" (*haḵi*="hawking") 3.11 n56

halloṯi="my weakness" (*ḥillah*="to entreat") 17.2 n10
(*ḥll*="to profane") 17.2 n12

ḥămuššim="armed" (*ḥamiššah*="five") 11.11 n32

ḥannoṯ="be gracious" (*ḥanah*="encamp") 17.1 n8

harim="mountains" (*horim*="Sanhedrin whose decisions instruct men as to what is just") 5.7 n38

harpu="let go" (*heref 'ayin*="wink of an eye") 24.12 n42

'hby="him that loves Me"
(*'alef*, [']*hby*=Abraham; *he'*, [*h*]*nh*=Isaac; *beṯ*, [*b*]*eṯ*=Jacob; *yoḏ*, *w*[*y*]*dy*=Moses) S1.20

ḥdš="month" (*ḥdš*="new") 5.11 n95

he'ĕḇalti="caused to mourn" (*heyḇalti*="caused to go down") 9.1 n3

hen="behold" (Greek *ena*="one") 9.6 n47, 24.6 n11

heres="destruction" (*heres*="sun"; *ḥeres*="sherd") 7.5 n20, 22

hḥzyr="bring back" (*hḥzyr*="restore to one's place") 1.1 n3, 4

Hilkiah (*ḥeleḵ*="portion"+*yah*="of the Lord") 13.12 n35

ḥmh="wall" (*ḥammah*="sun") 2.5

hn (*he'* 5+*nun* 50=55 "myriads of the completely righteous") S1.20

ḥnnk="bestowed upon them" (*hwnk*="substance given thee") 10.3 n10, 12

ḥoḏeš="month" (*ḥdš*="renewal") 12.19

holelim="arrogant" (*ḥolelim*="those whose joy has been mingled with grief") 26.3 n23
(*'olelim*="they who say 'alas, alack' ") n.24

ḥozĕrim="strain" (*ḥăruzim*="jewels") S5.1 n2

'ḥr="another" (*'ḥr*="delayed one") 7.2 n2

hšyḇ="brought back" (*mšyḇ*="brought back by being blown back") 24.11, 27.3

ḥtr="dig into" (Aramaic *'trth*="hole dug into the earth") 27.3

ḥtyrh="opening" (*wy'tr*, *wyḥtr*="entreated"; Aramaic *'tyrt'*="hole dug in the earth") 24.11 n31, 32

hywn (*wh*="wow!"+*wy*="woe!") 10.4 n18

'im="with" (*'am*="people") 26.3 n28

'immeḵa="thy mother" (*'ammeḵa*="thy member") 3.6 n46
(*'ummaṯeḵa*="thy people") 10.6

'iš="man" (*'iš*="spouse") S1.9

'iššah="woman" (*'iššeh*="fire") 17.7

Jeremiah (*yrmyh*=*yoḏ* 10+*rm*="journeyed up and away"+*yh*="the Presence"—in ten stages the Presence journeyed up and away) 13.11
(Greek *erēmos*="void, destitute") 13.8 n17
(Greek *erēmon*="destruction") 13.12

Jerusalem (*yr'*="fear"+*šlwm*="peace") 16.3 n19

'k="only" (*nkh*="spring upon") 26.1 n2

kaḏkoḏ (*kaḏ kaḏ*="this and that") 18.5 n11
(Syriac *kaḏkaḏyenon*="red") n12
kappoṯ="branches" (*kappaṯ*="one branch") 27.8 n37, 27.9
(*kofin*="sacrifice physical comfort") 27.9
(*kafuṯ*="tied together") 27.8, 27.9
Ḳarṭigna (Aramaic *ḳarta*="city"+Greek *gynē*="woman") 9.1 n10
ḳdḥ="bore, hollow out" (*ḳdḥ*="kindle") 18.5 n15
kĕḇaśim="he-lambs" (*kabbašim*="they that put out of sight" or "they that cleanse") 6.4
ḳfṣ="shut up" (*ḳṣf*="be wroth") 17.1 n7
kḥlnt="like those windows" (*khwt, khḥwnwt*="opaque" +*ḥlwnwt*="windows") 21.5
Ḳimḥith (*ḳimḥaya*="flour") 26.10 n59
klḳṭr (Greek *phylaktēr*="watchman") 5.18 n127
ḳll="to curse" (*ḳlh*="to roast") 24.15 n47
klt (*kallaṯ*="bridal"; *klwt*="brought to a conclusion") 1.1 n1, 11
1.2, 1.3
1.4, 1.5
ḳomah="stature" (*ḳomĕmiyyṯ*="go upright"; *ḳom me'oṯ*="a height of hundreds") 1.1 n8
'ḳrh="barren" (*'yḳrḥ*="root") 21.2
ḳrk="he met thee" (*ḳyrk*="he took advantage of the mischance which befell thee"; *ḳr'k*="he read up on thee"; *ḳyrḵ*="he called thee") 3.10 n52
'ks="beserpent" (*'eḵes*="anklet"; *'eḵes*="viper, serpent") 17.6 n26
ksh="appointed time" (*ks'*="not yet visible, throne") 23.8 n23
ḳṣyn="ruler" (*ḳṣh*="end, refuse"; *ḳwṣ*="to loath, despise") 14.3 n6
laḥaliḳ="to receive his portion" (*lĕḥalleḳ*="to portion out") 13.4
Laishah (*layiš*="the lion") 13.1 n2
lĕ-'aṭ (*lameḏ* 30+*'alef* 1+*ṭeṭ* 9=40 *se'ah*—minimum dimensions of pool for ritual immersion) 6.2 n39
leḥi="cheek" (*luaḥ*="tablet") S5.1 n1
'lh="oath" (Syriac *'elata*="altar") 26.1 n8
lh="to her" (*l'*="no") 16.1 n9
lhnḥyl="give" (*he'* 5+*nun* 50=55+*nḥl*="river") S1.20 n60
lirĕṣonḵem="that ye may be accepted" (*lirĕṣonḵem*="when you have all that delights you") 9.12 n57
l'mr="saying" (*l'w 'mwr*="negative prohibition") 4.4 n78
Mahol (*moḥlah*="pardon") 4.3
maḥtaṯo="his censer" (*mĕḥitaṯo*="his own breach" or "his own downfall") 26.8
mar="bitterness" (*mar*="lord, prime, first") 3.6 n43

marde'a="goad" (*moreh de'ah*="imparts an idea") 23.7
mašbir="selleth" (*masbir*="bestoweth unstintingly") S1.4 n17
maṭṭoṯ="tribes" (*maṭṭoṯ*="rods") 1.7 n54
mdbrh="wilderness" (*dbr*="speak") 17.1 n4
mdr dr="from generation to generation" (*mdrdr*="roll after, track") 3.16 n70
me'afa'="of naught" (*me'ah pĕ'iyyoṯ*="100 cries") 9.6 n44, 45
mĕḥayyeh 'et kullam="Thou keepest them alive" (*mĕḥayyeh lĕkullam*="Thou providest them with livelihood") 6.1 n4
mĕholal="mingled" (*mĕholal*="radiant") 26.2 n13
mĕḳareh="rafter" or "rafter maker" (*mĕḳorah*="well of her menstrual blood") 12.15
mĕlammĕḏeḵa="who teacheth thee" (*malmaḏ*="goad") 23.7
mĕ'oḏ="diligently" (*mo'eḏ*="season") 6.3 n45
mĕṣo'="be found" (*mṣh*="wring") S1.7 n22
mh="what" (*my*="who") 9.2 n23
mh="wherefore" (*mh*="not") 17.3 n14
mhwll="mad" (*mhwl*="mingle") 26.2 n11
mḥym="fatlings" (*mḥh*="remnants") 6.3 n57
midbar="wilderness" (*dbr*="to speak, to decree") 26.9 n55
miḏbareḵ="thy mouth" (*miḏbareḵ*="thy wilderness") 20.5 n7
miḳneh="cattle" (*ḳinĕ'ah*="jealousy") 13.10 n25
miḳra'="calling together" (*mĕḳora'*="one who is called") 23.7 n19
miḳweh="pool of hope" (*miḳweh*="pool of cleansing") 24.2 n4
Miriam (*mrwr*="bitterness") 5.9
moreh="teacher" (Greek *moros*="moron") 14.5 n11
'mrh="word" (Aramaic *'mr*="wool") 15.3 n5
mṣ'="find" (*mṣh*="settle") 24.17 n50
mskh="covering" (*mskh*="molten thing") 10.8 n30
mšl="rule" (*mšl*="utter a parable") 13.4 n8
mṣyṣ="he peereth" (*ṣwṣ*="chirp") 5.8 n47
m'wrwt="lights" (*m'rt*="a light") 5.1 n2
mym="water" (*nskyh*[*m*]+*wnsk*[*y*]*h*+*kmšpṭ*[*m*]) 28.f n13, 14, 15; 28.8
naḳai="clean" (*naḳai*="super-critical") 11.16 n64
naruṣah="we will run" (*rṣh*="be pleased, be satisfied") 9.1 n14
naśa'ṯa="forgivest" (*našiṯa*="forgettest") 25.2 n10
naṣu="they were banished" (*na'aṣu*="condemned"; *naṣu*="they became antagonists") 17.6 n35
nĕ'alim="sandals" (*nĕ'ilim*="closings") 28.e
nĕḡinaṯi="my song" (*miggen*="hath broken") 17.1 n2
nĕ'imoṯ="pleasures" (*nĕ'imoṯ*="those whose words of instruction are intoned") 27.2 n12
nešeḳ="battle" (*yaššiḳu*="contact") S2.2
nĕ'uraw="his youth" (*ninĕ'ar*="expelled") S3.2 n2
nfš="desire" (*nfš*="soul") 6.2 n43

nḥšlym="enfeebled" (*nḥ*="easy or feeble"+*šl*="cast out")
(*nḥšrym*="distilled, discharged") 3.12
niśśa'="lifted" (*niśśa'*="be sung to"; *maśśa'*="lifting in song") 21.4 n11, 12
'nky="I" (Egyptian *'nwk*) 12.24
'nky="I" (*'alef*=*'n'*, "I"; *nun*=*nfšy*, "myself": *kaf*=*ktbyt*, "I wrote"; *yod̲*=*yhbyt*, "I gave") 12.24 n77
(*yod̲*=*yhyb̲h*, "given"; *kaf*=*ktybh*, "writing"; *nun*=*n'ymym*, "pleasant"; *'alef*=*'mryh*, "its words") 12.24 n78
(*'alef*=*'n'*, "I"); *nun*=*nhwrk*, "thy light"; *kaf*=*klylk*, "thy crown"; *yod̲*=*y'wwtk*= "thy grace") 12.24 n79
noḳed="owner of herds" (*noḳed*="one who dots") 2.5, 6.2
nośe'="forgives" (*nośe'*="lifting up") 25.2 n7
(*nošeh*="forgets") n9
nšr="eagle" (*šrh*="abide") 26.3 n30
n'wh="comely" (*nwh*="residence, Temple") 20.5 n7
Pharaoh-necoh (Pharaoh *nkh*="sprung upon") 26.1 n2
pifiyyot̲ (*peh*="mouth" or "edge"+*fiyyot̲*="two mouths" or "two edges") 12.5 n25
piḳḳud̲im="precepts" (*piḳḳud̲im*="numbers") 6.3 n45
prś="separate" (*prś*="scatter") 10.4 n21
pšr="interpretation" (Aramaic *pšr'*="that which is dissolved") 4.4 n66
ranni="sing" (Greek *eirēnē*="peace") 20.2 n3
rdf (*rwdf*="fullness of the persecutor's power") 25.1 n5
Rephidim (*rfh*="let go"+*ydym*="hands") 3.a
(*rippu*="grew slothful"+*yad̲ayim*="hands") 12.15
rḥm="tender mercy" (*rḥm*="womb") 9.11 n53
ribbotayim="myriads" (*rbh*= "extend, enlarge") 12.22 n69
ruaḥ="air" (*rewaḥ*="space") S2.4
r'y="raiser of sheep in large numbers" (*r'y*="evil eye which knows no restraint") 6.2 n41
ša'af="gapeth" (*šuf*="bruise, crush") 8.2 n20
ṣab̲="covered" (*ṣab̲*="lizard"; *ṣb'*="decorated"; *ṣb'*= "equipped"; *ṣbh*="bent" or "arched") 1.8 n61, 62
ṣammim="snare" (*ṣamat̲*="to meet, to join") 8.2 n20
šanim="scarlet" (*šanim*="years") 6.4 n61
(*šĕnayim*="twice") 10.4 n15
šb'tym="7+7=14" (7 times 7=49) 4.2 n14
ṣdḳ="righteousness" (*ṣdyḳ*="righteous") 5.17 n123
ṣe'="get thee hence" (*ṣĕ'ah*="excrete") 13.2 n4
sĕ'assĕ'ah="full measure" (*sĕ'ah* for *sĕ'ah*="measure for measure") 11.4
šĕb̲i'i="seventh" (*mĕśubba'*="filled"; *šĕbu'ah*="oath") 23.9

ṣeḏeḵ="victory" (*Ṣeḏeḵ*="Jupiter") S4.3 n7
ṣĕḥoḵ="laughter" (Syriac *šeḥaḵa*="punishment or punishable") 26.2 n12
šĕlaleḵ="thy spoil" (*šellaḵ*="that which was formerly thine"; *šello' laḵ*="that which was never thine") S2.2
ṣĕlil="cake" (*ṣĕlil*="*bare* [of good deeds]" 8.4 n27
šĕliši="third" (*šališi*="to be trusted"; *šališim*= "three-decked") 12.12 n45
šĕlume="peaceable" (*hišlamti*="I completed, I turned over") 11.13 n46
śĕ'orim="barley" (*sar 'awon*="keep from iniquity") 5.10 n90
Šĕlomoh="Solomon" (*haš-šillum šello*="his private means of communication") 1.2 n12
(*hišlim*="to make peace" or "to cause to surrender") 1.3 n22
(*haš-šillum šello*="making himself surrender"; *šalom*="peace") 1.3
šĕṯiyah="foundation, spindlestone" (*hušaṯ*="was spun") 26.4 n34
Shealtiel (*huštĕlah*="newly set out") 24.11
śḥḵ="to play" (*šḥḵ*="to be ground") 6.1 n15
sḥrh="her merchandise" (*sḥrh*="her shield") 7.6 n32
šiḇyam="their captivity" (*šeb-ba-yam*="which is beyond the sea") 23.2 n7
śimḥah="gladness" (*šimhah*="desolation") S6.4 n3
šimšoṯayiḵ (*šemeš*="sun") 18.5 n14
šinĕ'an="angels" (*šĕnunim*="sharply intent"; *šenna'in*= "most radiant"; *ša'anan*= "comfortable") 12.22 n61, 64, 68
ṣinnim="thorns" (*ṣinnim*="shield" or "buckler") 8.2 n20
šlḥyk="thy shoots" (*šllwḥyḵ*="thy goings forth") 11.6
šlmh="complete" (*Šlmh*="Solomon") 16.1
šlyšym="captains" or "weapons"
(*šlšwm*="day before yesterday") 12.5
(*šlyšym*="made up of three ingredients") 12.12
smḥh="mirth" (*š'mḥh*="I will blot out") 26.2 n19
šn'n="angels" (*šnh*="to repeat") 12.22 n59
śoḇa'="fullness" (*šeḇa'*="seven") 27.2
śpḥ="scab" (*mšpḥh*="family") 17.6 n29, 31
(*šfḥh*="handmaid") n30
sr (*srs*="pull, tear apart"; *śr*="prince") 3.6 n44
ṣr="adversary" (*Ṣwr*="Tyre", i.e. Rome) 7.11
ṣrh="narrow" (*ṣrh*="rival") 10.8 n30
s'rh (*š'rh*="which is tossed") 18.2 n6
'śrwn="tenth" (*ytrwn*="profit") 8.1 n5, 6
stw="winter" (*syt t'h*="entice") 5.9 n75
surim="prison" (*sirim*="bushes") S3.2 n3

'ṣyrh="withholding of rain" (*'ṣrt*="holding of oneself") 28.3 n38
šyryw="song" (*šyyrw*="application thereof") 4.3
ṣywn="Zion" (*ṣywn*="sign") 1.3 n20
't="[another] along with"—the accusative particle rendered as an extending particle 1.4
taḥtaw="straightway" (*taḥtaw*="under") 4.2 n28
tammaṯi (*tamyaṯi*="my twin, my equal, my undefiled") 5.6
ṭebaḥ="slaughter" (*ṭabbaḥ*="slaughterer") 5.18 n133
teḥaṯ="to come down" (*teḥaṯ*="to be dismayed") 23.2 n6
'ṭf="fainteth" (*'ṭfym*="delayings") 27.3 n14
ṭhr="pure" (*zhr*="outshine") 16.1 n2
Tishri (*tišre*="remittest") 23.6
tiśśa'="accept" (*tiśśa'*="lift") 2.2 n8
(*taššeh*="lend") 2.7
tiśśa'="forgive" (*tiśśa'*="take payment") 24.19 n52
'tḳk="pluck thee" (*'tḳnk*="mend thee") 24.11
tnh="hire" (*ytnw*="recount, rehearse") 6.3 n53
torim="circlets" (*torah*="instruction") S5.1 n1
tšy="thou wast unmindful" (*tšš*="to weaken") 25.1 n3
tukku="wear themselves out" (*tukku*="are smitten") S1.18 n56
'tw="him" (*'wtw*="his mark") 26.1 n3
ṭwb (*ṭeṯ*=ninth letter; *waw*=sixth letter; *beṯ*=second letter—corresponds to *nfš* since *nun*=ninth from last letter; *fe*=sixth from last letter; *šin*=second from last letter) 24.19 n53
twr="turtle" (*tyyr*="turning") 5.9 n63
'ulah="sucking child" (*'olah*="burnt offering") 17.7
u-lĕ-'ummi="my nation" (*u-lĕ-'immi*="my mother") 1.3 n33
wayĕhi="it came to pass" (Aramaic *way*="woe," "and there was woe") 11.7 n15
way-yaḥălos="discomfited" (*ḥeleš*="lot"; *way-yaḥăloš*="and cast lots") 3.d n12
way-yĕzanneḇ="he smote the hindmost of thee" (*way-yĕzanneḇ*="he smote the hinder part of thee") 3.11
way-yišrĕṣu="increased abundantly" (*šereṣ*="small animal") 1.11 n34
wkḳp'wn=". . . and thickness" (*ykḳp'wn*="will be perspicuous") 4.7 n97
'wyb="enemy" (*'ywb*="Job") 16.6
wyḥlḳ (*way-yĕḥaleḳ*="and was divided"; *way-yaḥăloḳ*="and he divided") 7.5 n17
yamin="days" (*yamin*="right hand") 17.5
''ydk="forewarn thee" (*''dyk*="ornament thee") 16.3 n15
(*'d*="booty") n17
(*y'd*="to meet") n18
yĕḥakkeh="wait" (*ḥakkah*="to fish with hook") S1.3

yeḥolṣun="that they may be delivered from"
(*haḥăliṣenu*="deliver us [from wandering]";
yĕḥalleṣ="deliver us [from poverty]";
yaḥăliṣ="delivered [from weakness]") 17.5
yĕšallem="make peace" (*yĕšallem*="give up one's life") 11.1 n2
(*yĕšallem*="reward") n7
yhyh="shall become" (*yod̲* 10+*he'* 5+*yod̲* 10+*he'* 5=30
"righteous men") 11.15
yiškĕnu="shall dwell" (*yaškinu*="shall cause to dwell") 1.1 n9
yošeb̲="sitting" (*yašab̲*="sat") 5.8 n49
yšw'h="salvation" (*yš'*="gave heed") 28.5
yšwn'="was changed" (*yśwn'*="became a hater") 4.4 n76
zaddu="dealt proudly, acted mischievously"
(*zaddu*="cooked up, schemed") 11.5 n9
zamir="song" (*zamir*="pruning") 5.9 n60
'zbny="hath forsaken me" (*'z*=strength+*bny*="my
children") 17.6 n24
zeh="this" (*'z'*="to fire, to make hot") 2.10 n34; 6.4 n68
zh (*zayin* 7+*he'* 5=12, number of Tribes) 3.1 n30
zik̲ronek̲em="your acts of remembering" (*zĕk̲it̲em*="you
gain merit") 3.2 n34
Zion (*ṣywn*="sign") 16.3
zkh="pure" (*zkh*="profit") 3.4
zḳn="old man" (*zh šḳnh* [*ḥkmh*]="one who got wisdom") 27.9 n41
zoru (*zar*="stranger" or *zeyrta'*="fist") 3.1 n27